Winning Three Times

written by Jacobaris

iUniverse, Inc.
Bloomington

Winning Three Times

iUniverse books may be ordered through booksellers or by contacting:

iUniverse
1663 Liberty Drive
Bloomington, IN 47403
www.iuniverse.com
1-800-Authors (1-800-288-4677)

ISBN: 978-1-4502-9058-6 (pbk)
ISBN: 978-1-4502-9060-9 (cloth)
ISBN: 978-1-4502-9059-3 (ebk)

Printed in the United States of America

iUniverse rev. date: 3/7/11

Foreword by the Author.

In the early 1900's the Balkans were a powder keg. Before one problem was solved other problems had already appeared. Otherwise the world was seemingly peaceful. Many novel writers decided that they needed experience in warfare to write books and left for the Balkans to volunteer their services. They were eager to join before the conflicts would be settled and peace would be around for a long time to come. If that happened, opportunity would be lost; this was an opportunity of a life time not to be missed.

They were too hasty because in 1914 the First World War started and millions of people saw warfare involuntarily. Personally I lived through the Second World War and didn't have to go to the Balkans for war experience. My war experience was first hand. I could have done without the experience of this dreadful war but on the other hand I have a lot of material to write a book about. A lot of research went into this book and I have attempted to make it as factual as humanly possible.

Language Warning

At the best of times, people use course language. The war was by no means the best of times and naturally the language in this book is not the best English. It reflects what the people were saying and thinking. Therefore readers discretion is advised.

Contents

Introduction.

It was in The Netherlands in a town called Yselmonde, under the smoke of Rotterdam, that this story took place.

Arie de Kievit and his wife Ko lived with their 13 year old daughter Willie and their 10 year old son Adrie in a house that they had bought. Unfortunately, the Great Depression had changed a prosperous future into a poor one and had put Arie out of work for many years. He was forced to work in Dutch work camps in order to qualify for relief payments.

In spite that England, France and Germany were already at war for over half a year, the Depression still had a stranglehold on The Netherlands, but this was about to change.

A Rough Awakening.

On Thursday night May 9, 1940 Adrie went to bed as usual. Bed time came early at 9.00 p.m. because the next day was a school day. Before he was ten years old, bed time was at 8.00 p.m. When he became ten years old on March 23, 1940 he was allowed to stay up till nine. "Before the age of ten, small children have to sleep the clock around," his parents said. "When they do, they'll be wide awake during school hours." Adrie found this was a lame excuse that his parents used to get rid of the kids and get some quiet in the house.

This year, Whitsuntide was on Sunday and Monday, May 12 and 13. Whitsuntide was forty nine days after Easter and was, like Easter, always on a Sunday and Monday. It was celebrated in The Netherlands to commemorate the foundation of the Christian Church. Friday May 10th was the last school day before the Whitsuntide holidays which lasted ten days.

In anticipation of the coming holidays, Adrie had gone to bed excited. His mother didn't share in the excitement of having the kids around for ten days. When they were home they could get themselves into all kinds of troubles, she thought, and this knowledge was based on past experience.

On May 10th, 1940, with daybreak at 5.00 a.m., all hell broke loose. There were many planes flying low over the houses and cannons were firing at the planes. Adrie woke up because of all the noise and wondered what was going on. He got out of bed to see what was cooking. His father and mother were already up and people were gathering in the street in spite of the early hour.

Piet Brouwer from across the street had an audience gathered around him. He had been listening to the radio and there had been a message from the Government that Germany had attacked The Netherlands. According to the Dutch Government, The Netherlands were now officially at war with Germany. The Government advised everybody to stay calm because everything was under control and to stand by for news bulletins about the war.

Adrie was curious as to what was happening in the world and had read the newspapers daily. He had read all about Adolf Hitler and his attack on Poland. He knew that England and France had declared war on Germany and now The Netherlands had been attacked by Germany. The Netherlands was not neutral anymore and England and France had the same enemy. All of a sudden England and France were Dutch allies and became friends. There were a few questions he had no answer for, "How did The Netherlands get involved in this war and how did it start?"

Piet Brouwer had an answer to this question. He said: "This is the third war between France and Germany. The first war started in 1870 after years of tension between France and Germany. This war turned in favor of the Germans when in 1871 Paris was completely encircled.

The French couldn't break the siege and capitulated. An armistice was then concluded in which France had to cede the two ore rich provinces, Alsace and Lorraine, to Germany and they had to pay an indemnity of 5 billion Francs. As for insults, the German army had a victory march through the streets of Paris and the first Kaiser of a united Germany was crowned in the Palace of Mirrors in Versailles. Part of France was going to be occupied by the German Army until the indemnity was paid in full.

Thus the war in 1870 set the stage for another conflict which was brewing and which erupted in 1914. France had learned an expensive lesson and found an ally which was scared of a powerful Germany as well. England and France became friends for the first time in history."

"Shucks," Adrie thought, "I don't know anything about the First World War and the Second World War has already started. I have a lot of catching up to do."

When Adrie went inside, he wanted to know from his father everything about the First World War. His father had been a soldier in the Dutch army during this war and should know everything about it. And Adrie wanted to know it all.

His father cleared his throat and looked over his glasses as if he was staring into eternity before he started his long story: "I was drafted into the Dutch army and was only two months in training when the war started. All leaves were cancelled immediately and the army prepared for war. The training of the new soldiers was speeded up and the country prepared for defence of its borders.

The Netherlands is a country below sea level and most of the country can be inundated in a heck of a hurry. A large area close to the German border was inundated which was a powerful defence in those days. There were a few aeroplanes around but airborne troops were decades away. Only with amphibious troops could they attack The Netherlands and it was as hard to take as England.

At the same time the Dutch Government kept a neutral policy trying to stay out of the conflict. Nobody in the Dutch Government knew about the intentions of the German military command. All they could do was playing it safe and prepare for the worst.

It was a long war that ended when the Germans lost a major battle in France. To the German High Command it meant that the German border lay open to the Allies and that battles would be fought on German ground. For four years the battles had been fought in France and Belgium. Shelling of cities in those countries had caused a lot of damage with a lot of casualties among the civilian population. This same fate could be expected in Germany.

The German military command saw that the war was lost and suggested an armistice to prevent military occupation of Germany. It was revenge time for France when the Peace Treaty was signed. France took back the two provinces they had lost in 1870 and Germany had to make extensive repair payments. There were quite a few conditions that Germany had to keep according to the Peace Treaty. Germany was not allowed to have an army except for internal security and couldn't manufacture cannons, tanks, and warships."

Adrie had been listening with full attention to the story about the First World War and said: "Lucky for the Dutch people who were spared the horrors of war."

His mother commented: "The only problem we had was starvation. The Netherlands imported a large amount of wheat to feed its population and with the war on that came to a halt. Moreover the wheat production in The Netherlands itself had dwindled because of the large areas of agricultural land which had been inundated for the defence."

PRELUDE TO WAR.

Adrie was only ten years old but he was quite familiar with the events that had taken place before this war started. When he was only eight years old, he studied the daily events in the newspaper and the first front page head line that drew his attention was on March 1938.

AUSTRIA ANNEXED BY GERMANY.
Seys Inquart welcomes Adolf Hitler in Austria.

After reading the front page twice he wondered what it all meant. There was one way to find out. At night, groups of men assembled at the corner of the street discussing what was happening in the street, in The Netherlands, and in the rest of the world. Old Leen Willemstein was always leading the conversation, no matter what subject was tackled. He talked 80% of the time and only two other guys got a word in once in a while. The rest of the people were listeners like Adrie. Everybody was welcome to join and nobody minded that an eight year old boy came to listen. Most kids wouldn't come to listen to the conversation of the old geezers anyway. Old Leen Willemstein was selling gas for the few cars and motor bikes that were around in those days and had all the time in the world to do a lot of talking, and talking was his favorite pastime.

When Adrie arrived at the corner of the street there was quite a discussion on the go. Old Leen Willemstein was telling the people that war was in the making: "Adolf Hitler has gone a step too far. England and France aren't going to take this any longer because it is all in contradiction with the Armistice Agreement of Versailles. Wait and see, the French army will occupy the Rhineland and the Ruhr district where Hitler is making tanks and cannons."

Piet Brouwer had something to say too: "I went to the movies and they always show World News before the movie starts. This time they showed the rise of the Nazis in Germany; there were endless long torchlight parades and meetings in which the people were singing:

Deutschland, Deutschland uber alles,
Uber alles in die welt.

Piet Brouwer was so friendly as to translate that for the people who were not familiar with German. It meant "Germany above all, above everybody in the world." He added: "Those people mean business and the Germans are shouting 'Hail Hitler, Hail Hitler' for hours. It could mean major trouble.

The Nazi Party in Germany uses violent methods to attract new members, they don't take no for an answer. On the news release, they were singing:

If you don't want to be a comrade of me,
We'll bash your head in one, two, three.

Head bashing of the opposition was done by Nazis in black shirts using rubber hoses filled with lead. It's real scary with all the violence that's going on."

Adrie was studying the newspaper the following day and the day after but nothing happened. The old Leen Willemstein had it all wrong, which didn't happen often. Most of the time he could tell the future like a gypsy.

Half a year later, in September, Adrie read the paper and had another reason to go to the street to listen to the conversation of old Leen Willemstein. The headline on the front page stated in big fat letters:

GERMANY WANTS TO OCCUPY SUDETENLAND.

Adrie was good in geography and studied the atlas daily but he didn't know where Sudetenland was. When he read the article he found out that Sudetenland was a part of Czechoslovakia where many German people were living. Hitler wanted to be Fuhrer over all German people and had said: "One People One Reich!" (One people, one country.)

The next day the front page article said:

"MOUNTING FEAR OF WAR AS ENGLAND AND FRANCE WARN HITLER THAT WAR WILL BE DECLARED IF HE OCCUPIES SUDETENLAND."

"Wow," Adrie thought and ran to the street to listen to what old Leen Willemstein had to say about all that. From afar he could hear Leen Willemstein already and he hastened his step to join the lecture. Indeed Leen Willemstein predicted a gloomy picture for Europe and declared that war was now imminent. "Germany is a dictatorship and Adolf Hitler wants a war," he said.

Adrie had some questions for Leen Willemstein: "What is a dictatorship and why does Hitler want war?"

Leen Willemstein answered: "In a dictatorship only the nightingale sings and it's pretty quiet in the forest. Hitler is hell bent to revenge the Treaty of Versailles and make Germany powerful again. Ironically there is a German proverb that says 'The most amicable man can't live in peace if his quarrelsome neighbour wants to fight.' Unfortunately Hitler wants to fight and England and France don't. With Hitler in command of Germany there is no hope for Europe."

Adrie could hardly wait for the newspaper to arrive the next day. Because of the Depression his father was unemployed so his parents were poor. They didn't have a radio and were dependent on the newspaper to be informed about the world from day to day. Leen Willemstein had a radio and never missed a news broadcast so he was earlier and better informed than the victims of the Depression.

When the newspaper finally arrived, the newspaper boy didn't have to put the newspaper in the mailbox. Adrie almost ripped it out of the surprised boy's hand. The headline on the front page was:

"LAST DITCH EFFORT. CHAMBERLAIN SUGGESTS CONFERENCE AT MUNICH."

In the article, he read that Hitler had accepted the conference idea to solve the tension among the nations. Hitler had suggested inviting his friend Mussolini, Italy's dictator, to mediate in the conflict.

The next day's paper brought no relief to the people when the headline stated:

"WORLD IN ANGST WHILE IT AWAITS THE RESULT OF MUNICH CONFERENCE."

Leen Willemstein didn't believe that war could be stopped; he predicted: "Hitler will not stop, it is his way only."

After the conference in Munich there was hope for the world when the headlines read:

WE HAVE RECEIVED PEACE WITH HONOR.

A jubilant Chamberlain returned to England from the Munich conference declaring: "There will be peace in our time. Hitler is a trustworthy man and we have received peace with honor. We have agreed that Germany will occupy the Sudetenland because there are a lot of German people living there. In return Hitler has promised that this is his very last claim in his ambition to reunite the German people. He only wants to be Fuhrer over the German people and nothing else."

World tension eased slightly but in spite that Hitler was a trustworthy man, England and France took the necessary steps to prepare for war. The newspaper came on April 27, 1939 with a discouraging headline.

"ENGLAND REINTRODUCES CONSCRIPTION."

Old Leen Willemstein had something to say about that news, "I told you that we were heading for war and this confirms it. Why would England train more soldiers if they trusted Hitler?"

The worst news reached the world on September 1st 1939.

"GERMANY INVADES POLAND."

'At dawn the German Army marched into Poland and the German Luftwaffe has bombed Warsaw.'

A second front page headline informed the readers about the seriousness of the situation:

"FRANCE AND ENGLAND MOBILIZE THEIR ARMIES AND DEMAND WIHDRAWAL OF GERMAN TROOPS FROM POLAND."

England and France gave Hitler an ultimatum of 48 hours to withdraw his troops from Poland. If this ultimatum isn't met, war will be declared.

The Dutch, Belgian, Danish and Norwegian armies have been put on full alert by their respective Governments.

Leen Willemstein had no problem getting an audience that night; even people that had never attended his lectures were joining the nervous people. The question on everybody's lips was, "Can a war be avoided at this stage?"

Leen Willemstein had the answer to that question: "This is it, all hell will break loose after the ultimatum ends and before you know the corpses will be lying ten high."

It sounded terrible to Adrie who had lived a sheltered life so far; were all those people from around here going to die? September 2nd went by and the news was very discouraging:

"DUTCH ARMY ON FULL ALERT AS ADOLF HITLER SHOWS NO SIGN OF WITHDRAWING HIS TROOPS FROM POLAND."

Leen Willemstein predicted: "Tomorrow when the ultimatum elapses the world will be in World War II."

Unfortunately, the Gypsy was right again when the most dreaded news awaited the world on September 3rd:

"FRANCE, ENGLAND AND AUSTRALIA DECLARE WAR ON GERMANY AFTER ULTIMATUM ENDED."

The world was in shock and everybody was worried. Ko said: "We have to stock food because the First World War was a disaster."

There was only one problem; with the Depression nobody had any money to stock much food. However, Ko went to the store to buy 10 pounds of rice, she said: "Rice can be kept good if you store it in a dry place."

She had such a dry place in mind, there was a large steel storage container in the loft which could hold over 250 pounds of rice. "I will buy 10 pounds of rice every week till the container is full," she said. "At least we will have some food for a while."

Another headline attracted attention,

"DUTCH GOVERNMENT MOBILIZES ARMY BY CALLING UP ITS RESERVES."

It meant that all trained soldiers had to return to their war destination to defend the country. The next door neighbor Immerzeel was a blacksmith and worked with his two sons in the smithy. Both sons had to report for duty in the army which left the old blacksmith without help. He had a younger boy who was already 21 years old and was free from being drafted by the Dutch Government. If there were two boys of the same family in the army the third one was excused and had brother service. It meant that he was free of the draft. His younger son had done different work but now his father needed him he joined his father to help out.

Mrs. Immerzeel was quite nervous to see her sons go to the army now there was a war on. Old Immerzeel said: "Don't worry, I was for four years in the Army during the First World War and we never fired a shot other than during training manoeuvres."

As a typical mother she wasn't convinced at all and shared the worry of thousands of other mothers across the country.

Adrie ran to the mailbox as soon as the newspaper boy delivered the newspaper on the first day of the war and found that the war had indeed started. The first page read:

GERMANY SINKS BRITISH OCEAN LINER ATHENIA. 112 PEOPLE KILLED.

Leen Willemstein declared that those were the first victims of the war and that millions would die before this was all over. He also had comments about Adolf Hitler: "Attacking unarmed ocean liners is being a coward. According to the Geneva Convention only warships can be sunk without warning. All merchant ships and undefended passenger ships have to be warned before sinking the ships. The ship cannot be sunk until the crew and passengers have left the ship in lifeboats."

Every day there were headlines on the front page about the war.

"BRITAIN BLACKED OUT AT NIGHT."

In anticipation of air raids during the night, the British Government has taken steps to black out the country in order to deprive German pilots of navigational aids.

Another headline showed that civilians were suffering from the war as well.

"RATIONING OF FOOD AND GASOLINE STARTS IN BRITAIN AND FRANCE."

In view of expected shortages, because of the war, the British and French Governments have taken steps to secure a proper food distribution.

On September 6th the newspaper brought more news about the war,

"SOUTH AFRICA DECLARES WAR ON GERMANY."

This news was followed by news on September 10,

"CANADA DECLARES WAR ON GERMANY."

Leen Willemstein's gypsy kind of foretelling the future had come true and this war was turning into a global conflict.

Every day there was news about the war:

"LARGE AREA OF LAND INUNDATED AS GOVERNMENT PUT WATER BARRIER IN PLACE."

The Dutch Government has taken precautionary steps in preparation for the defence of The Netherlands. Dykes were opened today to flood the lands of the southern and eastern provinces. The Netherlands will be easier to defend against a possible attack.

On October 3rd there was bad news for the Allies.

RUSSIA TAKES NORTHERN POLAND. POLISH RESISTANCE CEASES.

Leen Willemstein commented that Stalin wanted part of the pie and had taken the opportunity when he saw that Poland had been defeated. There was a Non-Aggression Pact between Germany and Russia so it was in the interest of Germany to get this war in the East finished so he could take on France in the West.

There was also some news about The Netherlands in the papers.

"DUTCH GOVERNMENT PRONOUNCES NEUTRALITY IN CONFLICT."

The Dutch Government is taking no sides in the war between Germany against France and England. Through diplomatic channels the Dutch Government has asked the warring nations to respect and maintain the neutrality of The Netherlands.

Other Dutch news was about pending rationing.

"DUTCH GOVERNMENT PREPARES FOR RATIONING."

In spite of imports of grain and other foodstuffs which are almost non-existent because of the war, the Dutch Government announces that there is an ample food supply even for a prolonged war. As soon as war became a possibility, the Dutch Planning Department purchased and stored a four year food supply. This measure was taken in anticipation of a possible four years of war like in the First World War. Petroleum products will be rationed immediately and gasoline will be only made available for doctors and other persons who need gas to supply essential services to the public.

People don't necessarily believe Governments. Adrie's mother continued to buy 10 pounds of rice every week to secure an ample food supply just in case. Other people also started to store food in case The Netherlands would become a battlefield. It was noticeable that people were hoarding food, which caused shortages of certain articles in the stores.

The next headline in the paper dealt with the hoarding population.

"HOARDING OF FOOD OUTLAWED."

The Dutch Government announces that hoarding of food is contrary to the public interest and is therefore against the law. Hoarding is totally unnecessary since an ample food supply can be maintained. If this hoarding practise continues it will deprive some people of the needed supplies. People who are caught hoarding will have their illegal supplies confiscated and face imprisonment of half a year.

Adrie's mother warned: "Don't tell anybody that we have a rice supply because some people might be jealous and give us away."

In spite of the ample food supply, the Government announced:

"SUGAR RATIONING COUPONS ISSUED.

Because of the low production of sugar beets this year it might be necessary to ration sugar. The Government will issue sugar coupons to insure an efficient distribution if needed. Normally, if such a condition of low sugar supply existed the Government imported cane sugar from other countries. With the on-going war this is impossible so the Government will take appropriate steps to ensure that every citizen will get his fair share."

Of course this caused people to hoard sugar. If the Government had said nothing, nobody in The Netherlands would have figured that there would be a shortage of sugar. Apparently there was still enough sugar around and sugar distribution didn't start at once. There was a lull in the war which was more or less an armed standoff. With winter fast approaching it seemed that nobody was interested in starting a major offensive. Both sides were happy to be in the defensive position and planned their strategy for spring.

The month of December was remarkably quiet. There were only a couple of news items that surfaced and drew the attention. Sinking of the German Battleship Graf Spee in Montevideo was heralded as a great Allied success. So far, the Germans had had tremendous victories and success in the war had been very limited for the Allies. Another news item was the arrival of Canadian troops in Britain to shore up the defence of the Motherland.

At the end of the year there were the usual reviews of the past year. Both warring sides made up their balance sheet as to how well or how bad they were doing. In less than four months of war German U boats had sunk 114 Allied ships totalling 421,156 tons. The Germans had lost only 9 U boats and 75,000 tons of ships. This imbalance of lost ships was in favor of the Germans. Leen Willemstein's commentary cleared up the situation: "England has to be supplied across the ocean, from the United States, with oil, materials and food. The Germans are having a heyday attacking all those merchant ships."

The Belly Ache of Klazien

Nations go to war over the smallest things. People do the same, they fight about small potatoes and later they wonder why. During the summer of 1939 when the nations of Europe prepared for war, the neighbors started a private war with Arie and Ko. Talk about small potatoes, you couldn't even see a potato.

Kees Meuzelaar was Arie's next door neighbor. He had one son named Kees Meuzelaar. To tell them apart they were called the Old Kees and the Young Kees and when people talked about father and son they would talk about the two Keeses. The name of his wife was Klazien. She was scared that people would look inside her house and had put up defence works to prevent people from spying on her. The defence works consisted of a high fence between the houses to prevent her terrible neighbors from seeing what she was doing.

Between the front gardens was a high hedge and there was also a hedge at the front of the house which was only a foot away from the windows. It was about four feet wide and six feet high which made it dark in the bedrooms even in the middle of the day. If they went into the bedrooms in the day time they had to switch on the lights. They lived like hermits.

The hedge between the properties was growing wild and was never trimmed but that's the way she liked it. It looked like an impregnable jungle. On the other hand, Klazien loved to spy on everybody else. Her house was very close to the street and she had a spy mirror on each side of the living room window. When she was sitting behind her favorite spy window she could see whatever happened at both ends of the street. Every day, she sat behind her window to spy on everybody.

Not only were they spying, they were curious and wanted to know everything about everybody. One day when Adrie came home from playing with his friend, the Meuzelaars were standing in front of their house and Klazien asked: "Where do you come from so late at night?"

Adrie thought: "It's none of your damned business," but he knew better than to give her that answer. Instead he answered: "Oh, I come from nowhere!"

"Wow," Kees replied, "That's a long way out when you go all the way to nowhere! Does your mommy know that you go that far away?"

"They are getting nasty," Adrie thought, "It must hurt that their curiosity isn't satisfied."

One day Adrie was surprised to see his father get up early in the morning to trim the hedge. Adrie asked his father: "Why do you get up so early just to trim that hedge?"

His father's answer was: "I do that to prevent Klazien from getting a belly ache."

Adrie didn't understand a syllable about that remark and asked: "Why does Klazien get a belly ache?"

"Two days ago," his father explained, "I tried to trim the hedge because it's growing wild over our path. You can't walk to the door without walking against the wet branches of the hedge. When you have your good clothes on you get marks on your clothes. Klazien saw me trimming the hedge, she came up to me and said it was her hedge and I should leave it alone. When Kees came home a little later, she started to belly ache to Kees, whining: 'How can that terrible man next door touch my beautiful hedge?' I didn't want an argument so I quit trimming the hedge. Now I trim the hedge before she gets up so she doesn't see it."

Adrie thought this was crazy: "But when the hedge blocks the entrance to your door you should be able to trim it as long as you are on your own property."

"Never mind," Adrie's mother got into the conversation, "We sure don't want a fight with those childish people, they can and will make your life very miserable if they don't get their way."

His mother explained what she had been saying: "The woman who lived before in our house was Klazien's own cousin. Klazien got into an argument with her husband about a stupid little gutter that carried water from the roof to the back of the property. Klazien didn't like it, she got a lawyer who took it to court and they won. Her cousin had to remove the gutter and naturally she was madder than a hatter.

That wasn't the end of Klazien's wrath; she kept pestering her cousin with all kinds of little silly arguments and was always threatening her if she didn't get her way. She would simply say: 'I'll go to Court and then we'll see who is right!' Her cousin got so frustrated that she sold the house and now we have those terrible pesky neighbors. Klazien probably thinks that she won one round and she can run us out of town as well. Unfortunately for her, we are here to stay whether she likes it or not. In the meantime don't say anything back if they say anything to you. If you make them mad, they'll pester you long enough so that you don't want to live here anymore!"

Adrie didn't understand and asked: "What can they possibly do to pester you so that you sell your house?"

His mother replied: "Lots, but you better not find out." She added, "I know a better way to skin the cat, I'll kill that darned hedge and then we don't have to trim it anymore."

"How do you kill a hedge?" Adrie wanted to know.

"Every morning I'll throw a pot with piss where the roots of that hedge are and it will die. A tree or hedge can only stand so much manure and if it gets too much it will croak."

Adrie watched his mother for a year to throw a pot with piss around the hedge every morning but it didn't die. Emptying piss pots to kill a tree was an old home remedy that might have worked. Even dogs can piss a tree to death when they lift their leg daily to give the tree water. This hedge was different; it was very hardy and fast growing. It seemed to thrive on all the extra nutrients Ko gave it. Finally, Ko gave up and trimming the hedge early in the morning was the only alternative to prevent Klazien from getting a belly ache.

In spite of the precautions that Arie had taken to prevent an argument about that darned hedge an argument was coming anyway. If it's not one thing it's another. One day the young Kees and his friend, who was about the same age, were cutting the wire of the fence between the gardens with a pair of pliers. It was Arie's fence so he said: "You quit that right away." The boys were laughing at him so Arie got mad and threatened: "I'll tell the police about you and the police will throw you in jail."

The boys ran crying home to their mother and told her all about the evil man from next door. From there on if they saw Arie or Ko they said: "I'll tell the police all about you and the police will throw you in jail."

Arie and Ko pretended that they didn't hear it but they kept it up, they never quit. The neighbors would also pull their eyelids backwards to show the reds around their eyes when they saw anybody of the family. Adrie thought it was funny but his sister Willie got scared and came home screaming. Her mother consoled her and said: "Those people are terrible but don't say anything to them, just pretend you don't see them, so they don't have fun."

The Blitz Krieg.

In preparing defence, in case of a German attack, the Dutch Government hoped to avoid being drawn into the war and kept a strict neutrality policy. This had worked in the First World War and hopefully it would work again. General Reynders, the commander of the Dutch forces, was planning to defend the whole country with the cooperation of Belgium. He thought it impossible to defend The Netherlands without outside help. This was contrary to the Dutch Government's policy. The Dutch Government was fearful of infuriating Adolf Hitler and having to deal with his wrath.

Adrie found out about this friction on February 6th 1940 when the newspaper announced:

GENERAL REYNDERS SACKED. GENERAL WINKELMAN NEW COMMANDER OF NAVY, LAND AND AIR FORCES.
General Reynders policy of working together with the Belgian forces to defend The Netherlands was contrary to the neutrality policy of the Dutch Government. Therefore the Dutch Government has relieved General Reynders of his command. General Winkelman has been appointed as new chief of staff of all Dutch forces.

By assuming his command General Winkelman addressed his forces with a speech to explain why their commander had been fired. According to the new General the chance that The Netherlands would be attacked by Germany was minimal. There was also the possibility that France and England would invade The Netherlands to get at Germany. In case of a German invasion, General Winkelman was willing to sacrifice the south and eastern parts of the country and defend only the west and central part of The Netherlands. Only North and South Holland and Utrecht were behind the water barriers and were easier to defend.

It was a pretty cold winter and the water of the water barrier froze solidly. That wasn't much of a defence the Commander thought and ordered the soldiers to cut a very wide channel through the ice to stop the German soldiers if they came. People didn't mind having a large skating rink and young and old used the water barrier for their skating fun.

The newspaper announced:
"STALEMATE IN PHONY WAR."

Because of lack of action during the winter months the war was called "The phoney war." But Leen Willemstein said: "The war is not phony at all; just remember that the Germans have sunk 114 Allied ships with many casualties. And wait till spring arrives, then all hell will break lose."

The Gypsy forecaster was right on again. It was April 9, 1940 when the headlines in the newspaper indicated that the phony war had just ended to make place for a real war.

"NORWAY AND DENMARK INVADED BY GERMANY."

In the early morning hours Germany trespassed on the neutrality of Norway and Denmark and attacked both countries. German parachute troops that landed on the palace grounds in Copenhagen were killed by the Royal Guard.

Adrie wasn't sure what Norway and Denmark had to do with the war because they were neutral like The Netherlands. He had to check with old Leen Willemstein again for an explanation. Leen Willemstein knew it all, he never disappointed his audience and explained: "Germany is protecting his weak flank; if England and France land in Norway and Denmark they can attack Germany from those countries."

Well, that explained everything, Adrie thought. The next day there was some more news about this.

"DENMARK CAPITULATES"

Hitler promises painless occupation of Denmark. The Danish king is allowed to reign with the Danish Government in power.

And as seconds for news that day the newspaper read,

"NORWAY REQUESTS HELP FROM ALLIES."

Request for Allied help was granted which was reflected in the next day's news.

"ALLIES LAND IN NORWAY AT TRONDHEIM AND NARVIK"

In the early morning hours on April 14th English, French and the leftover of Polish troops have landed in Norway.

Even in The Netherlands it was obvious that there was a war on. There were several incidents during the night when Dutch cannons were shooting at foreign planes which were flying over Dutch airspace. It was not revealed what nationality the planes were because no plane was ever shot down. Dutch anti-aircraft defences were entirely inadequate. However, since The Netherlands was neutral it didn't matter whether it were German, English or French airplanes. They were violating the neutrality of The Netherlands and the Dutch Government had ordered to shoot at all foreign airplanes. According to Leen Willemstein they were German airplanes, they just were testing where the Dutch anti-aircraft cannons were situated. He probably was right.

April 26 brought some good news and some bad news. The good news was touted as a great Allied success.

"NARVIK TAKEN BY ALLIES."

The allied forces have taken Narvik which is the all-important vital port for shipment of steel to Germany.

The bad news was on the same front page.

"ALLIES PULL OUT OF CENTRAL NORWAY."

In order to consolidate the Allied forces the Allied command has retreated its troops from Central Norway.

Behind the scenes Germany was planning strategy. Hitler had wanted to start the attack on Western Europe right away after the declaration of war. His Generals weren't in favour at all and wanted to wait till next spring. Hitler set a date eighteen times and every time he had to cancel it because of unfavorable weather. His Generals couldn't be happier; they didn't want to fight until they were good and ready.

The German ambassador in The Netherlands had been called back to Berlin and intelligence had revealed that the Germans were planning to attack The Netherlands. The night before Hitler's campaign, the Dutch Prime Minister said in spite of the anticipated attack: "There is nothing to worry about, all citizens can go to bed and sleep peacefully." The people went unworried to bed alright but...

On May 10, 1940, the Dutch, Belgian and French people had a rough awakening when Hitler unleashed the Wehrmacht on its offensive against the West. German airplanes were flying low over the houses and cannons were roaring. It was plain intimidation to fly the airplanes that low over the houses; it scared the living daylight out of the people. Adrie had seen few airplanes during his life. The days of zeppelins were barely gone and few aeroplanes were flying over The Netherlands. Passenger service by airplane was very sporadic and was only affordable by the rich. When an aeroplane came over, people would run outside to look at the plane which was flying high and was hardly visible.

There were some countries in Asia and Africa that were largely covered with jungles. The natives of those countries saw planes before they saw cars. Without highways in the jungle, cars couldn't drive and when colonists needed supplies, they had to be brought in by ship or plane. On the other hand, in The Netherlands there were all kinds of highways for motorised traffic but planes were very seldom seen.

All people were running outside when the airship Hindenburg came across The Netherlands on its way to the United States in 1937. Half a year later, the Hindenburg was apparently hit by lightning and burned. Evil tongues had it that it was sabotage against Hitler.

The Hindenburg disaster wasn't the first disaster, it was the last. Before, England had an airship disaster in which over 200 people were killed. The airships were filled with hydrogen which is very flammable. When they started out they filled them with helium but helium was six times more expensive than hydrogen so they went cheap.

When Hitler came to power in 1933 he was interested in airships but the Hindenburg disaster changed his mind, he wanted nothing to do with explosive air bags and favored aeroplanes. An airship was just too clumsy; it took 200 men to bring an airship in.

This time, the Dutch people could have a good look at aeroplanes. It looked as if the planes would knock the chimney off the house when they were flying that low. To Adrie an aeroplane looked more like a big cigar with a piece of two by four across at the front, which were the wings. This sure was quite different of what he had seen before when they were staring at a high flying aeroplane. Adrie got quite excited and shouted to his sister Willie: "I can shake hands with the pilot."

Mrs. Immerzeel, who had her two sons in the Dutch army, started to scream at him: "This is no laughing matter, you should be ashamed of yourself to have that much fun, a lot of innocent people are getting killed today and you think this is fun?"

"What's the matter with her?" Adrie asked his mother.

"She is thinking about her two sons who are fighting in the army and could get killed," his mother explained.

Adrie thought it better to walk away from her and walked across the street where Piet Brouwer told everybody that The Netherlands was at war with Germany. Where was old Leen Willemstein who usually told everybody about this war?

It took a while before old Leen Willemstein surfaced. He hadn't been sleeping on the job; he had listened to the radio for some time to get more information. He said: "We are attacked by Germany and the Dutch Government has asked England and France to help us. The Government has also suggested we fill all containers with water because water could be in short supply if bombing or shelling starts. There is also the possibility of pollution of the water supply if too many corpses are floating in the rivers."

That Adrie had to tell his mother so she could fill all pots and pans with water. When his mother opened the water tap there was only a trickle of water coming out of the tap, it could take hours to get a pail of water. It seemed that the entire population had heeded the warning of the Government. Of course when everybody turns on the water tap at the same time the water pressure drops drastically.

The poor people who didn't have a radio were the last ones to know about filling containers with water. It really hurts when you are poor because much needed instructions can come too late. One thing worked favorably though and poverty became a bliss as well. Because of the Depression, Adrie's father had bought a rain barrel in order to save on the water bill. It rains a lot in The Netherlands and the barrel was almost full. Rich people would never dream about having a rain barrel but with the possibility of no water supply they wished they had one. To add to the water supply there was even a pail of water from the tap after a couple of hours. His mother put another pail underneath the tap which had slowed down from a trickle to fast dripping.

Thus water rationing was in order, and the pail of potable water his mother got from the dripping water tap and the water from the rain barrel were strictly for drinking purposes. All other water needed, including water for the laundry, had to come from the ditch. With sewers running into the ditch that water wasn't potable at all.

People who had a radio were listening for news bulletins from the Dutch Government and as soon as there was some news they would head for the street to tell everybody about it. However, there were quite a few conflicting reports from unreliable sources. One guy was saying that English and French troops had joined the Dutch army to fight the Germans. That would have been nice but unfortunately, the English and the French had trouble enough of their own. Other reports were that at the Grebbe and Peel Lines the fighting had been so severe that the hospitals were already full of wounded soldiers. The hospitals had run out of bandages to dress the wounded soldiers and had taken bed sheets from stores to dress the wounds. The rivers were full of floating corpses and cholera and typhus outbreaks were possible. A warning was issued by the Government to boil the water from the taps for five minutes at least before drinking it.

A confirmed report was that the Germans had taken the bridge at Gennep with the German Brandenburg Detachment, which was specially trained for that sort of mission. In the early morning hours, the Dutch post guarding the bridge saw a patrol of Dutch uniformed soldiers escorting a handful of German deserters, he thought. When they reached the bridge they opened fire and captured the bridge.

The Dutch army instituted a password right away to detect German soldiers in Dutch uniforms, who were dropped from the air for special missions. 'Scheveningen' was the password which is a Dutch city. Even if the Germans knew that password it wouldn't do them any good because they couldn't pronounce it properly. In Dutch the word is pronounced with a gurgling G sound which a German can't imitate. In critical situations when the password was asked and not given or not properly pronounced, the soldiers in Dutch uniform were shot at point blank range. According to the Geneva convention, 'A soldier in his own uniform, of the country he fights for, has to be taken prisoner of war but a soldier in civilian clothes or in a uniform of another country can be shot without trial.'

There Must Be Something We Can Do.

Across the street from the de Kievits lived a couple, Neel and Ver Echthuizen. They thought they were better than other people and pretended that the de Kievits didn't exist. Neel and Ver never talked to the de Kievits, it seemed below their dignity to talk to poor unemployed people.

Ko said: "Those people walk beside their shoes of cockiness and they think that their shit doesn't stink."

That was just about to change. War changed a lot of things; it changed especially the attitude of people. When there is a lot of trouble, people are more together and they need each other, even if it's just to talk about it. Neel knew that the de Kievits had no radio and had to hear the news from other people. Just before the regular news broadcast, she came over to ask them to come to their home to listen to the news. Arie said: "It looks like the natives are getting friendly. Let's take them up on their offer."

There was the news about the bridge at Gennep which was now in German hands. On the other hand there was some good news that the Venlo and Roermond bridges had been blown up to stop the German armies. The Germans had tried to take those bridges like the Venlo bridge to prevent the Dutch from blowing them up. This time the trick didn't work and when they couldn't deliver the password they were shot automatically and the Dutch blew up the bridges.

Special instructions from the Government followed the news. All wild animals in the zoo of Rotterdam had to be killed. With bombardments, dangerous wild animals like lions and tigers could escape and would be roaming the city in search of food.

Adrie had never thought to be confronted with a lion or tiger which might consider him to be the next meal. He could see that this precaution was necessary. All poisonous snakes, crocodiles, bears, wolves and other dangerous animals had to go too.

Since nobody went to work and didn't make money, there was also an order from the Dutch Government that all stores had to give credit to everybody. People needed supplies even with a war on. The Dutch Government would be responsible for the credit and would figure it all out as soon as normal conditions were restored.

A message from the Government that all schools were closed until further notice was the best news Adrie heard. He didn't hate school, there was no reason for that; he was a good student and was eager to learn things. On the other hand he didn't see the school as a blessing either.

Churches remained open for the people who wanted to pray for victory. The Reverend did just that, he prayed: "Oh Lord, Father in Heaven, let our troops be successful in battling the Nazis who have invaded our beloved fatherland. The Germans have better weapons than our soldiers and they are much stronger but that doesn't matter. Please give our weak troops victory over the Germans as you gave victory to David over Goliath."

A special message was broadcast in which the Dutch Army was praised for a great success. During the early morning hours, The Hague, the home city of Queen Wilhelmina and the seat of the Dutch Government, had been attacked. The German 22nd airborne division had taken the two airfields around The Hague and German troops had been dropped at the palace grounds of the Queen. A surprised Dutch Army had quickly recuperated; they had killed the Germans on the palace grounds and had retaken the Dutch airports.

General Graf von Sponeck, the German commander was seriously wounded. He had been dropped by the Germans, in his full uniform, for the purpose of asking for an audience with Queen Wilhelmina. Sponeck was going to ask for surrender and cooperation of The Netherlands. The 22nd airborne division was almost wiped out and over a thousand German prisoners had been shipped to England by the seaport Ymuiden. In view of the dangerous situation, Queen Wilhelmina had been advised to leave for England for security reasons. Ver Echthuizen remarked: "There goes the Queen for security reasons. Why can't I go to England for security reasons?"

Unfortunately there was some real bad news for the people of Rotterdam. The 7th German airborne division had taken Waalhaven airport of Rotterdam. A counter attack was prepared by the Dutch army in which they were going to try to recapture the airport.

Important news from England revealed that the English Government was in deep trouble. On the very day that Hitler unleashed the Wehrmacht on its offensive against the West, Chamberlain; the British Prime Minister was ousted and Winston Churchill took over the British Government. In his inauguration speech Churchill said: "I can promise you nothing but sweat, blood and tears but we shall fight the Germans on the beaches, we shall fight them in the air, at sea and in our cities till victory has been obtained."

After the news broadcast was over Adrie sauntered into the street to see if he could get any wiser. One thing he didn't understand, there were Dutch soldiers in the street who were just observing the low flying aeroplanes. They had a rifle on their back so why didn't they shoot the planes down? Adrie walked up to a Dutch soldier and said: "Why don't you do something?"

The soldier asked: "What do you think I should do?"

"Shoot down those damned German planes." Adrie replied.

"With an ordinary rifle it's hard to hit a fast moving aeroplane," the soldier explained. "Even if I would hit it, the damage would be minimal and not get the plane down."

"That's bologna, you have to shoot at the fuel tank," Adrie said disturbed. "If you hit the fuel tank the plane will come down."

The soldier didn't seem to be disturbed about a little boy who knew it better than him and replied: "I'll tell my commander what you are suggesting," and he walked away.

Adrie was furious about an attitude like that, he said: "There must be something we can do, you can't just stand there and let them get away with it!"

From the Schiphol Airport, the Dutch Air Force had taken to the air and was trying to do what Adrie had suggested to the soldier. It became a dog fight between Dutch and German fighters. Most of the bombers were accompanied by fighters and as soon as Dutch fighters came to attack the bombers, the German fighters would attack the Dutch fighters. That way, the bombers could proceed and bomb their targets while the fighters fought it out.

Everybody was watching the fight. A Dutch plane came out of a cloud unexpectedly and shot a German plane down. The German airplane went in a tailspin leaving a smoke plume behind and when the plane hit the ground there was a loud explosion. People applauded the Dutch pilot who had done that. Unaware of his applauding audience, the Dutch pilot made a loop to attack another German fighter. This time the pilot wasn't as lucky and his plane went down. There was no parachute which made the Dutch people very quiet. They realized that there was another dead Dutch pilot.

Adrie kept score; he was counting the Dutch and German planes which were shot down. According to his eye witness report, he came to the conclusion that the war didn't go good at all as there were more Dutch planes shot down than German.

It Takes a War to Get Peace
with Thy Neighbor.

Arie said: "The Dutch army is digging in to fight the Germans. We might as well dig in too. I'm going to make a bomb shelter to protect my family."

Adrie was all in favour of it and was going to help. His father said that the shelter had to be far enough away from the house; in case the house got hit it shouldn't fall on top of the shelter. That made sense; Adrie thought and helped his father dig a hole in the ground. The hole couldn't be dug very deep because groundwater levels are not very deep in The Netherlands. When the groundwater entered the hole they had to stop digging. His father said: "We'll put boards on the floor so we don't get wet feet."

The remainder of the necessary height for the shelter had to be obtained by erecting low walls from old lumber. During the Depression Adrie's father had built a hen house to secure an egg supply. It had been built from the wood of an old barn and there was lots of wood left. There were lots of solid posts to make sturdy walls and the roof was made out of heavy lumber. It had to be all heavy lumber that could carry the load of ground that had to be thrown on top of the roof for protection.

Purposely there was no door made in the shelter. In case of a direct hit the door shouldn't block the entrance. Instead there was an old blanket that would catch the shrapnel of bombs and shells. That was the best way to close off the entrance to the shelter, Arie said. The shelter was built with an angle entrance to enable everybody to sit without being hit by flying shrapnel, in case the old blanket failed. You had to bend to get into the shelter and couldn't stand straight up, which was alright, they weren't planning to stand up in the shelter anyway.

There was also a bench with enough room to seat all four of the family. Furthermore, food and water were brought into the shelter and extra clothes and blankets, just in case the stay in the shelter was for a prolonged time. Everybody of the family participated in the building and supply of the shelter. Willie, Adrie's sister, came with an oil lamp, candles and matches, just in case they had to dig out in the dark. An old pail with a lid on it had to serve as toilet whenever needed. Everybody had ideas and contributed to building a good shelter.

Building of the shelter had barely started when a curious neighbor Kees Meuzelaar came to see what their neighbors were doing. They were always watching their neighbors and nothing escaped their spying eyes. Arie said: "We are building a bomb shelter because we could be bombed or shelled."

Kees Meuzelaar replied: "That's a great idea, I'm going to make a shelter as well, you are so right that we could be bombed or shelled."

Ko had heard that conversation too and said: "That's a change of attitude, we never have been right before, it shows you that a war can make strange bed fellows."

Adrie and his father were way ahead of the Meuzelaars. When their shelter was ready for use, Kees Meuzelaar and his wife Klazien with their son Kees came to inspect it. They were sitting in the shelter for a while to look it over. Kees Meuzelaar said: "That's a very good shelter; we will build it the same way with an angular entrance."

For the next few hours everybody seemed busy and when the Meuzelaars were finished, Kees Meuzelaar threw some manure with straw on top of the shelter. He put even his pitchfork on top of the shelter and said: "When planes are flying over they can't see that it is a shelter, they'll think that it's a manure pit."

Arie said to Kees Meuzelaar: "I put a shovel and a spade in the shelter, just in case we are hit, we can dig ourselves out."

"That's another good idea; I will put a shovel and a spade in our shelter as well. But in case that your shelter or ours gets hit, we should help one another to dig each other out and help to dress wounds or get medical help if possible."

Arie took the olive branch which was handed to him and said, it was a deal. Arie and Ko were discussing the change of attitude of the Meuzelaars. Ko said: "All of a sudden they realize that they are alone and that they might need their neighbors for help."

"There is an ancient Dutch proverb that says: 'A good neighbor is better than a far friend,'" Arie remarked. "Of course if you have a mad neighbor you can't expect help when you need it. It is remarkable that it takes a war to get peace with your neighbors. Make that, it takes a world war to get peace with thy neighbors. At least the war is good for something."

At night, everybody was awaiting the news broadcast more than ten minutes before the scheduled time. Nobody was going to miss a word. Everybody figured to hear good news such as that the English and French army were running the Germans out of their country. Unfortunately, the news wasn't good at all; the news reporter said that the Moerdyk bridges had fallen into German hands without being blown up. The German 6th Airborne Division had the task to take the bridges and hold them until the German 9th Panzer Division had advanced enough to cross the bridges without delay.

The bridges had been undermined with explosives. However, there was an N.S.B. party in The Netherlands which was all in favor of the Nazis in Germany. Eight percent of the Dutch people were in favor of the Nazis, according to the way the people had voted in the last elections. The letters N.S.B. stand for National Socialist Beweging. (National Socialist Movement.) Members of the N.S.B. Party had even infiltrated the Dutch army and had removed the charges. The German Pantzer Division was successful in advancing fast because of the Gennep Bridge which was taken by the Brandenburg Detachment. The road to Shertogenbos was open to the Germans and they moved rapidly to the Moerdyk Bridges which were held by the German airborne troops.

Plenty of rumors surface fast with a war on the go, everybody is confused and when news goes from mouth to mouth the story changes. It was Whitsunday but not the Whitsunday people had hoped for. There was a rumor that French troops were marching towards The Netherlands to help the Dutch army fight the Germans. People were waiting in the streets to welcome them. Unfortunately, no French troops were sighted and the real news was far from good. The German Panzer Division had joined up with the German airborne troops which were holding the Moerdyk Bridges. The panzer division had crossed the Moerdyk Bridge and was on its way to Dordrecht. Dordrecht was a city 30 kilometres from Rotterdam and with the Panzer division fast approaching; fighting could be expected real soon.

If the Germans took Dordrecht, the next German move would be to move up with artillery to Dordrecht and shell Rotterdam. Four years back, the de Kievits were living in a one horse town called Yselmonde, just under the smoke of Rotterdam. The fast expanding city of Rotterdam gobbled up quite a few towns around and after being annexed, those insignificant towns were suddenly a world city. In spite of that, Yselmonde was still rural which would change in the years to come. For the time being there were quite a few farms around and Yselmonde had absolutely no military value to the Germans whatsoever. Even the two Dutch soldiers parading with their rifles on their back on the Hordyk didn't scare the Germans at all. Yet, if the Germans were going to shell Rotterdam, Yselmonde would be direct in the firing line of the German artillery, which could be a problem. The Meuzelaars and the de Kievits were glad to have a shelter they could withdraw in if all hell would break loose.

Shelling of Rotterdam could be expected on Monday May 13th. For the time being everybody was sitting tight. May 13th went by without the expected shelling and news had become scarce. At night everybody was glued to the radio when the news bulletin was broadcast. The news bulletin was far from encouraging. German Stukas had attacked the Navy Wharf De Helder and people around had been evacuated. The Dutch Army and Navy had everything under control. For safety's sake Queen Wilhelmina and the Princesses had evacuated the palace and had left for England. Leen Willemstein said: "Even though the Dutch Army and Navy have everything under control, the rats have left the sinking ship." And he meant the Royal family.

On Tuesday May 14th the situation deteriorated by the minute. An appeal to Britain for help had produced no results. They were trying desperately to get ready for their own defence. France had been asked for help as well but they were also attacked by the Germans and had enough problems of their own. The Netherlands had to go it alone to fight the Germans and the war became hopeless.

A City Without a Heart.

It was May 14, 1940, the war was in its fourth day and Hitler wanted a fast surrender. Germany demanded the surrender of Rotterdam before 2.00 p.m. or the city would be bombed at 4.00 p.m. In the centre of the city people became very nervous. They had seen pictures in the newspaper when the Germans had bombed Warsaw in Poland and feared the worst. The Government was going to have a meeting with the Dutch commander and the Mayor of Rotterdam to discuss the ultimatum and the serious situation. Because of the expected bombing, the prisoners had been released and were told to go home. There was no transportation with the war on the go. Only the ones who were living close to jail could get home.

The de Kievits were discussing the news with their now friendly neighbors and decided to put more food and water in the shelters. It looked that the suburbs of Rotterdam would become a major battlefield and heavy fighting, shelling and bombing could force the civilian population into their shelters for some time to come. Nobody could even guess how long the battle would last and where it would take place but nobody took any chances.

When two o' clock came it hadn't been confirmed that Rotterdam had surrendered. Conflicting reports came in. One report said that Rotterdam had surrendered and the next report said that it had not surrendered. What to believe? At 4.00 p.m. two squadrons of German bombers flew over towards the centre of Rotterdam. Everybody drew the conclusion that Rotterdam hadn't surrendered and was now being bombed to force the surrender.

In a special news bulletin it was confirmed that the centre of Rotterdam had been bombed and that there was extensive damage. At night when it was already dark, Neel Echthuizen came to tell the de Kievits that Rotterdam was burning. She said: "From the back of our house it is very good visible, if you people want to come over to see it, you are welcome to come to our place."

It seemed that everybody was watching the burning city. All people were remarkable quiet when they were watching this terrible sight. 'What would be next?' was the question on everybody's mind. Everybody hated the Germans already for doing all those terrible things to innocent and defenceless people. The entire horizon was blood red from the fire and flames could be seen shooting high into the sky.

Nobody slept very much that night and everybody wondered if more bombing raids would come. Everybody had heard the rumors that the English army had moved in to help the Dutch army in their fight against Germany. The fears were realized but the hopes were not. On Wednesday May 15, Neel Echthuizen hopped over to the de Kievits to tell them that there would be a special news bulletin from General Winkelman at 10.00 a.m. "If you want to come and listen you are welcome," she invited.

Everybody circled around the radio when the broadcaster announced: "The Commander of all Dutch Forces General Winkelman will now address all Dutch citizens. Here is General Winkelman!"

The silence became heavy in the room when General Winkelman announced: "Citizens of The Netherlands, as commander of all Dutch armed forces and being in charge of the defence of The Netherlands, I have grave news for you. Yesterday at 4.00 p.m., the German Luftwaffe bombed and destroyed the centre of Rotterdam with fire bombs. Over 25,000 houses were destroyed, rendering 78,000 people homeless. There were 35,000 people killed in this horror raid. In view of this immense suffering of the civil population of The Netherlands, I had no alternative but capitulate to Germany. With a deep sense of regret and great disappointment, I have signed the document of surrender at 9.30 a.m. this morning. I know that this is a great disappointment to all Dutch citizens but our army is no match against the superior German forces. Our forces have been fighting bravely while they were outnumbered by the German army. Total losses during this five day war are 2,100 killed and 2,700 wounded. My sympathy goes out to the families who have lost a dear one in this terrible war. I am very proud to have been a commander of such a brave Dutch fighting force and thank all of the members who participated. May God be with all of you."

It took a while before anybody spoke a word, after listening to this terrible news. Finally, Ver Echthuizen said: "This war can't last long, look how they destroyed Rotterdam, if this war lasts longer than a year there will be no stone left on top of one another. All cities will be in ruins and most people will be dead. For the time being, we are going to be occupied by Germany and can expect to meet the German soldiers any minute now."

Adrie walked back home with his parents and wondered if they would be enslaved by the Germans. From history he had learned that the victor of a war made slaves out of the defeated nation. The future had never looked that dark before. Even the Bible had a story about the defeat of the Israel army. They were driven to the land of their enemy with bare buttocks. "Luckily it was summer" Adrie thought, "If I have to walk in my bare ass to Germany, at least I won't freeze my balls."

He did a lot of thinking about the defeat of The Netherlands. What had happened to all the patriotic songs they were singing at school? One was about the lion in the Dutch weapon that didn't take shit from anybody and would help to fight the enemy. The enemy wouldn't get our land, we would never give it. Well, the Dutch people didn't give their country to the Germans, they just took it.

The water barrier which had served The Netherlands so well during the First World War hadn't been a barrier at all. Hitler surprised the Dutch with the first airborne assault in history. German airborne divisions were dropped behind this barrier. As soon as the Germans had taken airports with their airborne troops they landed transport planes. Motor bikes with side carriers were unloaded; two Germans jumped on the motor bike and set up German posts with machine guns at all strategic points. The Netherlands didn't have a single tank and the German tank divisions, with support of the Luftwaffe, were no match for the Dutch.

Everything had gone right for the Germans; the powerful Dutch Navy was guarding the Dutch Indies and the Dutch Air Force was outnumbered ten to one. In two days time the Dutch Air Force had been wiped out and after five days of fierce but futile resistance The Netherlands capitulated. The firebombing of Rotterdam which destroyed the centre of Rotterdam sealed The Netherlands' fate. The Netherlands had been defeated in and from the air.

Ver Echthuizen said that he had listened to the Dutch broadcast. They stated that Rotterdam had surrendered at 2.00 p.m. long before the deadline and that at 4.00 p.m. the Germans had destroyed the centre of Rotterdam. General Winkelman couldn't see that he could defend Rotterdam without having it destroyed by the Germans. He surrendered Rotterdam to prevent needless suffering of the civilian population.

The Germans apologized for destroying Rotterdam after it had surrendered. They had a lame excuse that they had tried desperately to call off the Luftwaffe. Unfortunately they couldn't get a hold of Air Command because of the war going on. Ver Echthuizen said: "Those rotten moffs, (A very unpopular name for Germans.) it was done deliberately so that The Netherlands would capitulate. They wanted to show General Winkelman what would happen to all the Dutch cities if they didn't surrender. And by golly it worked for them." Everybody agreed that it was a dirty trick; however, The Netherlands would have lost the war anyway.

The centre of Rotterdam had been destroyed by in cinerary bombs; it included the shopping districts with department stores, restaurants, cinemas, living quarters and City Jail. City Hall and the St. Laurence Cathedral were spared burning; they were built from solid rocks that didn't burn. With the centre of Rotterdam gone it became the heartless city.

(The first victim of the war is always the truth; already before the war starts facts are distorted. According to Radio London 35,000 Dutch civilians had died in the bombardment of Rotterdam. This was grossly overstated for propaganda's sake. England wanted to publish the brutality of the Germans and when there are 35,000 innocent people killed it sounds better than when you say there were 900 people killed which was the actual figure.)

At 4.00 p.m. on May 15th the first Germans arrived in Rotterdam. Henk Sturfs lived a few houses from Adrie and was a boy in Adrie's class at school. He came by and shouted at Adrie: "I have seen a moff."

His father who had been standing in the door opening heard that and came running up to him. He gave his son a poke in the ribs and told him to shut up and go home, unless he wanted to be shot by the Germans.

Adrie didn't know what a moff was and neither did he understand why Henk Sturf's father got mad. Adrie's mother explained that Germans are called moffs which is a bad name. It is similar to calling an American a Yankee. Nobody knew what to expect from the Germans but Henk's father figured that the Germans wouldn't be amused if they heard that they were called by their unpopular name.

It didn't take long for Adrie to see a moff as well; it was a German soldier with a pamphlet from his commander. The German commander of Rotterdam had some of his soldiers gluing bulletins on lamp posts and other obvious places. Half of the bulletin was in German and the other half was in Dutch. The German Commander announced:

Citizens of Rotterdam.

As the German commander of the city of Rotterdam, I like you to be calm and collected. The German army had no alternative but occupy The Netherlands. It was necessary to protect The Netherlands from the English and

French armies which were planning to occupy The Netherlands. Everything is under control and within a few days everything will go back to normal. The food supply is ample and there is no need to worry.

I expect every one of you to cooperate with the German occupation force which is in need of housing. Billeting of German soldiers will take place. Every Dutch citizen who has room is expected to put up some German soldiers. It is not necessary to feed the German soldiers as they have their own field kitchen.

German soldiers are well disciplined and citizens needn't fear them. Be nice to them and they will be nice to you. The German occupation of The Netherlands can be a good time for both parties involved.

From time to time new bulletins of orders will be issued and I expect that all Dutch citizens will obey my orders.

Your commander
P.P. Opperheimer.

Some of the teenagers wanted to tear the German bulletins off the poles. The older people prevented them, they said: "Let it be, if the Germans see you tearing up the bulletins you could be shot." There was also the commentary of the people such as: "This A hole of a commander says that everything is under control, I bet you if it wasn't under control he wouldn't tell us about it."

On May 16th, the day after the capitulation, the German Army moved in. They came fully motorized and with tanks. There was even a printing press which printed Dutch guilders. They had thought of everything. Now the German Army could buy anything that was for sale, including sex, with a piece of paper.

In the afternoon billeting of German soldiers started; everybody got inspection of his house to see if there was room to keep some German soldiers. A German soldier was accompanied by a Dutch citizen who acted as interpreter. Poor people like the de Kievits and Meuzelaars had only a small house. There was no problem to convince the inspectors that there was no room for German soldiers. The rich people who had a bigger house were so lucky to billet two soldiers most of the time.

At night German platoons marched through the street. They stopped at all addresses of the people who had been told that they had room enough to house German soldiers. The fieldwebel (German sergeant) shouted the names of the soldiers who had to stay at that address. The indicated soldiers left the platoon and entered the house.

Actually, the German soldiers were no problem, they were only in their room during the night and during the day they had duties to fulfil. There was a language barrier though. One of the German soldiers had to go to the bathroom but the bathroom was upstairs in the house. When he couldn't find the bathroom and the people didn't understand him, he turned his butt to the people, pointed with his finger to his bum and said: "Poop, poop!" That kind of language everybody understands and soon he could relieve himself.

On Friday May 17th, there was another bulletin with orders from the German commander. He ordered that everybody had to return to work and that the schools had to open on Monday. That didn't make him popular with the school kids who had been out of school for two weeks. *(This story had actually a very happy ending. The friendship between the Meuzelaars and the de Kievits lasted not only during the war. After the war the young Kees became a very good friend of Adrie who went every Sunday morning for coffee and a talk with the Meuzelaars. The city of Rotterdam was fast expanding and a lot of agricultural land was taken to build houses. The Meuzelaars were forced to give up their land on which they had been growing vegetables. They lost their livelihood and moved to Gorkum, a smaller city about 30 miles from Rotterdam. Old Kees retired and young Kees found a job with the city's park division. Willie (Adrie's sister) moved to Zevenbergen with her husband which was about 40 miles from Rotterdam. Adrie moved away the farthest of all, he went to Canada. Nobody was run out of town by terrible neighbors, everybody left voluntarily. Willie went often to see their old neighbors and Adrie visited them always, whenever he came to The Netherlands for a visit.)*

The Mother of the Fatherland.

At night Neel Echthuizen came to tell the Kievits that there was a news broadcast from Radio London at 7.00 p.m. and the news was going to be in Dutch. Before the war started the de Kievits never came inside the house of the Echthuizens, now they were there every day. All of a sudden people felt closer and also knew that they needed one another. Ko remarked: "It's amazing how many friends we have acquired since the war started. Even those terrible Meuzelaars are actually very nice people when you have them on your side."

"Yes it's really silly of people to fight about little insignificant things," Arie replied. "It's so much nicer when you are friends."

Everybody in The Netherlands thought that the English and French armies were going to defeat the Germans in the next week or so and that they would drive the Germans out of The Netherlands. However, the news broadcast from London brought little hope to the Dutch citizens. According to Radio London, a critical battle was fought in France at the Meuse River. Nine German panzer divisions were pitched against eleven French divisions. The Germans were better equipped and superior in fighting compared to the French. The German Army had broken through the French lines at Sedan and the French Army was in retreat to consolidate their positions.

Worse news came from Belgium. A reinforced Belgian Army with English troops had lost a critical battle. Brussels, the Belgian capital, and Antwerp had surrendered to the Germans. King Leopold of Belgium had said: "I will fight to the last man and will not leave my country; I will die with my people."

Queen Wilhelmina and most of the members of the Dutch Government had left The Netherlands and here was a king who stayed with his people. This was impressive to the Dutch citizens who felt kind of deserted by the Royal family and the Government.

At the end of the news bulletin there was a speech from Queen Wilhelmina who addressed her beloved citizens from a safe place in London. The announcer said: "And here is Queen Wilhelmina, the Mother of the Fatherland."

Queen Wilhelmina said: "My beloved Dutch citizens. With deep regret in my heart, I had to flee The Netherlands to escape our enemy so that I could continue to fight against tyranny from England. The Dutch Government in exile will fight the German invaders until they are defeated and driven out of our country. In those trying times I think about my people in The Netherlands all the time and live with you dear people who now live under oppressive conditions. May God bless us in our efforts to succeed in our fight against oppression and injustices."

Most people didn't buy the speech of the Queen and Ver Echthuizen said: "This Mother of the Fatherland can talk very nice while she has her ass safely in England and we are here under the Germans to be shot for all we know. I have a lot more respect for King Leopold who stays with his people."

Adrie had to think about this for a while; he had been taught at school that the people of The Netherlands were lucky to have a Queen like Queen Wilhelmina. The Queen was the best thing that had happened to The Netherlands. Willem of Orange had helped the Dutch citizens in an eighty year war against Spain and the thankful Dutch people let him run the country. In 1813 The Netherlands had become a kingdom and the Dutch rulers were Kings and Queens. However, a Queen who leaves her country and lets the Dutch citizens alone is not much of a Queen, Adrie thought and he sided with Ver Echthuizen.

Even the Dutch Navy saw the Queen that way. Adrie had an Uncle Henk who served in the Dutch Navy and was in Indonesia all the time. For the first time that Henk had been in the Tropics he had six weeks leave. The fifth week he was called back because of war threat. He was placed on a mine sweeper which was not much more than a soup can. It was made out of four millimeter thick steel and an old seven and a half centimeter cannon, a machine gun from the First World War and rifles for the men model 1895 were the defense.

Several reasons had caused the Dutch Army to be so ill equipped to fight a war. With the Depression in full force, successive Dutch Governments were always economizing especially on defense. There were also hordes of Socialists who were advocating not having war and were wearing buttons on their coat with a broken rifle and slogan, "Never war again!" or "Give us butter, not cannons." Of course, most of the Dutch citizens agreed with those slogans but when war came they had no modern weapons at all and were shooting with weapons from the First World War that they had retrieved from the museum.

When the war started there wasn't much they could do with their antiquated weapons against the modern weapons of the Germans. On the second day of the war, the Queen left with all the gold for safe keeping in England. It never came back. When on the fifth day of the war The Netherlands capitulated, the captain was ordered to sail back to the harbour and surrender their ship in good order to the Germans. The order was ignored; the men took all their personal belongings with them and went in the life boats. After the valves were opened the ship sank slowly but surely to the bottom of the sea. When they reached the shore they surrendered to the Germans.

When the Germans entered Amsterdam, Colonel Rost van Tonningen ordered not to shoot. A Captain shot the Colonel and ordered to shoot. Against the overwhelming German Army it was no use and they were forced to surrender. The Colonel survived and the Captain was put in a mental institution.

When the war started the Queen had addressed her military forces and had said in her speech: "Do your duty I'll do mine."

Escaping to England didn't look that she was doing her duty at all. The Mother of the Fatherland left her children behind. A Captain of a ship is the last one to leave the ship and here was the Queen, she was the first one to bail out. Navy personnel didn't think much about it and saw it as cowardice.

The Dutch Army had surrendered to the Germans and the soldiers were temporarily put into concentration camps. Dutch people who had sons or brothers in the Dutch Army were wondering if their loved ones were among the casualties of war. Travelling by train or bus hadn't been restored yet. The only way to find out was to bike to the concentration camp, in the area where the boy had been fighting, and ask to see the list of prisoners.

Immerzeel, the next door neighbor of the de Kievits had two boys in the army and the youngest boy Jan Immerzeel went by bike to get some information to find out whether the boys were dead or alive. When he finally came back, his mother jumped up to him before he could get off his bike and screamed: "Are they alive?"

When the answer was affirmative, she cried with relief. Everybody was glad for her, including Adrie, who had received a scolding when he shouted when the planes came over that low. Two weeks later, both her boys came home. The Germans were in firm control of The Netherlands and wanted all the boys to go back to work so they could make war material for the Germans.

A rumor went around that the Dutch army was unprepared for the war because the ammunition didn't fit the machine guns. All the soldiers that had returned from the war had quite some stories to tell. Adrie was listening when Leen Immerzeel told his experiences and besides listening he also had a question. Leen Immerzeel had been fighting at the Grebbe Line, he should know if the ammunition didn't fit their guns.

Leen answered: "That's plain hogwash, the war was hopeless from the beginning but the ammunition was good. We didn't have modern weapons but we shot quite a few Germans; every time that I shot a German, I carved a notch in the wooden handle of my rifle. At the end of the battle, I had seven notches in my rifle which accounted for seven dead Germans. In spite of that, the German Army was superior and we were no match to their modern equipment and well trained troops. They had a lot more planes than we did and we had hardly any flack to shoot the German planes down. That's where the Dutch Government has been wrong; they economized too much on the Army and figured that they were safe behind the inundated land."

How Does a War Start?

A little boy asked his father: "How does a war get started?" His father straightened his back to get ready for his explanation: "Suppose that England

and the United States have a disagreement and declare war."

His mother interjected: "You are a complete idiot to suggest that England and the U.S. would declare war on each other."

The father replied: "I said, suppose."

The mother said next: "I don't care what you are supposing, it's a hell of a way to educate a child with stupid supposes."

The little boy then said: "Oh, don't bother anymore I already know how a war gets started." And as usual, the little boy was right.

The chapters in different print are explanations why things happened and how. They are pure history while the book itself is the story how the de Kievits lived through the war and how the war influenced their lives.

Troubles between France and Germany go back as far as Napoleon. When Napoleon gobbled up most of Europe in less than no time, Germany wasn't in being yet. There were a lot of German independent States and Principalities which were no problem for Napoleon to overrun.

Over five million people died in the Napoleonic Wars. After the defeat of Napoleon, the German States figured that they should unite into one country and that way they would have a sizable army to keep intruders out. France was not amused at all to have such a powerful neighbour and tried to prevent that from happening.

Prussia was the largest and most powerful state of Germany that wanted to unite all of Germany in one country. Problems between Prussia and France led to war and a lot of German States joined Prussia to beat France.

France took a beating and sued for peace. Peace came at a high price, the conditions of the Peace Treaty included that France had to hand over its two best ore rich provinces, Lorrain and Alsace, to Germany.

Of course France was looking for revenge and to

take back the two best provinces it had lost. United Germany was too powerful to tackle for France by itself so they looked for an ally. That ally they found in England that was equally opposed to a powerful Germany and Russia was supporting France as well. Germany found some allies in Austria, Bulgaria and Turkey. The stage was set for an all-out war; all it needed was a spark to ignite and all hell would break loose.

The killing of the Austrian Crown Prince was the spark that set off World War I. Germany had a plan in place to get at France. After the 1870 war, France had learned a lesson when Paris was encircled by the Germans. In order to prevent that from happening again, they had built the Maginot Line between France and Germany which had to keep the Germans out.

The Germans weren't going to fight the French fortifications, they attacked Belgium and through Belgium they crossed into France. The French, Belgian border was hardly defended, France wasn't scared that Belgium would attack France and consequently the Germans met little resistance. Yet, the Germans didn't move fast enough to Paris and got involved in all out trench warfare. Actually, the Maginot Line had helped the French and Paris wasn't taken. It cost Germany the war.

Horses outnumbered machine guns in the First World War and both sides tried to come up with new weapons. When the First World War started the machine gun was the ultimate weapon; it could fire 600 rounds per minute and stop the infantry. It meant that a company had the firing power of a regiment.

The English had an answer to that, they came up with the tank which was supposed to win the war and was a weapon against the machine gun.

The Germans came up with the Zeppelin airship. Zeppelin had spent a lot of money to develop his airship in 1910 and was convinced that it would win the war for Germany. Later on, the airplane had gone from the state of invention to the state of usefulness. In the beginning it was solely used for spying but soon the planes were flying over to dump explosives on enemy troops.

The English blamed the Germans for bringing gas into the war; later on they used it themselves and even improved on it by making deadly mustard gas. One tiny molecule of mustard gas on your skin will act as a cancer and eat your skin away. The gas cape was invented to protect the skin from the deadly mustard gas.

The Battle of the Somme is well known to be the worst battle that took place during World War I. It was commanded by English General Haigh who believed that if you keep attacking, the front will waver sooner or later.

Before the attack took place he fired over 100,000 shells and figured that 99% of the Germans were dead. Unfortunately they weren't, the Germans had remained in their underground trenches and most of them had survived. As soon as the shelling stopped, the Germans came out of their underground trenches and with their machine guns they stopped the advancing army right in their tracks. More troops were employed and the corpses were piling up to the level that they were a hindrance for the storming troops that had to climb over the piles of corpses.

Many soldiers objected to the command to keep storming the German lines that didn't move. They were shot for refusing a command and their family would receive a letter from the Government: "We would like to inform you that your son has been shot because of cowardice."

You could try to survive the assault or you would be shot by your own. More than 200 Canadians and over 1000 English and Australian soldiers were shot for failing to follow up a command.

When finally at night the attack was stopped over 2,000 Canadians had died and many thousand others. A total of more than 500,000 dead were the result of the infamous Battle of the Somme. At the end a little gain of three kilometers was the result. It was questioned if the English tactics were worth it to conquer a few muddy German trenches at the cost of so many men.

Up to the beginning of 1918, the Allies didn't get anywhere; they had only conquered a few hundred meters of shell holes and had found nothing but death. That changed in August 1918 when the Germans lost an all-important battle. It was a great turnaround of the war for the Allies and a black day in German history.

This disaster was followed by the collapse of Bulgaria, Austria and Turkey, the three German partners in this war. With more and more U.S. troops coming across the Atlantic to fight the Germans, the situation became hopeless and Germany asked for an Armistice.

The Armistice ended the war but it didn't end the killing. W.W.I had a long time of repercussions after it ended. Two tons of ammunition had been dumped on France and 2000 miles of trenches had been dug in France and Belgium. For four years, day after day shells were shot, mines were laid and hand grenades were thrown. Many mine fields weren't cleared and unexploded hand grenades were left. The worst of the post war problems were the shells that had been fired for four years and had not exploded.

The warring nations had fired 20 million shells and one in eight shells hadn't exploded. When the war was finished there were still two and a half million unexploded shells on the land and in people's gardens. They kept taking their deadly toll. Every year 200 farmers and children died due to unexploded shells, mines or bombs. Tens of thousands of those shells were gas shells. For many years 10,000 calls came in per year from people who had an unexploded shell in their back yard. At the rate they are going it will take another 500 years before all the shells, mines and bombs are cleared from French soil. Long before the shells, mines and bombs were cleared World War II started.

When the war is suddenly finished what are the warring nations doing with ammunition that hasn't been used? The English dumped 30,000 ton of mustard gas into the ocean off the Nova Scotia coast.

An agreement was reached between the warring nations that all hostilities would cease at 11.11 a.m. on November 11th 1918. After the last shot of the war was fired came the difficult task to hammer out a Peace Treaty that would spell out the conditions of the Armistice.

After lengthy conferences between the major powers the Treaty was ready to be signed by Germany. As was expected, the Treaty was a revenge Treaty in which France would benefit the most. It was a 448 Article Treaty, all of them designed to hurt Germany and make it impotent to ever start a war again.

For a starter, the Treaty stated that Germany had started the war and was therefore responsible for all the damage that had been done which meant that they had to pay for it. The two provinces of Alsace and Lorraine that Germany had taken from France after the defeat of the 1870 war had to be returned to France. Moreover, Upper Silesia with its rich coal deposits and other significant areas of Germany were taken by Poland, Belgium and Denmark. The total loss for Germany was 12% of its agricultural production, 10% of its manufacturing and 75% of its iron ores.

Germany had also to deliver 25 million tons of coal to the Allies for compensation and the Saar was given to France for 15 years to exploit. All German colonies in Africa were lost and Germany had to pay $3 billion each year for 35 years. Since England had lost quite a number of merchant ships due to German submarines torpedoing them, those had to be replaced by Germany and England took most of the German merchant ships they possessed.

To make it impossible for Germany to have military ambitions in the future they were restricted to a very small army of 100,000 troops for home security and a small navy of 36 war ships not larger than

30,000 tons. Germany wasn't allowed to have any war planes, tanks or submarines.

In case the conditions of the Treaty weren't kept, the Allies had the right to occupy the Rhine Land. That would fix Germany's wagon for good the Allies figured. The Treaty was a horror for Germany but they had lost the war and had no choice. If they didn't sign it, Allied troops would move into Germany which would be worse.

With all the loss of land Germany had sustained, Germany had a hard time to make the repair payments. On three occasions when the payments weren't made, French and Belgian forces occupied the Ruhr to enforce payment. At one time they stayed for over a year.

Consequently, Germany ran into hard economic times because of the high international payments they had to make. The German Bank had to print more and more money which wasn't backed up by anything. There was severe pressure on the German Mark until it finally collapsed in 1923 when it dropped to 160,000 for one Dollar.

The Mark kept falling until it was so inflated that it took 4200 billion Marks to buy one Dollar. It took one billion Marks to buy a loaf of bread and 300 billion Marks were needed to buy one pound of apples. Bank notes were printed over before they could be put into circulation, they were worth nothing.

In less than one year the middle class was totally wiped out and Germany was completely bankrupt. Only people who had invested in real estate did alright. The losers were the ones that had sold their real estate holdings before inflation started. People who had to divide an inheritance which included the house of their parents had to sell it so the estate could be divided. They ended up with nothing except worthless marks. Germany couldn't make any more repair payments and the Allies re-negotiated the Treaty. Germany paid only $36 billion of the $105 billion they were supposed to pay.

The Treaty was signed but it created the seeds that were sown for another war. It was right there and then that the Germans vowed that this would never happen again. In case there was going to be another war, they would fight to the bitter end instead of being humiliated with a Treaty that kept Germany poor.

This other war was in the making right after the Treaty was signed. Losing a war is a disaster; you don't only lose the war, you are also expected to pay for it. In Berlin, the German Government didn't know they were beaten and started to work on revenge right away. Insult, humiliation and discontent made Germany act right away in spite of the fact that they weren't in any shape at all.

The token military force of 100,000 men that Germany was allowed according to the Treaty was commanded by Hans von Seeckt, a great unknown to the Allies. That's how the Allies got fooled, Hans von Seeckt didn't show it, but in reality he was a real militarist who regarded losing World War I as an unfortunate accident. His belief was that there would be a few World Wars but Germany was supreme and was going to win in the end.

Consequently, he started to rebuild Germany's Army to make it possible for Germany to fight the next war and win. Long before the world had heard about Adolf Hitler, Von Seeckt was rebuilding Germany as a military power.

During World War I, Germany had helped Lenin to return from Switzerland to Russia to start a revolution. Lenin had been successful and was ruling Russia which made it payback time. Von Seeckt made a secret deal with Lenin to help him to get ready for the next war. He believed that the Air Force was going to play a significant role in the next war and started a secret Military Air Force in Russia. He even had a Junker aircraft factory near Moscow and new German designed aircraft were built and tested in Russia.

Hundreds of German airmen were trained in the

1920's. Whenever young airmen were killed in training accidents they were shipped back to their family in Germany in crates stamped 'Machinery Spare Parts.' Even the Civil Air Line Lufthansa was involved in training military pilots for the Luftwaffe. They trained a lot more pilots than they needed and the surplus pilots were destined for the Luftwaffe.

Moreover, several ammunition plants were erected in Russia and even Krupp had a large manufacturing plant in Russia to make heavy war material. Von Seeckt had already a War Department in place as early as 1920, it was known as the Department of Veteran Pensions. In reality they were collecting information from all over the world and were studying the potential of Germany in the next war.

With the runaway inflation that took place in 1923 in Germany, the country became a chaos. All kinds of new political parties were started which made the German Government plenty worried. They ordered Adolf Hitler to spy on the National Socialist Party to see if they were plotting for an insurrection. The German Government sure picked the wrong guy for that job, when Hitler attended one of the meetings he was so impressed that he became a member himself.

It didn't take Hitler long to become the leader of the National Socialist Party and in 1923 he tried an insurrection. This attempt was a total disaster as Germany was still too prosperous and wasn't ready for National Socialism. The insurrection was doused in a hail of bullets in which 16 prominent Nazis were killed. Hitler himself was wounded and was jailed. It was a miracle that he survived, the world could have done away with Hitler but miraculously he escaped death again.

During World War I he was seriously wounded twice but he survived. When he was fighting in the Battle of the Somme in 1916, he was hit by a piece of shrapnel that hit his penis and surrounding areas. He lost one testicle and was hospitalized for half a year before he could piss against a tree again.

The story went that Hitler had lost his penis and they had given him a silver penis. This was not true at all, he only lost one testicle.

In October 1918 just before the end of the war, Hitler was hit in the eyes in an English gas attack. His eyes were burning and turned into glowing coals. When he was hospitalized he had no idea if he would recover. For the second time he brushed death to the side which made him boast that His Almighty had saved him to lead the German people.

During the early years of the Depression when Von Seeckt met Adolf Hitler, he was impressed and figured that Hitler could be the very man to lead Germany in a victorious Second World War.

In the aftermath of Germany's run-away inflation Hitler had gained some support from the German voters. Then Hitler had an unsuspected present when the Depression started. Hundreds of thousands of Germans became unemployed and were dumped into poverty. They were willing to listen to this Bohemian Corporal who said that he had a solution to Germany's problems.

Hitler took advantage of the post war chaos and played his cards right. So far he had accomplished very little, nobody was interested in what he had to say and few people had ever heard about him. Once the world got in turmoil, more and more people were listening to him. He was a great orator who could speak to the mass and impressed rich and poor alike. More and more people voted for him and he gained momentum. In 1933 he became Germany's Reich Chancellor. Never in the field of human history was so much owed by a Bohemian Corporal for doing so little.

When Hitler came to power, he surprised the Allies with a Military Air Force second to none in the entire world. Even the R.A.F. ranked second to Hitler's Luftwaffe. Hitler had 20 squadrons of military airplanes with well-trained crews plus a great military force.

At this stage, the Allies could have stepped in to stop Hitler by occupying Germany. Instead they did nothing and believed that Hitler was an honorable man who wanted only peace and prosperity for Germany. After Hitler had added Austria to Germany to make it the Greater Germany, which was contrary to the Treaty of Versailles, Hitler tore up the Treaty and prepared for war.

Although Hitler was supposed to be a peaceful honourable man, he took the Sudetenland and attacked Poland. England and France weren't ready at all for a war but gave Germany an ultimatum to withdraw their troops from Poland or war would be declared. As soon as the ultimatum ended, England and France declared war. The opening act of the Second World War was when Germany attacked Poland.

Up to May 1939, five months before war started, England had only five divisions to defend the Homeland and 13 divisions to defend its world-wide possessions. Those divisions were all volunteers but with the threat of war England introduced conscription three months before the war started. It was too little too late; it takes considerable time before you have troops well trained to participate effectively in a war.

After the fall of Poland 'Everything was quiet on the Western Front' so it seemed. Neither the Germans nor the Allies seemed to be interested in making the first move. The Allies were in no position to make any move at all and Hitler was anxious to get started with his great offensive. His Generals wanted to wait till spring when the weather would be better for full scale warfare but Hitler wasn't willing to wait that long, he wanted to hit the Allies before they could improve on their hopeless condition.

Hitler had planned to start his offensive on November 15th but to the relief of his generals the weather was so bad that the plans were on hold. Several more times a date was set, but the weather didn't cooperate with any of the plans so a great scale action was postponed till spring.

In April 1940, the Germans used the red herring

tactic to confuse the Allies. They attacked the heavily fortified Maginot Line between France and Germany with no intention of conquering anything. England and France thought that this was the major offensive and when the Germans withdrew their troops, the Allies thought that the Maginot Line was holding.

Germany only had withdrawn their troops to make them ready for the real spring offensive. So far, the Germans had tried to prevent supplies from the U.S. going to England with the 57 submarines they had. If England didn't have food, weapons and oil, they wouldn't be able to do much harm.

Of course, the Allies had plans, too, to make it difficult for the Germans to fight a war. Production of planes, tanks, cannons and other war materials is a race for which you need a lot of steel. Germany's steel supply came from Sweden where it was shipped to Norway and from the Norwegian harbour Narvik the steel was shipped to Germany. If the Allies could cut off Germany's steel supply, it would bring the German Army to its knees.

That was a great idea but Norway was a neutral country and wasn't willing to let any foreign troops on its soil. They were like all other countries that wanted to stay out of the war. If the Allies were serious about cutting off Germany's steel supply, they had to take Norwegian strategic positions by force, which would bring Norway into the German camp.

Hitler got the wind of the Allies evil plans and beat them to it. The Allies had a problem with the neutrality of Norway but Hitler didn't have a problem at all about using brute force. Denmark, a little country between Norway and Germany was in the way, so Hitler decided to take Denmark as well.

On April 9, 1940 the Germans invaded Norway and Denmark. It took only one day to take Denmark but Norway took longer. With aid from the Allies they battled the Germans successfully. In Northern

Norway the Allies managed to take Narvik, the vital port for the steel supply of Germany. The Allies' campaign was a great success, they had cut Germany's steel supply, exactly the way they had it planned.

Not for long were the Allies celebrating victory. On May 10, 1940 while they were still fighting in Norway, Hitler unleashed his Wehrmacht on Western Europe. He attacked The Netherlands, Belgium and France at the same time. The Germans moved so swiftly that right from the start France was in trouble which made it necessary to pull the troops out of Norway to prop up the defence of France.

Crime and Punishment.

Ko had an aunt who lived on the Hordyk, about a five minute walk from her house. Her name was Jacoba Sint Maartensdyk and Adrie's mother called her Aunt Ko. She was married and had three daughters and two sons.

Her husband Dammes was a real weirdo. He had a taxi but wasn't much of a taxi driver and drove his taxi company right into the ground. On one occasion, Arie's mother was going to come over for a weekend. It was a twelve mile distance which could be travelled by bus easily if you were in good health. As she was very old she decided to take a taxi. Favoring family, Dammes Sint Maartensdyk was in the family so he got the job.

Dammes was supposed to pick up Adrie and his mother first. That way Adrie's mother could help grandma to get into the taxi and Adrie could come along for a taxi ride. He never had a ride in an auto before so this was an opportunity that didn't present itself very often. Ko was always trying to give her kids some pleasures during the meagre Depression years. Dammes had to pass the house anyway, so it wouldn't cost any extra money.

Dammes managed to bungle it all; he didn't pick up Adrie and his mother and couldn't find the address where the grandmother lived. He phoned his son who came to tell Ko that his dad was lost. Now Arie had to go on his bike, peddle 12 miles to tell the nincompoop where his mother lived. Arie took Adrie along on his bike so he still could have his taxi ride. Thanks to the nincompoop it was now only a one way taxi ride. Arie remarked: "If you have to get things from your family you always seem to have trouble."

That was bad enough but there were a lot worse things. Dammes was in love with his own daughter. When they went to church or going home from church, he had his arm around her waist holding her tit. His daughter had her arm around his waist and they walked as if they were deeply in love. And they were. All church going people condemned him and thought it was a shame.

His daughter always had an excuse to get her father into her bed; she complained about a tummy ache and asked her father to come in bed to rub her tummy. Ko had witnessed that a few times and didn't want to visit her aunt anymore.

One day when Adrie came home from school, the kids were yelling that there was a fire in Sint Maartendyk's house. Everybody was going to see the fire. When Adrie came to the house; flames and smoke came out of the second floor window. Soon after, the fire engine came and put the blaze out.

Two days later Aunt Ko was arrested for setting the fire and claiming fire insurance. When the Fire Marshal asked her how the blaze got started, she said: "I was cleaning some pants and tried to get the stains out with gasoline. All of a sudden there was a flame and before I knew it the house was ablaze."

"Nice story," the Fire Marshal thought but he didn't buy it and asked: "How do you explain that in two bedrooms the beds were ablaze and that the fire got started with lots of gasoline? There were two fires at the same time how do you explain that?"

Finally she admitted that she had doused the beds with gasoline and had put a match to it. She was promptly arrested and put in jail. When the police were probing for the reason for the blaze she got quite confused and finally told her story. Her husband was having incest with her daughter, everybody in the neighborhood knew it and she didn't know what to do anymore. Finally she decided to burn the house.

After a thorough investigation, the police found the story to be truthful. The police arrested her husband and set her free. Dammes was now in jail for incest with his daughter, he had received a five year jail term. However, he only served two months of his jail sentence.

When the war broke out, he had been in jail for only two months. With the German ultimatum that the city of Rotterdam had to surrender or it would be bombed, the city set the prisoners free and told them to go home. That was easier said than done. Some prisoners lived close to the jail and made it home. Dammes who was living in the suburbs of Rotterdam didn't make it. There was no transportation because of the war. All he could do was stay in the city till transportation would be available.

When the bombs destroyed the centre of the city, Dammes was among the casualties. Aunt Ko came to tell Adrie's mother the news and added: "The Lord has punished the scoundrel, five years in jail wasn't enough punishment for what he has done. Seldom has the punishment of heaven come so swiftly after the crime as in this case."

DER KRIEG IM WESTEN IST BEENDIGHT.

(The war in the West is finished)

For a few days there were no newspapers printed. After the capitulation of The Netherlands, the newspapers weren't sure where they were standing. That situation was solved in a bulletin from the German commander who ordered that everything had to go back to normal, which included the printing of newspapers. Of course the press was now under control of the Germans and censorship was introduced right away.

Before The Netherlands was attacked by Germany, the Dutch people were more pro-German than pro-English. When The Netherlands was attacked by Germany, all of a sudden England and France were friends. That was something new in history. For the longest time all three countries had been competing for the colonies. The last time that The Netherlands and England were friends had been when both were at war with Spain and the English defeated the Spanish Armada.

After that they started to wrestle a few colonies away from The Netherlands including South Africa. Dutch settlements were started in South Africa in 1652 and the English came much later. South Africa was a big country; there was plenty of room for English and Dutch both but the English wanted it all.

In 1899 the Boer War started and a bright young man named Winston Churchill was in the army, at the same time as he was war correspondent for the London Morning Post. Within a month after his arrival he was captured by the Boers. When he escaped from a prison camp in Pretoria, he became an instant hero overnight.

In a critical battle, the Boers were driven back on the Table Mountain. When they were cornered, the English refused to take prisoners and drove the Boers off the mountain into the sea. In 1900 the English captured Johannesburg from the Dutch and took so many prisoners that they didn't know what to do with them. Churchill knew an answer to the problem; he was the inventor of concentration camps. Many settlers had to be moved to make South Africa English and Churchill put them into concentration camps. The Boer War lasted for three years and is still remembered by the Dutch.

When the war ended in 1903, Churchill wrote a couple of books and gave lectures about the war. With the money he made he was able to enter the English Parliament. Members of Parliament were not paid in those days, which was a handy way to keep the poor people out. Even today while Members of Parliament are being paid, the politicians still manage to keep the poor people out of Government. Who can afford an election campaign?

Naturally the English and Churchill were not admired by the Dutch. This was aggravated when the English supported the separation of Belgium from The Netherlands. Even during the First World War, the Dutch stayed neutral while the English were at war with Germany. They were neither friends of the Germans nor the English. Now that Germany had taken The Netherlands and England was at war with Germany, suddenly England and The Netherlands became friends.

All cities prepared for air raids and built air raid shelters every four blocks. There was no door in the entrance; the entrance was closed off with a blanket. That was the safest, they said, against shrapnel from bombardments. Indeed, it was very smart if you don't figure that people will steal the blankets. It was only a matter of time until there was nothing in the entrance, which didn't matter all that much because the real shelter was around the corner.

Despite the fact that the Germans were winning battle after battle, the Dutch people didn't believe the successes of the German Army that were loudly touted on the Dutch radio and in the Dutch newspapers. Every Dutchman and his brother thought that the German victories were tremendously exaggerated and that the war would turn around in favor of England and France.

Nobody wanted to believe in German victories though the German and English news broadcasts pictured a bleak future. Every day there were new successes for the Germans and on May 28th Belgium capitulated after an 18 day battle. The Belgians had lost 7,500 killed and 16,000 wounded.

Faithfully, every night at 7.00 p.m. the de Kievits went to their newly acquired friends, the Echthuizens, to listen to the news from Radio London. Unfortunately, the English news was similar to the German news. Nothing but German victories and Allied retreats. On June 7th English and French troops were pulled out of Norway to defend France.

There was a message from Radio London on June 10, 1940 that Princess Juliana had arrived safely in Canada with her three Princess children. That way the Royal family was well protected and the Germans couldn't touch them. If they had thought that this would make the Dutch people happy they were wrong. Ver Echthuizen said: "Princess Juliana took some safety measures, she expects heavy bombardments of England and perhaps an invasion is in the offing. She is now in Canada, enjoying the good life and we have to put up with the war."

June 10th was also a disaster for the war effort of the Allies. Norway had capitulated and King Haakon, his government and the Norwegian gold reserves landed all safely in Scotland. If that wasn't bad enough, Italy went to war to support Germany and attacked France from the South. The Italian army was on its way to the French Riviera.

Leen Willemstein said: "So much for France, now they are in a squeeze. It will be a matter of days now until France capitulates. With their out-dated equipment and out-dated Generals they are certainly no match for Hitler's modern fully equipped Wehrmacht."

It looked as if Leen Willemstein had it right again. On June 14th the German press heralded the surrender of Paris. For the second time in 70 years Paris had fallen in German hands. The first time was in 1870 and now in 1940. The German broadcast boasted that France and Germany were negotiating a peace settlement but the British press denied it. Of course, the brave Dutch citizens believed Radio London and thought that the Germans were lying. Too bad that faith can't change an unpleasant situation!

June 24th was another black day for the Dutch people and for a lot of other people in Europe. The German press announced that France had been defeated and that an Armistice had been signed with France. It was no capitulation; Hitler had worked out a fast deal with France to get them out of the war. Hitler was so good to occupy only the Northern industrial part of France which included Paris. The southern part of France would be Free France under an independent French Government. There were lots of conditions and if they weren't met, the Germans would occupy the Southern part of France as well.

Disappointed people tuned in to Radio London that night to hear the sad news from England. Radio London acknowledged the French defeat and tried to restore hope to the millions of people who had seen the Allies as the only hope they had. General de Gaulle had escaped with his French army to England; he said that France had lost a battle but not the war. He would continue to fight the Nazis from England.

Furthermore, the English broadcast announced that 9 British divisions and 110,000 French troops had been evacuated from Dunkirk. More than half a million men had reached England and were ready to take on the Germans if they crossed the Channel. No matter what the English broadcast said, the Dutch people were irreconcilable and feared the worst. The nice dream to run the Germans out of their country had been shattered. The Dutch people had learned a new word 'Blitzkrieg,' it wasn't in the dictionary yet but everybody knew what it meant.

In the German camp there was every reason to celebrate the victory which had come in a six week campaign. There was a special program on the radio with a victory speech from the Fuhrer. He shouted: "Our German Army is the best army in the world. We have dealt a devastating blow to our enemies from which they cannot recover. The Krieg im Westen ist beendight. (The war in the West is finished.) And let me remind Sir Winston Churchill, across the English Channel, that in spite of the evacuation of 13 English divisions, victories are not obtained by evacuations and retreats."

The German victory broadcast was concluded with the German Army singing their favorite song "Wir gahn fahren, gegen England." (We are sailing against England.)

Fighting with Beer Bottles.

There was a great celebration in Berlin. Leading a candle lit parade; Hitler was standing in salute in his open Mercedes Benz, followed by his other leading Nazis, Hess, Goring and Goebbels. They were driving between the jubilant German people to the Brandenburg Gate. When Hitler climbed onto the podium, he received an astounding ovation from the German people who were shouting "Heil Hitler" (Hail to Hitler) to no end. Hitler was in no hurry to make his speech, he obviously enjoyed his success.

When he finally raised his hand to quiet the people for his blaring speech, he shouted: "Der Krieg im Westen ist Beendight." (The War in the West is

Finished.) Before he could shout another word, the people started to shout again "Heil Hitler." When the people were listening again Hitler shouted: "Wir haben der krieg nicht gewillt, das haben die Juden. (We didn't want the war, the Jews wanted it) Those Jewish Imperialists are responsible for the First World War and the Second World War as well. Only the Jews were responsible for us losing the First World War and that we had to endure the indignity of the most hated treaty, 'The Treaty of Versailles.' But we Aryans cannot be defeated; His Almighty wants us to rule the world and we will do so. Deutchland Uber Alles. Uber Alles in die Welt." (Germany above everything. Above everything in the world.)

At this time the brass band started to play 'Deutchland uber alles' and all people were singing with fervor. After the singing of this German National Anthem, the crowd started to shout 'Heil Hitler' again. Hitler had his right hand raised when he left the stage and drove back to his headquarters in his Mercedes Benz.

On the other side of the Channel, Winston Churchill was tuned in on Radio Berlin to listen to the German celebration and what Hitler had to say. Churchill had nothing to shout about; before the war started British politicians had boasted that Great Britain could never be conquered. However, the war had turned for the worst and Churchill knew that Great Britain's number was up next.

Finally Churchill had accomplished what he always wanted, he was the Prime Minister. Unfortunately, it was the worst of times to be the Prime Minister. It was an eye opener for Churchill that the world power England had ignored its defense against the enemies. Almost all the English troops were in the English colonies and very little defense was left for England itself.

Becoming Prime Minister was a disaster; he had heard nothing but bad news in the five weeks that he had been in power. Obviously, Great Britain was in deep trouble and so was he. Tomorrow the Armistice would be signed between Germany and France in the same railway carriage that had been used in 1918 and on exactly the same place Compagnie. Hitler sure had a way of revenge and humiliation for the Allies.

Churchill didn't want to think about it; he was like a drowning man grabbing a straw. Tomorrow was a big day when he had to face his cabinet for a strategy meeting. What strategy could he possibly offer? Germany outnumbered the British divisions four to one and half of his divisions were only armed with a rifle and a bayonet; all other weapons had been lost in the Battle of France. Most of his soldiers were in desperate shape; they had been waiting for three or four days in the rain without food till they were evacuated.

The cabinet meeting was a disaster; as soon as the meeting was called to order, Chamberlain suggested: "Churchill should sue for peace with Hitler. If we don't we will be defeated in the Battle of Britain which is just about to begin. Germany conquered six countries in nine months. Poland took 26 days, Denmark 24 hours, The Netherlands 5 days, Norway 28 days, Belgium 18 days and France 35 days. We cannot stop the supreme German Army."

Churchill had been too late to save France but could he save England? Eventually he gained control over the House of Commons; even Chamberlain had shut up reluctantly. There was one more urgent thing to do; he had to prepare the English population for the worst of times. In spite of the hopeless situation for England he had to psyche the people up and instill courage into them.

A pep speech for the poor citizens of Britain was in order. There was no television yet so he spoke on the radio in his all-time famous speech: "Citizens of Britain, France has capitulated to the mighty German armies but we shall never surrender! I'm not denying that a very grave situation exists for England. And if you are looking for leadership, I can offer you nothing but sweat, blood and tears. But victory will be obtained at all cost, victory

in spite of all terror, victory, however, long and
hard the road may be; because without victory there
is no survival for the British Empire. We will fight
the Nazis on our beaches, we will fight them in the
streets and in our cities; we will fight them on
land, at sea and in the air until victory has been
obtained."

Churchill did by no means conceal the terrible
future England was facing but in return he offered
the promise of victory. *(Victory at all cost meant
that after the war was finished Britain was bankrupt
and lost all its colonies.)*

Churchill wasn't all that sure about fighting the
Nazis on land, at sea and in the air. As soon as he
put down his microphone after his speech, he added:
"By God, I hope that the Germans don't come because
if they come we have to hit them with beer bottles;
that's all we have. The Gods of Olympus must be
roaring with laughter over the shape we are in."

Churchill had promised victory, but the question
was;'how were they going to win this war?' Everything
went wrong for the Allies and everything went right
for the Germans. Compared to the Germans, the
British Army looked naked. Before the war started,
German manufacturing plants had worked around the
clock seven days a week. While England was making
toys for Christmas and tennis balls, Hitler was
making cannons, tanks, planes and bombs. Now the
war was on, the British were far behind compared
to the German Army which was well armed.

It was too bad that he couldn't employ the
Scottish soldiers to win the war for him. There was
a movie in which the Scottish Army had to defend a
pass in India.

The Scottish soldiers were known for wearing
nothing under their kilts. When they were storming
the enemy lines with their bayonets and their kilts
high blowing in the air, it was such an awesome
sight that the enemy got the hell out of there.

As it was very cold in the pass, the Scottish
soldiers started to wear long underwear. When the

enemy got to know that, they no longer ran away when the Scottish soldiers were storming their lines and the Scottish regiment was defeated.

The commander found out that his soldiers were wearing long underwear and figured that was the cause of their defeat. He ordered his army not to wear long underwear anymore in battle so they could defeat the enemy.

In the next battle, the enemy wasn't impressed at all and figured that they were going to beat the Scottish again. However, when they saw the Scottish with bayonets and their kilts blowing high in the wind with no long underwear, they took to their heels and were wiped out.

(It makes me think of a lady who asked a Scot: "Is there anything worn underneath your kilt." The Scot answered: "Don't you worry lady everything under my kilt is in perfect condition.")

Too bad that things like that only work in the movies. Churchill was right that they had only beer bottles to hit the Germans. When he inspected the coastline defense they had only six rounds of ammunition for each gun and there were only three anti-tank weapons for five miles of coast.

It looked as though the British Sun had set and Germany uber alles would be founded on the ruins of the British Empire. King George of England looked at the hopeless situation of his country under siege and thought that only a miracle could save Britain. He prescribed a day of prayer to ask the Big Boss for a miracle to defeat the Nazis.

Lord Halifax, a prominent member of the Government, had secret meetings with the Swedish Ambassador to keep the lines open with Germany in hope of negotiating a peace settlement.

Even President Roosevelt seemed to think that all was lost when he suggested that Canada house the entire British merchant fleet just in case that with a German invasion, Britain would be defeated and the Germans would take the entire British fleet. Roosevelt knew that if Britain would fall, the war would turn into a war of continents - America against Europe. England was the last stronghold and it was far from strong.

On the other hand Churchill had a lot of unwanted advice; there were all kinds of cooks that wanted to tell Churchill how he could win the war. Churchill had no time to listen to those useless suggestions; he had better things to do.

All kinds of measurers were taken in England after the declaration of war. In less than no time 38 million gas masks were distributed to the English people. Nobody knew if the Germans were going to use gas bombs when they were going to bomb England. It was against the Geneva Convention to use gas but that didn't mean anything. When there is a war on the only thing that is considered is winning no matter what you have to do. Luckily Hitler was against using gas; he had been seriously injured in an English gas attack during World War I and almost lost his eyesight.

The English, however, were contemplating using gas when their position became hopeless; they thought that using gas might reverse their desperate position and turn the fortunes of war around for them. Luckily they changed their minds because that would have made them very unpopular.

Rumors in England had it that Hitler had a flying tank as a secret weapon which they were going to use with the expected invasion. Hitler never had flying tanks but he had amphibious tanks he was going to use in the invasion. The tanks would drive on the sea bottom with a snorkel for air and come up on the English beaches. It was tested in Kiel, Germany and it worked.

Churchill had an answer to that, he made a fort of England and had thousands of gallons of gasoline ready to set the sea afire. Church bells were silenced, only to be used if an invasion took place and Churchill ordered not to be awakened unless there was an invasion.

Traitors and Collaborators.

In the daily newspaper there was a picture of Hitler against the backdrop of the Arc de Triumph in Paris. The English broadcast called it 'A picture of Evil.'

From the newspaper, the Dutch people learned that The Netherlands was going to be governed by Seys Inquart, the Austrian traitor. He was responsible for bringing the Nazis into Austria and Hitler hadn't forgotten. Hitler had a good job for him, away from his own country where he was called a traitor.

Leen Willemstein said: "It amazes me that Anton Mussert with his aunt didn't get the job."

Adrie knew that Anton Mussert was the leader of the National Socialist Party in The Netherlands, he was a Nazi and a traitor as well but what had his aunt to do with it?

When Adrie asked, Leen Willemstein answered: "This Anton Mussert was a real bright boy. He had a very high I.Q. Mussert wanted to study to make something of his life. Unfortunately, his parents were very poor which translated in no money for studies. Fortunately, Anton Mussert had a rich aunt who could easily pay for his studies. But his aunt didn't hand the money over without a condition and the price was high. His aunt had a proposal. (Sounds familiar, there are a lot of women who have a proposal, Adrie thought.)

Mussert's aunt was an old maid and was desperate to get married. 'Marry me and I will pay for all your studies,' she said. It was a deal, if they could get permission from the Queen. You can't just marry relatives; that causes inbreeding and a weak race. Mussert's aunt was already 47 years old, so the Queen must have thought that there wouldn't be any babies and gave her permission. Anton Mussert had all kinds of university degrees and got into politics. When the Nazis took over in Germany, he started a Nazi Party in The Netherlands which makes him a traitor."

Adrie had listened with attention and thought that there was nothing wrong with marrying your aunt; he had a few aunts who looked alright. On second thought it wasn't a very good idea, Mussert had married his aunt when she was 47 years old. By the time that Adrie's aunts were 47 years old, they would be old bags too he thought, and who wants to marry an old bag?

Seys Inquart arrived in The Netherlands and made some startling announcements in his inauguration speech. "It has been brought to my attention that the poor people of The Netherlands are discriminated against. It is shameful that poor people have to buy a bike license for one guilder each year. A bike is the poor man's transportation and isn't taxed in Germany or

Austria. Therefore the bike taxes are immediately cancelled. If you buy a bike you don't need a license anymore."

As it was already July, most people had bought their bike license. Unfortunately, Seys Inquart didn't offer a refund but it was a good thing for next year. Leen Willemstein commented: "This Austrian traitor is trying to win the Dutch people over and offers a lot of carrot. Let's be careful, there can be a lot of stick behind the carrot."

Seys Inquart's second revelation was that a lot of poor Austrian kids needed a holiday. In the near future they would be coming to The Netherlands to stay for a month. He trusted that a lot of good Dutch people would open up their houses for those poor unfortunate Austrian kids.

Leen Willemstein had no friendly words for the new Governor Seys Inquart, he commented: "If that traitor thinks that I'm going to have an Austrian kid in my house, he ought to be kidding. Austrian kids are Germans too; they are part of The Greater Germany. I know who is going to take Austrian kids into their houses; it will only be Nazi sympathizers."

Anton Mussert also had some good ideas to please the Nazis. In Germany there was a Hitler Youth Organization where they prepared the growing kids for Hitler's army. As soon as a kid was eleven years old he joined the Hitler Youth Organization and was taught discipline, shooting and to be faithful to the Fuhrer. If a kid wasn't poisoned yet with Nazi ideas of owning the world, they were sure learning it fast in the Hitler Youth. The Dutch desperately needed an organization like that in The Netherlands, Mussert said and all members of the Dutch Nazi Party had to send their sons of eleven years and older to the organization.

Anton Mussert thought it a good idea for the National Socialists to make some propaganda. He had giant posters made up with a good Nazi slogan and the members of the party were supposed to put the posters in their window. Besides the propaganda, it also showed the Dutch people who the Nazi supporters were. Everybody had a good idea who supported the Nazis but the members hadn't shown their true colors yet. A Nazi sign in the window would give them away and the Dutch people would know for sure. Mussert had quite an ego which was evident in the first poster. The poster said: "With Mussert Hoorah."

When Adrie came out of school he saw some posters on the houses of the National Socialists and wondered if Mr. Koekoek had one on his window. Mr. Koekoek lived a few houses from the de Kievits and everybody believed he was in the Nazi Party but nobody was sure. The proof came that very day; when Adrie came closer to the house he could see from far the giant poster in the window. No doubt about it, Koekoek was a traitor.

A week later there was a flag flying from all the houses which were occupied by Nazi supporters. It was a flag with two horizontal banners 'one red banner and one black one.' There were also rumors about some people who didn't fly the Dutch Nazi flag and didn't display their posters, that they were Nazi sympathizers in secret. That made it worse, if you know who your enemies are you can avoid them. When you are dealing with secret traitors, you can't trust your own people anymore and you start to live in fear of being betrayed. It's hard enough to fight the Devil you know, fighting the Devil you don't know is even harder.

The National Socialists weren't the only collaborators with the Germans. There were quite a few girls who were dating German soldiers. Some of those girls were plain ugly and hadn't attracted Dutch boys. Those girls had the idea that if the Dutch boys don't want us we'll take a German soldier.

German soldiers didn't care if a girl was ugly or stupid. To them a girl was a girl, they were living with death in their shoes every day and their philosophy was 'There is a time to love and a time to die. Let's love today because tomorrow we might be dead.'

Not all the girls who dated German soldiers were ugly; some of them liked the German soldiers for their money which they spent readily on the girls they loved. To the Dutch people those girls could be dangerous as well. It wasn't sure that the girls talked to their lovers only about the moon and roses, they could also talk about people who were underground and betray them.

A Reign of Terror.

Terror didn't start right off the bat after the Nazis had occupied The Netherlands. The Germans tried first the friendly way but it was the German way. Unemployment had ended with the Germans in control, they had work for everybody. It was very evident that it was going to be an industrial war in which the outcome was decided by the number of tanks, cannons, and planes a country could make. It was also very important to replace lost battle ships and submarines. There were quite a few Dutch shipyards and the Germans had orders for all of them. Other industrial plants received lots of orders too. Cannons, guns, ammunition and other warfare materials were now manufactured in The Netherlands.

General de Gaulle had said after his escape with his army to England, "We have lost a battle but we didn't lose the war." It looked as if The Netherlands had lost a battle too, but not the war. The Dutch soldiers had ceased fighting the German Army; instead the fighting was done underground. Many acts of sabotage were committed by the Dutch Underground. Most of the underground work was organized from London where the weapons came from.

The Dutch were not amused to make warfare material for the Germans and started to sabotage the manufacturing. This time the Germans weren't amused and took tough measures.

The now unfriendly German Commander had some news, too. He announced on his poster:

Dear Citizens:
"It has been brought to my attention that many Dutch citizens are listening to the broadcasts from Radio London. Those enemy broadcasts are poisonous to the people of The Netherlands and promote hatred against Germany. Therefore, it is strictly forbidden to listen to enemy broadcasting in any language. Severe punishment is in place for offenders of this law."

The German Commander didn't say what the severe punishment was. That way he could punish the way he saw fit from imprisonment to shooting by a firing squad. Whatever the punishment might be, it didn't deter the Dutch citizens at all. You could tell when it was time for the news bulletin from Radio London. Five minutes before news time people disappeared into their houses even when it was nice weather. Five minutes after the news broadcast, everybody was outside again to discuss the news with their friends and neighbors. A lot of people listened to Radio London together and would discuss the news after the broadcasting. Nobody was interested in German news; they wanted to hear what they liked to hear. Unfortunately, nobody really heard what he wanted to hear. There was no good news from the Allied side.

The B.B.C. (British Broadcasting Corporation) was jammed with extra broadcasts; they broadcasted news in all languages of the occupied countries. Before the broadcast in Dutch, there was a broadcast in Polish. When the people tuned in on Radio London, they usually heard the end of the news in Polish before they could listen to the news in Dutch.

If you wanted to listen to Radio London, you had to find a station that the Germans didn't scramble with noisy interruptive sound. The Germans were broadcasting it on the same wave length and most of the stations from Radio London were scrambled so much that you couldn't hear a word that was said. Usually the short wave had British Broadcasting stations with clear reception of Radio London. Rado London was broadcasting the news on ten different wave lengths on the same time to make sure that the people in the occupied countries could hear their news bulletins.

English broadcasting also provided news in coded messages for the Underground Forces. After the news broadcast they would usually say: "And now a look at the London Market. Today the radishes were selling for 9 cents a bundle, carrots went for 10 cents, turnips for 16 cents and potatoes for 8 cents per lb. It presented the prices of the commodities alright but it also provided the underground the telephone number of a secret agent. In the next broadcast they gave the prices of flowers.

Some Dutch citizens started a pirate radio broadcasting station called 'The Flitspuit.' They broadcast news the way they received it from England and had all kinds of national programs. It was a matter of days before it was declared illegal to listen to Dutch illegal radio stations and other pirate stations. That added one more illegal activity most of the Dutch people got themselves into.

Nobody was deterred by the German threats; everybody wanted to listen to news from the Allied side. The broadcasts of the Flitspuit illegal radio station weren't always regular. Whenever they were broadcasting, the Germans tried to cross tune the station from two different points. That way they could find the location of the Flitspuit. When the Germans got too close for comfort, the broadcast was halted and quite often the station was moved. People knew about the station from others, the word was spread from mouth to mouth.

On July 1st, the Germans took the English Channel islands and everything showed that they were preparing for the invasion of England. Hitler had been thinking that it was going to be a short war with the Allies totally unprepared and was now pretty sure that the ultimate victory was in sight. He offered peace to Churchill: "Let's face it; the German army outnumbers the English army four to one. There is no possible hope that the English army can stop the Germans when they land. Therefore, there is no reason for any further shedding of blood. Let's have peace!"

Radio London also acknowledged Hitler's peace offer and broadcast Churchill's answer. "I will deal neither with Hitler nor Mussolini. If we can stand up to Hitler, all of Europe might be free. We will brace ourselves to our duties and we will not surrender."

There was one piece of news that was very encouraging. With the threatening German invasion of England, the English Queen had taken lessons to shoot a revolver. People in The Netherlands were joking about it that the Germans wouldn't dare to invade England now with the extra fire power the English had with a shooting Queen.

Life Goes On.

In sickness or health, poverty or wealth, war or peace, life goes on. Calamities are overcome by the survivors; they simply learn to live with them. If they don't, they wouldn't be long among the survivors. War became part of daily life.

Dutch history starts with 100 B.C. The Frisians and Batavians entered The Netherlands. It was a spectacular entry. They came down the river Rhine in hollowed out tree trunks, for the simple reason that the steamboat hadn't been invented yet. The Rhine is one of the great rivers in Europe.

Those Frisians and Batavians were both of German descent. However, in 100 B.C. The Netherlands was not defended because nobody was living there as yet. It was about 2040 years later, in the year 1940, that the real Germans came to occupy The Netherlands. They didn't come in hollowed out tree trunks, they came in tanks. At that time, The Netherlands was defended but the defence was no match for the intruding Germans.

After all the devastating news that the Germans were in firm control of Western Europe, except England, the Dutch citizens had to accept that the Germans were to stay in The Netherlands for some time to come. They unwillingly accepted the fact that the Dutch were not boss in their own country anymore and had to put up with the German nuisance. Dutch citizens made the best of it and went on with living in their occupied country. What else could they do? They didn't have to like it and could only hope that some how the fortunes of war would change to their advantage.

Many religious people were very disappointed that they had lost the war against Germany in spite of the German army outnumbering the Dutch in soldiers and equipment. They never lost their confidence that they could beat the Germans because David had won from Goliath in spite of his inferior being. Unfortunately, it was not to be, the Bible story wasn't going to be repeated in The Netherlands. When the people came to worship in church on Sunday, the Reverend had a problem convincing the people that God would eventually destroy the Germans. He said: "It can take time but good will always win over evil. Tomorrow will prove that good will trump bad. Evil forces do everything they possibly can to prevent tomorrow from taking place. For the time being I can only forecast a dark night but the dark night will be followed by a very bright dawn."

Life wasn't exactly the same as before the Nazis occupied The Netherlands. Even at school there were drastic changes. First of all German language lessons became compulsory at the elementary school. Everybody received a German text book to learn German. The text book started with learning how to count in German. The second lesson consisted out of rhymes and the first rhyme was about counting off to see who is it; when you play a game.

We count off:
Ich bin Peter, I am Peter,
Du bist Paul.   You are Paul.
Ich bin fleissig, I am ambitious,
Du bist faul.   You are lazy.
Eins, Zwei, Drei, One, two, three,
Du bist frei. You are free.

When the new history books came out one could see the German influence. The old history books had as last lines:
1929 Stock Market Crash.
1930 Beginning of the Great Depression.
The new books had some additional lines:
1937 World jamboree in The Netherlands.
1939 Beginning of Second World War.
1940 The Netherlands occupied by Germany.
One Dutch history item had been omitted by the Germans. In 1938 Princess Beatrix was born. Obviously the Germans didn't care for the Royal family and pretended there was no Royal family.

Before the war there had never been phys. ed. at school. This was changed by the Germans who made it compulsory to have twice a week one hour of physical exercises. For about ten minutes there were exercises with hands and feet and rope climbing. Next there were soccer matches and broad and high jumping contests. Adrie loved all of it; that was right up his alley. He didn't like the German language because the Germans were the enemies. Actually, that's where he went wrong. It had been always his hope to learn English, French and German. However, the English language was number one on his agenda. With the Germans in The Netherlands there was no room for learning English, the Germans wouldn't allow it. Nobody took learning German seriously and very little German was learned. It could have been a start to learn the languages he wanted to learn but that opportunity was lost.

One of the first things the Germans did to the people was the issuing of identity cards. Everybody of 16 years of age or older had to carry an identity card. The picture of the bearer and the thumb and index finger print were on the identity card. It was done to fight the underground activities of the Dutch.

Jews were Hitler's worst enemies, they were forced to wear a yellow Star of David to show everybody who the Jews were. Later most of the Jews were transported to Germany to death camps. Anyone who had the misfortune to be born Jewish was in trouble in Nazi occupied territory. All of a sudden it had become a crime to be a Jew and Jews were not allowed to marry. The Germans didn't want more Jews, they wanted to eradicate them.

Children who had a Jewish parent and a parent of a different race were considered to be only half Jews. Therefore they could tear half of the Star of David off.

Fresco who lived close to the de Kievits was wearing a whole star; he was married to a German woman but he himself was a full blooded Jew. Being married to a German woman saved his bacon, he was the only Jew on the Hordyk who wasn't transported to Germany.

As far as Kees Meuzelaar, Adrie's neighbour, was concerned, they could ship Fresco to Germany and kill him. Fresco was a kind of a friend of Kees Meuzelaar and always came to listen to Radio London. At one time he bought some potatoes from Kees and Fresco was going to pay him at the end of the week. When no payment was made Kees asked for the money and Fresco said that he had paid him when he took the potatoes home and he wasn't going to pay twice for the potatoes. That kind of dishonesty made Kees furious and he told Fresco to get out of his house and not return. When Fresco left, Kees shouted after him: "You rotten Jew, I hope that the Nazis ship you to Germany so we are rid of you."

There were other things which had changed in The Netherlands. Before the war started people were singing about the beauty of The Netherlands, the dunes, the green meadows and beautiful flowers. That had changed dramatically; there were now songs about war, destruction, dead people and the mass burial place Rhenen where several thousand soldiers had died when they were fighting the Germans. There was also a dramatic love song about a young couple where the boyfriend had to go to sea. They were going to get married when he came back. However, his ship hit a mine, he died at sea and they didn't get married. His girlfriend returned to the beach staring at the cruel sea. It sounded like a dramatic opera.

There was no doubt in Hitler's and Churchill's minds that Hitler could land a hundred thousand troops or so in England. There was only one problem for the Germans; a fighting army needs a lot of supplies. If the army doesn't have fuel, ammunition and food, it won't be an effective fighting force. As long as the R.A.F. controlled the air, it would be very difficult to supply the troops and supplies could easily be cut off with disastrous results. As soon as the R.A.F. was wiped out, a landing could be most successful. Without air supremacy over the Channel and the British coast, the planned invasion became a risky venture.

The Battle of England was fought in the air; it was a battle to destroy the R.A.F. after which an invasion could take place. For the remaining part of summer everybody thought that England would be invaded and fall prey under the murderous machine of the German Wehrmacht. At this stage nobody thought that England could be saved. Even President Roosevelt wrote England off.

Roosevelt expected England to fall within a couple of weeks and that the defeat of England would be the most important news after the death of Christ. Reporters were dispatched to England to cover the defeat of England and its surrender. In spite of all the German victories they lost the most important one, 'The Battle of Britain,' which was fought in the air.

The battle lasted three months in which Hitler lost 1400 planes and the British lost 700 planes. The battle favored the British because the Germans could only stay over England for half an hour, after that they had to return to Germany for fuel. Also British damaged planes that had to make an emergency landing could be repaired and used again while German damaged planes were lost when they made an emergency landing.

The Germans failed to get air supremacy and consequently the invasion was postponed. It was the first defeat of the Luftwaffe and the first victory for the English. Churchill hailed the R.A.F. victory in the House of Commons with the immortal sentence: "Never in the field of human conflict has so much been owed, by so many, to so few."

On August 24 London was bombed for the first time. One week after the bombing of London there was some good news that Berlin had been bombed. The German press admitted that Berlin had been bombed and added that there was only minimal damage to houses of the German people. Hitler didn't think it terrible to bomb London but didn't like it a bit when bombs were falling on Berlin; he called it a cowardly attack.

Hitler had great plans for Berlin; he made plans with his architect Alphred Speer to make a Greater Berlin with a Reich Chancellery (Government building) with a dome sixteen times the size of St. Peter's Cathedral in Rome. It was going to dominate Berlin, a capital never seen before in the world. Speer had a model of this New Berlin. Unfortunately bombs started to fall on Berlin and eventually artillery reduced it to rubble.

Leen Willemstein said: "Finally, the moffs are getting a dose of their own medicine; I hope that they level all German cities."

Despite that there was only minimal damage to Berlin, Hitler was furious for it hurt his pride. In a shouting speech he announced that the English would pay for the bombing of Berlin and ordered London destroyed. Hitler tried very hard to make good on his threat to destroy London, he had London bombed for 57 consecutive days.

Bombing of Berlin appealed to the Dutch people who were promptly singing a song to praise it.

An English torpedo hunter,
Was flying over the German coast.
He said "I'm going to ask Hitler
If he likes bombs instead of toast.
In the bright moonlit night,
We bomb Berlin out of sight.
With all our planes and might.
Only Berlin in ruins makes it right."

When the English started to bomb military targets in Germany and the occupied countries, the Germans ordered a total blackout from half an hour after sunset till half an hour before dawn. When it started to get dark the radio played Lily Marlene and announced:
Before you continue to listen,
Take care to darken your window.
The lights went out and the bombs came down. If you didn't close off your window adequately, you would get a warning from the German patrol. A second offence was punished with the Germans throwing a rock through your window to smarten you up. Blacked out cities were necessary, the Germans said; they didn't want to aid the English pilots with their navigation. In spite of the black outs, the English pilots found their target anyway by using radar.

'Lilli Marlene' was a German song which was soon translated in all languages. The English version is:

Underneath the lantern by the barrack gate,
Darling I remember the way you used to wait;
It was there you whispered tenderly,
That you loved me, you'd always be,
My Lilli of the lamplight,
My own Lilli Marlene.

Early September, a busload of Austrian kids pulled up in the street. The bus stopped at Koekoek's place and two kids disembarked. Leen Loekoek and his father welcomed them with open arms. Leen Willemstein commented:

"Nice going, thanks to Seys Inquart the kids of our enemy have a free holiday at our expense."

Arie who had been unemployed for several years prior to the war now had steady work. Everybody was now working for the German war effort, including Arie who was forced to make concrete bunkers at the coast for the defence of The Netherlands against a possible invasion from England.

Before the war started, Arie had worked in labor camps of the Dutch Government in land reclaiming projects. And now the war was on he had to stay in labor camps to work for the Germans. Again he came only home every two weeks for a weekend which meant that Adrie had to do a lot of garden work when his father was gone.

There was one basic difference between the labor camp of the Dutch Government before the war and the German labor camp during the war. At least, the Germans paid him very well for his work which made it more attractive. The Germans had lots of money, the printing press could print a lot of Dutch guilders and there was lots of paper to do it. For the first time there was a surplus of money after food, clothes and other necessities had been paid for. After the surplus of money had accumulated, Adrie's parents decided to have a radio.

There were two options; they could have radio distribution which came into the houses by cable. Under normal circumstances there were four stations available - Hilversum 1 and Hilversum 2 were the Dutch radio stations. Before the war they had also the B.B.C. from London and radio Belgium the Flemish station that spoke Dutch. With the Germans in control of everything, the B.B.C. had been removed from the radio distribution system and Radio Berlin had taken its place.

When they inquired what the cost would be they found out that they couldn't get it. The radio distribution cable couldn't be attached to the power and telephone poles. Instead the cable was attached to the back of the houses and it went from house to house. There was a problem with home owners who didn't want the cable attached to their house. From both sides there was no cooperation from the home owners and it could only cross the street at designated places.

Consequently radio distribution was out. Actually that was no problem. Things were looking up and Arie had enough money for a brand new radio. "Just as well," Arie said, "With a real radio we can listen to Radio London."

Adrie and his sister Willie had seen radios in other people's houses. If they ever attempted to touch the radio, they were told to leave the radio alone. With a radio in their own house, a fight broke out as who would tune in the radio to a radio broadcasting station. Ko said that the kids had to take turns to find a radio station which was attractive to listen to. Of course, every five minutes, the kids decided that the program was lousy and that they had to turn the knob of the radio.

At that stage of the war, most people were doing better than during the Depression. The Depression had ended but oppression had started. A radio had never been a possibility for the many unemployed people who were struggling to have food on their tables. In spite of the improvement of living conditions, few Dutch people appreciated the Germans. Some Dutch people who were impressed with the Germans joined the Dutch Nazis.

Now that there was a radio in the house, the de Kievits didn't need to go to the Echthuizens anymore to listen to Radio London. It was actually better that way; it was very obvious when you go every night to somebody's place, just about ten minutes before the broadcast of Radio London. Ver Echthuizen said: "With Nazis in our street you can't be careful enough. On the other hand it was nice to come together and discuss the war. There is no reason that we can't continue to come together but not always when Radio London is on. That is too suspicious."

After the novelty of having a radio wore off, Adrie didn't have to fight his sister anymore to tune in the radio. He became a radio freak and was always busy with the radio. When it was time to listen to Radio London or the Flitspuit he was always in time to put the program on. Indonesia, a Dutch colony, was also broadcasting news in Dutch and there were also broadcasts from Radio London for Belgium. Since Belgium was speaking French and Dutch there were also broadcasts in Dutch. Adrie didn't miss even one of them.

All this illegal listening to enemy and secret broadcasts brought a scare to people when they were really threatened. Koekoek, the Dutch Nazi in the street, had a son at school who was in the same grade as Adrie. His name was Leen Koekoek and he was a plain numbskull. He was two years older than Adrie, yet he was in the same classroom. He had failed one grade and had managed very little. That didn't deter him from boasting about his Nazi career. Probably, for the first time of his life, Leen Koekoek thought he was real important and was a gift from God to the world.

He went to the Hitler Youth and was taught shooting of rifles. He also had taken an oath to fight for Adolf Hitler. He said: "We have the same oath of allegiance to Hitler as the S.S. We swear: 'Adolf Hitler, leader of the Germanic peoples, I swear loyal faithful obedience unto you and those that you place in authority over me unto death. So truly help me God.'"

Whenever the boys were playing soccer, Leen Koekoek wanted to join. That was a problem for Leen Koekoek; everybody had been turned off because of his Nazi career. There wasn't even one of the boys who wanted to play with him and they called him a traitor and a Nazi. Leen Koekoek always replied that he would report the boys that said this to him, to the German authorities in order to be punished.

One day, Leen Koekoek was bragging to Adrie that his father was studying for Mayor. The Germans had a special crash course for Dutch Nazis to become Mayor; they wanted all towns and cities run by Nazi sympathizers and many Dutch Nazis went for it. Before the war the Mayors were appointed by the Queen, they were not elected as in the States and Canada. Now Anton Mussert the leader of the N.S.B. did the appointing of Mayors.

Leen Koekoek went on by saying that he was already a leader in the Hitler Youth Organization. Adrie got fed up with his bragging and said angrily: "Just wait till the war is finished; they'll hang you on the highest tree for treason."

Leen Koekoek replied: "If I were you I would be very careful with what you are saying to me. Your father and mother are already on the list of people who listen to enemy broadcasting."

Adrie said: "What in the world do you mean, we never listen to English radio stations."

Leen Koekoek replied: "When Radio London is broadcasting in Dutch, we are listening at people's windows to see if they are listening to enemy broadcasting and your name was on the list."

It scared Adrie and he tried to end the conversation by saying: "You are absolutely crazy and you are wrong."

Leen Koekoek countered: "Just wait till the Germans come to arrest all of you."

As soon as Adrie came home he told his mother what Leen Koekoek had said. His mother said: "We'll have to be more careful. Hopefully it is not too late. Whenever we listen to the English broadcast, I will be sitting at the window to watch if anybody comes to listen at our window. After the broadcast you can tell me what you have heard."

When it was dark it meant that Adrie's mother was sitting behind the heavy drapes, which had to be on the windows, to prevent light from shining outside. Adrie's mother passed the information, about the listening Nazis, to Echthuizen and the Meuzelaars who were also listening to Radio London. Adrie was scared for a couple of weeks that the Nazis would come to arrest his family but it didn't happen. They had received a fair warning and Adrie's mother kept sitting behind the heavy drapes to see if anybody would come near the window. The German reign of terror was maintained by using Dutch traitors. You never were sure who would give you away and turn you in. (Adrie's mother never detected anybody listening on their window.)

The passion for pigeons ran high in Holland. Every week there were two pigeon race contests, one short race of fifty miles and one long distance race from the Riviera which was a thousand miles. There were a lot of people in The Netherlands who were keeping carrier pigeons. Before the war it was a sport to participate in pigeon flight contests. The longest flight by a pigeon was 2300 miles; a thousand mile flight was just routine. Pigeon racing people were members of a carrier pigeon club which organized flights from the French Riviera, England and other faraway places. If you participated in a race there was the cost of shipping the pigeons and an entrance fee from which cash prizes were awarded to the winners. The club banded all the participating pigeons with a rubber counter mark and released them all at the same time from a designated place. As soon as the pigeons were released the race was on and the pigeon which returned first was the winner.

As soon as the pigeon returned, the owner took the band off the pigeon's leg and deposited it in a special time clock that stopped as soon as the band was deposited. That way the club could determine whose pigeon was the winner.

The winner would get a medal and a generous cash reward. Some pigeon owners had a whole rack with medals from their winning pigeons. Those pigeon racing contests weren't exactly cheap. First of all you had to have good pigeons which could be very expensive. As much as $300 in today's money was paid for a good pigeon. Thousands of dollars were spent on breeding the right pigeons and thousands of dollars were bet on the birds. Sometimes quite expensive pigeons didn't return, they could have lost their lives when they met predators on their way home or got lost in a thunderstorm. When one of the pigeon owners was complaining about his lost pigeons, one of the smart kids asked; "Why don't you cross your pigeons with parrots so they can ask the way home when they get lost."

Pigeons could meet predators on their flight home but there were some pigeons that would meet predators at home. Willemstein had a real hunting cat; besides rats and mice she also ate quite a few birds including expensive pigeons from the people who were flying pigeons. The pigeon owners had complained about it because the cat would sneak around in their yard and grab some of their expensive pigeons. They wanted Willemstein to pay for the pigeons the cat ate but Willemstein dismissed their claim: "I can't help that the cat catches your pigeons, it's the nature of the animal to catch birds and the cat doesn't see any difference between a sparrow or an expensive pigeon. If she comes in your yard, club her to death. In vain, they tried. The cat was smart enough not to be caught or clubbed to death.

All the participating pigeons were released at a time so that they would return on a Sunday morning. Nobody worked on Sunday except the Reverend who had to deliver the Sermon on the Mountain. That way people had time to await the return of their pigeons and clock the time.

Every Sunday morning, you could see and hear the pigeon owners who were waiting impatiently for their pigeons. A pigeon which had returned was only good if it got in its cage. As soon as that happened, the owner could take the band off its leg to clock it. Some pigeons would sit in the tree for a while before entering their cage. The owner would whistle to his pigeon and stand with a tin box of food in his hand. He would shake the tin box with food to make enough noise to draw the pigeon into its cage. The pigeons weren't fed before the race so they were very hungry and willing to enter the cage for food.

One trick was played all the time by the pigeon owners. Whenever they had a pigeon with young ones they would enter that pigeon for sure. That pigeon was a good prospect to win a prize. As soon as the pigeon was released, the worried pigeon flew itself half to death, to return to her young ones, in order to take care of them. Cruelty never entered the mind of the pigeon owners, winning was the only thing that counted.

The Germans had a good look at all those carrier pigeons and didn't like it a bit. It was a way to get messages across to England or other places. Carrier pigeons went a long way back, they were already used by the Sultan of Baghdad in 1150 and Genghis Khan used pigeons as well to deliver messages. The American Army had been using pigeons for a long time to get the messages across. Nothing was faster than a carrier pigeon.

In less than no time, keeping pigeons was outlawed by the Germans. Of course, there were some pigeon owners who didn't comply with the German wishes and kept their pigeons. Those pigeons had to go underground to prevent the Germans from taking them. Another illegal activity was possible, keeping of pigeons and it meant all pigeons. The Germans weren't going to argue which was a carrier pigeon and which one was not.

(After the war the pigeon sport was revived but it wasn't the same as before. People had different interests besides flying pigeons.)

The Germans pretended that they took good care of all their people in the occupied countries. "Winter Help The Netherlands" was introduced for poor people during the winter. All German collaborators went from door to door to collect money for the poor people, to get them coal and warm clothes for the winter.

With the war already in its second year since September, it had been a war of German victories and successes. Oh yes, the Allies had sunk a few German ships and submarines which was an insignificant success, since the Germans were responsible for sinking 1059 Allied ships with a total tonnage of 1,471,000 tons during 1940.

The Germans had 57 submarines to do all this damage and they were building more submarines at an alarming rate of four per month to replace the lost ones. The Germans sank more ships than the English could build to replace them. The Atlantic was England's life line and they were struggling to keep going.

Hitler had a different plan to beat England after he chickened out of invading it. He was going to starve that island with a moat around it. That was less costly and less risky than a full scale invasion. All he had to do was sink the ships that were supplying England and he had it made. The submarine menace was like a pack of wolves among a herd of sheep. It looked that Hitler was succeeding in starving England.

When a year comes to an end, we look back at the accomplishments we have made and the good things we have experienced. There was nothing good that could be said about 1940 unless you were on the German side. The Germans could look back at a successful year. By the end of 1940 Britain was a beleaguered fortress, France had been driven out of the war and the coast of Europe was in German hands from the North Cape to the Pyrenees. They had all of Western Europe firmly under control and they were very confident that, when spring came, they would take England as well.

Radio Berlin touted the great successes the German Army had during 1940. Leaders from around the world had their usual speeches and Adolf Hitler didn't miss the opportunity. He warned England that they were toast as soon as spring came. Hitler boasted that he didn't even have to invade England; he would starve them to death. He boasted: "The blockade of the British Isles has been completed, 10,000 tons of shipping is being sunk every day and this will be increased during 1941."

Hitler himself was very happy with the way 1940 had turned out; his power had never been greater, he was Germany's dictator and ruled most of Europe after his victories. There was no doubt in Hitler's mind that he had won the war; all what mattered now was to end it as fast as possible.

For the people that were on the Allied side, the only good thing you could say about 1940 was that it was finally over. As for New Year's wishes, the people of The Netherlands were hoping that the fortunes of Germany would change into misfortunes.

The year 1940 had been a disaster for the Allies. They had lost Denmark and Norway for a starter and The Netherlands, Belgium, and France shortly after. It had been like shooting rats in a barrel. At the beginning of 1941 the situation for the Allies was desperate; all they could hope for was for the best and the best looked terrible. Spring was coming up fast with a new summer offensive for the Germans. The spring of 1940 was fresh in the mind of the Allies when most of Western Europe had changed hands. The only good thing for the Allies was that England hadn't been invaded yet but that could change in the spring of 1941. A German invasion could be expected with the outcome that England, the last stronghold in Europe, would fall prey to Hitler.

Hitler's blitzkrieg had given him control of Western Europe except for England. He was planning to take England come spring. When spring came Hitler changed his mind, invading England was a too risky venture. He could starve England with his submarines in the Atlantic and conquer the remainder of Europe in the meantime.

Kees Meuzelaar said: "The war is going so bad that I'm willing to mount a horse and charge the Germans in spite of my piles."

Everybody thought that the Germans would be running out of steam; they hadn't taken England and a counter offensive must be forthcoming next spring. Churchill had his pep speech for the Allies and Queen Wilhelmina spoke also a few words to her enslaved Dutch citizens. The Dutch people weren't exactly amused; they couldn't forgive her that she took off to England during desperate times.

German news broadcasts were always broadcasting victory after victory. It was always stretched that the Allies had lost so many men, ships or planes while the Germans had lost hardly anything. Even the English broadcast had some distorted figures so as not to show how serious the situation was. When England lost more and more ships due to the German sub marines, Churchill put a ban on reporting the losses.

The Dutch people were fed up with the German successes without losses that they fabricated a bragging story too, just to show how ignorant the Germans were. They would say jokingly to other Dutch people to imitate the German bragging: "Ich und meine Bruder Heinrich und zwanzig andere mutige Deutche soldaten haben eine Kranke Hollander ganz kaput geschossen." Translated it says: "I and mine brother Heinrich and twenty other brave German soldiers have one sick Dutchman shot to hell."

German broadcasts always had a program of German soldiers singing. A popular German song was "I have to write my mother. The time goes so fast." Dutch people replied to that singing: "I always thought that assholes had no mother and those assholes are singing that they are going to write to their mother."

There was one song they always were singing at the end of the broadcast: "Wir gahn fahren gegen England." *(We go sailing against England.)* The Dutch people improvised and made it: "We are drowning in front of England."

When the Wehrmacht was singing "In the heimat, in the heimat, There is always sunshine." The Dutch were singing 'In the heimat there is no fressen more.' *(In the heimat, in the heimat, There is nothing to eat anymore.)* Those jokes and songs weren't meant for German ears.

In spite of the censorship graffiti appeared on the walls. It was anti-

German and anti-Nazi. Hallo meant Hang All Lousy Land Occupiers. People were singing:

> The Netherlands has fallen by treason.
> For absolutely no good reason.
> England our friend came too late.
> Because Hitler was an ass
> As there no other was.
> The Netherlands has fallen by treason.

In spite of the singing German soldiers, it wasn't much fun to be in Hitler's Army. You couldn't fail a mission. If you didn't deliver you were removed from your unit to be transferred to the Penalty Battalion. Once you were there you weren't more than cannon fodder. You had to go ahead of the tanks with Molotov Cocktails to destroy the enemy tanks when there was a tank battle on the go. You either led the tanks to victory or you died.

On the home front things were changing as well. The jubilant German people who had been shouting 'Heil Hitler' to no end received more and more messages that their husband or son had died.

It was in Hitler's plan to take on Russia in spring but his friend Mussolini screwed him up. Mussolini was going to take Greece which was a cake walk he thought. He had severely underestimated the Greek Army. Not only did they repel the Italian Army, they conquered some of Albania which was occupied by the Italians.

Hitler had to postpone his invasion of Russia to help out his clumsy friend. In order to get at Greece, Hitler had to take first Yugoslavia. In spring 1940, Hitler unleashed his Wehrmacht on Western Europe and in spring 1941, he unleashed his Wehrmacht on Eastern Europe. It was another Blitzkrieg. On April 6, 1941 Yugoslavia was attacked and in 12 days' time it was defeated. Hitler didn't pause for a moment and attacked Greece which was defeated in 13 days. The Island of Crete, which was heavily defended by English troops, fell on June 2nd. Again the English were booted out of Europe. In 1940 they were booted out of Western Europe and in 1941 out of Eastern Europe. It was a second Dunkirk; the English troops lost all their equipment and barely escaped themselves.

When this was all over, the postponed invasion of Russia took place. Hitler had boasted that the war in the West was finished but the war in the East had to start yet. Right from the beginning Hitler disagreed with his Generals. Von Rundsted, one of Hitler's top Generals wanted to take Moscow first but Hitler contradicted him; he wanted to take Leningrad first which was the breeding ground of Communism. Von Rundsted screamed to his aids:

"What does this Bohemian Corporal know; he has an enormous moustache but tiny brains. If we go for Moscow now, we will have it; this might be our only chance.

According to Leen Willemstein, Adolf Hitler had made a vital mistake. He said: "Napoleon was defeated in Russia and Hitler will perish as well in that vast country."

It looked as though Leen Willemstein had it wrong this time. The Germans were quite successful in Russia. Despite that the Russians had 20 million armed men and the Germans less than 4 million in Russia, the Germans made fast progress.

In five days of fighting the Germans were 200 miles inside Russia and had taken the city of Minsk. The Russian Air Force had been destroyed and 300,000 Russian soldiers had surrendered. Moreover, the German Army was on its way to Leningrad.

The Red Army had been crippled by Stalin himself; after he came to power he was scared that the Army would take over and killed all his Generals except three. Those were mediocre Generals but they were faithful to Stalin and that's all that counted. After Stalin's killing spree Lieutenants were now commanding divisions instead of Generals. The result was disastrous.

Fabulous German successes were reported. In less than a month, the Germans had destroyed three Russian Armies and a week later they cut off 43 Russian divisions. Half of the Russian Army had been obliterated. The Germans captured 2600 tanks, 1500 guns and 3000 armored vehicles. It was hard to believe that the Russians could continue the war after their front was smashed.

There was one thing Adrie didn't understand. In 1939 when Russia attacked Finland, the whole Western World was in uproar and condemned Russia for aggression. The western press printed stories about the cruelty of the Communist regime. Churches were closed and mass murders had been committed. According to the press there were churches full of corpses and many mass graves had been found in the Soviet Union. The Reverend of the church, where the family the Kievit worshipped, had said that Stalin was the Anti-Christ.

Now, with the German invasion of Russia, Churchill had pronounced that Russia was an ally, the Russians were our big brothers and Joseph Stalin, the Russian dictator, was Uncle Joe. On the other hand, Adolf Hitler said that the German invasion was a crusade against Bolshevism and Communism; he added that the German Wehrmacht had found many mass graves and churches full of corpses. Churchill denied all this and said: "It's only German propaganda aimed at the people of the occupied countries to get them on their side."

When Adrie confronted the war specialist Leen Willemstein with his observation, Leen said: "That's a very good observation; the Western World has changed its opinion about the Russians now they are fighting the Nazis. England will never be a friend of Russia but in the hour of need it's good to have an ally to fight a common enemy."

Churchill had never liked Russia with its Communism and he was certainly no friend of Stalin. However, a common enemy makes a forced friendship. When Churchill was asked about his change of attitude he answered: "The friends of my friends are my friends but their enemies are my enemies. If Hitler wants to invade hell, I should at least make a favourable recommendation to the Devil."

With the favourable recommendation of Churchill, Hitler did remarkably well in Russia. After the heavy losses, it was up to the U.S. to re-supply the Russian Army across the Atlantic. Many more supply ships were torpedoed and went down to the bottom of the ocean.

Churchill couldn't have been happier with the German invasion of Russia. Finally there was a second front and a reprieve, for the time being, that could be used by England to get back in shape. After the defeat of Yugoslavia and Greece, Britain became isolated off the shore of a German held continent. Britain was the only part of Europe still holding out against Hitler. Ringed by U boats and suffering heavy air attacks, Britain had no other means of hitting back except by bombing Germany.

There was a strange incident on May 10, 1941. Rudolph Hess was number 2 in Nazi Germany. He had been more than anybody else responsible that Hitler came to power and Hitler had rewarded him for that. After the German successes with the Luftwaffe; Goring became number 2 and Rudolf Hess was demoted. Moreover, Hess didn't agree with Hitler to attack Russia, he thought that it was a grave mistake. Apparently he was cheesed off enough that he took a German aeroplane and parachuted down in Scotland. He asked for an audience with the English King but was promptly imprisoned and put in the Tower of London for safe keeping till the war was over.

Hess was a pilot himself and took quite frequently an airplane to fly so nobody expected that he would fly away from Germany to England. Hitler was devastated; it was the first split among the Nazis. With damage control he tried to cover up stating that Hess was mentally deranged. Stalin looked at this strange incidence with suspicion; he thought that Hess had gone to Churchill to arrange a pact to destroy Russia.

Radio London didn't do only news broadcasts for the occupied countries. They also had a cabaret every Saturday night, at 8.00 p.m., which was brought in the Dutch language. They called the show "Radio Orange." Few Dutch citizens missed the cabaret on Saturday night. This time there was a humorous song about Rudolf Hess. According to the song he had thought "There is trouble in Germany. So I better get the hell to Britain. Because you are much better off with an Englishman than with a Nazi."

Radio Orange had a message for the Fuhrer as well: "Dear Adolph Hitler; Your top Nazi Rudolf Hess has safely arrived in England. Don't you worry a bit; we'll take good care of him. Greetings from Radio Orange. Over and out."

There were all kinds of comical songs on Radio orange relating to the war. One of them was related to General Rommel who was fighting in the Libyan Desert.

What is this with that Rommel wizard?
Fighting up there in the Libyan Desert.

With all the Dutch National Socialists studying for Mayor in the New Order, Radio Orange had a new song in their cabaret program. It was all about the New Order and the refrain was:

In the New Order of today,
You can become a Mayor hip, hip, hooray.

Fighting Germany was mostly done by bombing raids on Germany by the English. In the beginning, the English made the mistake of trying precision daylight bombing of German cities. Without fighter protection the English lost a considerable number of bombers. Fighters did not have enough range to protect the bombers when they were flying over Germany. However, The Netherlands was closer to England and fighters were assisting and protecting the bombers during daylight. More and more bombing raids took place on the dockyards in Rotterdam. As soon as a new warship was launched the English bombers came to sink it before it could be put to use. The Dutch Nazis contributed to the German propaganda against Russia. A giant poster appeared on the houses of the traitors stating:

"The English and Bolsheviks,
Are dancing to the pipes of the Jewish clique"

On July 8th Adrie listened to the German news broadcast. The news was very good for the Germans but not for the hopeful Dutch people. The Germans boasted that they had destroyed 89 of the 164 Russian divisions and that the Russian defence was practically wiped out. According to the German news the Germans were now 440 miles into Russia and only 200 miles from Moscow. Before winter the war in Russia would be over.

Adrie wondered if the Germans were going to win this war and listened to Radio London that night. He hoped that the German news broadcast was only lies and that the English broadcast would set the record straight. He hoped in vain, there was no good news on any front; it seemed that there was no magic bullet that could turn the fortunes of war in favor of the Allies. It looked as if the Allies were going to fight another day but at the rate they were going, were they going to fight another month and how about another year? The Germans seemed unstoppable with their Blitz Krieg.

When the paper came there was another bolstering of the German forces announced.

"FRANCO SENDS BLUE SPANISH DIVISION TO RUSSIA TO HELP HITLER.

Leen Willemstein knew all about it and said: "Hitler and Mussolini both helped General Franco, in the Spanish Civil War, by bombing targets of the Spanish Government and now General Franco owes Hitler one. This is pay off time!"

There were daily advertisements in the Dutch newspapers which were controlled by the Germans. The Germans asked for Dutch people to enlist in the German Waffen S.S. to fight in Russia. Hitler had organized the S.S. in 1931 and in 1932 it had a strength of 30,000. When the war started there were quite a few S.S. divisions and now Hitler was so gracious as to let the occupied countries join in. In order to keep them separate from the Germans he called the volunteers from the occupied countries the Waffen S.S.

Giant posters appeared to get people interested.

"THE WAFFEN S.S. CALLS YOU.
People of the Netherlands. For your honor and conscience. Join us in the fight against Bolshevism and Communism."

It didn't take long to get enough Dutch volunteers to form a division to fight with the Germans in Russia. Most of those volunteers were sons of

Dutch Nazis and there were also some young Dutch boys who were nothing but a bunch of adventurers. There was also the Siegherheids Dienst, marked on the uniforms S.D.. It was another way to serve the Nazis. They were mainly chauffeurs to transport ammunition and troops for the Germans. Quite a few adventurous Dutch boys joined and became truck drivers or tank commanders.

After two months of vigorous advertising in the Dutch newspapers and on the radio, 50,000 Dutch volunteers had joined the S.S. The Germans heralded this success in the newspaper:

"DUTCH S.S. DIVISION FORMED."

The German Command is happy to announce that a full division of Dutch volunteers has joined the S.S. to fight for a New Europe against Communism and Bolshevism. They will receive a three month military training in Germany to make them ready for battle. After their training they will be shipped to Russia to join their German comrades in their fight against Stalin.

Koekoek had three sons, the oldest son Joe Koekoek volunteered for the S.S.. Before he left for Germany to receive his training, he came home for three days to say good bye to his family. He was showing off his brand new S.S. uniform by parading on the Hordyk. When Leen Willemstein saw this show off he said: "Luckily we have only to put up with that traitor for another three days and then he'll be gone, for good we hope. It's not very likely that he will return when he goes to fight in Russia."

Three months later the newspaper announced:

"NEDERLAND DIVISION FINISHED TRAINING."

The Dutch S.S. Division of volunteers is now ready to be shipped to Russia and will be assigned combat duties on the Eastern Front.

Leen Koekoek had all praise for his brother Joe who was fighting against the Bolsheviks for a New Order in a New Europe. Theus de Haan said: "You are only a bloody traitor, I hope you f... off to Russia like your brother and never return."

Leen Koekoek replied: "I'll remember this, after Hitler wins the war there wouldn't be a place for you in the New Order that is going to be established in Europe."

Theus countered: "There will be a New Order alright, but it will be an order without you because we will knot all you bloody traitors on the highest tree after we win the war." The school bell announced the beginning of the lessons which luckily ended the heated argument.

German propaganda had reached other countries as well and the next announcement in the paper told the Dutch people all about it.

EUROPEAN CRUSADE AGAINST COMMUNISM VALUABLE.

Germany is not alone in its struggle against Communism and Bolshevism. Belgium has joined the Germans with an S.S. division of Belgian volunteers.

Before Hitler attacked Russia, Stalin had occupied Latvia, Estonia and Lithuania. When the Germans took those countries from Russia they saw the Germans as liberators. The newspaper told the Dutch people all about it.

GERMAN ARMY WELCOMED WITH FLOWERS AND KISSES.

The German liberation forces are welcomed in Latvia, Estonia and Lithuania. Thousands of women came out to shower the German liberators with flowers and kisses.

The Ukraine and Belorussia had also been added to the mighty Russian Empire involuntarily and were also seeing the Germans as liberators.

CRUSADING VOLUNTEER S.S. DIVISIONS REACH 8 DIVISIONS.

Latvia, Estonia, Lithuania and Belorussia each contributed one S.S. Division to fight the Russians, and the Ukraine has volunteered two fine divisions to fight the aggression of Stalin. Many more divisions from European countries are in the making. Together with the German Army they will wipe out Communism and Bolshevism for good."

Propaganda was Hitler's strongest weapon. There were daily stories in the newspaper about life in Russia. There was a story about Moscow where the Communists had built a high wall around a block. Everybody had been removed and nobody knew what was going on behind the high wall. A young boy climbed the wall and when he was on top of it he was grabbed and pulled behind the wall. When his father went to investigate, he was told that he was misinformed and if he didn't stop making false accusations, they would arrest him and keep him behind the high wall.

Another story was about families who had to work the land in Russia. When the woman was pregnant, she was forced to keep working. She delivered her baby at a corner of the field and after the delivery she got up to resume her work.

There was also a story about a very old woman who was forced to work when she was dying. She died on the land she was working on and her family buried her where she dropped.

The cleverest story to get Christians on the Nazi side was the story about a Christian family in Russia. It was put on the radio as a play: "After the Communists had taken over, the churches were closed and the Russian people weren't allowed to worship anymore. Lenin had said that religion is the opium of the poor people and prayers at school and in the houses were outlawed. The Communists wanted to educate the children to be Atheists. In spite of all the repressions there was still a Christian family that had maintained values and were teaching their son to say Grace at the meals. As there was never enough food on the table, their son went to school hungry most of the time.

One time the Commissar of the Communist Party was visiting a school in Moscow. The children had been trained beforehand in order to make a good impression with the Commissar. When the Commissar entered the classroom, all children stood up and said in unison: 'Good morning Commissar.'

The Commissar asked the children questions. When the Commissar asked a Christian educated boy: 'Who takes care of the people?' the boy answered: 'God takes care of the people, Commissar.'

That was the wrong answer, the right answer was: 'The Communist Party takes care of the people.'

The Commissar asked the boy: 'Are you hungry?' When the boy admitted that he was hungry because of food shortages at home, the Commissar said: 'You were saying that God takes care of the people. If that is so, why don't you ask God for food? You are hungry ain't you?'

While the boy kneeled on the floor to pray for bread, the teacher and commissar were talking about those stupid Christians, who stubbornly refused to follow the teachings of Marx. The Commissar said: 'The churches are already closed for a long time, yet there are still some people who teach their children from the Bible.'

As soon as the boy had finished his prayer, the Commissar turned to the boy and asked him: 'You asked the Lord for bread, so where is it?'

The boy answered: 'I don't know!'

Now the teacher turned to the boy stating: 'You can see now that God doesn't take care of you. Why don't you ask the commissar for bread?'

The boy asked the commissar: 'Dear commissar I'm very hungry. Please give me some bread.'

Next, the commissar gave some bread to the boy. He also wrote down the boy's name and address for a report to the Communist party.

At night when the family had their meagre supper the boy refused to say Grace. His father got very angry but his mother said: 'Something must have happened at school.'

She asked her son why he wouldn't say Grace. The boy answered: 'I asked the Lord for food when I was at school but the Lord didn't give me anything. Then I asked the commissar for food and he gave me bread.'

That night there was a knock on the door and the people were arrested for conspiracy against the state."

All those plays and stories about the cruelties in Russia were geared to get religious people on the Nazi side. It's hard to say how much impact it had on the people of the occupied countries. One thing is for sure, that a lot of people had difficulty seeing the Russians as their allies.

During the summer of 1941 more and more articles were rationed. Meat, butter, milk, flour and sugar were in short supply and could only be bought with coupons. At that time the rations were almost adequate. There were enough vegetables and potatoes to make up for the shortage of bread and meat.

Coffee, tea and cocoa didn't grow in The Netherlands and were not available. Shoes and clothes were also distributed and more and more articles were added all the time.

When the Germans occupied The Netherlands, the German soldiers would buy all kinds of food, clothes and other articles for their family in Germany. They would send packages to their families all the time. However, when shortages became more frequent in The Netherlands, the Germans would say: "In the heimat (In our country) there is lots of everything and here in The Netherlands you can't buy anything anymore. Bei uns ist alles besser. (Everything is better by us.)"

One of the store owners said: "We had lots of goods here too, until you Germans shipped everything to your heimat, that's why there is a lot of stuff in your heimat and we have shortages."

The German soldier said: "The heimat is superior to any country in the world."

Quite cheesed off with this nonsense, the store owner replied angrily: "If it's so good in the heimat and everything is better why don't you F... off to your heimat and leave us alone?"

It was now the turn of the German soldier to be cheesed off, he shouted with a loud voice: "Nobody is telling us to F... off, we are here to stay."

His wife, fearing the worst in this exchange of words, said to the German soldier: "You are very lucky to live in Germany and to have it that good. We are less fortunate in The Netherlands."

A little more quietly, the soldier replied: "We sure are better off than you people and don't you forget it." He then left.

Of course there were some good Germans and there were some bad Germans, contrary to the belief of the Russians that the only good German was a dead German. On several occasions German prisoners of war had to march to their concentration camp and the Russians would simply shoot them in the back.

Hitler did his darnedest to force a victory; he tried to starve England with his U boats in the Atlantic. On the other hand England tried desperately to turn the war around. Their tactics were mainly based to cut off the Nazis from their oil supplies. A modern army needs oil and if they could just wipe out the German oil supplies the German Blitzkrieg would peter out.

With the tremendous German war effort, energy was in short supply. To remedy this problem, Germany was boosting its oil production with synthetic gasoline which was made from coal. There were quite a few coal mines in Limburg, one of the Southern Dutch provinces. With the increased demand for energy, the Germans took most of the produced coal to make gasoline out of it. Consequently, there was not much coal left for the Dutch people. Meagre rations of coal indicated that the people could expect cold houses during the coming winter.

There was no natural gas or oil in The Netherlands, everything was geared for coal. People heated their houses with coal and they cooked mostly on coal gas. As there was no natural gas in The Netherlands, it was made from coal. Coal was put in giant cylinders with no air supply. Next, the cylinders were heated from the outside to release the gas present in the coal. The gas, formed that way, would escape in big tanks where it was put under pressure. From there on it could go through the gas lines to the consumers.

Not too many people were allowed to drive a car. Only doctors and a few other people who provided essential services were still driving. Pony taxies were used more and more by people who had a car but no gasoline to drive it. They just took the motor out of their car and put a horse in front. It was exactly like the Depression when people couldn't afford to buy gasoline anymore and put a horse in front of their car. The horseless carriage had been heralded as the greatest thing on earth, yet, it had a terrible struggle to survive. There always seemed to be horses needed to pull it.

Before the war all oil supplies were imported from Rumania, Russia and the U.S. As soon as the war started there wasn't any oil imported from the U.S. and Russia. All the oil that entered The Netherlands came now from

Rumania which was a German ally. The Germans needed more and more oil for their army and took steps to limit the oil needs for The Netherlands. One of those steps was to convert busses for public transportation to coal gas. Now that the Germans had other uses for coal gas, they reduced the rations to the Dutch people who were cooking with gas.

Taxis had to use coal gas too; they were equipped with a gas balloon on top of their taxi which was filled with gas. The gas balloon was almost as big as the taxi itself, which created a problem when the taxi drove out of town. As soon as the taxi increased speed the big gas balloon made the taxi very unstable. Only for city traffic could gas balloons be used.

Buses used two gas cylinders which were mounted on a little trailer that was towed by the bus. All those converted buses had to go to the gas plant to fill the cylinders to keep driving. Trucks for transportation and the few cars that were left were also converted.

Gas cylinders on a trailer worked for buses that operated near the cities, where there was a gas plant to fill the gas cylinders. Trucks and buses which were used in the country were equipped with a trailer which had a wood gas generator. There was enough room on the trailer for a box with wood logs to enable the vehicles to travel quite a distance. Amazingly the wood gas generators worked quite well and did the job. The only setback was that it was dirty to stoke the wood gas generators and the generators had to be cleaned of soot from time to time.

Adrie thought that those little trailers behind the bus were made for him, to provide the necessary transportation when he went to school. He waited patiently like all other people at the bus stop till the bus came. When the bus stopped, the waiting passengers went into the bus except Adrie. He boarded the bus but he had standing room only on the little trailer. Adrie's friend thought that free public transportation was real cool. And he was right, standing in the open with rain and wind wasn't exactly comfortable. Soon there were two boys standing on the little trailer between the gas cylinders.

One day that Adrie and his friend were riding the bus, they had a spell of bad luck. To get on the bus trailer depended on the bus stopping at the bus stop. If there were no people getting on or off the bus, the bus didn't stop and there was no bus ride. That was no real problem, other than that the two had to walk to school. Well, they got on the bus alright but how did they get off if the bus didn't stop? The bus didn't stop at the stop which was only half a block before the school. That was already a disaster in itself.

Another disaster happened when they were driving past the school, they saw the Principal in the schoolyard and of course he spotted them on the trailer. He always saw things he wasn't supposed to see. There were just no people to get off the bus or to get on, except Adrie and his friend. This darned bus wasn't designed right at all; it didn't have a bell cord on the trailer to make the bus stop when they wanted to get off.

Because of the non stop trip, the bus had gained quite a speed which made it hard to jump off the trailer. However, when the bus didn't stop they had little choice but jump off a riding vehicle like a Commando Trooper. They didn't have the training of a Commando Trooper which made the landing more than a little rough when they landed in a hedge that had probably been put there with Adrie and his friend in mind to break their fall. Their school clothes were kind of green from the hedge which made them look like tramps instead of school boys. That free bus ride didn't do them any good; they had to walk further back to school than they had to walk to school in the first place.

Luckily they made it back to school before the bell signalled the beginning of the lessons, or else they would have been in deep trouble. That was all the luck they were going to have. First of all, the Principal wanted to see them to give them a lecture about the danger when jumping off moving vehicles. It was also noticeable that things had gone wrong. Of course, the Principal had something to say about their dirty school clothes and their bloody knees. They had to stay after school and had to write one hundred lines: "It's dangerous to ride on moving vehicles."

Now came another hard part when they went home. Adrie had to explain to his mother how his clothes got ripped and green. "There was this terrible big bully who pushed me right into the hedge and the hedge was freshly painted I guess because my shirt is all green."

When winter came they remembered that it was dangerous to ride on moving vehicles. They had written it a hundred times so they knew. There was a lot of snow on the road and when Adrie was playing with his sleigh the bus stopped. He had a better idea; he laid down on his belly on the sleigh and grabbed the bumper of the trailer. Another free ride was obtained but now on his own sleigh.

His friend didn't have a sleigh which was no problem at all. Pretty soon they were lying on the sleigh on top of one another. Unfortunately that ended in tragedy when the bus came on a stretch where they had cleaned the snow away from the road. The sleigh didn't slide very well on the rough road and both tumbled on the street. Luckily there was no damage done this time and no lines to be written.

At the beginning of December 1941 there was a special German broadcast. German troops had reached the outskirts of Moscow and were 22 miles from Red Square. Hitler had one of his shouting speeches. He shouted: "A European Crusade against Bolshevism and Communism has been successful. Moscow is in my palm and to celebrate the greatest victory of all times, I have sent a special train with granite, to Moscow, to make a giant Arc de Triumph on Red Square. I myself, as Fuhrer of the German race, will unveil the monument. This is the end of Russia. Russia is dead! Russia is dead! Russia is dead!"

The German people were shouting: "Sich Heil, Sich Heil," for a solid five minutes. They believed in their Fuhrer. The Germans went from victory to victory; it was hard to believe that it would ever end. Luckily, on December 5, 1941 there was good news from Radio London for the first time since the war had started.

"This is Radio London. There is no news from the Western Front but great news has reached us from the Eastern Front. The Russian counter offensive, which started yesterday with fresh troops from Siberia, has been a great success. In one day of fighting the Germans have been driven back more than 12 miles and have sustained heavy losses. Seventeen German divisions have been completely destroyed. Stalin has ordered that the beleaguered city of Moscow has to be freed at any cost and to kill all German soldiers who are on Russian soil without mercy."

All Dutch people were sure that this was the turning point in the war and that Hitler would be defeated like Napoleon in Russia. It looked as if history was repeating itself and that Hitler had found his master. The German blitzkrieg had brought the Germans into the outskirts of Moscow. But that's where the blitzkrieg ended; the Germans didn't take Moscow before the winter of 1942. The element of surprise had gone which gave the Russians time to reorganize and put up defences. Hitler's Russian campaign came to a screeching halt, he hadn't blitzed fast enough and had over extended his military abilities. Winter came early in 1941 and winter was on the Russian side, it was like having another ally. It looked as if the disasters of 1940 and 1941 had come to an abrupt halt and that 1941 would turn into a good year after all. This was the break that everybody had been waiting for.

It was not to be; only for two days did the Dutch people live in hope of a turning point in the war. On December 7, 1941 the glimmer of hope of a favorite conclusion of this terrible war disappeared completely. When the Dutch people were listening to the news on their own stations, which were controlled by Germany, they heard:

"Radio Berlin has announced that Japan has declared war on the U.S. In the early morning hours of December 7, 1941, the Japanese fleet has attacked the U.S. Naval Base Pearl Harbour in Hawaii. The U.S. fleet has been totally destroyed. Battleship Arizona, Oklahoma and two other battleships have been sunk and are on the bottom of the Pacific Ocean. Six other U.S. warships have been heavily damaged. The entire U.S. air force which was stationed on Hawaii has been destroyed. In a daring Japanese raid on Hawaii more than 350 U.S. aircraft in all were lost. The Japanese lost only 29 airplanes.

Furthermore, the Japanese have also attacked Hong Kong, Malaysia and the Philippines. It also has been reported that Singapore was bombed by the Japanese Air Force."

Radio London said that night: "Washington has confirmed that the Japanese have cowardly attacked the U.S. naval base in Hawaii and that heavy losses have been sustained by the Navy and Air Force. The Japanese Government declared war on the U.S. 55 minutes after this cowardly attack. President Roosevelt said: 'This day will go down in infamy.' President Roosevelt has also asked for an emergency meeting with Congress in which he will ask it to declare war on Japan."

Indeed, the next day the U.S. declared war on Japan. England also declared war on Japan because of the attack on Hong Kong and the bombing of Singapore. On December 10, 1941 Germany and Italy declared war on the U.S.

It looked as if another blitzkrieg had developed in the Far East. On December 14, 1941 the Japanese captured Guam. On December 17 they landed on Borneo which was a Dutch colony. The Dutch Government, which was in exile in London, promptly declared war on Japan. And on December 20 the Japanese captured Hong Kong.

After another disastrous year for the Allies; 1941 came to an end. It had been the darkest year in history. For the Americans Hawaii had been a Paradise for romance, hula girls, flower leis, entertainment and pineapples. While the U.S. Navy was enjoying all of it, the Japanese fleet was on its way to bring a devastating blow to the U.S. fleet and change this peaceful Paradise into hell.

Europe was already two years at war and the U.S hadn't been involved other than supplying England. The U.S. Congress figured that Hitler and his Nazis were the responsibility of Europe. Well, Hitler had all of Europe except one island. Churchill declared Pearl Harbour a blessing; it finally brought the U.S. into the war.

During 1940 World War II had been largely contained to Europe but during 1941 the war had escalated to a World War which had spread to all regions of the world. Even countries which were neutral were somehow involved in this global conflict. Russia, Japan and the U.S. had entered the war. They were all industrial giants with a tremendous production. Every belligerent state was now run on a war economy and an ever increasing mobilization of war industry to out produce the enemy.

Radio London was looking for good things to say when they reviewed 1941. Actually, the only good news about 1941 was again that it was finally over. Was there ever going to be a good year for the Allies? They could only come up with two notable items. On May 27th the greatest battleship ever, the German Bismark had been sunk. Radio London forgot to say that four days before the English battleship Hood had been sunk by the Bismark. However, it was a great accomplishment. The Bismark had sunk quit a few Allied ships which made Churchill say: "Sink the Bismark!" An all-out hunt by the English Navy accomplished what they were ordered to do.

The only other good thing that could be said was that Germany hadn't taken Moscow and Hitler had to postpone unveiling his Arc de Triumph on Red Square until spring. However, Hitler had said that because of the severe winter in Russia the German Army had faced a temporary setback. As soon as spring came he would finish Russia and take England right after.

Hitler had figured that Russia would have been in his palm before winter came and hadn't supplied his troops with winter equipment. The Russians had white uniforms which were a good camouflage in the snow. The Germans with their green uniforms were like sitting ducks.

In order to cover up their green uniforms, the Germans robbed the Russians in occupied territory of night caps, night dresses and white underwear. Most of the German soldiers looked like grandmothers instead of Herren Folk of the German Reich. The Russians had special oil to oil their rifles when temperatures were 40 below and the Germans didn't. When the German rifles froze, the soldiers would urinate on them to keep them going. It was Hitler's biggest mistake not to plan for a war in winter.

In spite of Hitler's blunder, the Germans didn't have to look for good things in 1941. In 1940 the German U boats had sunk 1059 Allied ships. In 1941 they improved significantly on that and sank 1299 ships totalling 4,328,500 tons. U.S. supplies that reached England were at their lowest ever. At the end of 1941 England had only oil for about 14 days, and very little food and ammunition. The docks of South Hampton had been totally destroyed and unloading the ships that hadn't been sunk by German sub marines was very difficult. Hitler had applied the choke hold to England. The Germans had also taken Yugoslavia and Greece during 1941 and had almost succeeded in taking Russia.

As for the Dutch people, they were even more disappointed than in 1940. The Dutch colonies were now also involved in the global conflict. Nothing good could be expected when you have to fight a supreme Japanese military force. Another Dutch defeat loomed in the near future.

THE NEW COMMANDER OF AIR, SEA AND LAND FORCES.

Adrie was glued to the radio; he listened to German and English broadcasts and read the newspaper from the beginning to the end. All he could think about was the war. He also observed the German Army when they were marching by. That must be real cool to be in the Army and go to different countries, that way you could see something of the world.

On a nice summer day, Adrie said to his friends: "Let's play soldier." His friends were all in favor of it but didn't know how to play this new game. Luckily Adrie knew all about it and lectured: "First of all we have to have an army with soldiers and the soldiers have to have rifles."

"Where do we get rifles?" was the question.

Adrie knew it all: "At Gerritje the Goat's place."

Gerritje was an old woman; she kept a few goats and the boys said she looked like a goat herself. Nobody knew her real name but everybody knew Gerritje the Goat. She was living in a small old house right beside a pasture where she kept her goats. In a corner of the pasture was a pile of sticks which she used for climbing beans which she was growing.

Those sticks were useful because a boy could put one over his shoulder and pretend it was a rifle. Of course, Gerritje the Goat didn't volunteer to supply this new army with rifles so they had to be swiped. That was no problem; the German Army stole everything under the Sun and never asked for anything. What the German Army did could be copied, so the sticks were swiped. They learned fast.

It took quite some doing to get a solid, straight stick looking like a rifle for all the new soldiers. A crooked stick wouldn't do because you can't shoot with a crooked rifle. Finally everybody was happy with his stick rifle and the army was ready to go into training. Adrie started out pretending he was the sergeant, he made some sergeant stripes of old rags and put them on his arm. Everything was ready and the new army was marching on the Hordyk.

Most of the boys living on the Hordyk had voluntarily joined the army but the boys from the Petersely Dyk never played with the boys of the Hordyk. That was a different group of boys who weren't really welcome in Adrie's army. "No problem," the boys from the Petersely Dyk said and formed their own army. A few of the boys who were living on the Hordyk, close to the Petersely Dyk, were renegades and joined the Petersely Dyk army. It was an opportunity lost and Adrie missed out on that possible reinforcement.

It was decided to have a singing army like the Germans and soon the new army was marching and singing like the German soldiers. Usually the German soldiers were singing "Wir gahn fahren, gegen England." Adrie was a copycat alright but he didn't want his army to sing that song, he had his army sing "Blond Marie has a heart of barbed wire." It sounded good and it looked great.

> Blond Marie has a heart of barbed wire.
> You can stay at home, barbed wire.
> All the boys were trying to melt her heart away.
> They better stay home, barbed wire.

It all started very innocently with a group of singing boys, marching on the Hordyk with sticks on their shoulders, pretending that they were rifles. Little they knew that this army game would grow on them, until a day that bloody battles would take place, injuring several boys with bruises and holes in their head and that windows of houses would be shattered.

This new game was an instant success and more and more soldiers joined the ranks of Adrie's army. With more soldiers there were more rifles needed which meant another visit to Gerritje the Goat's place. Even the German soldiers were watching the boys play and had all kinds of comments.

Something was missing, Adrie thought, there should be a Commander of Sea, Air and Land Forces. He had learned about the existence of such an important person when the war started. The Dutch commander had been sacked by the Dutch Government and General Winkelman had been appointed. General Winkelman had to fight the Germans and after the bombardment of Rotterdam he capitulated to the Germans.

Adrie never forgot a thing which came in handy when you play soldier. All the other boys agreed that there should be a Commander of Sea, Air and Land Forces even when there was no Air Force. The sea forces were actually insignificant but the Hordyk had a small raft two boys could stand on. The raft was pushed with sticks through the channel and the sticks came of course from Gerritje the Goat's place. She was lucky to have the contract for all supplies that the army needed. She was even luckier when the boys from the Petersely Dyk copied the army idea and also needed rifles.

There was only one person who knew the task of a commander of all forces. When Adrie said that he would be the commander, everybody agreed; there was no competition for the job because nobody else knew what to do. Adrie didn't know much about an army either but he closely watched the German Army and read the newspaper from A to Z which gave him a lot of knowledge. Compared to the other boys who knew nothing, he was a bright shining star in the firmament if it came to military matters and naturally, 'in the land of the blind, one eye will be king.'

Nobody was opposed to Adrie's promotion so he didn't have to shoot anybody. During a war when lots of under officers and officers are killed one can make fast promotion. But it was the first time in history that somebody who was sergeant for only three weeks was promoted to Commander of Sea, Air and Land Forces. It was a fast promotion, unequalled in history.

"It took Hitler longer to be promoted from Corporal to Fuhrer," Adrie's father said when he heard about the important job his son had. He added: "Winston Churchill said in the House of Commons that never during human conflict had there been a faster promotion than this one." Everybody was laughing except Adrie; he didn't think it was funny at all.

Kees Meuzelaar, the neighbor, heard about the new commander and said jokingly that it was about time that they had a new commander of all forces because the war didn't go good at all, maybe the new commander could make a difference.

Leen Willemstein said: "The new commander is coming too late for The Netherlands but maybe it can make a difference to the Hordyk. With the expertise and talents of the new tactical commander, the Hordyk could emerge as the most powerful street."

Adrie ignored all this smart talk; he had better things to do. The German soldiers commented on the competition army of the Petersely Dyk and asked when the Hordyk was going to go to war. That was a brilliant idea Adrie thought, the Hordyk could fight the Petersely Dyk which meant real war. However, there was one problem, there had to be an incident to cause a war. The big powers had never the problem of finding an incident to go to war about and neither did the Hordyk. Opportunity knocked at the door when the army from the Petersely Dyk was marching on the Hordyk. That was trespassing across the border line and Adrie's friends said: "Let's beat the hell out of the Petersely Dyk army; they think they can get away with murder."

That's not the way Adrie wanted to play the game; you have to play it right or don't play it at all. He said: "First of all we have to declare war on the Petersely Dyk and then we'll have a surprise attack like the Germans have done."

At night Adrie was busy writing a declaration of war which had to be delivered to the Petersely Dyk before the fight could start. Adrie called his army together the next day, and read the declaration of war. "Last week we saw that the Petersely Dyk army trespassed on Hordyk territory. This is a violation of the neutrality of the Hordyk and will be met with drastic action. Therefore, as Commander of Sea, Air and Land Forces I have no alternative but declare war on the Petersely Dyk."

He hand delivered the war declaration to Joh Kraak who was the sergeant of the Petersely Dyk army. Sergeant was the highest rank in the Petersely Dyk army; those kids didn't know from Adam and had no idea that an army needed a general commander of all forces.

When the important document was handed to Joh Kraak, he said: "What the hell is that?"

Adrie said: "You can read, can't you?" and left Joh Kraak alone. Joh Kraak didn't know what hit him and obviously didn't mobilize his army.

"Those boys have a lot to learn, they don't know squat," Adrie said to his friends. Everybody agreed and thought they were onto something big. This was the best game they ever had played.

After school the Hordyk army marched on the Petersely Dyk. They did a lot of shouting and screaming to intimidate the Petersely Dyk army and went to Joh Kraak's house. The world had never seen anything like this before. When Joh Kraak came outside, the Hordyk army was going to make him a prisoner of war. That attempt was unsuccessful because Joh's father interfered. He came after the boys who were trying to imprison his son with a long stick. When the boys started to run, Joh Kraak's father ran after them and hit them on their legs. It must have been a dry stick because it broke and there was minimal pain. However, the Hordyk army withdrew and regrouped on the Hordyk.

It was very obvious that the Petersely Dyk had a secret weapon. Their weapon was an angry Jaap Kraak who was Joh Kraak's father. One can always learn a lesson from any encounter and the Hordyk learned its lesson well. It was dangerous to venture into enemy territory.

Victory went to the head of the Petersely Dyk army. Of course, how much a victory is it when you call in your big brother or your big father to beat up on you? The next day when Adrie was eating, the war broke out. The Petersely Dyk marched on the Hordyk singing and shouting. They were rattling their sabres and beat up on every boy of the Hordyk they saw.

When this all happened the Commander of Sea, Air and Land Forces was eating. His friend came to bring the sad news that the Hordyk had been invaded. In the old days you would shoot the messenger when he brought bad news but Adrie was relying on his messenger so he let him live.

All of a sudden the Commander wasn't very hungry anymore and wanted to leave the table. The Commander's mother insisted he finish his supper first before attending to the war. She declared that the war could wait till he had finished his supper. Adrie argued that they could lose the war but his mother was bigger and stronger so the argument was lost in spite of Adrie's much higher rank.

Oh those mothers! As soon as supper was finished, the commander left the table to view the situation. He was very cautious not to show his face on the street because the enemy was in firm control of the Hordyk without firing a shot. From behind a hedge, Adrie spied on his arch enemy the Petersely Dyk. It was an insult to see the Petersely Dyk troops marching, singing and shouting but there wasn't much they could do about it. They had been caught with their pants down or with their Commander having supper.

Finally, the Petersely Dyk army returned home disappointed, they had been looking for a fight which didn't happen. The commander called all his staff officers for an emergency meeting. The Commander said: "It's disgusting how long it takes to get our army mobilized. It took us almost as long to get mobilized as England when they declared war on Germany. That's why the Germans took all of Europe and the Petersely Dyk took control of the Hordyk."

Piet Hermans said: "We don't take shit from anybody, we need an early warning system so we know when they are coming and we have to have a secret route to come together."

Jaap Hoogland lived about half way up the Hordyk. That was a good place to assemble so his basement was designated to assemble the troops. In case of a Petersely Dyk invasion everybody would avoid the street and take a route through the pastures. That way nobody would run into the Petersely Dyk army before the troops were at full strength.

It also had been decided that the weapons had to be improved. Some boys had sticks which were too short to fight a fully modernized army like the Petersely Dyk. Because of this another visit to Gerritje the Goat was necessary for re-arming purposes.

Gerritje the Goat had noticed that she had lost a lot of sticks and kept an eye on her property. As soon as the boys were selecting their sticks, she came running out of the house and called the boys thieves. She also demanded that the boys leave her property at once. Piet Hermans said: "As soon as we have enough sticks we will leave your property, don't you know there is a war on, damn it!"

Gerritje said: "We'll see about it, I'll go to the police." She walked into the street to the house where one of the policemen lived. Apparently she was lucky that the cop was home because she came back with him. By that time nobody was on her property anymore and the stolen sticks had been hidden because the writing had been on the wall. The policeman went after the boys right away and told them he had received a complaint that they were trespassing on Gerritje's property.

Piet Herremans, who was known for rough language, said: "That Gerritje the Goat is imagining things, if we only look at her sticks; she thinks we are going to swipe them."

The policeman asked: "Well, do you?"

"Are you kidding," Piet Herremans replied, "that old corpse of a woman can keep her sticks, we don't need them, what would we do with sticks anyway?"

Gerritje the Goat had walked up to the group of boys who were having the discussion with the policeman and had caught the last remark. She got furious and shouted at Piet Herremans: "For your information, I might be old but I'm not a corpse yet and I am very much alive, you big mouth."

The policeman warned everybody and told Gerritje that he would keep an eye on her property. Adrie didn't need a stick from Gerritje the Goat either; he had a much better idea. At the blacksmith's smithy, he had seen an iron rod which could be the ultimate weapon to secure a victory. Sticks break but iron rods don't and you can even break sticks if you hit them with an iron rod. At night the blacksmith was an iron rod poorer and Adrie was a good weapon richer.

The following day was a good day to try out the iron rod weapon. Another invasion of the Petersely Dyk took place and this time the army was mobilized in record time. In spite of the superior weapons of the Hordyk, the Petersely Dyk seemed to have the upper hand in the fight. They had quite a few more soldiers and outnumbered the Hordyk. It didn't take long for the Hordyk to acknowledge defeat and to run for their lives. They ran for Jaap Hoogland's basement with the Petersely Dyk army in hot pursuit. Jaap Hoogland bolted the basement door to keep the enemy out. The Petersely Dyk soldiers did a lot of shouting and banging on the basement door but as soon as Jaap Hoogland's father came to have a look at what all that noise was about, they withdrew to their heimat.

Disappointment followed the defeat and another meeting was scheduled. It had been noticed that the larger army of the Petersely Dyk had given them victory. Furthermore, there were also soldiers of the Dortse Straatweg in their army. There were about 25 soldiers in the Hordyk army and 35 in the enemy army. Adrie said: "What they can do we can do too, if not better. The Kerkedyk and the Smeetlandse Dyk are playing soldier too but they never went to war. Well here is their chance, I'll ask them to be our ally and we could end up with about 50 soldiers. We are going to teach the Petersely Dyk a lesson which they will never forget. We will fight the Petersely Dyk with our new allies until victory has been obtained."

It sounded much like Churchill's speech when he tried to bring hope in England's darkest hour. Adrie had heard this speech when he had listened to the forbidden English broadcasting. This was the darkest hour for the Hordyk and the disappointed soldiers needed much encouragement to continue fighting. Adrie borrowed a few lines from Churchill's speech and accomplished the same as Churchill had accomplished. Immortal words go a long way and after listening to Adrie's pep talk, everybody figured there were better days ahead and they would beat the Petersely Dyk.

It took some time to convince the neighboring streets to participate in fighting the Petersely Dyk and a few boys backed out, they didn't want to have a part in fighting, a boy could get hurt they said and my mother won't allow me to fight. It meant a smaller army than had been figured but there would still be about 43 soldiers. With a little luck they could outnumber the Petersely Dyk by about 8 men which should be good enough.

For a few nights, the Petersely Dyk had the pleasure of marching on the Hordyk, from beginning to end, with no resistance. But the day of reckoning was coming; it was all prepared in Jaap Hoogland's basement. Adrie said: "Strategy is important, our tactic will be to lure the Petersely Dyk army into a trap and then we'll ambush them." Adrie had studied the war all the time and used big words from world leaders and his soldiers were impressed.

It was the eve of the great battle and a fast mobilization of the army was prepared. Every night, the Petersely Dyk army had marched on the Hordyk at about 6.30 p.m. so all soldiers had to be on their post not later than 6.00 p.m. About half of the army would fight the Petersely Dyk army and the other half would be in hiding. Adrie said: "As soon as the Petersely Dyk marches on the Hordyk I will meet them at Waterloo."

That sounded interesting, he had borrowed that sentence from General Wellington who was fighting Napoleon in 1815. From there on everybody of the Hordyk army knew where Waterloo was, it was the critical point where the armies were going to meet. With half of the army fighting it had to be an orderly and fast withdrawal. After the Petersely Dyk had passed the hidden half of the Hordyk army they would attack the Petersely Dyk from the back and the fleeing army would stop running and attack from the front. The result would be "Total Ambush."

The Commander had supper at 5.30 p.m. but he was plenty nervous that he could not make it in time to the battlefield. His friend who had earlier supper was already whistling outside which made Adrie turn on his chair uneasily. His mother watched Adrie wolfing down his food and said: "Take your time to eat, London and Liverpool weren't build in one day either."

Adrie cared less about London and Liverpool, he only cared about the Petersely Dyk which could be marching on the Hordyk any time and he had to prepare the ambush yet. There were other soldiers who had trouble getting away from the dinner table in time but at 6.30 p.m. everybody was at his post. Nobody wanted to miss this historical battle, everybody wanted to be part of it and go down in history.

One more soldier was added at the last minute before the battle took place. It was Anton Jongenotter. He was the newspaper boy and wanted to help to spill the blood of the Petersely Dyk army. Anton lived on the Achterweg, which was a gravel road with a couple of houses. He was just a little independent country with no army but he wanted to fight and offered his services to the cause of the Hordyk. It was a deal and he asked to be in the group that would tackle the Petersely Dyk army as soon as they were advanced far enough.

It was already 6.45 p.m. with no enemy in sight. Maybe the Petersely Dyk got tired of marching on the Hordyk every night with no enemy to fight. But suddenly loud singing and shouting testified of the approaching enemy army. Within no time a bloody confrontation took place. Anton Jongenotter had his bike with bags of newspapers with him and when the Hordyk withdrew he almost lost his bike with newspapers to the Petersely Dyk. That would have been a disaster with dire consequences.

Everything went as planned; Joh Kraak headed the hot pursuit of the withdrawing Hordyk army. He was sitting in an old baby carriage which he called his tank. On the outside of the baby carriage he had painted a red cross for disguise. That's what the Germans used to do in transportation of war material, they had trucks with red crosses painted on them to avoid bombing from the air. Joh had made a couple of little wooden guns with an elastic with which he was shooting pebbles. The Petersely Dyk was inventive alright but to day they were heading for a total defeat, Adrie thought.

As soon as the Petersely Dyk had passed Waterloo, the hidden group of the Hordyk attacked them in the back. The fleeing Hordyk army made a stand and in no time the situation was reversed. The Petersely Dyk was trying to flee but they were enclosed and only a few lucky ones got out of the massacre.

Joh Kraak in his tank, which was pushed by one of his soldiers, passed a hedge where Hordyk soldiers were waiting with a pile of rocks which could have annihilated the entire German army. Joh was sitting in his tank looking over his two wooden pistols with his squinted eye ready for the kill but when the bombardment of his tank started; his aid took to his heels and never looked back at his sergeant who was imprisoned. His baby carriage tank with the Red Cross was booty for the Hordyk. There were eight prisoners of war including the sergeant of the Petersely Dyk.

The prisoners of war were tied to a tree but there were two boys who were considered to be traitors. They lived on the Hordyk close to the Petersely Dyk and also had friends who were living on the Petersely Dyk. They had crossed the floor and were renegades when they joined the Petersely Dyk army. Those two were brought before the Court Marshall. The Commander condemned their treason and said: "You two have been found guilty of treason which draws the death penalty in time of war. Therefore you will be executed by a firing squat at sunset and your corpses will be left in the field to be eaten by buzzards."

It wasn't sunset yet but that didn't matter. The condemned traitors were put against an old barn, four Hordyk soldiers formed the firing squad and when the commander shouted, 'Fire,' they said "Bang you are dead."

One thing went wrong, the dead traitors were still standing up but that was no problem, the commander poked them with his iron rod in the ribs and said: "Play dead if you love your life."

They got the picture and dropped to the ground. From a distance the Hordyk soldiers watched how the dead traitors came to life again and were running as if the devil was running after them with his pitchfork. Joh Kraak and the other prisoners were pardoned and could return to their heimat. That concluded the most devastating battle the Hordyk had ever witnessed.

Not everybody was enthusiastic about the great victory of the Hordyk army. As for starters, the parents of the soldiers who came home wounded with holes in their heads and bruises were furious. The traffic on the Hordyk had been halted for over fifteen minutes while the mother of all battles took place. In hot pursuit the fighting armies didn't watch for bikers and some of the bikers fell and sustained injuries.

In hot pursuit of the Petersely Dyk army, the soldiers never watched the bikers who were victimised. The cars had been honking their horns in vain and the bell-ringing bikers didn't get anywhere either. Some of the bikes had been hit by the bombardment of rocks and had lost some spokes from their wheels that had to be replaced. Even the bus was delayed because it had to wait about ten minutes before the Hordyk was safe again before proceeding. Moreover, one of the rocks had missed its military target and had shattered a window.

There were also a lot of complaints from newspaper readers who had their newspaper delivered over an hour late. Anton Jongenotter had the same attitude as Adrie: "Those people can be glad that they received a newspaper at all, sometimes when there is a war on people don't get their newspaper."

Adrie got cheesed off about this behaviour of the civilian population and said: "When there is a war on there will be casualties and of course some civilian property will be damaged by the shrapnel of our rocks, do you think this is a perfect war? Even the English damage civilian property when they are bombing military targets."

Most of the time the boys were playing football or hide and seek. This was something new the civilian population wasn't ready for. "Warring Streets!" The police were flooded with complaints and decided to let the Principal of the school handle this incident. Only the sixth and seventh grade students had participated in this all out war and were told to stay after school hour.

98 *Jacobaris*

For openers, the Principal faced Adrie stating: "I've heard that you are the commander and got this war started."

"Me?" Adrie said innocently, "what gave you that idea?"

The Principal continued with stating: "You have been seen running behind boys, with an iron rod, hitting them. This is sheer barbarism and it must stop immediately."

"The Petersely Dyk was trespassing on Hordyk territory and was beating up on us!" Adrie defended himself. "All what we did was defend ourselves!"

The other boys of the Hordyk agreed that it was Joh Kraak's fault and he was the instigator of the war. Joh Kraak defended himself: "That is a bloody lie, a couple of weeks ago the Hordyk army came and was trying to capture me."

It was exactly the way the Principal had seen it, nobody would take the blame for anything and there were a thousand excuses. First of all he had to disarm the army and told Adrie to get his iron rod and hand it over to him. Adrie would never hand over his superior weapon to the Principal and luckily he remembered that he had lost the iron rod in the battle. He said to the Principal: "I don't have the iron rod anymore I lost it last night in the battle."

The Principal saw that he wasn't getting anywhere. He took a deep breath before he said resolutely: "Those bloody confrontations of fighting boys have to stop right away. Why can't you boys play normal games like hide and seek. The police are monitoring the serious situation on the Hordyk and will arrest anybody who is fighting. You have been given a fair warning, is that understood?"

Joh Kraak, who had all kinds of bruises which were a result of the famous battle he had lost, wanted revenge and wasn't convinced that this was the end of the war. With a smaller army he marched on the Hordyk again to see if he could spill some blood the next day. He didn't get very far; before the Hordyk got its army assembled the police came out in full force. They confiscated the sticks of the Petersely Dyk army and told them to go home or they would be arrested. "Why don't the police tell the German army to go home or they'll be arrested," Adrie rebelled, but he went home the same as the Petersely Dyk.,

It seemed the end of a nice game which had developed into bloody confrontations. It wasn't even safe anymore just to march with the army, so the soldier game had to be suspended indefinitely. Adrie had another bright idea; they could play war with catapults. With nails they fastened a few old newspapers between the trees and shot them full of holes with pebbles. The newspapers were fortress Tobruk which was attacked by the English army at the time. When the newspapers had been shredded by the pebble stones, fortress Tobruk had fallen. After fortress Tobruk had fallen twice, the gunning soldiers decided that it was enough and they were better off to play another game. No game was as nice as the now forbidden game. What else can you play during the war but war games?

The night after the winning battle against the Petersely Dyke, Adrie took the newspaper out of the mail box and expected fat head lines on the front page of the paper:

HORDYK DEFEATS PETERSELIE DYK.
Hordyk conquers Red Cross tank from Petersely Dyke.

It was a disappointment that the victory of the Hordyk hadn't made the headlines. The German commander was the only one who got the news on his desk and he wasn't impressed. This war game had dire consequences. The German soldiers had watched the warring streets with great interest but the German commander wasn't impressed at all. It didn't look good when the youth went out of control so he had to take the necessary steps to secure a peaceful district. A curfew was ordered for children up to fifteen years of age. After 8.00 p.m. no children were allowed in the street and the local police were in charge of enforcing this curfew.

At 8.00 p.m. the police would bike through the streets in order to send all kids home. Adrie played with his friend Jaap in the basement or in the garden and around 9.00 p.m. he went home avoiding the street. He didn't have to walk on the road at all. From his friend's place he went out of the back yard across the pastures to his own back yard. As former commander he had gained experience about how not to run into trouble.

The War Goes On.

Almost every night English and American bombers were flying over on their way to Germany. Whenever the Germans detected enemy aircraft, they sounded air alarm and flack tried to shoot down the enemy aircraft. Search lights and anti aircraft guns were operating the better part of the night keeping citizens awake. Because of the nightly shooting of anti aircraft guns there was a lot of shrapnel from the exploding shells that came down. It was very dangerous outside; the heavy pieces of shrapnel could make a nasty hole in your head if you were hit.

Adrie started a collection of shrapnel; he would look for pieces in the pastures. It didn't take him long to have a large collection. Most of the pieces were steel fragments but there were also aluminium pieces. Leen Willemstein came to look at his collection and said: "You have at least 25 kilos of steel there. Don't show it to the Germans; they might want it back to make more grenades and shells."

That statement could have become true with the Germans always looking for supplies of materials. When the war started The Netherlands had silver guilders, quarters and dimes. That was the first thing the Germans could use. Within no time, the silver coins were replaced with less important materials. There were now paper guilders and the quarters and dimes were made out of zinc. Soon the nickel and copper pennies were replaced with zinc coins as well.

Zinc coins were very dirty when you handled them. Adrie delivered the weekly church news leaflets for which he had to collect five cents from the church members. He had his pocket full of zinc coins and when he had to give change he had to dig deep into his pockets. When he came home at night, his hands looked as if he had worked in the coal instead of with money.

More and more stuff came down from the air. There was a lot of tinfoil dumped into the air, by the R.A.F., whenever they were flying over. That was done to bugger up the German radar so that they couldn't detect the bombers which were flying over.

Quite often the R.A.F. would drop paper bombs with a lot of leaflets from the air. Most of the time, it was news or propaganda against the Germans telling the Dutch citizens what cruel beasts the Nazis were. One of the leaflets was most outstanding, it pictured Adolf Hitler in lederhosen (a traditional Bavarian pair of leather shorts) holding his penis and saying: "What you have you hold." It was well known that Hitler never wanted to withdraw from any occupied territory and he always told his Generals to fight to the last man adding: "What you have you hold."

Everybody liked the leaflet except the Germans who weren't amused at all. Promptly, they made it illegal to pick up those leaflets. The German commander stated: "The leaflets that the R.A.F. drops are full of lies and do nothing else but poison the people's mind. Therefore it's in the interest of everybody that those leaflets are left alone and not to be read."

When the Nazis found out that the Dutch citizens picked up the leaflets in spite of its illegality, they started to drop leaflets too. They probably thought that the citizens wouldn't know the difference between English or German leaflets. All the people had to do was read the leaflets and they could tell who the author was.

The Ticking Clock.

Whenever Hitler made a speech, he would always shout about the New Order in Europe. Hitler's propaganda minister Joseph Goebbels advertised this New Order in all kinds of ways. Joseph Goebbels was a sick looking short guy who never amounted to anything until he met Hitler. Hitler could use him and made Goebbels Minister of Propaganda. He was number four of the Nazi clique and that's where he stayed.

Goebbels had appointed Nazi supporters in the occupied countries for propaganda purposes. In The Netherlands there was a special radio program on the Dutch radio which was called "The New Order by Max Blockzeil." Every week he would speak and advertise this New Order. He started out by telling the Dutch people about the book "Mein Kampf" which was written by Author Adolf Hitler. According to Max Blockzeil, the book was published in 1925 and the sales had made Hitler a millionaire. It was second only to the Bible in sales and at weddings in Germany the new couples were presented with Hitler's book 'Mein Kampf.' In the New Order, this gesture of giving young couples Hitler's book on their wedding would be practised in all of Europe. Everybody was joking that they could hardly wait to receive a free copy of this stupid book which was written solely to destroy the Jewish race.

Another broadcast yielded some more information about Hitler, who said in 'Mein Kampf',' "We Aryans not only spare the life of those we subject; we are giving them a fate that is better than their previous so-called freedom." Only the Dutch Nazis believed all that bull, the rest of the people went for freedom instead of favors from the Aryans.

After enough good things had been said about Hitler and his book, Max Blockzeil started to preach about the New Order. One week he said: "People of The Netherlands, why don't you join the New Order before it's too late? If you join now, you will benefit right away and if you don't join us, you will be left in the cold when the war is over. Hitler will remember the people who didn't support him during the war, they will be known as the bad people. For people that are supporting the Nazis while the war is on, the post war world will be a Utopia." Luckily for the Dutch people, Max Blokzeil gave everybody a chance to join the New Order. He ended his broadcast with stating "This is the eleventh hour but there is still time to join us and prepare for a new Europe."

Adrie wondered what would really happen if the Germans would be victorious in this war. Hitler was known to kill everybody he didn't like, especially Jews. However, Hitler killed Gypsies and others as well and they might kill the Dutch people for not joining. It is unknown if some people joined the Nazis because of his speeches. Max Blockzeil was a Nazi collaborator of the worst kind with his low Nazi propaganda hitting people right below the belt. His following program included all the victories of Germany and all the good prospects of a new Europe in the New Order. At the end of his program he said: "It's still the eleventh hour but the clock is ticking. It is now 11.30 and there is very little time left." His programs became known as "The Ticking Clock Programs."

When the following week came, he said: "It's now five minutes before twelve, if you still want to come aboard you have to be fast." The week after he said: "Time is running out, it's one minute before twelve."

And then came the clincher: "The first stroke of the ticking clock, announcing the hour of twelve, has already been heard. Time has run out, you'll have to join the New Order right now or you'll be left out. If you still want to join the New Order, it's now or never."

He sure gave the Dutch people a last chance to get into something good. He could make it sound like heaven and hell, something like a crusade, "Accept Christ as your Redeemer or you'll end up in the eternal fire."

Not many people fell for this propaganda, they just laughed about his ticking clock that could end up being a ticking time bomb. When Max Blockzeil started his speeches about the New Order, the Germans were victorious everywhere. Undoubtedly there were some people who thought that the Germans would win the war, they wanted to be on the winning side and joined. This meant that you could help the Germans by joining the Waffen S.S.

Max Blockzeil figured that his deceiving advertising had a great impact on the Dutch population. He heralded the recruiting of the Waffen S.S. and claimed that those people had made their choice. They had made the right choice and had joined 'The New Order.' Probably, the Dutch newspaper made him think that way.

SUPPORT FOR CRUSADE AGAINST
COMMUNISM VERY SUCCESSFUL.

In 1941 there were 8 divisions of volunteers who joined the Waffen S.S. In 1942 another 17 divisions of volunteers have joined the fight against Communism for a better world.

Most of the news about the war had come from Europe. After Japan entered the war there was alarming news from Asia as well. The Japanese forces had a heyday like the Germans had in Europe. It was another blitzkrieg. The year 1942 started badly for the Allies. What else was new? The Dutch Indies were easy prey for the well trained and equipped Japanese troops. On January 11 Borneo and Celebes fell into Japanese hands. Those huge islands were part of the Dutch East Indies. The only islands which were still in Dutch hands were New Guinea, Java and Sumatra.

On January 21 there was some more bad news, Manila was taken by the Japanese and the U.S. was badly beaten in other places of the Philippines.

February 15, 1942 Singapore fell after a fight of 7 days.

On February 27 there was the Battle of the Java Sea. The Japanese were on their way to take Java and Sumatra and Karel Doorman, the Dutch commander of the Dutch fleet, was ordered to intercept the Japanese fleet. When he met the Japanese fleet, he signalled to the other ships: "I attack, follow me."

Despite that he was courageous enough; his 5 cruisers and 9 destroyers all went down to the bottom of the Java Sea. It sealed the fate of Java and Sumatra, both fell into Japanese hands on March 10. All of the Dutch Indies, except New Guinea, were now controlled by the Japanese, who needed the colonies to supply raw materials and oil.

When Darwin in Australia was bombed, there was no doubt about the intentions of the Japanese, the next target was Australia. Only one hurdle had to be overcome by Japan to invade Australia, it was New Guinea. After they had New Guinea, they would have supply and bombing bases to invade Australia. It was MacArthur who decided to defend Australia in New Guinea. As long as Japan didn't have New Guinea, the Americans would use it for bombing raids against the Japanese.

The first half year of 1942 was the grimmest period of the war for the Allies with the heavy losses to the Japanese. When the Japanese started in the 1930's by taking parts of China, nobody was worried about it because they were only yellow men killing yellow men and there were lots of yellow people, too many in the opinion of the Americans. That had changed for the worst and yellow man was now killing Americans and English on a great scale with great success.

There was a bit of good news on April 13, 1942. Tokyo was bombed. The Japanese had conquered all surrounding islands around Japan and felt pretty secure behind the large perimeter that was controlled by Japan. They thought that bombing of Japan was impossible since there were no long distance bombers yet. What the Japanese could do in Hawaii with carriers, the U.S. could do to Japan. The U.S. bombers took off from a U.S. carrier. Very little damage was done to Tokyo which didn't matter; it was only to show the Japanese that they were vulnerable as well.

This little bit of good news was overshadowed by a lot of bad news. On May 6th the final surrender of the U.S. army took place on the Philippines which were now also in Japanese hands. The Pacific had become an ocean of Allied defeat. It was the darkest hour of the war, the Axis had now more than one third of the entire land of the world under their control. At this time it was hard to believe that a reverse of the war was possible. Whatever the Axis touched became gold and what the Allies touched became shit.

Again there was some good news and a lot of bad news. As for the good news which was brought by Radio London. "The U.S. Navy and Air Force have dealt a heavy blow to the Japanese. In a Japanese attempt to take Midway the fleet was intercepted and great losses were sustained by the Japanese. The Japanese lost 2 carriers and 3 other naval ships together with 332 planes. U.S. losses were 1 carrier and 147 planes. This is the first major victory against the Japanese." The Dutch people couldn't believe that this so called great victory would change the outcome of the war, especially when the bad news came in. On June 6, 1942, the German summer offensive had started and on July 9 the Crimea Peninsula in Russia was taken. The lot of Russia was hanging in the balance.

On July 10, Malta, a stronghold British island in the Mediterranean had been destroyed by the Luftwaffe. Malta was an English stronghold in the Mediterranean and Hitler probably was planning to take it.

There was also important bad news from the Western Front. While Hitler was busy in Russia, the English were going to test Hitler's Atlantic Wall with a Raid on Dieppe. It was in the planning to occupy Dieppe for twenty four hours and then withdraw.

On August 19, 1942 Allied troops, mostly Canadians, landed. Unfortunately, this whole venture ended in a very costly defeat. German intelligence had revealed that the English were coming and they had a welcome committee right in place. The Allied tanks never made it ashore and from the 4950 Canadian troops that participated 3350 were killed, wounded or imprisoned.

It was very disappointing news; the Dutch had hoped that this was the invasion everybody had been waiting for. Now, with this commanding defeat, there was no hope that an invasion of Western Europe was in the offing.

To top off all the bad news, the German Army commanded by General Paulus entered Stalingrad on August 31st. The Russians put up a good fight; they fought for every street and building but in the end they had to yield to the German forces.

Leen Willemstein said: "This Hitler looks a lot like Attila the Hun. Attila was known as the 'Scourge of God' and was the worst Barbarian ruler the world had ever known. He tackled the Roman Empire and even attacked Gaul. They couldn't stop Attila in the year 450 and they can't stop Hitler in 1942.

Control over the Mediterranean was in everybody's mind. The Americans were going to do something about it by taking Morocco, Tunis and Algiers. Those were French colonies and still under the rule of Free France. If the French colonies were getting involved in the war, the Germans had the right to occupy Free France according to the Treaty.

It had to be a surprise and also a Blitzkrieg. Once the Americans landed, the Germans would move in their troops quickly in order to prevent the Americans from taking them. It was a risky operation with 100 U.S. ships participating in the landing. The U.S. fleet had to cross the Atlantic which was frequented with German sub marines. If the fleet was discovered by the Germans they would have more than a heyday and the invasion couldn't take place.

General Patton landed in Morocco on November 7, 1942. French Marshall Petain who was running Free France was furious. President Roosevelt had tried to explain that it was a protective occupation to prevent the Germans from taking it. Petain called it forceful occupation and the pretext of protective occupation didn't hold. The honor of France was at stake and he was going to defend it. Petain had been fighting side by side with the English and now he was opposing the Allies. The French troops resisted the invasion for only four days and an Armistice followed.

Hitler was completely surprised; it was the first U.S. involvement in the European war. Consequently, Germany occupied Free France because the Treaty had been broken.

Everything went well for the Allies, in three days they had conquered Casablanca and Algiers. All what was left to do was to take Tunis and Africa was theirs. As the U.S had feared, German troops had moved into Tunis to defend it. That was a setback for the U.S., they had figured to wrap up that operation before the end of 1942.

Another year of World War II was drawing to a close. The Axis had plenty of material to brag about, they could boast victory after victory. When the

U.S. entered the war the Germans had another heyday sinking U.S, ships. In the first half of 1942 alone, they sank 360 merchant ships in American coastal waters. They had the largest kill ever; with 1664 ships totalling 6.3 million tons sunk by German sub marines in 1942. The Atlantic was infested with German submarines extracting a heavy toll of the Trans-Atlantic convoys and the Pacific was a Japanese lake.

Good news had been scarce for the Allies in 1942. However, there was a step; albeit a baby step in the right direction during 1942. The Russian winter offensive had stopped the Germans for the time being and Moscow was still in Russian hands. The U.S. could say that they had prevented the Japanese from taking Midway. If the Japanese had taken Midway, their next step would have been to take Hawaii. And the Americans had taken Morocco and Algiers from Free France. At least that was promising.

＊ ＊ ＊ ＊

Bombing Germany was a setback in the occupied countries. Whenever there were shortages in Germany, they took more supplies from the occupied countries. Actually, the occupied countries suffered more from the Allied bombing than Germany. Everything was rationed now and quite a few articles were in short supply. Shoes and other leather articles were hardly available.

Each person was allotted 25 points of leather ware per year. The major problem was that a pair of shoes needed 100 points. That meant that every person had a ration of half a shoe per year. If you needed a pair of new shoes, this was only possible by combining the points of the family and taking turns. A family of four would have a pair of shoes, for each member of the family, once every four years. Of course children who outgrow their shoes can't wait four years for a pair of shoes.

Luckily there were some wooden shoes available but even those were rationed. To make them last longer people nailed a leather sole underneath the wooden shoes. When there was no leather available anymore people made their own leather from old auto tires.

Arie cut some rubber soles from an old auto tire and nailed the heavy soles underneath the wooden shoes. He thought those heavy rubber soles would last a long time. Adrie was always running to school which was impossible with those heavy soles and he couldn't get excited at all that he had long lasting wooden shoes. Even if you walked normally you could break your foot Adrie said. It never mattered what Adrie said, things didn't change.

When Adrie couldn't keep up with his running friends because of his heavy footwear, he took his wooden shoes off, kept them in his hand and was running as fast as his friends. His father had been right in assuming that his wooden shoes would last a long time, with the heavy leather soles. As a matter of fact you could hardly see that his wooden shoes had been worn.

On the other hand, his socks didn't last long at all when he was running on them. Soon Adrie's mother found out that his socks were full of holes. She had an idea and made socks from old corduroy pants. Those lasted a long time even when you ran outside with them.

At that stage of the war there were no new bikes available at all. If you wanted to keep biking you fixed your old bike to no end. Tires were the main problem in keeping your bike going. For a while bike tires needed a permit, which was only available if you needed your bike to go to work. When the resources dwindled in Germany there were no bike tires available at all. Only the black market could provide tires if you had an awful lot of money.

Old auto tires came in handy; there had never been much use for old auto tires. When shortages became more and more critical, the people had lots of uses for the old tires. Besides making rubber soles for shoes and wooden shoes, people started to cut bike tires from the old auto tires.

Most of those self cut solid rubber tires were flat, though some people kept carving on the tires until they were round. It was kind of a bumpy ride without air in the tires, especially in Rotterdam on the big cobble stone roads. It wasn't too bad when you were riding on asphalt roads. At least it was better than riding your bike without tires. If you did that your wheels didn't last very long, the spokes got lose and broke pretty fast. The best tires were made of rubber watering hoses, at least they were hollow and there was some air in. It was easier to cut a bike tire from a garden hose than from an auto tire. All you had to do was cut it at the right length and splice the ends together. Unfortunately, the de Kievits never had a garden hose; they couldn't afford a luxury item like that. Instead they used a watering can when it was dry and hot. Poverty lasts a long time; it always catches up with you.

The frustrated Dutch people had to clutch at straws. There were many defeats and hardly any victories those first three years of the war. It seemed though, that the blitzkrieg had finally petered out and that the Allies had consolidated their forces. However, this was winter, it was anybody's guess what was in the offing when the Germans started their summer offensive again.

By the middle of January 1943, there was some good news from the Eastern front. The Russians had launched a counter offensive and had General Paulus completely surrounded. Even better news came on January 30. General Paulus had surrendered to the Russians with 91,000 men including 24 generals and 2,500 officers. Most of the Dutch people had their confidence restored with this great German defeat and thought that this was the long awaited turning point in the war. It also restored the sinking confidence of the Allied soldiers who were now changing their view of a probable victory.

There wasn't real good news to report from the Far East. However, the Japanese blitzkrieg had slowed down and the Americans kept their own. For the first time the Japanese were on the defensive.

British Intelligence revealed that no immediate invasion of England was in the planning. That gave the Allies a break and they decided to go from defense to offense. It gave them a chance to launch an offensive in Africa where Italy was threatening the Suez Canal. Whenever the British were fighting the Germans, they always took a licking but fighting the Italians was quite a different story. The Italians had no guts, were poorly organized and had no discipline. Morale was low in the army and it wasn't hard to beat them.

It was a cake walk, Montgomery conquered Tobruk for the British in one day and in February he conquered all of Ethiopia which was an Italian colony. Italian power was broken in North West Africa. It was the first British victory and Hitler wasn't amused, he had wanted to control the Mediterranean and the Italians just blew it.

Hitler sent his best General, Rommel, to Africa with two divisions. Rommel was very successful; he re-took Benghazi and encircled many English troops who were taken prisoners of war. Rommel was advancing fast and was attacking El Alamein which is only 50 miles from the Suez Canal.

While the English were busy burning all their files in Cairo to get ready for a fast exodus, Hitler was waiting for a telegram from Rommel that he had taken Cairo and Mussolini got all excited, he got ready to make a triumphal entry on a white horse in Cairo. It would have worked beautifully for him; he would have had a large crowd welcoming him. Egypt, the land of the Pharaohs wanted to be independent and they could hardly wait for Rommel to liberate them from English rule. It didn't happen.

With new supplies from the U.S. and additional troops, Montgomery counter attacked and beat Rommel badly. When Rommel wanted to withdraw his troops in order to save them from being butchered, Hitler wouldn't hear about it.

The outcome of the battle was a disaster for the Germans; English bombers attacked Rommel's tanks and destroyed all of them, the German Army was surrounded and thirty thousand Germans were taken prisoner. Rommel lost also 300 tanks, 1000 guns and 25,000 soldiers were killed. For a change the God of all Battles was on the Allied side. It was the first significant win for the Allies.

Rommel wasn't used to being beaten; when his aide reported that all his tanks had been destroyed he said: "This is not possible; the only things that the Americans are able to produce are razor blades."

His aide replied: "If I were you I would try to get some of those American razor blades."

The Free Trade Agreement.

When Brian Mulroney, our prime minister, came up with a Free Trade Agreement with the United States in 1989, he probably figured that he had invented the white yarn before the black yarn had been invented. For his information, Adrie already had a Free Trade Agreement second to none in 1938 and was more than 50 years ahead of him. Mulroney didn't even exist yet when Adrie had it all in place. No pact was signed and neither was there a 1500 page White Book to spell it all out. In spite of that, the Pact worked to the benefit and satisfaction of both parties, which cannot always be said for the pact between Canada and the U.S. Let me tell you all about it!

When you are at school for a few years, you start to find out who the dumb and the bright kids are. Luckily, Adrie belonged to the bright kids; he had a photo copy mind and excelled in arithmetic. Some people are good in remembering telephone numbers. They only have to hear it once and remember it for the rest of their lives. Other people can see a car go by and they can tell you what make and model it is. They can even tell you what year it is. Whatever turns your crank you'll be good at. Unfortunately, you can't be good at everything. If Adrie had been good at everything he would have been an Einstein. Since he wasn't an Einstein he had to settle for top student of the class.

History and Geography were mastered quite well. If they told him something, he never forgot it. He even failed to forget useless information. Behaving in order to stay out of trouble was the only thing he kept forgetting. Several teachers had tried in vain to make him behave. They always wasted their energy. Somehow, he always seemed to forget the things he wasn't supposed to do in the classroom. But then he didn't have a big head like a dinosaur, his brain seemed to be pea sized, which wasn't his fault.

In spite of his problem with behaving, he did quite well especially with arithmetic where he seldom made a mistake. On the other hand, all classes have the usual blockheads who'll never learn arithmetic and have a lot of trouble with it. Two boys in Adrie's classroom, Kees Kraak and Joh Kraak, who were the sons of the greengrocer, didn't manage arithmetic at all. To the teacher those two boys were known as 'The Kraaks.' Kees Kraak, the oldest of the boys, had failed a grade. That's how he ended up in the same classroom as his younger brother Joh Kraak.

Joh Kraak was of the same breed as Kees Kraak, the 'numskull breed.' He didn't have the foggiest idea how to solve arithmetic problems but on the other hand, he was slyer than his older brother Kees, which was the reason that he made all his grades with the help of Adrie. Joh Kraak knew that there was more than one way to skin a cat. If you can't figure it out yourself you let somebody else figure it out for you.

That he was so good at arithmetic was very pleasant for Adrie; he never had to worry about his mark. It was always good. However, there was another pleasant spinoff of his skill in arithmetic. The answers to the arithmetic problems were valuable and could be sold to an interested party, such as Joh Kraak.

Joh Kraak was seated in the bench behind him. He tried to peek over Adrie's shoulder to obtain the answer to an arithmetical problem. Not that Adrie was childish, but he had no intention of letting him copy his answers and shaded his paper with his hand so Joh couldn't see the answers. After school, Joh wanted to talk to Adrie, but first of all he gave him a big juicy pear. That was an example to let him taste the merchandise he had for sale. His father sold fruit and veggies so he could obtain all the pears, apples and plums he ever wanted.

He gave another pear and an apple to Adrie and said: "Here, that's all for you, if you give me the answers to the arithmetical problems tomorrow. If we have a deal, I'll bring some more fruit for you tomorrow."

Adrie had never figured that his skill in arithmetic was so valuable that he could sell it but he learned fast. Isn't there always somebody peddling apples like the snake in paradise? Like Adam fell for the apple, so did Adrie. The Free Trade Agreement was sealed and delivered the next day.

Since he had eaten from the apple (and the pears), the next morning it was Adrie's turn to keep up the bargain. No problem, instead of shading his paper he put it so that Joh could easily see to copy the answers. Joh sometimes brought turnips and carrots; they were all items on Adrie's menu. It was a deal that one hand was washing the other. He was holding a good hand of cards and finally started to play them right.

The Free Trade Agreement worked well for both and they were happy with the deal. As usual there was a spoiler who didn't like Joh Kraak copying Adrie's answers. How did you know it was the teacher? Am I telling the story or are you?

Adrie's arithmetic was perfect but no matter how perfect it was, sooner or later he was going to make a mistake and consequently he would have the wrong answer. It didn't bother him a bit that he had made one mistake in an exercise. He still scored in the 90% and what's wrong with that?

It was a different story for Joh Kraak who copied the answers and had also copied the wrong answer, which made the teacher suspicious. How could it be that two boys, who are sitting one behind another, have exactly the same wrong answer? Soon he had figured that two wrongs don't make one right so there must be something screwy going on. The teacher had no problem figuring out who figured out the problems and who copied the answers. He knew his students.

Some scribbling paper was used for calculating the arithmetic problems to get the answers. The teacher said to Joh Kraak: "Show me where you have calculated that arithmetical problem."

"I had a piece of scribbling paper but I threw it in the waste paper basket."

The teacher replied: "The wastepaper basket hasn't been emptied yet; if you threw it in there it still has to be there. Look it up because I want to see your calculations."

Joh Kraak had his act well together. He went to the wastepaper basket, took the papers out piece by piece and studied them very carefully before going to the next piece of paper. He tried to find the missing link. (Manuscript.) It was worse than looking for a needle in a haystack. It's hard to find a needle in a haystack but at least there is a needle. How can you find a piece of paper that doesn't exist? So the magic manuscript was never found.

The teacher seemed to have as much fun as the class had. Everybody knew that he had copied the answers and was just stalling. After 15 minutes of fruitless search the teacher asked: "Didn't you find it yet?"

Joh Kraak kept the honor to himself and kept up the show. He replied: "No sir, I can't find it; I don't know what happened to it because I threw it in the waste paper basket yesterday!"

The teacher said with a grin on his face: "That's a real pity; I surely would have liked to see how you arrived at the answer of that arithmetical problem."

Everybody in the classroom knew how he had arrived at the answer, including the teacher. He just had copied it from Adrie but nobody mentioned it and nobody asked Adrie to produce the piece of scrap paper to see his calculations.

The teacher thought he had it figured out that Joh Kraak didn't get his answers to that problem by himself but he sure missed something. He hadn't figured that Joh Kraak had paid for the wrong answer. Even having paid for the wrong answer, Joh Kraak didn't complain since 95% of the answers he bought were correct.

That was the first business Adrie had in his life and it was very successful under the Free Trade Agreement they had. He had all the fruit he could eat and Joh Kraak had all the answers he needed to pass his grade. Joh Kraak was as good as Adrie was when it came to arithmetic. If he had 95% so had Joh. He also stumbled over the same arithmetical problems as Adrie and had the same wrong answers. It makes you wonder how the teacher could figure that Joh Kraak copied the answers from Adrie. This Free Trade Agreement was so successful that Brian Mulroney would have been green with envy had he seen it.

It is also very remarkable that when Kees and Joh Kraak got older they helped their father with the selling of vegetables and fruit. They never made a mistake if it came to money in spite of their poor performance in arithmetic at school. They could figure out when they sold 3 kilos of apples at 20 cents per kilo that they had to collect 60 cents. They also could give the proper change if they were paid with a guilder. Nobody would cheat them in their business but don't ask them: "If a father is twice as old as his son plus two years and the combined number of their ages is 77. How old were they?"

(If you don't know your arithmetic either, you could copy my answer. The price is two juicy pears. "The son was 25 and the father was 52 years old. If you keep copying my answers, you might even pass your grade but be prepared to look for the piece of scribbling paper if by accident I made a mistake and you have the same wrong answer as I have.)

Open Up Your Mouth For a Worm.

In The Netherlands, the Seventh Grade was the last grade of Elementary School. After the Seventh Grade you followed secondary education or rolled up your sleeves and went to work. The Principal taught the Seventh Grade and in order to get some more free time to play Principal, he sent the Seventh Grade students to the Sixth Grade for singing lessons. That way he was rid of his students for an hour and had some time to spend in fulfilling his Principal duties to work for the school instead.

With the voices the growing boys had those singing lessons were probably a total waste of time. In spite of the good intentions of the teacher, the Princess Juliana School never produced a Caruso. All that the school produced were a bunch of billy goats and little birds with their mouth wide open waiting for a worm.

Singing lessons were not enjoyed by most of the students mainly because of their bad voices which was aggravated by a hard to please teacher, Mr. Stoep, who thought that his students should at least sing like canaries that were born to sing and were taught singing by the Lord himself to sing flawlessly. Adrie's favourite subject was arithmetic and he had no problem ever getting a good mark on his report card for it. Luckily singing wasn't marked; if it had been he didn't even want to guess what his mark would have been.

At one of the singing sessions they were practising a song which didn't go over too well and the teacher got somewhat crabby about it. After the class had sung it repeatedly to get it to his liking, there was no improvement in their trials. Mr. Stoep was raising hell to about half a dozen pupils of the Seventh Grade, who were singing like billy goats according to him. One of the billy goat singers was Adrie, of course.

Well, that wouldn't happen anymore, he knew a solution to the problem so the teacher wouldn't bellyache anymore about his singing. He simply wouldn't sing anymore. That way his singing wouldn't bugger up the song. Of course, he could figure that he wasn't getting away with simply not singing. He could pretend that he was singing but in reality he just would open his mouth and snap for air. The song was doomed anyway. Even after Adrie quit singing it still wasn't good enough. Here was the proof that it wasn't his singing that buggered up the song.

The teacher got really ornery and threatened, "Come hell or high water or both you aren't going home until you sing to my liking." The class started to get really tense and nervous and the more they tried the worse it got. It was so bad that even Adrie could hear the billy goats in the classroom. The dingbat would have been better off to take dingbat lessons, there was just no possible way they were going to sing for him like nightingales no matter how mad he got. The only way that was possible was if he changed his students into nightingales, or the other option he had was to castrate them. He certainly was an incompetent teacher for it seemed that he had little knowledge about the anatomy of the human being. When boys grow up, they change from boyhood into manhood and this amazing feature of the human being is coupled with a few changes in the boy.

In the first place, the boy who reaches puberty undergoes quite a transformation. Though the age of puberty is generally believed to be fourteen for boys and twelve for girls, some of the transformation of the body starts around the 13th year. In the Seventh Grade, the boys were all around that age and of course one boy starts earlier than the next one. This explains why some boys didn't have trouble with singing as yet.

The ones whose body started to transform to adulthood started to show several symptoms which included growing hair underneath their nose and on their chin. This means you have a choice; you either shave, or you grow a moustache and a beard. If you are lazy and don't like shaving, you might be tempted to grow a beard and moustache. Even if you do, there is still extensive grooming to do, unless you don't mind looking like hell to the opposite sex.

It was Adrie's decision not to have a cookie duster underneath his nose since the cookies he ate were never dusty and a beard he didn't want either since he would hate to lift his beard when he had a leak. Moreover, he wasn't planning to play Santa Claus so why have a beard?

A growing boy who reaches puberty will also grow hair on his genitals, so he can do exactly what the poetry on the toilet door suggests. "Some come here to shit and write on walls. Others come to scratch their hairy balls." The most inconvenient thing about reaching puberty is that your voice starts breaking. That makes singing for the birds as the students and teacher found out. They should have left the singing to the birds instead of trying to sing like nightingales.

The school roster suggested that they had singing lessons. So there you are, they tried to sing but all they did was squeak. One cannot fight nature; even an angry teacher can't. When the changing of the voice takes place in the boy's fast changing body, his voice changes from a shrill boy's voice to a firm man's voice. Once the transformation is completed, he can sing again but while the transformation is taking place, he is well advised to keep his mouth shut when it comes to singing. Of course, the boys didn't know all this but the teacher should have known better if he was any teacher at all. For the boys, not understanding what takes place made it worse to cope with the problem. All boys tried hard but they just couldn't sing anymore. In The Netherlands they called the breaking of the voice, "a boy is getting his beard in his throat." That will do it, if you have a beard in your throat, it will prevent you from singing like Caruso. Many changes take place in a boy but luckily he doesn't grow a beard in his throat. He just grows a beard on his chin but the saying suggests that he is growing a beard even if he shaves himself.

The boys in the Sixth Grade were a full year younger than the boys of Grade Seven and didn't have that problem. Consequently Grade Seven got the blame when the singing turned sour. The girls have no problem with beards, period. Period indeed! They start to get their monthly periods but fortunately, for the teacher, that didn't affect their singing.

During the 18th century, castration of choir boys was common. It was done to preserve the soprano of their voice. All the choir boys of the 'Vienna

Boys Choir' were castrated. They prevented the beautiful soprano voices of the boys from turning into tenor voices. It was a high price to pay to be deprived of manhood in return for a soprano voice.

In Italy, during the 18th century, famous opera singers were missing their testicles. They had been castrated well before puberty to save their beautiful soprano voices. In those days women weren't considered to sing in an opera at all but today those parts of the opera are sung by women. Two balls for one soprano voice, the price was outrageously high. For the seventh class students it was already too late anyway, since their voices were already breaking.

Adrie wasn't the only one to gasp for air instead of singing. There were two other boys who had been scolded for singing poorly. They had found the same solution to the problem as Adrie and tried to escape the furor of the teacher by pretending that they were singing. It was very noticeable that from the outer corner not much noise was produced. The teacher came to check what was going on, he came to eavesdrop and listened if they were singing. His investigation indicated that three of his students were mutes when it came to singing.

By now, he was really cheesed off and the three that weren't producing sounds had to come in front of the class to sing. With voices such as they had, because of their beards being in their throats, they had no intention of singing and being the laughing stock of the class. He ought to be kidding! They were just standing there motionless and not even their lips were moving. There was no need to pretend that they were singing at this stage.

The teacher got really angry and said: "You boys are just sitting there in your bench and instead of singing you are just like a bunch of little birds, which are sitting with their mouth wide open, waiting for their mother to return to drop in a worm. This is a singing lesson, if you don't sing, out! He pointed angrily with his finger at the door. The three boys beat it and were relieved to get away from this nincompoop teacher.

However, they didn't get very far in the hallway. The Principal had a knack of always being in the wrong place at the wrong time. When they were walking down the hall, there was the Principal who had the bad habit of being curious. He wanted to know where they were heading and why they weren't singing. They told the Principal that they had tried to sing like Caruso but had failed miserably.

They had been wondering what they were going to do during the whole hour of singing. The Principal solved their problem: "Go and water the flowers."

Watering the flowers took five minutes and the remaining part of the singing lesson was spent playing football in the classroom. The Principal was apparently not planning to return and took advantage of the situation by instructing them to ring the school bell at 3.30 p.m. to signal the end of the classes. Instructions like that they could handle a lot better than singing in front of the class. Actually, they didn't mind this singing lesson at all; they sure had a lot of fun.

They only had an hour of singing once a week. After a week they all had to report again to the teacher of the Sixth Grade, for some more Caruso singing lessons. They were wondering what the teacher would say after their refusal to sing in front of the class. It wasn't hard to figure that he wouldn't exactly receive the lost Carusos with open arms. Such a gesture didn't occur in his repertoire.

As soon as the teacher spotted the famous singers he came to tell them: "If you figure you can come into my class to gasp for air like a fish out of the water, you can forget it. Get lost!" This teacher sure had a way with words, first he compared his singing nightingales with little birds and now suddenly they were dying fish on land. The message was loud and clear so back they went to their chore of watering the flowers and playing football.

For three weeks, the teacher sent them out of the classroom. The singing lesson had turned into a joke for the class that was anxiously waiting to see what the teacher was going to do with his famous singers. Probably, the Principal had recommended the three boys to replace Caruso and Mr. Stoep had a change of heart and let them participate in the famous choir of the hoarse chicken singers. Never again did the teacher come close to the boys to listen to their beautiful voices. He probably had given up on the idea of a perfect singing choir for the Princess Juliana School. In spite of the fact that after some time the voices of the boys improved to sing tenor instead of soprano, they never managed to come even close to Caruso.

Coup De Grace.

Language Warning. "It's strongly recommended that the innocent, the weak, feeble minded and uninitiated outsiders, take into consideration that: "Though, this epistle is entirely written in the English language, it is not necessarily that the same words, expressions and phrases are used, as are in use at the Sunday School."

The last year of the elementary school was more or less the crown on a disaster. Adrie had no problem with any of the subjects the teachers taught him; it was all a piece of cake to him. From time to time he had experienced some problems with goofy teachers, but in spite of a few minor incidents, he had maintained his position as star student of the class. And he had earned the respect of his teachers because of his qualifications.

In the seventh grade, the situation changed without warning. This was the result of a miserable relationship that developed between teacher and student. The reason that this happened was a combination of a stupid system which was in place and an ignorant, inefficient Head Master.

The education and labour laws stipulated that all children were subject to compulsory education, from ages six till thirteen. Nobody was allowed to work before his or her thirteenth birthday. It didn't matter what grade you were in, on your thirteenth birthday you could leave school and take on a job if you so desired.

When Adrie started his Fifth Grade, there was one boy who only was one month in that grade when he became thirteen. The day before his birthday was his last day at school. He was some kind of a slow learner and had managed to pass grade one in one year but he had to take all other grades for two years before he passed. Even then his marks were actually too low to pass but they put him in the next grade anyway. There was no school for slow learners, so the boy just suffered and never learned a thing.

Adrie's case was different, in those days you couldn't go ahead. You were tied to your class and had to go the tempo of the average student. This had caused some problems but in the seventh grade it became a disaster.

The seventh grade was actually a grade which wasn't necessary for your education at all. Whenever you wanted further education, all that was needed was to complete the sixth grade successfully. There was also a stipulation that you had to be 12 years and 8 months of age before you could be admitted to any other school.

This is where Adrie's problem came in. He went to school in his fifth year and he was planning to go to the Technical School. He had very successfully completed the sixth grade but unfortunately he was only twelve years old. Eight months short on his age for admittance. This meant that he had to go through grade seven.

Since grade seven was a necessary evil, it was a repeat from grade six. There was a difference all right. In grade six they had to solve problems about a grocer who bought 100 lbs. of sugar at 10 cents per pound. He sold it for 18 cents per pound. If he lost 5% of the sugar by over-weighing, how much percentage was his profit?

Grade seven was different. Here it was a butcher who bought a 300 lb. cow for which he paid 20 cents per pound. When he took the bones out, he lost 20% of the weight. The meat was sold for 40 cents per pound. How much was the percentage of profit he made?

In those days the children of rich people took High School and the poor man's kids went to the Technical School or went to work without further education. High School prepared you to be a white collar worker. You had to take English, French, German and of course Dutch. Furthermore there were a host of other subjects, such as Physics, Science, Algebra, Geometry etc.

The Technical School taught a lot of practical work and for theory they taught Physics, Algebra, Geometry and there was also Drawing. They were glad to get some kind of an education but after two years of day school, all further education had to come from night school.

The system was actually geared so that all the good paying jobs went to the children of the rich man who could afford to pay for education. It made a difference in your life. When later, Adrie was drafted for the Army, the kids with high school diplomas were trained to be officers or under-officers. The children who had gone to the technical school or had only elementary school were automatically soldiers. It was a system to keep the rich, rich and the poor, poor.

Most of the poor people were of the opinion that seven years of elementary school was enough education. There was no money for further studies so it was time that the children started to work to bring in some money. Other children had their pockets full of school, teachers and home work. Of course, not every rich man's child was a success and not every poor man's child was a failure but it helps if your parents are rich and pay for your education. Adrie considered himself lucky to get two years of Technical School but after that he was holding a job and was forever attending night classes. It really hurts to be poor but on the other hand, life is more challenging and struggling makes you strong.

Thus the Seventh Grade class was a combination of kids who were calling it quits, but had to stay at school till they were 13 years of age. And kids who shared Adrie's position; who had to waste some time till the required age was reached to be admitted to a school for further education. For Adrie, boredom set in when he had to repeat education which he already completed.

The Head Master taught the seventh grade. His real name was Mr. Haspels but he had a bunch of nick names. The most common one was 'Baldy.' That nick name he didn't receive because of his head of beautiful curly hair. As a matter of fact, it was easier to find hairs on a frog than on his head. If he walked underneath a lantern at night, his shining bald head reflected the light to make people think that the moon came up. Another well-deserved nick name was 'Billiard ball.' However, whenever the students talked about him to the other teachers, they would call him 'The Head Master.'

The problem of the head master was that he was part time teacher and part time Principal. The grammar book was very convenient for the Principal; whenever he had to attend to his Principal duties, he would assign the students some problems in their grammar book. He would end his instructions by telling the students that if they experienced problems with their work, he would attend to it when he returned. Quite often he returned just before the end of the classes and attending to the problems had to wait till the next day.

There was a big fat girl in Adrie's classroom by the name of Bridget Fresco. Her mother was German, her father was a Jew and she was stupid. She was the oldest girl in the class but she was as stupid as the rear end of a pig. Bridget was well built for her age; her boobs looked like the head lights of an old model T Ford and the Principal favored her; she was his pet poodle. She took advantage of that position. Whenever the Principal left, she bossed everybody around and if she didn't get her way, she would hit you or kick you.

She hated Adrie most of all; she probably was so frustrated that she was stupid and couldn't stand Adrie because he was the star student of the class. One time she kicked him in the shin, which he didn't appreciate. He was just about to make a kicking horse saloon out of the classroom and kick her back. At that very moment, the Principal returned and revenge had to wait till the next opportunity.

When the Principal left again, Adrie was going to get even. On second thought, after thinking it over, kicking her would definitely backfire. She would be crying and with a bleeding heart she would make her complaint to the Principal. The Principal wouldn't even listen to Adrie's explanation that she deserved what he gave her, he would beat the hell out of him and she would be laughing.

It looked better to insult her and make her the laughing stock of the classroom. There was a song which was very popular in those days; it was part of the operetta 'Violetta.'

Hear my song Violetta.
Hear the song I made for you.
Hear my song Violetta.
Hear my song that sings for you.

Adrie thought he could improve on that song and sing it to his sweetheart Bridget. After he had made significant improvement to the lyrics, it looked great.

Hear my song my dear Bridget.
You are always full of shit.
Hear my song my dear Bridget.
With your model T Ford heavy tit.

That would do the trick, Adrie thought; the way he made his famous poems, he could be competition for Robert Burns. The kids of the classroom thought it was a good poem, they were all laughing, but there had to be one spoiler who didn't laugh. Exactly, it was Bridget Fresco, she started to cry. Her problem was, she didn't have enough tears till the Principal returned. After a while she quit sobbing. However, as soon as the billiard ball returned her eyes got wet again.

At first Adrie thought she was quite moved by his famous song, which he had especially composed for her, so tears came into her eyes. Like always, he had that wrong again. Her shoulders were shaking and she wept hysterically. Baldy went straight up to her; he put his arm around her shoulder and asked with his slimy voice: "What happened to make you cry?"

Her crying increased dramatically; tears rolled over her cheeks and onto the floor. Baldy had to back up or else he would get wet feet. She played her role like a born actress in Hollywood. Baldy was at his wits end that he couldn't console his pet poodle and punish the evil creep who had brought sorrow to this lovely girl. This whole thing started to develop into a melodrama; she couldn't lose and Adrie couldn't win.

Baldy pleaded with her to reveal the identity of the person who had hurt her. Between the sobs she started to mention Adrie's name. The billiard ball looked furiously in his direction; it looked like he had it coming. When she told him that Adrie had insulted her with a dirty song, Baldy insisted that she repeat the song. Adrie figured that Baldy liked dirty songs; why else would he like to hear it?

Sobbing with tears in her eyes, she repeated the beautiful song on which Adrie had copy rights. The class was sitting on pins and needles; they tried very hard not to laugh. They liked the song and recognized his talents but judging by the looks on Baldy's face, he wasn't an admirer of the poetry. Adrie had to recognize that he couldn't please everyone so he might as well please himself. After all, the other pupils of the class loved his accomplishment and that was very important to him.

Baldy was infuriated and came running to Adrie's bench. He started to spank his ears and told him to go and stand in the hall; he couldn't condone filthy and vulgar language. It was against all moral standards in a Christian school. He had to throw that Christian school in when he condemned Adrie for his outstanding song.

All of a sudden Adrie was standing in the hall, trying to figure out 'Where did it all go wrong?' What was so filthy and vulgar about a tit, little babies take it in their mouth to suck. Of course, Baldy wouldn't know about that, he had a childless marriage and he had never seen a baby sucking a tit.

If this incident had happened fifty years later, Adrie could have gone to the Human Rights Commission, complaining that his civil rights had been violated. This was definitely an obstruction of freedom of speech and expression, which we all should enjoy according to the Charter of Rights. Unfortunately, it happened fifty years earlier, so he was doomed and punished without recourse.

If the Principal thought that he was using filthy, vulgar language, he had it all wrong. He was a Sunday School teacher compared to Piet Hermans who was also a student in Adrie's class. Piet Hermans had been corrected several times for his bad language. Adrie couldn't compete with him; he had one up on him because he had older brothers, who initiated him in the use of the Dutch language. He used words and expressions nobody knew existed, until he revealed them to the class.

One time, he had to go twice to the bathroom in half an hour. The Principal said: "What's the matter, can't you get rid of your egg?"

Piet Hermans answered: "The first time I went to the bathroom, I had to piss like a stud stallion but now I have to shit like a seagull."

Adrie wasn't sure what he meant by a stud stallion; the studs he knew were used to frame houses but he never had seen a stallion equipped with wooden studs. Of course, Baldy wasn't amused at all, he called it vulgar language and Piet Hermans had to stand in the hall.

Adrie had learned his lesson not to argue with Bridget Fresco. He didn't have to carry a torch for her, but on the other hand he could keep a safe distance and pretend she wasn't there. She probably figured she had subdued him so she looked for another victim. Her next target was Piet Hermans.

Piet Hermans took her childish behavior for a while but when she said that he was stupid, he blasted: "Look who is talking; if I were a total failure like you I would shut up. Your only hope is to be re-fucked with a feeble prick. Your father used the wrong semen to put you together; he should have flushed you down the toilet; it would have saved us all a lot of f...... trouble."

Never in his entire life had Adrie heard such a language. He had just learned a few new words and expressions. As far as he could tell, he had hit the nail right on the head because Bridget started to cry again. Piet Hermans said: "You are a total f... up, the only thing you are good at is crying."

"Right again!" Adrie thought.

When the Principal returned to the classroom, he found his sweetheart crying with no let up. He couldn't calm her down no matter how he tried. Finally he took Bridget to his office for a formal interrogation. Five minutes later she returned to the classroom with a look in her eyes as if she just had slain the dragon. She probably had because she said triumphantly: "Piet Hermans, you have to come to the Principal's office."

Piet Hermans didn't return that day, he was sent home with a letter to his parents, asking them to come to school to discuss the immoral conduct of their son. Next day he was back at school, after he had been reprimanded and told not to use indecent and vulgar language at school.

Piet Hermans had learned his lesson; he didn't say anymore vulgar and immoral things in the classroom, he wrote them on the blackboard instead. One day it said on the blackboard: "Free screwing lessons by Baldy. Every Wednesday 3.00 to 4.00 p.m. in the gymnasium. Register here."

He was as smart as a whip; he wrote it when there were no girls around who could give him away. When Baldy entered the classroom, the boys were chuckling with joy. Baldy was late as usual and in the rush, he missed the announcement on the blackboard. When he finally noticed it, he asked a silly question: "Who wrote that vulgar language on the blackboard?"

An eerie silence followed; you could hear a pin drop, if anybody had dropped it. Baldy looked around the classroom, his eyes rested briefly on Adrie. Next he looked at Piet Hermans and asked: "Did you write that on the blackboard?"

"No sir", was the polite answer. He addressed the class and asked once more who had done it. When no volunteer came forward he said: "I'm getting to the bottom of this; the culprit can come forward before tomorrow 3.30 p.m. I also encourage other pupils who know who is responsible for this, to tell me. If I don't have the identity of the scoundrel tomorrow, the whole class will have to stay after school for one hour."

He used the same dirty tactics as the Germans did during the war. Sometimes the Dutch Underground blew up a bridge or shot a German general. The Germans had imprisoned a lot of young Dutch men to use as hostages when needed. The German commander issued an ultimatum and declared that the culprit had three days to come forward. And he invited other Dutch citizens as well to betray the person who had been responsible for the incident. If they didn't get the culprit, they would shoot twenty innocent Dutch hostages.

Baldy had as much success as the Germans had during the war, there were no stool pigeons. The Billiard Ball made good on his threat, except he modified the punishment. He said that he was sure that the girls were not responsible for writing filthy things on the blackboard, so why punish the girls? They could go home but the boys had to stay. Actually, he was right that the boys were responsible for it, but it was only speculation, which wouldn't stand up in a court of law. The boys objected but Baldy overruled them.

(Baldy should have seen what went on in a different school. During lunch hour somebody had written on the blackboard: "Jimmy has the biggest cock." The teacher asked Roger if he had done it but Roger denied it. Next he asked a few more likely suspects but everybody pleaded not guilty. So he asked Jimmy if he knew who had put it on the blackboard. Jimmy said: "I did it, sir."

The teacher said: "Why on earth did you put that on the blackboard?"

Jimmy replied: "Well, sir, I have to advertise my merchandise.")

EATING CAULIFLOWER AND PICKING STRAWBERRIES.

Adrie lived in the outskirts of Rotterdam in a rural surrounding. There were a lot of farmers and produce growers who were growing strawberries which was very profitable. People were consuming a lot of fresh strawberries, but the jam plants also bought a lot of strawberries to make strawberry jam.

There was only one problem; the strawberries had to be picked and strawberry pickers were needed. Before the war, during the Depression, there were all kinds of workers available. The war had changed this; the Germans had all kinds of work. Many young men were transported to Germany to work in the German war production plants. Older men like Arie were sent to the coast to make concrete bunkers for the defense, because an invasion was expected.

Nobody liked to work for the Germans but it was an offer one couldn't refuse. Refusal could net you a bullet. When the strawberries were ripening, strawberry pickers were in short supply. If the strawberries weren't picked they would rot in the field. The authorities had decided to get the school kids of the seventh grade involved, to help out.

One day an official of the school board came to visit the school and proposed that the students of the Seventh Grade could get six weeks leave from school to pick strawberries. They could only get free from school if they had a boss to pick strawberries for. They didn't want to give the students an extra holiday to horse around in the street. The official left a bunch of forms behind which had to be filled out by the bosses who hired students. That was to keep everybody honest.

It was attractive to pick strawberries, it was all piece-work. The strawberry pickers were paid 15 cents per basket and if you were a good picker you could pick three baskets of strawberries per hour. You could make 45 cents per hour, which was pretty good pay because grown ups were paid forty to sixty cents per hour.

Most of the pupils of the seventh grade took a form and went looking for a boss. It was attractive and looked a good idea; Adrie went for it and took a form home as well. When he told his mother that he was going to make money, she was all for the idea, which meant that he had cleared another hurdle. All he had left to do was to find a boss.

When the official of the school-board explained the situation, it had sounded like those bosses were really up the creek without a paddle. Adrie expected to be received with open arms and was going to be a national hero for saving the strawberry crop.

At the first place he asked for a job, the man said that he had already enough strawberry pickers for the time being but he could check with him in another week. It happens that people quit their job. "That won't be necessary," Adrie thought, there were about twelve strawberry growers and he expected to be hired at the second place.

After the eighth grower turned him down, he wondered about the shortage of strawberry pickers. It was the competition that buggered him up; there were a lot of young women who wanted to make a few bucks and tried their luck with strawberry picking. Evidently the bosses liked young women better than a 12 year old school kid.

Adrie's father used to have that problem during the Depression when bosses would hire a young guy. Whenever his father told them he was 40 years old, they rejected him and said: "Forty years is way too old for that job." They rather would hire a young guy in the early twenties than an older person. Adrie's problem was different; he wasn't too old, he was too young. You just can't win in this life.

This incident made him understand what his father went through when he was rejected everywhere. His problem was worse than Adrie's; he had to put bread on the table for his family and Adrie was merely looking for a way to make some dough. However, this was cold comfort to him; he thought to make a lot of money but instead he had to go to school to repeat grade six.

It made him think that he was too young for everything, he was too young to go to the Technical School and also too young to pick strawberries. He wished he was grown up! A kid always seems to think about being grown up and being older but only up to a certain age. When you are old, you wish that you were eighteen again.

It wasn't only that he was too young; there was another problem; his reputation was catching up with him. For many years, most of the boys would steal apples and pears to satisfy their ferocious appetite. Many farmers and growers had tried to catch the boys, probably to beat the hell out of them. They never caught Adrie but now they got him and had the last laugh. Ha, Ha! Adrie couldn't see the fun of it.

There was one grower by the name of Kees Wensveen; he only lived seven houses from Adrie. That was the only grower Adrie didn't go to ask for work. He knew he didn't have a snowball's chance in hell that he would hire him. When the boys were growing up during the lean years of the Depression, they went never hungry but the quality of food left much to be desired. That was one of the two reasons they stole apples and pears. The other reason was; it was a dare and an adventure. They didn't stop at stealing apples and pears; they liked turnips, carrots, sugar beets and cauliflower. Raw cauliflower was their favourite; they could eat it every day.

Adrie's parents never grew cauliflower because of the white butterflies which laid eggs on the leaves. The cauliflower was infested with green cabbage worms and insecticides were the only way to combat them. Adrie's parents couldn't afford to grow them and they couldn't afford to buy them, so they did without.

That his parents didn't grow cauliflower was no problem; he knew where to get it. Kees Wensveen had a very long piece of land in the polder. He had a narrow railway for transportation of his produce and in the middle of the land was a huge barn for tools, fertilizer etc. Past the middle of his land, behind the barn, was a large piece of land designated to growing cauliflower.

For a couple of nights, Adrie and his friend Jaap had each taken a cauliflower for direct consumption. Kees Wensveen must have noticed that he had visitors at night and from there on he was sitting on his balcony with a pair of binoculars to keep an eye on things. It was far enough away that it was impossible for him to see who was way at the back of his land but he could see that something was going on.

Whenever he saw the boys going to his cauliflowers, he would come out with his bloodhound to chase them. He would run down the narrow railway path hoping to catch the boys but could only hope. Long before he was behind the barn, the boys had already disappeared with a cauliflower. Actually, with his cauliflower.

Kees Wensveen was hard to get along with; the boys appreciated his quality cauliflower, they were regular customers and yet he was chasing the boys with his bloodhound. This game could have gone on forever or as long as there was cauliflower on his land, if it hadn't been for the ingenuity of Kees Wensveen.

In order to protect his cauliflower he made a plan like a real General. He didn't put land mines on his land but he prepared an ambush for the boys. One night that they were out for cauliflower again; one of his workers was hidden in the barn and was watching the boys between the cracks of the boards of the barn. The boys had seen Kees Wensveen with his binoculars on his balcony but that didn't worry them a bit, they had an early warning system in place, they could see him come with his hound a mile away.

Of course, the boys were not aware of the danger so near. They took their sweet old time to inspect the cauliflower. They wouldn't take any cauliflower, the cauliflower had to be white as snow and be a good size, or it wouldn't be worth their trouble. After all, they were regular customers, which gave them the right to be picky.

All of a sudden the worker came running out of his hiding place and it looked like he wasn't happy at all with the business the boys were giving to his boss. The boys weren't worried at all when his worker came after them; they had been chased by cops, farmers and other people before. All of Kees Wensveen's planning would have been in vain, if it hadn't been for a lucky coincidence which benefited him.

There was a weak link in their chain; Adrie and Jaap were always with the two of them but that night they had a guest and were with three boys. Piet Herremans was just another boy who was fond of cauliflower and had joined Adrie and Jaap in their quest for the favorite vegetable. They had no objection; there were more cauliflowers than they could eat anyway.

The boys looked at the back and saw Kees Wensveen with his bloodhound, running in their direction. They couldn't make their normal get away because their regular escape route was blocked by the worker, who came running from the right. So they were in for a dilemma. Ha, ha. This is a joke so laugh!

(An adventurer was telling about his adventures in dark Africa. His speechless audience was hanging on his words. The adventurer said: "One day I was walking in the jungle when I suddenly came face to face with a big tiger. When I looked back I saw a roaring lion running in my direction, I was standing for a dilemma."

One of his female admirers asked: "Which one of the three did you shoot first?")

To get back to the story, the boy's dilemma was nothing to laugh about; it was a classical example of being caught between the devil and the deep blue sea. The deep blue sea was represented by a wide channel on their left. They couldn't go forward because their escape route was cut off by the worker who came from the right. It seemed that the only escape route was to the left.

Their freedom was on the other side of the channel, all they had to do was jump across it and they had it made. They were sure that Kees Wensveen and his worker wouldn't jump across the channel and the dog was no problem. The dog did always a lot of barking but luckily there is an Old Dutch proverb that says: "Barking dogs don't bite."

The boys hoped that the dog knew that Dutch proverb too and that he kept it. A proverb is a proverb; the dog shouldn't change it, especially since it is such an old proverb. Adrie and Jaap were running for the channel; they jumped and came safely across. They didn't have to run anymore, but where was Piet Herremans? He could jump ditches but the channel was too wide for him; he tried to run parallel with the channel but was cut off and caught with his cauliflower still under his arm. He should have destroyed the evidence; when you are caught without cauliflower there is no evidence that you stole cauliflower. He could have said that he was admiring the cauliflower.

When the chase was on, Adrie and Jaap had dropped their cauliflower when they were jumping across the channel; they didn't need the extra ballast. Their mission had been unsuccessful; there was no cauliflower on their menu for that day. They made their retreat and wondered what would happen to Piet Herremans. For no money in the world would they have liked to change places. They wouldn't even have liked to change places for any cauliflower in the world.

They had a reason to be happy and were laughing about this stupid Piet Herremans, who had always a big mouth but was caught because he couldn't jump the channel. Not for long were they laughing, after a while they saw Piet Herremans coming with his cauliflower under his arm. Kees Wensveen had said: "You might as well take the cauliflower along and eat it; I can't sell it anymore anyway, no use to waste it."

That was good news; at least they had some cauliflower to eat for all the trouble they went into. For the bad news, Kees Wensveen had asked who his friends were. He didn't even have to turn the thumb screws on or drive bamboo slivers underneath his nails; he gave the information in return for his freedom. Now Adrie and Jaap were in deep shit; they could count on it that Kees Wensveen would go to the complaint department which was staffed by their parents. It wasn't hard to figure out that their parents wouldn't be amused at all when they heard that their sons were stealing cauliflower. No, they weren't going to be proud of their boys.

All they could figure was that on this beautiful day of our Lord, their luck had run out and their beloved parents would be very disappointed in them. Those people were so naive that they thought that their sons were such a sweet, innocent, well behaved boys. They sure had that wrong. They should never have taken that Piet Herremans along; he was just a big mouth who had betrayed them. Some friend that was!

Adrie could hate himself whenever he figured there would be complaints to his parents. He was always right and the complaints were always made. He wouldn't have been disappointed at all, had he been guessing wrong just for once. At night he was playing in the street and all of a sudden he saw Kees Wensveen walking to his house. It wasn't hard to figure out that the natives weren't going to be friendly, so he disappeared in a heck of a hurry.

Everything had gone wrong but Lady Luck was on his side for a change; his father and mother weren't home and the complaint department was closed. It didn't make him all that happy because tomorrow was another day and Kees Wensveen would be back, guaranteed! If you have to face the firing squad, you might as well face it today and get it over with. Whatever his punishment would be, he might as well know and suffer.

This time Adrie could love himself because for a change he was wrong in his predictions. Kees Wensveen never made his complaint; he probably got over his anger and didn't return. Maybe, he put in practise what he had learned in church. He went to the same church as Adrie did and the Reverend always prayed the Lord's Prayer. "Forgive us our trespasses, as we forgive who trespass against us." Adrie could say: "Amen" to that. Kees Wensveen had to forgive him for trespassing on his land and stealing his cauliflower.

It seemed that he had to face the firing squad sooner or later. Now he needed a job; he couldn't even go and ask him. On the other hand, he had been to the other eleven places and they didn't need any help so why should Kees Wensveen need any help? Even if he needed help, he wouldn't hire him, Adrie would be the last resort for him. To hire Adrie would be as bad as putting the bad wolf in charge of Red Riding Hood. Nobody in his right mind would do that!

The pigeons come home to roost they say and they were right. At night his school friend came to see Adrie. He knew that Adrie had been unsuccessful in finding a boss to pick strawberries for and said: "Kees Wensveen is asking for strawberry pickers."

Well, wouldn't you know; there were twelve strawberry growers and only Kees Wensveen was looking for strawberry pickers. It looked as if the devil was playing with it, how else could that happen? First the devil made him do it and now he buggered him up.

Adrie's mother said: "You can go to Kees Wensveen and see if he hires you."

He could do that alright but that would be entering the lion's den; that would be really stupid. In order to find an excuse not to see Kees Wensveen, he said: "It's already late, I'll see him tomorrow."

By now, he could see that the Reverend and the teacher at school were right; sooner or later you are punished for your sins. In Adrie's case it was later, he could have had a job but he had that buggered up a long time ago. The price of cauliflower was high he found out; it buggered up his career in strawberry picking, he could have made a start in making his first million Guilders.

Adrie wasn't planning at all to go to Kees Wensveen for a job, that would be presenting himself on a silver platter to give Kees Wensveen the opportunity to chop off his head, like they had done with the head of John the Baptist. He always could tell his mother that he had asked him but darned, he already had enough strawberry pickers. Of course, that also could backfire. Kees Wensveen went to the same church as his parents did and there was a good chance that his mother was going to try to help him to get a job. She probably would say to Kees Wensveen: "Too bad that you already had enough pickers, my son was really disappointed."

One way or another, the shit was going to hit the fan blade. How was that saying about that tangled web we weave? The next day he was tempted to go and ask him for a job, at the worst he could say 'No,' but there was also a remote chance that he would say 'Yes.' Adrie was as bold as brass but this was the extreme of boldness. The extreme of boldness is to piss a policeman on his shoes and ask where the urinal is. He was sure that Kees Wensveen wasn't going to hire him; his past was hanging as a shadow over his future. On the other hand, it was already more than a year ago and the statute of limitations for such a petty crime couldn't be more than one year.

He might not even remember that Adrie stole his cauliflower; maybe he had Alzheimer's. Adrie mustered all the courage he had together and was going to find out what the man would say. It looked as if he had lead in his shoes; his legs didn't move very well; he had to encourage himself to see this through. He walked past his house; it looked more like a castle with a dragon in it. This reconnaissance flight was more or less a security check; he had to get familiar with enemy territory. He had learned that from the war books and this knowledge came in handy.

The second time he walked past his house; he felt like marching home and call it a day. He could see tigers and lions on his way like the hunter in Africa and not to forget all those dilemmas. On the other hand this was a real challenge; he had never passed up a challenge but of course there is always the first time. He never was punished for his sins but this must be it.

It says in the Bible that God punishes the sins and that the sins of the fathers will be punished to the children, up to the fourth and fifth generation. This was uncanny; just to think that the children of his grandchildren were going to be punished because he had stolen cauliflower. Could those poor kids help it that he had a taste for cauliflower and that the Devil made him do it? A lot of time was spent on reasoning but all reason seemed to be lost.

Finally, he got cheesed off with himself; now was the hour that he had to bell the cat. A cat is a curious animal and curiosity can kill the cat, but was the cat scared? Well no, a cat has nine lives to back him up. If he had nine lives he wouldn't be so scared either; if Kees Wensveen was going to kill him he still had eight lives left. Unfortunately poor Adrie had only one life. As soon as he moved on Kees Wensveen's territory his life was in jeopardy. Even Lloyd's of London wouldn't insure his life; they would turn him down because he was a bad risk.

He had one more look at the sinister house and decided to bite the bullet instead of horsing around. The sooner he got this over with the better so he could carry on with the rest of his life i.e. if Kees Wensveen hadn't killed him. Everything looked quiet on the Western Front so he had to make his move now.

Carefully he opened the gate because he didn't want to damage it. Just in case the cavalry had to withdraw in a hell of a hurry, he left the gate wide open. As a panther he was sneaking through the banana fields. Finally he was on the doorstep and rang the doorbell very shortly. If he made a hell of a ruckus by ringing the doorbell, Kees Wensveen might think that there was an idiot on his door step. Actually, he would have hit the nail right on the head, only an idiot would do something stupid as he did, to ask a guy for a job after stealing his cauliflower.

After he had ringed the doorbell, time seemed to be standing still; it took ages before the door was answered. They say that when you are facing death, your entire life will pass before your very eyes in a matter of seconds, as if you were looking into a kaleidoscope. Indeed, in the few seconds that it took Kees Wensveen to answer the door, Adrie's life passed before his eyes.

He hoped that Kees Wensveen wasn't home or that his wife would open the door. All his hopes vanished when the door opened finally. Kees Wensveen himself was standing, towering, in the door opening. He was much too close for comfort, all he had to do was stretch his long arms, grab Adrie and squeeze the life out of him. He was sure big for his age, Adrie never knew he was that big but then he never had seen him that close up. He was that kind of a guy with whom you were better off to dine, than to fight him, especially when there was cauliflower on the menu.

In spite of his desperate situation, Adrie started his speech which he had repeated to himself so many times. "I heard that you are looking for strawberry pickers. Could you use me for that job?"

He looked at his expressionless face, in order to decide whether he was going to stay or run for his life. Kees was just looking Adrie over and when his mouth finally opened, he said: "So you are that kid that used to steal my cauliflowers!"

Adrie knew it; Kees was like an elephant, never forgot anything and it looked like it was time of reckoning. It occurred to Adrie to cheer him up, by telling him that he had the best cauliflower in town. On second thought he'd better get the hell out of there while the getting out was still possible. He turned around to head for home just when Kees Wensveen cleared his throat and said: "Just wait a minute, you asked me a couple of questions, give me time to answer you. Yes I need strawberry pickers and yes I can use you, have you got a form from school?"

This could be a trap; if he handed him over his form, he had to come closer to him which would make it easier to grab him. Adrie decided to give him the benefit of the doubt and trust him, if he buggered him up, he had to answer to God in the here-after. In that case, both would go to hell; Kees for false pretence and Adrie for stealing his cauliflower. Adrie handed him the form, Kees filled it out and gave it back to him and said: "We start Monday morning at 7.00 a.m., come to the barn in the middle of my land."

Holy smokes, Adrie had a boss! He never had thought that he would hire him after the cauliflower incident. On the other hand, he had good reason to hire him, because he knew that Adrie knew his stuff. Didn't he always steal his best cauliflowers? No, he had nothing to lose; any job doing was worth doing it right, even stealing cauliflowers. He was so happy, he could have jumped over the gate, but unfortunately he had left the gate open in case that a hasty retreat was necessary.

It was a good thing not to jump over the gate anyway; he wanted to show him that he had hired a mature person to pick his strawberries and not a wild kid. It was as Adrie had thought; he hadn't forgotten the cauliflower incident, but he had forgiven him. He probably understood kids because he had been a kid himself and gave him a chance to prove himself.

Kees never regretted the chance he took on Adrie; he worked hard and did a good job. What else could he possibly want? Adrie had learned early in life to do a good job; his uncle used to grow some strawberries and he had helped him out before. He wanted to be grown up and do a good job. When people were happy with your work, you were grown up! Adrie was a fast worker but that wasn't important to Kees. When strawberries were picked he paid the pickers for the number of baskets they had picked. Kees sold strawberries to vegetable stores; they were sold for consumption but he also sold strawberries to jam manufacturing plants. When they made strawberry jam out of the strawberries, one thing was important. The petals had to be removed from the berries, since nobody appreciates green leaves in the strawberry jam.

When Kees delivered strawberries to the jam factory, the berries were dumped on a conveyor belt. The berries were checked and if there were petals on the berries, they were removed. If there was more than one petal in a basket of strawberries, he was docked 10 cents per basket. He always had over a hundred baskets per day to deliver; it could easily cost him ten Guilders per day if his merchandise was not in the required shape.

Some people wouldn't care less if Kees got less money for his strawberries, but Kees cared; it came out of his pocket book. He was constantly dumping the baskets on a cloth to check that there were no petals on the berries and of course he would raise hell if you bungled all the time. After he had checked Adrie's baskets for a couple of days, he never found one petal, so he said: "It's no use to check your baskets, you do a perfect job." That made Adrie proud when he gave him a bouquet.

When the strawberries were picked for the jam factory, Kees paid the pickers three cent more per basket because removing the petals slowed down the pickers. You sure had to have a knack to pick the berries without the petals. If you squeezed them too much the juice would drip out of the berries and when you lifted the basket, the bottom would be red. Again, the jam factory would give him less money for his berries. Adrie's bottoms were never red; he didn't squeeze the berries.

Between the first and second pick of the strawberries, there was about a week that there were no berries picked; the berries had to grow and ripen. The best pickers were asked if they wanted to do different work for a week. Adrie had to thin out the sugar beets and pick weeds; there was always something to do.

After the strawberries were picked, everybody had to go back to school but at the end of July there was a month of summer holidays. Just before the summer holidays started, Kees came to see Adrie. He asked if he would like to pick beans for him, during his summer holidays. All of a sudden Kees saw Adrie in a different light; from a mischievous boy he had transformed into a good worker and he liked him so much that he wanted him again.

After his career as a strawberry picker, he became a bean picker. His mother came along as well; she wanted to make some money too. They were paid five cents per kilo and if the beans were good, Adrie could pick 300 kilos per day. That was about fifteen guilders per day, which was a good wages for that time. His mother was also a fast bean picker but probably because of Adrie's youth, he picked about thirty kilos more than his mother. There was only one bean picker who picked as many kilos as Adrie. It was a young girl about his age; she made sure that she had the row of beans next to him. She said: "When you are a fast picker, you go way ahead of the other pickers and you are sitting all by yourself." It was obvious that she didn't like to sit alone.

When she was sitting beside Adrie they went at the same speed and kept each other company. They didn't talk much when they were picking beans; there was no time for talking when they were concentrating on making money. During lunch time they did all the talking but when they worked, they worked. If you think that a romance blossomed, you think wrong. They were very good friends but were only twelve years old. Adrie was fast in picking beans but slow in dating girls.

There came a day that Adrie wasn't that happy anymore. Something had gone wrong; he just couldn't make much money, no matter how hard he worked. Kees had another piece of land with beans. In order to get two crops off the land, he had planted Brussels sprouts between the beans. The Brussels sprouts had been growing like cabbage and the beans were dwarfed between the high sprouts.

There was another problem; it rained a lot and the Brussels sprouts were wet all the time. Walking and bending over between the high sprouts, to pick beans, made everybody wet all day. Luckily he wasn't made out of salt, so he didn't melt, but on the other hand he only picked 90 kilos per day instead of the usual 300 kilos. His income had dwindled to one third of what he was accustomed to and that made him very unhappy.

Kees brought his pickers to his land in the morning with his truck, and at night he picked them up. He brought a bascule to weigh the beans and marked the weight in his note book. At the end of the week he added it all up and knew how much he had to pay everybody. That night he found a very unhappy worker who told him: "You need a lantern to find the beans between the sprouts; I can't even make enough money to buy the salt for the porridge."

Kees replied: "Did I ever short change you?"

"No, you never did."

"Don't you worry, I'll make it good with you; I know darned well that you can't pick as many kilos when there is a second crop planted between the beans. The Brussels sprouts were growing too fast with all this rain, so you really have to look for the beans."

Indeed he didn't sell Adrie a bum steer, at the end of the week he paid as much as if he had picked 300 kilos every day. As you see everything worked out for the better and this story should have had a happy ending. The ending could have been, 'The bean grower and the bean picker lived very happily ever after.' They lived long alright but the end wasn't exactly happy. This whole bean picking business ended with a hell of an argument in which the police were involved. But that is the next story.

FROM A SHIT HOUSE, A TRAITOR AND AN INNOCENT VICTIM.

Kees Wensveen and Adrie were very happy with each other, that wasn't the problem. He never mentioned the incident with the cauliflower anymore and he never told his parents. His future looked rosy, but roses are known to have nasty thorns. The proverbial fly landed in the ointment as usual. There are always people around who are born A holes, they manage to spoil good things and are known as "The Spoilers."

September signalled the end of the summer holidays, which meant Adrie had to change his job for the dusty old school books. Kees said: "I've still a couple of weeks of work for you, if you are interested."

Ko knew a solution, she said: "I'll go to talk to the Principal to see if you can stay out of school for a couple of more weeks. The Seventh Grade is only a repeat of the Sixth Grade, so you gain nothing by going to school but you can gain a couple of week's wages."

Ko was right but the Principal didn't buy it. He said: "Your son is liable to compulsory education, he has to come back to school right away, that is the law and I have to enforce this law."

Adrie was baffled that he had gained that much in popularity; all of a sudden everybody wanted him. Kees Wensveen wanted Adrie to work for him and the Principal wanted to educate him. All those people seemed to have honorable intentions with him.

There is a Dutch proverb, which says: "If two dogs fight for the same bone, a third dog will take it." The third dog was probably the police, who had the last word when this conflict seemed to erupt into the Third World War, long before the Second World War had ended. It was strange that Adrie had to suffer because of his own popularity. His star had finally risen but it could very well be the rise and fall of an empire.

Actually, this whole incident shouldn't have escalated at all, but somehow it did. Almost opposite to Adrie lived a National Socialist with his family, which is equivalent to a Nazi. They were Dutch people who sympathized with the Nazis and to the Dutch people they were a bunch of traitors. Those people went by the name of Koekoek, and Leen Koekoek, their son, was in the seventh grade, like Adrie.

He was educated in the Hitler Jugend (Hitler Youth) and was seldom seen at school even though he was liable to compulsory education. Instead of an education, he was trained in the so-called New Order, to be used as cannon flesh and die for his Fuhrer. In the Hitler Jugend they put a rifle in the hands of 14 year old kids and let them play Kid Soldier. Those people had thrown away their Bible and read every day a piece from 'My Kampf' written by Adolph Hitler. If it hadn't been for Leen Koekoek, Ko would have taken it that the Principal enforced the law. However, what's good for the goose is good for the gander; if Leen Koekoek wasn't forced to attend school, why should Adrie be? When Ko mentioned it, the Principal got cheesed off and called it a pretext. Ko fired back and said: "If this is a pretext, why don't you go to that traitor and tell him what the law is. You wouldn't dare, you are just a shit house." (A coward in unorthodox Dutch slang.)

Although that Adrie never had heard his mother use such a language, he thought that it was very well said. After being called a shit house, the Principal got mad too. There were two angry people; Ko and the shit house, which actually was the Principal. The Principal said: "If your son is not at school tomorrow morning, I'll have him picked up by the police and delivered to school."

Ko fired back: "Why don't you have Leen Koekoek picked up by the police and delivered to school? You wouldn't dare because you might end up in a concentration camp."

The Principal threatened: "I warn you, your son has to be back at school tomorrow, this is the end of our conversation."

Ko said to Adrie: "Let that baldheaded Principal go to hell; he thinks he is so important, there is nothing wrong with making a few bucks."

In spite of the threat, Adrie kept working for his favorite boss. For a week everything went alright and it looked that it had been an idle threat. However, it takes time to get the authorities moving, the law works slowly but thoroughly.

The second week, on Monday morning, the police came to the door, but unfortunately for the police there was nobody home. Adrie's mother had gone out and Adrie was working. Fortunately, the neighbors had been looking from behind their curtain at what was going on. As soon as Ko came home, the neighbor lady came to tell her that the police had called. Of course she had hoped that Ko would have told her what the police wanted from her. Ko said: "I haven't got the foggiest idea what the police possibly could want."

Ko made sure that she wasn't home the next morning when the police called again. She repeated the same strategy on Wednesday and Thursday, when the police came there was nobody home. The police knew how to solve the problem and returned Thursday night at 9.00 P.M. and this time the birds were in their cage.

The policeman cleared his throat and said solemnly: "We have received a complaint from the Principal of the Princes Juliana School. Your son is liable to compulsory education and has to attend his classes. If he is not back in school tomorrow morning, he will be picked up and taken to school. Furthermore, if your son is not back in school tomorrow morning I will write you a summons to appear in court, in order to be dealt with according to law."

That would have been really interesting, if Adrie had been picked up by the police. The whole neighborhood would have been behind the curtains to watch the scoundrel being arrested. He would have created more interest than the Queen. Actually, Adrie had been doing alright; he had worked an extra eleven days and there was only a few days work left.

The next day he headed for school, bright eyes and bushy tailed, to resume his studies. If he had figured to pick up where he had left off, he had that quite wrong. The attitude of the Principal had changed considerably; he had been called a shit house and he did his best to act like a shit house. After all he couldn't disappoint Ko and call her a liar.

As soon as the classes started, the Principal looked triumphantly through the classroom and when he discovered Adrie, he looked satisfied that he had won the battle. After being called a shit house, winning the battle didn't satisfy him; he had it in for Adrie. Whenever something happened in the classroom, he was automatically the culprit who had to be punished. He never had said an indelicate word in this incident, yet Adrie was the object of his revenge. Ko had told him the truth and the truth was not appreciated.

He started the classes with the usual prayer, grabbed the arithmetic book, told the students to solve the next ten problems and disappeared. As soon as Baldy had disappeared, the circus started. The boys played with the football in the classroom and did all kinds of crazy things. Simon Vanderwild, who was a favorite of Baldy, became a wanton boy, as soon as the Principal had lifted his heels. He put his bench in the front of the classroom and was standing right on top of it.

That was the right moment for Baldy to return to the classroom. Simon Vanderwild hastily put his bench in the right place and pretended he was busy with his arithmetic. This incident looked very funny, the entire class was laughing. Simon Vanderwild expected to be punished but to everybody's surprise, the Principal passed Simon and came straight up to Adrie.

He spanked his ears and said: "Go and stand in the hall, I'll teach you a lesson for your misbehavior when I'm gone."

When Adrie told his mother what had happened at school, she was furious and said: "Stay home this afternoon; if he says something tomorrow tell him you had a headache after he spanked your ears. And tell him also that if he touches you again, I'll go to the police to lay charges for abuse and using unnecessary force."

Indeed, the next morning, the Principal asked Adrie why he hadn't attended school in the afternoon. He told the Principal that he had a headache after he spanked his ears and he also delivered the message from his mother. The Principal showed his true colors and acted like a shit house, he said: "You'd better start working on your arithmetic before you get a headache again."

The message of Ko had come across; he used every opportunity to belittle Adrie but he didn't use his hands on him anymore. The next opportunity to take it out on him came three days later. There were a lot of gun powder sticks around during the war, which were highly inflammable. The boys used to throw them on the stove in the classroom. As soon as they reached combustion temperature, they flamed up.

Of course they did those things after Baldy had left the classroom. However, Joh Kraak thought to have some fun and throw the sticks on the stove while Baldy was in the classroom. He walked to the waste paper basket to throw a piece of paper away and when he passed the stove he threw a handful of gun powder sticks on the stove. He had figured to be back in his seat by the time the flame would occur.

Baldy saw him throw something on the stove and asked: "What did you throw on the stove?"

Joh Kraak answered: "Nothing Sir."

At that moment, a big flashing flame on top of the stove made him an instant liar. The entire class was laughing and to the surprise of everybody, he ignored Joh Kraak, ran up to Adrie and said: "If you think it's funny, go to the hall and do your laughing there."

He didn't hit him, he probably remembered Ko's warning and didn't want to provoke her to make good on her threats. Adrie had learned a couple of things and knowing that his mother was on his side, he went straight home. When Ko heard about the incident, she wasn't amused at all and went straight to school for an audience with the tyrant.

She said: "I thought you wanted my son at school because he is liable to compulsory education. Why do you send him to the hall? He won't learn anything in the hall!"

The tyrant said: "If he doesn't behave, I have to discipline him."

Ko replied: "Right now there seems to be only one pupil who misbehaves and needs disciplining which is unfair. Try that once more and I'll go to the School Board to tell them all about you."

From there on, Adrie didn't get any more spankings and he wasn't sent to the hall anymore either. The Principal knew Ko well enough and didn't want to provoke her; his job was at stake and he knew it. An unpleasant atmosphere remained in the classroom, it was something like an armed peace accord and it was only a matter of time for another round of clashes to erupt. He wanted

Adrie at school but once he had him there he cared less for him than a fly on a pile of shit.

This conflict was actually just in its infancy shoes, if he couldn't hit Adrie or send him to the hall, there must be another way to get satisfaction. The Principal was forever teasing Adrie about his headache and found all kinds of ways to make his life very unpleasant, but somewhere this had to come to a head-on collision.

Once a week the students had phys. ed. And Adrie loved it. However Baldy had to spoil it and turn the phys. ed. into a nightmare. The playground for the little children of Grade One and Two, was at the back of the school. In the middle of the playground, they had lifted out quite a few tiles, in order to get a giant sand box for the kids to play in. That was a good idea, except there was a violent storm that blew the sand all over the playground.

The Principal knew a way to clean it up. When the students had phys. ed., the Principal said that sweeping and shovelling sand was a good exercise. Instead of playing soccer, the students had to sweep the school yard, shovel the sand in pails and dump it in the sand box. This was probably not allowed by the School Board but he did it anyway.

It wouldn't have been so bad if he hadn't been a hemorrhoid. He was a constant pain in the butt. He ran behind Adrie like a dog in heat and had all kinds of hateful remarks. First Adrie didn't sweep right, "Have you got a headache again?" he jeered.

Next Adrie had to shovel sand in a pail and carry it to the sand box. As soon as he walked with the pail of sand to the box, he ran behind him. Adrie thought he was keeping him company but that was wishful thinking; all he wanted to do was insult him. He said that he walked slower than a snail uphill, he was plain lazy. Adrie's blood started to boil but he restrained himself. The Principal never stopped with his hateful remarks; apparently he wanted to get him mad.

Next, the Principal remarked: "The way you work, it will take years before the sand is back in the sand box; I've never seen a lazy bones like you in my entire life."

The last remarks worked like throwing oil on a fire, Adrie was fed up with the insults of that bald headed idiot. He replied: "Oh you never saw a lazy bones like me before; I'll show you a sluggard who does absolutely nothing."

He dumped the pail of sand on his shoes and kicked the empty pail through the school yard. Next, he seated himself in the sand box to study the effect of his action. Looking at the shit house's face, it looked like thunder. He walked briskly up to the sand box, probably to give him a lecture but Adrie cut him off before he could start. "Accordingly to you I am no good, so the best thing for me is to play in the sandbox like my little sister. You know how to do everything, so why don't you do it yourself, that way you don't have to shout at me. Besides I'm a lazy bones!"

The Principal's face was now red with anger when he screamed: "I order you to pick up the pail; fill it with sand and dump it in the sandbox, or else I'll pull you to the pail by your hair."

Adrie was completely calm and completely in control during this argument. The Principal had wanted to make him mad but the only one to get mad was Baldy. Adrie replied nonchalantly: "I am a lazy bones; do it yourself; lazy bones don't work and for your information, if you touch my hair, I'll go to the School Board to ask if sweeping the schoolyard is physical education. It doesn't look like phys. ed. to me; it looks more like a hard labor camp."

Actually, he was surprised about himself that he dared to say this to the Principal but he asked for it. The other boys of the class were watching this episode as if it was the best Hollywood movie of the year. However, as soon as the School Board was mentioned, Baldy backed off. It seemed that he had forgotten something because he turned around and said: "Nothing good will ever come out of you, there is no room in society for lazy people like you, you are even too lazy to sleep."

He didn't give Adrie a chance to answer, he probably had heard enough; he disappeared and let him alone. Though, the Principal had been put back in his place, the situation got worse instead of better. What else can you expect of a shit house? Actually, this whole episode had given him more ammunition to insult Adrie; he went as far as gossiping behind his back and told the other teachers that he was the extreme of laziness. If he had told that to Kees Wensveen, who pictured Adrie quite differently than this bald headed idiot, he would have been told differently.

The End of a Milestone.

The children were educated to be true patriots, something like the Canadian National Anthem pictures. Where we have "True patriot love, in all thy sons command." Past heroes were heralded as the saviours of The Netherlands and there were all kinds of songs to honor them. One of the past sea heroes was Piet Hein. In Spain he was known as a sea pirate but then Spain was the enemy of The Netherlands. There was a song about Piet Hein in which he was described as the greatest guy since Adam. According to the song: "Piet Hein his name was short. His deeds were great. And he won the Silver Fleet." That winning of the Spanish Silver Fleet was just a polite word for stealing. You just can't teach at school that he stole but in reality he was just a privateer who captured merchant ships. However, he did it for the good of the order, the Dutch order. In spite of his blood drenched boots he was a great guy according to the song because he robbed the Spanish treasury of a silver fleet.

The Netherlands was in an Eighty-Year War with Spain. To finance this war, the Spanish robbed their South American possessions in Peru and Columbia of all their gold and silver. From South America it had to be shipped to Spain over the high seas. Once at sea it was up for grabs and easy prey for pirates such as Piet Hein and associates. One of those silver fleets was intercepted by Piet Hein. Since the Dutch ended up with all the silver, they had something to sing about, while the Spanish cursed Piet Hein.

The way it was, the Spanish stole the gold and silver from the Aztecs in South America and Piet Hein stole it from the thieves. Piet Hein was some kind of a Robin Hood with only one basic difference; you could say that Piet Hein stole from the rich but forgot to give it to the poor. In the Dutch song they sang that Piet Hein won the silver fleet and in Spain they said that he stole it. That's quite a difference of opinion.

You can argue about those things till the cows come home; it probably is in the eyes of the beholder. Even in "The Mutiny on the Bounty," the mutineers said they didn't steal the ship, they just borrowed it. Of course, Captain Bligh didn't agree with that statement because they took his ship and put him ashore.

Since The Netherlands was a seafaring nation there were lots of sea heroes. There was Michiel Deruiter who was born in poverty. He had to turn the spinning wheel by hand in one of the weaving factories. From the shop where he worked he could see and hear the sea. Being quite cheesed off with his non career job, he swore that he would sail the Seven Seas.

Finally, they hired him as a deckhand on one of the merchant ships. When the ship on which he sailed was attacked by pirates, Michiel showed courage and skill in fighting. He was rapidly promoted and became the Admiral of the Dutch fleet. Michiel was surely doing all right for himself.

England had been a long-time ally of The Netherlands during the war against Spain. After the Spanish Armada was defeated at sea, the Spanish withdrew from The Netherlands and the allies became enemies in a dispute about the colonies.

One of the English sea heroes was Drake, according to the English history books. That's not the way the Dutch history books pictured him, they described him as a pirate and a sea robber. In a different country they surely see things differently; it all depends who tells the story. It doesn't matter if you steal and murder as long as you do it for a good cause that is all that counts. Wait till you read what the English history books write about the Dutch sea heroes and the Dutch people. You could feel ashamed to be a Dutchman. The Dutch weren't worse than the Spanish or the English but when it came to war they surely weren't any better. Everybody is proud of his or her ancestry and ethnic origin but greatness is usually measured by how many enemies you kill and how much money you can bring in.

There were some other interesting stories in history. Jan Vanschaffelaar jumped from the tower in Dokkum when he was surrounded by his enemies. Evil tongues have it that he didn't jump off the tower voluntarily. No, his enemies threw him off the tower to get rid of him.

Then there was Hugo Degroot, a statesman who was imprisoned in a castle. To keep him busy he was allowed to read, so they brought him a wooden box with books from the library. After he had read the books they picked up the box with books and brought him another box. On one of those occasions, when they picked up the books, Hugo Degroot had crawled into the wooden box. When they picked up the books, they carried him out of the castle to freedom, while the guards were watching.

Learning history doesn't make much sense; it usually is learning about a bunch of battles and other things that took place with the year attached to it and the reason why it happened isn't taught. The excuse for having to learn history is so that they can learn from the mistakes made in the past. Unfortunately people learn nothing from history; the only thing they ever learned from history is that they learned nothing from history.

Dutch history wasn't the only history that was taught in the Princes Juliana School. They taught a lot of Jewish history. The Bible is nothing but Jewish history, the land of the Bible being Palestine. With full attention, the children listened to heart-warming stories in which Moses magically parted the water of the Red Sea. The Israelis didn't get wet feet but when the Pharaoh and the Egyptians tried to walk through the Red Sea, they got a lot more than wet feet. Evil Moses let the water go back to its original place, so that the Egyptians with their Pharaoh all drowned in the Red Sea.

There was another heart-warming drowning story in the Bible. This happened when Noah with his family sailed off into the sunset leaving screaming sinners struggling in the water.

Since it was a Christian School, the students had to learn all the Bible books and the names of the Apostles of Jesus by heart. Knowledge like that isn't likely to benefit the student during his life unless he becomes a Reverend or a Priest. It will never happen when you are applying for a job that the boss hires you because you know all the Disciples of Jesus and the Bible books by heart.

Adrie's education made it possible that he knew all the Bible Books and Apostles of Jesus by heart but he had never heard about dinosaurs. They were only terrible lizards as their name suggests and they didn't fit in with the Bible at all, so don't talk about it.

His education lacked a lot of things; he didn't even know that he was a Caucasian. Does that make sense? When he was 17 years old there was a lecture by a professor in ethnology. Since he was interested in everything that was around him and wanted to know everything - if that's possible - he decided to go to the University to see if he could learn something. Indeed he learned something! According to the professor, the Caucasian race was the least numerous race. Yet, they were top dog and ruled the world for a long time. They had accomplished more than all the major races in the world together.

Now, he wasn't so stupid that he didn't know that he didn't belong to the Negroid or Mongolian race, but was he a Caucasian? He was very curious but didn't dare to ask. People would think that he was stupid in which they were right, even if it wasn't his fault. Very quietly he went home and the first thing he did was look up in the encyclopedia what kind of a guy he was. For the first time in his life he came to the startling discovery that he was a full-blooded Caucasian.

Students were drowned with history, there was even Church History taught in which the students learned that early Christians were thrown to the lions so that the big cats could have Christian steaks on their menu every day. Other Christians were considered to be martyrs in spite of the Roman Catholic Church calling them heretics. After those Christians told the Pope to shove it where the Sun doesn't shine, they grabbed them and burned them at the stake. They just made charcoal out of those people.

The Roman Catholics were branded as a bunch of savages who burned people because they didn't do what they were told. Of course, that's where the history teaching stopped. Wisely, they forgot to mention that later on, the so called heretics persecuted the heretics.

Marten Luther was the rebel against the Roman Catholic Church and he was the one who founded the Lutheran Church. However, a couple of hundred years later, Calvin, a church leader, rebelled against the Lutheran Church. He said the Lutheran Church was astray of the Bible, so he reformed the Lutheran Church and made a Christian Reformed Church. The Lutheran Church leaders said that he was a rebel and a heretic (Look who is talking!) and threw him right out of the church. It seemed that history was repeating itself.

A lot was learned about different countries but ethnology was lacking. There used to be a travel song with some really stupid lines in it.

I came to Honolulu,
Deep in the Land of the Zulu.

Who ever made up this dumb song must have had his geography mixed up. Zulu Land used to be an independent country but is now part of South Africa which is a far cry away from Honolulu. It didn't make any sense but it rhymed, that was all. There are probably a few Zulus living in Honolulu and also a few Canadians. To call Honolulu the Land of the Zulu is absolute pure nonsense and ridiculous.

Education was biased and prejudiced. Children were taught to be racist. It was so bad that when a Negro kid came to school, the children were very careful not to touch the black kid, lest they would become black as well. They probably thought it was contagious. When one of the kids accidentally, touched the Negro kid, he looked fearfully at his hand, afraid that some of the black had rubbed off on his hand.

Roman Numerals were also taught at school. This knowledge didn't benefit anybody unless the students were looking at clocks with Roman Numerals or buildings dated with Roman Numerals. Actually Roman Numerals are very practical; they were used for over two thousand years. The advantage is that you only have to memorize four letters V, X, L and C.

I is one.
II is two.
III is three
IV is four
V is five
VI is six.
VII is seven.
VIII is eight.
IX is nine.
X is ten.
XI is eleven.
XII is twelve
C is Centum (Hundred)
M is Mill (Thousand)
L is fifty

If you never have studied Roman Numerals they look kind of complicated. Nothing is less true, it is our numerals that are complicated. It is much easier to see three in III than in our number 3. The V was used for five because the hand has five fingers. The hieroglyphic V represented a hand. It's all so simple. Take the X, it is actually two fives, one is upside down. Two fives make ten. An I before a V means one less than five so IV means four. When the I is behind the V it's added so it means six.

Certain people see other things in Roman Numerals, which is explained in the next anecdote:

"At a Girl's College, a professor had been teaching Roman Numerals. The next lesson he was checking how well the students had perceived it. He wrote on the blackboard LXXX. Turning around to face his class he scanned the students, settling on a good-looking girl in the front row. He asked, 'Miss, I'd like you to tell me what it means.'" She smiled and said: "Love and kisses."

Dutch language is important, especially when you live in The Netherlands. That's why they had to learn the longest word. "Hottentotten-soldier-tents-exhibition." That was in Dutch, in the English language the longest word is "Disestablishmentarianism."

All languages spawn funny sentences which are real tongue twisters like "Sheila sells seashells on the seashore." There was one sentence which was comparable to the English sentence: "Peter Piper picked a pack of pickled peppers but if Peter Piper the pickled pepper picker picked a pack of pickled peppers, where is the pack of pickled peppers that Peter Piper the pickled pepper picker picked?"

Besides, "Peter Piper couldn't have picked a pack of pickled peppers, because pickled peppers aren't picked, you pick the peppers first before they are pickled."

There was a sentence which contained all the letters of the alphabet. Comparable in English: "The quick brown horse jumped over the lazy, grey fox". There are many funny things in a language. Leave it to the kids, they'll find them. Such as, the spelling of Mississippi. It is spelled MI-SSI-SSI-PPI. Everybody went for those oddities because they were funny.

In spite of the many short comings in his education, it was sufficient to continue his further education at the Technical School. Completing the Elementary School is surely reaching another mile stone when you are heading for further education. Of course, before you step into the wide world, it is proper to say 'Good bye' to all those lovely teachers. Before the students could walk out of the school door for the last time, leaving this cheerful place behind with melancholy, they also had to listen to a farewell speech from Baldy.

It had been a long year. Actually, the year hadn't been any longer than the others, it only looked that way; even this year had counted 365 days. However, a year seems to last longer when you are enjoying yourself.

There were six other grades with six other teachers. That meant one had to shake six hands and tell six times the same story. When teachers asked what his next step was, Adrie answered proudly that he was going to the Technical School.

Goodbyes can be tearful but not in that case; all students were all too glad to say goodbye so they could go on with their lives. It was noticeable that the bald headed Principal had done a lot of gossiping; he had pictured Adrie to the other teachers as a lazy bum who refused to sweep the schoolyard. One of the teachers said: "Beware, at the Technical School you really have to work, you can't loaf around like here." Guess where he got his information?

Time would tell that everybody had it wrong. The elementary school years ended in a complete disaster but at the Technical School Adrie surprised everybody including himself. Tell somebody he is a lazy bum and what can you expect? At the Technical School the teacher said: "I frankly don't give a damn whether you work hard or not; it's your future which is at stake."

All gloomy forecasts about his future by the idiots at the Princes Juliana School were proven wrong. He thought about going to Baldy to show him his diploma; to show him how wrong he had been but he couldn't stomach him and there were better things to do.

Let's return to the wrap up of Elementary School. After all the handshakes, there was one more duty to fulfil before Baldy would release his precious students from his protecting wings. The boring speech that the students were subjected to looked more like a commercial of the Princes Juliana School and was intertwined with good advice and good wishes.

And now for the Head Master's speech:

"Dear students of the Princess Juliana School. It has been a real pleasure to me, to teach all of you the best Elementary Education available in The Netherlands. The Princess Juliana School has always excelled in Elementary Education and has always been far ahead in the education field. You can consider it a great privilege to have received such a great Christian education of this calibre.

As past students of the Princess Juliana School, you'll discover fast that you are far ahead of other students, who had their education elsewhere. According to a Dutch proverb, "A good start is half of the work." Though you all have a lead over other students, you cannot rest on your laurels. On the contrary, you'll have to work hard in order not to lose your lead.

However, you are on the right track; this good Christian education will cling to you as shit to an Indian blanket." (Oops that's not exactly what he said, though he meant it. He said neatly and formally.) It will cling to you as a burr. This is why students of the Princes Juliana School outshine other students all the time. Also, later in society you will always benefit from the excellent education you have received.

With melancholy, we always see our children, who we have had for such a long time under our protective wings, leave the Princess Juliana School. However, we are all convinced that with what we have taught you and what you have learned, you are able to conquer the world and you will be able to meet the challenges of today's society!

Hereby, I wish you all the best of luck and success in your further life. I am convinced that you will look back many times, with much gratitude, to the enjoyable time you have endured while studying at the Princes Juliana School."

This whole speech was an ode to the Princes Juliana School. It looked like the word of the sponsor by a first class bull-shitter. Adrie could have seen the Princess Juliana School in a different light after the information he had just received. The Principal had pictured everything just great.

This Princes Juliana School, which he always had seen as a stupid school, was actually the best school in the country. He started to wonder what the other schools were like, if this was the best. And to his shame he heard that all those teachers, who he always had seen as a bunch of ruthless dictators, had been courageous, hardworking teachers, who had only the best for the students in mind. They really went all out to give everybody the best education in the country. (How nice of them.)

Adrie always had seen the headmaster as a baldheaded tyrant, and had called him a nerd, jerk or a wimp, whatever suited the moment. Whenever he was cheesed off with him, he had called him an A hole. He should be ashamed of himself; this good man had worked his knuckles to the bone to prepare him for the cruel world. He should have praised and appreciated him instead of calling him a dink.

The way he saw it now, he had been misled and had been walking with a board in front of his head, so he couldn't see the good qualities of those fabulous teachers. Yes, that speech was an eye opener.

I once was lost but now I'm found,
I was blind but now I see.

Nazi Trouble at the Tech.

Time doesn't stand still not even when there is a war on. That time stands still happened only, in the Bible, when Joshua was fighting a battle. Joshua had almost won the battle when the sun was setting. Very cleverly, he put his staff underneath the sun to prevent it from setting and Joshua won the war. All according to the Bible.

Adrie had successfully completed Elementary School and was now ready for further education. Ever since he was a boy, when he was riding with his mother in the bus, he wanted to become a bus driver. Of course, a 13 year old boy can't be a bus driver; you could only get a driver's license when you were 18 years old. His mother said: "You should go to the Tech to take up motor mechanics. That will give you an edge in your later life when you become a bus chauffeur."

That was an excellent idea and Adrie was all for it. He thought that repairing cars was nice and interesting work and a good trade to be in. There were two Technical Schools in Rotterdam, one was public and the other one was a Christian Technical School. The Reverend who didn't mind his own business said: "You have to go to the Christian Tech. A boy who comes from a Christian family cannot go to a public school."

Ko didn't agree with the Reverend at all. The Christian Tech was on the other side of Rotterdam and the Public Tech was in the Southern part. Since they were living on the outskirts of the city, the Tech in Rotterdam South was still a considerable distance. It was about a forty minute walk. There was no bike available for Adrie, the Germans cared less that he had to walk to the Tech, their only interest was to make guns, tanks, planes and submarines. If Adrie had to go to the Christian Tech, he would have to walk almost an hour and a half. The Reverend said: "You don't have to walk, you can go by bus and tram."

Ko replied: "Do you know how long that takes. The bus here goes only once every hour and then he has to take a transfer on the tram. That will take him about 2 hours to go to school and another two hours to come home from school. Four hours of travelling is just too much for a studying boy. School starts at 8.00 a.m. so he has to leave his house at 6.00 a.m. in the morning.

The Reverend played his last trump and countered: "What do you think the Lord will say on Judgement Day, when you tell him that the Christian school was too far to walk?"

Ko stuck with her guns and said: "You always tell us that the Lord understands all of us and that he forgives all our sins. If the Lord doesn't understand our problem and we commit a sin we'll have to pray for forgiveness but I don't think so, there is a limit to what people can do!"

It was still possible that the Reverend would get his way. When Ko tried to enrol her son, she was told by the Principal that there was a severe shortage on facilities for technical education. One of the Technical Schools was occupied by the Germans and those students had been transferred to the other Techs. She could fill out the necessary registration forms and the admittance would go by the rule of "First come, first served." The Christian Tech had less enrolment than the Public Tech said the Principal. He would let her know as soon as possible if he could take her son. If not, she could still enrol her son at the Christian Tech.

Luckily, the mail brought a favorable reply and Adrie was admitted to start his training on March 1st 1943. There were two other boys of Adrie's class, who went to the same church and the parents of those boys had their sons registered at the Christian Tech. The Reverend never gave up ridiculing Ko because she had her son in a public school.

Even the Principal of the elementary school had been informed about the choice of the Public Tech above the Christian Tech. When he made his speech to the children, who were going to leave school, he suggested that two of his pupils were going to the Christian Tech for their education. Unfortunately one of his pupils went to the Public Tech which had inferior education compared to the Christian Tech.

With great expectations, Adrie walked his 45 minute walk to the Tech that first morning. Wow, he was going to work on cars and motor bikes and soon he would be able to repair cars, bikes and buses. As soon as he entered the Tech, he was met by giant posters from the Safety Museum. One famous one was the one that said: "A piece of paper is good, washing hands is better." Some people, who eat their lunch, don't wash their hands and take a piece of paper to hold their sandwich. The Safety Museum suggested that washing hands was better.

Next, he noticed signs which indicated what way the electricians, motor mechanics, carpenters and steel workers had to go. Soon he was among future motor mechanics. There were 54 boys who were taking motor mechanics which was way too many pupils for one classroom. Half of the pupils went to class 1 A and the other half went to class 1 B. Adrie was in the A class because his last name started with a letter which was in the beginning of the alphabet.

The first lesson was to get acquainted with the technical school procedures. Everybody was handed a sheet with the rules of the Tech and the teacher read them to the new pupils. After the reading he asked if there were any questions and next he held some kind of a pep speech to encourage the new students to give it their best shot. "You unlucky people, you are males which make you dependent on your own ingenuity to make a success of yourself. If you fail you are up the creek without a paddle. Females have two chances, they can make a success of themselves and if they fail they can still marry a success but you poor creatures have only one kick at the cat and that's it. Failing means working as a laborer for minimum wage or to become a scavenger, so take your pick. Since you have to work on your success, I expect you to give it your best shot and so will I."

In the afternoon there was a theory lesson in Material Knowledge. That was number one disappointment to the students, they had figured to study gasoline engines. Instead they had to learn how steel, cupper and other materials were made in smelters. The teacher made it interesting by giving some history on automobiles. He said: "You people have chosen a very interesting and promising trade. Motor mechanics is also a young trade. The automobile as you see it today wasn't invented. Many people have worked to make a horseless carriage possible.

Different ideas surfaced in different parts of the world to propel the automobile. One of the early tries was a vehicle which had windmills mounted on a mast. The windmills wound a set of springs which could be unwound to propel the vehicle. It worked like a toy car in the toy store, you wind the spring and the car will go.

A very successful attempt was a car running on compressed air. Instead of gasoline stations, a grid of compressor stations was necessary. Steam automobiles seemed to be the future. By 1800 there were steam buses running in Paris. They went at the incredible speed of 6 miles per hour. By 1900 that had improved significantly and the speed record of a steam race car was 100 m.p.h.

It was in 1875 that the first gasoline engine was tried for propulsion of cars. There was no clutch which made it hard to start the car. A strong man had to hold up the rear wheels to make it possible to start the engine. Once the engine started, the strongman would drop the rear wheels on the ground and the car would jump forward. Because of the sudden load the engine had to pull, the engine stalled many a time. By 1900 Ford and Mercedes Benz were building cars with the driver sitting in the open.

There are not that many cars driving now with the war on. After this war is over, the automobile will take off and really conquer the world. The post war world will have lots of work for motor mechanics. You guys are going to need sun glasses. That's how bright your future looks."

The teacher continued about his own venture with automobiles. "After the First World War, I wanted to study auto body repair but my father said: 'There are not enough people here driving cars that have accidents.' Later on I studied hard to become a teacher at the Technical School, to give me the opportunity to teach young people motor mechanics and auto body repair."

There were practical and theory lessons. The practical lessons had also blacksmithing and sheet metal working. However, when Adrie went to the practical motor mechanics class, he expected to start working on cars and motors. He must be in the wrong class room, he thought, where were the cars and motors? All he saw was a room filled with work benches, a lathe, drilling machine and a grinder.

There was no mistake, the teacher said: "Before you can work on cars, you first have to know the fundamentals to become a good motor mechanic and you'll have to know how to work metals."

Everybody received a piece of iron seven by four inches and about three quarter inches thick. Within no time everybody was busy filing the piece of iron to the thickness of five eighth of an inch. It also had to be square and once it passed inspection, everybody had to make a square hole in it. When that was done, a smaller piece of metal was given which had to be made fit in the square hole. One of the students said: "Why don't they make up their mind, first they want you to make a square hole in the piece of iron. When you have that accomplished, they want you to close the hole by putting a square piece in it." Before this was all done three weeks had passed.

This motor mechanics course was a great disappointment to all the boys who had expected to start working on cars. The first and second class were metal working only and only in the third and fourth class would there be working on motor bikes and cars.

In spite of shortages of materials, the Germans supplied the technical schools with materials. There was iron, steel, sheet metal and even coal for blacksmithing. The Germans needed lots of skilled workers and the technical schools could provide them.

There were also drawing classes and that's where Adrie ran into trouble with a Dutch Nazi supporter. When the pupils entered the classroom for the first time, the teacher let the students select their own place. Adrie didn't know anybody, he talked to everybody he saw. There was one particular friendly boy whose name was Cor Vanderzande. He seemed a nice boy to be friends with and Adrie took the drawing board beside Cor.

As it turned out, Cor was a Nazi sympathizer and when he found out that Adrie wasn't, the short friendship came to an end. That wouldn't have been that bad if Cor hadn't threatened Adrie. "You are making a bloody mistake; it won't be long now for Hitler to win the war. And when this war is over I'll report you to the German authorities for not being friendly to the German cause."

Adrie had dealt with Leen Koekoek who was even in the Hitler Youth and found it wiser not to say anything. Cor didn't like the silent treatment, he got mad and scratched with a hard pencil on Adrie's drawing. Normally if there was an account to be settled between the students, they invited each other to Sand Square for a knockout boxing match. That was the place where fights between students took place and where accounts were settled such as who was boss. Adrie didn't think it was wise to invite him to Sand Square for a fight. Cor could be a sore loser if he lost and make good on his threats.

Enough was enough, Adrie thought and waited till the end of the class. When all the students had left the classroom, he walked up to the teacher and told him what was happening. The teacher said: "We'll have to do some changing of places the next time and we also will have to be careful when we are talking. It's too bad that we have traitors."

It was a good thing that this incident didn't happen in the classroom of Adrie's Algebra Teacher who was a Nazi sympathizer himself. This teacher's name was Teunissen but the students called him conveniently 'Uncle Teun.' He had a white moustache and deep wrinkles in his forehead which made him look as if he was 150 years old. To keep order in the class room he had a backup in the storage room where he kept a big round table leg which he used as a club. Whenever things seemed to get out of hand, he went to the storage room to get his ultimate weapon to help him out. A loud booing of the class was heard but as soon he came out of the storage room the class was silent and waiting the reprisals that were following.

At one time when he saw one of the students throw carbide in his inkwell that made the ink boil all over his bench, he hit him right in the face with his club screaming: "I'll teach you to throw carbide in the inkwell."

The student had a bleeding nose and was awfully quiet after this incident. Uncle Teun always started his lesson with reviewing the war and had a reasonable explanation for the things that were going on. Most of the time he spent half of the lesson on politics before his lesson in Algebra started. He was a good politician but a bad algebra teacher.

On the other hand he wasn't all bad, he taught his students how to arrive at the date that Easter would be. Easter is always on the first Sunday in spring when there is a full moon. So the date will always be between March 21st and April 21st. With an algebra formula it worked perfectly.

(Adrie kept the formula for many years but when he emigrated it got lost. Without the formula he couldn't figure it out by himself and had to look at the calendar to see when it was going to be Easter, like everybody else.)

Uncle Teun had a certain outlook on life which made the pupils laugh. On one occasion he said: "What God makes is beautiful and what man makes is no bloody good. God made man and if you put two people together, a male and a female, sooner or later there will be a little man called a baby. Now take what people make, they make a car but no matter how many cars you put together, you'll never see that one day there is a little car produced by the other cars."

This baby making business versus car making business came up when they studied Dutch language. Mr. Derooi was a very good teacher; he had a natural way of teaching which appealed to all students. Whenever he was teaching, he spent the first half an hour on jokes and stories. He started the Dutch language lesson by stating: "In English every noun is headed with "The", in French some nouns are headed with "Le" when they are masculine and if they are feminine they are headed with "La". Now if you think I'm going to teach you English or French you got that wrong because the roster suggests that I teach you Dutch. I just mention this to explain the Dutch language which has Feminine Nouns which are headed with "De" and Masculine Nouns which are headed with "Den". But there are a lot of nouns that are neither masculine nor feminine; they are neutral and they are headed with "Het" It is 'de door' and 'het window.'"

The question popped up how we can see that the door is feminine and the window is neutral, how do you sex the objects? The answer was: "You can't, you have to learn that in your study of the Dutch language."

One smart student asked the teacher about the car which is feminine according to the Dutch language and according to the Algebra teacher can't produce any small cars. That was right on Mr. Derooi's alley who thought of a joke. "There was a stinking rich oil sheik who bought a brand new Ferrari. He was very superstitious and asked the Reverend, the Priest and the Rabbi to bless his new car. The Priest came, threw some water over the Ferrari and said 'I hereby baptize you in the name of the Father, the Son and the Holy Ghost, Amen.'

Next the Reverend came who stretched his arms out over the car and said 'The Lord will bless you.'

As last the Rabbi came and he cut a piece off the tail pipe."

Mr. Derooi paused briefly to see the impact of his joke and continued: "As you can see gentlemen, the Dutch language has it all wrong because the Rabbi found a little dink at the back of the car. This also confirms your algebra teacher's observation that cars don't reproduce like humans do. As you notice gentlemen, cars don't reproduce because they are all men. How could cars possibly reproduce when they are all males? You always need a female and a male to reproduce.

This brings us to the question: 'What does the Rabbi do with all those pieces of foreskin he cuts of the penises of the little boys when he circumcises the male babies?' Nobody had any idea so the teacher said: "They make dinky toys out of them."

There was a roar of laughter in the classroom. It didn't make the Dutch language any easier but a good laugh promotes the study. That was not the best teacher the Tech had to offer, the best teacher was the Principal himself. He had been a teacher in motor mechanics and whenever a teacher got sick, he filled in. One day that he was teaching, he impressed everybody.

There was always a little problem in figuring forces with different supports. A bridge has two supports with a load in the middle. A crowbar had a support in the middle with a force on one end and an opposing force on the other. A seesaw had a support in the middle with a force on each end. He added: "You all know this; you played this seesaw game with your little sister when you were growing up. Of course you still play this game but now with a different girl." He could make it plain to remember things.

All motor mechanics saw the glass motor he had in his office. One of the boys had brought a little gasoline, which was hard to get during the war. After he started the motor, you could see through the glass how the valves opened and closed. Even the ignitions in the four cylinder four stroke motor could be observed.

One morning when Adrie was walking to the Tech, he heard a horse behind him. It was a milkman who had a horse to pull his milk wagon. He had made a deal with one of the farmers to have his horse grazing in one of the pastures behind Adrie's house. Every morning, the milkman picked up his horse with his bike, and at night he took the horse back to the pasture. If he rode the horse, he had to walk to the pasture and at night he had to walk back after he had delivered the horse. The milkman asked Adrie: "Do you want to ride the horse?"

That was a silly question; of course he wanted to ride a horse. It was much easier than walking. The milkman had his milk shop a few blocks away from the tech. When they had arrived at his milk shop, the milkman said: "If you want to take my horse back to the pasture tonight you'll have another horseback ride."

Well, what could Adrie say? At night he picked up the horse and received a bag with some oats in order to catch the horse the next day. With a bag of oats it wasn't hard to catch the horse. From there on Adrie went to school on horseback. He could never have imagined that he would go to school riding a horse.

One day was spent in the Safety Museum. They had to go by train to Amsterdam and saw all kinds of examples how people were mangled by machines. There was the scalp of a guy who had been scalped when he was drilling and had looked closely at the drilling process. The bit had grabbed his hair and twisted off his scalp.

Quite frequently there was an air raid during the lessons. When that happened, the lessons were stopped and all students had to sit in the halls on the floor. The Tech was four stories high and when you were on the top floor you had to go down two floors. At that time bombs were not heavy enough to go through two concrete floors.

* * * *

July 1943 was the month when hope was restored in the hearts of the freedom loving Dutch people. When Adrie tuned in on Radio London on July 10, 1943 the news was encouraging: "This is Radio London. There is great news from the Western Front. The Allies have returned to Europe today. In the early morning hours, Allied troops invaded Sicily and have established two beach heads. Good progress has been made."

More encouraging news came from Italy on July 24, 1943: "This is Radio London. The Italian Fascist Party has ousted Mussolini and replaced him with King Victor Emmanuel. King Victor Emmanuel has summoned Mussolini to his palace and has placed him under arrest. American troops have made good progress in Sicily and expect to have the island under control in the next two weeks."

On August 16, 40 days after the Allies had landed in Sicily, it was confirmed that Sicily was taken by the Allies and on September 3 the Allies landed on the Italian mainland. That was the good news but unfortunately there was bad news as well. Messerschmitt, one of the greatest German aeroplane builders, had introduced jet fighters and jet bombers that would soon be bombing England. That could change the superiority in the air which could also spell disaster for the invasion of the Italian main land.

Uncle Teun, the algebra teacher, was good enough to explain how a jet engine worked. He said it was very simple; all you really needed was a cylinder which was open at the back. When you inject jet fuel in this cylinder and ignite it, the pressure of the explosion will escape on the back and will push the front forward.

Adrie asked Uncle Teun: "If it's that simple why we had to invent the piston engine first with all its complicated pistons, driving rods and crankshaft?"

Uncle Teun explained: "It was mostly the fuel which wasn't available in the beginning and needed an evolution to make it work in a jet engine." After everybody knew how a jet engine worked, the teacher spent some time teaching algebra.

There was more bad news on September 12, 1943. Adrie took the newspaper out of the mail box and saw on the front page in big fat letters,

ADOLF HITLER FREES MUSSOLINI IN DARING COMMANDO RAID.
Mussolini installed as President of the Italian Republic.

Everybody had hoped that when Mussolini was removed the new head of state King Emmanuel would take Italy out of the war. It was the intention of King Emmanuel to do that and ask for an armistice with the Allies. However, there were quite a number of German divisions in Italy and more were arriving all the time. And now with Mussolini back in action the war in Italy would continue.

Like a Thief in the Night.

During the summer of 1943, rations were cut drastically in half and later they were cut in half again. It became obvious that there was going to be a great shortage of food stuffs. Lots of items had disappeared completely from the store shelves. Amazingly coffee was kept going for a long time though it was surrogate coffee. The Dutch coffee came not from Brazil, during the war, as Max Havelaar wrote in his book "Coffee In Brazil." No, the Dutch coffee came from the tulip fields during the war. There are lots of tulip fields in The Netherlands which gave an adequate supply of coffee surrogate to the Dutch people. Tulip bulbs were dried, roasted and ground into coffee surrogate. The outcome of this procedure was called Pitto Coffee. According to the advertising "Pitto is best" and actually it was. Of course it's not hard to be the best if that's the only coffee there is. It was not real coffee but it tasted rather good if you had nothing else.

With the deteriorating food situation, the tulip fields were now used to grow grain. It meant that no more coffee surrogate was available until they found a way to make coffee out of dried and ground acorns. A popular song came about:

The coffee that they give us, is just fine,
They make it out of acorns and tastes like iodine.

Jan Lems was a small time farmer; he had some pastures on which he kept about 10 milk cows. He kept a pig for his own use and had some chickens for the egg production. Furthermore he grew some beets for his cattle which were consumed during winter time. And he was growing wheat which was in great demand during the war.

Farmers were allotted to keep some of their produce for themselves. Those quantities left little room to help out the relatives and friends. If they did, they would be short of food themselves. Of course, the Germans couldn't tell how much milk the cows would give from day to day, or how many eggs the chickens would lay. That gave the farmers a chance to sell some milk and eggs to their friends. During the Depression when Arie was unemployed, Ko was getting two litres of milk every day from the farm, at half the price that the milkman charged. That was a great help and this was continued during the war. When Jan Lems butchered his pig in fall, he gave every member of the family some pork. This was all illegal and could be done only within reason. Those extras from the farm were all supplements to the lean rations people got from the Germans.

Coal was rationed too and the rations were not half enough to heat the house for the entire winter. Everybody was heating the house with a coal stove and a lot of people like the de Kievits cooked their food on this very stove as well. People were worried that in the coming winter that they would be sitting in a cold house and worse yet, that they couldn't cook their food. That was, if there was going to be any food to cook. Nobody knew what the coming winter would bring, it looked very grim. Cold and hunger could be expected unless one could supplement the meagre rations.

Supplementing rations could be done, with a lot of money, on the black market. Most of the people didn't have that kind of money and had to find another way to keep eating and staying warm. There was a lot of coal arriving in the harbors of Rotterdam every day, of course, not as much as before the war. The holds of the ships were unloaded on railway box cars, trucks and also on smaller river boats. This was done with big cranes which scooped a lot of coal in their buckets and swung the bucket to the smaller vessels, box cars or trucks. Some of the coal fell in the harbors when it was moved with the cranes. Nobody cared about that little bit of coal that was lost. When this goes on from year to year the bottom of the harbor becomes a coal bed. With insufficient rations some people were dredging the coal out of the harbor. They used that coal for themselves, sold it on the black market, or used it to barter for other goods in demand.

It was in the time that The Netherlands had colonies in the East and West. With one of the geography lessons, the Principal had invited a planter from the Dutch Indies to teach the students about the Tropics. According to the planter; living in the Tropics exposes you to a lot of diseases which is aggravated because of poor hygiene. There were terrible unsanitary conditions in the Tropics. People were building settlements around the river and it was very common that you saw a guy shit in the river while the people downstream were drinking from it. *(Those were not the precise words the planter used.)* According to the planter, this was very unsanitary, it caused dysentery and all kinds of other sicknesses were the result.

What puzzled Adrie was; what made him think we were any better? The rivers in The Netherlands were open sewage channels and were so bad that no life could be found in the polluted water. When the water wasn't potable at all anymore they used chlorine to kill the bacteria, with the terrible consequence that you couldn't make a decent cup of tea. When you drank tea it tasted like chlorine. There was a solution to the chlorine problem; one of the newest techniques to make water potable was to use aluminium. The result of that experiment was that the water contained too much aluminium which could cause brain damage. It is believed that aluminium causes Alzheimer's disease.

People thought we had made progress when we got rid of the cess pit, but the same time that we made one step forward, we made two steps backward. The night soil which we used to dump on the land, where it was recycled into the system, went now into the river where people were drinking from. Nice going!

Before the war there was a wide ditch behind the houses on the Hordyk. This ditch was made to carry the surplus water to the river; it also carried all the sewage to the river. The houses had a flushing toilet. When people flushed the toilet, they flushed their excrement into the ditch. When it hit the water it would sink to the bottom. It would decay at the bottom and after a few days it would come up, floating on the water like a dead body.

When it came up floating on the water, the color had changed; it wasn't the usual brown anymore, it was black. There were always a lot of little black islands drifting in the ditch; they were carried off to the river and from there to the ocean. The rivers died; there was not a living critter to be found in the rivers. The rivers were nothing but open sewage channels, combined with other pollutants, like oil from ships.

At one time Adrie was catching salamanders and stickle bass between the little black islands which were the remains from human excrement. It all came from the flushing toilets of the houses on the Hordyk. The cess pit wasn't invented by Edison, but it was a great invention, which cannot be said of flushing toilets which created a lot of pollution. Look who was shitting in the river?

When more and more houses were built the situation deteriorated, there were not just little black islands drifting in the ditch, it became an open sewage ditch. The smell became unbearable and the Germans found that all that raw sewage in the rivers was unhealthy. Germany was far advanced with the many big cities they had. Their rivers were reasonably clean and to make the water potable wasn't that hard to do. They took it up with the authorities of the City of Rotterdam and proposed a modern sewage plant in which the sewage was changed into fertilizer. Sewer pipes had to be installed to carry the sewage to the plant.

The city was going to construct a sewage line beside and parallel with the ditch. The problem was that the land was owned by the home owners. Everybody wanted a sewer but they were against the city expropriating the land. The city wanted to buy the needed land from the owners at less than half the value.

Many owners didn't want to sell the land at all; they wanted compensation for damages. After the sewage line was installed it was covered with ground again and you could easily do some gardening on top of the sewage line, they reasoned. There had to be inspection holes but they were covered with a concrete lid anyway.

The city reasoned differently than the land owners, they wanted access to the sewage line at all times. After negotiations failed, the city sent a letter to all land owners with a deadline. Nobody sold the land to the city and the city expropriated the land. The city paid not a nickel more for the land than they had offered because it was in the public interest, they said.

After the sewer had been completed, it was covered with ground and the land was restored. However, that land belonged to the city and the city proposed to make a walking path out of it. This idea almost created a riot; with the ditch in the rear of the gardens the properties were only accessible from the street. With a walking path, it would attract kids stealing apples and pears from the trees. And since there was shortage of food, even potatoes and other produce might be stolen.

The people organized and marched on City Hall, demanding to see the Mayor. They told the Mayor and City Council that they would block the path with barbed wire and prevent people from using the walking path, even if it would take violence. As usual, the Mayor wasn't impressed, but apparently he saw the writing on the wall and scrapped the walking path.

The city never gave up making the people mad. Next, they sent a letter to the former land owners telling them that they could rent the land back and then they could use it for growing produce. The people were furious; the rent was set very high so that in about eight years time the purchase price of the land would have been repaid. After eight years it would be straight profit and a source of revenue. To add insult to injury, it was stipulated that, if for any reason the city had to do maintenance work on the sewer, they had the right to do it without reimbursing people for damage to their produce.

It must have been a great disappointment for the city that people didn't go for their profitable schemes. The next thing was that the city planted a hedge to indicate where the property line was. With dwindling rations, everybody used the city land which they had owned before expropriation, to grow potatoes. When the entire polder was flooded by the Germans at the end of the war to prevent landing of airborne regiments, the hedge was under five feet of water. Consequently, the hedge died and was never replaced after the war.

When the sewer line was trenched; a lot of peat came out of the trench. Peat was formed in the time that The Netherlands was still a wooded area. In the Southern provinces it was coal because the land was older. The Western provinces were formed later when the sand from the ocean was pushed up to form high dunes. People from the Northern provinces had been burning peat to heat their houses, for a long time. Around Rotterdam coal was burned, it was less dusty and more convenient.

When Adrie watched the trenching, he saw that big chunks of peat came out of the ground. Now here was fuel for your stove, peat burns very well, he thought. The peat was quite wet which was hardly a problem. In the sun the peat would be dry in no time at all and once it was dry the peat could be stored in the shed.

Adrie went home to get a wheelbarrow to transport the chunks of peat and told his mother that he had found fuel for the stove. It didn't take long for other people to see that here was a good deal. The price was right; all it took was hard work. People would transport the peat even in baby carriages.

If you are facing a cold and hungry winter, you will be surprised how fast you start thinking about how to solve your problem.

Within no time there were piles of peat at the back of the house. Peat burns rather fast which necessitates a large supply. People would even burn potato peels in the stove, anything to get heat. However, with the dwindling rations people couldn't afford to burn potato peels anymore. They just scrubbed the potatoes clean and cooked them in the peel.

In the meantime, that the sewer lines were dug, they built a sewage treatment plant. When it became operational most of the people had a tour to see what was accomplished. It was very impressive to see how at the beginning of the plant raw sewage entered and at the end the sewage had become white powder that could be used as fertilizer. Adrie could figure a lot of things but this he couldn't figure. How in the world could they make white powder out of brown shit?

Adrie was confident that the house would be warm during the coming winter but would there be enough food? In spite of the bag of wheat they had received from the farm and the potatoes they were growing in the rear garden, it was doubtful that those supplements were sufficient to keep the family fed. It became more and more obvious that money had no value; you couldn't eat it or drink it.

Willie had taken on a job in house keeping two days a week and was fed by the people on those days. Adrie didn't think he would be able to get a job in housekeeping, nobody would hire him. There had to be a different way to get food, he thought. He was eying at the wheat fields in the polder. The wheat was ripening and soon the farmers would take it off the fields. After the wheat was in the farmers' barns it was too late. He had to get his share before that.

It wasn't hard to figure out that he couldn't swipe some wheat in the day time. The farmers and the Germans wouldn't go for that. This job had to be done when it was dark. In the dark you can't see very much but Adrie could. Luckily he didn't need cat's eyes, yet he knew where everything was in the dark. When he was going to elementary school, he played in the polders with his friends every day. He knew every ditch, barbed wire fence and gate even if he didn't see them.

It was completely dark around 9.30 p.m. and when it was dark it was dark. There was a total black out during the war and there was also a curfew; that lasted from half an hour after sunset till half an hour before sunrise. That way the Germans could keep an eye on the people, they didn't like to have people sneaking around in the dark. Nobody was allowed to go out in the dark, which didn't deter Adrie, he wasn't going on the street anyway and it was unlikely that there were Germans in the polder in the dark.

On a moonless night, it was as dark as in a Negro's ass which made it perfect for Adrie's honorable plan. However, on the first night of his mission, to secure food on the table for the coming winter, it wasn't dark. The atmosphere was clear until a quarterly moon set shortly after 10.00 p.m.; then the sky became partly overcast and the night was pitch black.

"It was exactly what the doctor had ordered", Adrie thought. He took a gunny bag and a pair of scissors and disappeared like a thief in the night. Only the channel parted him from the fields with food supplies. That was no problem to Adrie, all he had to do was to cross two yards of his neighbors to reach the bridge. He climbed over the gate and started his walk in complete darkness. The first three fields were pastures followed by a field with beets for cattle fodder and then came a wheat field. There was one ditch to jump and that even went perfect in the dark. Adrie just sat down in the wheat field and started to clip the wheat heads into his gunny bag. It took quite a while to get the bag full with wheat but that didn't matter, he was still young.

Everything went without a hitch, he didn't see anything and didn't hear anything either. It was a perfect heist; he had never thought that he would be sneaking around like a thief in the night to steal wheat. Usually it was the devil that made you steal but this time it was the war that made him do it. He wasn't going to sit like a lame duck and do nothing. No, he was going to fight to keep food on the table for the family and he knew how to do it. He was capable to do a job which nobody had asked him to do. A kid has to grow up fast during depression and war, there was just no time to be a child, he thought.

The next day came the hard work; the wheat had to be threshed. Adrie had no threshing machine; he had never threshed grain before with or without a threshing machine. It seemed that there was only the ancient way to get his wheat threshed. Luckily, he had read about how it was done in the early days. What they could do then he could do now, he thought. It was a windy day which came in handy for wheat threshing. First he bashed the gunny bag with a club to get the kernels out of the heads. When that was done he spread an old carpet on the ground, took a shovel and threw the wheat into the wind. The chaff blew away and the wheat kernels dropped on the carpet. 'This really worked,' Adrie thought, he had read about it in books that people threshed their wheat that way. It never had occurred to him that one day he would do something like that. During a war people go back to basics, progress has stopped and everything is done the hard way again.

There was a lot of hard work to be done to get bread on the table. First you had to steal the wheat in the dark, then you had to thresh it and after it had been threshed it had to be dried in the oven. When the wheat was dry enough, it was ready to grind in the coffee grinder. Nobody cared how long it took, as long as there was something to eat.

Adrie had been brought up to be honest and not to steal. He had a conscience that would string him up high if he took one penny of someone else's money. In spite that his parents were very religious, his mother asked at night: "Are you going out again?"

Now here was a question, going out at night in the dark with a curfew? She knew what he was doing and in spite of her religion she was glad he did it. Surviving this horrible war was all that people could think about and conscience and religious rules were put on the back burner. Only the law of survival counted as in the animal kingdom. When you are going to be starving there are no civil or Bible laws. Manna wasn't coming from heaven so you had to get it yourself.

Going out at night to steal wheat became a way of life. There were only four or five weeks to get a winter supply. After the wheat was swathed and put in stooks on the land to dry, the farmers would take it off the land as soon as it was dry enough to put in the barn. Luckily, all the wheat hadn't been seeded on the same day and would mature on different dates. There were quite a few wheat fields which meant that there was wheat to be had for some time.

Not every day was a perfect day to steal wheat. When it was a moonlit night, a German patrol might detect you and arrest you. Sometimes, Adrie had to wait till the moon was gone. Instead of at night he went at 4.00 in the morning to raid the wheat fields. There were also a couple of nights that it was raining which didn't deter him; he wasn't made out of salt so he couldn't melt.

There was another danger which could come suddenly, almost without warning. Every night hundreds of bombers were flying over to Germany, except when the weather was bad. For a solid two hours, the sky was filled with the constant drone of Allied heavy bombers all going the same direction to Germany. Search lights poked frantically at the bombers and puffs of anti-aircraft fire detonated with some hits.

After a couple of hours it became quiet but all the noise of airplanes returned a few hours later when the bombers returned to England, after they had dumped their destructive load on targets in Germany. The skies were never still, the R.A.F. and U.S. Air Forces ruled the skies over Europe with their Armada.

When English bombers passed over on their way to Germany to bomb the German cities, search lights were used to detect the planes. There were quite a few search lights from all directions to light up the sky and unfortunately also the fields in the polder. When that happened, all he could do was sit at the edge of the ditch till the planes were gone and the search lights went out. Adrie knew about the time that the planes were flying over to Germany and the time that they returned to England and scheduled his nightly trips accordingly. Sometimes the planes came earlier or later, it depended on the targets they had and the flying time it took to reach those targets. Quite frequently his all-important work was interrupted.

The Germans were also shooting at the English planes and the big pieces of shrapnel that Adrie had found in the fields indicated that it wasn't without danger to be outside when the shooting was going on. For security he put a big old pan in his gunny bag which he used as helmet when they started to shoot.

Adrie was prepared for all dangers which might occur, he thought. To his surprise, there was one danger he hadn't figured on. When he returned with a full bag of wheat one night, he heard a voice suddenly. Adrie froze instantly and heard the voice say: "I think I heard something."

Another voice answered: "I don't hear anything it must be the wind I guess."

Adrie recognized the voices; they belonged to Henk Sturfs and Nelis Mouthaan, two boys from his class when he still went to elementary school. Henk Sturfs and Nelis Mouthaan were raising rabbits to get some meat on their dinner plate. Rabbits have a bad habit of eating and they were cutting grass for their rabbits. The farmers and Germans wouldn't like to see people cutting grass in the pastures. Therefore that job was moved to the dark hours of the night as well.

Adrie was pretty close to the two boys. It was a good thing that they started talking; else he might have stumbled over the grass cutting boys. For an instant Adrie was thinking to startle them. If he sneaked up a little closer, he could jump right in front of the boys and say: "Stickem up boys, I got you!"

That would be fun; the boys would shit their drawers for sure. On the other hand, you could never tell what the boys would do when they thought they were caught. Besides, Adrie didn't want anybody to know that he was stealing wheat. It was far too dangerous to get others involved, they might tell others and before you knew it the Germans might be waiting for him. He didn't even want to work with somebody else. If you were alone there was less chance of getting caught, there were always people who couldn't shut up and would talk about it. Adrie knew where the two boys were and very carefully he walked in a large circle around them. He was the only one who knew what they were doing. Fortunately, nobody knew what he was doing during the dark hours of the night, counting out God.

After a few weeks of ventures in the dark, Adrie had quite a winter supply. Wheat was very important; you could make bread and pancakes from it and even wheat porridge. After a while, he was looking for a change of menu. He had stolen some peas to make pea soup which went over very well. That opportunity was lost when the farmer took the peas off the field to put them in his barn. That put him right behind the eight ball and Adrie was back to stealing wheat again.

A field of oats he had seen gave him an idea. From oats you can make oatmeal and a plate of oatmeal would be a welcome change in his dull menu. Thus one night he sneaked through the darkness to the field with oats. You could steal oats at the same time that you could steal wheat, he thought. That was good thinking except when it came to make oatmeal out of the oats.

After beating his gunny bag with oats, there was a big surprise coming. Hardly any kernels of oats had separated from the chaff. No matter how hard and how long he beat the bag with his club, most of the kernels stayed within their protective shell. Rubbing the oats between his hands wasn't successful either. Probably, the oats had to be dried some more in the sun. Even after four days in the hot sun the oats were very stubborn, it helped a little bit and that was all. In the end, he was peeling the kernels one by one to separate them from their shell.

That was not the end of the trouble when you wanted to make oatmeal out of the kernels. The kernels had to be flattened which was another job and a half. There was only one way to flatten the oats. He put the oat kernels on the anvil and started to flatten them one by one with his hammer. When Adrie's mother came to look what he was doing, he said: "I remember an advertising about Quaker oatmeal and what Quaker can make I can make too. The advertising said:

Johnnie eats Quaker Oatmeal, hot and cold.
And grows like grampa strong and old."

Adrie's mother asked: "How does it go?"
"Not very good," Adrie replied. "I have to take the oat kernels out of the shell almost one by one and have to flatten them on the anvil with my hammer. The way this is going, I'll be old long before I have a plate with oatmeal in front of me and if you are ever that lucky to eat Adrie's oatmeal you'll be old too."

It took him an entire afternoon to get one plate of oatmeal for the family of four. Luckily they had milk from the farm or they would have had to cook the oats in water. Finally, after a gruelling afternoon of oat threshing, the family was enjoying a delicious plate of oatmeal. It was delicious and time doesn't count when you are working on the food supply during a war. However, Adrie thought that he could get more mileage out of stealing wheat and left the oats for the horses and the Germans.

∗ ∗ ∗ ∗

The war in Russia was a bloody war; nearly a quarter of a million Germans had died in the assault on Moscow. By the end of 1943 the Russians had lost 11.3 million men including prisoners and to the Germans it had been costly as well with a loss of 1.4 million killed and wounded. German General Paulus had been doing alright with his summer offensive in Russia. He went for Stalingrad which was a city of war production and it also had the name of Hitler's arch enemy Stalin.

Before Paulus entered Stalingrad, he had it bombed till only ruins remained. That back fired, the ruins became a fortress from which Russians would fire anti-tank weapons at the Germans and ambush German troops. With very heavy fighting and losing many of his men he almost had taken all of Stalingrad.

With winter on his side, Stalin launched a counter offensive and beat the Germans badly. The Russians were fighting the Germans in the sewers between the excrement and were fighting room to room in destroyed houses. When the war turned nasty, Paulus asked Hitler permission to withdraw from the trap the Russians were setting in Stalingrad. He still could get out but if he waited any longer, they would be encircled and destroyed.

Hitler didn't want to hear about it and ordered that every inch of ground the Germans occupied had to be defended to the last man. Paulus was infuriated with a stupid decision like that and told his aides that he wouldn't be able to win this war that he had to fight on two fronts; against the Russians and against Hitler.

When breaking out of the Stalingrad pocket became impossible his army was butchered. Stalin said that every second a German died and time was running out for the Germans. Paulus could see the truth of that statement and when he was completely encircled he surrendered to the Russians with 91,000 men, including 24 Generals and 2500 officers, 6,000 guns and 60,000 motor vehicles. The Battle of Stalingrad was the bloodiest, most decisive battle and the turning point of the war.

It was the first time during the war that an entire Army with its Field Marshall had surrendered and Hitler wasn't amused at all. He screamed for a solid hour to his Generals: "There is no honor in Paulus at all; he is nothing but a coward. There is never an excuse to surrender as long as you have a revolver with a bullet in it you can blow out your brain."

The Stalingrad Battle was the most expensive battle for the warring parties; it had yielded 147,000 dead Germans and 47,000 dead Russians. Paulus surrendered and the dead bodies remained in the field. They served as food for the ravens and the crows that had a feast. Paulus Army accounted for 91,000 prisoners including Paulus. Only 5000 survived including Paulus. If it hadn't been for Paulus, nobody would have survived.

To the Russians it was a great victory; it also proved that the mighty German Army could be beaten. For Hitler, Stalingrad shattered his dream of world domination. After Stalingrad, it was a steady retreat for the Germans.

Hitler had made a great mistake; he couldn't blizkrieg a vast country with winter temperatures of under 40 below. Hitler tried to keep the Germans going by awarding medals. Paulus wasn't impressed, his troops were not supplied and were hungry; they couldn't eat medals. Stalingrad became the graveyard of the German army.

Hitler despised his Generals because they couldn't give him victory in Russia and his Generals started to hate Hitler, they blamed him for the heavy losses of the Army. They didn't have any use for the shouting Bohemian Corporal who shot his Generals if they didn't perform to his wishes. Hitler wouldn't listen to his Generals, his policy was to attack and fight to the death.

Hitler had the best Generals in the world and he was generous in awarding them the Iron Cross, the highest decoration in the German Army. Rommel and Kesselring were promoted to Field Marshalls. When things went sour, Hitler killed his best Generals for not obeying impossible orders.

Hitler had much praise for his Generals as long as they won battle after battle. As soon as the shoe was on the other foot when his Generals started to lose battles, he was furious. Generals who withdrew against his orders were dismissed and quite often executed. More and more of his Generals conspired against him and tried to get rid of this stupid Bohemian Corporal before he got rid of them. They said to each other that they didn't need the Bohemian Corporal anymore now they were losing battles. Blowing out Hitler's brain seemed to be a logical thing to do to get rid of the tyrant. When Hitler visited the Russian front on March 13, 1943, it was an excellent opportunity to kill him. A bomb was planted in the airplane he was using. Unfortunately, the weather was bad and the pilot had to fly at higher altitudes which made the trigger mechanism freeze up and nothing happened. Three more attempts were made to kill the monster but Hitler escaped because of changed schedules.

The Great Turn Around.

Slowly but surely, the Americans came to grips with the war and started to put its industrial might into gear. They could make three times as many planes, tanks and ships as the Japanese. It helped to change the tide in the Pacific. The U.S was finally ready to make the Japanese held territory shrink. The first attempt was Guada Canal; it was a start to take back what the Japanese had conquered. Unfortunately, what the Japanese had conquered so easily was extremely difficult to take back. At the rate they were going it would take another ten years if not longer to end the war. The landing at Guada Canal was easy. Nothing else was. The Japanese were waiting out the shelling and let the Americans land to meet them right after.

Finally in November, the Americans booked another victory and took the Gilbert Islands back. It didn't impress the Dutch people very much. Very few people had ever heard about the Gilbert Islands and a victory in the Pacific was a long way from a victory in Europe. Adrie looked it up in his atlas in spite of the seemingly insignificance. That was a long way from home but a victory is a victory, he decided.

In 1943 there was still some entertainment. The movie theatres in Rotterdam were still open and in the neighboring town Barendrecht they had a great night of entertainment. First of all the brass band would play for 45 minutes. Next the boys club was giving a few skits and the final entertainment was a German movie called "Wir machen musik." (We make music.) There was only one problem, the tickets were sold out. That left Adrie and his friends without tickets. "No problem," Adrie said, "There are all kinds of ways to get into a building."

Transportation costs were cheap, there was a closed farmers wagon going to Barendrecht. It looked like some kind of a chuck wagon. There was hardly enough room for all the interested youngsters to have free transportation. Boys and girls went all together which provided enough entertainment for a starter.

After arriving at the building, the boys and girls who had tickets went inside. Adrie, with his three friends, tried to pass the control without success. Without tickets it seemed impossible to gain entrance to the show. They didn't give up that fast and scouted around the building. Their reconnaissance revealed that there was a flat roof from where one could get inside the building through the bathroom window. Only one problem, to get on the flat roof they had to climb a drain pipe. Climbing trees or climbing drain pipes, what's the difference?

Soon they were in the building and from there it wasn't hard to get into the auditorium. The auditorium was packed and getting a chair was out of the question. Without tickets there was standing room only. When the brass band was finished they left and all of a sudden there were lots of chairs. A free ride back in the chuck wagon signalled the end of a beautiful night. And the price was right. That was the last entertainment for a long time to come. Right after, all forms of entertainment and congregations of more than five people were outlawed by the Germans.

The year of 1943 came to an end. It was the first year that wasn't all disaster. After the Allies had defeated Rommel in Africa, they had taken

Tunisia, Morocco and Algiers. They also had taken Sicily and there was the landing in Southern Italy. Although that the Allies didn't progress much in Italy, it seemed that there had been a turn around of the war. By the end of 1943 Hitler was withdrawing in Russia, Africa and the Atlantic. Finally the fortunes of war had turned and the Allies were planning an invasion of Europe.

Hitler had another shouting speech at the end of the year. He said: "We will break terror by terror with our secret weapons and London will be levelled to the ground forcing capitulation of Britain. Then we will have a thousand Jahren Reich." *(A thousand years empire)*

In spite of Hitler's bragging and shouting, he knew that an invasion of Western Europe was imminent and appointed General Rommel to take charge of the Atlantic Wall. Adrie was the lucky boy to see General Rommel when he was inspecting the Atlantic Wall.

Aunt Joh was suffering from rheumatism, and was lying in bed all day. She never got married and was living with her crippled old father. Ko went twice a week to do the house cleaning and Aunt Ploon did the laundry for them. Adrie was in charge of the transportation. He would pick up a suitcase of dirty laundry on Monday and return it, clean, on Wednesday.

One day when he was returning from his grandfather's place, there were all of a sudden German motor bikes with side carriers coming down the street. All traffic was halted and everybody had to get off the street because General Rommel was coming to Rysoord for inspection of the defence works.

Adrie was just standing with his bike at the side of the street until he was allowed to proceed again. There were quite a few German cars with all kinds of German officers and finally there was a car with the German red flag with a swastika. Inside the car was General Rommel. "Big deal," Adrie thought and was glad to continue his trip.

A change in the war was noticeable. Since early 1942, English and American bombers paid nightly visits to Germany in an attempt to cripple Hitler's war industry and destroy the cities. The blue sky over Germany turned lethal from 1942 to 1945. The Allies struck at railways, aircraft plants, ball bearing factories, oil depots and power stations as they tried to beat the German military into submission.

U.S. and English airplane manufacturers were hell bent to produce long range bombers and escort fighters to penetrate deep into Germany. In the beginning of 1943 the U.S. came up with new Liberator bombers. They had a range of 2,100 miles with a 4,000 pound bomb load. A round trip required about 12 hours in the air. Older bombers weren't going to last very long, they would be shot down before too long, and were used on shorter runs. Neither a bomber nor a fighter made many missions. Flak took its toll and many bombers and fighters were shot down over The Netherlands.

The Germans were proud of the many planes they shot down over The Netherlands; they never removed the wrecks of the shot down planes. That way the Dutch people could see that it cost the Allies dearly to bomb Germany.

During 1944 the bombing raids on Germany intensified and dozens of German cities were almost completely destroyed. Munich, the former headquarters of Hitler was completely destroyed with 66 days of continuous bombing.

The Allied strategy sought to destroy Germany's industrial military muscle before Allied forces could attempt to invade Europe. The Allies were boasting that with a thousand airplane raid on Cologne, they had destroyed over one third of the city. It was very obvious that the war had turned into an air war. Over 20,000 American airmen died in those bombing raids over Germany.

It was well known that the German factories had moved underground. Old coal mines were used to make factories in and the Germans had dug underneath mountains as well. Hitler could make tanks, cannons, submarines and ammunition but with the Allies bombing railways and other communications centres, Germany had a problem to get the needed supplies to their destination.

Another Allied tactic was to level all German cities in order to demoralize Germany's civilian population. There were good bomb shelters underground for the Germans when Allied raids took place. In spite of that, many thousands of Germans got killed including women, children and even babies. When you are throwing bombs, you cannot select who is going to die. Besides, generals don't care about babies; they figure that today's baby is tomorrow's soldier.

There were 90 English and 120 U.S. airbases North East of London; it was closest to all the important targets in Germany. All the bombers en route to Hamburg, Berlin, Bremen, Cologne, Essen and Dortmund were flying over The Netherlands.

There was little fighter opposition over The Netherlands; almost all German fighters were defending Germany when the bombers came to destroy their cities. It looked like a regular milk run but it wasn't. Quite a few British and U.S. planes were shot down over The Netherlands which was no surprise with the great number that were flying over.

Pilots from the R.A.F. returned quite frequently with heavily damaged planes wondering if they would make it back to their home base. They were singing a song when they saw the white cliffs of Dover: "I'm coming in on a wing and a prayer."

One night an airplane that was shot down crashed less than a block from the de Kievits home. The plane was on its way to Germany and was loaded with bombs. After the crew had bailed out of the airplane with parachutes, the plane crashed with the bombs aboard. Adrie was fast asleep when the plane and bombs exploded. It sounded as if doomsday had come, he didn't hear the Angel Gabriel blow his trumpet but that could be next.

He jumped out of bed and ran for the door. They could have been hit by a bomb. Luckily that wasn't the case, the only damage there was were a couple of broken windows. The only injury in the house was sustained by Adrie. It was summer and pretty hot in the house. To get a little draft in the bedroom he had opened the bedroom door when he went to bed. Of course, when you are in dreamland and rudely awakened, you don't think about the bedroom door you had left open on purpose. Besides, it was dark and the big bang had startled him. He crashed right into the open door which gave him a bleeding nose and a fat lip and he also mumbled something about a stupid idiot who had left the door open. A guy could get wounded in this blasted war he thought. The next day he went to look at the crater which was formed by the explosion.

In January 1944, Hitler became desperate; he had lost quite a few divisions in Russia and ordered every able bodied German between 16 and 60 years of age to the front. Factory workers in charge of the war production had to go as well. Hitler said: "The old people can be in charge and all other workers have to be replaced with workers from the occupied countries. I want 8 million men from the occupied countries, to work in the German factories on warfare production."

Adrie's sister Willie, was dating a boy by the name of Wouter Fioole. He was 18 years old and was notified to come to the train station for transportation to Germany. Of course, Wouter and Willie were both very upset. Every night they heard hundreds of planes flying over to bomb Germany and in spite of the bomb shelters they had, it was plenty dangerous.

There was little that Wouter could do when he was notified. Some of the young men who were notified to work in Germany went underground. This was even more dangerous than going to work in Germany. If they didn't report on the specified time, they could expect that the Germans were coming to look for them. And if they were found they might be shot or imprisoned. Nobody knew what the Germans would do to disobedient people. Wouter decided that it was too risky to go underground, he couldn't take the chance.

Willie went with Wouter to the station to see him off. It was busy at the station; the Germans were going to have an entire train with young men from Rotterdam and surroundings transported to Germany. Once Wouter was inside, Willie went home. She came home crying and said: "I might never see him again." Her mother tried to comfort her but she was inconsolable.

About 8.00 p.m. at night Wouter came home. At first everybody thought that he had decided to go underground and had escaped. When he was asked, Wouter said: "Not at all, they sent me home because I got sick and started to vomit."

He had trouble with his stomach and if he didn't eat in time his ulcers started to act up. When one of the German officers saw what kind of a shape he was in, he said: "Go home; we can't use sick men in Germany."

As soon as Wouter heard the magic words 'Go Home' he felt better already and almost ran home. His ulcers were a problem at times but now they had turned into a blessing. Even sick and disabled people counted their blessings that they were spared from working in Germany.

Everybody was glad for Wouter and Willie that he didn't have to go to Germany. At night, Aunt Ploon came to see him. She had heard that he had returned and said: "Nice to see that you are back. Luckily I am married to an old man so I don't have those kinds of problems."

Adrie's neighbour, Kees Meuzelaar was in the next train load to be transported to Germany. For a while he had managed to be excluded from work in Germany because he was working in The Netherlands on the food supply. His luck had run out when Hitler demanded eight million workers from the occupied countries to work in German factories. Hitler was going to make soldiers out of every German who still could walk. Kees was almost 20 years of age and the Germans wanted him on Adolf Hitler's orders. Adrie was only 14 years old and too young to work in Germany. This made Adrie say: "I'm glad that I am young so I don't have those kinds of problems."

Sometimes he had wanted to be older as he was always too young for everything and consequently excluded from all kinds of excitement. However, this time he could very well do without the excitement.

Uncle Jaap was notified as well and they all left to work for Hitler. After Uncle Jaap had been gone for a month, his wife, Aunt Johanna, said that she was pregnant. She had only one daughter and being pregnant in a normal time might have been great news. With her husband in Germany and rations slashed all the time, this news was worrisome. Milk rations were very meagre and although babies had extra allowances, it could very well be that there was no milk at all by the time her baby was born.

Adrie was the church paper boy. Every week on Friday night and Saturday he had to deliver a four page church bulletin to the members of the church. It told the members what Reverend would be preaching on Sunday. Furthermore there was other church news and a message of the Reverend that God still loves you. Adrie was awarded with 10% of the haul for his trouble. It wasn't a very big haul with the people paying only five cents per week. There were about 160 papers to deliver, that were paying customers which accounted for an 80 cents reward per week. It took him about eight hours to deliver the papers which meant that he made himself 10 cents per hour. There were fifteen people who had a free church paper because they were too poor to pay for the paper. Among the non-paying customers was the Reverend, he was not exactly poor but he was the servant of God and you can't charge God for a church paper.

Adrie saw it different, he thought the Reverend was a cheapskate; he contributed nothing to the church. With the collections in the church they never went to the Reverend and he had a house free from the church. There was one thing he contributed to, it was for missionary work. He always preached doom that the people didn't give enough for that worthy cause because they had to bring the Gospel to heathens in Asia, Africa and elsewhere. If not, all those people would go to hell because they were not going to be saved by Jezus and Jezus himself had said to bring the Gospel to all people on earth. If we didn't do that we would be disobeying Jezus.

Once a week the members of the boys club were going from door to door, of the members of the church, with a collection box for donations for Missionary work. The Reverend always stated that the people didn't give enough and because of them many heathens didn't go to heaven. The deacons who were in charge of the collections wondered how much the Reverend himself gave to Missionary work. They had one of the boys going to the Reverend's house first with an empty box and after the Reverend had made his donation the boy had to come back so they could check what the Reverend gave. When they opened the box, there was only one penny in the box which was the Reverend's contribution for Missionary work. The Reverend sure didn't live by what he preached.

His wife wasn't any better; they were a well matched pair. With New Year's Day the printer had printed some cards that said: "Happy New Year from the church paper boy." Most of the people would give him ten extra pennies for his New Year. That netted him close to 16 guilders. Adrie was hand delivering the New Year's card to the Reverend to see if he could get 10 cents out of him. His wife opened the door and when Adrie handed over the New Year's card, she gave him a hand and said: "Happy New Year to you."

However, there were some fringe benefits with his job. A lot of houses had no door bell. Knocking on the door made the people answer the door. Sometimes people didn't hear the knock on the door and you had to use other means to tell them there was somebody at the door. In those days, the doors were seldom locked during day time so you just opened the door and shouted: "Anybody home?"

One time when he opened the door there was a naked girl washing herself at the sink. Adrie never saw naked girls except his sister, so he looked her over. The girl started to yell for her mother: "Mother the boy is looking at me." Was that naked girl silly that she thought he was going to close his eyes when there was something to see? When her mother came she was just laughing, she couldn't blame him for watching the show.

With the curfew, it wasn't possible to deliver any papers on Friday night. During the winter it was dark at 5.00 p.m. which resulted in paper delivery on Saturday only. To get the paper route finished in time before curfew, he had to start right away after the curfew was lifted on Saturday morning. He always picked up the papers on Friday night, at the printer's place, to have an early start on Saturday morning. Arie Mulder was the printer, who was a numbskull as far as Adrie was concerned; he never had the papers ready when he came.

One weekend, the papers weren't ready on Friday night. Arie Mulder said he had some trouble and to come back on Saturday morning. On Saturday morning Adrie still had to wait twenty minutes. Adrie never went home to eat; he was just going to finish his route before curfew time. There was quite a bit of wind which slowed him down on the bike. It was already dark when he delivered his last paper and he still had to bike 15 minutes home.

As the way home passed a German commander post, he was sure to be stopped. He had guessed that right; a German soldier stopped him and told him that it was curfew time. Adrie said: "I know but I'm delivering papers and was slowed down by the wind." He showed the soldier one of the left over papers.

The soldier looked at it and said: "Nach hause immer schnell." (Go home very fast.) That wasn't bad at all, the German soldier could have said: "In sperren." (Take him prisoner.)

It was very easy to be arrested especially during curfew time. When you had a pair of eyes you could be a spy or an enemy agent. People who didn't meet curfew time were usually interned for the night and if they weren't on the most wanted list of the Nazis, they were released the following morning. Of course, you never knew if the Germans would shoot when they saw somebody in the dark. Most of the Germans were very reasonable when they were dealing with young persons who posed no threat to them. If Adrie had been a couple of years older, the Germans might have looked more suspiciously at him.

Ko wasn't too happy when she heard what had happened, she went to the Reverend and told him: "If the papers aren't ready on Friday night when my son comes for them, you can deliver the papers yourself. He shouldn't have to break curfew and take a chance that the Germans will lock him up for the night." It helped, from there on the papers were ready when they were supposed to be.

One time when Adrie was delivering the church papers, the Reverend came by on his bike and stopped to talk to Adrie. He said: "You are doing good work for God and you will be rewarded in the hereafter."

Adrie didn't think so, if he wasn't getting paid, he wouldn't do it. You can't make a living on rewards that you'll get in the hereafter. The Reverend didn't do that either, he got paid handsomely and was always trying to get a better paying place to be Reverend.

The Roman Catholic Churches are run by Bishops that appoint Priests to the churches. The Protestant Churches follow mostly the Presbyterian system in which the church itself finds a Reverend. When a church is in need of a Reverend they ask different Reverends to come on a Sunday to preach in their church. When they find a Reverend that they like they ask him if he wants to be their Reverend. Most of those Reverends already are taking care of a church so if they accept, that church will now be out of a Reverend.

The reason for accepting a different church is if he gets paid more money or that he goes to a bigger city. Sometimes the reason is that his wife was born in that town or city. Another good reason is to leave the church, where a Reverend is preaching, when he has been too long in the same church. He can be finished preaching to his flock, he has said it all. There is nothing wrong to leave the church where he is taking care of for better conditions or more money. Everybody looks out for himself.

What Adrie didn't like was that whenever he had such a request from a different church that he announced it, on the pulpit, to the people of his congregation. He added to that announcement that he was praying for guidance to find out if God was calling him to that place. To Adrie that was sheer bologna because he was just trying to find out if he could do better. It always happened that God was calling him to that church if he was getting better.

There was one Reverend who would hit the pulpit with his fist when he was preaching. They never asked him to come to their church because they were scared that he would make firewood out of the pulpit.

Arie was in a German work camp working on the never finished Atlantic Wall. After General Rommel took command of the Atlantic Wall and the defence of Western Europe, a lot more concrete bunkers had to be built on the coast. Arie was lucky; he was at least in The Netherlands and came home for a weekend every two weeks. And Adrie was too young to work for the German war production. Even Wouter had escaped transportation to Germany thanks to his ulcers. All those favorable things didn't mean that the family was free from troubles.

After the Allied landings on Sicily and the Italian mainland, the Germans expected another invasion in Western Europe. Nobody knew where the invasion was going to be, it could be in France or Belgium or perhaps in The Netherlands. One thing was for sure that an invasion, wherever it took place, would be accompanied by a lot of bombing and shelling. This would kill many soldiers and also civilians. Even if the landings were elsewhere, eventually there was going to be war in The Netherlands to be liberated from the German yoke. Many lives would be snuffed out and those people wouldn't see the end of the war.

By far the worst news came with a poster of the German Commander in May 1944. The poster read: "General Rommel has ordered that in defence of Western Europe it has become necessary to inundate the fields around Rotterdam. All fields to the South of the Hordyk will be flooded. The river gates will be opened 7 days from today. Fields North of the Hordyk will be defended against airborne troops by putting posts in the field, which will make landings virtually impossible."

This drastic step by the Germans to flood the lands was a disaster. Adrie lived with his parents on the South side of the Hordyk which meant that the house and garden would be inundated. The newer houses were all built at the same level as the top of the dyke and escaped flooding. Unfortunately, the older houses used to be built on the level of the land and were all going to be flooded.

Arie was home for the weekend and the German commander had said that he could have a week to take care of his family because of serious circumstances. All owners of the low lying houses decided to make a dam around the house to keep the water out. Arie was going to build a dam as well. There was one problem; it had to be a rather long dyke for it had to be connected to the Hordyk on both sides. On one side of the de Kievits there was Kees Meuzelaar and the house next to that was from Willemstein. Those houses were on dyke level and consequently free from flooding. That left them out of dyke building. If they had had to build a dyke too, the de Kievit's could have worked together with them. Arie had to build a dam around his house connecting to the Hordyk.

On the other side of the de Kievit's house, there was Immerzeel the blacksmith. There was a house in which he was living with his family and the smithy was built against the house. The lot on which his house and smithy were built was more than twice as wide as the de Kievit's house. Consequently he had to build a dyke twice as long as the de Kievits. Immerzeel with his two sons were going to build a dyke around their house and smithy and were going to join up with the dyke of the de Kievits. That was a help, it meant a shorter dyke for both parties.

Quite a few houses and farms that had been built in the middle of the polder couldn't be dyked in. All those people had to be re-located which aggravated the shortage of housing for the Dutch people. Those people had to move in with relatives or friends. This inundation tactic of Rommel was the last nail in the disastrous Dutch food supply. There was hardly any food in The Netherlands and now all those fertile fields would be under water and out of food production.

There was no time to waste, in seven days the gates would be opened and after that, it wouldn't take more than a day for the water to start flooding the land. To make the dyke high enough, a lot of clay had to be wheel barrowed from the back of the garden to the front. The dyke had to be at least two feet higher than the water level to prevent water washing over it in a storm. Everybody worked like horses, yet it became questionable if the dyke would be ready when the water was going to rise. Immerzeel came the third day to say that he was not going to make it with his two sons and was going to move. He needed time to move his blacksmith business so he couldn't wait.

Arie said: "Without their help we can't make it either and we'll have to move out too." That was easier said than done. You can move if you have a place to move to. However, because of the war there was a shortage of houses and there was no possible other house that they could rent.

Jan Lems the farmer said: "I still have that little old house on the farm where the farmhand used to live in. It's very old and also very small. Actually the house is derelict; it has only one small room and no bedrooms. If you can live in that small one room house during the daytime, you all can sleep on the loft of the farm."

That was the only offer there was which made it easy to decide. Jan Lems lent his horse and transport wagon to Arie to move everything to the farm. He said: "Don't leave anything behind; if you do it will all be stolen."

He had given Arie a very old horse which was easier to manage than the younger horses. The only problem with the horse was that it was actually too old and it was always sleeping. It didn't hear when somebody was shouting "Go." Adrie took the horse by the bridle and led it for a bit. As soon as he thought that the horse was awake and walking, he jumped on the wagon for the ride. When the horse wasn't led by the bridle anymore, it started to walk slower and slower until it had completely stopped. No matter what Adrie shouted at the horse, the horse wouldn't budge until he led it by the bridle again.

In spite of the sleeping horse most of the possessions were moved that day. People didn't have much furniture and other possessions in those days. A few things that were left could be moved the next day.

The loft of the farm was rather large and completely open. Normally it was used for storage of all kinds of things. Now everything was moved to one corner and the three beds had each a separate corner. Everybody slept together in the large loft and had his or her own bed in his or her own corner.

The next day, Adrie's uncle had a job for him to do. Between the cities Rotterdam and Dordrecht there was a highway, which ran across the polders that were going to be inundated. The Germans needed that highway for transportation of troops and equipment. They were working to build a dyke on each side. It was a stretch of about 25 kilometres and they were behind. Most of the work horses had been obtained from the large farms. With the tight schedule, they needed more horses. Jan Lems had received a notice that he had to deliver one horse to the work site. Guess what horse he was going to deliver? Of course the sleeping horse.

He said to Adrie: "Take my bike and deliver the horse to the work site of the highway dam. Don't sit on the horse because they need horse riders as well to ride on the dam, to make it more compact. If they tell you to ride the horse tell them you can't ride a horse."

Adrie took the horse by the bridle and led it to a mere trot. Quickly he jumped on the bike and the horse stopped as soon as it wasn't led anymore. Even yelling at the horse made no difference; the horse just nodded his tired head and slept away. When he tried again to get the horse moving, the horse stepped on his foot. It felt like all his toes were laying lose in his shoes. Adrie said a few friendly words to the horse which don't lend themselves to be repeated.

It was just great the way that things were going, it meant that he had to walk about an hour to the dam site with his horse. Luckily help was on the way, a boy from the neighborhood asked if he could ride the horse. That was an offer he could not refuse, it was a deal and finally they made it to the work camp. Adrie went to the office to have the paper signed that the horse had been delivered. The horse with the boy were driven right away on top of the dyke to tramp the clay solid and Adrie jumped on his bike and went back to the farm. At night the neighbor boy came back with the horse. The Germans had said: "Go home with that sleeping horse, it is unusable, we need work horses here." Everybody was happy that the horse came back, even if it was only an old horse and the horse itself couldn't be happier back in his warm stable with some fresh hay.

The flooding of the polder was delayed for a few days. It took the Germans longer than they had expected to finish the dykes to protect the highway. However, when the gates went open the water came fast. In no time the de Kievit's house, Immerzeel's house and quite a few others were flooded. The water came as high as the windows. Jan Lems was lucky to have only one small pasture inundated. Others weren't that lucky and had all their agricultural land flooded. It was the livelihood of the farmers, yet there was no compensation for the flooded lands. The Germans couldn't care less.

With the flooding of the land there was another severe problem. The sewer line was under water which put it out of commission. All the people, who were still living in their high houses on the dyke, couldn't use the bathroom anymore. The city of Rotterdam found an old honey wagon to collect people's waste. They distributed large cans, which looked like large garbage cans. The lid could be closed to avoid most of the stench in the houses. All the people needed was a plank with a hole and the shitter was ready. When you had to go, you opened the lid of the poop pail, put a board with a hole on the pail and did your business.

It seemed that this shitty problem had been resolved. Once per week everybody had to put their pail on the street and the honey wagon came to collect the contents of the can. It worked like garbage collection; the only difference there was that they collected shit. The honey wagon they used was an old honey wagon. It had seen better days and was quite rusty. On a fateful day the honey wagon burst open and all the contents went flowing through the street. It seemed that there was no end to shitty problems. To clean this mess up, the city had to dispatch another honey wagon and a cleaning crew.

The Beginning of the End.

In spite of the German defense of Italy, after eight months of war with heavy losses, the Allies entered Rome on June 4, 1944. Rome had been declared an open city because of its historical value. It wouldn't be bombed and no fighting would take place in the city. On June 4th the Germans withdrew and the Americans moved in. It was the first big city to fall into Allied hands and also the first Axis capital.

Most of the people didn't understand this open city business. Jan Lems was explaining to his willing listeners what had taken place and added: "It's amazing that Hitler gave up the capital of Italy. Usually he fights till everything is in rubble before he pulls out. He possibly had to make peace with His Almighty because he had chosen Adolf Hitler to rule the world. Rome has no military value but if fighting had taken place, little would be left of all the historical sites. Vatican City with its St. Peter Cathedral would have been destroyed. No Christian would ever forgive him. Such a city can be declared to be an open city, which means that it is completely demilitarized and left open for military occupation in order to gain immunity from bombardment and attack, under international law."

Italy was quickly gobbled up by the Allies and Mussolini and his mistress were trying to escape to Switzerland. They were turned back at the Swiss border and were arrested and shot. The bodies were taken to Milan where they were hanged upside down on meat hooks in the Plaza. Mussolini was an opportunist, he could have been a modern Caesar but now he was hanged. Every Dutch citizen could handle news like that.

Mussolini hanged in Milan,

The underground newspaper reported. German newspapers never mentioned it but the word went around in The Netherlands. All Dutch people, except the Nazi supporters, agreed that justice had been done and they could hardly wait till they hanged Hitler.

Much greater news was in store for the desperate Dutch citizens, when they tuned their radios to listen to the illegal broadcasting of Radio London. "This is Radio London. In the early morning hours General Eisenhower landed on the beaches of Normandy. The Allies are holding five beachheads in Normandy and heavy fighting is reported."

Radio London didn't give much detail for security reasons. With the Germans trying desperately to throw the invaders back into the sea it became a touch and go situation. Everybody was glued to the radio the next day and for a welcome change, Radio London didn't disappoint its listeners. "This is Radio London. From the Western front comes exciting news. The beachheads have joined together and instead of five beachheads there are now only two much larger beachheads. In spite of heavy casualties the Allied landing forces have endured, everything is going well."

Radio Berlin gave quite a different picture about the invasion. "This is Radio Berlin. The Allied forces that have landed on the beaches of Normandy have sustained heavy casualties. Normandy's beaches are paved with the skulls of thousands of Allied invaders. German reinforcements are on the way to Normandy. General Rommel has ordered three panzer divisions to Normandy to drive the Allied invaders back into the sea. This will be done in the coming three days and all what will remain of the invasion are the tens of thousands of Allied dead bodies on the beaches. The Fuhrer has announced that new German secret weapons will be deployed in the next couple of weeks which will destroy London."

Adrie counted his blessings that he was too young to fight this silly war.

War is vindictive and wasteful of life and property. Thousands of young lives are wasted every day. Young soldiers think of dying all the time, at an age that nobody should be thinking of death. He could also see that in Normandy a lot of civilians would be killed. It is nice to be liberated but it can come at a high price.

With the move to the farm, Adrie couldn't listen to the commentary of Leen Willemstein anymore. However, there was a good replacement. Adrie's uncle had news letters from the Dutch underground. At night he asked the de Kievits to come inside the house for a cup of coffee. He got the underground newsletters and said to Adrie: "You can read those loud so everybody can hear it."

Adrie felt mighty important; it felt like he was the news broadcaster. After the news was read, the atlas came out on the table and everybody was bent over the atlas to see what progress the Allies had made.

On June 13th there was more exciting news. "This is Radio London. From the Western Front comes still very good news. In spite of the slow progress because of heavy German resistance, the Allies have reached their goal. The two large beach heads have joined together and there is now only one beach head 42 miles wide. The war goes well for the Germans. On June 6 there were five beach heads, on June 7 there were only two beach heads and on June 13 there is only one beach head."

From Wireless to Radioless.

Radio Berlin countered the Allied successes with their own translation of the war. "This is Radio Berlin. German reinforcements have reached Normandy and are engaged in heavy fighting with the Allied landing force. General Rommel declared that it will be a matter of days to clear Normandy of all Allied soldiers, except the dead ones. In the first ten days of fighting the Allies have lost 23,000 killed and 97,000 wounded. The secret weapon which our Fuhrer had promised is now officially in use. It is a flying bomb which is called V1. The V stands for Victory for Germany. Several V1's have been fired on London and have caused extensive damage. London will be flattened and this will bring Britain under submission."

Radio London admitted that the Germans were shooting flying bombs to London which were called V1's. They gave some details about the flying bombs. They said: "The V1 is an unmanned airplane, powered by a simple pulse jet engine, going at the speed of 350 miles per hour and it has a range of 100 miles. The V1 carries a 2,000 lbs. warhead in its nose. Some of the bombs have reached London but most of the V1's have been shot down before they could reach their target."

That was the last time that everybody listened to Radio London. Everybody had to go to a depot the next day to surrender their radios. This taking away of radios from the Dutch people had been in the planning for a long time. When the Germans abandoned bike taxes, as soon as Seis Inquart started his reign over The Netherlands, the Dutch people were rather happy. Only a year later when the Germans introduced radio taxes nobody liked it. Instead of paying the one guilder per year on bike taxes, everybody who had a radio had to dish out one guilder per month on radio taxes. Leen Willemstein's commentary was: "The Germans gave a little and take a lot." They took even more when the radio taxes went up to one and a half guilders per month.

To make everybody comply with the radio taxes, the Germans put a scare into the Dutch citizens. For every radio you had you needed a listening permit. The listening permit was a card divided into 12 squares. At the beginning of each month, the people had to stick a radio stamp in the appropriate square on the permit. Radio stamps were available at the post office. Moreover, this permit had to be right beside your radio. That way the Germans could inspect the radio permit whenever they liked. It entered everybody's mind not to have a permit. That of course could cost you if you were caught.

The Germans had severe penalties in place; if you were caught they would confiscate your radio and put you in jail as well. If you didn't get a permit, you had to hide your radio and took a chance you would be betrayed by some Nazi supporters. As it was too dangerous to keep a radio without a permit; most of the people paid their one guilder per month to have peace of mind. Few people dared to risk having an illegal radio. Little did people know at the time that there was something greater behind the radio permit.

With the war going bad for the Germans, they didn't want the Dutch people to know about it. They knew that most of the Dutch people were listening to the illegal British broadcast and wanted to stop that. To them that was very simple, they knew exactly who had a radio with the radio listening permits in place. They just announced that the Dutch people had to turn their radio in to a German depot. They gave the people three days to comply and after that an illegal radio could mean imprisonment or perhaps a bullet. One never knew what the Germans would do to you once they caught you. Everybody agreed that this had been in the planning by the Germans. First they made it law that you had to stick a stamp on a listening permit every month. And now they were calling in all radios and they knew exactly who had a radio.

For the good news, the radio taxes were abolished because nobody had a radio anymore or they weren't supposed to have one anymore. And so things came full circle. For the first time in their life the de Kievits had a radio. The Germans had made it possible, they gave it and then took it away. All what was left of the radio was a paper that said that the radio had been received by the Germans. All that the paper was good for; it gave you peace of mind. In England they call a radio a wireless because the radio waves go through the air instead of a wire. It seemed that the Dutch citizens had gone from wireless to radioless.

Nobody dared not to deliver the radio to the depot. The Germans knew who had a radio. If they didn't receive it they would come for it and the disobedient owner might be shot for all one knew. The de Kievit's radio was only two years old and now the Germans had it. With tears in their eyes the de Kievits saw their good as new radio go. On the other hand the risk was too great to keep the radio. If the Germans grabbed you, you could be dead and a dead man doesn't listen to his radio very well.

Only aunt Pietje kept her radio. Uncle Henk was in Germany and she decided not to give her radio up. She put it in the root cellar underneath the potatoes. At night she rolled out the extension cord to connect the radio in order to listen to Radio London. Actually, it was a very stupid thing to do rather than a brave thing; if she had been caught the consequences might have been terrible. Besides confiscating her radio, the Germans could have arrested her and put her in a concentration camp. With four little children that would have been terrible. What she did was very dangerous. *(Lucky for her she got away with it. Apparently the bookkeeping of the Germans wasn't what it used to be. She was one of the very few people who had a radio after the war.)*

Although people couldn't listen to Radio London anymore, they still heard all the news. Underground newspapers were distributed and passed from one person to the next. Even that was illegal and therefore dangerous. On June 27 the underground newspaper brought some good news that Cherbourg, the first harbor city, was taken. Everybody was viewing the atlas again and decided that the Germans wouldn't be able to drive the Allies back into the sea, no matter what they said.

This was confirmed on July 9 when Caen fell into Allied hands. Progress was slow but steady. Everybody looked at the atlas again and decided that the war would take another two years with the speed the Allies came to The Netherlands. The Dutch people were very happy with the successful invasion; they knew there was a lot at stake. Had the landing in Normandy failed, the

Russians might have to liberate all of Western Europe which could have made a hell of a difference in the post-war world.

The Invasion.

The invasion of Western Europe had come a long way. It had been discussed way back in 1942 between Roosevelt and Churchill. Stalin wanted a second front to take the pressure off Russia but Churchill was in no mood to fight the Germans on a scale like that. He had lost the Battle of France and he also had taken a licking in Greece. Although he wasn't going for it, he promised Stalin that he would start a second front. That satisfied Stalin but Churchill also thought that this second front business would also be reported to Hitler by his intelligence. In that case it would tie up some German divisions in France.

The Atlantic Wall was an entire fortified coast defended by a strong German Army, the powerful Luftwaffe and the Atlantic full of submarines. Churchill was in favor of destroying Germany's war production and also bombing the cities to break the morale of the German people. Once they were mortally wounded, he would go in for the kill.

Roosevelt was thinking about a second front because he wanted to keep the Russians in the war. If Russia was defeated, a Channel crossing for an invasion would be out of the question with the German defense concentrating on the Atlantic Wall. An invasion was planned though the Allies were in no position to make a successful landing. Eisenhower considered an invasion at that time sheer madness and military suicide.

Early in 1943 the Allies had their first conference

in Casablanca. Their thought of a possible victory
had improved, they were now thinking about a sure
victory. They decided that only unconditional
surrender of Germany and Japan would be accepted
and nothing less. With the Armistice after the First
World War, the Germans always had claimed that they
really weren't beaten by military forces. This time
they were going to be.In Germany and Japan they
made propaganda from this decision; they told their
people that they didn't have any choice but to fight
to death because slavery would be the only other
option they had.

It was also agreed between the Big Three that
Germany had to be beaten first; the rest of the
Axis would follow soon after Germany was finished.
An invasion of Western Europe was discussed but
Eisenhower stated that it would require a lot of
preparation or it would fail.

Roosevelt had concerns about postponing the
invasion when he looked at the development in
Russia. It seemed that the Russians had the Germans
licked and were ready to move into the heartland of
Europe. That could spell disaster if the Russians
were going to liberate Europe. Once the Russians
had occupied Western Europe, how was he going to get
them out? Roosevelt knew that the Russians were the
next enemy, yet the Germans had to be defeated first.
Even Hitler had figured that the Allies wouldn't get
along and would break up.

Preparation for an invasion started right after
the Conference. First of all the war against the
German submarines had to be won. As long as the
submarines were in control of the Atlantic an
invasion wasn't possible. Secondly, the German air
force was too powerful and had to be destroyed.
Without air supremacy, a landing would be impossible
and end in a costly failure.

There also had to be sufficient well trained men
backed up by tanks and air force to make it work. In
the year 1943 more than 700,000 Allied troops landed
in England to take part in the invasion. The Queen

Mary and Queen Elizabeth ships could transport 15,000 men each per crossing and there were also a few smaller ships. All those ships went too fast for the German submarines to sink them.

Logistics was the most important thing after the landing force was ashore. It doesn't matter how many divisions you put ashore, they need food, weapons and ammunition and if they don't have all of that the invasion is doomed. Southern England became a large military camp with three million soldiers, together with sixteen million tons of cargo that had been shipped from the States.

Tanks went only half a mile on a gallon of diesel oil. They needed a lot of fuel. If there was no fuel you might as well not have a tank. It was in the planning to roll out gas lines across the Channel to provide gasoline and diesel oil.

With the Raid on Dieppe, the Allies had learned that the Atlantic Wall was hard to penetrate and the Germans were too well armed and too mobile. The Romanian oilfields supplied more than one third of Germany's oil. At the beginning of the war the Allies had tried unsuccessfully to cut off Germany's steel supply and now they were contemplating to cutting off Germany's oil supplies.

Destroying the Romanian oil refineries was a must but it took four missions to accomplish it with a heavy loss of Allied airplanes. After the oil refineries were destroyed, German oil production was down by more than a third and severe shortages of oil hampered German mobility.

Another daring plan was to destroy the ball bearing plants in Schweinfurt that produced over 50% of the German ball bearings. This mission was equally successful. Slowly but surely German power was waning. Besides the heavy losses of men, the industries couldn't supply the armies with proper armament and Germany was losing its power as Popeye would lose his power if he ran out of spinach.

Another plan was to destroy the German cities and break the will power of the German people. Hitler had destroyed a significant part of London with his bombing raids and Churchill figured that if he was meaner than Hitler, he could win the war. On May 30, 1942 a thousand bombers went out to destroy Cologne. They dropped half a million incendiary bombs on Cologne which destroyed 50,000 homes, killed 500 people and wounded 6,000.

Most of the German submarines were built in the city of Hamburg. In a mission called Gomorrah, a large air strike was launched in July 1943 with 800 bombers to destroy Hamburg. After the city was burning the bombers returned for two consecutive days. The city burned for a solid two weeks, it looked like Dante's inferno. Hamburg was totally destroyed. Over 40,000 people were killed and 27,800 houses were destroyed. All that remained of Hamburg were some charred ruins.

According to the Geneva Convention civil air attacks were not allowed. Hitler started to bomb Warsaw, Rotterdam and London. In return, the English and U.S. bombed German cities. Thousands of innocent women and children were killed. Military targets were important but civil bombings were thought to end the war. It became important to kill the people who contributed to the war effort. Night after night bombers seeded death and destruction on civil properties. Since World War II had started there was a new kind of warfare, slaughtering people on a great scale.

Essen was the home of the Krupp factories that employed over 20,000 workers. It was the largest armament plant in the world. In a spectacular air raid, the Allies dropped over 8000 tons of bombs on the plants which reduced them to a bunch of smoking rubble. When Alfred Krupp saw the ruins of his city, he had a heart attack. It saved the Allies putting him on trial for war crimes; he probably would have ended up with a noose around his neck for making all the war material for Hitler. Hitler called the air strikes 'Aerial Terrorism,' while he himself had tried to destroy London.

Destroying military targets and cities was an expensive proposition for the Allies. On most of the bombing raids, the R.A.F. suffered 40% losses quite often. In three months' time they had lost 850 planes and 5800 airmen. Bombing Germany to destroy war production was a must before an invasion of Europe would be possible. War production was hampered more and more which rendered the Germans less powerful.

Manufacturing plants of German aircraft had to be destroyed. With 4000 bombers that were protected by 4000 fighters the Allies were bombing the German factories that made aircraft. It cost them dearly on lost planes and crews but the result was significant. The Allied Air force had a superiority of thirty to one over the Germans.

As soon as it was decided to go for invasion, there were a lot of questions like, where, who and when? First of all the General had to be picked who would be in command of the invasion forces. Hitler thought that President Roosevelt was going to pick General Patton but Roosevelt picked General Eisenhower. Next, Normandy was picked for the place of landing and the date was going to be on June 5 or June 6 when the tide was going to be good.

Normandy was a beautiful place with the nicest beaches in the world until Rommel filled it with barbed wire, concrete bunkers, cannons and other war material. Before Rommel came, it was beautiful and quiet, people were swimming in the ocean and some French couples were mating on the fine sand of the beach.

It was also decided that the attack would take place in day light to make sure that the landings would be in the right place. A Naval bombardment of half an hour would precede the landing, followed by flotillas that crossed the Channel under the cover of darkness and the landing would take place soon after dawn. 'Overlord' was the code name for the invasion and 'D Day' was the date. Churchill called D Day, 'Deliverance Day,' and others called it 'Dooms

Day.'The beaches where the landings were going to take place had also code names; Utah, Omaha, Gold, Juneau and Sword. Caen that had to be taken on the first day of the invasion had the code name 'Poland.' Everything was coded to prevent the Germans from figuring out what was in store for them.

Of course Hitler knew about the invasion plans of the Allies but that's all he knew, he didn't know the place of landing and neither did he know the date. Hitler thought that the invasion was going to be in Norway but Von Rundsted, one of Hitler's best Generals thought it was going to be in the Pass of Calais, the shortest distance between England and France. General Rommel wasn't sure where the landing would take place; his main concern was to get his troops to the beachhead soon after the landing so he could drive the invaders back into the sea. After strengthening the Atlantic Wall significantly, he was confident that he could repel the invasion force within 48 hours.

One more important thing had to be done before the invasion could take place. All communication and transportation means had to be knocked out to prevent the Germans from moving troops and supplies to the place of landing. Day after day, the Allied bombers bombed railroads and bridges in Germany, France and Belgium. By the end of May all railroad traffic in France and Belgium had virtually come to a halt. Furthermore, many planes were assigned to keep the submarines out of the Channel while the invasion took place. Five divisions had to land on the first day of the invasion.

The Germans had problems with transportation with the Allies controlling the air. They painted a red cross on their trucks to get supplies to their destination. The Red Cross is a symbol that only can be used to mark hospitals, ambulances etc. Therefore what the Germans did was a war crime.

Verner von Braun was making rockets to put on the moon. When Hitler visited the site in Peenemundi, Hitler told von Braun: "Don't bother putting a man on the moon, you don't have to go that far, all I want you to do is to make one that goes to London."

The Germans always seemed to come up with a new secret weapon to change the outcome of the war. Von Braun did as he was ordered and was working on a project that should flatten London. Allied intelligence had revealed that the Germans were working on missiles at Peenemundi. There was no doubt in the Allies mind that this could make an invasion difficult if not impossible so the plant had to go.

On August 16, 1943 Allied bombers dropped 1500 tons of bombs on the German installations at Peenemundi. It was a great success and German rocket launching was delayed for many months.

There were other Allied bombing successes when the English blew away some massive dams that were in place to hold water to generate electricity. To make one ton of steel 200 tons of water was needed. Massive dams were in place to generate hydro electricity. If there was no dam, there was no electricity and no production of war material. Wallace worked on it for three days to find a way to blow away the massive dams. When it was accomplished German war production was severely disrupted.

A conference between the 'Big Three' took place at the beginning of 1944 at Teheran. Instead of a probable victory, they were sure to win the war by the end of 1944.

Finally the Allies managed to make long range fighters that could out maneuver the German fighters and support the bombers to any target in Germany. The Allies barely had their superb long range fighter when the Germans trumped their ace. They now had a jet propelled fighter that could out-maneuver the Allied superb fighters.

At the end of 1943 the menace of German submarines was under control; they still inflicted heavy losses, but thanks to the invention of centimetric radar the German losses on sub marines were significant. There were 237 German submarines lost during 1943.

The feared submarine that had been hunting the U.S. convoys was now hunted. Only one out of four men that served on submarines survived in their iron coffin. It was rare that a submarine made more than two missions.

By the beginning of 1944 the Allied Air Force had control over the air. Everything that had to be done before the invasion could take place had been accomplished. 'Exercise Tigre' was the code name for the final rehearsal of the invasion which was so real that even German submarines were present sinking two American landing crafts with a result of 750 American dead bodies. German submarines had slipped past the English defences and attacked the Allies that were training for the big day. It seemed like a bad omen that 750 people were killed in the rehearsal; the real Mc. Coy would be a lot bloodier than that.

All troops were ready for the invasion, all that was needed was good weather and a lot of luck; both proved to be in short supply. Altogether there would be 5400 ballooned ships taking part in the invasion. The balloons were to protect them from bombs and shells. Five divisions had to land on the first day of the invasion. Everything was set to go except the weather. A gale had moved into the Atlantic and the North Sea making it impossible to go ahead with the invasion. The invasion could be postponed for one day and could still take place on June 6th. If it didn't take place on that day, the invasion had to be postponed for three weeks before favourable tides would make it possible again.

The sea was still rough on June 6th but General Eisenhower gave the go ahead. It was just too much trouble to disembark the troops again. Moreover if there was a three week postponement, the Germans might get the hang of it and they could possibly surprise the surprise party.

It was a very rough crossing and many men in the landing force were seasick. It seemed that the weather benefited the Germans but on the other hand the foul weather was a blessing. The Germans hadn't thought that an invasion was possible with that kind of weather and even General Rommel had gone home to celebrate his wife's birthday.

Over a thousand planes dropped 13,000 Para troops behind the beaches of Normandy before the landing took place. Their task was to blow up bridges and railways to prevent the Germans from shipping in supplies. A half hour shelling took place before the first troops landed.

It was a very slow crossing with a speed of six miles per hour due to mine sweeping delays. Everybody was frightened and quiet, even the noisiest soldiers didn't say a word. Everybody was busy with his own thoughts and wondered if tomorrow he would still be alive. Only praying was heard.

Even the Generals wondered if an invasion of this magnitude was possible and they expected that their men would do the impossible, breaking through the Atlantic Wall. President Roosevelt was also in doubt if the enterprise would be successful and prayed on the radio for the soldiers who were participating in this dangerous mission.

General Eisenhower had his doubts as well that the invasion would be successful. On the eve of the invasion he typed two different statements for the press. One was that the landing had been successful and the other that it had been a failure.

It was a historical moment for an invasion force of a magnitude never seen before in history. It was also a historic command that was given: "Land the landing force," when the landing force approached the beaches of Normandy. Nobody knew if it could be done. The Atlantic Wall was a most awesome barrier built to keep the enemy out. Right in front of the beach was a mine field followed by steel obstacles that were designed to rip open any landing craft. Right after the landing, the beach was nothing but mines covered by guns.

When the historic command came the soldiers had no choice but to obey. The officers had been instructed to shoot anybody who didn't jump ashore when the command was given. It was seen as cowardice and was a bad example for the other soldiers. If you were part of the landing force you had no choice, you had to jump ashore or you would be shot by your own officers. All a storming soldier could do was to shut down his brain and do what was commanded.

Fifty Canadians died by Canadian bullets for desertion. Shell shocked soldiers lost their nerve. If they didn't do what they were ordered to do, they were facing a firing squad. On D Day they had to run into a rain of enemy bullets, if they hesitated they were killed by friendly fire. With bullets coming from the front and back their life wasn't worth a plugged nickel. During preparations, some nervous young men shot themselves right through their hand to be ousted from the operation.

After the rough crossing, most of the soldiers managed to get ashore. Many of them were seasick and were in terrible shape. There was no time to think about being sick, if they didn't get moving fast, they would be dead instead of sick.

When the first wave of 34,200 men landed on Omaha Beach, over 300 boats capsized before they reached the shore and the soldiers that managed to get ashore were greeted with machine gun fire, exploding shells and nothing but mines that took a heavy toll. Young men dropped like ten pins, they were so young and never had a chance to live. The Germans weren't waiting with coffee and cookies; instead the Allied soldiers were welcomed by machine gun fire and thousands of exploding shells all around them. The water turned red from the blood that was spilled on Normandy's beaches. In no time at all, the beach was covered with dead bodies. Fortunately, some of the soldiers got through; the Germans couldn't shoot fast enough to kill everybody.

The Germans were standing their ground and the landing forces didn't manage to get off the beaches. It became so crowded that it hampered progress and landing of more troops had to be stopped until the beach could be cleared.

It was a touch and go situation all the time but by the evening of June 6th, the Canadian and English beachheads had been united and they were holding an eight mile long area half a mile deep. It was an expensive piece of real estate that came at the cost of 120 planes and 4,000 dead bodies.

Fighting for freedom had a very high price. There were five beaches where landings took place Utah, Omaha, Gold, Juneau and Sword. The Germans stayed in their bunkers where they were safer than going on the beach to fight the invaders. From their bunkers, they could extract a heavy toll with their machine gun fire and artillery.

Amazingly, all landings were most successful except the one on Omaha Beach. Naval bombardment hadn't destroyed all German batteries and some were still shooting when the troops went ashore. Landing of amphibious tanks was also a disaster with the rough weather, 27 out of the 32 tanks never made it to shore which gave the infantry little support.

When Rommel returned from his wife's birthday party, the Atlantic Wall had four holes in it. In spite of the air supremacy and the bridges and railways that had been knocked out before the landing, Rommel managed to move in three Panzer divisions within a few days.

The only thing that made the invasion work was the total supremacy in the air. General Eisenhower said: "If you see any planes, don't worry, they are ours." It was hell for the Allies but also hell for the Germans who were constantly bombed. The Allies were supposed to take Caen the first day of the invasion. Unfortunately, there was a German tank division in place that prevented them from reaching that objective.

On the first ten days of the invasion, the Allies landed 650,000 troops, 950,000 vehicles and 250,000 tons of supplies. Everything looked good for a change until another storm hit the area and played havoc with the supplies.

The Allies had towed artificial concrete harbours across the Channel to unload their supplies. Normally, unloading supply ships was done with small boats that unloaded their precious supplies ashore. Some of the artificial harbours were lost together with 800 cargo ships and hundreds of millions of dollars of war material. A severe shortage of ammunition was the result and ammunition had to be distributed which benefited the Germans. The elements were surely favoring the Germans but when sunshine returned the Allies got going again.

The Germans always had another surprise. Eight days after the landing in Normandy, the first V1 missile hit London on June 13, 1944. A total of 8500 V1 missiles were launched against London from which 2400 reached their target. Hitler said the V of the V1 stood for Victory. The English learned to live with the new destructive weapons the Germans had come up with. The V1 could be tracked by radar and shot down; they only went 350 miles per hour with a range of 100 miles.

However, the V1's that reached their target did a lot of damage to London until the Germans came up with the V2 that went 55 miles above the earth at a speed of 3400 miles per hour, faster than sound, with a range of 200 miles. They carried a ton of explosives and couldn't be tracked with radar or shot down. When the first V2 hit London on September 8, 1944 the Germans had a heyday destroying London with their supersonic strikes that came without warning.

With the great success the V2 had destroying London, Hitler ordered 30,000 V2 rockets. Luckily, that insane order couldn't be delivered. Industry could make six fighters in the time that they manufactured one V2. London was burning again after a short reprieve when the Germans had been concentrating on Russia. There were many V2 launching pads that were well hidden and production was done underground so bombing German cities had no effect on the production of V2's.

An even greater threat to the Allies was the atomic bomb the Germans were working on, that was Hitler's bomb. The Americans were working on it too but the Germans were half a year ahead of the Allies. If the Germans would get an atomic bomb ready and deliver it with a V2 rocket, it would have ended the war in favour of the Germans

By the beginning of July more than a million soldiers had landed in France who needed to be supplied with food and ammunition every day. A permanent harbour was needed and the Allies were eying at Cherbourg. It took six divisions and two tank divisions to take the harbour on June 26th. As expected, the harbours were completely demolished. All cranes were lying on the bottom of the harbour, ships had been sunk and the harbour was full of mines. Scorched earth was all that the Germans had left.

It took some doing to make the harbour operational again. In an all-out effort the Allies managed to clear the harbour in three weeks' time and on July 16th the first cargo ship was unloading precious supplies for the troops. That was quite an improvement for the cause of logistics but more harbours were desperately needed to satisfy the needs of the troops when they took on more real estate.

Logistics was the big thing in the invasion. Only three out of every ten soldiers had combat duties, the rest were involved in supplies. Thirty six hours after the landing, the troops needed a re-supply of 300,000 gallons of fresh drinking water. They couldn't drink the salt water from the sea. Once they were farther inland they could obtain water from the rivers, but on the beach was little water, if any.

Supply trucks were driving night and day to get the goods to the soldiers. By transporting 135,000 tons of supplies per month, the trucks were wearing out 35,000 tires per month.

By the end of August 60,000 Allied soldiers had died and an estimated 240,000 Germans. It wasn't a Sunday School picnic at all; it was a cruel war for both sides! According to the Geneva Convention, 'A soldier is supposed to kill the enemy but if the enemy waves a white flag or comes out with his hands in the air, you are supposed to take prisoners and not shoot them.' With the Allied landing there was no time to take prisoners. All troops had been instructed that if taking prisoners would delay them, to hell with the Geneva Convention; delays could be too costly, which could cost their own life.

The Germans were even worse. According to the Geneva Convention, a prisoner is supposed to give only his name and rank to the enemy and for the rest he is supposed to shut up and not reveal any military plans. If the Germans were unsuccessful with their interrogation of prisoners, they tortured them and even shot them. War crimes are only prosecuted by the winning side. The winners might have committed the same crimes as the losers but that was alright. They were the winners that decided what was right and what was wrong.

General Rommel wrote his last report to the Fuhrer. He stated that an Allied break through was imminent which would have grave consequences. He was right; when the breakthrough came the Allies were unstoppable. At the beginning of the invasion, the Allies were far behind on their time table due to heavy German resistance. That had changed for the better; after they broke through there was no stopping and the Germans withdrew faster than the Allies could advance. They were now way ahead of their time schedule. The Allies were only slowed down by enthusiastic French people that wanted to shake the hands of the soldiers and French girls who wanted to kiss the liberators. It seemed that the end of the Nazis was in sight and also the end of the war in Europe.

The fast advance of the Allies caused supply problems for General Patton's Army that used 400,000 gallons of gasoline per day. As soon as their fuel tanks were empty they came to a screeching halt. Taking Paris also caused a food shortage among the troops. There were a lot of hungry mouths to feed in Paris by the tune of several millions and all those starving people were looking to the Allies for food.

November 4, 1944. The Canadians captured Antwerp undamaged. With the supplies lines getting longer all the time, the capture of Antwerp improved the Allied position a lot. The harbour could handle 40,000 ton a day.

There was a great rivalry among the Generals; Eisenhower had a hard time to please them. Montgomery was the worst, he objected that this war started out as an English war and now he was commanded by a U.S. General. He didn't like Canadian General Crerar at all, he said that he was appointed to lead the Canadian Army at noon and five minutes after twelve he already had made his first mistake. All Generals wanted to take Paris but Eisenhower gave the job to French General de Gaulle.

Slaying the Dragon.

Although the Allies were seemingly winning the war, it took too long for the desperate people under Nazi occupation. It looked as if a very dark and hungry winter was in the offing. Rations were cut and cut again and more and more items were not available anymore.

"Rommel wounded in air attack and possibly killed,"

said the underground newspaper on July 15.
Great but disastrous news came on July 20, 1944 in the newspaper that
night:

HITLER SURVIVES ASSASSINATION ATTEMPT.
The Fuhrer only slightly wounded.

It was amazing that an assassination attempt was possible. Hitler's
headquarters Berghtesgaden was well protected by mountains and mine fields
and his underground bunker could resist a heavy bombardment. In spite of
all those precautions it was possible because the attempt came from within,
from his closest Generals.

The next day there was a shouting boasting speech from the Fuhrer:
"Providence has protected me so well from all harm that I can continue to
labor on the great task of victory. The criminal element in this country will
be destroyed without mercy. We shall settle accounts with those people in the
manner we National Socialists are accustomed to."

Radio London replied to Hitler's speech about Providence that had saved
him. "If Providence has saved the Fuhrer to continue this bloodbath, why then
is Hitler's empire shrinking?" Most of the Dutch people had to hear this from
the underground Dutch newspaper since they didn't own a radio anymore.

Details of the assassination attempt appeared in the newspaper and also
the punishment that Hitler brought to the plotters.

PLOT TO KILL HITLER FAILED.

A bomb exploded in Hitler's bunker killing 5 German Generals but the
Fuhrer escaped. Wrath of Hitler kills 200 suspects among them 17 German
Generals. All 200 suspects were hanged this morning on meat hooks."

Hitler was very happy that he was saved by his Maker. On the other
hand the Dutch people were not impressed with the miraculous saving of the
Fuhrer. They all were very disappointed in His Almighty who had saved this
monster so he could continue his evil. It was just no use to pray to the Lord
'Deliver us from Evil.' All the Lord had done was save evil.

The Reverend had been approached by several members of the church
who said: "Hitler has survived several assassination attempts. If there is a God
why doesn't he make the people succeed in the plot to kill him?"

The sermon of the Reverend was based on the doubt that had entered the hearts of good Christians. He preached out of the Book of Job, he read a few versus on which he had based his sermon: "There was a man in the land of Uz, whose name was Job; and that man was perfect and upright, and one that feared God and eschewed evil. Job had 7 sons and 3 daughters; he also had 7,000 sheep, 3,000 camels, 500 yokes of oxen and 500 she asses."

The Reverend read another verse when he said to Satan: "Hast thou considered my servant Job, that there is none like him in the earth, a perfect God fearing man?"

When the Reverend got to his sermon he gave the answer of the Devil. The Devil said: "No wonder that Job worships Thee because thou has blessed them to no end. Take everything away and he will curse Thee instead of praising Thee."

Anyway the Devil was allowed to take everything away and Job said: "The Lord has given and the Lord has taken it away, Blessed is the Lord."

When the Devil was allowed to smite Job with sore boils from the sole of his foot unto his crown, Job cursed the day that he was born and said: "Let the day perish wherein I was born. Why died I not from the womb? Why did I not give up the ghost when I came out of the belly?"

Then his wife turned to him and said: "Why don't you curse God and die?"

Job's answer was: "Why should we receive good at the hand of the Lord and shall we not receive evil?" This was the message of the Reverend to his congregation. The Dutch people had received many blessings and much good from the Lord, such notables as Queen Wilhelmina and freedom. And now, the people were receiving evil things named Adolf Hitler, oppression and occupation of their country. The Reverend stated that at the end of his ordeal Job received from the Lord twice as much as he had before. According to Adrie's calculation Job had at the end 14,000 sheep, 6,000 camels, 1,000 joke of oxen and 1,000 she asses. Wow!

As always, the Reverend read a supporting verse from the Bible which stretched the message of his sermon. He had chosen Romans 8 verses 28 "And we know that all things work together for good to them that love God, to them who are the called according to his purpose."

The grand finale of the sermon was when the Reverend closed stating: "This senseless war can test the deepest faith. Our view of the world and our view of God are shaken to the core with the atrocities that are going on against people."

Of course, the Reverend sang the old song in his closing argument that God will in due time deal with the Fuhrer. "And God's ways are mysterious but only God knows what's good for us. It says in the Bible 'And God saw everything that he had made, and it was very good.' So who are we to say that it isn't? We have to trust God that in due time God will destroy evil. We are tested to the limit but we are not alone in our suffering. Righteousness will triumph in the end and tyranny will lose even if it doesn't seem that way. There isn't much else we can hold onto today."

The Reverend had brought no consolation and very little hope to the disappointed Dutch people. They felt like Job when he was tested to the limit and when he broke he cursed his birthday. And this all happened to Job because God wanted to show the Devil that he was a God fearing man. People said: "If we are doing evil things God punishes us according to the Reverend, and if we are like Job we are tested because God wants to show us off to Satan that we are that good. It really doesn't matter whether we are good or bad we get the same treatment anyway. And Hitler is saved by Providence, what a bull this is."

Even preaching a sermon against the Germans could be dangerous. There were spies everywhere, even in the church. The Germans had Dutch Nazi sympathizers going to church, to listen so that the Reverend didn't say anything nasty about the Germans. On one occasion when Hitler attacked Russia, there was a Reverend who had preached from the Book of Revelations in the Bible. The verse he had taken for his sermon was verse 1 of chapter 13. "And I stood upon the sand of the sea, and saw a beast rise up out of the sea, having seven heads and ten crowns."

According to the preacher, Hitler was the beast and the seven heads of the beast were Hitler's partners in crime. Among them were Hess, Goering, Goebbles and Himmler. And the ten crowns were the ten countries Hitler had taken or attacked. They were Czechoslovakia, Poland, Denmark, Norway, Belgium, The Netherlands, France, Yugoslavia, Greece and Russia. Russia would be the last one Hitler attacked. Hitler would be defeated like the dragon in the book of Revelations. This dragon with his ten crowns was beaten and reduced to poppycock and Hitler would face the same lot. It sounded to Adrie that somebody was going to beat the crap out of the evil dragon and the dragon would be reduced to milled doll shit. Of course the Reverend had to use more civilized words in his position, although he meant the same.

That was good preaching, most of the people thought, it was exactly what they wanted to hear that Hitler was going to be defeated. Unfortunately, the Nazis didn't like that kind of preaching in which the Reverend had called Hitler the beast and had suggested that the top Nazis were criminals. The Reverend was promptly arrested. He was lucky that after two weeks internment, they gave him a warning to smarten up and let him go.

Churches were watched continuously by the Nazis. They figured that the leaders of the churches could cause trouble and outlawed all meetings except strictly religious ones. The Reverend could preach his sermon on Sunday provided he didn't say that Hitler was the Beast which would be defeated. Of course, there were a lot of other things which the Reverend wasn't supposed to say.

All churches got a letter from the German commander outlawing meetings of church groups. The churches had Boys' Clubs, Girls' Clubs, Young Men's Clubs, Young Women's Clubs etc. All were outlawed by the Germans. Church leaders asked to be allowed to have Bible Study Groups for the young people. It was allowed on one condition, no separate boys and girls clubs. If there were Bible study groups, only mixed groups were allowed.

One Sunday morning after the sermon, the Reverend announced that there was a meeting of all young boys and girls. At that meeting the Bible Study League was formed in order to comply with the German wishes. Actually, the church leaders didn't mind this at all, the Reverend was always preaching that Reformed boys should look for a good Reformed girl to date and to marry. Of course, the trouble is that if you can't find such a good Reformed girl what are you going to do? With mixed meetings there is a very good chance that boy sees girl, they get married and live happily ever after. The Reverend loved it.

The Leader of the Bible Study League suggested that the members of the league would make a day trip to the Grebbeberg. The Grebbeberg had been the scene of a severe battle between the German and Dutch army when the war started. Dutch authorities had made a Memorial Garden honouring the many dead soldiers. There was one part where the Dutch soldiers were buried and a part where the German soldiers were buried. It was very impressive and an eye opener to all visitors. One thing was very noticeable that everybody visited the graves of the Dutch soldiers and not those of the German soldiers. Why should they? If the German soldiers had stayed in their heimat this wouldn't have happened. Even the Reverend who was always preaching forgiveness from the pulpit wasn't interested in the German section at all.

The Great Conspiracy.

With the war going bad for the Germans in Russia, Hitler had shown his true face. As long as his

Generals were winning battle after battle he decorated them and loved them. Once they started to lose battles he had very little use for them if any and blamed his Generals.

He sacked several Generals and executed some of them because they had withdrawn their troops before they were wiped out. Whenever Hitler's Generals had asked permission to withdraw their troops in order to save them, Hitler had refused those requests and ordered them to fight till the last man.

Rommel had experienced the same when he was fighting in Africa. When they were being surrounded, Hitler had ordered him to defend every inch of ground. He lost most of his army because of that.

Rommel had never agreed with this kind of warfare and he knew that Hitler would indeed fight to the last man and till the last bullet had been fired. He would never surrender and would make his last stand on the rubble of a totally destroyed Germany.

Many German Generals, including Rommel, saw the writing on the wall that the war was lost but Hitler would never see it that way. When you are beaten you try to make the best deal possible with your enemy. More and more Generals who had loved Hitler in the beginning started to hate him and blamed Hitler for the heavy losses of the army. This Bohemian Corporal was telling Generals what to do and for the least disobedience of his orders, he executed them.

Some of Hitler's top Generals figured that Germany still had a chance to play an important part in a post war world. Though the Allies had only one thing in their mind to destroy Germany, not everything was well. Stalin was making plans to make Russia a country never before experienced in history and was very inflexible in the post war planning.

If they could make a deal with the English and the Americans to end the war between Germany and the Allies and then go together to defeat Russia, Germany would have a future. (This probably wouldn't have worked because the Allies had agreed that they would accept nothing less than an unconditional surrender from Germany.) In order to try to make such a deal, they had to get rid of Hitler first and take over Government. When that was accomplished, Rommel with some other top Generals were going to try to make a deal with the Allies to fight Russia together.

Colonel von Stauffenberg was one of Hitler's top planners in strategy. In the beginning of the war he had great faith in Hitler but at this stage he wanted to get rid of him to save Germany. There was going to be a very important meeting in Hitler's bunker on July 20, 1944 with at the top of the agenda a plan to throw the Allies back into the sea. Colonel von Stauffenberg thought it a great opportunity to get rid of Hitler. Although he was a staunch Roman Catholic he saw nothing wrong in killing Hitler. According to him Hitler was the Devil himself and nothing was wrong in blowing up the Devil.

Everything went wrong; it was already a great disappointment that Goebbles and Himler weren't present at the meeting. They were the ones to take over if Hitler died. It meant that they had to find another way to get rid of those two after they had blown up Hitler.

For this occasion, England had supplied two bombs to blow up Hitler in his bunker. Unfortunately, there was the problem of setting the time of the explosion in the washroom. The conspirators were disturbed and consequently they had only one bomb ready to blow up the bunker. It was a powerful bomb so it should do the trick.

Von Stauffenberg had no problem to put the bomb underneath the table with the maps where Hitler and his Generals were bending over. He had a report for Hitler and when he handed it over to Hitler he put the bomb underneath the table. Next he got a phoney phone call and pretended that he had to go to Berlin to get some more information on the report. Once outside the bunker he waited for the explosion. When he heard the explosion, he thought that Hitler was dead and left for Berlin to take over Government.

It was not to be; five of Hitler's top Generals were killed by the blast but Hitler escaped again with the closest brush with death that he had ever experienced. Hitler had a shouting speech in which he boasted that His Almighty had saved him again to lead the German people. He was shouting: "Providence has protected me so well from all harm that I can continue my mission in the great task of victory. The criminal elements in this country will be destroyed and we will settle accounts with those people in the manner in which we National Socialists are accustomed to."

Indeed Hitler's revenge was terrible; Colonel von Stauffenberg with 17 other Generals and a couple of hundred other conspirators were killed and hung from meat hooks. More than 4900 people died in Hitler's revenge and Hitler could continue his despotism for another nine months in which another fifteen million people died because the conspirators had failed to kill the beast.

Lady Luck seemed to be forever on his side. It was Hitler's luck that one of his Generals had kicked against the bag with the bomb. The bag fell over and was resting against an oak table leg which took the brunt of the explosion and Hitler himself escaped with only minor injuries.

General Rommel, the German's people most famous General was in the conspiracy as well and consequently he must die. To cover up and to prevent embarrassment, the German people shouldn't know that Rommel had been in it.

Two German officers visited Rommel to give him two choices, he could either be arrested as a traitor and killed by the Gestapo or he could take a cyanide capsule in which case his death would be announced as a heart attack. If he decided to kill himself, he would receive a State Funeral and they would take care of his wife and son with a handsome pension.

The two choices he had were to die or to die and he chose to die by his own hand. He said good bye to his wife and told her that he would be dead in half an hour. Next he left with the German officers to take his cyanide capsule.

Everything went as promised, at his State Funeral there were wreaths from Hitler, Goering and Gobbles and Rundsted read the eulogy. (Rommel's family was taken care of and his son became a politician after the war. He served as mayor of Stuttgart for over 25 years and retired in 1995.)

Mad Tuesday.

On the Eastern front the Germans took a licking as well. The Russian Winter offensive had started on December 24, 1943 and the Germans were in full retreat. Even when it became spring the Russians didn't slow down. The best news was brought by the underground press.

Wehrmacht in Trouble in Russia.

The Russian Red Army has broken through the German lines. The gap caused by this breakthrough is 185 miles wide and 28 German divisions have been completely surrounded.

The next night the underground newspaper brought some more news from Russia. Almost all the 50,000 Dutch young people who had joined the Waffen S.S. were dead. No good Dutch man wept a tear when they heard the news, they were just traitors anyway and it would save them the trouble of punishing them when the war was finished.

NEDERLAND DIVISION WIPED OUT AT LENINGRAD.
After enduring a siege of 880 days the Red Army has freed Leningrad. In the process the fast advancing Red Army trapped

the Nederland S.S. Division which was completely wiped out. Only 500 prisoners were taken, the rest are presumed dead.

People started to figure that there was really something about the sermon from the book of Revelations. And it looked as if the Beast was going to be defeated by the tenth crown he had taken on.

On August 1 it seemed that the Red Army wasn't to be stopped.

"Red Army drives Germans out of Latvia and Estonia and advances into Poland." In the last six weeks the Germans have lost 60 divisions.

All this good news made the Dutch people look at their atlas continuously. The Dutch people concluded that it was a long way to Tipperary and it was equally a long way to go before The Netherlands would be liberated.

By August 1, 1944 the Russians moved into Poland and by October 1 they had control over Poland. August 31ˢᵗ was another mile stone for the Russians when they conquered the Romanian oil fields. Between June 1ˢᵗ and August 30ᵗʰ the Germans had lost over one million men killed wounded or imprisoned. Hitler was fast running out of German divisions. At the end of 1944 the Red Army moved into Germany.

The faraway war with Japan had changed for the better too i.e. if you can call being hit by kamikazes an improvement. The Japanese tried to reverse the war to their advantage by introducing kamikazes. They loaded an old plane full with explosives and a pilot dived his plane on a U.S. war ship. The success was tremendous; one old airplane could sink the biggest war ship.

It took the Americans a while before they caught on to the kamikaze attacks which started in October of 1944. The first time that this happened, it looked like a Japanese airplane had been in trouble and the pilot had landed it on the warship. When they figured out what was going on they thought that there would be only a few, nobody in his right mind would be so stupid as to make a bomb out of himself.

The Americans had it all wrong, kamikaze pilots were told to focus on the target and never close their eyes on impact. As soon as they died they would see their ghost flying to a much better place than it had ever been. Over 2500 kamikaze pilots destroyed over 400 U.S. war ships killing over 7000 U.S. service men. Plane, bomb and pilot were one and the kamikaze always hit its target; the only defence was to shoot them down before they made their final dive on the ship. That wasn't as easy as it seemed because there were a number of kamikazes escorted by Japanese fighters.

In order to protect the big war ships the Americans sent little ships like mine sweepers ahead of the fleet. That way, they only lost little ships and the big ships were saved. It was known as the Shepherd Tactic. A shepherd sends his weak and sick sheep ahead to protect his strong herd when he is attacked by a wolf pack and loses only his sick and weak sheep.

The U.S. was also bombing air bases where the kamikazes came from. The Japanese had an answer to that problem; they hid the kamikazes in the jungle and put plywood models on the runways. U.S. pilots reported that they had destroyed many kamikazes but they had only destroyed plywood models.

It was a heavy blow for the Germans when the Allies finally succeeded in blowing up the Romanian oil fields. A modern army without oil won't go very far. To remedy this disaster, oil supplies to the occupied countries ceased altogether. Even coal supplies to the people of The Netherlands came to an end. There were more important things for the Germans to do than to worry about the Dutch people who were facing a coming winter without heat in their houses. Moreover the gas supply for cooking purposes was cut off as well.

All of a sudden people couldn't cook their food anymore on gas. It was no problem for Ko because she never had used gas for cooking. She cooked on the stove in winter and in summer when it was hot she cooked on an oil burner. That wasn't really a help because the coal supply had stopped and oil was not available for a long time. Everybody was in the same spot, how to heat the house in winter and how to cook the little food they had.

The Germans were good enough to set up soup kitchens. If you wanted, you could go to the kitchen, hand over your ration coupons and you could come every day to receive your ration of cooked food. It was usually a dish of soup and a couple of spoonfuls of mashed potatoes with some vegetables in it and never any meat. Meat had disappeared from the Dutch menu. It was totally insufficient to keep the people alive but the Germans didn't care.

All kinds of wood burners were constructed of old metal. This didn't completely solve the problem. If you didn't have a property with trees on it you wouldn't have wood. Of course, people would go out in the dark and saw down a tree from another yard or a tree that belonged to the city. There were quite a few people who had a tree on their property and when they woke up the next day it was gone. Somebody in need of firewood had taken it during the night. All this in the dark business was very dangerous with the curfew in place. As you couldn't steal in broad daylight, people didn't have a choice.

On August 3rd 1944 the German press announced that General Rommel had died from a heart attack and Germany's top general was given a state funeral. In spite of Rommel being a great General, there wasn't even one good Dutchman who mourned his death. The de Kievits couldn't care less, Rommel was the A hole who had flooded the polder and their house. Why should they care at all?

With the war going bad for Germany, Hitler became crueller by the day. When the German army had victory after victory, the Fuhrer was much obliged to hand out many medals for bravery and skill. Now that German victories had changed into defeats, the Fuhrer changed the medals for bullets. Generals, who withdrew their troops in order to save them from annihilation, were shot.

On August 15, three American divisions landed at the French Riviera in the South of France. It didn't move the war tired Dutch people at all. They were living North and the Allies landed in the South. Nice going!

However, on August 26 the Allies started to move Northward. After a break through in Normandy the underground paper reported:

"General de Gaulle Liberates Paris."

Well, that sounded like music in the Dutch people's ears. A lot of times the news was about seemingly unimportant places the Dutch people never had heard of before. This time it was about the liberation of Paris. Everybody knew Paris; it was only 400 kilometres from Rotterdam. According to the underground newspaper, Hitler had ordered that Paris be completely destroyed when the German army moved out. An unwilling German General saved the city, he couldn't see that it would do any good for the Germans; the only thing that would be accomplished was to destroy priceless architecture.

Jan Lems had something to say about that: "That damned Hitler; he saved Rome because it was the Christian headquarters but Paris he wanted destroyed. Twice during the last 70 years did the Germans conquer Paris and for the second time they had to give it up. If he couldn't have Paris, nobody would. Luckily for the French, Hitler's orders weren't carried out."

August 31ˢᵗ was Queen Wilhelmina's birthday. The R.A.F. gave a daring fire works display for the Dutch citizens to celebrate the Queen's birthday. All major Dutch cities were given a free fireworks display to honor Queen Wilhelmina. It was a dazzling display of exploding firecrackers with colorful stars. It went on for half an hour and concluded with a royal crown and a W of Wilhelmina on top of it. The R.A.F. had complete air supremacy in Western Europe and the Germans could only watch the display.

There was good news every day now. On September 3

"Dieppe captured by Canadians."

It was up to the Canadians to take Dieppe. In 1943 with the debacle of the raid on Dieppe, the Canadians had taken quite a licking so they had a stake in that place.

On September 4 Ghent was freed and Luxembourg was liberated on September 5. Most of Belgium was overrun by the Allies and they moved into the Southern part of The Netherlands. The German army was in disarray and everything became a complete chaos. It set the stage for 'Mad Tuesday.'

A shortage of supplies for the Allied Armies made their rapid advance come to a screeching halt. With the Allied armies in hot pursuit of the retreating Germans and the Allied forces liberating Eindhoven in the Southern Province of The Netherlands, everybody thought the war was over. Arie was working on the coastal defence works when all this good news reached the workers. Happily, they decided to throw in the towel and go home. Arie came home with good news: "The war is over; everybody quit working for the Germans."

It was not to be, the worst was yet to come. This day would go down in history as 'Mad Tuesday.' With all their available means, the Germans tried desperately to stop the Allied advance. They retreated behind the big Dutch rivers, blew up all the bridges and were making their last stand.

The exiled Dutch Government in London ordered the railway workers to go on strike. On September 17th, 30,000 railway workers in The Netherlands went on strike. It meant that the Germans had to bring in people from Germany to keep the railways going for troop transportation. In retaliation, Seyss-Inquart forbad food transportation to the West of The Netherlands where more than four million people were living.

There was little activity on the railways; there was no passenger transportation anymore. Only German warfare material and troops were transported on the railway. There were a few freight trains that transported the little food that was available in The Netherlands. Most of those food transports went straight to Germany. With the railways on strike it deprived the Germans of one of the few transportation means they had left.

With the laborers quitting and the striking railway workers, the Germans were far from friendly to those Dutch people. All those people, including Arie, had to go underground for safety's sake. That was very dangerous too but there was no other solution. The Dutch people had shouted victory too early and had to pay for it.

There was a rumor that all German records of the coastal defence had been destroyed but nobody knew for sure. If they had been destroyed no one would know where the striking people lived. What if they hadn't been destroyed and the Germans were going to round up all those disobedient people? It was natural that they would go to where they lived, where else could they go?

Everybody had to have his or her identity card with them. If you were stopped by a German patrol and you couldn't identify yourself you were arrested on the spot. Thus the people going underground had to stay away from the streets and had to hide when the Nazis came to search the houses. Several times, a person came rushing on an old bike, shouting: "There is a German patrol coming and they are searching houses."

There was one question in everybody's mind "How many people could be underground hiding from the Germans?" There were the Jews that went underground to avoid being shipped to the death camps in Germany. Hiding Jews was a crime punishable by death. Moreover, the Dutch underground had also people who were known to the Germans and they were on the list of most wanted criminals. Their crimes were usually raids on food storage places or stealing ration cards. Underground raids were usually done with a baby carriage containing a baby. The mother would push her baby carriage and underneath the baby was a machine gun ready to use if needed.

Some Dutch boys who didn't want to go to Germany to work for the Germans were also underground and now there were hundreds of people added who had quit working on the German defence works at the coast plus the railway workers who were on strike.

Many people were hiding in The Netherlands and the Germans had nightly raids to round up those people. The Dutch had unique hiding places between floors or walls, they slept normally in their beds and when a raid took place they moved into their hiding place. Other people who were living in the same house had to cover up the tracks of the people who were now in hiding. Their beds had to be made in a hurry and the mattress had to be turned around, if it was warm the Germans could figure somebody had slept in the bed. In the hiding places there was a bottle of water and an empty bottle to pee in. When you got to go you got to go and if you had to pee on the floor, it might seep through to give the hiding person away.

At a farm there are lots of hiding places but most of the people hid in the hay. There were always three people who were hiding at the farm of Jan Lems when German raids took place. All crawled deep into the hay. The thought was that the Germans wouldn't take all the hay out of the barn to look for wanted people. If they thought that people were hiding in the hay they might shoot a couple of shots into the hay and leave. The chances that you would take a bullet in a big hay barn were there but you had a fair chance not to be hit.

There was another problem; when Arie came home, he didn't have ration coupons. When he was working for the Germans they fed all their laborers from the camp kitchen and when they went home for the weekends they gave them ration coupons, just for the weekend. However, when the workers ran away they didn't have ration coupons. Every Dutch citizen could pick up the ration coupon cards on their identity papers. When you were underground hiding from the Nazis, you couldn't go for your ration coupons. That was just too dangerous; they might arrest you on the spot. With the very meagre rations it was difficult to keep food on the table and now there was one more person eating who had no ration.

With the war going bad for the Germans, they couldn't care less about the Dutch people. In spite of the railway strike the Germans had the railway going again. The striking railway workers were replaced with Dutch collaborators and many of the striking railway workers were rounded up and shot. Moreover, the railways were now off limits for any transportation of food for the Dutch people. The Germans always thought that those stubborn people had to be taught a lesson.

I Won't Be Home For Christmas.

It was a beautiful sunny late summer day on September 7, 1944. The air was filled with the sound of hundreds of aeroplanes. Adrie decided to investigate what was cooking and found everybody and his brother watching the sky. Hundreds of aircraft were towing giant gliders with troops inside that were flying over. The Dutch people had never seen gliders towed by aeroplanes. Nobody could even speculate what it all meant but one thing was sure, something very big and very important was taking place.

At night, the Dutch underground newspaper had nothing to report about the great number of planes which had passed over. For security reasons the English press didn't release any details either and the Dutch people were left in the dark. However, the next day sketchy information came to the Dutch people about a giant operation at Arnheim. In spite of the few details that were announced, the Dutch people sensed that it was a matter of life and death. Besides the military battle against the Germans, there was even more at stake for the people of The Netherlands. If the Allies succeeded to cut off the Germans in the three western provinces from Germany, the West of the Netherlands could possibly be liberated in the next week or so.

While the two Southern provinces of The Netherlands were celebrating their liberation, and were marching through the streets of Eindhoven singing "Orange for ever, Long live the Queen," the greatest airdrop in history took place at Nymegen. Montgomery had planned this short cut to get the troops home before Christmas. It was not to be; the Allies took a terrible beating. They had used 2800 aircraft and 1600 gliders. Of the 10,000 airborne troops that had been dropped, only 3,000 returned from the operation. The rest were dead or imprisoned. Of course, the German press boasted a smashing defeat for the Allies and it was.

If the battle of Arnheim was a smashing defeat for the Allies, the Dutch didn't fare any better. When the city of Eindhoven was liberated the Dutch people hung their flags out and were celebrating. Of course, the Dutch people in Arnheim and Nymegen did the same thing; they welcomed the Allies and celebrated.

After the Germans defeated the Allies at Arnheim they were not friendly to the Dutch population. Hitler sent the Hitler Youth out to teach the Dutch people a lesson they would never forget. The Hitler Youth consisted of a bunch of fanatical very young Nazis; they had been taught they were Arians and the master race. They confiscated everything that was usable in Germany; furniture, clothes, and decorations. What they couldn't take or use, they destroyed. Next they painted swastikas on all the houses and the short lived celebration, with Dutch flags on the houses changed into a bunch of robbed people with swastikas on their houses.

For a few days there had been hope for the desperate Dutch people, they thought that they saw the light at the end of the tunnel. After the Allied defeat, it seemed that the tunnel had become longer and stretched. Once more hope turned into hopelessness. After the fruitless attempt to liberate The Netherlands, the darkest time of the war was yet to come for the unfortunate Dutch people, who had thought for the second time that the war was over for them.

Good news wasn't on the program anymore, it seemed. Instead, there was the very bad news that the Germans were using a new secret weapon. The first V2's were hitting London on September 8, 1944. German propaganda told the Dutch people that the V2 was Hitler's vengeance weapon which would turn the war around in favor of the Germans. All details possible were provided in order to impress the people, showing them that the Germans were going to win the war. The V2 went 55 miles above the earth at a speed of 3400 miles per hour, which was faster than the speed of sound. The V2 had a range of 200 miles and could carry a ton of explosives. Hitler vowed that no two stones would be left standing on top of one another in London.

Especially that the V2 was going faster than the speed of sound was praised all the time. However, besides light that goes much faster than the speed of sound, there is the whip which is the first man made invention to break the sound barrier. The crack from a whip is actually the tip of the whip travelling faster than the speed of sound emitting a small sonic boom.

Adrie was impressed with the missile launching pad near Rotterdam. He would see the missile trail of vapour go and right after he would hear the sound of the launching. It proved to him that the Germans weren't lying that the missiles went faster than sound. It was kind of scary that the Germans kept coming up with forever new secret and powerful weapons. Adrie wondered if the war would turn around in favor of the Germans. Those Germans were sure masters at making deadly and destructive weapons.

A Black Day of the War.

The Allies were closing in from the West and the Russians had driven the Germans out of Russia. They were now on their way to Germany. Oh, those Russians, for the second time in the last 130 years they had chased the enemy out of Moscow and destroyed his armies. Napoleon in 1813 and Hitler in 1944. The Russians were on their way to the Nazi home base. It made the Germans real ornery especially when strikes from the Dutch Underground occurred.

The Dutch Underground had become a mighty force to be reckoned with; two percent of the Dutch people were working in underground illegal activities. Killing a German General or killing Dutch Nazis wasn't exactly legal and there were also acts of sabotage against the Germans. Blowing up bridges and railways was a favorite pastime of the Underground. Those actions did a lot of harm to German troop transportations.

Hitler had wanted to include The Netherlands in his Thousand Jahren Reich. At first when the Germans started to run The Netherlands, they treated the Dutch citizens with velvet gloves; they were trying to get the Dutch people to cooperate. When Underground activities started the German gloves came off, Hitler would kill and torture in revenge.

One time when an important railway bridge had been blown up by the Underground, the Germans rounded up ten Dutch men at random. They had to dig their own graves and while they were doing this, there was an opportunity for the culprits to come forward or for the Dutch citizens to turn them in. When this didn't happen, everybody had to face the consequences and the men were executed by a firing squad. Other Dutch men were engaged to cover up the dead bodies. All people were held responsible and accountable for what happened in their neighborhood

The bullets were free contrary to the bullets that were used in China to execute people. Whenever this happened in China the family had to pay for the bullet. "Why waste good bullets?" In China they used one bullet and shot it through the back of the head. The Germans used a firing squad.

A firing squad consisted out of six soldiers. There was only one real bullet and the other five were dummy bullets. All six soldiers of the firing squad fired at the condemned man's heart and the real bullet killed him. The dummy bullets did no harm. Nobody knew who had shot the real bullet and who had killed the guy. That was done on purpose, as some people might have their conscience bothering them if they knew they had shot a man. Now it was a chance of one in six for everybody.

Adrie was in the third class of the Technical School and was 14 years old. Classes at the Tech were from 8.00 a.m. till 5.00 p.m. To have that long a day at school was done on purpose; it was figured that after Tech the students were going to work. When they made a long day at the Tech, the students would get used to getting up early. Apparently the Minister of Education had thought of everything to make the students ready for the world of working.

On the other hand the lunch break was from 11.30 a.m. till 1.30 p.m. which made it a two hour lunch break. Most of the students were not living that far from the Tech so they took an electric tram home for lunch. Where Adrie lived there were no electric trams and it was too far to walk home for lunch break. With a couple of friends of the neighborhood, he took lunch along to eat at school. A two hour lunch break is too long to eat all the time which left plenty of time to do other things.

After the lunch was devoured, Adrie and his friends killed the time with window shopping. There was very little for sale and moreover they had little money to buy things. It didn't matter; they had to kill a two hour lunch break, what else was there to do? Sometimes they went to the market and if they had nothing to do they would sit on the steps of the school. Every day 10 minutes before classes would resume, there were a dozen men leaving from the school building. Those men were no teachers or students so what were they doing in the school? Adrie cared less; it was not really his business but somebody had made it his business.

One afternoon when Adrie was waiting for the gate of the Tech to open for his afternoon education, he saw a dozen German soldiers moving towards the gate with rifles in front of them ready to shoot. "Holy cow," he thought, "I'd better get the hell out of here." He turned around to leave not knowing what was going to happen; all he knew that he didn't want to be part of it. When he turned around, he saw more German soldiers coming out of the side streets who were encircling the school completely. Adrie's heart was bouncing in his throat; he had never seen rifles pointed at him. One thing he knew for sure, he had to get away from this before the shooting started. He didn't run or shout, he just walked up to the Germans. When he was close to the Germans; the Germans opened up a bit to let him get out. There were a few more students who had to break through the German cordon. It wasn't difficult because the Germans weren't after the students; they were after the Underground people.

Adrie went home not knowing what he just had witnessed. The next morning he returned to see if there was going to be school. There was a note from the Principal on the door that the Tech was closed for three days. Teachers and students alike came to check about the conditions. One of the teachers provided details of what had taken place. The Tech had been used for Underground activities; there had been a printing press for Underground newspapers and they were also printing ration coupons and falsifying identity cards. When the raid took place, the janitor and stoker, who were leading figures in the Underground, tried to make their getaway. They were shot in their attempt, together with four other Underground workers. Five more people had been arrested and their fate was unknown. The Principal and Vice Principal of the Tech apparently had no knowledge of what was going on. They were taken in for questioning but miraculously the Germans had released them at night.

Some people from the Underground left for England, to fight on the English side, in order to free The Netherlands. Jan Dejong a relative of the de Kievits had suddenly disappeared. His father and mother knew of his Underground activities and assumed he had left for England. It was usually done with little motorboats from a desolate piece of beach. There were lots of German patrols to guard the Dutch coast on land and also German patrol boats were sailing up and down. It certainly was a dangerous mission, especially when the weather wasn't cooperative. Many escapees had a rough ride making the crossing to England.

That wasn't the only danger for the escapee. The family that remained behind had to face the Germans if someone was missing. For this reason, Jan Dejong had told nobody that he was going to disappear and where he was going. That way, his family knew nothing when they were cross examined by the Germans. It was very obvious that people were crossing the Channel to England, but a guy could disappear for other reasons. However, the Germans had to be convinced that the family knew nothing. And if they knew nothing they couldn't say anything to give him away.

His father and mother went through all his stuff to make sure that nothing could connect him with the Dutch Underground. To avoid reprisal from the Germans they had to report that he was missing. They waited about three days to give him time to make his get away and then reported to the police that their son was missing for two days. A little lie about the last day he was home gave him an extra day to make his get away. If they had waited longer than two days, to report his disappearance, it could have looked suspicious. The Germans were always suspicious and might have thought that the people were in cahoots with the Underground. It worked rather well and nothing was heard after an investigation.

Not everything went well in the Underground. There was the matter of the England Spiel (England game) by the German counter espionage. The Dutch Underground had radio connection with the English; they supplied valuable intelligence information to England. And the English in return were supplying the Dutch underground with weapons, ammunition and explosives for sabotage purposes. They also sent Dutch agents to reinforce the Underground movement.

A Dutch traitor had infiltrated the Dutch Underground, which resulted in a German raid whereby the Germans arrested several important members of the Dutch Underground. The Germans also impounded a Dutch Underground transmitting station with which they maintained contact with London. There was a key code to make connection with England; if you didn't know the code you couldn't transmit to London. That's where the arrested people came in; Huub Lowers, the head of the local Underground, was forced to send messages to London pretending that he was still free.

A warning was sent by the Dutch underground to England, that the Germans had taken over the transmission station and they should stop transmitting on that wavelength. The English didn't acknowledge the warning and kept transmitting. Consequently, the Germans knew when secret agents were arriving and when ammunition drops were to be made. All the Germans had to do was to arrest the secret agents and when a drop was made at a pre-arranged place, the Germans were there to receive the delivery.

(Why the warning was ignored by London remains a mystery and has never been resolved. The administration in London was either extremely stupid and incompetent or they were using the agents to make the Germans believe that the invasion would take place in The Netherlands. They could have sacrificed fifty Dutch agents just to confuse the Germans. After the war when there was a probe to discover the truth, the headquarters in London that contained all the information mysteriously burned down and all the files were lost.

The German counter espionage agent who managed to arrest 50 English agents and took delivery of weapons as well, wrote his memoirs which were published as a book, "I played the England Spiel.")

Over fifty Dutch agents were captured by the Germans. Most of them were executed in German death camps. One of the agents escaped to London and warned them not to send messages over that wave length. To his dismay the interrogators in London didn't believe his story and detained him as a suspected double agent.

An interrogation of secret agents by the Germans usually started with a form with ten questions that had to be answered. After the form had been completed the answers were checked out and if they weren't satisfactory they used more persuasive ways to get the answers they wanted.

The Gestapo used cruel methods to get information; they would stick a guy's head in a tub with water till the lungs filled up and wack him on the buttocks. They also would hit his testicles till they were bleeding. Often they smashed their fingers and broke their knees. Few people could endure the torture and talked under terrible pain. For that reason all people of the Underground had nicknames. Nobody knew the real names of the people he was working with and could never give anybody away. If there was trouble, nicknames could be changed.

That was not the only trick the Germans knew to round up the Dutch Underground. The Dutch Underground was also heavily involved in supplying aid to English pilots who had bailed out over The Netherlands, when their plane was shot down. There was an escape route for flyers that were shot down through Belgium, France and the Pyrenees back to England. Every night, for hours, the drone of thousands of airplanes was heard over The Netherlands. Many planes were shot down and the Dutch underground picked up many pilots and managed to get them back to England.

All British flight crews that were involved in the bombing of Germany, or strategic positions in the occupied countries had a parachute and an escape kit to escape capture by the Germans. This escape kit consisted of a map of the areas they were flying over. Very conveniently the map was printed on silk so it didn't matter if it got wet. Moreover one button of their jackets was a compass and aircrews were also taught different languages they might run into. All aircrews could say in those languages: "I'm British, can you hide me." Or "I'm Hungry" (or thirsty). Emergency rations were also included in their kit which were mainly concentrated food and chocolate bars. There were also pills to purify the water and money for each country. The aircrews were also instructed to try to get back to England and if they were captured they had to try to escape because "Your Country Needs You."

It was easier said than done to return to England after they had bailed out of their burning aircraft. But help was on the way from the Dutch Underground that assisted many of the British aircrews to return to England. Of course the Germans, who were themselves trying to round up the English aircrews, were not easy on Dutch people who helped British airmen. If caught aiding a British airman you would be shot, period.

The Germans had another trick up their sleeves to catch the Dutch Underground red handed. They dropped Gestapo agents from the air in English uniforms, pretending they were shot down. Of course they were speaking English and they even had proof that they were shot down. They were dropped when a lot of British planes were flying over and several planes had been downed. There was also an English parachute to prove it. Lots of English aircrews bailed out over The Netherlands and the Germans collected the parachutes. If the Dutch underground doubted their word, they had buried an English parachute for the Underground to find.

After several successes of the Germans with this scheme, the Dutch underground got more careful and had interrogators to question the supposed English airmen. They were questioned in English and insulted in German, in a way that only a real German could understand. The insults were so gross that if they had been Germans they would have reacted.

The Dutch Underground used all kinds of means to battle the Nazis. If a prominent leader of the Underground or a British airman was arrested, they had a few tricks up their sleeves to get him out of jail. Usually they swallowed an open safety pin that would get stuck in their throat to cause an inflammation. Once the prisoner was sent to the hospital it was easier to free him. One time this procedure backfired when the safety pin passed the throat and got stuck in the intestines. The British airman got out of jail alright and into the hospital to die on the operating table.

Since this safety pin method had proven too dangerous, they invented a safer way to get a prisoner into the hospital. They simply gave the prisoner a 'Diphtheria Sandwich' to get him out. An orderly in the hospital, who was an Underground worker, collected diphtheria germs from a patient's throat. They put the germs on a sandwich and smuggled it to the prisoner they wanted to get out. Once the prisoner had diphtheria the Germans sent him to a hospital and from there on the underground freed him. The Germans were very afraid of this disease and were quick to get the prisoner to the hospital.

"Power comes from the barrel of a gun," Hitler said. "You shoot as many people as you have to, to make them heel. After that people will do what they are told."

The Waffen S.S. was Hitler's most brutal force. It was a criminal organization of elite troops that Hitler called his finest army. They left behind them a trail of towns in which they killed the entire population because people had moved against them. The Allies saw all soldiers of the S.S. as war criminals.

One of the most horrifying stories took place in the village of Lyson a few miles from Prague. Heinrich was the top Nazi who had to take over when Hitler died; he was put in charge over all of Europe and was well known for his cruelty against Jews. The Underground, together with London, had decided that Heinrich had to go.

Heinrich lived on an estate close to Prague and drove every day to his office. His cavalcade was attacked in an effort to assassinate him. It didn't go all that great when the rifle that had to kill Heinrich jammed but fortunately the backup plan to throw a hand grenade in his car worked and Heinrich died. That was the only good luck they were going to have. When Hitler heard the news, he was furious and ordered the town of Lyson totally destroyed. All men and women had to be shot and the town had to be totally leveled so it would never be on the map again.

Because of the hostilities of the Dutch Underground, the Germans were taking Dutch hostages. All important Dutch people were imprisoned, they had committed no crime, yet they were taken prisoner for the sole purpose of retaliation. On the other hand the Dutch underground force would not quit battling the Germans in spite of the danger. They preferred to drown in blood rather than to live in shit.

The German commander warned that if acts of sabotage should occur, he would shoot a number of Dutch hostages according to the seriousness of the act. By the end of September, the Dutch Underground killed a much hated German General, who had been responsible for the transportation of many Dutch Jews to German death camps. There was a terrible price to pay for that one German General.

The German commander announced that the culprit could turn himself in to be punished, which undoubtedly meant a bullet for him. Moreover, the Dutch people had also the opportunity to turn in the murderer. However, if after a week the culprit hadn't been found, the Germans would kill one hundred Dutch hostages. There was a last call to turn the culprits in 24 hours before the time had elapsed. It didn't produce any results so the Germans got even.

It was a black day of the war. At night, the newspaper came out with a black one inch margin line all around the front page. The German commander made known to the Dutch citizens:

"Today, at twelve noon, one hundred prominent Dutch citizens have been shot in retaliation of the killing of the German General Luffing. Anymore incidents against the German occupation force in The Netherlands will be met with the execution of innocent Dutch citizens. The following innocent Dutch citizens were executed today."

All the names of the unfortunate Dutch citizens were published. Among them were the Commissar of Police Mr. Staal of the city of Rotterdam and the Commissar of the Queen in South Holland. Even this bloodbath didn't stop the Dutch Underground from fighting the Germans.

Most of the time, when something went wrong, the poor people got it in the neck but for a change it was the rich and important people who suffered. Adrie was really glad to be too young for playing soldier and that his parents were insignificant poor people. How lucky can you get?

Stealing Wheat Again.

With the land inundated around Rotterdam and other important cities, food production was much less than the year before. In spite of the little food the Dutch produced, the Germans robbed an even greater share from the Dutch crop. Adrie couldn't go at night to steal wheat anymore after the Germans had flooded that polder. However, he was heavily involved in the food production. His uncle Jan asked him if he could give him a hand. Of course he could, he helped to get the wheat and hay in the barn.

The Netherlands has a lot of rainy days which doesn't help harvesting. First the wheat had to be stooked and when it was dry it had to be loaded on horse drawn wagons. Arriving at the farm, the wheat had to be put in a big barn where it would stay until such a time that the threshing machine arrived. Adrie had to throw the sheaves to his uncle so that he could put the wheat heads on the inside of the barn. It was all important for the wheat to stay dry, with the damp climate in The Netherlands, if it got wet it could easily mould.

Harvesting was quite a job in those days. In The Netherlands most of the farms were too small to have their own threshing machine. *(Of course there were no combines in those days.)* Some people who had a threshing machine did custom threshing and they went from farm to farm. Jan Lems was a small time farmer who had to wait till such a time that the threshing machine would arrive.

One day the threshing machine arrived, complete with German inspectors. The inspectors would count the bags of grain and would mark the number in their book. They would give the farmer a letter stating how many bags of grain he had to deliver to the German authorities. And if he didn't deliver the demanded number of bags of wheat, he would be in deep trouble.

First of all, his uncle needed Adrie to take all the sheaves out of the barn. After the threshing had been done, the wheat would be in bags and the straw had to go back in the barn for the cows and horses. His uncle needed him with the threshing as well. He took Adrie to the side and said: "I am going to steal some of my own wheat under the very noses of the German inspectors. As you seem to get along pretty good with the Germans, your task is to keep them occupied as long as you can, with the coffee break. You call them to the living room when the coffee is ready and help your aunt to serve them coffee. Keep them talking to give me and my farmhand time to hide some of the wheat."

Wow, stealing wheat again but this time it was in broad daylight. Adrie knew how important his job was to give his uncle and the farmhand ample time to steal some of the wheat. Some of that stolen wheat would be given to his mother. It was not difficult to get the Germans into the living room for their coffee break and to keep them talking was the easiest thing in the world. Most of the German soldiers had children in Germany and they loved teenage boys. When his uncle entered to get a cup of coffee, Adrie knew that the task of stealing wheat had been accomplished. A repeat of this scenario took place in the afternoon.

Most of that stolen wheat was to give away to family and friends. Before the war, farmers had few friends other than people who worked in agriculture. People living in the cities couldn't care less for farmers; they saw them more or less as second class citizens. With the war on, this changed and all of a sudden the people saw the importance of farmers. Everybody tried desperately to secure a food supply and become friends with the farmers. Those friends counted on the farmers to give them food. Of course they were more than willing to pay for it; that was not the problem.

The problem was that the Germans were in control of food production and the farmers had to deliver all their produce to the German authorities. They were allotted a certain number of bags of wheat for their own use. That allotment was barely enough to keep enough food on their own table. If the farmers wanted to satisfy some of the needs of their relatives and friends they had to steal their own wheat.

The war changed everything, people got a different look at life; even Tryntje, Ploon's sister had second thoughts. When Ploon had to get married because of a baby that was coming, she didn't think much of her sister who had committed a deadly sin and figured that Jan Lems who was one year older than her own father, was an old buck that wanted a green leaf. One day when Tryntje was visiting Ko she said: "It really was something with Ploon that she crawled in bed with an old man and had an illegitimate baby. Now, after all, the entire family benefits from it to get some food from the farm. The Lord sure has provided."

Jaap Dalm, who was conveniently and unrespectfully called "The Fat Dalm," for a reason that wasn't hard to guess with the weighing scales topping 300 pounds. Jaap Dalm was married to a sister of Adrie's father. He was no family of Jan Lems but they knew one another. When there was a birthday at the de Kievits place, Jaap Dalm would go to the birthday party and so would Aunt Ploon and Uncle Jan. That's the way they met each other, which would have been alright if Jaap Dalm had not hated farmers and had made some disrespectful remarks about them.

On several occasions when the family was together, Jaap Dalm was blabbering off his mouth. He did a lot of talking about those fu..... farmers while Ploon and Jan Lems were present. Jan and Ploon never said anything at the time but they would remember in due time. Due time was when Jaap Dalm ran out of food and had changed from 'Fat Dalm' to 'Skinny Dalm.'

When he got hungry enough, he suddenly remembered, "Oh yes, there was that cholera farmer Jan Lems on the Hordyk. (*In The Netherlands all kinds of plagues were used to describe a person they hated. Cholera farmer or Typhus farmer or other persons were used frequently.*) At one time he had said when Ploon was present that he had seen that cholera farmer standing on the dyke. All of a sudden, he didn't see him as a cholera farmer but as a relative who could help him out by selling him some food. Jan Lems had known him for a long time so he was sure he could sell him some wheat.

Jan Lems and Ploon knew him alright; they knew him so well that they remembered that in his eyes they were cholera farmers. When he asked Ploon if he could buy some wheat from them, Ploon said: "Why are you coming here to a bunch of cholera farmers and why do you want to buy food from those fu..... farmers? You seem to hate us so much."

Jaap Dalm tried to explain the unexplainable; he told her that he never really meant what he had said.

Ploon said: "It's too late for apologies, you don't get anything here. In your eyes we are cholera farmers and cholera farmers don't sell wheat to people like you."

"But I didn't mean it that way," Jaap tried once more.

Ploon cut him off, "Yes, you meant it but now the shoe is on the other foot, you have regrets. Buzz off and leave those cholera farmers alone."

All Jaap Dalm could do was going home and go to bed with a hungry stomach, thanks to his cursing of farmers in general. It seemed that the ghost of Farmer Beet had come back to haunt him and got him right over the barrel.

The Dark Ages.

A long time ago in our history, we had "The Dark Ages." It seemed that things came full circle and that the dark ages had come back. In the past, dark ages were meant figuratively. This time they were dark in all aspects. Not only did the people have to darken the city against air attacks, they also got the message that no electricity was going to be provided. Only urgently needed facilities, like hospitals and workshops that worked for the Germans, were going to be supplied with electricity. Everybody else had to do without.

For a long time electricity had been rationed and rations were low. They allowed only a few kilowatt hours, just enough to burn the lights in the house. Of course, the rations of electricity became lower all the time. To bolster the low rations of electricity, people bypassed the meter which wasn't hard to do if you knew how. Overhead wiring was easy to rig, you just bared the copper wires and with a cord and clamps you could bypass the meter. As with everything, you could get caught and again you never knew what they would do to you.

If you used more than you were allotted, they gave you a fine and if it happened again they cut off your electricity. This time electricity was cut out completely for everybody. It was dark at five o'clock during the winter. People tried anything to get light in their houses. Some people who were skilled workers took old generators from cars and sometimes from bikes. They made a windmill out of it and they had at least some light at night. Other less talented people had a bike with a light in their living room. They took turns to peddle the bike, to give the others a chance to do something. Usually they were reading the underground papers aloud so everybody could hear the news.

When you are a farmer you have always some things to barter. Jan Lems got a hold of some sunflower oil and when it got dark, the de Kievits came to his living room as usual. He put a little dish with the sunflower oil on the table, put a little floating wick in the centre and lit the wick. It was a very small flame which only spread very limited light. Adrie was the news broadcaster again to read the Underground bulletins. Everybody else was listening, hoping to hear some good news that this terrible war would soon be over.

While Adrie was reading the news bulletins from the Underground, his mother, aunt and sister did some handwork. Adrie's mother was forever knitting. She took the still good wool of old worn out socks and sweaters and made other socks and gloves out of it. Jan Lems was just sitting in his armchair listening to the news and after the news; he would open the atlas close to the little dancing flame on the sunflower oil. Everybody would look at the progress the Allies had made i.e. if there was any progress.

With the war going badly in Italy for the Germans, they withdrew their troops from Greece after they had scorched the earth. They had totally devastated anything that the Allies could possibly use. The beautiful harbors in Athens were completely demolished and many public buildings were blown up. All Dutch people envied the Greek people that they were finally rid of the Germans. When they heard that the Communists from Russia tried to take over and that a civil war had erupted between Communist people and people who didn't want to have anything to do with the Communists, they pitied the Greek people. They were rid of the Germans but peace had not been achieved.

At this stage of the war, very few things were available and if they were they were rationed. Jewish soap was distributed as well. They were little pieces of soap that floated on the water and there was hardly any foam. The story went that this soap had been made from Jews in Germany. The Germans gassed the Jews and made soap out of them.

With the dwindling rations of food, no coal, gas or electricity, the Dutch people became desperate. Facing starvation and cold, dark houses during the coming winter, everybody was on the go to secure some food before the winter would set in. People went with baby carriages from farm to farm to beg for food. Aunt Ploon, who had nothing to give away anymore, usually gave them a slice of bread. At least it was something. People wanted to buy food at any price but the farmers couldn't sell it. They were forced to deliver everything to the Germans.

There was a field of potatoes which was owned by Koos Vryland. He didn't dare to sell some of the potatoes to the hungry people out of fear of the Germans. When the people got hungrier and hungrier, they didn't take no for an answer anymore. Hundreds of people went to the field with a spade or a fork and dug up potatoes. When Koos Vryland found out what was going on, he went to the field and told the people to get lost because they were stealing. The people said: "We are not stealing potatoes, we are only digging them up and we'll pay you for the potatoes we take home."

Koos Vryland overlooked the situation; he knew how desperate the people were and figured that it was no use to try to stop them. He could have gone to the German authorities to force the people off his potato field but those were his own people who were very hungry. He decided to let the people dig up their own potatoes and to charge them for the potatoes they were taking. It was a large field of potatoes and before he knew it there were at least a hundred people digging potatoes. Within no time at all the last potato was taken. He went to the German authorities to report that all his potatoes had been stolen.

The Germans had a lot of other problems to solve, which were associated with the safety of the Germans, so little was done about it. They probably figured to cut the rations of the Dutch people some more to make up for it.

One of the problems the Germans were facing was that people were sitting in cold houses and had cut down most of the trees that could be stolen. At that stage it didn't stop at cutting trees, the desperate people cut down the telephone posts, which the Germans had erected in the polders which weren't inundated. Rommel had figured that it was hard to drop airborne divisions on a field if there are a lot of telephone posts.

During the darkness of the night, people went to saw down the telephone poles for wood and heat in their houses. Of course, the Germans weren't very happy when they noticed that the telephone poles were disappearing. They knew how to handle troubles and made the Dutch people responsible for it.

All eligible men who were still around in The Netherlands and were living around the fields where the telephone poles had disappeared, were notified that they had telephone pole watch duty. A German corporal came to tell them what duty they had. They had to report to the German Command Post for duty every night and were assigned a certain time that they had to patrol the field. They only had to patrol one hour every night. The involuntary watchmen were responsible for seeing that no poles disappeared during their watches. If a pole disappeared during that time they were in trouble.

Of course, there were many telephone poles on a field. It was hard to tell when it was completely dark, if there were poles missing when you started your watch duty. There were no lanterns to take along for the watchmen so how could they see anything. (*The only lanterns there were in those days were oil lamps and carbide lanterns. Lanterns with batteries were introduced during the war, but were only available to the Germans.*)

Arie had no watch duty; he was underground and non-existent to the Germans. Piet Fisher was a neighbor when the de Kievits were living at the farm. He had to go four times a week on watch duty for an hour. At one time he was walking in the dark with two other watchmen. When they heard a sawing noise they went to investigate and found two guys sawing one of the telephone poles. He said to the wood thieves: "What the hell are you doing there?"

One of the thieves answered: "We are stealing wood to heat our house; I have three young children and a baby who are freezing. Tonight I'm going to come home with wood whether you like it or not. So what are you going to do about it?"

Piet had a problem on his hand. The Depression years had made people frugal and the following war had made them hard. He wasn't going to fight with the two guys and wasn't going to turn them in either. "They are your own people," Piet said, "and they aren't really stealing, they are fighting for their family to ensure that they don't freeze. The guy was right, what was I going to do about it?"

When the night had passed, the Germans checked the telephone poles and found that there were two poles missing. They questioned the patrols in vain; they couldn't determine which shift had lost the poles. All the people who had been on watch duty that night were held responsible. The Germans told them where they could get telephone poles and gave them two days to replace the poles. With horse and wagon, the people had to pick up the two poles that had been lost during the night. Once they had the poles at their places, they had to dig a couple of holes by hand and erect them. That wasn't bad after all; it could have been a lot worse.

Piet Fisher had some terrible times. First he lost two telephone poles, next he had to pick up and replace the poles. Then one night when he came home after his watch duty, he was very hungry and looked in the cupboard for something to eat. When he saw a dish with porridge he ate it all. The next morning his wife asked him: "What happened to my curtains that were in that dish?"

Piet said: "What do you mean by curtains in that dish, I thought it was a dish of porridge and ate it."

His wife said: "You stupid ass, you ate my curtains." *(This might sound like some kind of a joke but it wasn't. During the war there was a shortage of linen and other fibres. Curtains were made out of paper and if you had to clean them, you had to soak them very carefully lest they dissolve. This is exactly what happened and to a hungry guy it looked like a dish of porridge.)*

Before the war started the Dutch press had published horror stories about Russia. All kinds of stories, how the people were living in fear of the knock on the door during the night which could mean Siberia. When the Germans invaded Russia the Dutch people heard the same stories from the Germans. Eventually, with all those Dutch people underground, the German Gestapo now checked houses with a knock on the door in the middle of the night.

A lot of Dutch people had a knock on their door during the night. When there was such a knock, nobody knew what would be next. One could be arrested or shot; it was a time of uncertainty. With the end of the war in sight and the Germans desperate, it wasn't sure for anybody that he or she would survive the war.

The Gestapo was looking for Jews in hiding, striking railway workers, underground workers and people like Arie who were considered to be deserters by the Germans. Jan Lems could have been shot for harbouring deserter Arie.

One night there was a knock on the door in the middle of the night.

When Jan Lems opened the door, very luckily it wasn't the Gestapo to arrest somebody, but it was Germans though. Most of the time the Germans were looking for bikes, handcarts and even baby carriages to transport their weapons. Whenever they found something that they could use they took it. They even took paintings and valuable books from people to transport to Germany.

During the middle of the night there were lots of German troop transports. It was unsafe for the Germans to move during daylight hours with the Allies in control of the air. In the day time, British patrol planes were shooting at German columns all the time. One night a German column had reached its destination. They woke up Jan Lems demanding a sleeping place. Jan Lems said they could sleep in the hay. The German sergeant said, they had girl friends with them and they weren't going to sleep in the hay, they wanted beds.

Jan Lems said: "There aren't any beds I can give you."

Of course, the Germans didn't believe him and demanded that they had to check the farm. Downstairs was only one bed where he was sleeping with his wife and there was a crib for his little daughter. They wanted to check the loft too. When they saw the three beds where the de Kievits were sleeping in, they told Jan Lems to throw the people out because they wanted to sleep in those beds with their girl friends.

Jan Lems argued that he couldn't throw people out of their bed but the Germans insisted. Luckily some unexpected help arrived. With all the noise the Germans had made everybody woke up. Willie had a bad cold and was coughing very bad when she woke up. Jan Lems had an idea, he said: "Those people are very sick, the girl has tuberculosis and the other people are coughing too, you can't throw sick people out of their bed."

The German sergeant said: "You are right, those people can stay in their bed; we don't want to sleep in their bed and get sick, too."

On November 4 there was great news that the Allied forces had finally taken Antwerp. The Germans had defended this very important harbor city with all the might they had left. Antwerp could be valuable for Allied shipping; it could handle 40,000 ton per day. It had to be defended at all cost Hitler had said. When it finally fell to Allied hands hardly damaged, Hitler ordered an attack on Antwerp with V2's. The V2's were shot from a site close to Rotterdam, which attracted Allied bombers to destroy the launching pad.

It was very much evident that the power of the Axis was waning. Industry couldn't feed the armies with proper armament and they would lose their power as Popeye would lose his power if he ran out of spinach.

Some important news for the de Kievits was received with mixed feelings. During summer, the Rotterdam Polder Works had put a dyke around the de Kievit's and Immerzeel's properties. They still had a lot to say about the use of electricity and had managed to pump the water out of the houses. While nobody had electricity anymore, Rotterdam Polder Works still pumped with an electric pump. Rain water and water that leaked through the dyke had to be pumped out daily to keep the houses dry.

With the houses not in the water anymore, it could be an attraction for desperate people to go in there and take doors and other wood out to use for heating their house. In many houses people kept one small room intact to heat and the other walls and doors were broken out for firewood. Many houses started to collapse when people took support walls and beams out. Nobody cared, when you are cold you don't think about little details like that.

Arie wasn't happy with this kind of help, he said: "Why don't they leave things alone, we were alright at the farm. Now, we are forced to move back into the house or people will demolish it. And if fighting comes to The Netherlands, the Germans could blow up the dyke and we'll be in the water again."

And so, in the beginning of December the de Kievit's moved back into their house. There had been four feet of water in the house and everything was muddy. It took some doing before it was liveable again, especially since there were no cleaning supplies available anymore. Most of the cleaning had to be done with brush, broom and muscle power. Adrie didn't like it at all, he had been happy at the farm and he missed his uncle.

They had barely moved back into the house when trouble started. The electricity which drove the pump was cut and the electric pump was replaced with a hand pump. When Adrie's father raised hell about the situation, the polder management said: "The dyke protects three houses, if you want to do the pumping, we'll pay you for it at the going labor rate of 60 cents per hour. Your son is welcome to work to, also for sixty cents per hour. Just keep track of your and your son's hours and hand in your time sheets once a week."

Arie wasn't all that happy with money, there was very little you could buy with it anyway. The stores were empty and all the people got for rations was 'one loaf of bread, one pound of potatoes and two pounds of sugar beets per person per week.'

Nothing else was available, no milk, sugar, cheese or meat. People made sugar syrup and candy from the sugar beets and the remaining pulp was used to mix with the potatoes and vegetables if there were any. Ko mixed the beet pulp with some flour and made pancakes out of it. She did that to make the flour last longer. Nothing that was edible was wasted. The de Kievits had still some hoarded food supply which was stretched to the limit. Nobody knew how long this situation was going to last and if there would be food at all during the coming winter.

Normally, people never worried about sugar beets. The farmers grew them and when they were harvested in fall, they transported them to the sugar plant where the sugar was extracted for consumption. The remaining pulp was shipped back to the farmers to feed the cattle and horses.

Many people in the cities saw sugar beets for the first time in their lives. Everybody was involved in the sugar and candy making business. The sugar wasn't crystallized, actually it was not sugar at all, it was only molasses. If you wanted to make something sweet you just put a spoonful of molasses in it. Nobody cared, it was sweet and that's all that counted. People sliced the beets in very fine cubes and cooked the beets in water till the sugar was out of the beets. The water was boiled until enough was evaporated so that only molasses was left.

The next step was to make candy out of the molasses. Some more water had to be evaporated to do that. When enough water had been evaporated the molasses got heavy. That's where the water evaporation had to stop or the candy would burn. The thick heavy molasses was poured into forms and when the molasses cooled down it was hard and one could call it candy, syrup candy. You could cut it in pieces of the size you wanted and eat it as candy.

Ko had still some Pitto surrogate coffee left. She made a cup of coffee and put a spoon of molasses in it to make it sweet. It was delicious. There was even a candy, made from sugar beets, with the coffee. Everybody appreciated things that never had been attractive before. The battle was survival and everybody knew it.

One loaf of bread per week was the ration for everybody. It was very poor bread, even if you cut it with a sharp knife; it would stick to your knife as shit sticks to an Indian blanket. In the beginning bread was made from a mix of wheat flour and flour that was obtained from grinding bones. The Germans had received an order that all bones had to be delivered to a depot; they would grind them and make aeroplane glue out of them. Other substitutes had to be found to mix in with the flour for the bread. Straw was the new substitute; it was ground very fine and mixed with the little flour there was.

The tobacco plant is not endemic to Europe. Before Columbus discovered America nobody in Europe knew about tobacco. Once Columbus showed the European people how to smoke, some countries started to grow their own tobacco. There is very little agricultural land in The Netherlands; they can't even grow enough wheat for their densely populated country. Therefore most of the farmers went for growing wheat and for pastures to get dairy products. Some other agricultural land was used to grow tulips and other flowers. Nobody was interested in growing tobacco.

When the war started it was a disaster for smokers; all of a sudden there was rationing of tobacco. The tobacco rations were 20 cigarettes per week per man. Women weren't considered to be smoking in those days; they would receive candy rations instead. The tobacco rations were cut by 50% and after that they were discontinued. Whatever tobacco there was went to the German Army.

At first people saved the butts of their cigarettes and rolled cigarettes from the butts. After that they rolled cigarettes from the butts of the cigarettes that had been rolled from butts. Finally there were no butts anymore; the last butt had been smoked.

The climate is alright for growing tobacco in The Netherlands and soon people who had a garden started to grow their own tobacco. It was a lot of work, the tobacco had to be dried, cut and fermented for taste. Nobody was deterred by all the work that had to be done; if you wanted to smoke, work didn't bother you. Of course growing your own tobacco didn't mean that you were going to smoke. Anything that was outside overnight could disappear. There were other desperate smokers who had nothing to smoke. They could easily steal your tobacco overnight. Nobody could sit outside during the night to watch the tobacco plants. You were never sure that you were going to smoke until you had the tobacco in your pipe.

Inventions were limitless during the war; somebody came out with surrogate tobacco. The surrogate cigarettes were called 'Blazertjes' (Little Blowers). They looked like little cigarillos but smoking them was by no means the same. As long as you didn't inhale the smoke it wasn't too bad. If you dared to inhale you would choke and cough your lungs out. They probably were made from hay or some other crap. The Dutch people called the surrogate tobacco 'Fleur the mattress' (Aroma from an Old Mattress), indicating that it was made from old pissy mattresses. It sure tasted like it.

Of course there was lots of black market tobacco available at a price. The black market was illegal for seller and buyer, if you were caught you would be arrested and after that it was anybody's guess what the Germans would do to you. Most of the black market tobacco was Belgian tobacco that was bought by the Dutch people. People thought that Belgian tobacco was good smoking until they got sick. When the authorities investigated, they found out that the Belgians used horse piss to ferment the tobacco, probably for lack of something else. When that practise became known, a lot of people switched to the home made tobacco of The Netherlands.

At the beginning of 1944, people were still thinking about smoking and grew some tobacco. Now with winter approaching, few people thought about smoking tobacco, everybody got his mind on eating food. It was going to be a long winter before anything would grow on the land again. If you can't buy food, you can try stealing. The fear of hunger was so deeply rooted that no law by Government or Bible could prevent the people from stealing. Nobody wanted to work for money anymore; you just can't eat money and can't survive on it. The society as it was known before the war had ended; it had been replaced with a straight barter society. If you had nothing to barter you were shit up the creek without a paddle. It was impossible to survive on your rations which meant that you had to have other sources to get food from.

Ice cream had disappeared for a long time; it was replaced by fluffed cream which was made from sugar beet water. There wasn't much in it but when you are hungry you eat anything. At one time Adrie had bought a paper cup of cream for twenty five cent; he left the store eating his cream. He only had taken one lick when a boy ran past him and snatched it out of his hand. Adrie thought about chasing the boy, but on second thought, it wasn't likely he was going to retrieve his cream cup. The boy must have been very hungry so let it be. There was a lesson to be learned; the next time he bought cream he ate it inside the store.

The de Kievits were lucky to secure some food from the farm and other sources. It was a struggle to keep food on the table but they were never hungry. Many hungry people would get malnutrition and many of those unfortunate people died during the hunger winter. People like the de Kievits also developed symptoms from lack of nutritious food. They filled their stomach mostly with inferior food. Adrie and Willie started to develop big lumps in their necks. They became as big as a tennis ball and then they would burst open. The doctor said: "Young bodies need vitamins and nutritious food to develop and if you don't have that you'll develop those lumps. The puss that comes out of those lumps is an unhealthy substance which is pushed out by your body."

Willie was a seamstress; she could make dresses and other clothes. At that stage of the war there was no supply of clothes or material to make clothes from. All that was left to do for a seamstress was to repair old clothes or make something else out of old clothes. That is, if you had hoarded some thread, which was an item that was also taken off the market. If you hadn't hoarded thread you couldn't even sew a button on your shirt or coat. Willie still had some thread and there were still people asking for her services. She would work an afternoon and get a free meal out of it. Nothing else. But that was good; it was one more meal she didn't have to eat at home.

Good or not, she decided that she could do better and went asking at farms around if they needed somebody to work. She made a deal with Huib Zwaal; his wife needed somebody to help her in the household work. When he heard that she was a seamstress she was hired. There were two small children and there are always a lot of chores to do at a farm. She worked six days a week and was free on Sunday. Huib Zwaal didn't want her to work for just food, he paid her some money and for the rest she would eat at the farm. When she was finished on Saturday, he gave her a loaf of home made bread and some potatoes to take home for Sunday. That made up for her father who didn't have ration coupons when he was underground. Underground or not, the man still had to eat.

People were telling Willie that she was working for a silly, nutty guy. Huib Zwaal was a stupid bugger who talked crazy. Willie didn't care what people said, she had a job and was fed, what else did she want?

Ko tried also to do work for food. She found an old man by the name of Tilleman who needed somebody to clean the house twice a week. He was willing to feed her those two days when she worked there. Nobody knew where he got the food from and nobody cared either. Mr. Tilleman had been a teacher at the Seamen Officers School. Since he was well to do he could have bought food on the black market.

When she had been working at Mr. Tilleman's place for a month, he had two male guests staying with him. He introduced them to her and said: "Those are two friends of mine; their names are Ted and Carl. They lost their house in a bombing raid in Rotterdam and are going to stay with me for a while."

Ko didn't doubt him at all; there were many people who had lost their house that way when military targets were attacked. Sometimes the bombs missed the target and hit civilian houses.

One day she was working all alone in the house, she hadn't seen the guests and Mr. Tilleman had gone out. When the doorbell rang she opened the door. There was a man out of breath shouting: "Are Ted and Carl gone?"

She answered: "When I came this morning they weren't here."

The man said: "There is a search of the house coming up! Clean up their room so that it isn't noticeable that anybody has stayed here." Then the man left in a hurry.

Ko got busy taking the clothes that were left out of the room and made it look like the room hadn't been occupied for a long time. When she came into the bathroom she saw some shaving equipment. Mr. Tilleman with a beard and moustache wouldn't use that kind of equipment. She took it all out of the bathroom and put it in a box which she put on a shelf. She even cleaned the furniture and door posts to make sure there were no fingerprints of the guests.

Two Germans came in the afternoon. They asked for the owner of the house. She said: "I'm just working here. When I came this morning, he wasn't in and I don't know when he will return."

One of the Germans said: "We have to search the house."

"Go right ahead," Ko said and in order to do something, she went back to work. She was very nervous about the situation; you never knew what could happen in a situation like this. After the Germans had searched every room they asked: "How many people are staying in this house?"

"Only Mr. Tilleman," she said. "He is a widower."

One German said to the other: "No use to ask her questions, she doesn't know anything."

When Mr. Tilleman didn't return, Ko thought that somebody had tipped him off about the coming house search. As soon as she had finished her work, she locked the house and went home. At night she said to Adrie: "I think I know where Mr. Tilleman is. He is always going around with Doctor Meerkerk. And if he isn't there Dr. Meerkerk will know where he is."

Adrie said: "You better be careful, they didn't search the house without a reason."

When Ko came to Dr. Meerkerk's house, the girl who did the medicines for him opened the door. Ko asked: "Is Mr. Tilleman here?"

"No, there is nobody here," the girl answered.

Dr. Meerkerk came to see who was at the door and said to the girl: "It's alright; she works for Mr. Tilleman and can be trusted."

He said to Ko: "Come in and I'll get Mr. Tilleman for you."

Mr. Tilleman was glad that everything had been cleaned up and said; "I know tomorrow is not your usual day of work but can you check the house and see if everything is alright."

(Some stories have a happy ending and this is one of them. Ko checked the house for a few days and luckily the Germans didn't come back. Mr. Tilleman moved back into his house and nothing happened to him. He lived to celebrate VE Day. Apparently, the Germans had received a tip that Underground workers were harbored at his address. However, another tip was received by the Underground workers that a German raid was coming. The workers left in time before the raid came. Mr. Tilleman had been intercepted by some friends when he was on his way home. He was told that there was trouble and moved in with his friend Dr. Meerkerk.)

There was a little bus company three houses away from Adrie. Before the war the three busses they had were used for a host of different things. The schools had a once a year school trip and there were excursion trips. During the war the Germans wouldn't allow pleasure trips that consumed gas. The busses were solely used for workmen transportation. Mr. Ringelberg was the owner and needed some help to get the wood gas generators cleaned of soot. He knew that Adrie was studying motor mechanics, and asked Adrie if he could help him. Ringelberg said that he couldn't give food for his work; instead he would take Adrie to the Island Hoeksewaard. On Saturday afternoon, he had to pick up workmen and take them back to Rotterdam. Adrie got paid some money and for that money he could buy food on the island. Who cares that it was a dirty job, anytime that food beckoned, it was a deal.

There was a slight problem. The island was off limits to all people except the ones that were living there and the ones who were working on the island. The Barendrecht Bridge was the only access to the island. Everybody was stopped at the entrance of the bridge by the German patrol and turned back.

Around Rotterdam and other big cities, the farmers didn't have any food to sell anymore. Still there were hordes of people on the way to find food; they didn't care how far they had to walk. For that reason the Germans had closed off the island to prevent people from the city getting to the island in order to buy or to steal food. They wanted to keep the food of the island for their own use.

Anybody living on the island could cross the bridge to get off the island. They had to have proper documentation for their return. It was no problem to get Adrie on the island with the bus. Ringelberg crossed the bridge every day with his bus. In the beginning, the Germans stopped the bus and searched it. When he came to the island to pick up people the bus was empty when he crossed. After the Germans had seen the empty bus a dozen of times, they didn't bother anymore; it was just an empty bus they thought.

The German control was right, it was just an empty bus but not on that Saturday afternoon. When they came close to the bridge, Adrie moved to the back of the bus and was lying on the floor between the benches. For the German patrol it still looked like an empty bus. Ringelberg slowed down when he reached the patrol. The watchman had to open the gate to let the bus through. When he saw the seemingly empty bus he opened the gate right away. When the bus slowed down for the control, Adrie wondered if he would get away with this illegal crossing.

No sweat, everything went as planned. As soon as the crossing was made, Adrie could sit in the front of the bus again. There were about twenty minutes left before the return trip would start. It gave Adrie time to buy potatoes, some beans and cabbages from the farmers. The de Kievits had always been growing most of their own potatoes and vegetables but now their garden was inundated they had nothing. There was no problem with the trip back. The bus was leaving the island which was alright.

NO FREELOADERS PLEASE.

With all the problems that people had to keep food on the table, visitors weren't welcome to stay for supper or lunch. Everybody was thinking about his own stomach and didn't want to share with others, not even when it was family. There are always some people who will try to stay for supper, welcome or not. The stepfather of Arie was known as Father Penning. When his father died his mother had remarried to this greedy man who knew exactly his rights and the law. When a woman marries the second time there is the problem of the inheritance. In those days the law was that the inheritance had to be divided and that the man got half plus a child's share. So he got most of it. After Arie's mother died, Father Penning still kept visiting. He was no blood relative; he only had been married to Arie's mother.

Father Penning was retired, which gave him plenty of time for the 45 minutes bike ride to the de Kievits. He started to come frequently for visits and always around four o' clock in the afternoon. The de Kievits were eating at five and he made sure he was there. As soon as supper was over, he would say: "I should get moving to be home before dark."

It's difficult to say to a relative: "We are going to eat and you get nothing."

The first time that he visited, nobody objected that he stayed for supper. When he came steady as clockwork, once a week, Ko said: "We'll have to tell him to bring his own food with him when he visits us."

The next time that he came, he ate with the family as always. After supper when he was ready to leave, Ko said: "Say Father Penning, we are very short of food, when you come again you'll have to bring your own."

He made all kinds of apologies stating: "I had no idea that you were short of food, it wasn't the idea at all to eat at your place while you are short."

When he came again a week later, he had brought his own food. He had two slices of bread in a paper bag which he ate at supper time. The de Kievits were eating mashed potatoes with lettuce and he was looking with hungry eyes at the food. After he had finished the two thin slices of bread, he said: "Actually I'm still hungry."

"Well, the next time you come you'll have to bring more food with you," Ko replied.

"I certainly will," he said and left in a hell of a hurry after supper.

"What a nerve," Ko said, "he was just trying to get something from us in spite of what I told him."

Now there was nothing to be gained by visiting Ko, he never came again.

However, on one occasion when he had to visit his sister, he asked Arie to come along for the ride. When Arie picked him up, he was making a couple of sandwiches for himself to take along. He asked if Arie had also sandwiches with him and when he said that he hadn't, Father Penning didn't offer even one sandwich after he had eaten so many times at Arie's place. Arie hadn't been planning to stay for supper at his sister's place in the first place but was invited with Father Penning to stay for supper. Father Penning said nothing about the food he had with him and enjoyed another free meal.

From Blitzkrieg to Snail Krieg.

Adrie had lost his horseback ride to the Tech. The milkman said: "There are only rations left for little babies and I can't even earn the salt for the porridge." Besides, the Germans had confiscated his horse. Slowly but surely the Germans were squeezed to the limits and army trucks were now all running on wood gas, just like the bus used to. The busses weren't running anymore, they also had been taken by the Germans for troop transports. More and more horses and farmers wagons were taken from the farmers to replace the trucks lost in bombing raids. The former German Blitzkrieg Army was now moving at a snail's pace.

When the war came to The Netherlands, everything was motorized, the Germans moved fast in their blitzkrieg. They were well prepared and well trained; the Germans had the best army in the world. Before the war started, Hitler had studied why they had lost the First World War and had come to the conclusion that a long trench warfare was the cause of losing the war. This time he wasn't going to have trench warfare.

He was going to have a Blitz Krieg with sudden swift and large scale warfare intended to win a quick victory. All those overwhelming attacks brought confusion among the defenders. Bombing the civilian population brought terror and was aimed for quick surrender. Poland, Norway, Denmark, The Netherlands, Belgium and France, went under with the German blitzkrieg. A combination of tanks, infantry with good air support, bombardments and shellings brought all of Western and Eastern Europe under Nazi control.

Finally, the German blitzkrieg had petered out when the Allies applied the choke hold. Hitler's army had seen quite a change, now they were moving trucks with wood gas generators. The army trucks had a limited supply of wood. When the truck ran out of wood gas, the driver had to chop down a tree and cut it up in sizable pieces to shove it into the generator. The wood was wet and green most of the time, which meant a lot of smoke but no gas. There was quite a delay before the army truck was moving again.

To top it off, the Underground was throwing shingle nails on the highway to slow down the German Army. At this stage of the war only doctors and the Germans were driving a car. Other cars and motor bikes were hidden by the owners lest the Germans would take them. Doctors were usually driving in the cities and stayed away from the highways. The only ones to get flat tires were the Germans. There was no blitzkrieg anymore, just a snail krieg.

There was always a lot of homework to do when Adrie went to the Tech. As always, he was sitting at the table which was shoved against the window. That way he had plenty of light to make drawings and do his calculations. All of a sudden he heard half a dozen planes flying low over the house. They opened up their machine guns when they were over the house. The English gunners were aiming for a German train which had left Rotterdam. It came so suddenly that there was little time to get to a safer place. Adrie didn't hesitate a second, he took a dive underneath the table for protection. He was barely underneath the table when a few heavy explosions occurred which blew all the windows out of the house. The glass of the broken window, where Adrie had been sitting, was lying on top of the table. If he hadn't taken his dive underneath the table he could have been seriously cut by the glass.

When everything was peaceful and quiet again, Adrie went outside to check what had happened. The English bombers had aimed for the train alright but they had missed. They had tried to shoot the steam kettle of the train full of holes and had thrown a few bombs at the moving train. After the planes were gone the train continued its journey. The houses on the other side of the railway had taken the brunt of the exploding bombs, and were heavily damaged.

For bombing targets the Allies used the Nordon bomb sight. The Americans bragged that they could hit a barrel of pickles with the Nordon bomb sight during day light hours and the British claimed that they could hit a barrel of pickles at night, using the Nordon bomb sight in combination with radar. Why could they hit a barrel of pickles and not a train was the question?

Luckily there was still glass available to replace the windows. No sooner were the windows replaced when another attack on a train took place. Adrie was sitting in front of the window again and when he heard the planes coming, he took a dive under the table as he had done before. He was sitting more underneath the table than at the table. All the windows were shattered again. The people on the other side of the railroad had heavy damage again and were wounded this time. They decided to move elsewhere before they would get killed. This time the train didn't move anymore, the steam kettle was full of holes and three bombs had hit the train.

One more train was hit when it left Rotterdam. The R.A.F. controlled the sky and was patrolling all the time. Even German troop movements were attacked in the day time. The highway from Rotterdam to Dordrecht was cleared by the R.A.F. every day. Fighters would just land on the highway, taxi some distance and take off again. As there were no German fighters in The Netherlands anymore, the Germans couldn't do anything about it.

There were several occasions that houses were hit by bombs when military targets were missed. Then one day, the British hit a wing of the Southern Hospital. German propaganda kicked in and called it British brutality to bomb hospitals, which were clearly marked with giant red crosses. Troop transportation during the daylight hours was murder for the Germans. Consequently they quit moving troops and trains during the daylight hours. Everything was now moved during the night.

When the oil supplies dwindled, it had a dramatic effect on the German war power. Planes weren't flying, tanks stood still and at last there wasn't even gasoline for the limousines to transport the German big shots. On a moonlit night the Germans were moving a lot of troops and equipment over the street. Adrie woke up when he heard horses neighing and walking on the street. When he got out of his bed, his mother was sitting behind the drapes of the living room watching what was going on. Adrie joined her to see for himself. There were no trucks anymore, just horses and wagons. Most of the Germans were walking and others had bikes which they had stolen from the Dutch citizens. There were also a lot of baby carriages in use to transport equipment.

Adrie's mother said: "The once proud German army that came fully motorised with tanks and trucks has now to resort to horses, wagons, stolen bikes and baby carriages."

"It looks like it's the end of the line for the Germans," Adrie replied. "They look more like spiritless sheep being led to the slaughter."

All of a sudden a German soldier stopped and turned to the window where Adrie and his mother were watching. Adrie's mother closed the drapes fast and they both left the window in a hurry. You never could tell what he might do, he could shoot at you if he didn't like that you were watching. Whenever they heard troop transports after this incident, they just stayed in bed.

The Hunger Winter.

After taking big losses in Russia, Africa and Italy, the Germans were fighting for survival. In spite of their hopeless position, their morale never diminished. They still figured that Hitler would come up with a secret weapon that would win the war for them.

The Germans had been fighting a very long war for over five years. At this stage, all of Europe was running out of everything. Nobody could have figured that the war was going to last that long. Even the people in Germany were now cold and hungry. The Germans knew a way to remedy that problem in the heimat. They simply stole more food from the countries they had occupied. Moreover, they demanded that every family must give two blankets for the cold people in Germany, plus a complete outfit of men's and lady's clothes. A horse and wagon came to collect; if you gave the requested items the Germans put a sticker on your door. If you didn't have a sticker on your door, the Germans came back and took a lot more.

Everything seemed to end in that hunger winter. The Underground had to cut down on news bulletins as well and had a bulletin every second day now. With no newspaper and no radio it was the only news people had. And only the people who had connections with the Underground would receive a news bulletin. One had to be very careful with those Underground newspapers, if you were caught with them on you or in your house, you were arrested. That's the way the Germans found out sometimes who was printing those papers. After your arrest you were questioned as to where you got the papers. If you ever had illusions that you could fool the Germans you had it coming. The Germans could be very persuasive; they went as far as torturing the people to get information.

St. Nicholas Day on December 5th was on hold. It was a memorable day in The Netherlands when people exchanged gifts with one another and it was a big day for the kids. There was nothing to celebrate and certainly there were no gifts at this stage of the war. All the Dutch people were at a very low ebb of life and the only present possible was food on the table.

Being very inventive was also a way to survive. People cooked 'Stinging Nettles,' the recipe was simple, you cooked them in water. It looked like spinach but tasted quite different. Even grass was cooked to have something to eat. That was in summer but when winter came, the fields were covered with two feet of snow; and you couldn't even find nettles or grass to cook for food. During winter people baked bread from tree bark, they stole a tree and used the wood to heat their house and baked their tree bark bread.

People were starving and desperate. They were all thinner than Gandhi. (Gandhi was the President in India and when he didn't get his way he went on hunger strikes. Consequently he was just skin over bone.) Many hungry people were foraging for food in a bare winter landscape; they were walking the streets with a gunny bag and took home whatever they found on the garbage dump.

All services had been discontinued because of lack of transportation. There was no garbage collection anymore and people started to dump their garbage on the street corners. People who weren't able to get additional food to supplement their meagre rations were very hungry. They would search the piles of garbage to see if there was anything edible in them. If you had a cabbage or a head of lettuce, you took some dead or half rotten leaves off and threw them on the pile of garbage in the street. Those half rotten leaves would disappear within the next five minutes. Somebody would comb the garbage and put them in a gunny bag to cook them at home.

Every cat and dog had been consumed and people caught birds and mice to eat. Grass, nettles and everything else green had been eaten. Some people would scout in the day time for food to steal during the night. They broke into stores and houses if they thought there was something to eat.

To keep the houses warm without coal was a job and a half. People cut down trees, hedges, gates and everything that possibly would burn. They even took some walls out of their house and the houses were nearly collapsing.

The Germans were in the same boat, they were taking the church bells for copper and even from buildings they took any metal to make bombs and shells. People were told to take all the copper they had to a depot.

The de Kievits were anxiously waiting for the news bulletin and hoped to read that the war would soon be over. December 16th brought the opposite news that the war would last longer. There was a German counter offensive in the West; it was 'The Battle of the Bulge.' The Germans boasted that they would drive the Allied forces back into the sea at Antwerp.

It was a master plan designed by Hitler and his planning General Yodel. Logistics was the weak point of the Allies, if the Germans could retake Antwerp, Allied supplies would be in jeopardy. The attack took place in the worst possible weather to prevent the Americans from launching a counter attack with the support of their Air Force.

Small groups of English speaking German commandoes in American uniforms were dropped behind the American lines. That was quite successful in the beginning until the Americans figured out what the Germans were doing. Those were the condemned soldiers; if they didn't obey their orders they would be shot by a German firing squad and obeying the orders meant to go against the rules of the Geneva Convention which stipulates that if soldiers wear the uniform of the enemy, they can be shot without a trial.

December 18th brought some more bad news. The Germans had managed to advance 20 miles in two days, the town of Bastogne was completely encircled and could fall into German hands any minute. There was also a little epistle about the U.S. commander Mc. Auliffe who was approached by the Germans to surrender. He refused and his reply was "Nuts." That was heroic in his deplorable position. Adrie didn't get it at all, he said: "Are those damned Germans ever going to run out of steam?

People in The Netherlands were starving and had lost their faith. They asked the question: 'On whose side is the Lord?' That always had been a leading question during the war. Hitler always was bragging that His Almighty had saved him again so he could rule the German people and the world. When two Christian warring nations both pray to the Lord and ask for victory, who is going to get it and on whose side is the Lord? Both countries think they are right. Unfortunately they can't both be right.

General Patton was equally disgusted with the German successes and ordered his Chaplin to write a prayer for him that he could use when his counter attack took place because he wanted His Almighty on his side. When his troops got ready for the counter attack he prayed for victory so that righteousness would return to Europe.

General Patton counter attacked on December 19th without the support of his snow bound planes. However, on December 23rd the fog miraculously lifted and was replaced by sunshine. Immediately, 2000 bombers escorted by 900 fighters attacked the German positions and food and ammunition supplies were dropped over Bastogne. On Boxing Day December 26th, the siege of Bastogne was lifted and the Germans withdrew. It took till January 30th, about six weeks after the attack had started, to regain the positions the Allies had before the Germans had attacked.

It had been a costly battle for the Allies with a loss of 77,000 men, 705 tanks and 600 aircaft. For the Germans it was costly as well, they had lost their last reserves 120,000 men, 325 tanks and 320 aeroplanes in their quest to drive the Allies back into the ocean.

The Battle of the Bulge had far reaching consequences. When the Allies liberated the countries, they rounded up the traitors and put them in jail. With the Battle of the Bulge, as soon as the Germans were re-taking some of the lost ground they let the traitors out of jail and locked up the Underground workers. The Underground workers were freed again after the Allies re-conquered lost territory.

Everybody was disappointed with the turn of the war but kept hoping for better news. It seemed that the Allies were making headway again; the

French troops had reached the Rhine. They now attacked Germany's West Wall of the defence system. It was the Siegfried Line which now came under attack. During the war, the Germans broadcast an entertaining program on Sunday afternoon. They would always sing "Why don't we hang the laundry on the Siegfried Line." The soldiers that had reached the Siegfried Line had a lot of fun in doing just that.

With no coal supply at all, the de Kievits were down to burning just wood. For a long time they had burned coal with peat and wood with peat. Now the peat was gone, the wood supply went pretty fast. Adrie had gone quite often to the railway to collect the pieces of coal which had fallen off the locomotives. In the beginning there was quite a bit of coal but other people walked the railway too for coal. You just had to be lucky that a train had gone by and had lost some coal.

In spite of that, one day he decided to test his luck and went to walk the railway. Actually, it was forbidden to walk on the railway. It wasn't only dangerous; the Germans didn't want anybody on the railway, period. They were afraid of sabotage. Several times the Underground had blown up railways.

Adrie had walked for twenty minutes on the railway and had only five small pieces of coal. If the situation didn't change fast, they would be sitting in the cold. There must be another way to get fuel for the stove, he thought.

While he was thinking about other supplies, he hadn't noticed the German patrol which was riding on the railway. They had a flatbed car which was moved by hand. There was a train coming and the Germans were checking if the railway was safe for the train and that it wouldn't be driving over a mine. When Adrie heard some noise behind him he saw the German patrol. It was too late to run away, you can't outrun a bullet, he thought.

A German fieldwebel (sergeant) jumped off the car, his gun pointing at Adrie. He shouted: "Was machen sie dahr?" (What are you doing there?)

Adrie answered: "I am collecting coal for our stove, the house is cold and my mother is sick." It was a lie that his mother was sick but he had had a good learning school. His uncle told the Germans that the people in the beds were sick and they left.

"How much coal did you find?" the fieldwebel enquired.

Adrie answered: "Hardly anything," and he showed him the five small pieces of coal. In the meantime the train had arrived at the spot and was waiting for the Germans to clear the railway.

The fieldwebel said to the machinist: "Throw some coal down from the locomotive for this cold boy."

The machinist dropped a few big pieces off the locomotive and the fieldwebel said: "Here is coal, fill your bag, go home and light the stove for your krank (sick) mother."

Adrie got busy and the Germans left. He waved at the Germans and they waved back to him. Those were the good Germans Adrie thought. When he came home with his bag full of coal, his mother couldn't believe it, she asked: "Where did you steal all that coal?"

When he told her that he didn't have to steal it because the Germans had given it to him, his mother said: "That was a good day."

To make things worse in this miserable war with no food and fuel supplies, the winter started early. It was snowing every day and the temperatures went down to 20 below. That was low for The Netherlands and also extremely cold with the very damp climate. It was a disaster. The house, which had been flooded with water up to the windows was very wet and wouldn't dry out during the winter.

Adrie and his sister were sleeping on the loft. His father had made a little room for his sister and Adrie inhibited the rest of the loft. When he went to bed, three foot long icicles were hanging from the beams. There was no insulation in the roof. The loft consisted of beams with planks nailed over them and then the roof tiles. It was almost as cold as outside, except there was no wind. With the moisture of the house and the breath of the people in the house, icicles formed. Adrie pulled the blankets over his ears to prevent them from freezing and looked at the icicles. That was something to remember, he thought, he could tell his grandchildren about it later. That's if he was going to survive this miserable war and winter.

His mother came upstairs to look over the situation. She went and got some old rugs and coats to put over the blankets for extra insulation against the cold. Normally there were two woollen blankets which would do the job for most of the year. When it got too cold, old coats supplemented the blankets to secure some extra heat.

With a cold and miserable winter the bag of coal which Adrie had obtained with the assistance of the German Fieldwebel, didn't last very long. When there is snow on the railway you aren't apt to find coal and it wasn't likely that the good German would turn up to give him another bag of coal. Adrie had a better idea to keep the stove burning; he thought that winter could be helpful in getting a supply of wood. There was an old highway between Rotterdam and Dordrecht; it had a row of giant elm trees on each side of the road. The elm trees were huge, even their branches were sizeable trees. That was good wood he thought. Adrie had looked at the extensive wood supply before but he lacked transportation means. Once the roads were covered with a layer of snow, he knew exactly how to secure a wood supply.

Adrie said to his dad: "Let's get some wood from the Dordrecht Highway."
He grabbed a long rope, a stone, a string, a sleigh and a saw. It was a cold day
with some snow falling. There was no snow cleaning anymore, with the result
that there was a good layer of snow on the road. Even the Germans didn't
attempt to clear the roads. Willie asked what Adrie and his dad were up to
and said that she would come along to pull some pieces of wood home over
the snow. Everybody was thinking how to get food and fuel for the stove.

It was only a ten minute walk to the tree highway. With hundreds of trees
to choose from, Adrie picked a tree with not too heavy branches. He had only
a handsaw and a hatchet to cut the branches to sizeable pieces that could be
pulled home over the snow. When he saw a good sized branch that he could
handle, he tied the stone on the rope and threw it over the branch. All he had
to do was give the rope enough slack, to make the stone come down by its own
weight. Next, he put a knot in the rope and pulled the knot up. Now there
was a rope hanging from the tree. All that was left to do was to climb the rope
and he would be in the tree. Adrie had no problem with rope climbing; he did
that all the time in Phys. Ed. at the Tech. It came in handy that he managed
this ancient art to secure a wood supply.

Once he was in the tree he dropped a string down and his dad tied the
handsaw on it. After Adrie had pulled up the saw he started to saw the limb
he wanted. The saw was very sharp and soon the branch started to make
squeaking noises. It became obvious that the branch would break soon.
Adrie's dad had to make sure that nobody was passing on the road when the
branch came down. The branch fell across the road and now there was a road
block which had to be cleared as soon as possible. There was very little traffic at
that stage of the war. The few bikes that were using the road could go around
the obstruction, but you could never know if a German patrol would turn up.
They wouldn't be very happy to see the road barricaded.

As soon as the limb was cut up, the sleigh was loaded with the small pieces
and the long, big pieces were dragged home. It was heavy, tiring, important
work to get heat in the house and nobody thought about getting tired. In the
afternoon they returned for a second branch. This time they weren't alone,
there were a few more people who copied the de Kievits.

Jaap Kraak was looking for wood too. His problem was that he didn't
have a monkey to climb the tree. He left and returned with his friend Koos
Groeneboom and a draw saw. He said: "Why take only a limb if you can take
the whole tree?"

That was good reasoning but the result was a disaster. When the tree fell
down, he didn't shout timber because he had no timber. The tree fell sideways
into the neighboring tree. Adrie said to his dad: "We are doing much better

with our branches, it doesn't take as much effort to cut them in sizeable pieces for the stove and our pieces are easier to transport."

Jaap Kraak and Koos Groeneboom encircled the tree as the Indians encircle the wagon camp. They decided to cut down the next tree so they would have two trees. Well it didn't work that way because of the weight of the tree which had fallen in that tree, the tree fell to the side into the next tree. Now the third tree had to go as well, they decided. When finally all the trees came crashing down, they didn't fall across the street. Unfortunately, they fell the other way, right across the telephone wires. That brought the Germans out when the telephone quit working. They needed communications for their army. When they saw all the struggling people to get wood, they luckily didn't think that it was sabotage. However, the law was laid down, the harvesting of trees had to stop and if any more trees fell over the telephone lines there would be trouble.

A German patrol checked to see if people were obeying their orders. Adrie and his dad kept cutting branches out of the trees. The Germans had said: "No more cutting down of trees," and those were only branches. A few weeks later the telephone service came to a halt as well. There was no gas, electricity or telephone anymore. The German Army used field radio and couriers for communication and the Dutch people could only deliver a message personally on foot or on an old bike with solid tires.

There were no newspapers other than the Underground ones and no radio. The Underground still managed to print their news bulletins with hand presses which they had recovered from the mothballs. Now that the de Kievits weren't living at the farm anymore, Ko would pick up the bulletins from Jan Lems, at least they could keep up with the progress of the war.

When telephone services were discontinued totally, the Germans didn't care how many trees fell over the telephone lines and people continued the harvesting of trees. The twelve mile double row tree stand disappeared completely during that winter and all the beautiful trees were gone. However, there were a lot of Dutch people who had a warm home during the hunger winter.

How On Earth Can You Lose A Shoe?

That was a good legitimate question, especially when it's war and you can't buy any. It did happen and unfortunately Adrie had to answer the question. It wasn't his fault, but he got the blame anyway.

The inundated land provided an excellent ice surface that winter. In spite of the misery of hunger, some people were skating and Adrie decided to do some skating too. It was a huge skating rink with no end in sight. He saw his two cousins Henk and Mary playing with a sleigh. They asked if he could pull them. No problem, Adrie gained speed and everybody had fun. Then he saw a real nice smooth area coming up. "Terrific" he thought but when he hit that smooth area it was far from terrific.

The reason that the ice surface was that smooth was because of the wind. A strong wind had kept that area as open water. When the wind died down, it finally froze and became very smooth ice. Only one problem, the ice surface was very thin. When Adrie and his cousins came on this smooth thin surface, they all went through the ice. Luckily it wasn't above a channel, yet, Adrie was standing up to his middle in the water. His shorter cousins were unluckier, the water reached almost to their neck.

Adrie tried to get out but the ice kept breaking. He had a better idea and decided to get out from the way they came. That ice was holding them before and should provide them a way to get out of the cold water. It worked; soon they were all standing on the ice with shattering teeth from the cold. Adrie said: "We better hurry home to get dry clothes on."

Marie started to cry: "I lost my shoe."

Unfortunately, they had gone through the ice where the land had been used for produce. It was clay and when she tried to get out, her shoe got stuck in the mud and she lost it. Adrie looked at the large area of broken ice where they just had come out. The only way to retrieve her shoe was to get back in the freezing water and reach deep down. It would be very difficult; he would almost have to dive for the shoe. Besides, the shoe would be hard to find in the mud, which made it very unlikely that he would successfully recover the shoe. He was also cold and started to freeze up. "The heck with it," he thought, put his cousins on the sleigh and pulled them home.

Aunt Pietje didn't say: "The heck with it," she was very unhappy when she found out that Marie had lost her shoe. She said: "Those were new shoes for Pete's sake; she only has worn them three times. I bought them a little too big for her so she wouldn't outgrow them that fast."

Adrie replied: "That's why she lost her shoe because they were a little too

big and when she was standing in the clay under water, the shoe came off."
If Adrie had thought that this was a good excuse to get him off the hook, he
had figured wrong.

Aunt Pietje kept up her crying saying "This is a complete disaster; new
shoes won't be coming any more until the war is over. You were wet anyway,
why didn't you go back into the water to get her shoe?"

Adrie answered: "The water was just too deep to reach down to find a shoe
in the mud. I have to go home now to get dry clothes on."

At this stage of the war there was no footwear available at all and shoes
could only be bought on the black market for a lot of money. Old shoes were
fixed to no end, they couldn't be replaced. Luckily, there was a very good shoe
maker; he was a mute and an excellent tradesman. He had stocked up a large
supply of materials to repair shoes before they ran out and used parts of old
shoes to fix other totally worn out shoes. But no matter how good he was, he
couldn't replace the lost shoe of Marie.

Some people don't want any children because they are too young, too
poor or business wasn't very good. When everything is right for a change they
say: "This is not much of a world to put children in." The "hunger winter" was
certainly no time to bring a baby into this hostile world in which people were
starving every day. In spite of the terrible timing, Aunt Johanna had her baby,
it was a boy. She lived in Rotterdam city and not in the outskirts like the de
Kievits. There were no more milk rations, not even for babies. Aunt Ploon said
to Adrie: "Can you bring her two bottles of milk twice a week?"

There was nobody else to do the job so Adrie took it on. On a bike with
solid tires, riding on the cobble stones in Rotterdam is quite a job but in
a snow blizzard it's a disaster. It was freezing and there were a lot of snow
drifts. This had been going on for two solid days with no let-up in sight. Aunt
Johanna's baby needed milk even when it was snowing. As there didn't seem
to be a break in this horrible weather, Adrie decided to go anyway. Normally
it took half an hour biking to get there. This time he had to walk more than
bike. When he hit a snow bank, he fell and could hardly get up. He was cold
and tired, and felt like throwing in the towel. But no he couldn't do that, what
would his aunt's baby drink?

Other people who had been walking on the sidewalk gave him a hand to
get up. When they pulled his bike out of the snow bank, Adrie got worried
that the bottles of milk would break. They were packed in woollen blankets
to prevent them from freezing, if they broke, all his effort would be in vain.
When he told the people to be careful because of the bottles of milk, they
thought that he had managed to buy some milk and said: "It's terrible weather
but luckily you have some milk to take home, that makes this terrible weather
easier to bear."

Adrie said: "No it's not my milk; it's for my aunt's baby."

People got the wrong idea: "Oh, you are a farmer's boy. You are lucky; at least you have something to eat when you come home."

Adrie gave up trying to explain; however, in a way he was lucky and continued his delivery trip. He was almost frozen when he came at his aunt's place. His aunt couldn't believe that he could get through in this adverse weather. She was very happy and couldn't thank him enough. When Adrie came home, he felt worn out and exhausted. It felt like he had been doing a day's work and settled himself right in front of the stove. At least they had wood to burn and could keep the house warm during the winter. It had been a lot of back breaking work to secure a wood supply. Now it paid off with a bad winter like this.

It was the darkest and gloomiest Christmas ever for the Dutch people. They still were singing of Peace on Earth and Goodwill to men. It didn't make any sense at all, singing about peace when the cannons are roaring and talking about good will to men when everybody is starving. The Germans were rounding up people from the underground every day and shot them without a trial. Many young lives were snuffed out during the war, many had been hardly lived. The faith of the people took a licking again. They reasoned "If there is a God, how can he allow all those terrible things to happen." Maybe they were stupid but it made no sense at all.

People who were wanted by the Germans, and managed to escape the German raids, saw their houses emptied by the Germans. The Germans came with a couple of wagons pulled by horses and loaded all the furniture and other possessions up. All this stuff was sent to Germany with a big sign on it "A gift from The Netherlands." After the house was empty the Germans would simply burn it in revenge of the non supporting stubborn Dutch people.

The Dutch people lived in a harsh and often brutal world where survival was a daily struggle. No, nobody could see Peace on Earth and Goodwill to men while thousands of people were killed every day. Desperate people who were still singing of Peace on Earth made it sound more like a prayer instead of a belief. There was hope in people's heart but every time this hope was tested.

The church was cold; there was no heating and no light. People were sitting in the church with their coats on and the Reverend was standing close to the window. He had abandoned his pulpit when the light was inadequate to read. There was no electricity; the electric organ had been replaced by an old pedal organ. The church service only lasted 30 minutes because of the cold. It was not a merry Christmas at all in 1944. When the year of 1944 drew to a close, all Dutch people would wish each other 'A Happy New Year.' Everybody hoped that peace would be restored during 1945 and that during the 1945 Festive Season people could really sing about peace on earth.

(Whatever is written or shown in movies about this time, it cannot describe the misery people went through.)

When the Second World War started, it certainly didn't make much sense any more to sing "Peace on Earth," and preach "Good will to man," while soldiers were aiming guns at one another. Peace on earth is a farce most of the time and even a Roman Catholic Priest had his doubts about it and made a poem during World War I.

Peace on earth we sing it.
It took a hundred thousand priests to bring it.
All that ever accomplished was,
That we got a lot of gas.

This was in reference to the gas war of World War I. Nerve Gas was poisonous, colorless and odorless; it caused paralyses of the respiratory and central nervous systems. And there was Mustard Gas, the most deadly gas of all. Any contact of the skin with this gas caused extreme irritation, blistering and disabling effects. The defence against mustard gas is a gas cape that protects the skin.

On the first Christmas Day of the First World War, British and German troops quit shooting for a while and walked through no man's land to the trenches of the enemy to shake hands, wish them a Merry Christmas and light some Christmas candles. They found that actually their enemies weren't that bad after all and wondered why they tried to kill one another.

The soldiers had a good time but their Generals were shocked, they figured that fraternizing with the enemy could kill the will to fight. A High Command order was issued stating that fraternizing with the enemy was absolutely prohibited. The Germans didn't do any better and an Army order forbade fraternization as it was high treason. Soldiers were supposed to hate the enemy instead of loving them.

No fraternizing between the opposing parties ever took place during World War II. The aim was to kill as many people from the enemy, including civilians by means of air raids. There didn't seem to be an end to the war and not to the winter either. One had to do with the other. Because of the long severe winter there was little progress. The Allies were looking for a break up of winter to start their spring offensive, in order to deliver the deadly knock out punch to Nazi Germany.

The Good Looking Girl Was a Guy.

Black market prices were more than inflated. One pound of potatoes, which were sold on the ration coupons for 10 cents per pound, went on the black market for 4 guilders per pound. Meat was not available at all and was worth its weight in gold on the black market. The price of meat had skyrocketed to 50 guilders per pound. Not too many people could afford to buy at the black market. Considering that the average wage was 24 guilders per week you had to work for two weeks to get one pound of meat. Old people were most vulnerable and many who had saved for their old age saw their entire life savings disappear, when they bought food on the black market, during the 'hunger winter.' It didn't matter, you can't eat money and when you are hungry survival is the name of the game.

There are always people who take advantage of the misery of others. Food is man's most essential commodity and as it became scarcer there were lots of farmers who decided to become rich by selling food on the black market. Some farmer black market racketeers wouldn't take money, they wanted gold.

A teacher of the Tech found that racketeers were abundant when he bought two pounds of meat for 100 guilders. The teacher had a couple of houses which he rented out and he also was paid for teaching at the Tech, otherwise he wouldn't have been able to buy meat. When he came home he weighed his meat and found that he was one and a half ounces short. He complained to the black market guy who had short changed him. The guy got real mad and said: "Are you telling me that I cheated you? Well that's fine; don't come to me anymore for meat. I only tried to do you a favor. You should be ashamed of yourself to accuse me of dishonesty."

The teacher was in a bind with the little there was available on the black market. You also had to know where to go; if you lost your contact you were finished buying on the black market. He said to the cheater: "Don't get mad, I don't accuse you of any wrong doing, maybe my scales weren't accurate. And I appreciate it very much that you are doing me a favor." The teacher said: "What could I do? I have to eat to stay alive."

Adrie was luckier in obtaining meat. He was watching the cook of the German field kitchen fry a lot of meat for the soldiers. It smelled so good that he started to drool. The German cook asked him: "Are you hungry?"

He looked at the cook with his great big, blue eyes and answered: "Yes, I'm very hungry."

The cook took a piece of paper and rolled a big piece of meat in it and said: "Go home with it and don't show it to anybody."

Adrie was by no means a German collaborator but if it came to food he accepted anything, even from Germans, especially if it was meat. Besides he didn't have to do anything for it, he just said: "Thank you" and went home.

That piece of meat was nothing compared to the pieces he got from butcher Pypers. Butcher Pypers had to butcher cows and pigs for the German army. One night they were picking up the deboned meat. It wasn't wrapped; it was thrown on the floor of the wagon. Pypers was loading up the meat while the Germans were talking in his butcher shop. Adrie licked his lips; it was quite a while since he had eaten meat. He looked with interest at the meat but couldn't figure out a way to swipe a piece. Butcher Pypers guessed his thought and said to him: "Here are two slabs of meat, you and your family might as well eat it instead of those damned Germans, get the hell out of here before the Germans come out of my shop."

Although Adrie could hardly carry the two slabs of meat, he wouldn't leave one behind for anything in the world. He was like a stubborn captain who would go down with his ship. His mother couldn't believe her eyes when she saw all the meat; it was the greatest thing she had seen for a long time. Real meat and quite a bit of it.

About a month later Adrie ran into some more good luck. He still went to the Tech and during the winter it was almost dark till 8.30 a.m. It started to dawn in the East but it was still twilight. When Adrie walked with his buddy Kryn Visser, on the Smeetlandse Dyk on his way to the Tech, he saw something move at the ditch. On closer inspection he saw that there was a horse lying near the ditch with a broken leg. Apparently there had been some troop transports during the night and one of the horses had broken a leg. The Germans had just left it there without finishing it off. They probably had better use for the bullets than to shoot a horse. Adrie said to Kryn: "Let's go home fast to get some big knives to butcher the horse."

Kryn said: "Are you kidding, what if the Germans come back?"

"Don't be stupid," Adrie said: "The Germans won't be back for the horse, they left it here because it broke a leg. Now do you want to eat horse meat tonight or not?"

They went home fast to get some butcher knives. Adrie took a saw as well to cut the bones. When they returned Adrie cut the throat of the horse to kill it and bleed it at the same time. They just cut pieces off the horse. An old baby carriage served for transportation. They had learned that from the Germans. They brought the meat home and returned for a second load. In the meantime other people had arrived to obtain some meat. Everybody was hacking at the dead horse and in no time at all the last bones of the horse had disappeared.

Adrie figured that he had at least 75 pounds of meat and Kryn Visser had also that much. At 50 guilders per pound that was a fortune. He was doing a lot better than his teacher at the Tech. Nobody had fridges or deep freezes at the time which didn't matter. Ko had always made beans and endive for the winter. She had big earthen pots to put her vegetables in. Then she put a layer of salt on top to keep it good. Granted, freezing of meat is superior when you want to keep meat; especially for taste. Salted meat has to stand a night in water to remove most of the salt, otherwise it is not edible. But that piece of horse meat tasted better at that time than the fresh meat out of the deepfreeze of today. When you are hungry everything tastes good.

Even Ko managed to get some meat. Actually she stole it in spite of her religious beliefs. Well, this was war and praying to the Lord for food didn't bring food on the table. Everybody had heard the play on the radio about the kid in Russia that prayed to the Lord for food. When he didn't get it he asked the Commissar of the Communist Party and received some. Well, there was no Commissar here that was so good to prove the point that the Communist Party takes care of the people instead of God.

Don't tell Christian people that they can't steal when they are hungry. Necessity is the mother of invention. Ko was baby sitting at the farm when her sister and her husband went to church. The girl was seven years old and went to Sunday School. She had to leave for Sunday School shortly before her parents came home. Ko sent her away early enough to have sufficient time to cut a piece of the bacon that was in the cellar, underneath the brine in an earthen pot. She had sewed a little pocket under her clothes to put the bacon in. She couldn't take much or it would be noticeable but even half a pound of bacon can make a difference on your dinner plate.

When you are starving you try anything to get food including dangerous things. Stealing food was dangerous, yet there were things which were more dangerous than that. Sjoerd the Ruiter was a seventeen year old boy. Luckily the Germans didn't get him to work in Germany at this stage of the war. There was no transportation of any kind anymore and Germany's ravaged cities were hard to reach.

Sjoerd had very little to eat and was hungry all the time. He figured he could get some food from the Germans. Stealing food from the Germans seemed impossible which called for a different plan. He said to his dad: "They are going to give it to me." He had long hair and when he dressed himself up like a girl he looked like a girl. Moreover, he had a high shrill voice which could be from a girl or a boy.

The next step was to get a date with a German soldier and ask for food. It was easy enough to get a date. Most of the German soldiers had been a long time away from their heimat (home land) and realized that they were walking with death in their shoes. They cared less for their wives in the heimat and were looking for the little pleasures which were available.

Sjoerd dated a German soldier for a couple of nights and complained about the hunger he experienced. The generous German soldier got some bread and potatoes and gave it to his sweetheart, he thought. On his third date this scam backfired. The German soldier wasn't willing to be a food supplier for a handshake and a couple of kisses at night. 'Tonight is the night,' the German soldier thought. When the odd couple was kissing and hugging, the soldier grabbed under his skirt. Sjoerd knew he was in trouble and tried to prevent the German soldier from doing that.

The German was fed up and tried to rape the girl he thought and pulled the panties of his ass. They both had a surprise coming. Sjoerd hadn't thought that the soldier would grab for the cookies that fast and the soldier hadn't figured that there was a penis in the panties. This deception made the soldier mad and he pumped two bullets into him. His father found Sjoerd lying in his own blood the following morning.

His father told the sad story. "I told him he couldn't get away with it, but Sjoerd didn't listen. He said that if the Virgin of Orleans could get away with dressing up like a boy, he could get away with dressing up like a girl. I told him that there was a vast difference, the Virgin of Orleans was leading soldiers to war and Sjoerd was leading a soldier to believe he was a girl."

Going Fishing.

Finally in March, the ice on the inundated land had melted. There was one thing that the water had brought; all kinds of fish that used to be in the river were now on the inundated land. When the gates were opened to flood the land the fish came with the water. There were a lot of pikes in the water that attracted many men, who were fishing from the shore. Adrie started to fish too. He got a couple of bamboo sticks for a fishing rod and a couple of old corks for a float. All he had to buy was a few treble hooks, and his fishing equipment was ready.

Using lures was outlawed in The Netherlands, only bait fishing was allowed. That made it necessary to catch some small bait fish in order to catch a big fish. It wasn't hard to catch small stickle bass. Most of the people took a worm to catch stickle bass. That was time consuming Adrie thought, and took a short cut. He took a rake and threw a lot of weeds on the land. Small fish hide in the weeds and all of a sudden there were all kinds of bait fish.

It took him about a day to catch one pike. He could do better he thought, if he would build a raft. From some old planks he built a raft and when it was finished he launched his raft without a bottle of champagne. Adrie had never drunk champagne in his life and it didn't look like that this situation would change in the near future. With no end of the ordeal in sight, he spent a lot of time fishing.

It was only a small raft. Without rubber boots, he had to stand barefoot on it. It didn't matter; he could get at the channels and ditches where most of the fish were. The only setback he had was that if the pike wasn't firmly attached to the hook, it fell on the raft and with water on the raft; the pike didn't have much trouble returning to its element. "Never mind," Adrie thought, he caught quite a few fish every day now that he could reach the channels and ditches. Soon he had more fish than his family could eat, which came in handy. His surplus fish could be bartered for coal. There was a man who was dredging for coal in the harbor who was quite willing to trade for fish. Adrie even managed to trade some fish for a sink pail.

The Germans had a better way of fishing than Adrie, they came with hand grenades. They threw the exploding hand grenades in the water and all the fish came drifting to the top of the water, belly up, from the concussion in the water. All they had to do was scoop the fish out of the water. Adrie was watching them closely and checked the water as soon as they left. Usually there were still a couple of fish floating on the water. He could scoop fish out of the water too, that was even easier than fishing with bait.

One day when a German soldier was fishing with hand grenades, Adrie was watching. The German soldier pulled the pin and kept the hand grenade in his hand too long. The grenade exploded while he was throwing it, smashing his hand and it also made a nasty hole in his tummy.

Seriously injured, the German soldier screamed like a pig that's being butchered. He was also alone with his fishing expedition; there were no other Germans on the dam. Adrie didn't know what to do, he sensed trouble. A German soldier being wounded could be explained as sabotage by the Germans.

One of the neighbours came out when he heard the screaming, he assisted the German soldier as well as he could and said to Adrie: "Go to the German Commando Post and tell them that there has been an accident."

Adrie wasn't exactly tickled to death with this all important job. There used to be a time that they would shoot the messenger if he brought bad news. Luckily it wasn't that bad anymore, yet he still wondered how the Germans would react when they heard the news.

At the commando post he went straight to the soldier who was on watch duty. Adrie addressed the soldier: "There has been an accident on the dam, a German soldier is wounded."

The German soldier said: "Come to the commander and tell him."

The commander asked: "What happened?"

Adrie answered: "A soldier was fishing on the dam with hand grenades; the grenade exploded and injured the soldier."

The commander said: "Come with us and show us where the accident happened."

At the place of the accident the commander said to the other soldiers who he had taken along: "Quickly, load him up and take him to our doctor." The Germans didn't even ask any questions, after Adrie told them what had happened, they saw it and believed it.

Manna From Heaven.

It was January 1945; Hitler had still 109 divisions in the West and 64 in the East. The Russians had 527 divisions and the Allies 70. The Russians couldn't be stopped and were heading for Berlin. Hitler did nothing to stop them because he had to defend the West.

When the Russians entered Prussia, panic broke out among the population. They knew they had it coming and could expect retaliation. The German invaders had destroyed Russian cities and had behaved beastly in Russia by raping women and even children.

Whenever the Germans had to clear mine fields, they chased cows over the mine field. When they ran out of cows they took the dogs from the people. Dogs were walking in front of the soldiers to explode the mines. They also destroyed tanks with the aid of dogs. The dogs were trained to eat only underneath a tank and before a tank battle erupted, the dogs were starved. When the tank battle started, the dogs were released with a bomb on their backs. They would head right away for the tanks because they expected to find food underneath the tanks. A little antenna that rubbed against the tank would set off the explosion and the tank and dog were no more.

Whenever the Germans ran out of cows and dogs, they took Russian people, preferably women and children, to cross the deadly mine fields. They warned the Russians "You put up mine fields; you'll clear them with your life." All those atrocities were remembered when the Russians entered Germany. The Russians had no mercy, not even for the civilian population, it was payback time.

Moreover, when the Germans had conquered Russian cities, they rounded up all the girls and women to rape them. Women who resisted were hanged. The Russians remembered and got even. They had been away a long time from home and were so sex starved that they raped everything that was female. Five and six year old girls, mothers, grandmothers and even great grandmothers of 90 years and older were raped by the Russians. Some women were raped 25 times per day. Over 100,000 instances of rape were reported and many more were never reported. They also stole whatever attracted them. They liked watches and some Russians had fifteen watches on each arm.

With the cold and the snow, there seemed to be a lull in the war during the winter. As early as March, the Allies went on the offensive again. March 6 brought great news, the Americans had taken Cologne. That wasn't far from the Dutch border, though the Northern part of The Netherlands remained occupied by the Germans.

There was daily news about Allied successes. On March 7th the Allies had some good luck by taking the bridge at Remagen across the River Rhine. The River Rhine had provided a natural barrier, it was Hitler's last defence; once the Rhine was crossed the road to Berlin was open. Capturing of the bridge, intact, shortened the war by at least two months.

"Remagen Bridge taken undamaged,"

The underground newspaper reported. The Germans had figured to stop the Allies at the river by blowing up the bridge. The General in charge was holding out as long as possible so the retreating German troops could cross the river and hold the front. When the General gave his orders to blow up the bridge they failed because of a shell that had hit the wire that was supposed to ignite the dynamite. It cost him his life, when Hitler heard the news, he was outraged and called it incompetence. He shot the commander who was responsible for the destruction of the bridge and ordered the bridge destroyed at any cost to prevent the Allies from crossing the Rhine. When shelling and bombing failed to do the job, Hitler ordered that the bridge be attacked with V2's. All efforts to destroy the bridge failed, to the annoyance of Hitler.

Ten days later the Remagen Bridge was in the news again. This time the news wasn't that good.

REMAGEN BRIDGE COLLAPSED.

The bridge collapsed by itself. Shelling and bombing had weakened the structure of the bridge and overloading of the bridge also had a lot to do with the collapse. Quite a few Americans lost their lives when the bridge collapsed. In the meantime the Americans had managed to put two pontoon bridges across the Rhine. At least the troops that had crossed the Rhine could still be supplied.

There was also news from the Eastern front. The Germans launched a counter offensive again. They never quit putting up resistance and there was always another counter attack.

At night the underground newspaper announced:

"BELGIAN S.S. DIVISION COMPLETELY DESTROYED.
In the Battle of the Oder, the Belgian S.S. Division trying to stop the Russians in their drive to Berlin was completely wiped out. Very few escaped the murderous Russian onslaught."

THE END OF A NIGHTMARE IN BLOOD.

Hitler had failed in his counter attack in the Battle of the Bulge in the West. On March 10, 1945, Hitler went on his final counter attack in the East with the intention of re-taking the Rumanian oil fields. He used 22 divisions, which were massacred by the Russians.

The Russian onslaught on the Eastern front was spectacular. Once they crossed the Oder there was no stopping them. Four million troops supported by 150,000 tanks and 200,000 cannons were heading for Berlin. It was the largest army ever assembled. It was a bloody battle and the Germans inflicted heavy casualties. For every German killed there were five dead Russians. It never stopped them, soldiers and supplies were inexhaustible.

Hitler would never quit, he always had another plan to turn the war around for the Nazis. Slowly but surely his options were running out, he was commanding forces he no longer had and was waiting for His Almighty to interfere. He said: "The Germans are not worthy of my genius, when I go I want the whole world to go with me."

During the last weeks of the war, millions of people died because of Hitler with his insane orders. When the Russians moved into Germany, the Jews in the concentration camps were marched south so they weren't going to be liberated.

When freedom beckoned for the P.O.W.'s in the legendary Stalag 3 camp known for the Great Escape, Hitler ordered the camp closed and the P.O.W.'s had to march south out of reach of the Russians. They shouldn't be liberated either.

On January 28th in the middle of the worst winter in a decade the P.O.W.'s were marched south, they were underfed and weak and winter took a heavy toll with frostbite. More than a thousand of the 10,000 didn't make it. Nothing was prepared for them, no food, no shelter and no destination, just out of reach of the Russians.

Hitler ordered a total scorched earth tactic. All transportation and communication means had to be totally destroyed before the Germans withdrew. Generals Kesselring and Speer sabotaged Hitler's orders, the war was lost and destroying everything would only aggravate the possibility for Germany to exist in a post war world.

On March 10, 1945 the Russians approached Berlin. Things seemed to come to an end for the Third Reich, there were new successes every day for the Allies on the Western and Eastern fronts. At one time, not too long before there had been nothing but German successes. The German successes had come to an abrupt halt and instead there were nothing but Allied successes.

On March 30th Heidelberg was taken by the Allies and the Russians had Berlin encircled. They got ready for the Grand Finale. The situation became hopeless and the Germans withdrew from all occupied countries except The Netherlands. Freedom had beckoned several times but every time it didn't happen. Moreover, the Dutch were very low on the battle plans of the Allies. It was suggested to liberate The Netherlands so the hungry people could be fed. The Allied command suggested that it would prolong the war, they had to defeat Germany and then The Netherlands would be liberated automatically.

While Europe was in flames and starving, the Americas weren't experiencing any of this. The U.S. and Canada had many of their young men fighting overseas and gasoline was rationed but they didn't know any hunger. In the meantime, the poor people of The Netherlands, who hadn't managed to get extra supplies beyond their rations, were now thinner than Ghandi; they were nothing more than walking skeletons. The starving people could hardly get up to walk. People who got up too fast; passed out, they had to get up slowly hanging onto something. With the rations being that low in The Netherlands, the people barely existed and had no resistance at all.

Finally it was left to the Canadians to liberate The Netherlands. On April 6 the Canadians liberated Zutphen and Almelo, and four days later Groningen and Leeuwarden. On April 28 the Canadians finally liberated Arnheim. However, Great City Holland missed the boat again. Great City Holland consisted of three provinces with all the big cities Rotterdam, Amsterdam, Hague, Utrecht etc.. That was the part of The Netherlands that was really starving, with millions of people and not much agricultural land. And that was the part which was occupied the longest by the Germans.

When the Canadians reached the Zuiderzee the Germans started to inundate the rest of The Netherlands. General Crerar, who was in charge of the Canadian troops, managed to secure a ceasefire with the German commander Blumentritt. In exchange British and American aircraft were allowed to supply food and medical supplies to the starving people of The Netherlands.

English and American planes were dropping supplies by parachutes on pre-selected fields. It was a sight that one never will forget, food coming down by parachute. The Red Cross was in charge of collecting the food supply and distributing it among the starving people. There was flour to bake bread, crackers, biscuits, egg powder, cans of meat and even chocolate.

All the Dutch people were outside to view the miracle "Manna from heaven." Jaap Kraak was also viewing the parachutes coming down. After a while he needed a leak and decided to piss in the ditch. One of the parachutes that were dropped didn't open and instead of on the field it crashed into the ditch close to Jaap Kraak. Jaap Kraak was as white as a bed sheet and ran away from the ditch with his penis still out of his fly. No, he wasn't arrested for indecent exposure; that was in nobody's mind.

Everything that came down by parachute was used, including the parachute itself. The linen of the parachutes was excellent material to make blouses and silk stockings for the ladies and shirts for the men. Everything was usable, even the shells of the cannons were collected by the Dutch people. People would make ashtrays and copper lamps from the shells.

Baking bread from the flour was a problem, the bakers didn't have coal for their ovens; they didn't even have salt to put in the bread. All they had was rock salt which was, as the name suggested, as hard as a rock and had to be soaked overnight to make it usable. They had to go out to get wood from trees before they could start baking. There was no electric light, so the work had to be done with candles and oil lights. Both were in short supply, if they were available at all. Somehow the bakers managed to make bread from the manna from heaven and the people enjoyed it.

For many Dutch people the food droppings came too late, they had already died. Even some people who hadn't died yet didn't make it; their body couldn't recover from malnutrition. Over 16,000 people died from starvation that "hunger winter." There were even people who died from consuming chocolate bars. This chocolate was concentrated and one bar was a complete meal. Soldiers were supplied with those chocolate bars, just in case there was no food supply because of shelling and bombing. They would eat just a bar of chocolate to survive. People who ate more than one bar of chocolate experienced severe stomach cramps when this chocolate expanded in their stomach. Some people died, their stomachs weren't used to much food anymore, and kind of exploded.

On April 11th the Allies received very sad news that President Roosevelt had died of a stroke. What was bad news for the Allies was great news for the Axis. Hitler saw it as the best news he had heard for a long time and delivered his last speech. He said: "Our enemy Roosevelt is dead. It's like a long awaited providential miracle and a divine intervention. We will now defeat the Russians at the gates of Berlin and destroy the English and American armies and I will remain Germany's Fuhrer."

On April 25 the news bulletin announced in fat letters:

Germany cut in two.
The Russian and American armies met and Germany is cut in two.

Great news arrived every day and Hitler made the headlines all the time. On April 26,

Hitler takes charge to defend Berlin

It showed everybody that the clock was ticking and the end of this terrible monster was in sight.

April 27, **Hitler fires Herman Goring and Heinrich Himmler for trying to negotiate a ceasefire.**

The Final Curtain.

While the people in The Netherlands were starving and hoping to hear that the war was finished, Hitler was sitting in his concrete bunker with his Nazi buddies and his long time mistress Eva von Braun. Berlin had been surrounded by the Russians and bombs and shells were exploding every second. Hitler's bunker was deep underground so he was safe from being hit. The Berlin people were also safe in their concrete bunkers, while the remnants of the German Wehrmacht were fighting the Russians from house to house. A standard joke went around among the fighting soldiers: "You had better enjoy the war because the peace will be terrible."

Hitler had ordered the 12th German army to free the city of its siege. On April 30 Hitler got the message that the 12th Army had been destroyed and the city was doomed. There was no escape for the Fuhrer of all Germans; he knew that the collapse of Nazi Germany was imminent and prepared for his final act. He ordered a city official from Berlin to his bunker to get married to his long time mistress Eva von Braun. Hitler never had wanted to get married; he liked being desired by the German women who were shouting at him: "Say Fuhrer, I want to have a baby with you." He liked pretty women but they had to be pretty in more than one way, they had to be pretty stupid as well because he didn't like smart women.

Hitler always figured that he was more popular with the German women when he was single; he never wanted to marry Eva von Braun. Now, with the day of reckoning fast approaching, and his popularity running out, it didn't matter anymore. Now the end was near Hitler wanted to reward his faithful mistress and married Eva von Braun on April 28. Just before the marriage Hitler had killed Eva von Braun's brother for abandoning his post.

Hitler had a present for the ones that attended his wedding; he gave them each two cyanide capsules. Marrying Eva von Braun was a reward for her being faithful to the end. Right after the wedding ceremony on April 30th, Hitler took a cyanide capsule and fired a shot with his revolver in his temple. The worst beast of Germany dropped to the floor lying in his own blood. He took no chances and was making sure that he was dead before the Russians found him. A dozen times, His Almighty had saved Hitler so he could kill himself in the end.

There was no wedding night for Eva von Braun, as soon as she saw that her husband of less than an hour was dead, she took a cyanide capsule to join him. Hitler's aids doused both bodies with gasoline, burned them and buried them in a shallow grave.

On special orders from Stalin, Russian troops stormed the bunker to take Hitler dead or alive but where was Hitler? All they found were two charred bodies in a shallow grave, a female and a male with one testicle. It was in the nick of time that Hitler killed himself to escape being captured and hanged. The Russians were 400 meters from his bunker when he married Eva von Braun; he had no time to lose.

May 1. That night there was great news in the Underground news bulletin.

Hitler commits suicide.

A crowd was gathering in the street. Good news travels fast and the good news was that Hitler was dead. Leen Willemstein said: "Hitler always has boasted that he was saved by His Almighty whenever he escaped death. Now His Almighty couldn't save him anymore, he had to kill himself or be hanged and mutilated like Mussolini."

With the monster finally dead, his successor Grand Admiral Donitz could now come to grips with the defeat of the Master Race and negotiate a cease fire.

This was announced in the Underground bulletin the next day on May 1st:

Grand Admiral Donitz in charge of Germany.
Grand Admiral Donitz, who fought the Battle of the
Atlantic, was chosen by Hitler to succeed him.

The Dutch people didn't know if this was great news or not. 'He couldn't be worse than Hitler,' they thought. 'That was pretty near impossible.'

The Dutch People's Finest Hour.

On May 5th 1945 very great news.
"German Commander Blumentritt and Canadian Commander

General Crerar Sign Unconditional Surrender Of All German Forces In The Netherlands."

Was it really true that the war was over for the desperate Dutch people? There were at least five occasions that the Dutch people had thought that the war was over and every time they found out it wasn't. There were no newspapers anymore and few people had a clandestine radio. Most of the news was spread from person to person by mouth. The Dutch people were slow in grasping that this time it was really true that the war was over.

All of a sudden there were Dutch flags flying from the houses. As long as the Nazis were ruling The Netherlands all nationalistic feelings were depressed and flying a flag was prohibited. Now the war was over, flags came out by the thousands; Adrie had never seen that many flags before. Ko came home with a flag too; it was given to her by Mr. Tilleman where she worked. It was the first time that the de Kievits had a flag; they had never needed a flag because there never was a reason to fly a flag. Before the war, during the Great Depression, nobody in his right mind would fly the Dutch flag. It was a terrible time and nobody was in the mood to fly the flag. However, now the war was over, everybody was in the right mood to fly the flag and there was nobody to tell people they were not allowed.

Everybody was wearing orange buttons and the girls had orange ribbons in their hair. For five long years wearing of orange buttons and ribbons was outlawed by the Germans. During the war, on the Queen's Birthday, people would carry an orange in their hand to fool the Germans.

Adrie with his two friends were wearing orange buttons too. They were walking in the street when a German soldier came up to them. The German soldier was walking with his stolen bike in his hand and had his rifle on his back. Adrie and his two friends had the shock of their lives, wearing orange buttons had been forbidden for such a long time and now this German soldier was coming up to them. This could be it, all it took was a sore head of a German soldier and bang you are dead. Adrie saw his entire life go past him in the next three seconds but luckily it didn't happen. There was still fear of the Germans. Maybe this German soldier didn't like to see orange buttons and he still had his rifle with which he could shoot if he wanted. There were some die-hard soldiers who didn't want to give up. On the other hand, most of the German soldiers were glad the war was over and they were looking forward to returning to their heimat.

The German soldier asked: "Is this the way to Barendrecht?" Adrie told him that he was on the right track and the German soldier continued his way. Barendrecht was the place where all German soldiers had to report and surrender all their weapons to the Canadian depot. From there they were transported to camps until transportation could be supplied to ship them back to Germany.

After they continued their walk, Adrie and his friends met a bunch of girls who were in a festive mood. They were dancing and singing and came over to the boys, embraced them and kissed them. Adrie thought: "It's better to have kissing girls coming towards you than a German with a rifle on his back. What a crazy world this is," Adrie liked it already. For five years there had been misery and nothing to celebrate, there had been only the struggle to stay alive but now they were free. The Dutch people could finally shake the yoke of the Nazis and say: "Nazi go home!" Everybody thought that a better world was in the offing, the world was a bowl with cherries and all you had to do was eat one by one and spit the stones out.

Now the war was over, there was no curfew anymore and people celebrated till far after midnight. There was dancing in the streets all night. People provided the music with an accordion, mouth organ or other music instrument. Sometimes the music was provided by a few men playing their mouth organ. People danced and were singing to the wee hours of the morning. As Winston Churchill suggested "This was their finest hour."

The Party of the Century.

With the massive food drop by parachutes, people would receive tin boxes of crackers, a couple of loaves of bread per week, a can of beef, corned beef and even a bar of chocolate per person per week. Now the war was over in The Netherlands, convoys with food supplies were brought in over the road with big G.M.C. army trucks.

There was nothing to drink except water. There was no beer or other alcoholic beverages; there wasn't even tea or coffee but people celebrated. You don't have to get drunk to have a good time. If you have real reason to celebrate you celebrate. This was the "Party of the century." There were lots of lovely girls to kiss and the girls were willing. There wasn't much to eat yet but the young people lived on wind, sunshine and love.

Adrie with his friend Gerard Ploeg arrived at the Zevenbergse Street where all young people of the whole neighborhood seemed to have assembled. They weren't dancing; instead they had a game on the go. All young people joined hands and formed a circle. In the middle of the circle were a boy and a girl. The circle started to move around clockwise and everybody was singing:

"Kissing kissing falderalderiere.
Kissing kissing falderaldera."

Then the two in the middle of the circle would kiss each other. Next, the magic circle started to move counter clockwise and everybody was singing:

"Choosing, choosing falderalderiere.
Choosing choosing falderaldera."

Then the boy would leave the circle and the girl would pick a nice boy she liked. The circle would move again clockwise and the two would kiss again. Next the girl would leave the circle and the boy would pick himself a girl he liked to kiss. There were a lot of kisses exchanged that night and all young people had fun. *(In today's world, games like this might be asking for trouble with Aids and other sicknesses around. However, this was long before Aids was invented.)*

Adrie looked at this spectacle for a while but didn't think he wanted to participate in the kissing game. They were all older women of seventeen and eighteen years old and what boy of fifteen years old would want to kiss those old bags. No, he preferred young women of his own age, about fourteen or fifteen.

His friend Gerard Ploeg had walked away for a while when Adrie was observing if he could learn something from those old men and women. Gerard came back and said: "The younger boys and girls want to make their own kissing circle and they ask us if we want to participate."

Well, here was an offer he couldn't refuse. When they arrived at the magic circle of young girls and boys they were already turning around. As soon as the boys and girls saw the new arrivals they graciously opened up the circle to let them in. The more souls, the more fun was the general thought, especially when you are celebrating "Liberation Day."

During the "hunger winter" there were no marriages and even dating was very sporadic. Everybody was busy trying to survive: you can't live on kisses and sunshine for long. Now the war was over everybody was suddenly interested in the opposite sex. And with this kissing game there was ample opportunity to taste the merchandise. It was an opportunity a young boy wouldn't want to miss, he could choose a girl that he never would have a chance to kiss but it was a go if he picked her. And the girls? They enjoyed it as much as the boys; or they wouldn't have been there.

Before the war there was a similar game in which young girls and boys participated. There was the same moving circle but instead the participants would sing.

In Holland stands a house.
In Holland stands a house yah yah,
From tingeling tingeling hopsa sa.
In Holland stands a house.

In the house there lives a man.
In the house there lives a man yah yah,
From tingeling tingeling hop sa sa.
In the house there lives a man.

And the man chooses a wife.
And the man choses a wife yah yah,
From tingeling tingeling hop sa sa.
And the man choses a wife.

And the man kisses his wife.
And the man kisses his wife yah yah,
From tingeling tingeling hop sa sa.
And the man kisses his wife.

You guessed it; at that time there were the kisses. But they had to sing four verses before somebody would get a kiss. Some great inventor had invented the short cut to sing "Choosing choosing falderalderiere" and right after "Kissing kissing falderalderiere." When you cut out the bull shit, you got more kisses and you didn't have to wait that long before it was your turn to get a kiss. Yes, that was progress. The invention of this short cut was classified at the same importance as the invention of the wheel. It probably saved the species.

Spin the bottle was another favorite game. A girl spun the bottle and if the bottle pointed at you, the girl had two options; she could kiss you or give you a nickel. Some boys got rich and others didn't have a nickel to spare.

Around two o' clock after midnight, everybody was well kissed and the party started to break up. People were still walking through the street and everybody was happy, even happier than a pig in the shit. And that is happy when you can beat the pig in happiness when he is in his element.

Powerhouses were still closed after the war. They didn't have coal to fuel the steam kettles that had to turn the generators. Consequently, there were no street lights. Instead, people brought out the old oil lamps, which were fuelled with oil that came from the defeated German army. It didn't give much light which the young people didn't mind, who needs light when you are necking with a beautiful girl? And in case you are necking with an ugly girl you don't need light either for obvious reasons. In the dark they all look the same.

Most of the people slept long the next morning. They hurried to eat some food to get ready for some more celebrations. A lot of people were gathered on the Hordyk. When Adrie inspected what was going on, he saw that people were playing 'Crown and Anchor.' A little farther they had some kind of a wheel of fortune. There were only numbers on the wheel. You could buy a ticket for a quarter. The wheel man would announce what the price was going to be, next he would turn the wheel and if you had the number on your ticket you would win. Most of the prizes were cash prizes that started to appeal to the people again now there were a few things that one could buy. Yet, the favorite prizes were a frying pan or other valuable utensils which weren't even available in the store.

All of a sudden, Adrie came face to face with Henk Sturfs who had been cutting grass, in the dark, with Nelis Mouthaan, when he had returned with a bag of wheat that he had stolen. Now here was a rare opportunity to have some fun.

"Aha!" Adrie said, "I caught you red handed with your hands in the cookie box."

"What do you mean?" Henk Sturfs asked.

Adrie replied: "How soon we forget, I saw you cutting grass with Nelis Mouthaan, in the pasture of Koos Vryland, in the dark."

"How can you possibly see us in the dark?" Henk Sturfs asked.

Adrie said teasingly: "You thought it was dark and nobody could see you. Wrong assumption! The Lord and I see everything, even if you think you can get away with stealing in the dark."

Adrie sauntered away, leaving a puzzled Henk Sturfs behind.

Everybody had to go home to eat, there were no restaurants open yet because of lack of food supplies. There wasn't even a stand to buy ice cream or a hamburger. (*Who in Canada would like to go to a party like that at this time? That was a different time and all people in The Netherlands loved it, they had been without fun and in fear for too long.*)

AGAIN: " DER KRIEG IM WESTEN IST BEEINDIGT." (The war in the West is finished.)

On May 8 people had more reason to celebrate. The daily news letter from the former underground announced:

"V.E. DAY IN EUROPE."
Grand Admiral Donitz signs unconditional surrender of Germany. Joseph Goebbles kills all his six children and he himself and his wife commit suicide."

For the second time during the 20th Century, the krieg im Westen was beeindigt. Hitler said it on June 1940 after he had defeated France. Almost five years later, Hitler didn't say that the Krieg im Westen was beeindigt. Hitler was dead and had nothing to say, yet, the krieg im Westen was now finished for good. The entire world rejoiced and celebrated V.E. Day in Europe, except the Axis of course.

The Allies and the Germans both had been using the sound of Beethoven's Fifth Symphony in their propaganda broadcasts. "Dit-dit-dit-dah." It was the same sound as the "V" in Morse had and the V was standing for victory. The problem was that there was only one victor and the other party was the loser. Luckily the Dutch people were on the winning side. Luckier yet, this was the second time that they came out as winners. First with the First World War and now with the Second World War. How lucky can you get? Germany was a second time loser.

Adrie saw a couple of Canadian soldiers who were talking to the Dutch people. They were actually Dutch men who were liberated earlier in the Southern provinces of The Netherlands. They wanted to help to liberate their country and had joined the Canadian army. One of the soldiers said: "Europe has suffered severe damage to communications because of Allied air attacks and systematic demolition by the Germans. All the cranes for unloading ships have been blown up and are lying in the harbors and the railways are pretty near destroyed. It will be very hard to get everything going again without electricity and telephone. It is impossible to do business without telephone, it takes too long if you have to use couriers."

Adrie didn't quite catch that part of the story, for the last eight months of the war, that's all the communications they'd had. If you wanted to talk to somebody you went to his house or business. And even before the war there were only a few telephones around. The only phone call you would get before the war was if something bad had happened. Most of the time if you got a phone call, somebody had died in the family and they informed the family when the funeral would take place. There was a radio store about half a block away. Piet Westdyk sold radios, lamps, fuses etc. He also was an electrical contractor and of course he had a phone. Everybody in the neighborhood used his phone number but only in emergencies.

With the war over in Europe, the city of Rotterdam had appointed a Feast Committee. Most of the members of the committee were school teachers or city counsellors. The idea was to have all kinds of contests. A large pasture was selected for the feast. There was a lot of work to be done before the pasture was ready to receive the feasting people. All the telephone poles that had been put in the pastures to prevent troop droppings from the air had to be removed and the holes had to be filled. Furthermore there were cow plaques in the pasture which had to be removed.

Adrie studied the program and decided to participate in sprinting, broad jumping, the obstacle race, and gunny bag racing. He managed to win the first prize in sprinting and broad jumping. His training had been achieved in the polder when he was still going to school. He also got the second prize on the obstacle course. That was all; he didn't succeed with gunny bag racing. Running while standing in a bag wasn't his cup of tea. You can't be good in everything was his philosophy.

His prizes were a charcoal drawing of the food drops by parachute, a thin book about the liberation of The Netherlands and a little chest of drawers in which he could save his jewels. First of all he was going to bring those valuable prizes home to safety where he couldn't lose or damage them. *(I can hear a lot of people say: "Wow, big deal." However when you have been deprived of everything, for a long time, you really appreciate the small things of life. People had all kinds of money but there was nothing you could buy with it. Only the rations, which were increasing to a level which would sustain the people, could be bought.)*

When he returned to the feast pasture, he decided to try to climb the greasy pole. On the top of the pole was a wagon wheel on which envelopes were attached. In the envelope was a piece of paper telling you what you had won. Adrie was good at climbing but this slippery pole was too much for him. He climbed to the top and as soon as he reached for an envelope, he started to slide down.

He watched the other people do it for a while. There was one guy who had no trouble climbing the greasy pole. When he was at the top he took his sweet old time to open up all the envelopes to select his prize. He then shouted down: "Is Mr. Hoving there?"

Mr. Hoving was a farmer who had his cousin living with him. When Mr. Hoving replied that he was there, the man on the pole asked which prize he wanted. He read all the pieces of paper to him. There was a little painting, a colorful box, an etching, a vase, a loaf of bread and a bar of chocolate. Mr. Hoving shouted to him: "Take the loaf of bread; you can always use a loaf of bread."

One woman behind Adrie remarked: "What a strange guy, what in the world does a farmer want a loaf of bread for."

One more thing drew Adrie's attention. It was a narrow railway on a steep hill. On top of the steep hill they had a flatbed cart which was pushed down the hill. Going downhill, the cart got quite a speed which was the idea. At the bottom of the hill was a ring hanging on a hook which was attached to a barrel of water. The idea was that when you had this bumpy ride you had to get the ring on your stick. If you missed the ring you would hit the barrel with your stick. The barrel would turn upside down and the driver would get all the water over him self. Adrie didn't get a prize this time but he sure got the barrel of water to make him soaking wet. Once more he had to go home, this time to get dry clothes.

When he came back for some more celebrations, he watched the older men and women play 'Musical Chair.' They had a bunch of fat women sitting on the chairs and another bunch of skinny men encircling the chairs while the music was playing. When the music stopped the men had to occupy a chair a fat lady was sitting on. There was one chair short which left one skinny man out of the game. Adrie couldn't understand that there were still fat ladies around after the "hunger winter;" however, most of those fat ladies came from the island where people were farming.

There was also a bandstand with a band playing brass music instruments and a dance floor.

At night Gerard Ploeg said to Adrie: "Everybody and his brother is here."

Adrie said: "I don't think so, I don't see Leen Koekoek." Leen Koekoek was the boy who had given Adrie a hard time at school, when he was in the Hitler Youth and Adrie hadn't forgotten this.

Gerard Ploeg replied: "You are right, I haven't seen him at all, he probably hasn't got anything to celebrate and is in hiding."

"I hope they let him celebrate in jail when they throw the key away," Adrie remarked sarcastically

Some people had heard the discussion which was going on and agreed that those traitors should be punished.

There never seemed to be an end to street parties, the happiness and excitement seemed to last almost forever now the war was over. Every street took its turn to have a street party and everybody attended. Never in history has there been a celebration like the celebrations at the end of the war in Europe. Red Square, London, Paris, Amsterdam and others celebrated to no end. All people of Europe rejoiced, except the people of Germany who were walking between piles of rubble, which had been beautiful cities before the war. Hitler was dead and the Nazis were imprisoned waiting for their trial.

After the Depression and the war, everybody in The Netherlands thought that a better world would be in the offing. The good guys had won the war and the bad guys were being punished. The war was over and prosperity and peace would return.

The Day of Reckoning.

No matter how happy the Dutch people were, the celebrations had to end. A lot of work had to be done to get everything back to normal. There was a shortage of food and everything else and the country was in ruins. And there was the day of reckoning.

The day of reckoning was coming and so was punishment. It took the authorities some time to handle all the surrendering German soldiers. They had to be put in camps and transported to Germany. It would take some doing to get rid of the Germans with no transportation. Only five days of warfare were needed in 1940 to get the German soldiers into The Netherlands and they came by themselves. It took five years of warfare to defeat them and months to get them back to their heimat.

As soon as the authorities had a camp organized for the traitors they were rounded up. A large wagon with a flatbed was pulled by a couple of horses through the streets. The wagon stopped at all the houses where the traitors were living. Most of the traitors had expected to be arrested; they came out with their suitcases packed and were ready to leave. A couple of men put up a fight and on one occasion the traitor tried to escape. Fast young men chased the traitor and soon he was under arrest. There were chairs on the flatbed and the traitors took a seat.

Some people started to throw rocks at the Nazi supporters. When those hostilities started the traitors used their chairs as a shield. The wagon was accompanied by people who had been fighting in the Underground. They had a band around their arm stating "Dutch Inland Fighting Force." There was also Dutch police but those people were added for safety and security during the transition period. An officer climbed on the flatbed wagon and said that the people had to stop throwing rocks at the prisoners. All of the prisoners were facing charges and would be judged by the courts.

People were in a hanging mood and started to shout: "Hang the traitors, they deserve it. They never were sorry for us when our people got shot by the Germans and they have betrayed many good Dutch citizens."

The officer shouted through his bullhorn: "We have fought the Nazis who were shooting our citizens. Now we are victorious we should not resort to their terrible methods of shooting people without a trial. Let's not be barbarians like the Nazis."

The crowd shouted: "An eye for an eye, string them up. Let's hang them first and give them a fair trial after."

The officer shouted back: "I agree; an eye for an eye but let the courts decide who should be hanged."

More officers were added for the security of the prisoners. The prisoners were brought into a camp and were punished according to the crimes they had committed. People like Koekoek who had been a mayor for the Germans, in some city, were treated as real criminals. Koekoek was arrested in the town where he had performed as vassal mayor for the Germans. Most of them had assisted the Germans in rounding up the Jews to send them to Germany. Others who had been only a member of the Nazi Party and had had a poster of the Nazis in their window were put in work camps. Everybody agreed that they should work for the Dutch people instead of doing nothing.

More reckoning was to be done by the Dutch people. There were quite a few Dutch girls who had been dating German soldiers. Some of the girls were hungry and dated the German soldiers to get food. Others like Betsy Lankhaar, who was as ugly as the night, so that no Dutch boy ever dated her said: "I need love and if the Dutch boys don't want to give it to me, I'll get it from the German soldiers."

There were also girls who liked the Germans. It didn't matter what reason they had to date the enemy, all good Dutch people hated the Germans and Dutch girls shouldn't love the enemy. The flat bed wagon was used again to round up the girls who had dated German soldiers. There were chairs for the girls to sit on the wagon and there was also a guy with a pair of scissors to clip their hair. When he was through with the girls they were as bald as Toby's ass. Since there were no wigs available in the immediate post war period it was quite a punishment for the girls. Most of the girls would wear a bonnet or a scarf to cover their bald head. After the girls were clipped they had to remain on the flatbed till all the girls who were implicated in dating the Germans were dealt with.

It was quite a spectacle to see the most hated girls become baldies. Everybody was following the flatbed wagon to enjoy the spectacle of proper punishment for loving the enemy. Adrie had nothing better to do than to look at what was happening. Most of the girls knew that they couldn't escape the fury of the Dutch people and came out of their house voluntarily. They climbed on the wagon by themselves and took the hair clipping ceremony with courage. All of them knew that they had it coming and wanted to get their punishment over with, so they could carry on with their life. Nobody was imprisoned for dating German soldiers.

When the wagon came to Betsy Lankhaar's house, she came out of the house right away. There was no hair clipping to be done on her head, she knew what was coming and had asked her father to clip all her curls. The people appreciated the fact that she had acknowledged her mistake and applauded her. She took her seat between the other bald girls.

There were now eight bald headed girls on the wagon. The next stop was at Mantje Verzyl's place who had dated quite a few German soldiers. This time it didn't go as easy and voluntarily as with Betsy Lankhaar. Rook Verzyl, the father of Mantje, opened the door and when he heard what they were coming to do, he called his wife and shouted: "Get me the hatchet so I can scalp the bastards before they cut the hair of my daughter."

His wife came with the hatchet and when Dirk van Vliet wanted to enter the house to get the girl, Rook struck him on his head with the hatchet. Blood splashed on the street; Dirk van Vliet was taken to the hospital and treated for a skull fracture. He was in the hospital for over half a year before he could return home.

A few big guys subdued Rook Verzyl and his daughter Mantje was forcefully taken out of the house. They had to hoist her on the wagon while she screamed and kicked at her attackers. They had to tie her to the chair for the involuntary haircut and after the haircut they left the ropes in place to prevent her from escaping.

Rook Verzeil was promptly arrested for cleaving the skull of Dirk van Vliet. They released him the next day and Rook came home. The judge ruled in favor of Rook Verzeil, only the police had the right to go into people's houses. When people forced their way into his home, he had the right to defend his homestead.

It seemed that Mantje Verzeil was embarrassed with her bald head. She always wore a scarf around her head to avoid people seeing her bald head. Even months after the incident, she was going to the centre of Rotterdam by bus for her outings. She was so embarrassed that she would wait in her house for the bus. The bus stop was right in front of her door. She would stand in front of the window and when she saw the bus coming, she still had plenty of time to catch the bus.

Adrie considered himself lucky again that he was only fifteen years old. During the war he was too young to be a soldier and too young to work in Germany. Now after the war he was too young to round up girls for the hair cutting ceremony. He was just a spectator. Just as well, he thought, a guy can get hurt when you try to cut a girl's hair.

The executioners of the haircut punishment were a little more careful after the blood bath. When the wagon reached farmer Hoving's place to get his daughter, there was another argument. Hoving went inside and came back with; you guessed it another hatchet, the weapon of the barbarians. He was standing in the doorway and threatened: "Anybody who comes on my doorstep will be killed. My daughter never dated a German and you are not going to cut her hair."

Two officers of the Internal Dutch Fighting Force arrived. They had guns and demanded respect even from the axe swinging Hoving. Hoving said that his daughter never had dated a German soldier, he could vouch for that. The officers ruled in favor of the angry Hoving and told the people that if they could prove with absolute certainty, they could cut the hair of the girls.

Adrie hardly knew the girl and he hadn't watched which girls had been dating German soldiers, he had better things to do. To him the only important things had been to get food on the table and coal and wood in the stove. It could very well be that somebody thought he had seen the girl with a German or maybe they didn't like the girl or her father. Somebody might have been jilted by the girl and was out for revenge. Only one guy has to say: "Let's go to Hoving, his daughter dated German soldiers too," and everybody will agree.

The peace keeping officers also stipulated to the men in charge of the barbering party that the girls had to be delivered home safely, they had received their punishment and they had been taught a lesson. There was one more girl clipped and then the wagon turned around to drop the girls off at their homes.

So, dating German soldiers was wrong but when the Canadian soldiers came to The Netherlands, dating Canadian soldiers was the thing to do. And the Dutch boys became second class citizens. The girls were crazy about sitting with a Canadian soldier in a jeep chewing on a bar of chocolate. There was a song that developed:

> Tracey has a Canadian,
> Together in the jeep and floor the gas.

It seemed that all women went berserk about the Canadians. When they entered The Netherlands some of the Canadians were kissed by over 200 women. As the Chinese proverb says: "That you may live in interesting times." How could you miss it when you were a Canadian?

Even born party poopers, loners and ugly Canadians didn't escape the festive mood of the Dutch girls who wanted to make love to their liberators. Not only the single girls dated Canadian soldiers, even married women went for it. There was a 35 year old woman, who had three children. She went twice every Sunday to church; if she could have gone three times she would have done so. Her husband was an elder in the church and both looked like respectable people. She jumped in the jeep with a Canadian soldier and returned two days later. Her husband wasn't exactly amused when she told him that she had been celebrating.

The Canadians didn't mind celebrating with the happy Dutch people. They were generous with their bars of chocolate, especially to the girls and women. They were also generous in sperm donations. Consequently, quite a few Dutch girls got pregnant. Most of the times when the Canadian was single, he married the girl and wanted to take her back to Canada, to mother. In England where the Canadians had stayed most of the war years, it was even worse than in The Netherlands. Thousands of English women had babies by the Canadians and got married. The Americans had participated too to increase the world population. Many girls got knocked up by the Americans and had married American soldiers.

The Queen Mary and Queen Elizabeth transported over a million troops during World War II. Now the war was over, the English authorities decided that they had to fulfil one more war duty. It was not allowed for the girls to go to Canada with a troop transport ship; they had to go by themselves. "Operation Baby Carriage" had to bring the war brides with babies across the Atlantic. All Dutch women with their babies had to travel to Southampton to make the crossing to Canada or the U.S.

Over 25,000 marriages took place between Canadian soldiers and English girls. More than 48,000 young women with 20,000 children left for Canada. The Canadian soldiers had done more than win a war. Most of the war brides were from England, where three divisions had been stationed for about three years, before the Canadians were given active war duties. Quite a few Dutch war brides and a few from Belgium all made their way across the Atlantic to join their husbands. Many of the girls were city girls who moved to the farm in Canada. They persevered in houses without electricity and without running water. They also had to get used to outhouses with temperatures of 40 below zero. It took quite an adjustment but most of the girls made it and started to love the country in which they lived.

In The Netherlands, the inundated polder had to be milled dry by a steam engine. However, there was no coal available right away. Again it only took a week to get all that water in the polders and it took many months to get rid of it. All supplies of everything had been exhausted and transportation was very difficult. After the electricity was cut, Adrie had done most of the water pumping with a hand pump. Every day he had to pump for two hours at least to pump the water out that had seeped through the dyke. If it rained he had to pump a full hour longer to keep the houses dry behind the dyke.

Now the Dutch authorities had decided that this work could be done by the imprisoned traitors. One morning, a wagon came by to deliver two men who were supposed to pump the water out. Adrie loved that idea, he didn't mind at all to get rid of this tiresome job. There was only one problem; the men didn't do much pumping. Adrie always pumped alone but those traitors were both holding the handle in the same time and moved it very slowly down. The pump wasn't even properly primed with their slow pumping. Adrie had been watching their pumping and went up to them to tell them that they had to pump faster. They gave him a dirty look while they were still pumping very slowly. Adrie got mad and told the men: "Watch me, I'll show you how pumping is done."

The men were just standing to the side with no interest in their job whatsoever. Adrie gave them back the handle and said: "Now pump like I do or the water will flood the houses."

They couldn't care less and kept up their slow pace all day. At night the men were picked up to be transported to the camp. Adrie told the officer in charge that the men were lazy bones and that he had to do at least an hour pumping yet. He said: "I can pump all the water away in two hours if it doesn't rain and those nincompoops can't do it in eight hours."

The officer said: "What do you want me to do about it, I bring them to their jobs and tell them what to do, if they don't work fast enough there is little I can do. You want me to hit them with a whip?"

"Yes that's what you should do. Our people had to work for the Germans too during the war and they had to work hard or they would be shot. You think that all the Dutch men that were transported to Germany could get away with work like that?"

"I know that, but we cannot use the Nazi methods, we must show those people that we are better than the Nazis."

"You are wrong; we must show those people how we were treated by the Nazis and give them some of their own medicine."

Whatever Adrie was saying didn't help a bit. After the men left he pumped for another hour to get the remaining water out. He was real pissed off and complained to the polder authorities. They sent a man to instruct the workers with no result. The best they did was to have a little pissy ray of water coming out of the pump.

After the unconditional surrender had been signed by the Germans, the German soldiers had dumped boxes with ammunition and other supplies in the water. Everybody was fishing for them to see what was in the boxes. Adrie raked through the water and fished up a machine gun band with bullets, a bayonet and a German helm. Adrie's mother wasn't very happy when he brought the band with bullets in the house but his dad said: "Bullets without a gun are alright they can't do any harm." *(For years to come he would treasure those souvenirs of the war. When he emigrated to Canada he sold his treasures. He didn't think the Canadian customs would allow him to bring those war treasures into Canada, especially the bayonet.)*

Kees Vanderlinden was raking for treasure as well. He raked up a sheet metal box with a hasp on it. It could have contained hand grenades. When the neighbor saw Kees going home with it, he called him back. Kees didn't want to give up his treasure and ran away. He had bad luck; two inland security guards were just biking by and caught him. They took his box and one of the officers told him: "You stay away from the ammunition the Germans dumped in the water if you don't want to fly around with the angels." Everybody quit raking because of the danger that was involved.

Trials against Nazi collaborators started and one of the trials was against Koos Speenhof who was a Dutch poet. Before the war he had a poem in the newspaper every week and during the war he was hired by the Germans in a radio cabaret. He made all kinds of poems and songs about the war and those were publicly broadcasted. One of the songs he composed had been insulting to Her Majesty Queen Wilhelmina. It was all about the Depression years when people were starving and all kinds of bad moves had been made by the Dutch Government. He sang a couplet and in his refrain he would sing: "Have thanks your majesty." He was found guilty of insulting the Queen. His sentence was one year in prison and he wasn't allowed to publish any poems or songs for five years.

Willemstein commented: "It's a good thing that the Allies won the war so they could punish Speenhof. If the Germans had won the war they would have rounded up all the people who were singing songs on Radio Orange about Mussert and his aunt."

In Germany, the Allied occupation force tried to make the best of it. Many of their comrades had died during the war but the war was over, the enemy had been beaten so what else was there to do? The Americans had plenty of cigarettes and chocolate bars to chew, however, men can't live on cigarettes and chocolate bars alone.

Many German soldiers, in their prime of their lives, had been killed fighting the war. Their death had created many young German widows. The U.S. soldiers had no problem crawling in bed with the enemy. The frauleins (German women) had a good pension from their fallen husbands and the U.S. soldiers had a good army check. Most single U.S. soldiers were ready to fill the vacuum caused by the ravages of war.

Orange Forever, Long Lives the Queen.

Before the war, most people didn't care much for the Queen. Many people were unemployed and starving while the church and school preached that the Queen was the best thing that had happened to The Netherlands. With 90% of the money in the hands of 10% of the people, those teachings were questioned before the war and it hadn't improved when the Queen left for England when the Germans occupied The Netherlands. That certainly didn't make her popular.

Whenever she was announced as "Here is the mother of the fatherland with a message for the Dutch citizens," people had something to say about the mother of the fatherland, who had her ass in England, while the Dutch people had to put up with the Nazis and went hungry. However, when the coast was clear, this mother of the fatherland returned to The Netherlands to sit on the Dutch throne and her throne was not in the outhouse, it was a golden chair with purple satin covering. People had been singing in the streets: "Orange forever, long lives the Queen." However, when the Queen was trying to pick up where she had left off, people had a second thought about the Queen and didn't want to return to pre-war conditions.

The mother of the fatherland had a speech for the happy people of The Netherlands. She said: "My dearest citizens of the Netherlands, it is a great honor to set foot on the land of our beloved country again. Five years have gone by since the Nazis occupied The Netherlands forcing the Dutch Government into exile. We in England have fought hard for the liberation of The Netherlands, with all our might and power, all the time. And now is the hour that we have succeeded to drive the tyranny out of our beloved country. Nobody shall ever forget what it was to live under the German yoke. Therefore we shall celebrate May 5th as Liberation Day forever."

Princess Juliana, who was the heir to the throne after her mother, had buggered off to Canada when the war started. She had to make sure that the Nazis wouldn't touch her offspring. Those Princesses were destined to rule the Netherlands in the future. She left with her husband Prince Bernhard who was Prince of the Netherlands and three Princesses. When she returned she had four Princesses. The Prince of the Netherlands had done a good job to ensure that there would be heirs to the Dutch throne, so that the Dutch people could sing; "Orange forever, long lives the Queen."

Prince Bernhard was heralded on his return; he had been faithful to his wife Princess Juliana and The Netherlands. Prince Bernhard was a smart guy, who knew on which side his bread was buttered.

There was a strange thing with this latest Princess. Her father and mother were in Canada and her mother delivered this last Princess in an Ottawa hospital. Yet, she was born in The Netherlands. Leave it to politicians, everything is possible. For some unidentified reason it wasn't very good that a Dutch Princess was born in a foreign country. Therefore the Canadian Government was so gracious to declare the hospital in Ottawa, where Princess Juliana was delivering her baby, Dutch ground. All of a sudden The Netherlands had annexed a small part of Canada. Right after the birth of this new Princess, the Dutch Government was good enough to give that piece of real estate back to Canada. The Dutch people were moved to tears when they heard about the cooperation among the nations that had made this all possible. A Dutch Princess was born on Dutch ground in a hospital in Ottawa.

Rebuilding a Devastated World.

When World War II started a reporter asked Churchill: "The First World War was called 'The Great War.' What do we call the Second World War?"

Churchill's reply was: "The Unnecessary War. If England and France had stepped in before Hitler became powerful this could have been avoided."

He was right; England and France could have prevented the Second World War from happening if they had grabbed Hitler in his first venture when he occupied the Rhineland. At that stage, he wasn't powerful at all but while France and England were making Christmas toys, Germany was making planes, tanks and cannons around the clock. Over 56 million people later, who had died during the Second World War and the mass destruction of Europe and a large part of Asia, the unnecessary war was finally over but not the problems.

The Axis had spent $422 billion during World War II and the Allies $746 billion; a total expenditure of $1168 billion by a world that was in the Great Depression when the war started. The big spenders won the war showing that money talks, though with the new secret weapons of Germany, the war could have turned easily in favour of the Germans.

It was Hitler, who made a mistake in his planning; that gave the Allies victory. The Germans were working on the atomic bomb and the V2 in the beginning of the war but Hitler didn't think that the war would last long so he shoved the programs on the back burner. When things went sour for him, he saw too late that the Allies could win the war. That made him change his mind in a hurry and he revived his new secret weapons programs. The V2 was very destructive but it didn't turn the war around for Hitler, it came too late. If Hitler had had the V2 before the invasion of Normandy, the invasion would have been doomed.

With attacking Russia he made a mistake as well, he over extended his military power and was clobbered by the Russians. If he had finished England first, the outcome of the war could have been different.

Britain came out of the war as a pauper while the U.S. had become an economic giant being the richest nation on earth. And Germany, the loser of the war, was in ruins. It was the end of the Third Reich. Hitler had promised a Thousand Jahren Reich but twelve years after Hitler with his Nazis had come to power, the country was in ruins and Hitler was dead. After five harrowing years of warfare, World War II, the most destructive event in history in bloodshed and destruction came to an end. An uneasy peace settled over the devastated world and no one claimed that World War II had been needed to end all wars, as statesmen did at the end of World War I.

Lester Pearson, the Canadian Prime Minister, said: "You don't get peace by simply silencing the cannons; peace has to be in the people."

He was right; cannons and tanks don't make war but people do. Cannons had stopped firing and bombs had stopped dropping; it was peace in a world full of hate. The losers hated the victors and the victors hated the losers for all the damage they had done. The most difficult task was to make the world a better place that everybody had been fighting for. It was going to be a challenge. Many disillusioned soldiers claimed their place in the post war world, some were wounded and maimed for life but they all had to live.

Deutschland uber alles (Germany over everything) was now divided among the Allied victors. Things that might have been, had Germany won the war, would never be. Trouble started from the onset when Germany was divided into four occupied zones, France, Britain, U.S. and U.S.S.R. Because of tension with the Russians the Allies united their zones.

With cities in ruins, millions of people uprooted and destitute, and with foreign trade at a standstill, the immediate prospects seemed grim indeed. Europe was in a bad shape, imports exceeded exports by 100%, the national debts were increasing by the day, and an inefficient, unemployed, disorganized Europe came out of the war.

It was a hopeless situation even to think about rebuilding. Quite a few Dutch polders were still inundated waiting for a coal supply in order to mill them dry. The coal mines in the Southern part of The Netherlands were closed by lack of electricity, and coal was needed to make electricity with steam engines. Everybody expected that the black gold from the coal mines would get the Dutch economy going again. Even when they got the coal mines producing again, transportation of coal was a problem.

The Germans had done a good job with their scorched earth policy. If they couldn't own the world nobody else would. All the bridges that connected the Northern part of The Netherlands with the South were lying in the rivers. The Allies had built some temporary Baily bridges which were hampering the ships. Baily bridges couldn't be opened to let the ships through and the ships couldn't get underneath to pass.

Major supplies had to come from the U.S. across a sea that was full of mines. Hundreds of thousands of mines had to be swept. Many mine sweepers worked around the clock, they had to cut the chains on which the mines were anchored. As soon as the mine floated, it had to be destroyed with a cannon that was on the deck of the mine sweeper. If they didn't manage to destroy the mine, the mine became a floating menace instead of a stationary one. It was a tedious task and in spite of the mine sweeping efforts, there were still lots of mines left which made shipping a dangerous job. Rotterdam's harbor was a mess, full of sunken ships and cranes that were needed to unload the ships.

Schools were still closed; they were scheduled to reopen soon. Luckily it was spring so the schools didn't need any heating. The Tech was still closed. It was expected that it would open up in September when the new classes would start.

People needed bikes, shoes and other clothing and most houses were in need of repair. A lot of houses were beyond repair. The inhabitants had taken every door and piece of wood out of the houses to keep the stove burning. Luckily the houses were mostly made out of masonry.

With the unorganized mess that Europe was in, it was difficult to start organizing. The first priority was to get enough food for the hungry people and also medical supplies. It was a slow process until momentum was obtained. From there on, it was a matter of time to come to grips with the problems.

When the war was finished it was not possible to travel. The railways were destroyed and the few cars that the Germans hadn't taken had no gasoline to drive them. Yet, over eight million workers of occupied countries had been taken by the Germans to work in Germany. It never deterred the people who were in Germany that there was no mode of travel. They were going home to their families. It was a long trip, most of the time they were walking and sometimes a farmer with a horse drawn wagon offered them a ride for a few miles. It became chaos as hordes of people moved to go home.

About three weeks after Germany's defeat, a man came running to the Meuzelaars. He shouted: "Your son Kees is coming home from Germany, he is sitting on a wagon which is coming through the street."

Indeed there was a wagon pulled by a horse and Kees was sitting beside the owner. It had taken Kees 18 days to reach his home. He had been lucky that he had been working in West Germany; a lot of people had to walk home from East Germany and took more than 5 weeks to reach home. But home was a strong pulling magnet; in spite of the long distance and little food to eat, they all managed to get home.

On the other hand few of the Jews who had been transported to death camps in Germany returned. There was a clothes store owned by an older couple who had been rounded up by the Germans and transported to Germany. They never returned. The only Jew on the Hordyk that survived the holocaust was Fresco who was married to a German woman. Actually, that was a miracle, usually the Germans wanted to keep their race pure on Hitler's orders. Marrying a Jew was the worst thing a German woman could do. Fresco was wearing a yellow Star of David, yet he was never imprisoned.

From the millions of Jews who had been transported to death camps in

Germany very few survived. They only survived by chance. They were no better or smarter, they had only been lucky.

The Netherlands had 140,000 Jews when the war started. In spite of the brave Dutch people who were hiding the Jews, only 36,000 survived. A sad story about a Jewish girl Anne Frank surfaced. She had been hiding with her family for over a year in an attic room in Amsterdam and the Germans had finally discovered her and her family. All of them were arrested and transported to Auschwitz in Germany. In view of the advancing Allied forces, Hitler ordered the Jews to be shipped to a different camp in the Southern part of Germany. A typhoid epidemic broke out; Anne Frank contacted the disease and died a week before the liberation.

There are many sad stories like this one where the liberation came too late. On the other hand there are also some happy ones where the Allies came in the nick of time, to liberate the people, before they were exterminated by the Germans.

The most remarkable war story wasn't a happy story at all. It was about the Great Escape on March 25, 1944. The escape took place from Hitler's top security Prisoner Of War camp, near the Polish border, after preparation of over a year.

Although the escape was well planned and nothing was taken for granted, everything went wrong. It took them more than an hour to break through from the tunnel to the outside, which put the escape two hours behind schedule. The escape hole was also short of being in the protective woods and was in the perimeter surrounding the camp. All they could do now was to wait till the regular search lights had passed and head for the woods a few at a time.

When Hitler found out about the escape he was furious and ordered ten thousand troops to recapture them. The now free prisoners had not much chance to be successful with that kind of a man hunt. They had very good papers obtained by bribing German prison guards. The papers were so good that the German patrol let one of the men go but with an old trick the guard took him. When he let him go he said: "Good luck" in English. The escapee answered in English: "Yes, thanks."

Only three made it home and fifty of the escapees were shot after they were captured. On their way back to the prison camp they were allowed to stretch their legs in the woods and were shot. To cover up the execution, it stated on their death certificate that they were shot for trying to escape.

Eighteen of the Gestapo that were involved in the shooting were tried for war crimes. The Gestapo Commander said in his defence: "It was an official order from the Fuhrer. Befel is befel. (An order is an order.) If I hadn't done it somebody else would have done it and we all would have been shot."

Thirteen of the Gestapo were sentenced to death and hanged.

Another problem in the liberated countries was that people were overrun by lice and fleas. Soap hadn't been around for a long time and there were no means to combat lice or fleas. The Canadians who occupied The Netherlands shared their cigarettes and chocolate bars with the Dutch citizens and the Dutch citizens gave some of their lice and fleas to the Canadian soldiers. Canadian army trucks were sent out with D.D.T.. They had a pump with which they blew D.D.T. powder through the clothes of the Dutch people.

Going Fishing Again.

After food supplies, the next priority was to get the polders dry. If they hurried up, the farmers could still put some kind of a late maturing crop on their fields and the pastures could be restored for dairy cattle that had to be brought in. There was a lot of work to do, yet people were unemployed because of lack of supplies.

Finally they had the steam engine going and the inundated polder could be pumped dry. It had taken a few days to inundate the lands but it took three weeks to get the fields dry again. That caused a concentration of fish in the ditches and channels. Fishing had never been that good anywhere in The Netherlands at any time.

Adrie tried his luck and caught one fish after another. He had already ten fish before he ran out of live bait. For a while he had to suspend fishing to catch some stickle bass. Actually he had more than enough fish to eat and didn't like to go to the small ditches where he could get small stickle bass for bait. Instead he decided to try something else and cut up a small pike into pieces. He put one piece on his treble hook and threw it in the channel. To his great surprise, the piece of fish barely hit the water when he had another bite. Before he knew it he had caught 20 fish. Besides pike and pickerel there were other fish to be caught as well. Adrie even caught an eel, every fish and his brother was hungry.

That was enough fishing he thought and walked past a smaller ditch to go home. He couldn't believe his eyes when he saw countless bass and pikes swimming, right on top of the water, gasping for air. There were far too many fish in the ditch and the oxygen supply was insufficient which made them surface. Bass wasn't easy to catch with angling; Adrie had tried it a few times unsuccessfully. Now here was an opportunity not to be missed.

He went fast home and returned with a large pail and a rake. He moved his rake underneath the fish and he threw them on the shore. When there were quite a few bass and small pikes lying on the shore, he decided to put them in his pail and call it a day. The muddy shore had made his fish kind of dirty. Some clean water would get rid of the mud, Adrie thought. It would be more effective to swirl the fish around with his hands, that way he would get them cleaner. When he was moving the fish around in the water, he felt all of a sudden a sharp pain in his hands. He lifted his hands out of the water and to his surprise two pikes were hanging on each hand.

Both hands were involved which prevented him from grabbing the pikes behind their gills, to remove them from his hands. Hitting the pikes on the ground didn't produce any result either, only some more pain in his hands was the result of that idea. The pikes were stubborn and didn't let go. What could he do to get rid of the biting pikes? When he saw his neighbor Kees fishing in the channel, he ran for help to be relieved of the aching pain. Kees didn't know what he saw when Adrie ran up to him with two pikes dangling on each hand. Another few painful minutes passed before Kees managed to remove the biting pikes.

Adrie had way too many fish to eat them all; they wouldn't stay good for more than a few days. It didn't matter, there was hardly anything for sale in the stores and food was still in short supply. Bartering for food and other goods still went on for quite a while after the liberation of The Netherlands.

After the water had been pumped out of the inundated polders it was quite messy. Trees and hedges that had been standing in the water had all died and had to be removed. Between the properties of Immerzeel and the de Kievits was a wide hedge. It also had died, except a couple of sticks that were close to the dyke. Arie removed the dead hedge and when he was just about finished Leen Immerzeel, already 25 years old, came to raise a stink. He said: "You have no right to take out that hedge; I was the one who planted it when I was young."

Arie replied: "It was dead, what do you want to do with a dead hedge?"

Leen Immerzeel said angrily: "It was my hedge, I was rather attached to it; you should have left it alone."

It was like seeing the same movie twice; first there was a hedge problem with the Meuzelaars and now with the Immerzeels. Arie said: "I'll put up a fence. At least it doesn't need trimming and its dead already."

At night there was a headline in the newspaper that Adrie didn't like.

DEPORTATION OF N.S.B's TO NEW GUINEA INHUMANE.

The Dutch Prime Minister has studied the possibility of deporting all members of the Dutch Nazi Party (N.S.B.) to New Guinea. In a plan for a major overhaul of the Dutch citizens and to clean them of all riff raff caused by the war, it had been in the planning to deport them all to New Guinea to help with the Indonesian agricultural project. It was suggested that this was a cheap way to get rid of those unwanted non Dutch like citizens. This way it would be not necessary to imprison them and they would be doing some good to society after doing damage for five years during the war. Prime Minister Drees suggested that this would be very inhumane just to satisfy our revenge.

Adrie wasn't the only one to be outraged, everybody had thought that as soon as the war was over, all those Nazi supporters were going to be adequately punished and deporting them was the punishment they deserved. All traitors and collaborators with the Germans should leave, those people thought that the Germans were great so let them bugger off.

People were outraged about the poor punishment of the traitors. On the other hand the soldiers who fought the war were mistreated. There was the usual medal rain after the war was finished. Soldiers were recognized for services provided beyond the call of duty. They had to pay seven guilders for their medal because the Government couldn't afford to pay for all those medals.

As always, the officers didn't have to pay a nickel for their medals. Only John with the cap paid and the officers received higher medals free. Officers are usually in a safe place while the soldiers succumb. Soldiers do all the dirty jobs to win the war for the Generals and the Generals receive a higher medal for which they don't have to pay.

Always Something.

On the Hordyk was a house with a motto in the front with big letters, "Always Something." One disaster after another had happened, first the Depression and next came the war. Adrie wondered if they ever would have a good time again. So far he hadn't seen any. There was hope that now the war was over, better times were lurking in the future and prosperity would be restored. Hopefully the de Kievits wouldn't be poor for a change and that an era of good times was looming for the family. That would be nice!

Early indications were that the family was going to have trouble to make good times happen. When the water was finally milled out of the polder, there was lots of work to do; the earth dam had to be levelled so that the gardens could be restored. The water state that had put the dam up was going to do all that and hired Adrie and his father to do the work. Adrie didn't mind working, but his father pocketed all the money; he never got a nickel from the money he made, which made it not attractive at all. As a matter of fact, he didn't even get any pocket money; his father said that he had to contribute to keep the family going and young boys didn't need any pocket money. They were fed and taken care of at home, what else did they want?

There was a lot of good fishing around when the land was dry again; all fish had retreated to the channels and ditches. Adrie had planned to go fishing one Saturday afternoon with his friends and had caught some little fish for bait the night before. It could have been a lot of fun if his father hadn't told him in the morning that he had to work on Saturday afternoon as well. When his friends came to call on him, his father said: "Adrie has to work for the Water State, he can't always play; there is a lot of work to be done."

That incident made the relationship with his father go down some more. There had been way too many incidents already. Adrie had his first unpleasant incident when he was only five years old. At that time, he was collecting caterpillars, lady bugs and a host of other things in metal boxes which were closed. He needed some little holes in the boxes so that his insects wouldn't suffocate and went to his father for help. Unfortunately, his father was in a bad mood and hit his box with insects so that it flew away over the yard. He told Adrie not to bother him with stupid things like that.

Of course his insects escaped and Adrie ran crying to his mother. His mother went to his father to give him hell for being so rude. His father went to Adrie after he had punched some holes in the box and he had caught a bunch of caterpillars in the trees which he had put in the box. That should make Adrie happy his father thought. On the contrary; Adrie wanted nothing to do with his father anymore and never went for help to him after this incident. Once hurt, twice shy.

The many times that his father sent him and his sister to bed for running around the house because he couldn't stand it didn't improve his thoughts about his father either. Even in the morning when they had to stay in bed till he was ready to get up was very unpleasant. Whenever they made too much noise in his opinion, he came out of bed to give them a spanking.

With an attitude like that Adrie and Willie saw their father as an old grumpy sour puss that had loose hands to spank them on every little occasion; they couldn't even play, or they were sent to bed. The straw that broke the camel's back came when for the first time there were clothes available. They were still rationed but everybody had enough coupons to buy some clothes. Adrie needed a new Sunday suit and his sister a dress so his mother gave them the money to go downtown by bus to buy it. Willie, his sister, being the oldest was in charge. When they were waiting for the bus at the bus stop, his mother came out to tell them that their father had made a big row with her and told her that the kids had to pay for their own clothes.

She had objected to his demand by telling him that they had no income and no pocket money so they couldn't. He wouldn't listen and said that the kids had enough money in their piggy banks to buy some clothes. In order to stop the argument that was going to turn into a fight, their mother had said that she was going to tell the kids that they had to pay for their own clothes. She didn't agree with this attitude at all and told Adrie and Willie to tell him that they had paid for their own clothes but she would still pay for it. "Don't tell your father," she warned, "because if he finds out that I paid for your clothes, he will take it out on me!"

That was the end of respect that Adrie had for his father. The money in his piggy bank was derived from working on the land for ten cents per week, from birthdays when his aunts would give him a dime or so and from delivering the church papers. His father had punished him even when he had taken money out of his piggy bank to buy candies so he could pocket some more money.

When Adrie made sixty cents per hour by working for the Water State and worked about thirty hours every week, his father wrote his time down and collected all the money, he never gave him a nickel and now he was supposed to pay for his own clothes. There would be nothing left in his piggy bank and that money was supposed to be for his future. The way it looked he didn't have a future at all. Adrie and his sister were infuriated with their dad, but they played along with their mother so she wouldn't get into more trouble with the old geezer.

Instead of having good times after the Great Depression and now that the war was finished, they were fighting each other. During the war and the Depression they had been a fighting unit to keep the wolves away from the door and to get food on the table so they would survive. For the first time things were looking up, they were still a fighting family but now they were fighting each other. As the house on the Hordyk suggested there was "Always Something."

The English Army was Driving on the Wrong Side of the Road.

There were all kinds of foreign troops in The Netherlands. Beside the Canadians there were also American and English troops. Most of the problems were caused by the English troops who were driving on the wrong side of the road. The tunnel underneath the Meuse River consists out of two tubes, one for each direction. That was done for safety and was a good idea. When the Americans were half way through the tunnel, they didn't know what they were seeing. From the opposite direction, came a column of the English army that was transporting some heavy equipment on flatbeds. The Americans were driving in the right tube but the English troops, being used to left hand traffic, had entered the wrong tube. All the English army trucks had to back up for a considerable distance to clear the tunnel.

With the war finished, the U.S. started to supply the liberated countries. Once the harbors of Rotterdam and Amsterdam were cleared it became easier. More and more ships unloaded their precious cargoes for the hungry people.

Besides food, the ships unloaded paper which was urgently needed for office supplies and to get the newspapers going again. Little newspapers consisting of two pages of standard office paper were available right after the war. Most of the news was about the progress which was being made in re-supplying the countries to get them back to normal. At the end of every week the newspapers reported how many ships had entered the harbor of Rotterdam. Every week this number was higher which indicated progress in the post war world.

There were two different newspapers. One was from before the war and was called 'The Rotterdam Newspaper' and the second one was from during the war. It was, during the war, an underground illegal newspaper. The name of the paper was 'Trouw,' translated in English it meant 'Faithful.' The name was chosen because they were faithful to the Royal Family. They were now advertising their newspaper "Trouw. First Illegal and now National." A lot of people who had read the illegal paper during the war years subscribed to Trouw.

After the war people were saying that:

England was strongest at sea,
The U.S. was strongest in the air,
Russia was strongest on land,

And Germany was strongest in the newspaper.

This was supposed to be a joke to show that the Germans were first class in distorting the facts. In the real world, the Allies did the same thing to cover up defeats and losses.

Monuments and Sour Grapes.

Rotterdam centre was destroyed in the beginning of the war. Now the war was over; the city of Rotterdam commissioned the artist Zadkini to make a sculpture expressing the destruction of Rotterdam center. He made a sculpture which looked like a monster without a heart. A big city without a heart. The only thing that was left of the old centre was City Hall, the General Post Office and the St. Lawrence Cathedral. The cathedral was severely damaged when other buildings were burning all around. The massive basalt blocks from which they had built the cathedral had saved the structure but internally it was burned out.

Rotterdam wasn't the only city that was bombed, at least it wasn't completely destroyed like the German cities. Goebbles had boasted at the beginning of the war that no R.A.F. bomber would ever bomb Berlin. The powerful German Luftwaffe would intercept any bomber on its way there. In spite of his optimism, there were 30 air raids on Berlin. Before the war Berlin was a beautiful city with 4.4 million people, when the war was finished only 2 million were left and the city was totally destroyed.

London had been the target of the Germans and had experienced massive destruction. Even the Royal Palace had taken a direct hit which made the English King remark: "It looks like Hitler wants to get rid of me so he can put my brother on the throne. *(His brother had been pro- German before he abdicated; he thought that Hitler with his National Socialist Party was doing a great job for Germany.)*

Russia had also cities that were completely destroyed. Stalingrad was a heap of rubble and Leningrad, one of the most beautiful cities in the world was reduced to ruins after an 880 days siege by the Germans. It was the longest siege of any city in the world. From the more than 3 million inhabitants only

750,000 were left. More than a million people had died by German shells, bombing and starvation and over a million people had been evacuated.

Japan had Tokyo in ruins and of course Hiroshima and Nagasaki. Confucius, the Chinese philosopher, said: "What you don't want them to do to you, don't do it to others." In 1937 Japan bombed Shanghai, it was the first air attack in history and in 1943 till 1945, Japan was the target of the U.S. Air Force. It was the same for Germany; they bombed Warsaw in 1939 and Rotterdam in 1940. They had it coming and many German cities were destroyed.

All countries were planning to rebuild their cities, but it was going to take time and of course an awful lot of money. Early plans were made to rebuild the centre of Rotterdam. Actually the City Fathers considered themselves very lucky. The old city centre had been built in the time of the horse and buggy. It consisted of narrow alleys, shaggy cafes and old buildings. The narrow streets were already quite a problem when the war started. In the post war years with the development that took place, it would have been a disaster. A blueprint for a modern city with wide avenues was easy to draw because there was a lot of room. In a way, if we forget about the brutality of the Germans, the open space in the centre of Rotterdam was bliss.

Another monument was erected in Rotterdam; it was in honor of Admiral Karel Doorman. He was the commander who was defending Indonesia against the Japanese. Against the overwhelming Japanese forces, he had lost the Battle in the Java Sea in which he died. The Dutch government considered him a hero and erected a monument for him behind the Coolsingel. Two weeks after the monument was unveiled, it was deliberately destroyed by vandals. During the night somebody toppled the statue and destroyed it completely. On the pedestal was a large piece of cardboard with the message, "If you want to honor your heroes. Make sure that your artists aren't dishonored."

Not everybody was happy that the war was over. There were a lot of sour grapes after the war among the losers. Apparently there was somebody who didn't like the monument and destroyed it. The monument was never restored and neither did they find the culprits.

During the last years of the war, no houses had been built. Moreover, many houses had been destroyed by bombing raids. This created a severe shortage of housing in post war The Netherlands. When rebuilding started it was obvious that there was a new style of architecture. It used to be that houses had gables which gave each house a character of its own. After the war all buildings looked the same, like oversized square shit houses. Houses were no longer built for eternity, but mostly for the need of the moment.

Because of the destruction of the old centre of Rotterdam most of the movie theatres, pubs and restaurants were destroyed. Alcoholic beverages were pretty near non-existent and eating in restaurants was out of the question shortly after the war. Everything was still rationed and entertainment was very scarce.

People needed entertainment although that most movie theatres were destroyed. Building more movie theatres would take a while with all the other priorities. It seemed that all Governments followed the same policy to rebuild the industry first to get the economy going. Next was house building, which left movie theatre building low on the totem pole in the rebuilding program. The centre of Rotterdam was a heap of rubble in very slow restoration.

People who were working had no time to buy tickets in the afternoon and when they wanted to go to the movies at night the theatres were sold out. If there is a shortage there is a black market. People who weren't working bought a lot of tickets in the afternoon and sold them at night for double the price. Who wants to work when you can make easy money by scalping? The theatres tried to combat this problem; they wouldn't sell more than six tickets to one person. But this person could go back half an hour later and buy six more tickets or he had his son or daughter buy tickets.

Next, the police grabbed the bull by the horns. Plain clothes policemen walked the movie theatre district to watch what was going on. They promptly arrested a few scalpers and confiscated the tickets. The scalpers had an answer to that problem; they took their son along with the tickets in his pocket. First of all the scalper would find a customer and next he would go to the side street to get the tickets from his son. If they arrested him he had no tickets in his pocket. Of course, the police got wise on that system; they followed the man to the side street and arrested his son as well.

No More Stealing.

During the five war years in The Netherlands stealing had become a way of life. When people are starving; 'Dire need knows no laws.' Now the war was over everybody had to face severe adjustment changes. The main problem was that there were severe shortages for quite some time and people helped themselves.

Uncle Jaap had also returned from Germany; it had taken him more than four weeks to arrive back home. For the first time, he saw his baby son and was thrilled to no end. He now had the perfect family a daughter and a son, what else could he possibly want? He wanted wood to cook supper for his family and he knew where to get it. When the polder was milled dry, there were still barbed wire fences standing on the land. Those fences had been put up to divide the pastures and were going to be used again. That is, if nobody swiped them. There were quite a few poles in those fences which made good wood for the stove.

With a saw, a claw hammer and a couple of bags, uncle Jaap arrived. He went into the pastures, took the barbed wire off the wooden poles and cut the poles to size for easy transportation in his bags. Koos Vryland was the farmer who owned the pastures. When he saw a guy taking his fences down for firewood, he went to Uncle Jaap to tell him that those were his poles and he couldn't take them.

Uncle Jaap was still used to war circumstances when everything was a go. "Why don't you shut up, you asshole, I need wood to cook my supper."

Koos Vryland went straight to the cops to complain. In the meantime Uncle Jaap had left with his wood and was planning to come back for more. He had asked Adrie if he could leave the saw in the bike shed till he returned. Adrie was home by himself and said it was alright. However, one thing uncle Jaap hadn't told Adrie was about the confrontation with Koos Vryland.

Koos Vryland had watched where uncle Jaap had disappeared to and figured that he was living there. A little later the police came, together with Koos Vryland, to the door to ask Adrie where the wood was that he had stolen.

"I know nothing about wood."

Koos Vryland said: "It wasn't him that stole the wood, it was an older man."

The police asked: "Was your father stealing wood in the pasture?"

"No, that wasn't my father, it was my uncle."

When the police asked where his uncle lived he said: "Somewhere in Rotterdam."

The police wanted to look in the shed and when they discovered the saw, they figured that this was the tool with which the crime had been committed. Promptly, they confiscated the saw and left. When uncle Jaap returned to steal more wood, he found out that he no longer had a saw. He was quite cheesed off and left in quite a hurry, just in case the police came back.

At night a letter was delivered to the owner of the property, that the saw which was confiscated could be claimed by its rightful owner. It was a trick to get the thief, but it didn't work. Uncle Jaap could smell the rat; he had no desire to ask for his saw and being arrested at the same time.

With more supply ships docking in Rotterdam the food supply became adequate. There was still rationing of meat, sugar and tobacco. Staple food like bread and potatoes were sufficient. In time, everything improved and small rations were increased. Even the newspaper had a normal size again with quite a few pages less than before the war. Adrie read the newspaper every night and on July 2nd, 1945 he read:

OKINAWA IN U.S. HANDS.

"U.S. Prepares For Invasion of Japanese Main Island."

It was almost unbelievable that there was still a war on at the other side of the world.

The Graduate.

Very slowly everything went back to normal and all the post war problems were dealt with. Adrie had been doing a lot of fishing while he was waiting for a letter from the Tech to advise him when he had to go back to school. That would be in September, Adrie thought, when normal courses would resume.

In the meantime, there were other things to do. There never had been an opportunity for him to learn swimming. Around where he lived there were no swimming pools. Consequently, learning to swim had been on the back burner. When he learned that the swimming pool in Barendrecht had started a swimming course, he registered right away. That was the opportunity of a life time. It was a 45 minute walk, which didn't deter Adrie. What else was there to do? While he was waiting for the Tech to re-open, he could learn to swim the Channel. That was perfect planning until the proverbial fly landed in the ointment.

In July, Adrie received a letter from the Principal of the Tech, telling him that he had passed and he could pick up his diploma. He couldn't believe his eyes, the last half a year of his course had been a disaster. With the "hunger winter," he only had attended classes for three months before the school was closed. There hadn't been any examinations which are always part of any curriculum. How was that possible?

If it hadn't been for the war, Adrie could have finished the Tech at the end of March. During March nobody thought about finishing the Tech, everybody was glad to be alive. May 5, 1945, the war ended in Europe and everybody had to face the consequences of the war years. The war had uprooted the lives of many people.

On the designated day, Adrie walked to the Tech. He still didn't have a bike that soon after the war. At the Tech he met his friend Cor Vanelst who also came to pick up his diploma. Cor was working as hard as Adrie, they exchanged technical books and were always together. Of course, 'Birds of the same kind flock together.'

Adrie and Cor were the only ones to receive a diploma from the 50 students in Motor Mechanics. There were also two students from the electricians, two from the carpenters, two from the metal workers and two from the painters. They had taken the best two students of each trade to qualify for a certificate. All the others had to repeat the fourth class.

From the over 250 students at the Tech, only ten graduated. That was only four percent of all the students. It was the worst performance ever and if Churchill would have heard about it, he certainly would have said: "At no other time in history, have so few of so many students graduated in such a long period."

The Principal was very nice when he handed the diplomas to Cor Vanelst and Adrie. It made Adrie think about the time that the Principal was furious when all students of the fourth class of motor mechanics had missed the afternoon classes.

Mr. Schuif was one of the two teachers in blacksmithing. He was very strong and all muscle. He could bite a penny into two peaces. If you wanted to see him do that you had to give him a bar of chocolate. Chocolate was hard to get during the war but one of the students had managed to get one. Indeed he managed to bite the penny in half and had some bleeding gums after the performance.

Biting pennies in half wasn't the only thing he was good at. All the students called him 'The Rules King.' There was a sheet with the rules of the Tech; it was quite extensive and would take you about half an hour to write the rules out. For punishment you might have to write the rules of the Tech four times. Mr. Schuif was very bad in punishing students. For any little thing that went wrong, the students had to write the rules of the Tech four times. It was plain ridiculous; even Adrie had to write the rules four times. His punishment was unfair and Adrie was furious.

One afternoon when he was blacksmithing there was a worker who was fixing the windows. The man asked Adrie: "Can you open the window for me?"

"Sure I can," Adrie replied and opened the window.

A little later Mr. Schuif came, mad as a hornet, to Adrie and asked him "Did you open that window?"

"Yes I did, because the worker had to fix the window."

Mr. Schuif said: "You have to keep your paws off the windows. Because of you there is one of the hinges broken. You have to write four times the rules of the Tech."

Adrie tried to explain that he had been asked by the worker and he had only tried to be helpful. The teacher didn't even listen. Adrie wasn't going to take this unfair punishment and didn't write out the rules four times. When they had blacksmithing again he was supposed to hand over the rules. Mr. Schuif said: "All the students who had to write the rules four times come to my desk and hand them over."

That afternoon there were nine students who had been punished to write the rules four times. Eight students came forward and Adrie stayed where he was. Mr. Schuif punished way too many students and hadn't written the names down. He couldn't remember who he had punished. It was Adrie's lucky day and he got away with it.

When Adrie was in the fourth class, he had blacksmithing by Mr. Dekeizer who was a nice teacher and never punished anybody. One afternoon when they had blacksmithing, it was known that Mr. Dekeizer was sick. This meant that Mr. Schuif would take his place. Nobody liked that idea, everybody hated the Rules King. It was decided to cut classes and go downtown instead of getting rules to write. The school skippers were waiting at the gate to catch all the pupils of the class. When they were informed that the Rules King would be teaching, everybody joined and went downtown.

Only one pupil of the 25 had attended classes that afternoon. He had been late and missed the message. The next day, the Principal visited the class and asked everybody where they had been. Most of the students used the standard excuse: "I had to go to the farm to get some food."

Obviously, the Principal was cheesed off and said: "The gentlemen will be very sorry for what they have done!"

When the Principal handed over the certificates to Cor and Adrie, he didn't seem to think of that incident but Cor and Adrie remembered the threat. On the report cards of Cor and Adrie it said on the fourth class page, "No marks because of war circumstances."

With his diploma in his pocket, Adrie could now try to find a job in a garage. That was easier said than done. The war was over only 10 weeks and there were very few cars left. With only doctors, lawyers and some business people having an old car, there wasn't much to do in the garages. Uncle Jan said: "I'll find you a job!"

First he tried to get Adrie in the military garage. Wouldn't you know it, he had to be 18 years old and he was barely 15. It looked as though in his entire life he was going to be too young. One night his uncle came to see Adrie and said: "Mr. Spoormaker lives on the Dortse Straatweg, he has a garage downtown. I have spoken to him and he said he has a job for you, go over and see him."

Adrie went with his diploma to see Mr. Spoormaker. Mr. Spoormaker looked at the marks on his report card and said: "Excellent, I got a job for you; come tomorrow to the garage and I'll tell the personnel manager to hire you."

The next morning, he went on his old bike with solid tires, to the garage and was hired. When he asked how much money he was going to make, the personnel manager said: "16 cents per hour. That's not bad for a 15 year old boy, don't you think so?"

Adrie didn't think so; he had made 60 cents per hour when he worked for the polder and considered it not more than a lousy tip. Apprentices were paid very little in those days; there was nothing anybody could do about that. The main thing was that he had a job and was getting experience.

In a way, Adrie had hoped that finding a job would take longer than it did. At least he could have learned to swim properly. He only had received a few lessons and swimming had to be postponed now he had to work.

Six o' clock comes early in the morning, Adrie thought when his mother woke him up. He had to start work at 7.30 a.m. and there was almost an hour of biking to get to his work. His bike was an old piece of rust with solid rubber tires which he had cut from an old auto tire. It wasn't too bad riding on the asphalt roads but Rotterdam had quite a few cobble stone roads and the cobble stones were real big which gave you a very bumpy ride.

His mother said she was going to try to get air tires for him. In order to get a tire permit, she had to fill out a bunch of forms and Adrie's boss had to fill out a piece on the forms as well. In vain she tried; you only could get a permit if you were employed in essential services. Adrie's mother said to the city official: "You mean to tell me that repair of cars is not essential?"

The man looked over his glasses at her and said: "Yes, repairing cars is essential but your son is just an apprentice so he himself is not essential at all. When he has his master certificate come again and we will give him some tires." That's the way it was with everything, you had to know the right person to get a permit.

There was one customer Adrie liked very much, his name was Mr. Merry; he had a shoe store and was very proud of his car. As soon as the Germans had occupied The Netherlands, he had hidden his car. Luckily for him, he got away with it and he was one of the few people to drive a car. When he came in he said to Adrie: "When my car is finished, you are one guilder richer, make sure to do a good job." That was a good tip when you make 16 cents per hour Adrie thought. He had to work more than six hours to make a guilder.

Mr. Spoormaker was a G.M.C. dealer and was a representative of Opel automobiles. The Americans were selling off war surplus and Mr. Spoormaker had acquired four big G.M.C. army trucks. He was going to fix them up and sell them. With the shortage of transportation means there would be no problem to sell them. Army trucks never had a key; that was just too clumsy when you are fighting a war. They just get lost. The army trucks were just parked in the street and anybody could drive them away.

When lunchtime came Adrie and his friend had a keen interest in the army trucks. It was easy to start the trucks, all you needed to do was turn on a switch and away you went. Driving up and down the street was the next thing and soon they were driving army trucks. Mr. Spoormaker wasn't impressed when he found out that joy riding was going on during lunch time. In no time he had starter keys put in all four trucks. That solved that problem and that was the end of the fun for Adrie and his friend.

Spoormaker used to repair a lot of cars for the Germans during the war. He had a garage and the Germans brought in cars. You couldn't say no to the Germans, they don't understand that kind of language. Whenever the mechanics worked on German cars they sabotaged them. Most of the time they put half a hand full of sand in the oil which made the engine wear out fast. Sabotage couldn't be overdone, that might make the Germans suspicious. Putting a hand full of sugar in the gasoline was a faster remedy; that made the motor seize up pretty fast.

Now the Germans were back in their homeland, Spoormaker had a lot of American army trucks to repair. All those American soldiers had lots of medals. One of the soldiers had three purple hearts. "Why three of the same medals?" Adrie asked.

The American explained: "You don't get a purple heart for bravery beyond the call of duty. A purple heart is given for being in the wrong place at the wrong time. That means that you are wounded. I was wounded three times during this war, once I was hit by a bullet and twice by shrapnel."

How Can a Particle of an
Atom End the War?

It sure did! After the Nazis had been defeated, there was still the other war going on with Japan. Actually in The Netherlands there wasn't that much interest in that far away war in Asia. Some of the news that was brought to the Dutch people about the war was about the destruction of Japanese cities. There was also an article in the paper about the kamikaze attacks by the Japanese. Adrie couldn't believe that kamikaze pilots were flying airplanes loaded with explosives and stayed with them until they hit their target. The Americans couldn't believe their eyes either when the kamikaze attacks started and were not prepared at all for this strange and deadly practice.

On the other hand, the English and American pilots who had bombed German cities didn't have much more chance to survive than the kamikaze pilots. Many missions had 40% losses and if a pilot was still alive after five missions, it was a miracle.

There were all kinds of riddles when Adrie read the paper. This time there was no headline, just a very little piece in the paper that stated: "The Allies defeated the Nazis in the nick of time. The Germans were working to split the atom and were half a year ahead of the Americans. Had they succeeded to split the atom before the Allies, the outcome of the war could have been different. With splitting the atom, the Nazis could have made a bomb of unequalled power and destruction, which could have altered the outcome of the war."

Adrie sure couldn't figure that one; he had learned at the Tech that a molecule is the smallest particle of an element. When the molecule is divided some more, we get atoms which consist of protons and neutrons. Those atoms you couldn't even see with the naked eye; how could they be that powerful when they are split? Besides, the word atom comes from the Greek word 'atomos' which means indivisible. Now if it is indivisible how can you split it? Although Adrie was good in Physics, this time he didn't have the foggiest idea what they were talking about. But then he happened to be no Einstein.

The mystery of the powerful atom deepened when on August 6 the entire front page was covered with news about the atomic bomb.

U.S. DROPS ATOMIC BOMB ON HIROSHIMA.

The atomic bomb which was dropped on Hiroshima today had a strength of 20,000 tons of T.N.T. and the bomb was more powerful than 20,000 normal bombs. Hiroshima has been destroyed, 86,000 people were killed and 61,000 wounded.

It seemed that the war in the Far East was coming to a conclusion as well. On August 8 the headlines in the paper read:

SOVIET UNION DECLARES WAR ON JAPAN.

On August 9 there was some more historic news.

NAGASAKI DESTROYED WITH ATOMIC BOMB.
26,000 Killed And 24,000 Injured.

August 10 saw finally the end of the most destructive war to hit the globe.

"JAPAN SURRENDERS."
Emperor Hirohito announced the surrender of Japan. People are weeping in front of the Imperial Palace.

It had been a savage war against Japan. The Japanese were smashing dead American soldiers with a sledge hammer on their face to get their golden teeth. The Americans were acting the same after they saw the atrocities committed by the Japanese. Those animals were no good, all you could do with them is kill them, so no prisoners were taken; even wounded soldiers were shot. The U.S. marines threw away the rule book, surviving was all that counted.

The Japanese military command was hell-bent to save Japan at the expense of the Japanese people who were willing to die for their Emperor. When the Americans started to bomb Japan, the Japanese didn't shoot at the bombers, they rammed their fighter right in the American bomber to get it down.

Fighting the Germans was quite something; no matter how much they were beaten, there was always a counter attack and they never gave up ground till the last man. The Japanese were worse; they would rather commit suicide than become a P.O.W. They fought to the last bullet and lined up to commit suicide. They waited till it was their turn, took the last dead Japanese soldier of the rope and hung themselves.

The Japanese were preparing the defence of their home land. People were told that the Americans were nothing but a bunch of derailed sex starved soldiers who would make sex slaves of the entire Japanese population, young and old. They had two choices; victory or slavery.

After all the severe battles in the Pacific, there was one major final battle looming, the Japanese main land. With all the kamikazes, suicide boats etc., the Japanese were going to use, the first wave of landing forces had no more chance to survive than the kamikaze pilots. It would be plain suicidal; Normandy had been bad but this would be worse. The cost of taking Japan was estimated to be over a million U.S. soldiers. Two atomic bombs forced the surrender of Japan and made a landing unnecessary.

The war in the Pacific against Japan was a costly war; 3854 ship wrecks are lying on the bottom of the Pacific including 23 carriers, 213 torpedo boats, 22 battle ships and 50 oil tankers. The ships are rusting and one after another is letting its oil out of the tanks. An ecological disaster is looming.

More than 12,000 U.S. men and 200,000 Japanese were killed. The civic population was reduced to 60%. 200,000 people died instantly with the first atomic bomb and 100,000 people died later from the radiation they had been exposed to.

Three months after Germany surrendered, Japan was defeated and surrendered. Finally the world was at peace and everybody could start to rebuild the devastated world. Peace came at a high price. More than 53 million people had died during World War 2. The Allies put the blame solely on the Nazis and Japanese. They were planning to bring those responsible for the greatest destruction ever encountered on earth, to justice.

Europe had taken the brunt of the war but Asia had seen some terrible destruction as well, especially Japan. Finally war production could be cut back and industry could start to rebuild the world and provide food and housing for the people. The first post war year was terrible; great shortages of everything prevailed and the Government instituted price control which stayed in force for a long time. If a certain job was done and the customer didn't like his bill, he could complain to the price control committee. The contractor had to supply a worksheet to show the materials he had used and the time it had taken to do the job. The committee's decision was final.

Everybody thought that there would be a combined effort to get the economy going. Unfortunately, that didn't happen. During the war there was an agreement with the Unions not to strike as it would only benefit the enemy. As soon as the war was finished troubles started. The Unions were determined to get hefty wage increases in order to keep up with the inflation, which happened because of too much money chasing not enough goods. In 1945 - in spite of the fact that the U.S. was for more than half of the year at war - there were over 40 million man days lost due to strikes. It tripled in 1946 with more than 120 million man days lost. This all happened while the competition for a job was severe in post war U.S.A. In the first post war year over 9 million U.S. servicemen were demobilized who all needed a job.

In The Netherlands, the Dutch people didn't understand all those strikes. They seldom had strikes in The Netherlands before the war. Most of the

Dutch people saw a strike as a losing proposition, you lose wages and jobs are lost to the competition. If you want to milk the cow, you don't kill it.

On the other hand the Americans didn't understand the Dutch system either. Before the war there were no holidays in The Netherlands other than for rich people. After the war this was changed; the Dutch people had now six holidays and six snipper days. Those snipper days could be taken any time when a person needed a day off for some reason. If you wanted you could add some to your holidays to get a longer holiday.

There were quite a few Americans in The Netherlands to help getting the industry going. From the U.S. came all kinds of shipments. There were a lot of machines that arrived in boxes that had to be assembled. One of the Americans had a crew of Dutch workers which consisted of mechanics, welders etc. After a few days working he missed John one morning. He asked the other guys: "Where is John?"

The answer he got was: "John has a snipper day."

He asked: "What the hell is that?" It took a little doing before he understood what a snipper day was.

Wouter Fioole, the fiancée of Willie, had lived in North Brabant before the war. During the war his parents had moved to Rotterdam and now the war was over they moved back to Brabant. They invited the family de Kievit to come over for a weekend. It was an eye opener for Adrie. The Germans had blown up the Moerdyk bridges. A couple of spans of the railway bridge and of the traffic bridge were still usable. They had put the usable spans in the traffic bridge and there was one span from a completely different bridge. The Americans had finished the bridge with a couple of Baily bridge spans.

That was the weirdest bridge he had ever seen with round spans and square spans. With the narrow pieces that they had used from the railway bridge, it was only one way traffic. The two directions had to take turns to cross the bridge and the railway bridge was not usable. The train went as far as it could go. From there on American army trucks transported the people across the traffic bridge and put them back on the train again, on the other side of the river, to continue their journey. No matter where you were travelling, it was time consuming. However, people put up with the inconveniences, they wanted to go places. Nobody had been anywhere for five years.

A Fireworks Nobody Had
Seen the Likes of Before.

There were lots of excuses to celebrate. First the liberation of The Netherlands followed by VE Day in Europe. Next was VJ Day, Victory over Japan. And last but not least there was a celebration of the Queen's Birthday on August 31st. For five years the Dutch Queen had been in exile but in 1945 the Queen was back in The Netherlands and celebration was in order.

All of Rotterdam was decorated with thousands of lampions and flags. When it got dark it was just beautiful to watch all the colorful lights. Adrie paused for half an hour to watch the water organ. When they played music, rays of colorful water went up in the air, it was astonishing.

What was even more astonishing were the fireworks that followed. The U.S. Navy was going to have a fireworks display. Everybody and his brother attended the celebrations and the fireworks. There were many U.S. war ships anchored in the harbor of Rotterdam. They were going to shoot the fireworks display in the air over the river. Over 15,000 people were watching the fireworks from the Maas Boulevard.

It was a colorful fireworks with loud bangs when the fire crackers exploded into the air. There were even quite a few unscheduled very loud bangs which were caused by explosions of cases of hand grenades, shells and other explosives. There were warships and they had lots of ammunition aboard. Somebody had bungled safety regulations; there were cases with ammunition on the deck of one of the ships. One box of ammunition was open and when a piece of firework exploded on the ship, the box with hand grenades exploded right after. That gave added fireworks and when the other cases of ammunition started to explode it created an air pressure on the Maas Boulevard. To top it off, there was shrapnel flying through the air hitting the spectators.

Especially the people in front were getting hit by the powerful explosions. They started to panic and tried to run away. That wasn't easy and shoving, pushing and shouting people turned into a stampede. The police on horseback tried to keep order but that aggravated the situation. People crowded the horses and the horses were standing on their hind legs neighing between the hysterical people.

About 40 people were trampled to death and several hundred people got seriously injured. It was a fireworks never to forget. Luckily, Adrie was not standing in the front row. When the cases of ammunition started to explode he got the heck out of there. He said to his mother: "A guy can survive the war and get killed in the celebrations."

Adrie and his friends had a little fireworks of their own going at night, actually it was only bangs. Before the war there were still some bikes that were equipped with carbide lanterns. Whenever there was need for carbide a visit to the blacksmith, who was selling blocks of carbide, was in order. All the boys knew the game thunder box. All you had to do was take an empty can with a tight closing lid and make a little hole with a spike in the bottom. Next a lump of carbide was put in the can and everybody spit in the can to make the carbide wet for gas development. At this time the lid was put on the can and the can was put on the street. One boy would put his foot on the can to prevent the can from flying away. Another boy would keep a burning match in front of the hole, which would ignite the carbide gas. Action came instantly with a big bang that made the cover fly away. That was fun, at least that's what the boys thought.

When the war was over, it took a while to restore electricity. Old oil and carbide lamps were brought back and one could buy carbide again at the Blacksmith's. Soon the boys brought the old thunder box back. Now the boys were bigger the thunder box became bigger as well, until a day when one of the boys swiped an old milk can from the farm. It could hold 100 litres of milk and it could hold a lot of carbide as well. That was exactly what the doctor ordered; it would sound like a real cannon.

With the inauguration ceremonies there had to be real water, spitting in the can would take for ever to develop gas. Everything went well as planned. Indeed there were some real loud bangs that made people think that the war had started again. Only for one night did they get away with the big bang show. The next night the police appeared to confiscate the milk can. They said: "Haven't you boys anything else to do than those dangerous games? You can easily get hurt with those war-like explosions."

When the police left one boy shouted: "Why didn't you tell that to the Americans, that people could get hurt when they exploded the atomic bombs in Japan?" Apparently, the police weren't interested in doing that and disappeared in the darkness of the night.

Rip Off Insurance.

You have very good insurance as long as you don't make a claim. When the war started, the insurance companies came up with War Damage Insurance. Because of the chance to lose your house in a bombing raid or shelling, everybody bought this insurance. You couldn't afford not to have insurance. Like most insurances it was a mutual insurance, which meant that in case of heavy damage the premiums had to be raised. In case of total destruction of cities extra premiums might have to be levied, to enable the insurance company to pay all the claims. Of course that portion of the insurance policy was in fine print and not understood by most of the people.

Arie had also War Damage Insurance. He had made about five claims during the war to pay for the blown out windows and they had paid those claims. However, when the house was inundated there was extensive damage too. Most of it was wall paper, paint and some wood damage. War damage is war damage Arie said and made his claim after the war. It took quite a long time before the insurance company replied to his claim. Unfortunately, there was no cheque in the envelope. To make up for that they had enclosed a bill, with a letter that explained why there was a bill instead of a cheque.

Dear Sir:

We are very sorry for the delay in processing your war damage claim. As we are receiving thousands of claims every day, we are handling the claims in the order they are received. As you can see in section 3C of your insurance policy, the War Damage Insurance is a mutual insurance and extra premiums will be levied whenever there is extensive damage. Heavy destruction in the western part of The Netherlands where Nymegen and Arnheim have suffered a lot, made it necessary to levy such extra premium.

You are required to pay an extra premium of 850 guilders to secure adequate funds for the insurance company to pay the claims. Enclosed is a bill for this premium. We are looking forward to receive this extra premium. As soon as we have received this payment we will consider your war damage claim.

Arie was furious: "If they think that I'm going to pay 850 guilders and then wait to see if they pay me my damage claim, they have something coming. They can go to hell. I will keep my 850 guilders and use it to paint and wall paper the house. At least I have something; if I pay them I might lose that 850 guilders too and get nothing in return."

That wasn't the only rip off insurance around. As a matter of fact, it seemed all insurances were a rip off. Before the war, during the Depression, there was a burial insurance. At that time a burial cost 125 guilders which was difficult to pay when you only got 10 guilders from relief. For 1 guilder per month you could insure yourself, with a family of four, against burial expenses. After paying this premium for 15 years the insurance was paid up which meant that no further payments had to be made.

Fifteen years later, the de Kievits had paid up their insurance which should entitle them to a free burial for the rest of their lives. Not so! When the insurance was paid up a burial didn't cost 125 guilders anymore. Due to inflation it cost now 175 guilders. The insurance company was so friendly to send a representative to talk about additional insurance to cover those 50 guilders. Ko got mad this time and called it a rip off: "When we took out the policy we were told that we only had to pay for 15 years and now you want more. I suppose when we have paid up that additional insurance a funeral will cost 200 guilders and we'll have to pay an additional insurance again. Why do you think we are going to pay our entire lives to get ourselves buried?"

The rep cleared his throat to explain. "But madam, those are outside influences which are completely beyond our control. There is nothing we can do about it."

Victory Parade.

When Adrie read the paper there was some hard to understand news.

ELECTION IN BRITAIN OUSTS CHURCHILL.

Attlee Takes Over.

How could the people in England be rude enough to throw Churchill out after he had won the war? Adrie didn't know enough about politics to understand it.

Many countries were struggling to get a stable Government again. The French Government resigned every month and a new Government had to be assembled. England under Attlee now, who was a Socialist, didn't do well at all. There was one strike after another especially in the harbors of London. First the dock workers went on strike, next the tugboats, then the crane operators. When finally all strikes were settled, the dock workers had to unload ship holds with meat which had spoiled during the strike. It smelled terrible and was enough reason for the dock workers to go on strike because of unhealthy working conditions. Rotterdam was benefiting from continuous troubles in the harbors of London and became bigger all the time until it surpassed London and became the largest harbor city in the world.

During the war there had been no elections in Britain. Churchill had shared power with the opposition parties to secure unity. Now the war was over there were elections in June 1945. Churchill had guided Britain through the most difficult time in history; he had won the war and figured that the people would vote for him overwhelmingly.

The contrary was true; people had no use for Churchill and now the war was over they dumped him like a hot potato. Attlee from the Labor Party won with a landslide victory. Actually, the people of England hadn't voted against Churchill personally, they had rejected the Conservative Party. The Conservative Party had been in power for a long time and the English people blamed the Conservatives for the Second World War happening. Moreover, the Labor Party had promised the English people cows with golden horns. Many Social Programs would be instituted if the Labor Party won. Unfortunately, the English people went for fake promises and Churchill lost the election.

Churchill was devastated. It was an insult which was hard to take for him, first winning the war and right after being dumped by the electorate. There were lots of other places in Western Europe where they admired him after winning the war. It proved that a prophet is seldom recognized in his own country. Churchill decided to have a victory parade in all the countries which had been occupied by Nazi Germany.

D Day was followed by T Day. (Triumph Day.) In September 1945 a victory parade was winding through downtown Rotterdam. Adrie worked in downtown Rotterdam and the boss had given all workers time off to see the hero of World War II. The main attraction was Winston Churchill, standing on a flatbed, with his hand high in the air and two fingers spread in the form of a V. He was displaying the V for Victory. All of the staff of Spoormaker garage was standing together for this rare occasion. One of the younger members of the staff asked: "Why does Churchill have his two fingers spread?"

One of the older mechanics replied: "He is waiting till somebody throws a cigar between his fingers."

The crowd was jubilant when Churchill passed, people were shouting as loud as the Germans did when Hitler paraded in one of his candle light parades. It could be said that this was everybody's finest hour including Churchill's.

Of course reporters wanted to ask Churchill some stupid questions. One of them was "If you had to do it over again would you do the same?"

Churchill knew how to answer questions, he answered: "I don't have to answer that because nobody gets a chance to do it over, but I have no regrets."

(Churchill made a comeback. On his 77th birthday Churchill became Prime Minister for the second time. Churchill had a grandson by the name of Winston Churchill who was elected to Parliament. It could very easily mean "Churchill forever.")

Even if there was a Churchill forever, there was certainly no British Empire forever. Before the war, England was the richest and most powerful country in the world. One quarter of the world was ruled by England and called London their capital. Adrie was very fond of geography; he studied the atlas all the time. He found that on the world map the areas controlled by England were indicated with a green color. There was an awful lot of green on the map, at that time the sun was never setting on the British Empire. Winning two World Wars did Britain in.

After the war had ended Churchill said: "Britain has undergone the crisis of defeats, the glory of her supreme resistance and the triumph of her returning might."

Victory had been obtained by spending five billion English pounds and 400,000 dead people. British returning might was in doubt, they were broke. Very little of the British Empire remained in the post war years. Immediately after the war, Gandhi started to wrestle India away from England. It became independent in 1947, with England losing its greatest possession.

East Africa demanded independence and when England didn't give it, an independence movement called 'Mau Mau' started a guerrilla warfare. They burned rural farms and killed all the people. Soon people left their farms and returned to England.

1954 saw independence for Egypt, followed by Cyprus in 1960. Rhodesia declared independence in 1965 and South Arabia and Aden in 1968. Hongkong was returned to China after the 99 year lease ended.

The only colony England is holding is Gibraltar which is little more than a rock in the Mediteranean. For the rest, England has returned to its normal size.

There was a soldier, a Scottish soldier
Who wandered far away and soldiered far away.
There was none bolder, with good broad shoulder
He's fought in many a fray, and fought and won.
He'd seen the glory and told the story
Of battles glorious and deeds nefarious.

The Scottish soldier and the English soldier came home, they wandered no more.

Equality At Last.

Many mottoes have served all kinds of causes. A much over used motto is 'Equality, Liberty and Fraternity.' Karl Marx had preached a classless society where everybody would be equal, with the Proletarian inheriting the power. It didn't happen in Soviet Russia and neither did it happen elsewhere in the world. After the Russian revolution, the Proletarians looted the liquor stores and were lying drunk in the gutter. They weren't even fit to inherit power. The ruthless Communist leaders killed millions of people as they saw fit and cared less for the people they had liberated from the clutches of Tzar Nicholas. Equality was a farce; everybody was poorer than ever before, yet, Lenin, the supreme leader of the Soviets, had eight Cadillacs with one specially equipped for winter driving.

The same happened in Cuba and China, where people were promised a Utopia on earth. It was plain hogwash which only served the leaders to gain power. As soon as the leaders had things under control the people were worse off than ever before.

However, once upon a time in Dutch history, everybody was equal and had only 20 guilders in his or her pocket. Even the very rich were reduced to 20 guilders. It was Communism at its best. Only one problem, the equality didn't last very long. But it did happen. How could this happen?

During the war the Germans printed as much money as they needed. Consequently, after the war there was way too much money in circulation. To make it worse there was very few goods that could be bought with this money. People had lots of money in their pockets and were wild for consumer goods.

Prices skyrocketed and a hefty inflation was the result. The Government had to straighten out its finances, which required making more goods and having less money in circulation.

Most of this bad money, which the Germans had printed, had ended up in the pockets of the black market dealers. Black market dealings were always cash dealings. Consequently, the black market dealers never paid any taxes on their ridiculously high profits. It was difficult to take this money out of circulation without hurting innocent people. Fortunately, the Dutch Government was lucky to have a financial wizard in its cabinet. He was the Minister of Finance Mr. Lieftink, who said in his radio speech:

"Now the war is finished, we have to clean up the financial mess the Germans left behind. Before the war started The Netherlands had 45,000 billiard guilders in circulation. At the finish of the war this number had doubled to 90,000 billiard guilders. *(In Europe they know 1 million which is like in Canada a one with six zeros. In Europe they know also a billion which is a large million. It is a one with nine zeros. A billiard in Europe is a one with 15 zeros.)* This 45,000 billiard guilders has to be removed. It is well known that black market dealers have taken advantage of hungry Dutch people and have made a killing in profits. All this money is hereby confiscated. The Dutch Government will introduce new money and all old money has to be deposited in a bank account. This money will remain frozen. Everybody who can prove to me that he or she has made this money in an honest way will get new money for the old money. When you deposit your old money, you will get 20 guilders in new money on which you have to live for that week. Your wages will be paid in new money and as soon as you have proven to me that the old money is honest money, I will release a certain percentage at a time. All excess money which couldn't have been obtained by honest work will be confiscated. I know that people don't like this Government intrusion but everybody should be happy that I didn't use the same steps as my colleague, the Minister of Finance in West Germany. He gave every German a chance to exchange 40 of the old marks for new ones and the rest of their money is worthless. I only punish the black market racketeers by taking all their money and people who got their money in any honest way will get all their money back."

It was a smart move; Mr. Lieftink killed two birds with one stone. He punished the black market racketeers and got rid of a lot of bad money. Furthermore, he also had a hand in releasing the old money to the honest people. There was way too much money for the few things that you could buy which resulted in inflation. Even honest money was out of circulation for the time being. When more goods became available he just released 10% of the old money at a time, until all the good people had been paid off.

Only the bank notes were taken in, the change kept its value. People who had way too much paper money accumulated during the five war years, tried to buy up as much change as they could get. They paid one paper guilder for one dime. That way they got at least 10% of their black market money back which was better than nothing. However, there was only a limited amount of change and people were hanging onto their change. While the black market racketeers were struggling trying to save some of the dishonest money they had obtained, Mr. Lieftink was laughing all the way to the bank, he got them.

It seems that there are always fish that escape through the net. The only people he didn't get were the farmers who had sold their wheat on the black market in exchange for gold. No matter what happens, gold always has retained its value.

Everybody had to fill out a form showing where he or she had worked during the war and how much they got paid per week. If you had made 5000 guilders per year you couldn't have accumulated 50,000 guilders during the five war years. If you could satisfy the Government that you hadn't made any money on the black market, you had very little problem to get your money back.

Trial of the Century.

People think that the trial of the century happened in Los Angeles in 1997, against O.J. Simpson, for murdering his ex-wife. It was quite a trial alright that took more than a year. It sparked interest throughout the world and made lawyers millionaires. This trial was nothing compared to the trial of war criminals at Nurnberg. Millions of people lost their lives and many more millions lost their homes and loved ones. There was an outcry that the people responsible should be held responsible and tried.

On November 20, 1945 the newspaper announced:

TRIAL OF NAZIS STARTS IN NURNBERG.

Herman Goring, Rudolf Hess, Seis Inquart, General Yodel and eight other prominent Nazis were indicted today at the Criminal Court in Nurnberg. Four judges provided by the U.S., Britain, U.S.S.R. and France will judge the defendants.

The defendants were charged with "Seizing power to institute a totalitarian system, Crimes against humanity, Crimes against other races and Atrocities against humanity."

All defendants pleaded "Not guilty. Befehl is Befehl" (orders are orders). Everybody stated that they were under direct orders of the Fuhrer who is conveniently dead. Rudolf Hess said "Nein" (which means 'No' in German.) The court entered a not guilty plea on his behalf.

Many films were shown by the prosecution about the atrocities of the Germans, especially the killing of millions of Jews. One movie about Auswitch, the infamous death camp of the Nazis, was shown, accompanied with this charge of the Prosecutor:

"Honorable Judges; When the Russians freed Auswitch in 1944 they found deplorable conditions with survivors weighing less than 80 pounds. For many liberated Jews it was too late, their body was gone too far and was shutting down already.

During the war, trainloads of Jews arrived daily in wagons like beasts. They had been rounded up in Germany and occupied countries and were told that they were going to be transported to work camps to make war material for Hitler. It was by no means a work camp, it was a death camp.

Thousands died because of miserable conditions but one and a half million died in the gas chambers where they were incinerated. There were five gas chambers with incinerators that incinerated 12,000 people a day, every day.

Auswitch is the world's largest graveless cemetery and still stands as a remembrance of world's darkest hour. Hitler, with his Nazis, had decided on the Final Solution and had put Himmler in charge of the program to wipe out the Jewish race. One and a half million Jews were killed at Auswitch."

The defence entered with a long speech and asked the judges: "Were only the Germans committing atrocities, were they the only ones who were cruel? And were the British and Americans all good? The Germans tried with terror bombing to destroy London and the English got even with destroying Dresden. Was destroying London a crime and was destroying Dresden alright because that was only revenge. Is revenge justified when the other party started it?

All that this trial is; is a revenge trial, the losers of the war are tried by the victors who committed the same crimes, but nobody talks about that. If Hitler had won the war he would have hanged Churchill and other prominent English and Americans. It seems that the victors punish the losers because the losers have all the war criminals that have to be punished. The victors were merely fighting for just cause. Honorable judges, this trial is a mockery of justice."

Goering and other prominent Nazis had as a defence that they only had taken orders from Hitler. Hess, who had gone to England, had been released to stand trial. His defence was that he had amnesia and didn't remember. Alphred Spear, who had been Hitler's Arms Minister, had a different approach to save his life. He broke ranks with his co-conspirators in his trial.

Alphred Speer said that he was responsible, but never admitted that he was guilty. He also stated that he never knew about the holocaust; if you look away from crimes committed you are guilty but if you don't know about it you are only responsible.

Speer also claimed that he had been in a plot to kill Hitler with poisoned gas to come through the ventilation system in his bunker. That was foiled when Hitler had ordered the poor ventilation system changed.

The prosecution claimed that this failed plot to kill Hitler was only a ploy to get a lighter sentence.

Judgement Day.

The trial at Nurnberg took 10 months with 216 actual trial days. It took the judges one month to go over all the evidence presented. On September 30, 1946 the sentences were announced:

12 NAZIS SENTENCED TO DEATH BY HANGING.

Herman Goring, Seis Inquart, General Yodel and 8 others of the German High Command were sentenced to death by hanging. Rudolf Hess and two others were sentenced to life imprisonment and 4 defendants were sentenced to imprisonment of 10 to 20 years. This is the verdict of the century.

With the execution coming up fast, the world got ready to punish the Nazis who had brought so much destruction and suffering. Goering still had a surprise in store to escape his execution by committing suicide. He was dead anyway but the world would have liked him to suffer for his crimes.

HERMAN GORING COMMITS SUICIDE.

Herman Goring, who was scheduled to be hanged today, committed suicide two hours before the hanging. Prison authorities state that his wife, who visited him the day before the hanging, had smuggled a tube with cyanide into his jail. In her last farewell kiss to the condemned Goring, she moved the tube with cyanide from her mouth into her husband's mouth. Goring hid the tube in his toilet bowl and used it two hours before his execution.

Alphred Speer was among the ones that had received twenty years imprisonment. During his imprisonment in Spandau Prison, he wrote a book titled "Inside the Third Reich." After he regained his freedom he didn't do any more architecture. He died at the age of 76.

Rudolph Hess was found guilty of atrocities against Jews and contemplating war with Hitler. He received life imprisonment.

After many years in prison, he became sick and the U.S. and England were ready to release him but the Soviets objected. Finally when he was 93 years old during the Gorbachev era, he was finally released. After his release he stated that he regretted nothing, he did what he had to do and owed it to the German people to put the greatest son of Germany in power. Shortly after his release he committed suicide.

Quite a few Japanese war criminals were tried later on. The main trial was with Toyo, the man who had brought Japan into the war. Toyo believed there were a red peril, Russia, a white peril, the United States, and a yellow peril, China. He had preached that the war was a liberation from the White Man. When the war went bad they sacked him and blamed all evils on Toyo. When the Americans came to arrest him, he tried to shoot himself and missed his heart by inches. The U.S nursed him back to health so they could kill him for crimes committed.

His defence was that the war was not aggressive, it had been defensive. He was found guilty and hanged. His body was cremated and the crematorium was ordered to turn in the ashes so the Japanese wouldn't honor him. The crematorium short changed the U.S. and didn't turn in all the ashes. They kept some of his ashes in a Buddhist temple.

Later on, a movie was made about Toyo in which he was praised as a war hero. The movie was a great success; it was shown for over half a year in Tokyo and millions of Japanese saw it.

Russia wanted to try Hirohito too as a war criminal but McArthur, the commander of Japan prevented it from happening. With the Emperor in his place Japan could become a peaceful country and if they hanged him the Japanese might resort to guerrilla warfare. Moreover, McArthur stated that Hirohito had only been a figurehead and wasn't responsible for the war.

Finally a <u>Christmas</u> With Peace On Earth.

The Bible says: "There will be wars and rumors of wars, but World War II was by no means a rumor, it was a full-fledged, devastating, killing war which killed 53 million people. Even during the war people were singing of "Peace on Earth," however, they were only hoping. Christmas 1945 was one of the very few Christmases that there was really peace on earth during the 20th Century of war. Unfortunately, there were already cracks showing in the peace on earth world that millions of people had died for. Severe troubles with Soviet Russia were developing at an alarming rate after Japan had been defeated. Winston Churchill had proposed to tell Russia the way it was going to be and in case they refused, the Americans could nuke Moscow. The U.S. wouldn't hear about it and wanted to resolve the differences through negotiations.

The Bible also promises a New Heaven and a New Earth without armed conflicts and cooperation between the nations. If we only could make a better world where millions of people had died for. After the First World War with its devastating effect, world leaders got together and agreed that there must be a better solution to the problems in the world. War is the last resort to settle anything. It can be avoided, and should be avoided, they said. At that time they decided to form the League of Nations to solve disputes. It didn't work at all with no army at the disposal of the League of Nations.

After the Second World War, the United Nations was formed in order to solve the problems of the world peacefully. However, it was the big countries that had the power in the U.N. The super powers had veto power; they could prevent any resolution from becoming effective. Moreover a country like The Netherlands didn't even have a vote. All small countries were put into groups of three or four and they had to take their turn to vote in the U.N.

If anybody had hoped for a Utopian World after the devastating World War II; their hopes went up in smoke. Many unsettled conflicts had to be resolved, preferably by the United Nations. In spite of the U.N., most of the conflicts weren't resolved peacefully; they were settled with bloody battles.

One of the first conflicts that came on the agenda of the U.N. was Palestine. After World War II ended the Jews wanted a home land, they were tired of being persecuted all over the world. Quite a few Jews had landed in Palestine which created hostilities between the Arabs and the Jews. The Jews stated that Palestine was the Promised Land and they had a right to it. On the other hand the Arabs told the Jews that it was their land and they were living in it.

When the conflict came on the agenda of the U.N., the U.N ordered an end to hostilities and voted in favour of an independent State of Israel. This step created over a million Arab refugees when they had to move for the Jews. Naturally the Arabs didn't like it and vowed to drive the Jews into the sea. The U.N found out the hard way that they had resolved a conflict in order to create a different one.

There was lots of food available in The Netherlands, but many articles were still rationed. Meat, sugar and tobacco were still in very short supply and rations were meagre. Everybody, women included, qualified for a candy ration card or a tobacco card. Not both, you either smoked or you ate candy. To qualify for a tobacco card you also had to be 16 years of age or older. As long as you weren't 16 years old you had to eat candies.

Adrie had smoked when he went to elementary school, when it was forbidden by his parents, because it was the smart thing to do. As soon as his parents allowed him to smoke, there was no fun to it anymore so he quit because it was the smart thing to do. A typical teenager.

When he was 16 years old, his mother asked him if he wanted a tobacco card. Adrie hadn't been smoking for some time and had no intention of picking up the habit again. Smoking was not good for his health and not good for his purse either. His mother was buying the candies and if he was going to smoke, he had to buy his own cigarettes. He had better use for his money than blowing it in the air. Instead, he had all kinds of plans to see the world which would cost him lots of money; he just couldn't afford to smoke. So Adrie opted for a candy card.

The euphoria that the war was over electrified the people; they were really happy and were looking for a better world like the one they had been used to. A better world came with the extension of the black market and cheating people who managed to take people's money in a dishonest way.

If you didn't want to be in the black market to make money, there was an alternative, you could always swindle the people. One of the swindlers was a barber in Een, which was a little town in the Northern provinces. He stated that he had a cure for baldness and guaranteed that the cure would work. To make it honest, he asked for the payment of the cure. This money was put in a trust account and would be repaid if the cure didn't work. It would take half a year to be successful and in this half a year he treated a couple of hundred bald customers. When, after half a year, some people wanted their money back, the baldhead specialist suddenly disappeared and when they checked the trust account, all the money had been withdrawn.

There were honest entrepreneurs who had ideas to make a lot of money. One of them was a guy who started to raise beavers for their hide. Adrie never had seen a beaver and observed the beaver's hideout till he appeared. He never contemplated at that time that he would move to Canada where there are lots of beavers in the rivers and lakes.

There was also a lock making outfit that had started to make props for ships that came in the harbour of Rotterdam. When the Willem Ruys, a big ship, needed a prop they made a beautiful prop for it but they had a problem with the transportation. The shipment got stuck in a little village where the roads were just too small for a transportation like that. They had to remove the corner of a house to enable the prop to get through. The owner of the house was paid handsomely and the prop got to its destination. Later on they moved the prop making business closer to the harbour to avoid more problems like that.

People were never more united than when there was a war on. As soon as the war was finished, people started to drift apart again and were fighting about silly little things. Even in the church the fight was on. It seemed that after the greatest conflict in human history ended, there was now room for little conflicts.

Ever since Christ founded the Christian Church, people have split up the church time after time. There was the English split from Rome, when the English king was told by the Pope that he couldn't divorce his childless wife. Then there was Luther who started Protestant churches and then there was Calvin who started the Reformed Churches. In all those splits, there was usually a lot of fighting and even killing, even though those people were Christians.

More and more splits occurred but the greatest split in the Christian Church had yet to come. It resulted in a fight that made 'Desert Storm' look like a training manoeuvre. (Desert Storm was the code name given in 1991 when U.N. forces invaded Iraq.)

There was Professor K. Schilder who was teaching religion according to the rules of the Reformed Church. All churches have a dogma what they believe in and what their teachings are. A few times Professor Schilder had preached in the church on the Hordyk. That was an eye opener, not that Adrie learned something he didn't know already. No, people from all over came to listen to Professor Schilder. At least twelve Reverends from other churches of the district came to listen. Adrie wasn't that interested in all the squabbling those religious nuts were doing. He could very well do without it.

A real argument developed in the Reformed Church about Article 31 of the dogma. Professor Schilder was teaching one way and the Synod of the church had contradicted him. As usual in those arguments, nobody backed down or made compromises and another split occurred. Now there was another war on about the real estate involved. When a church splits up who gets the church? Some of the churches had about an even split in members. In most cases the court had to decide which faction would get the church.

Of course, the party that didn't get the church was not very happy and all kinds of brawls erupted. I don't want to go into further details at this time about religion. I could write an entire book about it. Maybe some other day. I only wanted to show that during war and misery everybody seems to be content with one another, because they need one another. As soon as the common enemy is defeated we grab one another.

A major battle was looming in the U.S. between White People and Negroes. When the war started, the Negroes fought hard for the country that hadn't been very nice to them. Many died fighting for their Fatherland, but as soon as the war was over they found out that the White Man had won the war and they had won nothing. Before the war, they had to sit in the back of the bus and now the war was over they had to sit in the back of the bus again.

The general attitude of the Americans was that those people were only Niggers, who you can use when you need them and when you don't have any use for them, you shove them to the side. This time the Negroes were not going to be pushed to the side and under Marten Luther King they protested and demonstrated.

When real clashes occurred, some Americans suggested shipping all the Negroes back to Africa, that's where they belonged. Unfortunately for the White Man you can scramble an egg but once it's scrambled you can't unscramble it. The Negro was there to stay. Marten Luther King was assassinated but eventually the Negroes had the same rights as the other citizens of the U.S..

On May 5th 1946, it was one year ago since The Netherlands had been liberated. Everybody liked the celebrations and the extra day off that you got paid for. Celebrations started on May 4th at 8.00 p.m. At that time, everything came to a standstill, even the trains stopped dead in their tracks. Two minutes silence was observed for the fallen comrades that gave their lives so we could be free. There were a lot of children who knew their daddy only from a photo on the buffet. Their daddy had been a soldier or went working in Germany never to return. During the two minutes of silence the flags were flying at half-staff. As soon as the two minutes were over, all church bells started to ring, the flags would fly normally again and the celebrations could start.

Teen Age Problems.

"What is the matter with me?" Adrie wondered. He was working and had studied during the winter by taking night classes. When summer came around in 1946, he felt like doing crazy things. At night he went to his friends and crazy they were. One older man shook his head and said: "Can't you fellows ever behave, you act as if you were born in a barn and raised by wolves."

That lecture promptly created a wolf call. Teenagers probably can never help the way they feel and act, they are young and they think they know everything better. After the war it took some doing to stay in the harness. Too many young years had passed into oblivion without enjoying the benefits of being young. During the Depression and the following war years, survival demanded that all kids had to grow up in a hell of a hurry. Adrie had gone in the dark to steal wheat and had secured a wood supply, all for the family. He never gave it a thought and was proud to be of help to the family. Now the war was over, he couldn't help himself, he seemed to have missed something. Few people understood the teenagers who had virtually nothing to laugh about for a long time, and were now going to enjoy life to its fullest.

Actually the major problem was that he didn't belong to the kids anymore, but he wasn't an adult either, he felt he was neither fish nor fowl. At last Adrie overcame his problems and started to work for a bridge building company. Most of the bridges were lying in the rivers; they had been blown up by the Germans. A lot of work was out of town, it consisted mainly of supplying power for welders and other machines.

A bridge in Roermond was under construction. Whole sections were pre-assembled in the yard and transported with semis. It was quite a trip to go by semi with a wide load. There was also another river to be crossed with a single lane temporary bridge in place. During the day time the traffic flow was organized by the local police in a jeep. They just halted the traffic from one direction until the last car had passed and then the other direction could go. During the night there was no traffic, the police decided and went to bed.

When one of the main sections had to be transported, the bridge builder said to the semi driver: "Transport has to be done during the night when there is no other traffic on the road." Adrie had to go in the same time, to hook up some welding cables. To him travelling at night was alright, it sounded like fun.

There were still a lot of foreign troops in The Netherlands that moved about the country for whatever reason. Whenever there were major troop movements they were done at night when there was no traffic.

After the semi got far enough out of Rotterdam there was indeed no traffic anymore. Progress of the heavy transportation was good and it seemed like a piece of cake during the night. When they reached the single lane bridge, there was a long steep hill ahead of the bridge. The semi driver started to shift back timely as not to lose speed; he couldn't afford not to make it. When they came level with the bridge, a column of American troops with big G.M.C.s was coming across the bridge. "Holy smokes" said the driver, "Now what?" All traffic came to an abrupt halt and the driver jumped out to see what he could arrange. Adrie didn't think they needed his help but he got out anyway, just to see what was cooking.

There was an American captain who came to overlook the problem. He said: "I was told that there was no traffic during the night. We would encounter no problems moving our equipment."

The semi driver replied: "That's what they told me that there wouldn't be any traffic. There is only one problem; I can't back up with my semi that heavily loaded. Even if I could back it up, I would have to back it up for five miles to get enough speed to make it uphill."

"No problem" said the captain, "If you can't back up, we'll have to back up."

There were probably about 20 big army trucks that all started to back up in the dark. It took almost a full hour before the semi could continue.

On another job Adrie did some smuggling. It was made possible by stupid situations that had two Belgian fiefdoms in the southern part of The Netherlands. The highway went right through the fiefdoms; there was no other way unless you made a long detour. There were customs in the middle of the Netherlands.

Adrie brought some Belgian tobacco with him when he returned. Tobacco was rationed in The Netherlands but not in Belgium. That made it attractive to supplement the rations and smuggle a little. He didn't smoke himself but he could sell the tobacco with a hundred percent mark-up. Twice everything went right and the third time he was caught. The customs only confiscated his tobacco. If he had had 20 packages he might have been in more trouble. Four packages was smuggling alright but it was for his own use and not for resale with a large profit, the customs thought.

When bridge building became a little caught up, the company bought a landing ship which had served in the Normandy landing. They refurbished it to a small freight ship. It was the first time that Adrie worked on a ship and learned about wiring ships.

The Netherlands Annexed Part of Germany.

The Dutch Government requested from the Allies that they be allowed to take over part of Germany. This was supposed to be some kind of a repair payment for all the damage the Germans had done to The Netherlands. There was no objection from the Allies, they didn't mind at all to carve up Germany. To them a smaller Germany meant less danger for the future. The only one to object was Germany that had lost the war and had nothing to object about. And so little The Netherlands annexed part of Germany after the war. It was a piece of land about 25 miles long and 6 miles wide with two towns in it, Elten and Emmerick.

The German people didn't mind at all belonging to The Netherlands. To them it meant extra business when the Dutch people came with touring busses for a day trip. They were all smiles when droves of Dutch people came to their restaurants and stores. All Dutch people were interested in the region that the Dutch Government had acquired, and they wanted to see it. Everybody was happy with the arrangements, business was booming for the people of Emmerick and Elten and to the Dutch people it meant an outing.

'Love is a many splendour thing,' is the title of a movie. With the war on, very few people thought about love, especially the people who were starving. Even young boys and girls who were already going steady for a couple of years were holding off getting married. Other young people didn't think of romance, there were more important things to think about. Those more important things were to get food on the table and coal or wood for the stove to cook the little food the people had. Everybody was thinking about survival first and love later.

When the war was barely over and food returned to the tables and coal in the stoves, romance blossomed among the young people. There was only one problem; during the war many houses had been destroyed by bombardments and few houses had been built. The Germans were not interested in using up precious materials to the benefit of the people, if they could be used for warfare. Consequently there was a severe shortage of housing. Young couples who wanted to get married couldn't rent a suite; they couldn't even rent a room. Couples just got married and moved in with their parents which caused many problems.

Willie and Wouter, her boyfriend, had been going steady for five years. The year was 1947, two years after the war, and there was no hope in sight that they would be able to get a suite or even a room. Wouter was living in Zevenbergen, which was a small town. He had been looking around to see if anything had become available. One day he came across a derelict dwelling which had been declared not suitable to live in for the last four years. When he inquired with the owner if he could rent it; the owner said: "No, it is not fit for any occupation; the town council wouldn't allow it."

Wouter didn't give up that easy and asked: "If I get permission from the town council to move in, will you then rent it to me?"

The home owner replied: "Yes, if the town council approves it, I'll let you have it, as long as you don't expect me to make any repairs. Repairing a place like that would be a waste of money."

Wouter paid a visit to Town Hall to ask for permission to move into the unfit dwelling. He said: "I have a life to live and I want to get married. Would you let me move into that unfit for occupation dwelling?"

They agreed that the housing need was severe and there was no hope that it would improve in the next five years, perhaps ten years. Permission was hereby granted. Wouter was glad as a kid with a candy, at least he had something to start and they could get married. The rent was very low which was good. On the other hand the house was in a desperate shape which was bad.

Now they had a house to move into, they could get married. The happy event would take place on February 2nd 1947. There were few preparations since not much was available, yet Willie managed to get some light blue cloth on her rationing coupons. She had no problem to make a beautiful wedding dress from the material. For seamstress Willie it was a piece of cake. White material for a virgin bride was just not available at the time, not even two years after the war. White material for bridal dresses was very low in the priorities of the Dutch Government. They figured that there were few virgins that got married anyway. Deflowering of a bride on the wedding night was very rare. At least if a white dress was not available it kept the brides honest, they didn't have to pretend they were a virgin.

Nobody had a car; you couldn't even rent a car for such a happy occasion. Willie went to Ringleberg who had a touring bus company before the war. After the war he was merely engaged in workmen transportation. At this stage there were no trips of any kind for sightseeing. Ringleberg said that he would supply a bus for the wedding party.

Adrie got involved too; he was in charge of the bar which was a very good choice he thought. He went to Cafe Sport to see what he could get on alcoholic beverages for the wedding. He talked to Meeuw Vanderjacht, the owner of the cafe, who was willing to supply lots of beer, some gin and wine.

February 2nd was actually a beautiful sunny winter day; the temperature was about eight degrees Celsius which wasn't bad for a starter for the young couple. The entire family came together, nobody wanted to miss a party. There were even cousins at the wedding whom Adrie had never seen before. He knew they existed but they had never met.

As for entertainment, they had hired an accordion player who played all night for three guilders and at the end of the party he went around with the hat for tips. It was a good party, people were singing together and everybody had a little skit, a verse or a riddle in order to participate in the party entertainment.

After the wedding, the young couple moved to Zevenbergen to take possession of their brand old house. They asked all of the family to visit them in their humble mansion. The house was very small; it had a small living room, no kitchen and a cupboard bed on the main floor. As there was no garage, the cupboard bed was used for storage of the bike. Sleeping was done on the second floor which was an open space with a plank floor.

That soon after the war, there was little entertainment and no place to go for holidays or long weekends. Adrie decided to take them up on the offer to visit them. His neighbour Kees Meuzelaar was interested as well.

On a Saturday afternoon Adrie biked with his neighbour Kees Meuzelaar to Zevenbergen. Nobody was worried about sleeping place for the guests. When it was time to go to bed, the bikes were removed from the cupboard bed to make room for Wouter and Willie. That way Kees and Adrie could sleep on the top floor which had just enough room for one bed. It was one of the older very small houses where a guy had a family of ten and raised them all. You can keep a lot of tame sheep in one barn, they say.

It was raining all day which made the roof leak like a sieve. There was a simple solution to that problem; they had all kinds of old pots and pans which they put underneath the leaks. Several pots and pans were on the top floor to catch the water. The ticking of the raindrops could be heard all night on the roof and in the pots and pans. Nobody complained because that's all there was and that's all that the young couple had. They were glad to have visitors and Adrie was glad to see his sister. He really missed his sister; now he had to face his grumpy father alone. Monday was a working day which meant that Kees and Adrie had to bike back on Sunday night.

When a year later their first baby girl was born, it was even more difficult; they had to find a corner for the cradle. Even with one baby they didn't qualify for a suite or room. All they could do was to make the 'unfit for habitation' dwelling work. They had little choice, nothing else was available. In spite of the deplorable house, it was still a place to call home.

(Love didn't only blossom after the war; during the war all was fair in love and war. "An elderly Italian man went to the Parish Priest, and asked if the Priest would hear his confession. "Of course my son" said the Priest.

"Well, Father, at the beginning of the war, a beautiful woman knocked on my door and asked me to hide her from the Germans. I hid her in my attic, and they never found her."

"That's a wonderful thing, my son, and nothing that you need to confess," said the priest.

"It's worse, Father. I was old and weak and wanted more than anything to have sex with her so I told her that she had to pay for renting the attic with sexual favors," continued the old man.

"Well, it was a very difficult time, and you took a large risk. If the Germans had found you hiding her they might have shot you. I know that God, in his wisdom and mercy, will balance the good and the evil, and judge you kindly," said the priest.

"Thanks father," said the old man. "That's a load of my mind. Can I ask another question?"

"Of course my son," said the priest.

The old man asked: "Do I have to tell her that the war is over?")

Adrie had been taking night classes and had his diploma in his pocket. One day there was an advertising leaflet in the mailbox about a correspondence course in radio repair. That was the next project he could tackle and he was planning to fill out the coupon to ask for more details. It was fall; Adrie was busy with all kinds of things and forgot about the radio course. The radio school salesman was a good salesman; he could even manage to sell water to a drowning man. He knew how to attract new students and figured that a lot of people were planning to take the course but they needed a reminder.

A second leaflet came in the mailbox telling everybody how easy it was. Everybody could do it, there was even an eighty year old man who just had received his diploma and was now repairing radios. What an eighty year man can do I can do too, Adrie thought and registered for the course. Radio School Maxwell had adopted the name of the British physicist Maxwell, who had done extensive research in radio waves during the 18th Century.

At that time radios were not available at all and some people built their own radio. The course lasted one year and Adrie built a crystal radio with a crystal receiver, a coil and a variable condenser. It worked perfectly with a head telephone. His next project was a radio called 'Band Leader.' Soldering all the little resistors and condensers in their places was harder than he had imagined.

The end result was not entirely satisfactory; there was a lot of interference which he couldn't get rid of. Luckily Adrie had a friend who worked in a radio shop and had some instruments to detect the problem. According to his friend, the coils were the guilty parts and had to be shielded to eliminate the problem. Finally the de Kievits had a radio back in the house while most of the people were still without. The radio wasn't as good a radio as the Germans had stolen but it worked.

When he had written his test he received his Radio repair diploma. Of course there was another course which was for students who had followed the beginner's course. (*Later when he had finished that course they talked him into a television course. He had also the option to become salesman for the company, full time or spare time. At that time Adrie worked already as an electrician and became a part time salesman on commission. Radios and T.V's were readily for sale at that time. All electronic equipment was for sale and also sewing machines. Adrie managed to sell a few radios, record players and a sewing machine. His reward was 20%. Televisions were still black and white and very expensive; he never sold one and didn't even buy one for himself. In 1958 he left for Canada and was no longer a salesman.*)

The City of Rotterdam decided to get rid of the air raid shelters. During the war people had some good use out of the air raid shelters for protection. When the war was finished there was little use for the air raid shelters, other than for use by dating couples to do some heavy necking and have sex. Others used the shelters to have a crap.

In the city of Rotterdam there were only urinals for men. Women or people needing a crap had to sweat it out. Most of the time the urinals were used for a crap, if you got to go you got to go, either in your pants, or in the urinal, or now in the bomb shelter. With the accumulating piles of shit in the shelters the stench became unbearable. To get rid of those unsanitary outhouses, the city of Rotterdam removed them. And so pre-war times returned to Rotterdam, if you had to go you used the urinals. As long as you didn't step in the piles you were doing alright.

With the discovery of atomic energy, the first application was for warfare. After the war atomic reactors started to produce electricity and Rotterdam was one of the first cities in Europe to build an atomic reactor. The fission of one lb. of uranium yields 10 million kilowatt hours. When burning coal we need the combustion of 3 million lbs. of coal to produce the same amount of energy. It seemed a bargain, and it was thought that with nuclear energy an era of unequalled energy would change the world.

The Mayor of Rotterdam said: "With atomic energy we'll make electricity dirt cheap. Pretty soon we'll be able to pull the electric meters out and have free electricity."

(*Unfortunately this illusion never materialized. Not one nuclear power station has ever made electricity as cheap as coal fired plants. The Mayor and others had it all wrong but then what can we expect of a Mayor. What would he know about atomic power? In spite of all the optimistic predictions, the price of electricity kept going up. Atomic reactors also created a lot of trouble on Long*

Island and in the Ukraine. In the future, the cost of obtaining electricity from uranium will decline. Normally atomic energy is converted into steam and with the steam we drive generators to get electricity. In the future we will be able to cut out the middle man and we will have conversion of heat to electricity directly with thermo electric devices. No more steam will be needed and for the second time steam engines will disappear.)

With an extensive article on atomic energy they tried to sell it to the people. The paper touted that the peace atom can move mountains and can be used for extensive excavations.

August 31st, 1948 was a barn burner of a party. It was Queen Wilhelmina's 68th birthday and she had also been Queen of the Netherlands for fifty years. At this occasion she stepped down in favor of her daughter Princes Juliana. Queen Juliana said in her inauguration speech: "Who am I that I can do this?"

Adrie said to his neighbor Kees: "Who am I that I can't?"

Kees replied: "I haven't got the foggiest idea."

Colonial Problems.

Before the war, The Netherlands had quite a few colonies in the East and in the West. The East Indian colonies were quite extensive; they consisted of a chain of big islands; Java, Sumatra, Borneo, Celebes, Bali, Timor and New Guinea and a host of other smaller islands. The entire island group extended from East to West for more than 3,000 miles across the Equator. The total land area is 736,512 sq. mi., while the total land area of The Netherlands is only 14,000 sq. mi. There were 583 million people living on the East Indian islands which were ruled by a little over 9 million Dutch people.

The colonies in the West were very insignificant to the ones in the East, they only had a land area of 371 sq. mi.; they were only small islands. The colonies in the West didn't represent any problem; they were in the Caribbean and never had been involved in the war.

Before the war, the Dutch Government had promising people of the East Indies study in the Netherlands at the University of Delft. Sukarno was one of the students in The Netherlands and when he returned he had learned a lot. For a starter, he wanted to kick the Dutch out and declare the East Indies independent. Dr. van Mook, the Dutch Governor General, had him promptly arrested and thrown in jail. After serving his sentence he was involved in an uprising and Dr. van Mook threw him back in jail.

The Japanese had a problem which was that Russia occupied one sixth of the world's land and England ruled a quarter of the world. Moreover, England, France, Belgium and The Netherlands didn't have raw materials but they had solved that problem by occupying vast land masses which they called colonies.

Japan didn't have raw materials either and their country was heavily overpopulated. They were going to have colonies as well and captured part of China which wasn't welcomed by the U.S. They weren't amused to have competition in Asia and put an oil embargo in place. Japan needed oil and occupied the East Indies. When the Japanese occupied the Dutch East Indies, the first thing they did was to release Sukarno. They used the former rebels of the colony and gave Sukarno and Hatta administrative jobs. In the face of defeat, Japan told Sukarno and Hatta to prepare for independence when the Japanese withdrew. They told them: "If you don't manage to get Indonesia independent, they might as well bury you standing up. Your entire life you have been on your knees for those colonial masters."

The Japanese figured that if they couldn't have colonies, neither could England, France or The Netherlands. That was their revenge for losing the war. Withdrawing of the Japanese forces happened on August 17, 1945. All the Japanese weapon arsenals were handed over to the rebelling East Indian leaders. There was a power vacuum after the departure of the Japanese troops, which gave Sukarno and Hatta the chance to proclaim the Indonesian Republic. Japan had proved that the White Man could be beaten and they were going to do it.

Before the return of the Dutch army, Sukarno waged war against everything that was Dutch. They rounded up many Dutch men and kept them in toilets that served as cells. After a week of imprisonment they were turned lose on the square. Dutch East Indians were waiting with long knives and hacked them to death.

Chinese people who were living in the East Indies were told not to supply Dutch people with anything. Some Chinese, who did, paid with their lives and were hacked to pieces with axes.

When Dutch troops were landed in Indonesia, all the soldiers thought they were going to liberate the Dutch Indies like the Canadians had liberated The Netherlands. They had a surprise coming when they landed. There were no girls with flowers and kisses waiting, they were not welcome at all and were opposed by the Republicans. The Netherlands dispatched more and more military troops to the Dutch Indies and wanted nothing to do with the

Republicans. They were willing to go into an equal partnership but rejected independence ideas. The first 'Police Action' was the result. *(It was actually a military action but the Dutch called it a 'Disciplinary Police Action.' That sounded much better than a military action though it was exactly the same thing.)*

When keeping colonies became more and more costly to the tune that it cost more to keep them than they got out of it, the colonies were given back to their rightful owners. Sometimes peacefully, but a lot of times, as in Indonesia, not; it created a struggle for power as never had been seen before.

Most of the countries had followed the pattern of mobilization of an army by conscription when war broke out or when war threatened. There was always a regular professional army for internal security. With the Russian threat, all countries in Europe followed conscription. All young men of 20 years of age had to have at least one year of military training.

The Netherlands needed an army to restore authority in The Dutch East Indies. After the war had ended, the Dutch Government had put Military Conscription back in place to form an army again. After proper training, they were all shipped to the Dutch East Indies to re-establish law and order under the Dutch Government. When the United Nations got involved, the Dutch were ordered to end hostilities and negotiate with each other. The Dutch were under pressure of the U.S. which had a stranglehold on The Netherlands. They provided aid under the Marshall Plan and that could be cancelled if The Netherlands didn't dance to the pipes of the U.S. Consequently, the military police action ended and it went to the bargaining table.

Adie had witnessed all this commotion with mixed feelings. He never thought that negotiations would amount to much when you have to talk to rebels. In his opinion you don't talk to rebels, you don't even throw them in jail, the only sure way to deal with them is to shoot them. After Dr. van Mook had thrown Sukarno in jail twice, he was still a rebel and he was still around. Sukarno had even declared an Independent Republic of Indonesia. If van Mook had shot him in the first place, Sukarno couldn't have caused any more trouble.

All Dutch boys, who reached the age of 20 years, were drafted and trained for the Tropics to do service there whenever needed. Of course Adrie was too young to participate in any jungle warfare in the Tropics. He wanted to travel to see different countries and participate in actions that were going on in the world. It wasn't only his adventurous longing that made him think that way.

There was a real problem at home between Adrie and his father. Adrie's parents were very strictly religious and went to church twice every Sunday. Adrie found this a waste of time, he wanted to see the world and do things; you don't see much in the church. For a starter he wanted to go with his

buddies to the beach instead of to the church. Finally this battle was won by
Adrie but it didn't mean the end of hostilities. His father never forgave him
that he was disobedient and chucked the church. He was the father, and the
elder. The children had to do what they were told. Adrie's mother liked to see
that Adrie went to church. When he was 17 years old, her attitude was that
forcing wouldn't help the cause. It only would make him more determined
to break with the powerful church.

Jan van Delen was Adrie's friend; he was two and a half years older
than Adrie. Jan had been drafted into the Dutch army and was training for
service in the Tropics. When he came home for the weekend he started to
talk Malaisian. The people in the Dutch Indies speak very little Dutch and
in order to talk to the population they were learning Malaysian. Adrie wasn't
interested in learning Malaysian since it was not an important language with
which you could conquer the world. However, if it meant going to the tropics
he might be interested. Jan van Delen had learned quite a bit of Malaysian,
it was in rhyme too.

> Satu is one,
> Batu is stone,
> Rotti is bread,
> Matti is dead,
> Dapour is rocking,
> And Mekmek is fucking.

"These were about all the important words that you needed when you
went to Indonesia," Jan said. The next weekend Jan had watch duties on
Sunday at 5.00 p.m. That was a weekend that he couldn't go home. Adrie
said to some of his other friends: "Let's go and visit Jan. Pretty soon he will
be going to the East Indies."

Four other boys thought it a good idea and came along. Jan was in the
Frederick Hendrik barracks in the garrison city of s'Hertogenbos. It was
a 90 kilometre bike ride which would take about six hours of biking for
experienced bikers.

They left 6.00 a.m. and arrived around noon. They viewed the barracks
and even got supper at 5.00 p.m. Next was the long trip home. Two of the boys
started to get some saddle blisters and could barely sit on the saddle anymore.
With a lot of effort they all made it home.

A couple of weeks later Jan came home, he had ten days holiday before he
was going to the tropics. Adrie spent a lot of time with his friend and the last
day there was a farewell party at his home. When Adrie arrived, Jan's mother

was crying in the kitchen. He thought that was a typical mother to be worried when her son leaves home, to go far away to the Tropics.

"It is by no means a trip without danger" his mother said, "there are snipers and many outposts are destroyed by guerillas. Besides, the Dutch Government has ordered a second police action which means war."

Adrie tried to calm her down and said: "I know that if I were going to the Tropics my mother would be plenty worried too but don't worry Jan can take care of himself."

"I know he can take care of himself but he can't escape bullets if they are shooting at him," she wept. "We have had five years of war, what did we fight for? We have barely finished our liberation celebrations and there is already another war in the East Indies. Can we ever have peace to let people live instead of having them shot up in a faraway country? Many people die or come out of the war as invalids for the rest of their lives."

Adrie promised her that he would visit her whenever he received a letter from Jan and finally she calmed down to the relief of Jan and Adrie.

It sure left a vacuum now his long-time friend had left. He had other friends to go out with, yet, he couldn't help wishing he was a couple of years older, that way he could see something of the world too. Adrie was eighteen years old now and had to wait another two years before he would be drafted into the Dutch army.

However, there was a short cut possible. The Dutch Navy was asking for volunteers to serve in the Tropics. They took boys from eighteen years and older. Most of the boys, who volunteered for the Navy, wanted to see the world and thought that all nice girls loved guys in the Navy. Indeed there were quite a few girls who were uniform sick; they just loved to have a guy in uniform. Other girls figured that guys in the Navy were strong and healthy. Adrie's main reason was to get away from home and to see the world. If there were other fringe benefits attached to being in the Navy, like girls, he could easily handle that.

There was a catch to get into the Navy, you had to have permission of your parents and of course there was the medical and physical examination. But first things first, he could only apply if his father gave permission. With the hostilities going on, he wasn't even on speaking terms with his father, but he had to speak to him whether he liked it or not, or he could forget about the whole thing.

One night when there was a little conversation at the table, Adrie thought that it was the right moment to bring the Dutch Navy up. He said nonchalantly: "I wouldn't mind going to the Navy for a career, if I pick up a form would you give consent?"

Adrie observed the face of his father as if he could read some good news coming from it. His father asked: "What do you want to do in the Navy?"

"I probably could be a radio technician or so."

To his surprise his father said: "If that's what you want to do, it's O.K. with me; maybe they'll teach you some discipline."

"Yah right," Adrie thought. "He missed the opportunity to say that maybe the Navy will tell me to go to church."

He could sense that his father gave his permission to get rid of him; if he didn't dance to his father's pipes he had no use for him. Actually, Adrie cared less why he signed his application as long as he signed it.

It wasn't hard to get a form from the Navy and with the signature of his father on it there was no problem returning it. Now there was the waiting time for the call to come for his examination.

It was an all-day examination and it was very extensive; they tested him for hearing, sight and reflexes. Other tests were done to see that you weren't color blind and they told you to put your lips on your hand and blow. That way they could tell if you had a hernia.

The intelligence tests were even more extensive. Even if you were as strong as an ox and healthy, it didn't mean that they would take people with a low I.Q. It was important to the Navy to determine where they could use you, if they could use you. Adrie was sure that there were all kinds of jobs that he could handle. He had his diplomas for motor mechanics and he had also a diploma for radio technician.

It looked like another exam that he had to take in the trades in which he claimed to have proficiency. There was a complete test to check his knowledge on radios and a test for Morse code. At that time communications were mostly done in Morse signals and they needed lots of radio operators. Morse code is used by telegraph operators and comprises combinations of dots and dashes. To test if you were able to be a radio operator, they gave you three Morse code letters. The A, which consists of one dot and a dash .- The second letter was the I which consists of two dots .. and the third letter was the N which consists of a dash and a dot -. It wasn't hard to hear the two dots of the I but to keep the dot and the dash apart from the dash and the dot proved more difficult. Actually it wasn't hard at all Adrie thought and could see himself as a future radio operator. Soon he found out that he had thought wrong when they speeded it up. You sure could get confused and he was only working with three letters.

There was also an intelligence test in which all kinds of stupid questions were asked. One of the questions was: "Are you afraid of a tiger?"

Adrie hadn't expected a dumb question like that but knew that he had to be careful with his answer. He answered: "I never came face to face with a tiger so why should I be scared?" It was an evasive answer to a dumb question, but who cares?

There was a little wait before he had an interview with an official of the Navy. He was told that he qualified for mechanic and radio technician but he was not good enough to operate the telegraph. His test result was only 87% and that wasn't good enough the officer said. When there are important messages coming in they have to be at least 95% accurate, preferably 100%. The officer concluded that he hadn't failed the test but there are only a very few that score high enough to be useful to the Navy.

"No problem" Adrie thought, "I can just as well be a mechanic or radio technician."

"That will be all" the officer said, "We will notify you about the result of your medical examination and if everything is in order we will give you a date when you have to report."

It took three weeks before the letter from the Navy came. Unfortunately, the message wasn't good at all. The letter stated that everything was excellent except he had flat feet and only if this was corrected could they take him. They suggested going to the doctor for support soles in his shoes which would correct the problem, probably in a year.

It was a disappointment that he was doomed to stay home with his mounting problems. Of course, he could get the suggested support soles. It would take a year before he could re-apply for the Navy. Besides in another two years the Government would call him up for Army training. That wasn't quite the same as the Navy and he would only get paid one guilder a day instead of a good salary from the Navy.

It wouldn't do any harm to get his flat feet improved, they had never bothered him but he might as well give it a whirl. The doctor had a good look at his feet and asked: "Did you walk barefoot a lot?"

"Yes, I always played in the polder and never wore shoes. I only put on shoes when I went to school or to church."

The doctor looked over his glasses at Adrie and said: "Exactly, that's where the problem is. When you walk barefoot too much, your feet sag through and become flat instead of having an arch. I will refer you to a specialist who will take care of this little problem."

In spite of his support soles Adrie didn't think it would get him in the Navy. The problem was that after the war, many young boys tried to get a career with the Navy. With the Navy there was good pay, a steady job and there was the necessary adventure of seeing the world. It was everything that most young boys would go for. With the tremendous number of applicants, the Navy was very particular in weeding out the surplus. If they didn't get enough applicants they would have been a lot less fussy.

There was only one other way to get away from home and that was joining the Foreign Legion. He didn't even need the signature of his father, they took anybody who was willing to join, even murderers. If they had committed a murder or other serious crime, many men opted to join the Foreign Legion, instead of being apprehended by the police to end up in jail. Once you enter the doors of the Foreign Legion, the police can't get you so you are off the hook.

Pete Hendriks was a friend of Adrie and one night when Adrie called, his brother John had returned from the Foreign Legion. He had signed up for five years and when his five years were done, he called it quits and came home. John wasn't wanted by the police; he just had joined for the adventure.

Now here was a guy to get first-hand information from. When Adrie asked him some questions, John replied: "There are many misconceptions about the Legion, many of them are just myths. It seems you are interested in getting some information; I will give you all the information you need and then you can make up your mind if it is something you want to do."

Here was a guy who knew what his intentions were and he was going to tell him all about the Foreign Legion. Adrie stretched his legs and got ready to listen. John rolled another cigarette and blew some circles towards the ceiling after he lit it. He sat back in his armchair and started his story:

"The French Foreign Legion is called in France 'France Legion d'Etrangers'. It has a long tradition and was actually established in 1865 to get the foreigners out of France. Once the foreigners were out of France the rules were changed and the Foreign Legion could only serve out of France. France needed many soldiers to serve in its colonies in Africa. They had colonized Algeria, Morocco and Tunis and there was plenty of trouble which was to be solved by the Foreign Legion. When they were short of volunteers, they opened it up to foreigners who wanted to join for any reason. Some saw it as an opportunity to escape the past; they were in police trouble and wanted to sign up for five years to create a new identity. Everybody is asked if you want to become anonymous and change your name. Other young men saw the Legion as a way to get a military career or a way to adventure.

Before you sign the contract you have medical and mental exams. They don't want stupid people; you also get an I.Q. test. If you don't pass, it's back to civilian life. Once you passed and signed up for five years, you wished you hadn't passed. There is very rigid training and if you are two seconds late you are punished. They give you three weeks to learn the Foreign Legion Anthem. If you don't sing it to their liking, you have to climb a very steep hill.

If you join the Foreign Legion you better comprehend French pretty good because all commands are given in French and there is no interpreter to translate it for you. Severe punishments are in place if you don't understand a command.

There is a myth about the Foreign Legion; everything sounds fabulous which makes it attractive. The truth is that once you are in it, nothing in hell will be more pleasant. Adventure attracted me and adventure I found, lots of it. On the other hand I have been very disillusioned as well, it was very rough and a dangerous way of life. Several times we were ambushed and many of my friends got killed.

You have to be in excellent health to be able to take desert life in the Sahara. The desert is 55 degrees Celsius in the day time but as soon as the sun sets the temperature plunges to as low as 6 below zero which is well below freezing. There are seldom clouds in the sky and with a clear sky the heat escapes instantly after sunset. After the excruciating heat you are shivering in your sleeping bag all night, especially since you are used to a temperature of 55 degrees in the day time. Often I longed for sunrise to warm me up and in the heat of the day I wished the sun would set again. The Sahara is the worst place on earth, even flies can't survive. The hottest temperature on earth of 58 degrees Celsius was recorded in Lybia in 1922, that is the current world record. The sand absorbs a lot of heat and the temperature of the sand sears to 94 degrees Celsius which is only 6 degrees below the boiling point of water at sea level."

Adrie had listened with attention and had a few questions, he asked: "It sounds as though the Sahara is living hell when the temperatures soar that high. Don't they go for a siesta in the heat of the day and is the Sahara not beautiful?"

John replied: "The Sahara is the world's largest desert, it is about the size of the United States and it received its name from the Arabic word 'Sahra', which means simply 'Desert.' The Sahara is untamed and few people ever visit it. In a way it's beautiful that's if you like sandstorms, dehydration, venomous snakes and the threat of Arab guerillas that have only one thing in mind, to kill all of the French troops and take back the desert for their own.

If your commander can afford to take a few hours off at midday, when the blistering sun makes the desert an inferno, you are lucky. We always had sheets of canvas with us which we would spread across the roofs of the parked cars. This created the only shade for hundreds of miles. But if you have eye for beauty you can find it in the Sahara. You can see palm dotted villages between the endless sand dunes and craggy massifs rise from the 'bahr bela ma' which means 'the sea without water.'"

Adrie was learning a lot but he wanted to know more. His next question was: "Do you drink a lot of water with that heat?"

John answered: "You sure do! A person sweats about two gallons of water a day which has to be replaced. If you lose a gallon of water with no liquid to replace it, you'll become dehydrated and die fast. You'll be deader than the Dead Sea in no time at all. Water is so scarce that we had to wash our face with camel milk. Nobody in the desert takes a bath. A group of 25 soldiers received one litre of camel milk and everybody washed his face in it.

If you had a crap, there was seldom paper to clean your ass, most of the time you had to take your finger and clean your hand with desert sand. You always used your left hand to do that, you had one clean hand and one dirty hand. Muslims are severely punished if they steal. Most of the time the authorities cut off your right hand with an axe if you are caught stealing. That is double punishment, since the Muslims eat out of one common dish, also because of lack of water. They all use their right hand, the clean hand. Of course if they cut off your right hand you have no clean hand and you are not allowed to use your dirty hand. In order not to starve you eat mostly fruit after losing your right hand."

Adrie was thinking that if he had been living in Muslim country he would have lost his right hand for sure, he always was stealing apples and pears from the farmers when he was younger.

John Hendriks must have sensed Adrie's thinking and said: "Don't worry, if you are in the Foreign Legion you don't go by Muslim law, you go by French law."

"What a relief" Adrie thought, he almost could have seen himself with a stump instead of a hand.

John Hendriks was a good story teller and he had a lot to tell after he came out of the legion. He continued: "Water is not the only precious thing in the Sahara, salt is of equal importance. When you sweat a lot you lose a lot of salt which also has to be replaced or you'll die. Water and salt mean life in the desert, without them means death. They say that at one time gold and salt were traded one ounce gold for one ounce of salt. There are no salt mines or sea water which can be evaporated to get salt. Every ounce of salt has to be brought in from thousands of miles."

Adrie couldn't get enough of it and wanted to know if they were using camels in the Foreign Legion.

John said: "They sure do. Trucks are expensive to operate in the desert. After a few sandstorms the windows of the trucks turn milky and you can't see through them anymore. The paint on the trucks disappears fast, which means repainting. Camels can survive for more than thirty days on a little water and a little hay; you never have to repaint them and never have to replace their windows."

Adrie wondered if he could get one more question answered and asked: "Do they really take murderers and don't they hand them over to the Police?"

John answered: "Yes they take murderers, but you have to pass a rigid medical examination. If you don't pass they don't take you which is a good thing. Even if you are in good health, you wonder if you will make the end of the day, especially with the frequent sandstorms. Once you are signed on, the police can't touch you. As long as you are within the walls of the Legion the police cannot arrest you either, but if you are rejected they can pick you up as soon as you leave the building. Inshallah".

"What does that mean?" Adrie asked.

John replied: "Inshallah means 'If Allah wants it'. The Sahara is one of the harshest and most demanding environments on earth in which climate it can't hurt to have a greater Order on your side. The Arabs use it a lot. 'Tomorrow we will travel to the next oasis. Inshallah. Hopefully we are not going to be massacred. Inshallah.'"

This information was an eye opener for Adrie, it turned him off joining the Foreign Legion. He was better off to take all the shit that was flying around from his dad. Besides, he thought, "They very likely won't take me because of my flat feet."

Every four years before the war there were Olympic Games. The last time there were Olympic Games was in 1936 in Berlin. Adolf Hitler hosted the games in 1936 and in 1940 the war was on. That cancelled the games. In 1944 the war was still on, so the world missed two Olympic Games. After twelve years, the first Olympic Games were in London. Probably the Olympic Committee had chosen London because England had been the victor of the war.

Most of the countries participated and The Netherlands sent some very good athletes. Gold medals didn't come easy to a small country like The Netherlands. Bigger countries have more people and consequently they have more athletes. Nevertheless, there was one outstanding woman by the name of Fanny Blankers Coon who won three gold medals. In spite of the three children she already had, she was still the world's best in sprinting, hurdles and broad jumping. After all the hurdles she had overcome, she faced another hurdle on her way back home. Gold was not allowed to pass any border, however, there are exceptions and the Dutch custom official allowed the three gold medals to pass from England into The Netherlands.

The Cold War Years.

The U.S. saw the writing on the wall that a post war world in poverty, as it had been before the war during the Great Depression, would cause many countries to go over to Communism. In impoverished countries the lure for Marxism is great. Lots of people live in underdeveloped countries. They live in neighbourhoods of "Five no's". No sewers, no water, no electricity, no jobs and no hope.

"Land reform, take the land away from the landowners and collectivise the farms. Take from the haves and give it to the have nots." This is powerful propaganda for poor and hungry people, what do they have to lose? The problem is that once they elect a Communist Government, how do they get rid of it? In order to stem poverty, to stop more countries from embracing Communism, the U.S. Government brought in the Marshall Plan. That was the first move in the forthcoming Cold War.

The transition from war to peace hadn't been as easy as it had seemed in the U.S. With the termination of World War II there was a cancellation of orders to produce thousands of military aircraft. In 1943 and 1944 the U.S. produced about 29,000 bombers, 39,000 fighters and 33,000 miscellaneous types. With the surrender of Japan huge fleets of military aircraft were mothballed. Diminished needs to produce military aircraft got the aircraft industry in trouble. Many huge factories were shut down and thousands of workers became unemployed.

Even without hardly any need to produce military aircraft, the aircraft manufacturers were optimistic for the future. They continued to design new aircraft with jet engines and figured that post war prosperity would need thousands of planes to transport people in a peaceful world.

Moreover, the aircraft industry started to build small private planes and was forecasting "An airplane in every garage." High demand was expected, which would make up for the cancelled orders of military aircraft. These predictions didn't materialize. First of all there weren't enough airports to handle that many planes. Of course new airports could be built but most of the people couldn't afford a private plane. Private flyers found they could operate their airplane only in near perfect weather and in the vicinity of their home airports, unless they installed expensive navigation equipment that few people could afford.

There was more than enough need in the world to produce cars, radios etc. However, there was a problem, 'Europe was broke.' England the victor of the war was to its neck in debts and asked Uncle Sam for more money but Uncle Sam had multiple problems of its own. War production had to be transformed to peace production. Something had to be done to avoid another Depression.

Airplane orders weren't the only cancelled orders in the U.S. Tanks, submarines, bombs, shells, bullets etc. had very little demand in a world at peace. Moreover, millions of soldiers came home who needed a job. Most of the jobs were held by women who had gone into war production. In post war U.S.A. it became a major problem to keep everybody working.

'Make Love, no War' bumper stickers appeared on cars. Most of the people went for that advice but unfortunately the world leaders didn't. There had been all kinds of independence struggles in the former colonies of England, France, The Netherlands and Belgium and it looked as though this would go on for some time.

Other problems occurred between the former Allies. Adolf Hitler had predicted that during the war the Allies would split up. There were problems already with Stalin and it looked that post war relations with Russia would be strenuous at the best of times.

Hitler wrote in 'My Kampf',"People are only united when a common danger forces them to be; as soon as the common enemy is conquered and the danger is averted, the apparent harmony ceases."

When he wrote this he was sitting in jail for a failed insurrection. At that time he couldn't possibly know that his writing would be a prophecy, as he didn't know that a Second World War was in the offing. Yet, Hitler's writing became ever so true during the post war years.

It was early in 1948 when Adrie grabbed the newspaper from the mailbox. His eyes were instantly attracted to the fat headlines of the front page.

BERLIN CRISES COULD HAVE SERIOUS CONSEQUENCES.

Increased friction among the former Allies caused Stalin to act. He ordered all accesses of roads, railways and waterways leading to West Berlin closed. Only three small air corridors remained open to reach West Berlin. West Berlin has 2.3 million inhabitants who need 2,000 tons of food and other supplies a day. With no supplies entering West Berlin, its people will be starving within a week. President Truman and Prime Minister Attlee are stunned by the provocative action of the Soviet Union.

After supper, Adrie saw Leen Willemstein having a discussion with other people from the neighborhood. That could be interesting Adrie thought and joined the group. Leen Willemstein seemed to know it all again; he said: "The Russians want the U.S., England and France out of West Berlin. West Berlin is in the middle of the occupied Soviet zone. The only way to get supplies to West Berlin is to force a supply corridor. It seems that the defecation is about to hit the fan."

That was a neat way of putting it Adrie thought and asked: "When this defecation hits the fan what is going to happen?"

Leen Willenstein replied: "It could very well be that we are heading for a Third World War."

Adrie said: "That soon after the Second World War has ended; I thought we were going to have peace for some time?"

Henk Sturfs had joined the group of people who discussed world's problems in the street. He was about the same age as Adrie and asked Adrie: "What are you guys talking about defecation hitting the fan, why don't you say when the shit is going to hit the fan blade?"

Adrie explained: "Leen Willemstein's mother washed out his mouth, when he used bad language when he was growing up and obviously your mother has never done that to you. That's why you are talking about shit and Leen Willemstein says defecation."

Henk Sturfs replied: "I wouldn't say that, my mother washed my mouth out with soap as well but it helped f… all."

When Adrie came home from work the next day, he went for the newspaper as if his life was depending on it, which could very well be, if there was another war coming. The front page was secured for the Berlin crises it seemed.

U.S. AND GREAT BRITAIN HAVE STARTED TO SUPPLY WEST BERLIN BY AIR.

The U.S. and Great Britain are sending extra squadrons of freight planes to West Germany, in order to supply West Berlin with food and other needed supplies. Though the situation is very critical, U.S. officials believe that they can fly in enough supplies to keep West Berlin fed. If this situation is not resolved before winter, West Berlin will also need a significant supply of coal to keep West Berliners from freezing.

The next night there was more news about West Berlin in the paper.

U.S. SENDS TACTICAL STRATEGIC BOMBER SQUADRON TO ENGLAND WITH NUCLEAR BOMBS.

"The Western Allies are getting ready to defend West Berlin if necessary".

Leen Willemstein commented: "That's the only way you can treat the Russian bear by showing power. Luckily the Soviets don't have nuclear bombs or else we would be looking at a nuclear war. Now the U.S. will use nuclear bombs to keep the Soviets at bay. They call this a cold war."

"How can there be a cold war. No war has been declared and no shots are fired?" Adrie brought up.

"As long as no shots are fired we can call it a cold war. It's like playing chess, when the Soviets make a move; the U.S. makes a counter move. Hopefully this Cold War won't change into a hot war in which atomic bombs will be used."

When the discussion turned to the Communists in The Netherlands Adrie said: "I don't understand why the Dutch Government condones a Communist Party. First they allowed the Nazi sympathizers to form their own party which resulted in treason when the war started and now they make the same stupid mistake again."

Leen Willemstein knew it all again: "Nearly all attempts to exterminate a doctrine by force have failed. Most of the time the exact opposite is the result. The more repression of the doctrine takes place, the more hatred will occur. It was the only reason for the failure against Marxism. It was like hiring the wolf to mind the sheep. Also when they form a party we get to know who the members are. If we forbid them they go underground."

Actually Adrie already knew that it is not successful if you try to wipe out a doctrine by repression. He had learned at school that the Spanish Inquisition had tried to wipe out the Protestants. They were even burned at the stake for being Protestant. It didn't work; every time that the Roman Catholics burned a Protestant, they created a martyr which made Protestantism flourish.

Luckily in 1949 when Stalin saw that the Western Allies were able to supply West Berlin indefinitely by air and the threat that the U.S would use nuclear weapons, he called it quits and reopened the waterways, railways and rivers to supply West Berlin. The Berlin airlift had lasted for over a year and the Allies had transported 2.3 million tons of food and other goods within that time. People had learned to live with it. Now it was all over and the conflict had ended in a great victory for the Western Allies, people breathed a lot easier.

Not for long would people breathe easier. A month later the newspapers brought news that spread sorrow in all people's heart.

RUSSIA EXPLODES FIRST ATOMIC BOMB.

The Pravda, Russia's Communist newspaper, announced that Russia has tested and exploded their first atomic bomb and called the test successful.

The U.S. Press Agency has confirmed this report as correct. It means that the U.S. lost its monopoly on nuclear weapons and no longer will they be able to threaten the Soviet Union with nuclear bombs. If they do, the Soviet Union will have a reprisal in store for the U.S..

With the Russians being a nuclear power the entire world was in shock. As long as the U.S. had the monopoly on nuclear bombs, they could be sparingly used like on Japan, perhaps one or two or maybe four or five if it came to war with Russia. This was a calamity unheard of before. The world entered its most dangerous age in history and humans faced for the first time a total annihilation after they came to rule the world. They took over after the dinosaurs had been wiped out. Reptiles had ruled the world for millions of years. Supposedly their reign ended with a calamity when a meteor struck the earth. It certainly didn't look like humans would rule the world as long as dinosaurs had done.

The U.S. was more than alarmed and got ready for a nuclear war. They were caught napping after the Second World War started but they were surely not sleeping at the helm this time. Western leaders came together and so did the Eastern ones. People were petrified when a couple of months later the newspapers reported.

NEW YORK HAS ATOMIC DRILLS.

Drastic steps have been taken by the U.S. Government to be prepared for a nuclear war. The first atomic bombing raid exercise was held in New York City today. Most of the shelter was provided by underground subways. This training exercise was a great success. Busy New York streets were deserted five minutes after the alarm sounded. The U.S. takes the threat of a nuclear war seriously and acknowledges that the entire world is at risk. The speed with which the Russians developed their atomic bomb astonished the U.S. However, most of the Russian success came because of espionage.

Communications has come a long way from the time when Eve whispered in Adam's ear that there were good apples to be had. Drum, smoke signals and shouting from one hill to the next was also a way to communicate until radio and telegraph changed everything with wireless communications. Unfortunately, wireless could be as easily intercepted as the messenger who you could shoot if he had a bad news message.

Making airplanes, tanks, cannons and ammunition is very important in any war but there is a lot more to it. Planning and strategy is also very important in any war and if you know what the enemy is going to do it makes it a lot easier. Espionage and breaking the enemy code are very helpful in obtaining the information you need.

First the code was invented and next came the code breaker. It started by writing messages with invisible ink needing a chemical to reveal it. Next they had a code in which they changed the letters. A could be G and B could be H for all you knew.

Both of those systems were broken in no time. Experimenting with chemicals gave up the secret code and even the key to the code with changing letters was easily found. In a hundred letter message, the T is used about twelve times and the E fifteen times. Figuring out the number of occurrences in a message makes the secret code fall apart and it is no secret anymore to the code breaker.

Interception of radio messages made codes necessary i.e. codes that couldn't be broken. The Japanese code had been broken by the Americans and the Americans knew what the Japanese were planning, yet they let Pearl Harbour happen. It has never been revealed why they didn't take the appropriate steps to avoid this disaster. With the Battle of Midway, the Americans took advantage of their knowledge and clobbered the Japanese.

All countries had a code they thought couldn't be broken.

The English had a code that couldn't be broken. You had to learn an English poem of six sentences as key to the code and you had to know where to start.

The Germans had the enigma machine to code their messages. There was a book with the machine describing how to use it. The English had over a hundred people working to break the code. There were endless different combinations, as many as there are in D.N.A. They might never have broken the code if it hadn't been for some luck that came their way.

They captured a German sub marine that had the enigma code machine and users book. Once the English knew where the German sub marines were heading, it helped to sink a lot of them. Hitler never figured that the enigma code had been broken; he thought that the heavy losses were due to improved radar of the English.

The Americans had a simple code; they used the Navaho Indian Language. The Japanese tried to break the code but they never managed. It was so simple; a man was just speaking his own language.

The Russians had given all the words in the dictionary a number. Which would give a message:

Tank Division Will Move South
54 112 4700 88   912

Next the numbers were grouped in five digits   54112 47008   8912

Random numbers are added from the code book in the order they are printed.

54112	47008	8912
113	21890	199
54225	68898	9111

Does the message 54225 68898 9111 tell you "Tank Division will move South?" If you didn't have the numbered dictionary with random numbers you wouldn't be able to figure it out.

The Americans were going to try anyway; hundreds of typewriters were working night and day to reveal the secret code. (With the computers of today it could be done much easier in a lot less time.) It took them a long time but there were still some similarities they detected and soon they could read the secret messages that were sent by Soviet spies from the States to the Soviet Union.

The Soviet Union had a network of spies in the States as early as 1941. The atomic bomb was exploded by the Russians in 1949 much earlier than was expected. It appeared that the U.S. was rounding up the spies who worked for the Soviet Union. A few months later the newspaper reported:

ROSENBERGS ARRESTED FOR STEALING
SECRETS OF ATOMIC BOMB.

The Rosenbergs were U.S. citizens who had worked as spies for the Soviet Union since 1944, when the U.S. was working on its atomic bomb; they sent the atomic bomb secret to the Soviet Union. After the Americans cracked the secret code of Russia the Rosenbergs were caught and executed for stealing the atomic bomb secret and selling it to the Russians. *(The Rosenbergs were tried, found guilty of espionage and executed.)*

Even Canada had a spy school that could rival the K.G.B. in Russia. One of the men who wanted to be a spy had failed to become one. He said that they used all kinds of methods to make you fail. "I was at the end of the spy course when we had a test patrol. On the way there was a naked woman screaming on the beach for help. When I tried to help her they told me to mind my own business, spies don't need naked women when they are on duty. I was washed out."

That was by no means all the bad news that 1949 had to offer. News that shook the world came in the latter part of 1949 when the newspapers reported.

Communist Victory in China.

A four year civil war between Nationalist forces under Chiang Kai-chek and the rebel Communist forces under Mau Tse-tung ended with victory for the Communists. The mainland of China is inhabited by 583 million Chinese people and all those people are now under Communist rule.

The U.S. is taking a lot of heat that they let this happen. This is an all important victory for Communism. Marx and Lenin had predicted a worldwide revolution would turn the world completely to Communism. It seems at this time that their predictions make a lot of sense now that Russia, the largest country in the world and China the most populous country in the world, have both embraced Communism. The non-Communist world becomes smaller all the time.

Communists throughout the world had been convinced that the Red Dawn would come after the successful takeover of Russia in 1917. Thirty two years later when China became Red, dire predictions seem to come true. The non-Communist world faced the serious threat of being overrun by the Communists and they were uniting to make a stand in case of war.

Adrie was working in the harbors of Rotterdam. One day he was working on a Shell tanker where the crew was all Chinese except the officers. When he enquired about how it was in China under Communist rule, one of the Chinese said that Mao Tse-tung was a national hero. He said: "For the first time in the history of China the Chinese people aren't exploited and for the first time the Chinese people are fed."

Most of the Chinese agreed, except a couple of older guys who said that Mao was a traitor and the Chinese people would regret embracing Communism.

At the end of 1949, in December, there was some more devastating news. This time only the Dutch people, who lost most of their colonies, were affected. After the police action in 1946, an uneasy lull in the fighting had set in, which was followed by all out guerrilla warfare. Lonely outposts were ambushed, which took the lives of several young promising Dutch boys. In 1948 the Dutch Government launched a Second Police Action which took some more Dutch lives. With a total of 6,000 casualties and many more seriously wounded there was mounting opposition to the presence of Dutch troops.

Newspaper headlines spelled the news.

SUKARNO ELECTED AS PRESIDENT OF INDONESIAN REPUBLIC. HATTA BECOMES PRIME MINISTER.

The Dutch Government bowed under diplomatic pressure of the U.S. and the United Nations. Indonesia is now recognized as an independent country. Dutch troops will remain in Indonesia for the orderly transfer of power. After this has been accomplished the Dutch troops will come home. Sukarno made his first mark by changing the name of Dutch East Indies to Indonesian Republic. He also altered the name of the Capital Batavia to Djakarta. New Guinea is to remain under Dutch control.

Sukarno acted like all other revolutionists, by changing the names of cities and streets in order to wipe out the past and glorify the freedom fighters. Nobody in The Netherlands liked the way the Dutch Government had handled the problems in Indonesia. Many people had stakes in Indonesia and no matter how valuable they were; there was never compensation. The Dutch Government probably saw the writing on the wall that the many years of colonialism had come to an end.

Adrie was infuriated; it was a matter of another year before he would be drafted in the Dutch army. Now there were no Dutch troops to be dispatched to Indonesia anymore, the sting had been taken out of the army adventure. Every time that adventure beckoned and seeing the world seemed within reach, something changed and he missed the boat again. Serving in the Dutch army in The Netherlands wasn't all that attractive since the pay was only one guilder per day. With a salary like that you sure can't paint the town red.

Stalin moved fast to have Indonesia adopt Communism, he invited Sukarno for a state visit to Moscow. Sukarno was treated like a King in Moscow and he became a puppet of Stalin. Sukarno, as a Muslim, already had four wives plus a Japanese concubine, yet he brought back from Moscow another sexy blond, a personal present from Stalin.

If The Netherlands had thought to keep friendly relations with Indonesia they were quite wrong. In 1954 Sukarno expelled all remaining Dutch citizens and confiscated their properties. After 300 years of colonization 300,000 Dutch people returned to The Netherlands. Many of them were sick and weak.

Sukarno's next move was to add New Guinea to his country. He demanded that The Netherlands hand it over to Indonesia. When his request was denied, he severed diplomatic relations with The Netherlands and mobilized his army in 1961. Next he dropped airborne troops on New Guinea which brought the conflict in the U.N. Finally the Dutch handed New Guinea over to the U.N. which gave it to Indonesia the following year.

Sukarno was a Communist dictator, he suspended elections in 1963. This was followed with a declaration of the Indonesian Congress that declared Sukarno to be president for life. Hatta resigned and unrest and revolution attempts followed. In 1966 the Indonesian army took control, ousted Sukarno and put President Suharto in place. President Suharto outlawed the Communist Party and put Sukarno under house arrest. Suharto brought Indonesia back to the U.N. and brought back elections in Indonesia.

In 1960 Indonesia took possession of the Western half of New Guinea. They renamed it Iran Jaya - "Victorious hot land." The Dutch were ousted from the last of their East Indian colonies. The Irianese people did not embrace their new rulers, they hated them. Two independence movements were crushed by the Indonesian army. The Australian half, the Eastern part became Papua, New Guinea an independent state in 1975.

More than 6,000 Dutch soldiers lost their lives in Indonesia to guerrilla war fighters. Several monuments were erected in The Netherlands to honor the ones who gave their life, fighting to subdue the guerrillas. One of the monuments in the City of Leiden was totally destroyed by people who didn't believe that the soldiers died for an honorable cause. They said: "The people should honor the Indonesians who were killed by the Dutch troops fighting for liberty."

Luckily for the people in Indonesia Sukarno was unseated by Suharto who was not a Communist. To the people of Indonesia who were still poor it didn't make that much difference. After a few Presidents the Indonesian people said:

"The first President of Indonesia Sukarno went crazy for women. He was diagnosed to have died from Syphilis.

The second President Suharto went crazy for money.

The third President Habibi went crazy for everything.

And the fourth President Wahid made everybody crazy."

Party Time.

Jan Metselaar had a rubber plantation in the Dutch Indies before the war. When the Japanese came he was imprisoned in a work camp and was later transported to build the Burma Railway. After the Japanese left, Jan tried to pick up where he had left off but the guerrilla war made that impossible. Finally he threw in the towel and went back to The Netherlands. Adrie met him at his work and it didn't take long to get him talking.

Jan's story was full of hate for the Japanese. He described the cruelty of the Japanese in the prison camps, according to him there were no crueller people than the Japanese. He said that they were eating dogs and the preparation of dog was plain cruelty to the animal. They put the dog in a gunny bag and hit the dog in the bag, that way the dog had a slow death which makes the meat tenderer.

He also told the story about the Burma railway they had to construct for the Japanese: "We were transported under worse than animal conditions. We were packed like sardines and were only fed one time a day. The toilet pails from the train had to serve to get the food in. There was no water to even rinse the pails, they were just emptied and without cleaning, the food was dumped into the pails. The Burma railway was 400 kilometres long and went right across the jungle. Malaria and other tropical diseases killed about 75% of the people that worked the railway. It was disgusting; I don't know how I ever survived that ordeal.

Women were also put in concentration camps and the prettiest ones were put in convenience stations to be used by the Japanese for sex. Some pretty women were raped twenty times a day."

In the summer of 1949 another Jan came back from the Tropics, it was Jan Vandelen with other friends Gerrit Vandriel, Cor Vanderpoel and Gillis Hays who lived all on the Hordyk. They had been in the same draft as Jan and they came home all on the same ship. After debarkation they were allowed to go home for a four week holiday. As soon as the holiday was over they had to report back to their unit to be relieved from military duties.

Adrie had been working all day and while he had his supper, Jan his old friend came to see him. Adrie was so excited to have his old friend back that he had no more time for supper. Jan said: "I come to pick you up for the party at our home. We are going to celebrate."

Jan's parents had the whole house decorated in and outside for a whole week. Everybody was happy that he had safely returned from fighting in the

Tropics. Jan's mother was crying again but this time from happiness, she said to Adrie: "You were right, Jan could take care of himself; he came back."

The other three returned soldiers were also at the party. There was lots to eat and drink, and there was an accordion player which meant that all drinking songs had to be sung all night. Singing in unison with an accordion was very common in The Netherlands. There were quite a few tropic songs from the East Indies and one of the songs had a refrain:

When I'm dreaming in my klamboe,
I'm dreaming about my fatherland.

(A klamboe is a bed in the tropics with a mosquito net around it to protect you from all kinds of harmful mosquitoes that can give you Malaria and sleeping illness.)

Jan said: "That's not the way we were singing it in the East Indies, we had our own version.

When I'm dreaming in my klamboe,
I'm dreaming of my fatherland.
But on the other hand:
It's the baboo who you never forget.
You do everything with her and when you go to bed,
You saw the way she really was.
When you pulled down her sarong you saw her brown bare ass.

(A baboo was originally a native nurse but the word baboo was later also used for household help.
A sarong is a long strip of cloth, often brightly colored and printed, worn around the lower part of the body like a skirt in the East Indies.)

Jan told a lot of stories and he had a great audience. He told that they had a lot of trouble with dysentery. When they had dysentery they were only allowed to drink rice water for three days. After that they gave the patients dry toast and they had to deliver a stool sample in a little cardboard box to the medics every day. The medics would study the sample to determine if they were cured. One of the patients put a piece of toast in the cardboard box and gave it to the medic on duty. When the medic saw the toast he asked the soldier: "How come there is a piece of toast in your box?"

The soldier said: "What do you expect? I have been eating dry toast for ten days, how could I possibly shit meat."

Jan's mother said: "I knew that we were going to get some shitty stories but I am glad you came home to tell them."

When the conversation turned to religion, Jan said: "The people on Java don't believe in the creation as Genesis pictures it. According to them, 'God sculptured a model man and put it in his oven to bake. However, God took his model man out of the oven too early so the model man was still white. He put that model white man in Europe. Having bungled it, God made another model man and put it in the oven. This time he wasn't going to take it out too early but unfortunately he waited too long and when he opened the oven the man was black. God put that black man in Africa. God thought that he had experience now and he knew exactly how long his model man should bake to make him perfect. He put another man in the oven and this time because of his experience, he had the perfect man. This man was baked nice light brown and he put this man on Java.'"

Jan went to the bathroom and when he returned he said: "I'm missing the bottles of water in the bathroom. In the Dutch Indies they don't use a piece of paper to wipe their butt; they have a bottle of water which they squeeze. They don't think much about our habit of taking a piece of paper to look at the color of your shit, they consider it very dirty. When we arrived in Indonesia some kids were shouting at us 'Dirty Asses.' Since it was Malaysian we didn't understand it. It took some explaining before we understood what they meant. We always had thought that we were very clean and that there was no hygiene in the East Indies."

There was a lot of Malaysian to be learned when Adrie went out with his friends who had remained in the Indies. At one time when they were biking Jan said: "I see Poekie Ajan."

Adrie asked what that was and Jan's answer was 'a chicken cunt.' He saw a young girl of about twelve years old riding bike. With a gust of wind, her skirt blew up which revealed most of her bottom genitals. A young girl still has everything small so he called it a chicken cunt which wasn't that big either. Adrie learned a lot of Malaysian but he only retained the worst.

One of the other soldiers said: "To morrow night the party is at my house, everybody that's here is hereby invited. The other two soldiers indicated that there would be a party at their house the two days after that party. There was lots to celebrate and there was much happiness for the return of the soldiers after they had served for two years in the Tropics.

Four parties in a row was a lot of fun at night. Of course the morning after was a different story. Party or not, the boss demanded that you worked all day for a day's wages. Finally it was Saturday which meant that Adrie had to work only half a day. At night he was used to going to the corner of Cafe Sport. That was 'The Gathering Place,' where everybody was heading to on

Saturday and Sunday night. Only if the weather was bad would they go inside Cafe Sport to play pool and have a beer. If the weather was good everybody went girling or just biking around. If they returned early enough there was always time for a game of pool and a drink.

That Saturday night was different. When Adrie came to Cafe Sport, Jan was already waiting; he was on holiday so he was early. He said to Adrie, the other three soldiers, and a few more boys from the neighborhood: "Let's go inside Cafe Sport and have a party, the party is on me."

Adrie said: "That's all very nice of you but when can I buy you a drink?"

Jan replied: "What are you talking about. I was gone for two years, it's my party and I pay for it. I have lots of money because they paid me my Tropic Money."

Sunday was another party supplied by one of the other soldiers and the week after the other two fellows took a party turn. The week after that, Adrie said: "To night it's my party, you guys have been away for two years and in that time I couldn't buy you a drink but tonight I will." That was nine parties in a row and that should be it.

It happened that two weeks later was the Queen's Birthday which was always a celebration. Rysoord was always a very active town when it came to entertainment. There was a pasture set up for the celebration. After the necessary pooper scooper activities had been completed, a bandstand was set up for dancing and games. There were also some hotdog and hamburger stands and at the very beginning of the pasture there was a giant beer tent for the thirsty people.

There were about ten boys at Cafe Sport when Adrie arrived and everybody was heading for Rysoord. Before they entered the pasture, they had to go by a wicket where they had to buy their ticket. Admission was one guilder. There was an oompah band tootling Old Dutch tunes, but the boys had little ear for music, their attention was drawn by the beer tent. The sight of the beer tent made Jan thirsty, he said: "Let's first go for a beer." Since nobody objected, it was a deal.

When they entered the beer tent, there was already a table with six boys from the neighborhood. As soon as they saw the new arrivals, they invited: "Come and sit with us."

It was a very long table and everybody had a seat. As it was rather busy, it took a while to get a beer. Before anybody got a beer a few more boys came who wanted to join the table. This time a small table was moved to seat everybody. Finally the waiter came and Jan said to the waiter: "A beer for everybody." The waiter counted to twenty four before he was finished. A little later he came back with 24 beer and Jan paid.

When the waiter came in the neighborhood again Gerrit said: "Waiter bring us 24 beer." Cor and Gillis took a turn too ordering 24 beer. Adrie thought "That's very nice of you guys but my turn is next" and ordered 24 beer. Everybody caught on to take a turn to order 24 beer. The waiter couldn't carry the 24 beer orders in fast enough. He just looked at the table off and on and if somebody raised his hand he just brought another 24 beer.

The waiter had some other tables to serve as well which left him little time to take the empty glasses off the table. After a while the table was full of empty glasses and some full ones. When one of the fellows had to go to the bathroom due to high water levels, he didn't have sure footing and fell against the table. The table tipped over and all the empty glasses and some full ones fell off the table on one side. Jan caught most of the glasses in his lap and could have put them back on the table. Instead he threw them on the floor and kicked them under the tarp of the tent outside.

After everybody had a turn to order 24 glasses of beer it was time to go home but where was home? First they had to get their bikes and try to mount them. Adrie was finally on his bike after a few futile attempts. A few minutes later his stomach started to act up and he had to get off his bike to make his offering to Bacchus. After that incident he felt relieved and was in better shape to peddle home. Everybody had paid a guilder admission fee to get on the pasture for the celebrations. No one of the 24 fellows had seen anything but the beer tent and twenty four beer delivered 24 times to the table.

Playing Soldier.

After the celebrations for the return of the four soldiers of the Hordyk, they all went back to their unit for final preparations to return to civilian life. All of them went back to their former boss and civilian life made them think about getting a steady girlfriend.

Early in 1950 when Adrie was reading the paper, the headlines on the front page read:

FREE WORLD MAKES STAND AGAINST COMMUNISM.

The North Atlantic Treaty Organisation comes into being as Belgium, Canada, Denmark, France, Iceland, Italy, Luxemburg, The Netherlands,

Norway, Portugal, The United Kingdom, and the U.S. sign the treaty. It is a collective agreement with the purpose of defending Western Europe together. If anyone of those treaty countries is attacked, the other members will be automatically at war and will take appropriate steps to defend all NATO territory. General Eisenhower will be NATO's first commander.

(NATO was outnumbered by the Soviet Union in tank divisions by ten to one. Now the Soviet Union was also a nuclear power, threatening with atomic bombs made no sense. It would only attract a revenge by the Soviet Union. However, NATO made the Soviet Union believe that NATO would use atomic weapons and any belligerence meant technically to commit suicide.)

On a Saturday night when all the young boys came to Cafe Sport, which was the meeting place, an unwanted person came to join. It was Leen Koekoek who had boasted about being in the Hitler Youth and had threatened to disclose the people who were listening to Radio London. His father had been a vassal mayor for the Germans and his brother Joe Koekoek had volunteered for the Waffen S.S. to fight in Russia. Everybody had wished Joe Koekoek 'A never come back trip' to Russia.

Joe Koekoek had not returned from Russia but Leen Koekoek was still here. He was wearing the uniform of the Dutch Military Air Force and was already Corporal. Sjaak Heyboer was a Corporal in the Dutch Army too; he was present to hear some boasting from the former traitor. After Leen Koekoek left, he said he was going to report his past to the proper authorities. When they knew his past, they could kick him out of the Air Force.

Few people in The Netherlands could afford a car but they had to be motorised. More and more people resorted to the moped. Most of them were equipped with little auxiliary motors which needed additional pedalling when there was a bit of wind. As with everything 'the sky is the limit.' More and more powerful auxiliary engines came about, until the day when there was little difference between a light motorbike and a moped. That was a disaster with high speed mopeds riding between the bikes on the bike paths. They were ringing their bell to indicate that they wanted to pass. Most of the time they were ignored and the bikers didn't move. That caused some heated arguments on both sides.

Only a couple of months after Jan had returned to civilian life, Adrie received a letter in the mail from the Dutch Government that he had to come to Army Headquarters for medical examination. It meant that if he was in good enough shape they could use him for cannon fodder and he was going to be recruited for military training.

There was no escape from playing soldier unless you had two brothers before you in the Dutch army. They called it Brother Service. Apparently, the

Dutch Government could see the financial hardships to the family after two had been drafted. Before the war started, you needed only one brother in the army to be free. They would take every second boy from the family. With the international tensions, the Governments of the NATO countries wanted as many soldiers in NATO as Russia had.

Somehow along the line, there were young men who dodged military services. They claimed to have religious objections. It says in the Bible "Thou shall not kill," That's the word of God which you have to obey, they reasoned. The Dutch Government allowed that kind of reasoning to let them off the hook for military services.

To make it fair to the young men who were drafted into the army, those legal draft dodgers had to report to a work camp. They had to put the same time in as the soldiers and also got the same pay of 1 guilder per day. And they had the same leaves as the soldiers. There was no way to dodge the compulsory work camp. If they didn't report, they were treated the same way as the other young men who had no religious objections. They were all considered to be deserters; they were arrested and put in jail.

A cousin of Bina didn't want to be trained as cannon fodder and didn't report. He was seen as a deserter and put in jail. He was planning to get married but when he got out of jail after two years, he found that his brother had married his girlfriend and had emigrated to New Zealand. Ten years later his brother had a heart attack and died. His ex-girlfriend came to The Netherlands for a visit, she married him and both went to New Zealand. "Old love doesn't rust was his comment." Some stories have a happy ending.

In order to claim religious objections you had to be in a religious group like the Jehovah Witnesses to qualify. If you thought to claim your objection and joined the Jehovah Witnesses shortly before the draft, you had something coming. Only if you had been in that religious group for at least two years was your claim valid. If this hadn't been a condition, half of the young men would have joined the Jehovah Witnesses temporarily. If you wanted to go that route you had to plan it long in advance. After Adrie had chucked the church, he didn't think that he would qualify to have religious objections. Besides, he would rather be in the Army than in a work camp.

Playing soldier was a game Adrie had been quite familiar with since he was 12 years old. He had made it to the rank of Chief of Staff, Commander of Land, Sea and Air Forces. When he was 12 years old he liked playing soldier, it was fun. Now he was 20 years old, he had little heart for the army. It wouldn't have been as bad if he could have maintained his former rank and lead his troops to victory. Undoubtedly, there would be some loudmouth sergeant present to give him a bad time.

Some people were smarter than the average bear. There was no draft for them when they had the required age. They had simply buggered off to a different country with emigration. It used to be that all eligible young men for the army had to draw a number and if you had a high number you had a chance to be free of military conscription. With the increased possibility of war, this drawing of numbers was discontinued in 1938. When war became likely the Government wanted to increase its army and gave fewer breaks.

As a good obedient Dutch citizen, Adrie reported reluctantly to the Army Headquarters. First of all there were a bunch of forms to be filled out. There were some samples on the wall to make it more understandable. The samples had the same questions and some smart guy had filled them out. If they had taken the joker seriously they would have rejected him for sure.

When he came to the question "Have you ever had sexually transmitted disease and if yes what kind?" The joker had filled out: "Rotten dink only."

When it came to family history with the question: "Are there any mental illnesses in your family on your father's side?" The answer on the sample was: "Yes, my father is an idiot."

And his mother he described: "My mother is insane."

When it came to the question "Have you any mental disorders the answer was "Only retardation and stupidity."

Some young men tried to fake malfunctions to get themselves rejected. Few, if any succeeded. One of the prospective soldiers tried to be rejected by claiming deafness. They gave him a rigid test first. Next one doctor whispered to the other doctor: "Rejected, he is as deaf as a stone."

They watched him very closely. When he looked relieved after he heard the magic words; that was enough proof that he had heard and was not deaf at all.

Three months later Adrie received notice in the mail that he had to report for military duties in s'Hertogenbos by the Shock Troops. It was the same unit Jan had served under. When he told Jan that he was also going to be with the Shock Troops, Jan replied: "The only shock you will ever have is when you enter the building of the Shock Troops for the first time; you get the shock of your life."

For a soldier to be, the news was very discouraging on June 25, 1950.

COLD WAR HEATS UP IN SOUTH KOREA. NORTH KOREAN FORCES HAVE INVADED SOUTH KOREA.
An emergency meeting of the U.N. has been called for tomorrow."

As soon as Adrie came home the next day he grabbed the paper to read all about it. The news was a calamity for a future soldier.

SEOUL, SOUTH KOREA'S CAPITAL FALLS
INTO COMMUNIST HANDS.
U.N. condemns North Korea and calls for an immediate withdrawal of their troops from South Korea.

It was quite clear that they had to serve their fatherland to show the Russians a brutal military force against the Soviet bloc. All NATO countries had to contribute to stop the Russians in case they were coming. There was even a movie called "The Russians are coming." Though this was comical, the threat that the Russians were coming was real. The Russians outnumbered NATO with tank divisions ten to one. They could march faster to the North Sea than the Germans had done in 1940. NATO divisions didn't keep the Russians out, the atomic weapons kept them out. Luckily Stalin wasn't crazy like Hitler who wanted to take all of Germany with him if he couldn't rule it.

It seemed that the world was preparing for war when the news came the next day.

U.N. FORMS 'UNITED NATION FORCES' TO OUST
NORTH KOREAN FORCES FROM SOUTH KOREA.
General McArthur in command of U.N. troops.

A week later the news became more encouraging when the headlines of the newspaper reported:

GENERAL MACARTHUR LANDS TROOPS NEAR INCHON
IN NORTH KOREA AND RECAPTURES SEOUL.

It looked that General MacArthur had things under control in Korea; three days later he crossed the border and entered North Korea. He was not about to stop when he had chased the Communists out of South Korea.

One week after that, it looked as if the U.N. Army would win the war.

U.N. FORCES CAPTURE NORTH KOREAN
CAPITAL P'YONG YANG.
There were sixteen nations fighting under U.N. flag to battle Communism in Asia.

Adrie was only 20 years old and the year was 1950. Time goes fast and the day came that Adrie boarded the train to report to his unit for training.

He had picked up smoking a few weeks before. Every soldier smokes; if you want to be part of the bunch, you smoke. Some kind of "If you are in Rome you do what the Romans do."

When he arrived in s'Hertogenbos there were all kinds of military personnel awaiting one thousand new recruits. Soon he was lined up in his first queue up of the army, waiting for transportation. Big Army trucks were driving continuously to the military barracks. On arrival, the new recruits were all sorted out and directed to the company they were going to serve.

There was another line-up in front of the company building and more sorting to the platoon of the company. There were four platoons to a company, each existing of forty soldiers. Each platoon had its own room with forty soldiers occupying it. The platoon sergeant was waiting to give each new soldier a bunk bed. He said he didn't care who was sleeping on top of the bunk or at the bottom.

Adrie got a bunk bed in the corner beside the window. One chap by the name of Don Kleiweg was already waiting for his buddy sleeper to arrive. Kleiweg came also from Rotterdam; he said that he was quite restless and preferred to sleep in the lower bunk. That way if he fell out of his bed, the distance to the floor was shorter. That was fine with Adrie who favored sleeping in the top bunk; he liked to see more than the bottom of the bed above him.

The platoon sergeant came in demanding quiet to bring some good news, he said: "The first day of your military career is going to be designated to get the new recruits into uniforms. For your information that's all you are right now. You are only a soldier after you have completed your three months basic training and have passed your tests satisfactorily. As long as you are a recruit you will make only 75 cents per day. As soon as you have your status of being a soldier, after three months, you will get paid one whole guilder per day. If you ever become a First Class Soldier you will get paid 1 guilder and 10 cents per day. If you want more money than that, you will have to become a corporal in which case you will make 1 guilder and 25 cents per day.

I will take five at a time to go to the quartermaster sergeant to fit uniforms and other clothes. As soon as you receive your uniform, you will put your military clothes on and put your civilian clothes in your suitcase or bag. You'll take them home as soon as you go on leave. I do not want to see anymore civilian clothes here and no suitcase either in the barracks. This is a military establishment in which there is no room for civilian stuff other than your razor and your toothbrush. As soon as you put on your military clothes you are in the Army. When you go home for leave you wear your uniform; if you are caught in civilian clothes, your company commander will deal with you and punish you. Now proceed with getting acquainted with your brand new buddies with whom you are going to spend an awful lot of time. Don't forget, in the army your buddies depend on you and you depend on them."

Every soldier plays cards; what else is there to do? Some of the new recruits were already playing after they got to know some of their comrades. Adrie and his bunk buddy Kleiweg found a couple of other roommates who were interested in a game of cards. Soon they were playing for money and smoking like a chimney. They looked like real soldiers though they were only recruits.

At 5.30 p.m. the platoon sergeant came to announce that it was time for supper. All the new recruits received two mess tins, one for soup or porridge and the other for potatoes, vegetables and steak, the sergeant said with a false smile on his face. A fork, spoon, knife and a tin cup for drinking were also given.

Since the supper was mass produced it wasn't quite as tasty as back home. Because there was nothing else, you could live on it was the general conclusion. There was little variation in the menu, most of the time it was pea soup on Thursday and fish on Friday. About 30% of the people in The Netherlands are Roman Catholic and they are not allowed to eat meat on Friday. To accommodate the Roman Catholic soldiers the menu was fish on Friday, usually with carrots as vegetables. *(Quite a few years later, the Pope changed this meatless Friday with a Papal Bull that allowed eating meat on Fridays.)*

A popular song in the army was "Who has put sugar in the pea soup?

The quarter master sergeant had really outdone himself. At night everybody had a uniform on and wondered how long it would take before they could put the uniform back in the mothballs. Everybody was looking forward to get his army training finished. Then they could continue with their civilian life and work for their future. There was no time limit set for the length of the military service duties. The Government had to decide those little details yet.

Friendships are made easily in the army. Everybody was a stranger but not for long. A lot of talking was done that night and a lot of jokes were also on the repertoire. Of course a lot of jokes were soldier jokes. One joke was particular interesting; it was about the possible fate of a soldier.

When you become a soldier there are two distinct possibilities; you serve your fatherland during peace time or war.

If you are a soldier during peacetime you are lucky but if you serve during war there are two possibilities; you have to fight the enemy or you are assigned to other duties.

If you are assigned to other duties you are lucky but if you have to fight the enemy there are two possibilities; you survive the battle or you are killed.

Of course if you survive the battle you are lucky but if you are killed there are two possibilities; they burry you in a single grave or in a mass grave.

If they bury you in a single grave you are lucky but if you are buried in a mass grave there are two possibilities; they leave you where you are or they dig you up later.

If they leave you alone you are lucky but if they dig you up later there are two possibilities; they bury you again or they ship you to the paper plant to make paper out of you.

If you are re-buried you are lucky, and if they ship you to the paper plant there are two possibilities; they make writing paper out of you or shit house paper.

If they make writing paper out of you, you are lucky and if they make shit house paper out of you there are two possibilities; you end up in the man's toilet or in the lady's toilet.

If you end up in the man's bathroom you are lucky but if you end up in the lady's bathroom there are two distinct possibilities; they use you at the front or at the back.

Then there was the joke about the sergeant who was standing in front of the tallest guy of the company. He found everything wrong and started to give him supreme shit. The tall guy didn't move and looked straight forward which made it worse. The sergeant got mad and said: "Don't you want to look me in the eyes when I'm talking to you." The tall guy said: "Yes sergeant, but then I have to bend over."

Another joke was that if you got in the airborn troops you had nothing to fear. Of course you were depending on the girls that packed the parachute. If one string wasn't sitting right the parachute might fail. Of course you are allowed to check your parachute but you can't try it out to see if it works. (If the parachute doesn't open up when you jump it's called 'the parachute Roman Candles.' It means that you are dead.) You have nothing to fear because there is warranty on the parachute. As soon as you are on the ground again, you can exchange it for another one.

There also went around a joke about the United Nations. A U.N. army could win any war if they took the best that all countries had to offer. They should follow the Israel advice that attack is the best defence. Fight with German guns "Die schiessen wunderbar" (They shoot so wonderful). With American mentality; "We scare the shit out of them." With Dutch additional shit after eating brown beans with onions; "We'll let them smell some farts and the enemy will think that a gas war has started." Fighting should take place according to English politeness: "Please sir, tell us, which war has the highest priority!" And with French determination; "Apres nous le deluge! And with Spanish war screams "Ole!"

The Bishop came to the barracks in a brand new Ford Mustang. The soldier at the gate said to the bishop: "And then to think that your big boss was riding a donkey."

A veteran tells his story: "I have been hit by 30 bullets on different occasions and I'm still alive. One of the listeners asked "Don't you have trouble with all that lead in your body?" The veteran answered "Well no, the only problem is I can't swim anymore."

It was 6.00 a.m. the next morning when the platoon sergeant came in the room whistling like a steam locomotive and yelling: "Get up you lazy bums; nobody ever won a medal in bed. You are in the army now. Maybe you are used to being a boy, tough luck, in the army there is no place for boys. Men only! I want you spick-and-span with polished shoes that shine like a dog's dink in the moonlight, at 7.00 a.m. in front of the company building."

He made sure that his new recruits were there in time for breakfast. The sergeant said with a grin on his face: "I will appoint six volunteers to get your tea and bread from the kitchen. You six will do." He pointed at six recruits and off they went to the kitchen. Everybody received a cup of tea, five slices of bread, a slice of cheese, two slices of sausage, a bit of jam and a little cube of butter. The sausage was inferior compared to what people usually eat and most of the recruits threw it away. The cheese and jam was alright, it almost tasted like something you ate back home. Breakfast was barely swallowed when the sergeant shouted to get ready to meet the Company Commander Major Brown.

At eight o' clock sharp, the recruits were put in lines of three and a sergeant shouted "Report!" All four peloton sergeants marched in front of the company commander and stated to the commander that all men were accounted for. Apparently nobody had run away back to mother.

Of course, the company commander had something to say or else he wouldn't be a commander. "Most of you men were under care of your mother but now ... you are under my tender care. I am your mother, your father and your legal guardian; as long as you are here I decide what's good for you. By the way, 'Your mother doesn't work here so you clean up your own damned mess because I'm not going to do it for you.' I want all the rooms to be as immaculate as the Virgin Mary. By the way, if you treat me like you treat your mother, I'll kill you!

I saw you all stroll to the company square for your daily report. Tonight at 5.00 p.m., at the end of your normal duties, you all report here again. At that time I want to see an energetic bunch of people full of pep and vinegar. Today your platoon sergeants will teach you how to march and I want to see that you know how to be properly dismissed by tonight. Is that understood?"

Nobody said anything so the commander repeated "Is that understood?"

Most of the recruits shouted "Yes."

It didn't make the commander very happy, he shouted: "The answer is 'Yes Major'".

That very first day was spent on marching, learning how to stand at rigid attention and how to be dismissed properly. The platoon sergeant wanted everything perfect in one day, he kept yelling: "You guys can't do anything right, you don't even know what's left or right when marching. He expected that with marching everybody would swing his arms to shoulder height. This is very hard in the beginning, quite a few recruits had extreme trouble with that, and it took weeks instead of days.

A quick look at the muddy obstacle course concluded the day. It looked as if the war had started, there were swinging ladders to climb and artificial cliffs. There were also wooden and concrete walls to scale and barbed wire fences. "Some other day we'll have some fun here," the sergeant said.

An instruction roster was put up in the rooms to give everybody an idea what was up next. The new recruits were also taught how to make their bed; the blankets had to be folded exactly 37 centimetres wide. There was even a lesson on how to put on your beret; it had to be exactly two fingers above your left eye. A drawing was pinned on the wall showing how to put everything in your locker. All lockers were the same size with three shelves.

The top shelf was designated for the uniforms and sweaters.

The second shelf was for shirts and underwear. A pile of shirts on the left, in the centre undershirts and shorts on the right. All the items had to be folded neatly at the same width to make the piles even and square.

The bottom shelf had the mess tins and cutlery on the left, and the right half of the space on that shelf was for private stuff, soap, shaving equipment, toothbrush etc.

The sergeant said: "Whenever I pull open a door of a locker I want all of them to look identical, except the right hand side of your bottom shelf. Your beds all have to look the same as well. As for your personal grooming, you have to present yourself at all times clean and well shaven except when you are training in the mud. You are not allowed to wear a beard but a moustache is allowed, that is if it doesn't deface your countenance. Your commanders will decide if this is the case and if it does you have to remove your moustache."

Shoes had to be polished at all times and even the soles between the foot and heel had to be polished with shoe polish. That way the leather wouldn't dry out and crack, the shoes were supposed to last longer that way.

A gas cape was also supplied to each soldier; that was supposed to prevent mustard gas from getting onto your skin. "If mustard gas hits your skin it will eat your flesh away and you will die," the sergeant said.

"Don't we get a gas mask?" Adrie asked.

The sergeant said: "If we have war there will be gas masks, they probably come with white mice in a little cage. If you have trench warfare it happens that the enemy releases deadly gas to kill us all. An early warning system is supplied by white mice; that at the first sign of gas, start to act erratically. If the mice behaved that way the soldiers shouted "Put it on, white mice." Everybody knew what it meant and put on his gasmask. It saved many lives during the First World War when gas was used a lot.

There were a lot of theory lessons, some were given to explain how a certain weapon worked and how it had to be taken apart and assembled again. Everybody received a rifle which was a Lee-Enfield. The first lesson was how to take it apart and clean it. The sergeant said that they used to destroy tanks with a piat which was hard to handle because of the tremendous kickback it gave. Now they had the bazooka, which was much lighter to transport and to shoot.

Some theory lessons were a bunch of unnecessary crap; they were only on the roster for the Government to explain why soldiers could kill their enemies while the Bible clearly dictates: "Thou Shall Not Kill." In civilian life you can't kill the bastard either, so what changes when you are in the Army? All of a sudden you have a license to kill.

The Chaplain had a crack at it and said: "We all know that the ultimate answer to the world's problems cannot be found in armed conflict. However, we must realize that wars have been a way of life throughout history; and that this aspect of man's inhumanity to man will in all likelihood and for whatever reason continue.

We fought for five years to get peace and we thought we had it. Unfortunately, the defeat of the Axis powers in 1945 did not bring peace to the world. The Western Allies soon found themselves engaged in a new struggle with their former ally the Soviet Union. Freedom isn't free; it comes at a very high price.

You men were all too young to be involved in the fighting of the Second World War. You might be shocked that killing in action is forgivable. For nearly six years during the Second World War there were many millions of men who were decent law abiding citizens. They would have been ashamed to maltreat a child or an animal but during the war they were prepared to kill other men whom they didn't know. Wars breed cruelty but sometimes man has to fight for freedom and against oppression and tyranny. We must fight for what we believe in. When you have something precious in life, like freedom, you have to fight for it to keep it.

History teaches us that even the Jews were constantly at war. One of the great warriors was King David." The Chaplain kept beating around the bush for a little while longer and then asked if there were any questions.

Adrie had been listening attentively and could hardly wait for the question period. This stuff was right up his alley. He said: "Yes Chaplain, you mentioned the Jews who were constantly at war, I sure question the validity of their claim to Palestine. The Jews were in Egypt when God told Moses to lead his chosen people out of Egypt to the Promised Land. That Promised Land was inhabited by all kinds of people. What gave the Jews the right to kill all those people? In one of the battles which was led by Joshua, God ordered them to destroy all men, women and children and also all their sheep and other husbandry animals because they were evil. What did those animals have to do with the conflict and how can animals of certain people be evil?"

The Chaplain answered: "The Israelis were certainly entitled to Palestine, that's where they lived before they went to Egypt. And to destroy all animals was an order from God, we can't question God."

Adrie had heard this same stuff before but he wasn't finished with the Chaplin. He replied: "Abraham was born in Iraq and not in Palestine. Later on, he was sheep herding around the Mount of Olives where he offered his son Isaac to God. Jacob was the son of Isaac and he left for Egypt because of starvation. But there were only thirteen people at that time; they could hardly believe that all of Palestine was theirs. Even so, they left and a couple of hundred years later, when all of Palestine was occupied by different people, they wanted the Promised Land."

The Chaplain answered: "You sure know your Bible very well. However, this is not the time and place to discuss those things, when you come to the religious hour we can discuss this more extensively. This brings me to your training program which includes one hour of religion every week. I hereby invite all you young men to attend this hour of the Protestant Religious Group."

Adrie took it as a compliment that he knew the Bible that well. He wondered though if the Chaplain liked it that he was that well informed. Probably not!

It looked as if the Chaplain wanted to finish his speech impressively. He said: "Now you are in the Army you probably hate to be a soldier. Instead of being miserable that you were drafted to serve your Queen and your country, be proud to be a soldier. Never forget:

'It is the soldier, not the reporter, who has given us freedom of the press.

It is the soldier, not the poet, who has given us freedom of speech.

It is the soldier, not the campus organizer who has given us the freedom to demonstrate.

It is the soldier, who serves beneath the flag, who salutes the flag. Whose coffin is draped by the flag, who allows the protester to burn the flag.

It is the soldier, not the politician, who has given his blood, his body, and his life to give us all these freedoms.'

So be proud to be a soldier, we are all here to serve our fatherland, Long live the Queen." At that time he threw his beret in the air and expected the recruits would do the same. Although that his speech had been very impressive, there wasn't even one recruit who threw his beret in the air and nobody shouted "Long live the Queen." How could anybody expect to be enthusiastic about serving his fatherland and the Queen for seventy five cents per day? They ought to be kidding.

Of course there was the competition that moved in next. It was the Roman Catholic Chaplain who had a little speech as well. He refrained from trying to explain why all those young men had been drafted to kill other people. The Chaplin said that during the war their commando post was attacked by the Germans. He didn't want to kill in his position but he filled the shot empty magazines with shells. He even made a little joke about the time when he served in Indonesia when there were some problems with sexual contracted diseases. "If you ever have this kind of trouble you don't have to behave like the soldier who had contacted gonorrhoea. When I visited him in the hospital and asked why they had hospitalized him, the soldier said: 'I stumbled over a lady's bike.'

However, the doctor who is assigned to this unit holds 'Prick Parade' every two months, just to make sure that nobody has contracted V.D."

The Roman Catholic Chaplain seemed to have a better way with the soldiers; he called a spade a spade and seemed to be more understanding and less serious than the Protestant Chaplin. He invited everybody to the Roman Catholic Religious Hour.

Next it was the Company Commander's turn to explain a few things. First he told the recruits, "Some of you might consider military conscription to be a subordination of the individual to the state. Others think that The Netherlands is supposed to be a Democracy in which one should not be called to become a soldier. All this might be very true; if it wasn't that the state has enemies who want to destroy our Democracy. We lost our freedom for five years to the Germans; let's hope that we don't lose it to the Russians this time. Freedom doesn't mean that everybody is free to do what he wants, we have to protect it or we'll lose it. Many politicians believe that the Russians aren't people but the Russians might say that about us, too. Communists are stating that the Russians never nuked anyone and they are very peaceful. It doesn't matter what we believe, the bottom line is that we have to keep the Russians at bay. You have to defend your fatherland like your girlfriend's cherry."

That explained that but he had to explain a lot more. He continued: "You are in the army now and you are very lucky to be in the Infantry which means walking. A mechanized war doesn't mean that infantrymen have nothing to do but ride in trucks. Mechanized war merely means that there are more things to carry on your backs. Most Infantry men don't ride, they walk. It has always been the same: they have always walked. If there are still wars 100 years from now; super scientific wars, the infantry will still be walking, winning the wars. With the invasion of Normandy, it was the Navy and the Air Force that made the landing possible but it was the storm troopers that brought liberation."

There was a question by one of the recruits: "Why are we drafted when we are 20 years old? We have just started to make some money to begin our lives and then our fatherland needs us."

The Captain had an answer: "Would you rather be called up when you were 14 years old or younger? Mussolini had boy soldiers who were only 11 years old. And Hitler used 12 year old boys as well at the end of the war. One of the boy soldiers that we captured said, full of hatred: 'You bastards aren't even worth a bullet wasted on you.'"

The recruit answered: "Yes, but that was during the war. We have peace now."

The Captain replied: "Peace or war has nothing to do with it; even today there are rock throwing groups in Ireland. They are fighting an enemy they have never seen and they fight for a cause they don't understand. They are setting trucks ablaze and are looking forward to becoming 12 years old, when they get a rifle to shoot and kill with."

Now he had explained about the infantry prospect and why they had been drafted when they were 20 years old, he continued to explain what the draft was all about: "When a total stranger shoots at you, the natural incentive is to shoot back. Kill or be killed. That's why you are here; we will teach you to shoot back better than that total stranger. We will make you so good that your enemy will vanish like mice at the sight of a cat. Your total commitment is to fight for your Fatherland!"

That last sentence triggered a remark from Simon. He was one of the recruits who always had to say something. Jokingly he said: "Nice going, my father has no land, all he has is a little garden and a few chickens. When I go to war and get killed for my Fatherland, all that they will ever do is play the National Anthem and throw some sand over me. Besides, we can't all be heroes."

The commander stepped right in the trap and asked: "Why not?"

Simon answered: "If we are all heroes, who will sit on the steps to applaud us when we go by?"

The commander laughed about the joke as a farmer laughs with a toothache. There was an easy way out of all those embarrassing questions that he didn't manage to explain very well. He looked at his watch and said: "I see that it is coffee time."

That did the trick; all of a sudden there were no questions anymore and everybody was heading for the canteen. At night there was a lengthy discussion about the explanation that was given for the reason that the recruits were called up to train for war. Dick Brand worked for his father in an importing business. He listened quite frequently to radio stations in England and the United States. At one time Billy Graham, the Evangelist had said: "No sane person wants war but there comes a time we have to fight for peace."

An American General had heard that and had answered Billy Graham. "I've heard this before that countries or factions are saying that they are fighting for peace. Fighting for peace is plain bullshit, it is as stupid as saying that you are fucking for virginity."

That put the frosting on the cake in the discussion; every soldier understands talk like that. There also had been some talk about heroes in the war explanation session. One of the recruits had a journal that dealt with heroes. It asked the question "What makes a hero?" According to an old soldier who had been at war, 75% of the soldiers fell asleep when under attack because of fear and 24% called for their mother. The few remaining didn't think and became heroes.

Simon said: "There are always the leaders who sit safely in their bomb shelters and there are soldiers like us who are expected to be heroes. I bet you that most of those heroes have been buried. Bravery comes pretty close to being stupid. My personal belief is that 'He, who runs away, might live to fight another day.'"

There was also the discussion about the Protestant Chaplain who had said that everybody should be proud to be a soldier. It was generally agreed that being proud to be a soldier never puts more than one guilder per day in your pocket.

It was the next day at 5.00 p.m. sharp that the troops were standing neatly lined up in front of the company's building for report. Apparently all men were accounted for again and the company commander had a few messages. He also had an announcement and said: "Apparently we have some kind of a joker in our midst, who shits in the urinals of the bathroom. This nonsense has to stop immediately. If this happens again all of you will be assigned watch duty to see that this does not happen again."

Before playing cards that night, Adrie had a play to perform. He was going to copy his drill sergeant with his big mouth. Kleiweg, his sleeping buddy, was the drilled soldier who was doing the tiger crawl on the long room table. Adrie imitated his drill sergeant so well that he got the nickname Fieldwebel. (A German Sergeant.) For the rest of his military career, he was always greeted in his original platoon, with 'Hi fieldwebel,' even after he became a cook.

The next day the Company Commander was furious that somebody had shit in the urinals again. This time, he did a lot of shouting that he was going to get to the bottom of this. He ordered the Sergeant of the Week to assign men from the company to watch the urinals. If they saw somebody shitting in the urinals they had to report him to the Company Commander for punishment. He closed his speech powerfully remarking: "If somebody shits in the urinals when you have watch duty, you have to clean the urinal yourself. If you catch the culprit, he will clean the urinal and he will also be adequately punished for his dirty trick."

Adrie was not among the ones assigned to urinal watch duty but when he went to the bathroom for a leak, the watchman came to check if he was indeed leaking or shitting. That same night they caught the culprit who was brought before the Company Commander. It was a chap who lived on the island in the boonies.

When the Company Commander shouted at him that he was a dirty dog, the chap answered: "But Major I didn't know those were urinals, I thought they were very neat toilet bowls."

The major had heard it all but this was the first time he encountered somebody who didn't know the difference between a toilet bowl and a urinal. The major said: "You are not back at the farm where you piss against a tree. This is a military camp and we need hygiene. I realize that you didn't know what a urinal was, and therefore I'll take it easy on you. You are hereby assigned to clean all the urinals tonight. That way you'll remember what a urinal looks like. Dismissed!"

On Friday there was the religious hour. Everybody could go to the Roman Catholic or Protestant services by choice. Some soldiers went one week to the Protestant services and the next week to the Roman Catholic. If you didn't want to join any group that was O.K. too. In that case you were the designated hall scrubber. Nobody liked to scrub halls which made everybody instantly religious.

A soldier had 48 hours leave once per month. It meant that if you didn't have to perform watch duties or was punished for something, you could leave 1.00 p.m. on Saturday afternoon. You had to return with the last train Monday night. All other weekends were only 24 hours off. Once a month when you had a 48 hour leave, you would get free transportation; all the other

24 hour weekends you had to pay yourself. With the military identity card the soldiers could get half fare on all public transportation.

Adrie had to go by bus to the train station which cost him 25 cents half fair and his train ticket half fair was 2 guilders and 45 cents. That was one way; there were no return trips for weekends. If he had to go both ways by train and bus it cost him 5 guilders and 40 cents. As long as he was a recruit, he was paid 75 cents per day which netted him 5 guilders and 25 cent per week. To his knowledge he was 15 cents short every week. This playing soldier was not profitable at all. Everybody worked his butt off, was insulted all week and had to dig up 15 cents to cover the shortage. Of course Adrie had some reserves to pay for his tobacco and other things. The question was how long were his reserves going to last under those terrible financial conditions.

Once a soldier he would get paid 7 guilders per week which would leave him I guilder and sixty cents to buy shaving blades, shaving soap and tobacco. There was also fifteen minutes coffee time in the morning and afternoon. A cup of coffee cost only 5 cents, a package of tobacco cost 50 cents and cigarette papers 10 cents per package. Pretty near all soldiers were chain smokers and consequently needed some extra money to stay afloat. That once a month free transportation weekend had to make up for the disastrous other weekends.

To improve the critical financial situation, a lot of soldiers went hitchhiking home when it was still daylight. Coming back at night made it impossible to hitch hike in the dark. Hitchhiking was a problem; it was not that people didn't want to give a poor soldier a ride - there were just too many. Every Saturday afternoon there were over 2,000 soldiers released in the garrison city. It made chances for successful hitchhiking very poor.

That was not the only problem; the real problem was that the military command had outlawed hitchhiking for soldiers. Whenever you were hitchhiking you had to be very careful. The military police were patrolling the highways and could arrest you if they caught you. Not all soldiers were hitchhiking; there were a few soldiers who were subsidized from home.

A new draft of recruits didn't get any weekends off till they were in the military service for a whole month. For the entire month nobody was allowed out of the barracks, not even at night to go to the movies. After a month of service, there was a 48 hour long weekend with a free transportation ticket. Moreover if you wanted to go out at night you could ask for permission. Everybody had to be back in the barracks before midnight. Normally all soldiers had to be in their room at 10.00 p.m. The sergeant of the week came to check if everybody was in his room and had a list of the soldiers who had permission to be out till midnight. A soldier returning from his night permission trip had to report to the watch commander.

That first month of training was hard on everybody. The lieutenant provided some good news, he said: "When you came here you had still the softness of youth but we will make sure that you will spring from the ranks of the army with bodies as hard as steel. Your army training will make you all vigorous young men which will benefit you for the rest of your life."

For entertainment the recruits depended on the R.A.O. (Recreation and General Development.) It wasn't free though, it cost 25 cents per week. This money was deducted from your salary and handed over to the R.A.O. officer who organized everything. There were two movies per week and every two months there was some big entertainment night in a theatre, special and only for the military. English lessons were also provided once per week. All this was available for twenty five cents per week. The price was right for soldiers with a very limited income. Consequently, every soldier was a member.

It looked more like a jail than a military camp. Everybody was looking forward for the first month of service to be finished. A thorough inspection always preceded a weekend. If a soldier or recruit failed to pass inspection, they would give him a re-inspection at 4.00 p.m. It meant that the little time off was shorter.

Passing inspection wasn't easy either. The copper emblems of the unit had to be shined with copper polish, the anklets and belt had to be made green, the shoes had to be polished, the rifle had to be cleaned and personally a soldier had to be spic and span. That was a tall order, a soldier could work on his rifle all Friday night to have it spotless clean and quite often the sergeant would inspect it and say: "That's a piss poor job of cleaning your rifle, all the sand of the North Sea beach is still in your rifle."

It certainly took some doing to learn to pass inspections. Everybody was expected to have a sharp crease in the pants of his uniform which wasn't easy with a woollen uniform. There was a trick to accomplish it. You made the pants wet on the inside where the crease was supposed to be. Then you took a cake of soap and rubbed some soap on the inside where the crease was supposed to be. Next you put the pants on your bed, put a blanket over it and slept on top of it the night before inspection. If you moved around too much during the night, the crease might be in the wrong place which gave you a very good chance not to pass the inspection. At home, Adrie's mother always pressed his pants with the electric iron to make the crease stand up longer.

There were three recruits who didn't pass inspection. One of them was a total disaster; he had polished his copper emblems on his beret and uniform with copper polish. He never had polished copper before in his life and didn't know that he had to remove the emblems from his uniform. There was a red background behind the emblems and the copper polish had made it pretty black. He had to remove the red background and clean it with soap and water. Re-inspection came at 4.00 p.m.

Luckily, Adrie passed his inspection and could leave at 12.30 p.m. With his free train ticket, the first leave was on the house. It was civilian trains that had to be used. The railways would couple some extra wagons on when there was a weekend, just for the extra soldiers.

The electric train from s'Hertogenbos to Rotterdam had a couple of hundred soldiers aboard, who went home for their very first weekend after being cooped up for a solid month. When the train entered the station in Rotterdam, the platform was lined with beautiful girls who were picking up their sweethearts. Adrie had no sweetheart anymore; he had had a girlfriend for a while before he went to the military service but just before he had to report for duty he had decided that he wanted to be single while he was in the Army.

The main reason was that he didn't need help to spend the one guilder per day he made. Now he was watching all his buddies walking on the platform and suddenly a beautiful girl jumped forward embracing her sweetheart tenderly. "Wow!" he thought, "maybe it wasn't a good idea after all to give up love while in the Army." Almost all soldiers walked from the station with a beautiful girl on their arm, and Adrie was left alone by himself on the bus which would take him home.

When Adrie walked from the train station to the bus stop, all of a sudden he heard somebody shouting across the street. That somebody was an officer who expected to be greeted by that damned soldier. With his shouting he tried to draw Adrie's attention so he would greet him. Adrie had no choice but greet that ignorant officer or he would write a report to his Company Commander. It was just a bloody nuisance to be a soldier; it was as bad as in Russia where big brother is always watching.

A soldier had to greet all officers and the under officers of his own unit when he was in public. The only place you didn't have to greet an officer was in the train station. The military command found it too cumbersome to greet officers in the train station. While you were waiting for your train, you might bump into the same officer half a dozen times.

If you didn't greet an officer in public, the officer would come after you and ask for your identification card. Next he would write a report to your company commander who in turn would punish you for your evil deeds. Most of the time it would net you three or four days light arrest. (House arrest) That meant you couldn't go out at night and were confined to the barracks. It was the watch commander who was in charge of seeing to it that punished soldiers with house arrest didn't sneak out to go to the movies. When the watch commander had somebody blowing the bugle, you had to report immediately to the watch commander, if you had house arrest. One of the soldiers had a bad cold and wanted to go to bed but the watch commander wouldn't let him.

Adrie did not have much luck on his first long weekend. As usual, he had to wait a while for the bus. A little bored, he looked at the display in a store with his hands in his pockets. All of a sudden somebody tapped him on the shoulder. It was a sergeant who said: "Say soldier, if you are looking for your hands, I know where they are."

"I know that too, but thanks anyway."

That was the wrong answer apparently, the sergeant shouted: "It's a disgrace to see soldiers who are wearing the uniform of their country, with their hands in their pocket. Take your hands out of your pocket or I will write a report to your company commander!"

Right there and then, he made up his mind that whenever he was on leave, he wouldn't greet any officer and he would put his hands to his elbows in his pockets if he wanted to. Of course, he could only get away with that if he didn't wear his uniform. That was also a sin against the establishment, once a soldier you had to wear your uniform at all times. It wasn't very likely they would catch him, if he had no uniform on, nobody could see that he was a soldier. The only way he could get caught was if he bumped into an officer who knew him, and even then a guy looks different in uniform than in civilian clothes.

Adrie got the notion that a soldier has many problems and was pissed off to no end. 'What the hell did those assholes think they were, they treated him like a slave, for which he got paid a lousy tip of 75 cents per day? From that lousy tip he had to pay his travel expenses three times a month and to top it off, they expected to be greeted. No damned way that was going to happen. When he was in the garrison city, or on his way home, he had little choice, but once he was home they could go to hell. He was not going to put up with that nonsense.

At home his mother was glad to see him and of course she had to admire her son in his new uniform. Adrie's father had been in the army, and was interested as well. When Adrie complained that he only would get paid 75 cents per day instead of one guilder the first three months; his dad said: "What are you complaining about, when I was in the army I only got paid fifteen cents per day and if you peeled the potatoes every day you would get five cents extra per day. That's what I did because I needed those five extra cents per day."

"With your twenty cents per day, you could buy a lot more than with twenty cents today," Adrie remarked.

After supper there was work to be done. Adrie was into amateur photography. He did developing of films, printing and enlarging of photos for quite a few people. Since he had been gone for a month there were twelve films waiting for him to develop. Most of the photos were 9 x 6 centimetres and there were eight photos on a film. It meant that he also had to print 96 photos. Moreover he himself had taken snapshots from the barracks, his room and while receiving training in the forest and glens. He had taken three films of photos; many were of his buddies in his room who were all going to buy their photos.

At least he didn't have a steady girlfriend, and he could do whatever he pleased and didn't have to take her out on his miserable salary. For the first time, after seeing his buddies with their lovers, he could see that he had made the right decision to face military services by himself. It took about twenty minutes to develop a film. Next, the films had to be thoroughly rinsed in water to get the residue of the fixing bath removed. If this wasn't done adequately, the film would discolor in a short time.

When seven films had been developed, Adrie had enough of it. After being cooped up for a whole month, he wanted to go to Cafe Sport to shoot a few games of pool and play cards with his friends. For this occasion only, he decided to put his uniform on for the sake of his friends, who wanted to see him in uniform. After that, as soon as he came home, he took off his uniform and put his own clothes on. He found it more than a nuisance to have his uniform on. As soon as you had your uniform on there were unwelcome obligations.

There was another threat for soldiers when they were travelling home or back to the camp. The military police were at the train stations, they even went into the trains to check the soldiers. On the way back to the camp, it was pretty hot in the train. Some soldiers had taken off their military jacket and others had one button loose on the top which was a "no, no." All of them were reported to their company commander, who gave them four days light arrest, for going inappropriately dressed. According to the military police they were naked when they had one button loose at the top. It was another reason not to wear your uniform when you were back home. Without a uniform, nobody could tell you how many buttons you could have loose, and if you could take your jacket off, it was nobody's business.

Time for a soldier on leave goes fast and before he knew it he was back in the military camp. Because of the little rations of butter, cheese and sausage, Adrie's mother had given him a piece of cheese and some butter to supplement the meagre rations.

There was another very unwelcome training on the program, 'Night exercise.' Nobody knew when there was a night exercise except the officers who planned it. Adrie went to bed at 10.00 p.m. for a good night's rest after a strenuous day. At 12.30 a.m. the light in the room was suddenly switched on. A sergeant with a whistle in his mouth made a noise as if he was blowing the doomsday serenade. He shouted that in ten minutes time everybody had to be in front of the company building. He could have punched the whistle in the sergeant's mouth right into his throat. This was overtime for which he wasn't going to get paid. But then he already made so much money, why should they give him more?

The night manoeuvre lasted two hours; they were marched off to the forested area. A demonstration took place in which they showed that the light of a cigarette can be seen at a great distance and also that light is closer than you think. With no moon in the sky it was pretty dark in the forest. They must have done that on purpose to test your abilities in the dark. When Kleiweg walked through the forest he fell in a fox hole. Some soldiers had dug some holes for exercise and had failed to fill them in when they went home. Kleiweg said some adequate words to describe the soldier who had made this happen. Adrie thought that the sergeant came to help Kleiweg out of the hole but he had that wrong, the sergeant came only to give him shit for making noise on a night exercise. During war you could get killed if you make noise like that.

Kleiweg replied to that remark: "During war a guy could get killed when he makes noise and during peace time, a guy could break his bloody leg when stupid idiots don't fill in their fox hole."

"Keep quiet," the sergeant said, "This is serious business!"

Kleiweg had been leading the group when this incident happened. The soldiers who followed Kleiweg had been alerted when he disappeared into the hole. "Let somebody else lead the group," Kleiweg thought.

After the incident there were no volunteers to go first anymore. That made the sergeant mad who started to shout: "Come on you cowards, be a leader! Remember that the lead dog always has the best view, the others that are following see the ass of the dog in front."

"What's the difference," Kleiweg said. "I can't see the forest, a foxhole or an ass in front of me when it's dark. I had my turn, let somebody else lead."

On Monday there was always a march scheduled. It started with an easy march of four miles. In less than no time it became a march of fifteen miles and they were eying for a march of twenty five miles every week. It was all part of the training.

There was a concentration camp in Vught which was the next town from the barracks. It was still filled with Dutch Nazis who had been rounded up after the war. They had been tried for war crimes and collaboration with the Germans. Most of the prisoners were released fast if their only crime had been collaboration with the Germans. Others, who had been the Mayor of Dutch cities and had assisted the Germans in rounding up Jews to be sent to German gas chambers, were still imprisoned. There were still a couple of hundred prisoners, about five years after the war had ended.

When they came in the vicinity of the camp, the Dutch soldiers met a group of Nazi prisoners who were on a march as well. The only difference was that the prisoners marched to get some needed exercise and the Dutch soldiers were marching for their military training. Most of those prisoners had served in the S.S. and were used to marching.

When the war started, the German Army was a singing Army; the soldiers had lots of reasons to sing. They won battle after battle and were winning the war. Quite often when they conquered Russian occupied territory, they were welcomed by girls who gave them flowers and kisses. When the tide turned and it was obvious that they were losing the war, the Germans were still singing. This time it was compulsory, they had to show the world that they were happy soldiers that believed in their Fuhrer.

When they were in the S.S. they were singing songs and most of the time they were singing the S.S. Anthem. The men were allowed to sing when they were marching but singing the S.S. anthem was prohibited. They knew a way to circumvent this restriction and were singing the words of a Saint Nicholas song on the tune of the S.S. anthem. Instead of singing about the greatness of the S.S., they were now singing about the greatness of Saint Nicholas using the same tune as before. When they were singing their Saint Nicholas song, their chests were put proudly forward and one could notice; that inside of themselves, they were reliving their glorious past.

See there comes the steamboat, the steamboat from Spain.
It brings us Saint Nicholas, once more again.
I see his white horse run the deck to and fro.
When the ship docks, the horse is ready to go.

This showing of the former S.S. was considered as S.S. brutality. Dutch people complained to the Dutch authorities and asked them to stop it. It was difficult for the camp commanders to forbid the men to sing a Saint Nicholas song, even if it was to the tune of the S.S. hymn. Their hands were tied and they probably were happy as long as everything was peace and quiet on the Western front.

The Dutch Army wasn't a happy army at all; they were more a bitching army rather than a happy one. They all were young men who were forced, in the prime of their lives, to serve their Fatherland. They had been working on a career and now they had to train to become cannon fodder for the Russians who were threatening to overrun Europe. And who could be happy with the miserable salary of one guilder per day for which they had to do night manoeuvres and all kinds of training? You couldn't paint the town red with that kind of money.

Yet the Dutch Army was also singing in spite of the half a dozen blisters they had on their aching feet. It was the spirit between the soldiers that made them sing, it killed the time and made one forget about his sorrows.

It didn't take the Dutch army long to adopt the singing of the Saint Nicholas song when they were marching. In the beginning it was sung with the traditional tune. Later on, it was found that the S.S. tune was superior to the Saint Nicholas song and the Dutch army was singing like the former S.S. The military commanders had the same problems as the camp commanders; they couldn't outlaw the singing of a Saint Nicholas song. They probably were thinking along the same line as the camp commanders, as long as the troops were happy that's all what counted.

One of the marching songs was outstanding. It was also very long with eight stanzas. If you were singing about the steamboat of Saint Nicholas you were soon finished and had to think of another song. This one was long enough to keep you singing for a while. The song is based on a saga that was supposed to have taken place in Vienna. An Austrian soldier was court marshalled and condemned to death. Facing death, the condemned soldier wrote a letter to the Emperor pleading for mercy.

> Many soldiers are living in Vienna.
> They are living glad and happily.
> But one of those soldiers
> In prison wasn't free.

> Yes, soldier, you must die
> And you must become dead.
> For you there is no mercy,
> For you there is only death.

The emperor visited the condemned soldier and said:

> Four riddles I will give you,
> Four riddles it will be.
> If you can give the answers,
> My soldier, I'll set you free.

Tell me what is the water;
The water without sand.
Tell me what is a king
A king without land.

Tell me what is a mirror;
A mirror without glass.
Tell me what is the key
That fits all locks and let you pass.

Now it's up to the soldier, if he can solve the riddles he will gain his freedom and if he
can't he will die.
The soldier answers:

The water of your eyes,
Is the water without sand.
And the king of the cards,
Is the king without land.

The soul that is the mirror,
The mirror without glass.
And the money is the key,
That fits all locks to let you pass.

Those were the correct answers and the emperor keeps his word and says:

My soldier you have given
The answers to set you free.
Now go to your comrades
And live very happily.

There was a song that was outlawed for recruits to sing when they were marching. It was said to be the second National Anthem, in reality it was poking fun at a Dutch song.

He who put Dutch blood in a little pan,
And put it on the fire here,
Take care it doesn't boil over man.
Because Dutch blood is very dear.

Another song the recruits were singing to show their dismay of the army.

He who shot his father dead,
And poisoned his own mother
He is much better off,
Than soldiers with one another.

But once will come the time,
That we will leave those rotten officers.
Damned is the regiment,
And long live all the soldiers.

It wasn't that the honeymoon was over between the new recruits and the military cadre. There never had been a honeymoon. Officers and under officers alike thought the same way. They found that the new recruits needed to be disciplined.

There was a very steep hill in the forest which was said to be held by the enemy. The soldiers had to storm it with weapons and ammunition. When they had reached the top of the hill they were in no shape to whistle Yankee Doodle for the next ten minutes. Nobody asked them to whistle but the sergeant wanted them to run in hot pursuit of the imaginary enemy. One of the soldiers was tired out and was kind of slow with his hot pursuit of the enemy. The sergeant shouted: "Come on you lazy bones, we'll never win a war with the snail pace you have."

The recruit answered: "I can't run that fast man, I am beat and I have a headache."

The sergeant countered: "I have 50 men in my platoon. To me that means I have fifty headaches. But I have a good remedy for your headache. Tonight after the service, you can clean the company square with your toothbrush. There is a lot of grass and moss growing between the stones and I want that all out. That will give you a lot of fresh air and I bet you that you'll never have a headache again when we have a run." The only one who thought that it was funny was the sergeant; everybody else didn't go for crap like that.

One morning, one of the recruits didn't get out of bed after the sergeant had whistled. When the sergeant came back to check if everybody was out of bed, he found one recruit still sleeping. He woke him up and said: "Oh, sleeping ugly wakes up. That's just great because I have a lot of chores that have to be done tonight. You slept longer than the others, to me that means that you are well rested and qualify for the job."

When inspection time came, one of the soldiers was still smoking a cigarette. Hastily he put it out and discarded the butt in the hollow bedpost. Unfortunately the cigarette was still smoking in the bedpost and a curling smoke was the result. The sergeant looked at it and said: "I see the Etna is smoking again."

The soldier said: "I can see the Etna smoking too, and I also can see the future."

The sergeant said: "Me too, tonight you remove all the cigarette butts from all the beds in this room. Inspection at 9.00 p.m."

There were the necessary vaccinations against cholera, polio, diphtheria and tetanus. No shots against malaria were scheduled as the soldiers weren't scheduled to go to the Tropics anymore. The joke went around that instead of a malaria shot, the soldiers were going to receive a shot against frostbite because they were scheduled to fight in Siberia.

In spite of the immaculate rooms the soldiers had to keep, hygiene of the soldiers wasn't very good. The soldiers only had one shower per week. There were about 15 showers for over 1000 soldiers. A stoker was in place to provide warm water. There were five companies and each company had a specific shower night.

When you had your shower night it was compulsory. That created no problem since everybody loved his shower. In order to get all the soldiers cleaned up it had to go fast. Fifteen soldiers went to the shower with only shorts, sport shirt and gym shoes on. Bathing time was ten minutes. After five minutes the next group was already lined up to ensure that no time was wasted.

One time the sergeant had not counted right and there were 16 soldiers for 15 showers. That mistake wasn't noticed by the sergeant, who was already busy getting the clean soldiers back to the barracks. When one soldier didn't have a shower, his buddy said: "Come with me in the shower, we can share."

Everything went well until the sergeant returned to see that two soldiers came out of the same shower. Promptly he wrote a report about homo sexuality going on among the soldiers. The two soldiers had to appear before the company commander who said: "I hear that you two are active in homo sexuality."

One of the soldiers answered that charge: "It wasn't even our fault that the sergeant can't count; actually we only helped him out by sharing the shower."

The other soldier added: "What is that sergeant worried about? We are only friends and certainly no homo sexuals. We both have girlfriends, and besides we can't get pregnant."

The captain smiled when he heard that argument, he said: "Beware the evil eye that sees wrong things that don't exist."

Adrie kept his own in the military service. At this time he didn't enjoy playing soldier at all. He played soldier before when he was fighting the Peterselydyk. He had enjoyed that very much, but this was ridiculous. Why should he like it? He used to be the top commander and now he was demoted to less than a soldier. Right now he was only an apprentice soldier.

Matheis was the Platoon Sergeant; he was a professional who had no use for recruits who were drafted. He got Adrie's goat on an inspection on a Saturday. It was only a 24 hour weekend and he was going to hitchhike home. First there was of course the unavoidable inspection. The sergeant looked very critically at his rifle and Adrie expected to hear that the entire North Sea beach was in his rifle. Finally the sergeant gave the rifle back without saying a word. It looked as if he was hell bent to find something wrong. Very critically he looked in his locker and finally he opened his backpack which was on top of the locker. He removed the cork of his field bottle to smell the bottle and said: "If you have to drink out of a bottle like this you will get sick. Start cleaning it and you will have re-inspection at 4.00 p.m."

Adrie was furious; the field bottle had never been used for anything but water. That was plainly a crock that it smelled that bad, it was merely a way to intimidate him. Of course, if a bottle is closed for a week or so, it might smell a little stale. Rinsing with water didn't improve it at all, that's the way the bottle smelled.

However, he couldn't fail the inspection at 4.00 p.m., something had to be done. There were five corporals in the peloton and Adrie had made friends with one of them, Corporal Bakker. Sometimes at night he came to talk to Adrie about a host of subjects. Luckily Corporal Bakker was still in his room, he hadn't left for the weekend yet. When Adrie told him about his problem, Corporal Bakker said: "Sergeant Matheis is a professional soldier; he is tough and brushes his teeth with whiskey in the morning. Complaining won't help a bit; all you can do is making the field bottle smell good. If you want your field bottle to smell fresh, you squirt some toothpaste in it the night before inspection, fill the bottle with water, shake it and leave the water with toothpaste in it. Just before the inspection, you pour the water out and your bottle will smell like peppermint.

There was no night before the inspection thus the remedy had to be powerful. There was still three and a half hours before the re-inspection. Adrie squirted about half a tube of toothpaste in the bottle and shook it good. Ten minutes before the inspection he poured the water out and indeed the bottle smelled like peppermint.

A total of four recruits had been turned down by the inspection. Two of them had to clean their rifle of the North Sea beach sand and the other one had to polish his copper emblems better. After half an hour of cleaning their already clean rifles, the recruits said: "Piss on that asshole sergeant, the rifle can't be any cleaner and for his information the rifle has never been at the North Sea beach, so how can that sand get in my rifle?"

All four recruits were cheesed off to no end; if they had given a re-inspection an hour later instead of three and a half hours it wouldn't have been that bad. It was a dirty trick to deliberately bugger up the weekend for the recruits, just to discipline them.

Since there were four recruits, they could play a game of Klaverjassen which was a game that had to be played with four people. Adrie said: "If the sergeant had known we were going to play cards, he would never have turned down four people; he would have turned down only three."

With playing cards it didn't take long to finish the rest of the time. According to the sergeant the rifles and the brass emblems looked better and Adrie's bottle smelled better too. With his shortened short leave, he had to walk more than twenty minutes to the highway where he could try to hitchhike to Rotterdam. When he tried to get a ride, it looked as though it was just a useless day when nothing worked, he would have been better off to stay in bed but that would never do in the army. For some reason, nobody stopped to give him a ride home. It was already 5.00 p.m. and soon it would be dark, then getting a ride would be pretty near impossible.

He knew another trick to get a ride and walked to the highway crossing. There the trucks had to slow down significantly and he could jump on the back of a big truck. His plan worked and soon he was sitting on the back of a big truck. It was kind of cool which could be seen as part of the soldier training. The truck speeded up quite a bit; it took only about an hour and a half to drive to Rotterdam. Now he was facing another problem, how did he get off this fast moving truck? Adrie didn't want to go as far as the city; he wanted to jump off close to home. There was a hill, which was a slowdown for the truck he thought. Not this time, the truck kept going with the same speed. Jumping off was a disaster, he couldn't run fast enough and fell on his knee on the street. His knee was bleeding which wasn't bad, that would easily heal. The worst thing was that there was a hole in the knee of his good uniform and that hole wasn't going to heal. What a day this was, everything had screwed up like a whore's dream.

Adrie's mother fixed the pants as well as she could, but a hole is a hole. His uniform would never pass inspection anymore. Back in the barracks he tried to get another pair of pants for his uniform. The quartermaster said: "I cannot give you a new pair of pants without a note from your platoon sergeant." That was another disaster, the platoon sergeant Matheis said that Adrie was costing the taxpayers a lot of money, his uniform was worn about two months and it was finished. He got a new uniform alright, at a price. For punishment, he had to mop the halls every night for the entire week. A general dissent was the result of treating soldiers in an unfair indignant way. Of course, there was nothing anybody could do to improve the situation; everybody had to put up with this childish nonsense.

At one time Adrie got supreme shit from Sergeant Matheis during a field exercise. He hadn't understood the sergeant and did the wrong thing. Adrie said: "I thought that..."

He was cut off by the sergeant who said: "You don't think in the army, we do all the thinking for you. You have to keep your head cool and your feet warm but don't think."

There was little enthusiasm and even less skill during the training which seemed to go on forever. In spite of the indignities that soldiers had to endure during their training, they were happy among one another and played all kinds of tricks. It was noticed that some of the padlocks on the lockers had the same key in the same room. That was not a coincidence; everybody could use his key to get in three or four different lockers. There were no thieves around but there were plenty of jokers. When somebody left with night leave permission, somebody who had the same key would open the locker, put the neat piles of clothes and all other items on a few sheets of paper, tied a few strings to the paper sheets and the other end to the locker door. Now the soldiers were ready for the surprise that came when the soldier came back home, unlocked his locker, pulled open the door and all his clothes and other things fell on the floor.

Numerous funny things were going on in the soldiers' rooms. There were always soldiers who would go to bed early. One of the fellows seemed to be some kind of a poet. When he was dreaming, he would sit straight up in his bed and recite all kinds of poems. One of the poems he recited quite frequently, it must have been his favorite poem.

Everybody was circled around his bed to be entertained by the unknown poet in his sleep.

When I was riding on my fiery steed
Through fields with knee high weed.
My steed was snorting all along
While he kept going very strong.

One time, Willem, the soldier in the bed beside Adrie, had kicked away the blankets in his sleep and his shorts were hanging on his toes. It didn't take long for one of the soldiers to pull the shorts of his toes and throw them over the lamp cap. In the morning Willem was looking all over hell for his shorts, he asked Adrie: "Have you seen my shorts?"

"No I haven't seen them, did you take them off before you went to bed?"

"No I had them on when I went to bed and when I woke up they were gone."

Then his eye fell on the shorts on the lamp cap and he said: "Hell those are my shorts, how for Pete's sake did they get there?" The lamp cap was quite high, he had to move a bed underneath the lamp cap and take a broom to get his shorts back.

All soldiers seemed to play for money in spite of the 75 cent a day they were making. It didn't take much to lose a day's wages or more. One night Kleiweg and Adrie were playing partners as always. Losing a game meant that you had to pay ten cents to the winners plus other charges. If you played, you had to make more points in that hand than the opposition. If you didn't you had to pay five cents. And if the opposition took all the tricks, you were out another five cents. In one game you could easily lose twenty five cents.

That night everything went wrong and after three games Kleiweg and Adrie owed eighty five cents. That was more than a day's wages and there was enough time to play one more game. If that game went wrong as well it could cost them more than a guilder. Kleiweg said: "Double or nothing!"

This meant that if they would win the game they would owe nothing. However, if they lost, they had to pay double which was one guilder and seventy cents. It was the equivalent of more than two days wages. The opposition went for it with one stipulation in force. There would only be one game played 'Double or nothing' and then they had to pay the piper. This double or nothing trick can wipe out your debts eventually. The more games you play, the more likely it is that you are going to win at least one game. But even if you owe five guilders or more when you win a game you owe nothing. If you play long enough, sooner or later when you win a game, you are freed from paying up.

Both soldiers were sweating it out since there would be only one chance to wipe out the debt and if they didn't, they had to pay double. Luckily Lady Fortune was finally smiling on them and they won. They had played all night without losing or winning a penny.

There was another session of theory in which the soldiers were taught how to behave during war. The captain said: "It can happen that you are ordered to attack the fortified positions of the enemy. When your sergeant shouts 'Storm,' you get up out of your trench, without hesitation, and storm; even when the bullets are whistling around your ears." Little enthusiasm was shown by the recruits and nobody had any comments. It wouldn't do much good no matter what you said.

The Captain continued and asked: "When you were storming, you have reached the lines of the enemy. You see the enemies coming out with a white flag, what do you do?"

He got an answer: "Make them prisoners of war."

"Exactly" said the Captain, "And you treat them decently, don't kick them in the butt or beat the crap out of them. That's against the Geneva Convention."

"When the shoe is on the other foot," the Captain continued, "and the enemies are storming your position, don't surrender, you never can be sure that your enemy is taking prisoners. Even the Canadians didn't always take prisoners if it was not feasible. One time they gunned down the soldiers with a white flag and when the Captain came, the sergeant said: 'Sorry sir, I didn't see the white flag.' The Captain replied: 'O.K. but don't let it happen again.' There remains a question, 'Did he see the white flag or didn't he?'"

The Captain had another question to test the cleverness of his recruits. He said: "Suppose you are at war and you are the platoon commander. You have taken ten enemy prisoners who are Prisoners of War. Intelligence reveals that the enemy is going to launch an all-out counter attack and headquarters gives you an order to move out fast. It's impossible to take the P.O.W.'s along; they will slow you down too much when you move out. What are you going to do with the P.O.W.'s? You are not allowed to shoot them according to the Geneva Convention, yet you can't take them with you."

One of the recruits had an answer: "I would tie them to a tree."

The captain said: "That idea might fu.. up on you. When the enemy moves in, those P.O.W.'s will tell them all about you and your troops. With the necessary information, they could cut you off and kill you all."

Since nobody had a remedy, the Captain said: "Those are the problems that you are facing when in command. There are no easy solutions, you are damned if you do and you are damned if you don't."

Simon had some comment to that and said: "When it's you or them, you'll have to shoot them. What do you think your enemy will do if they hold you as prisoner? They won't think twice about shooting you."

The Captain said: "Then after the war you could be tried as a war criminal as the Nazis were after the war."

Simon replied: "Piss on the Geneva Convention, those guys make rules when there is peace. Once it is war nobody gives a shit about any rules and everybody tries to survive."

Apparently the Captain didn't want to reveal what he was going to do when he was in a bind like that and looked at his watch again. Luckily it was almost canteen time which was a good excuse to end the theory lesson. There was no opposition by the recruits to quit the lesson five minutes early. In less than no time everybody was heading for the canteen.

Great entertainment was supplied by the R.A.O. in the theatre for the first time. It was a two and a half hour show with the best entertainment available in the country. There was a comedian, singing groups and a tango and rumba orchestra. The reason that this all could be paid for with 25 cents per week was, that the R.A.O. had made a deal with a radio station. The first hour of the night was taped, sound only. *(This technique of taping shows was very new in those days. It was strictly magnetic sound tape which was used for the radio program. Video tape was not invented and even T.V. was very sporadic. For rich people only.)*

The director of the show explained what everybody had to do. After a performance he would put his hands high up meaning 'applause.' If he wanted it louder he would move his hands fast up and down and when he wanted the applause to stop he dropped his arms. It was all regulated for the taping of the show. The soldiers had to supply the regulated applause to make it sound good on the radio.

There was a play which wasn't interesting at all to look at. If you only heard the sounds it was quite good. When the doorbell went it was just rung from a table. The participants of the show didn't move at all, they just were saying their thing and making the necessary noises. All sounds and talk was supplied for the purpose of listening and not for viewing when it was taped. The tango and rumba orchestra of Malando played for about twenty minutes. It was excellent; the director didn't need to raise his arms to get an applause.

After the intermission, there was a full one and a half hour show for the soldiers with no taping. Since there was no radio taping, there was no director of applause. It wasn't needed, the applause came spontaneously. A great evening with superb entertainment made it worth your while to be a member of the R.A.O.

That weekend when Adrie was on leave, the radio station sent out the program they had taped in s'Hertogenbos. He listened and to his surprise, the play sounded great, it was much more interesting when you didn't see the stage with people sitting on a chair.

Learning to shoot a rifle was the first object of the military training which accounted for many trips to the rifle range. Soldiers had to be able to shoot a rifle in any position, lying down, standing up and kneeling down. The sergeant was giving the instructions. He shouted: "Aim! Target Wild Women, in the front terrain. Shoot!" There seemed to be plenty of wild women around, the target was always 'Wild women in the front terrain.'

Any soldier who hit the heart of the target most of the times was selected for sharp shooter. In spite that Adrie was a good shot, he scored only 75 percent of the bullets in the heart of the target. That wasn't good enough, to be a sharp shooter you had to have at least 95%. No sharp shooter career for Adrie. He didn't care at all about the missed opportunity. Sharp shooters operate a lot of times in enemy territory. They sit quite often in a tree, trying to shoot officers and under officers. Of course as soon as you shoot at the enemy, they try to find the sharpshooter's hiding place. Quite frequently the sharp shooter ends up dead.

One of the soldiers was talking about his gun to the sergeant. The sergeant said: "Don't you guys get it ever through your knuckle head that this is not a gun, it is a rifle. When people enter the Navy they are talking about their boat and they are told that it is not a boat, it is a ship. And here we have to tell you that you have a rifle instead of a gun. When I had my training in England, one of the soldiers who was talking about his gun received a punishment that cured him for good. After that punishment he never forgot that he had a rifle. He had to strip naked and was placed in the middle of the company square with his rifle. On his belly he had a huge sign stating:

This is my rifle and that is my gun
My rifle is for shooting and my gun is for fun.

There was an arrow from the sign pointing at his prick meaning that this was his gun." The sergeant said that he never mistook his rifle for a gun again. He didn't say if he was going to have soldiers naked on the company square with a sign if they talked about their gun again. Maybe his story was a fair warning.

An entire day was spent on artillery shelling. When you prepare for an attack, you systematically shell enemy terrain to make sure most of the enemies are dead. The sergeant said: "If you are under shelling you have to keep your cool, you hear the shells hit closer all the time in front of you. They are real close and then they fall behind you. Whenever a shell explodes close to you, jump in the hole. No shell ever falls in the same place twice. If you were saved from artillery shelling, you now have to kill the enemy attackers or they will kill you.

An early snowstorm in November surprised everybody. In spite of the cold, all training continued as normal. Phys. ed. was done in light sport shoes, the only garments that were allowed were shorts and a thin sport shirt. Cold or not there was no underwear or socks allowed and this was checked by the sergeant. Phys. ed. was usually done outside if the weather was reasonable. In case that it was raining or too cold, phys. ed. was done in a non-heated drill hall. At least you were out of the rain and wind.

It was Monday morning and phys. ed. was on the roster. With the snow on the ground phys. ed. was moved to the drill hall. The sport instructor was a young sergeant who was very unhappy that when he was on leave, he was called back due to a sick instructor. He told the recruits that he was in an extremely bad mood and they'd better do everything right or they would be sorry.

There was an exercise in which they had to stand on hands and feet to do push ups. It made some of the recruits think that they were cows and they started to moo like a cow. That made the instructor very mad, he shouted to the troops: "I warned you to do well; but all you people do is behave like a bunch of pregnant sparrows."

It didn't make sense what he said; nobody understood the connection with pregnant sparrows. He continued to shout at the recruits that they just had bungled it and instead of the inside drill hall, they now had to do sports outside. He marched the troops off outside the garrison. There was a high dyke with a ditch at the bottom that looked very discouraging. The ditch was filled with snow and thorny bushes were growing all around. When the sergeant ordered everybody down in the ditch, the recruits staggered through the undergrowth, noticing the sharp twigs and thorns which tore into their legs like malevolent claws.

At this time, the sergeant gave his next command screaming that the recruits had to lie flat on their belly, and commence the tiger crawl.

Not one of the soldiers followed the unfair order. The sergeant got really furious now and shouted that this was an order which had to be obeyed.

Frustrated recruits were now whispering to one another, deciding what to do with that screaming idiot high on top of the dyke. They decided to stand up, go back to the top of the dyke and stand at attention, in file, to wait what was going to happen. Adrie was in the middle of the first row of three.

The sergeant was now furious and said to Simon: "This is an order, go down and crawl the tiger crawl on your belly."

Simon answered: "It is an unfair order; we might all get pneumonia if we do that."

The sergeant now turned to Adrie telling him to go down and crawl on his belly in the snow.

Adrie replied: "My answer is the same, sergeant."

Next, Kleiweg got the same order to go down.

Kleiweg stated that he was of the same opinion as the other two recruits.

The sergeant said: "Very well then, you three are going on report to the company's commander and the rest will stay in their room till further orders."

The company commander said: "It seems that we have a discipline problem. You three have refused an order, which is very serious. If it was war you would be shot. During peace, normally you will go for a court martial to deal with serious offences like that. It usually means a month or more in the punishment camp. However, you are lucky that you are still recruits and only a very short time in the military service. Therefore I will just warn you that you cannot refuse to follow up on a command. If you think you are unfairly treated, you can write out your complaint to your company commander but you'll have to follow orders first. We cannot have soldiers determine what is fair and unfair. Understood?"

"That's very nice and dandy," Adrie replied. "When there is a war on, a company commander can bugger up and lead his company into a death trap. Who is going to complain after he got killed because of a stupid commander! Many booboos have been made during the war and thousands got unnecessary killed."

The commander said: "Hindsight enables everyone to know better after the war is over. But hindsight cannot reproduce the total flow of reports, correct or incorrect, which beset a commander at the time he must make his lonely decision."

Kleiweg thought that the commander was dodging the issue and said: "This incident didn't happen during the war, the real question is: 'Why do we have to follow unfair, ridiculous orders that were given because the sergeant was pissed off when he was recalled from his leave. If we had crawled through the snow we might all get sick or even die.'"

"At all times you have to obey orders," the Company Commander replied. "I warn you, if it happens again I won't be as tolerant in dealing with this."

When the three recruits returned to their room there was great interest by the other recruits as to what had happened. Kleiweg said ironically: "You know, I almost started to cry when the Major told that bullshit storey about the commander who has to make his lonely decision."

At night Adrie went to see his friend Corporal Bakker to tell him what had happened. Corporal Bakker said: "I know that it is stupid to follow orders in peacetime that might kill you, there is no need for that. Some under officers and also some officers can be terrible to the troops. When I got my basic infantry training it was a lot worse. We had English army training which was a hell of a lot tougher. Luckily for you guys that was changed to American training, about a year before you came into the army. We were standing every day with one foot in jail. Every morning, afternoon and night we had inspection. The Company Commander would walk between the lines with the Platoon Sergeant right beside him. If there was anything that was less than one hundred percent, he told the sergeant to put the soldier in jail for a day or sometimes more. Every inspection yielded two or three soldiers who went to jail. After the inspection, the Platoon Sergeant would run them to jail. It took less than a month to learn that we had to work on our equipment and ourselves, all the time, to pass inspection. Even then, you still would sometimes end up in jail."

Kleiweg said: "If we ever have to fight a war, the first bullet I fire is for that asshole."

"If there is a real war on things are different," Corporal Bakker replied. "If you have to storm the enemy lines you have little time for revenge and if you want to turn back your officers will shoot you. At night they will tell you how many of your comrades have been killed, just to get you angry. Then they have you over the barrel when you want to kill the bastards that did this to your buddies."

A week later there was another phys. ed. session by the same sergeant instructor. All soldiers could see a tough hour coming up. It was a nice day for a change, the sun was shining and the temperature was great compared to a week ago. The instructor marched the troops outside the garrison into the woods. On all soldiers' faces one could read: "We knew it that we would pay hell for not obeying him."

The question was 'what were they going to do if this A hole had more stupid orders that were hard to follow?' Disobeying was out of the question; that would land them in the punishment camp. They were warned by the company commander. It looked like they had to suffer first and complain later.

The troops walked normally between the trees for a while. When they reached an open spot with dead trees lying on the ground, they came to a halt. To everybody's surprise, the sergeant said: "Be seated, that's enough exercise for one day."

Nobody could believe that this really happened. The sergeant went to Kleiweg, Adrie and Simon who had not obeyed his orders. He was interested in what they were doing in civilian life to make a living. He listened what everybody had to say and had a few stories of his own. After the hour was over, they marched back to the garrison.

Back in their room the soldiers were wondering what had happened to the once so evil sergeant sport instructor. Adrie said: "He either was on the way to Damascus or he got supreme shit from the Company's Commander." Most of the soldiers thought that he never had been close to Damascus and settled that the Company's Commander had reamed him out.

Three days before the three months of basic training were fulfilled, it was examination time. A recruit had to show that he comprehended what they had taught him. Luckily for Adrie the Platoon Sergeant was not one of the examiners; that could have been a disaster. The Lieutenant and the Sergeant Major were the examiners. Handling and presenting rifles, parading, bayonet fighting and a host of other things were included in the examination.

Even Adrie gave it his best shot because a raise of 25 cents per day depended on it. Anybody who passed was a soldier and received one guilder per day. He passed easily; he could do it if he wanted to. There were three in the peloton who didn't pass, they were held on 75 cents per day. They had extra drills and duties at night to shape them up for a second examination. That time they passed as well and the entire platoon now consisted of soldiers only. Now they were soldiers, it meant that they had a license to kill in case of war.

In the three months of training the soldiers had learned a lot. Every soldier had also learned that a soldier never will stand up if he can sit down. And if he can lie down he won't sit down. And if there is an opportunity to sleep while lying down he will do that too.

There was a barn burner of a celebration scheduled with all the parents of the new soldiers. The parents were invited for a day, to see the parade which marched past the General. Pea soup dinner was included with the celebrations. There were over two thousand new soldiers, divided over ten companies.

There was, of course, a speech from the General. He said to his new troops: "It gave me great pleasure to view the new troops, they are so well trained and they look very good to me. As a matter of fact I have never seen a troop like that before."

That made everybody chuckle. In The Netherlands troop means troops like soldiers but the word troop has also a different meaning in Dutch. It means a hell of a mess. Thus when the General suggested that he had never seen a troop like that before, he could have meant that he never had seen a hell of a mess like that before.

While the new soldiers marched off to their garrison, the parents were invited to meet the military commanders. There were two garrisons, each with about 1,000 soldiers and each garrison looked after their own guests. Adrie's father and mother, together with all the other parents, were received in the auditorium. They were told a lot of hogwash and then some. The Colonel ended his speech by stating: "I am proud of my troops; they are the best soldiers possible. With those soldiers we will fight the Russians till hell freezes over and when that happens we will fight them on the ice."

After that there was time for questions. Most of the questions centred around the poor quality of food for breakfast and lunch. Most of the time supper was good, few complaints were about supper. The parents were told that there was a budget of one guilder per day, per soldier, for food and the purchasing officer did all he could. When they had asked the Government for more money per soldier, they were turned down. They advised the complaining parents to take this problem up with the Government.

Next, the parents were transported to the barracks of their sons where pea soup was waiting. Pea soup is always the best meal in the army. Nowhere is the pea soup better than in the army. Half a pig, lots of sausages and a variety of vegetables were among the ingredients of the pea soup. The pea soup was so good that soldiers and parents couldn't get enough of it. In order to be able to eat more, the men adjusted their belt an extra notch. The women had nothing to adjust and hoped that the elastic in their panties wouldn't break with the extra tension.

After lunch there were some demonstrations by the new soldiers. One of the demonstrations was bayonet fighting between groups of soldiers. To make it look real, some of the soldiers had bags of pig blood beneath their clothes. Behind the bags of blood was a steel plate to prevent injury to the soldiers with the spike bayonet. The idea was to puncture the bags of pig blood with the bayonet to make it look like the soldiers were wounded. A near panic broke out when a few soldiers collapsed from a bleeding wound in their chest, which was only pretence because the parents saw only pig blood. Some of the mothers fainted when the so called wounded soldiers were carried away on stretchers. To ease the worried people, the so called wounded soldiers returned rather fast. When they showed the spectators that it was only pig blood that had been spilled, the parents let go a sigh of relief. That part of the demonstration didn't go over too well with the parents. There were a lot of complaints about that one.

After the demonstrations there was an opportunity for interested parents to do some target shooting. Adrie's father participated as he had been in the army as well. Of course, the parents were allowed to see the rooms where their sons slept and were free to walk about the barracks.

All the soldiers were allowed to leave the garrison to go with their parents for a sightseeing trip in the garrison city s'Hertogenbosch. Downtown there was a huge cathedral from the 14th century which drew a lot of visitors. All together it was a successful day for everybody except for the bloodletting incident.

Now they were soldiers, they received one guilder per day but it didn't come free. Before they were soldiers they weren't allowed to stand on guard at the gate or at the ammunition magazine. That duty was performed by real soldiers and not by recruits. Now they all were soldiers; that duty became their duty and the older soldiers were moved back to their own detachment.

Every night there were ten soldiers needed to perform guard duty for security. When it was Adrie's turn there were field manoeuvres on the schedule of that day. It meant that the rifle would get pretty dirty and it had to be clean when the officer of the guard would inspect the rifles.

Watch duties commenced at 5.00 p.m. and ended 24 hours later at 5.00 p.m. If you had to perform watch duties, you were allowed to go to your room at 4.00 p.m. to shave, put your good uniform on and clean your rifle. That wasn't much time to do all that work and if your rifle was dirty enough, you couldn't clean it in an hour. Adrie knew a way to circumvent that problem. One of his roommates had watch duty the day before. When he came off watch duty Adrie commenced. He made a deal with his roommate to trade rifles when he came off duty. With that trick, he didn't have to clean his rifle which saved him a lot of time and agony. He should be able to get away with that, as the officer of the guard didn't know that he didn't have his own rifle. Wrong idea! It backfired.

Everything went right, the exchange of rifles was made with the changing of the guard and Adrie had a clean rifle without cleaning it. At least, so he thought. When the officer of the guard came in, he held inspection and rejected Adrie's borrowed rifle. He just couldn't get it that the rifle didn't pass inspection. Most of the time it had been standing in the watch room and the few hours that it had been taken outside shouldn't have made it dirty. And the night before it had passed inspection. The officer wrote a report to his company commander which would attract punishment for sure.

Three soldiers at a time had to stand on guard, one at the front gate, one at the ammunition magazine and one at the rear gate which was closed at night. Every soldier had to stand one hour on guard and was then two hours off. Those two hours he had to sit in the watch room and stay awake, just in case that the outside guards needed help. Sleeping was not allowed in the watch room. When the watch duties started everybody was already tired after a day of military duties. Yet, there were 24 hours of guard duties to fulfil without falling asleep.

Adrie had to sit the first two hours in the watch room with the other soldiers who were not guarding the barracks. In that time he ate and played cards with the other soldiers. Nothing to it. When it was his turn he had the post at the front gate which was alright too. There was a lot to see and do at 7.00 p.m. which makes the time go fast.

One of the main jobs he had to do was make sure that no intruders passed the gate. It was his duty to check everybody's credentials. Simon had watched the gate before Adrie and he had a run-in with the Colonel. The Colonel had tried to bike through the open gate and Simon had stopped him. When he asked for the papers of the Colonel, he said: "I'm your colonel, you know me."

Simon replied: "Maybe I know you and maybe I don't. It doesn't matter whether I do or don't, my orders are to check everybody's papers."

The Colonel said agitatedly: "If I were you I would be a little friendlier to my Colonel. I want to get in."

Simon countered: "As long as I haven't seen your papers, I don't know that you are my Colonel and if you try to get in without my permission I'll blow your bloody brains out."

That probably sounded convincing and the Colonel produced his papers. Simon checked the papers, saluted the Colonel and said: "Thank you Colonel, go ahead. I'm sorry for the delay."

The Colonel mentioned the incident to the watch commander and praised the soldier for doing a good job in checking everybody out. On the other hand he also complained about the rough language Simon had used. However, the watch commander said to Simon: "Good for you, I told you to check everybody which includes the Colonel. With his refusal to show his papers he had it coming."

At 9.00 p.m. the front gate was closed to make it easier to control.

At 10.00 p.m. it was Adrie's turn again to stand guard outside. This time he was at the ammunition magazine. At 11.00 p.m. he came off and had to spend two hours in the watch room awake. It became more difficult; even while playing cards it was hard to keep his eyes open.

It was 1.00 a.m. and he was standing sentry at the rear gate. By now he was quite exhausted and started to yawn. There was absolutely nothing going on, the gate was closed and nobody tried to climb it. What else could he do in this hour? He walked up and down a few times to stay awake and decided to stand in the sentry box for a while. He leaned against the wall and dozed off a little. What kind of a sentry am I, he thought, to fall asleep on watch duties. However, he was alert even if he took 40 winks while leaning against the sentry box wall. As soon as there was the slightest sound he got out of the box to check. It could be the watch commander to check up on him. If he found him with his eyes closed there would be hell to pay for doing a lousy job. But then the pay was lousy too, what a guy had to do all for one lousy guilder per day, it didn't give him any incentive to stay awake.

To stay awake from 2.00 a.m. till 4.00 a.m. was even worse. Adrie drank three cups of coffee to keep himself awake and was still sleepy. His card playing partners supported their heads with one hand and were dozing off. The card game stalled and everybody in the sentry room had his eyes closed. No sooner were their eyes closed when the watch commander entered the sentry room. He shouted: "Is that the way you guys are performing when you have watch duties, you look like little babies that need their sleep. If I see this again you will be reported to your commander."

Everybody took turns to walk outside a bit to keep awake. It was the longest night Adrie had ever encountered. Once it got light the sleepiness lifted and without further incident the sentry duty came to an end.

Luckily, sentry duties had been performed on a Tuesday. On Wednesday Adrie stood in front of his company commander, who had the report of the watch commander that he had reported for sentry duty with a dirty rifle. The commander called it negligence of the most important thing in the army and that his life could depend on his rifle. After this lecture, the company's commander asked him if he had something to say for himself.

It wouldn't do him any good but he tried anyway. "Yes major, you are right that my rifle is the most important thing and it should be kept clean. Believe it or not, I tried very hard to clean my dirty rifle after the field exercise. Unfortunately, there wasn't enough time to make it spotless."

As he had figured, it didn't do him any good, the Commander said: "Three days light arrest."

Adrie started to figure fast, that meant Wednesday, Thursday and Friday. At least he could go home on Saturday, provided that no other stupid incidents took place. He considered himself lucky that the commander hadn't found out that they had swapped rifles to avoid cleaning it.

One of Adrie's roommates Toon van Loon wasn't that lucky. When he had sentry duty three days later there had been a disturbance in the concentration camp at Vught. A dozen or so prisoners had escaped and the police were looking for them. It was feared that they would try to get weapons from the military camps by force. An alert warning was issued to the sentries to make them aware of possible problems.

Toon van Loon had gone on watch duty with five bullets in his magazine. Everybody received five bullets when he went on sentry duty. When your guard duties were finished you had to return five bullets. If you were missing one bullet there had to be a good explanation for it. Toon van Loon was a nervous person at the best of times and with added security problems, he was on edge. In the middle of the night, while he was watching the front gate, he thought that somebody was sneaking up on him. Toon van Loon took no chances and fired a shot in the air. Nobody was found but that one bullet that was missing was a disaster. Endless reports had to be filed to account for that one missing bullet. The company commander gave him six days light arrest. That included the weekend, so he couldn't go home.

After the three months of basic infantry training, there was selection for special units. Some of the soldiers were trained to be chauffeurs of army trucks; while others received technical training to build bridges to cross rivers during war time. There were also hospital soldiers needed and cooks.

Adrie had his driving license which was pretty good for those days. Very few people had a car or a driving license which made him think they would take him to be a chauffeur. He even had driven heavy trucks where double clutching was a must when you were shifting gears. It was all in his papers, it would save them the trouble to start teaching a bike rider how to drive a truck. Not such a luck; they took greenhorns instead of knowledgeable people. When Adrie complained about this to his friend Corporal Bakker, his friend said: "Most of the soldiers are with the infantry; that makes everybody's chance pretty good that you end up there."

It ticked him off that he was doomed to stay with the infantry.

The army needed also Commando Troops, a unit that had highly specialized training. They were very selective when it came to recruiting Commandoes. A lieutenant of the Commandoes came to visit the new soldiers to lecture them. He made it sound very attractive to volunteer. In his lecture he said: "For a good military career you have to start digging outhouses and clean toilets. There is always a chance that if you wait long enough that you become a General. While you are waiting to become a General, you could have a real interesting time if you join the Commandos. When you are a Commando you are the cream of the crop; you'll have to be able to drive a tank and a train and fly an airplane. Your duty is often to fight behind enemy lines. You have to have knowledge of all kinds of explosives to blow up buildings, bridges and ships. You have to be able to jump off a train or truck when it drives fifty or sixty miles per hour."

Adrie thought "Yah right, I tried that and when I fell; I had to clean the halls every night, for an entire week because there was a hole in my pants."

The lieutenant continued: "Most of the guerrilla war fighters are actually nothing but commandoes who attack lonely outposts and lightly defended areas. A successful commando avoids fighting strength and strikes weakness. The use of tactics based on deception, is the hallmark of success for any commando soldier.

In Indonesia guerrilla warfare was very successful, it brought them independence. Other successful guerrilla warfare was seen in Russia where they were called partisans. Behind the German lines they caused heavy damage. Not a day passed when the partisans blew up a train or a bridge. The Germans took revenge and killed ten Russians for every German who got killed. It was to no avail; the acts of sabotage by the partisans or commandoes continued. No matter whether you are part of a regular or an underground army your job will be destruction of enemy troops and equipment."

There was an opportunity to sign up which didn't mean that they would take all volunteers. They would simply look at your file and see if you would do. Toon van Loon volunteered too and was found too nervous for the Commandoes, they needed men with steel nerves. There was only one soldier from Adrie's room they took; he left for the training camp in Roosendaal.

Adrie had no intention signing up for anything. Playing soldier wasn't what it used to be when he was 12 years old. At that time he drove his mother up the wall when he had no time for supper and now he drove Sergeant Matheis up the wall. He had enough of those stupid buggers in the army and wouldn't volunteer for anything. All he wanted to do was mark time and get back to civilian life.

Sergeant Matheis was a real military man who always thought that the soldiers tried to dodge their duties. There was a real problem that made the unpleasant attitude of Sergeant Matheis worse. Adrie started to get real itchy feet between his toes and the skin was disappearing. A visit to the doctor revealed that he had Athlete's Foot. The doctor asked if it had started between his second and third toe from the left. "Exactly," Adrie replied, "How did you know that?"

"It's the area with the least room between the toes and that's where it is moister than between the other toes. It is caused by ringworm and is easily spread to other people who walk on the same area. When you take a shower dry your feet real good and make sure that there is no moisture left between your toes."

He gave him some ointment to put between his toes. It didn't improve at all, it only got worse. All his toes on the right foot were now infected and it had also spread to his left foot. Walking on high military shoes made it worse when his feet started to sweat.

Another visit to the doctor was in order. This time the doctor gave him some baby powder to make his toes dry. The doctor said: "It keeps the baby dry and it should keep your feet dry as well. As long as your feet are wet from sweating they can't heal."

There was also a doctor's order that gave him four days free from walking and standing duties. It meant that he only could attend theory lessons and when he walked to the room where those lessons were given, he had to use his gym shoes and not the high military shoes.

This incident happened on the very day that there was a twenty kilometre march scheduled. When Sergeant Matheis heard that Adrie wasn't going to participate in the march, he was furious and said: "You know exactly when to go to the doctor. There is a march and all of a sudden you have trouble with your feet, nice coincidence!"

Adrie replied angrily: "You always seem to think that we try to dodge our duties. Maybe you want to look at my feet and judge for yourself if I can walk twenty kilometres."

"I'm not interested looking at your feet I'm not a doctor;" Sergeant Matheis answered.

"Exactly, you aren't a doctor and the doctor will decide what I can do and what I can't in my condition. However, the doctor said that I have to let my feet heal before I can march again."

"We'll see about that!" Matheis replied and left the room.

The other soldiers of the room had listened in on the heated conversation and sided with Adrie. They said: "Why don't you tell that stupid sergeant to get off your ass unless he is a hemorrhoid."

Adrie replied: "I'd better not say that, he might throw me in jail for insubordination."

In those days there was very little the doctor could do. There was no Absorbine Junior to combat athlete's foot. To keep the feet dry with baby powder and walk on bare feet was the best remedy. As much as possible he walked on bare feet and treated his feet three times a day. After four days, the toes started to heal and Adrie resumed regular duties.

Perhaps he went back to regular duties too fast. As soon as he walked in the high closed military shoes, the toes started to deteriorate again. There was another march coming up and it didn't look like Adrie could walk twenty kilometres on those infected feet. At night Sergeant Matheis warned him: "Tomorrow there is another march, also for you. This time you are not staying behind in the barracks, I'll make sure about that!"

This was more than Adrie could take but he bit the bullet and thought: "We'll see about that!"

Instead of taking care of his feet, he kept his shoes on at night and walked downtown to see a movie. The result was remarkable, the next morning his toes looked like raw hamburger, just what the doctor ordered. Better this way than marching that far on infected feet, that would have made it worse he thought. Another visit to the doctor was necessary.

While Adrie was waiting in the treatment room for the doctor, he heard Sergeant Matheis coming into the doctor's office. He reported in military style to the doctor who was a lieutenant. The doctor asked: "What can I do for you?"

Sergeant Matheis said: "You have a soldier by the name of Adrie de Kievit on the sick list who is fooling the house. He pretends he can't walk but all he is doing he is trying to escape from his duties. Every time there is a march he is steady as clockwork on the sick list".

The doctor asked Sergeant Matheis: "Who is the doctor here in the barracks?"

Sergeant Matheis answered: "You, Lieutenant."

The doctor replied quite agitated: "You are so right that I'm the doctor and I'll decide whether he can do his regular duties or not. Don't you ever come busting into my office again telling me what to do. Your advice isn't needed at all. I can do very well without it. Just mind your own business and we'll get along very nicely."

Well, that was well said, Adrie thought. After a little wait, the doctor came in to look at his feet; he never mentioned the incident and probably didn't think that Adrie had heard the commotion. The doctor had a close look at his feet and said: "By golly that looks real bad, we'll treat it the same way as we did before. This time we'll have to give it more time to heal. Four days free of all standing and walking duties."

Sergeant Matheis didn't look very happy when he heard that Adrie was not going on the all-important march. His roommates cautioned him: "You'd be well advised not to come close to Sergeant Matheis, he is out to get you."

"That figures!" Adrie agreed.

It was obvious that on Monday morning there were always a lot of soldiers on the sick list. Nobody in his right mind would go to ask to see the doctor on a Thursday or Friday. In case the doctor gave a soldier free from standing and walking duties or sick in bed, the soldier couldn't go on leave. If the doctor specified Light Duties, a soldier was exempt from participating in marching and field manoeuvres. All duties within the gates of the barracks had to be attended. He also could go on leave which was considered to be a light duty. In reality it often wasn't.

In Adrie's case where the doctor could see a real problem, he would give him four days free of standing and walking duties which enabled him to go on leave on the weekend. Even if his toes were in a bad shape, he never went to the doctor on a Friday. That could be done on the next week Monday after the weekend. It meant that he had to participate on Friday in all duties whether they hurt him or not.

All soldiers knew the tricks of the trade and quite often faked illness and injuries. Whenever a soldier had to supply the doctor with a urine sample, the soldiers took their sweet old time and pretended that they couldn't go. They had to stay in the bathroom till they could go and the doctor told them to put their hands under the cold water tap to make it work. The longer it took the more time they spent away from military duties.

Tons of baby powder were used to keep Adrie's feet dry between the toes and if there was no march he usually managed not too badly that week. However, when there was a march his feet took a licking which made a doctor's visit necessary again. The doctor found out that a twenty kilometre march was a disaster for athlete's foot and gave him free from walking a march. Since the doctor was unable to cure the athlete's foot, he sent him to the military hospital in Utrecht for day treatment.

Any time that a soldier had to go to the hospital, he had to take his medical record and other records with him. Since Adrie had to leave right after breakfast, he had to pick up the envelope with all his papers for the doctor in the hospital the night before. When he got into his room he wanted to put the envelope in his locker. One of his roommates said: "Why don't you open it and read it?"

"It's sealed."

"So what, I can open and close it and nobody will notice. Why not take the opportunity to see your personal record while you have it in your possession?"

Adrie couldn't agree more and handed the envelope to his roommate for opening. His roommate took a pencil and inserted the point into the corner of the envelope. Then he started to roll the pencil, inserting pressure to open the envelope. It was only a paper seal which rolled open as well. Adrie checked everything that was in the envelope, which didn't really reveal anything that he didn't know. Everything was in the record, even that he had received three days light arrest for not having his rifle properly cleaned when he had to go on sentry duty. Nobody could understand what that had to do with his infected feet. With some paper glue the envelope was closed and sealed again. Adrie figured he had learned another trick of the trade.

In the morning, he picked up his free travelling pass for the train from the company office and was on his way to Utrecht. It was only an hour train ride and the military hospital was only a ten minute walk from the train station. The doctor gave him an injection in his feet and disinfected them. He also gave him a bottle with disinfectant to be used every day, and he was to return after a week for a check-up.

It was just before noon when Adrie was finished in the hospital. For obvious reasons he was in no hurry to get back to the barracks. Nobody knew how long it took in the hospital unless they phoned.

There was another soldier leaving in the same time and he wasn't in a hurry to go back either. Both soldiers had taken a lunch packet with them in order to have something to eat. They went to buy a bottle of pop and ate their lunch on a park bench.

Now there was a whole afternoon to waste. Instead of running back to their barracks they went to some department stores. They found a floor with all kinds of spring wound toys. Soon frogs and dogs were running and hopping across the floor. There were some young sales girls running the toy department who came to talk to the soldiers. Everybody had a good time.

The train went 4.15 p.m. which brought them back in the barracks around 5.30 p.m. just in time for supper. The next morning he had to go to the doctor to show him the letter from the hospital doctor. Four days of light duties was the result of that visit.

After those four days his feet looked reasonable and he could participate again with all duties. It was much nicer to be with the other soldiers than horse around in the barracks when his buddies left for field exercise. However, the athlete's foot came back and soon he had to return to the hospital in Utrecht.

It was November 1950 when the U.N. forces came close to the Chinese border and the North Korean troops withdrew into China. Perhaps China thought that the U.N. troops would chase the North Koreans into China and were joining the North Koreans to fight the U.N. troops.

300,000 CHINESE TROOPS JOIN NORTH KOREAN FORCES, TO DRIVE U.N. FORCES BACK.

That news brought some discussion in the army barracks. It seemed that the new soldiers were needed desperately after their initial training.

On January 4, 1951 one of the soldiers brought a newspaper in the room with the most devastating news. Everybody tried to get a peek into the newspaper to see where this world was heading for.

HALF A MILLION CHINESE AND NORTH KOREAN TROOPS CAPTURE SEOUL FOR SECOND TIME IN HALF A YEAR.

The Communist forces have been successful in their summer offensive to drive the U.N. forces out of Korea.

Toon van Loon said: "It looks that the U.N. is going to need us to drive the Communists out of Korea. Many countries have already sent troops to resist Communism."

Kleiweg replied: "That will be hard to do; you don't drive the Chinese out of Korea that easy. You can't win a war by killing Chinese; there are too damned many Chinese. There are over 585 million Chinese in Communist China who can make more Chinese people faster than we can shoot them."

Adrie got into the conversation and said: "When my friends went to Indonesia, I wished I could go too to see the Tropics. I always wanted to see the world but I sure hope that I don't have to go to Korea to be shot up, it's not worth it." There was no zest among the soldiers for any war and certainly not in Korea.

It was February and the garrison city S'Hertogenbos celebrated carnival on a great scale. S'Hertogenbos is in Brabant, the Southern province of The Netherlands, where 90% of the people are Roman Catholic and they celebrate carnival. The average person in Brabant drinks 15 glasses of beer and spends fifty guilders per day during the celebrations. (About five times as much in today's world.)

There were all kinds of celebrations and on the day of the Carnival's parade, military service was suspended for that one day. Everybody had a chance to see the carnival parade and at night everybody had permission to stay out till midnight. You didn't even have to ask for it.

Adrie went out that night with his sleepy Kleiweg who slept in the lower bunk. They both had a few bucks, just enough for a few beer. There was not even need for money in your pocket; there were all kinds of mini parades. They pulled Kleiweg and Adrie into the mini parade and soon the parade ended in a pub. All the people had saved the entire year to celebrate carnival. People had lots of money and they shared freely with the soldiers who had very little or no money. Before Adrie could order a beer, some guy from the crowd pushed a glass of beer in his hand and his friend Kleiweg received one beer too. You can't celebrate carnival with an empty glass people said and kept pushing glasses of beer into their hands.

Time flies by when you are enjoying yourself. When Adrie looked at his watch, he saw that it was time to mosey back to the barracks. It was 11.30 p.m., and a twenty minutes' walk should take them back to their barracks. That gave them ample time to be back in the barracks before midnight. Under normal circumstances it wouldn't have been a problem to get back in time but after drinking more than a dozen beer; straight walking was hard to do. Besides there were a lot of other soldiers on their way back to the barracks and they were in no hurry. They were back at 12.45 a.m. about 45 minutes late. That was late alright but nobody cared, it was later in China and nobody said anything because it was carnival.

Kleiweg and Adrie were back early, almost half of their roommates hadn't returned yet. The sergeant of the week came in to check how many soldiers were still missing. One of the soldiers was still in a festive mood; he hit the sergeant on his head with a clothes hanger and said: "Hello there, sergeant of the week."

The sergeant of the week left in a hurry mumbling: "I'll check tomorrow morning when you guys are sobered up."

It was a heck of a mess, quite a few soldiers had been puking in the hallway and others who couldn't make the bathroom threw up in the room. Kleiweg and Adrie went to bed too, they hadn't been puking yet and wanted to sleep it off. After Adrie had been lying in his bed for a while, he suddenly felt sick to his stomach. As it was too late to run for the bathroom, he puked beside his bed on the floor. Kleiweg and Adrie had their bed in the corner which gave them only one side of the bed to puke. When Adrie puked on the floor, Kleiweg was puking at the same time and Adrie puked on his head. Neither Kleiweg nor Adrie realized what had happened but the next morning it was visible. Kleiweg's head was covered with dried puke and some other roommates explained what had happened. Kleiweg went to the bathroom to clean himself up and never mentioned the incident. The other roommates never forgot and mentioned it all the time whenever they were talking about carnival.

Even the military authorities were in a festive mood, they never said anything to the soldiers who came back early in the morning, they were glad that everybody had returned. To complement the aching heads, they had changed the normal program to light duties and long coffee breaks.

Usually light duties were only given after inoculations. All soldiers had to be vaccinated against cholera, typhus, plague and a host of other contagious illnesses. One of the vaccinations caused a big lump in the armpit which was very painful when the arm was moved. For the rest, the military were merciless with cold and heat. At one time a Company Commander had the stupid idea to harden the soldiers. It was a little over 40 degrees Celsius and he wouldn't give permission for the soldiers to take off their woollen jacket. After five soldiers had fainted because of heat exhaustion, he finally backed down and let the soldiers walk in their summer shirts.

It wasn't until March 15, 1951 that the first good news came from Korea.

U.N. COUNTER OFFENSIVE PRODUCES RESULTS BY TAKING BACK SEOUL.

And in May 1951 the news was even better.

KOREAN WAR ENDS IN ARMISTICE.

The Korean War has been a war which nobody could win and therefore a negotiated settlement was reached between the U.N. Forces and the Communists. The armistice accord takes effect immediately as peace returns to Asia."

Kleiweg said to Adrie: "It seems that the U.N. doesn't need our services in Korea, we can stay in The Netherlands."

Adrie wasn't that sure: "Don't bet on it that the Cold War is over yet, they'll find another place to fight."

Between the doctor of the barracks and the doctor of the hospital in Utrecht, they didn't manage to eradicate Adrie's athlete foot fungus. They feared that other soldiers might be infected as well. Therefore, they decided to give him permanent light duties to keep the fungus at bay. It was stipulated that going on leave was permissible since he still could walk.

What was also permissible was to have watch duties in the ammunition fort. There was a corporal and a soldier needed to do that job. A canal surrounded the ammunition fort and there was an office to sit in. At their own discretion, the sentries could walk around to check up. To gain entrance to the fort there was a dam with a gate which was always locked unless a qualified person had to enter.

With an army truck, the Corporal and Adrie were transported to the ammunition fort. It was about time to eat the supper that they had brought with them when they arrived and after that they talked for a bit. To kill some time they started a card game. Before it got dark the Corporal decided to make a round on the inside of the canal. When he came back they played some more card games. It was going to be a long night, Adrie could smell it.

By 1.00 a.m. they were both very sleepy and ready for bed. The corporal said: "There is a mattress in the corner, go and sleep for an hour. We'll take turns to sleep, I'll wake you up and then I can sleep an hour. The corporal shoved his chair closer to the window, to have a better view of the gate and the path that led to the office. Only the officer of the watch had a key, besides the sentries. In case the officer of the watch decided to check up on his sentries, he could surprise them if they were sleeping. If that should happen, the consequences would be severe.

It doesn't take very long to fall asleep when you are that tired. After three hours of sleep Adrie woke up, he had to go to the bathroom from all the coffee drinking he had done. Looking at his watch it told him that he should have taken his turn to watch the gate two hours ago. When he looked at the corporal he saw him sleeping with his head on the table. Holy smokes, he thought, there could be real trouble if the officer of the watch found out. He jumped up; told the Corporal to lie down for a bit and he would watch the gate. After sleeping for three hours, Adrie wasn't tired anymore, so he let the corporal sleep until he woke up at 7.00 a.m.

At 8.00 a.m. the army truck arrived to bring breakfast and soon the sleepy night was forgotten. This was not bad for watch duty Adrie thought. It was even better than being in the barracks to do all kinds of silly jobs that the Sergeant of the Week dreamed up.

Light duties were sometimes hard to take; he didn't like it a bit. When the other soldiers left, he was alone by himself in the barracks. Moreover, when a soldier had light duties, he was put to work, when the other soldiers had duties he wasn't supposed to participate in. It was up to the Sergeant of the Week to assign work to the soldier with light duties. Usually, it meant that he had to mop the halls or clean the under officers rooms. That made him feel that he was the low man on the military totem pole.

When Sergeant Matheis was the Sergeant of the Week, he said: "Now you can be assured that you are going to do some work around here, you can start with cleaning the under officers room."

Adrie started to sweep the room and was in no hurry to finish. One of the civilian workers had become his friend and came over for a chat. Soon they were both sitting on a bed, smoking a cigarette and talking. As they were upstairs, they could hear if somebody came up the stairs.

All of a sudden they heard somebody running up the stairway. That brought instant action, the civilian guy left in a hell of a hurry and Adrie went back to sweeping the room. Both had been smoking and had extinguished their cigarettes. They had put the left over in their pockets and Adrie moved the blue air a bit. In spite of his efforts it was still noticeable that somebody had been smoking. The door went open and there was furious shouting Sergeant Matheis. "I knew that you would sit around when you are not watched, you have been smoking too. Not much good is coming out of your lazy bones, you are a misfit and not good for anything in society."

Adrie was fed up with this sergeant who couldn't see that anybody had light duties; he always saw conspiracy to get out of military duties. Those insults were just too much. Everybody has a breaking point, when you have reached it you snap and don't consider the consequences.

Angrily he responded to the insults: "Maybe I don't fit in military duties very well with my feet but I didn't ask to come here. I have a good trade and I made lots of money before I was drafted. All that you manage to do is shouting at soldiers. If they ever kick you out of the army, the only job you'll be able to handle is ragman."

In his fury he had said things which could easily be translated into insubordination. The sergeant seemed perplexed that somebody had told him the truth; he didn't say anything and left, to the relief of Adrie.

In finding jobs to do for a light duty soldier, there were some remarkably stupid ideas, Adrie thought. At one time he had to clean the windows with old newspapers and this time he was told to go to the Company Commander's office to wax his desk. He sure didn't need a stupid job like that, but what could he do?

After picking up some wax and rags for the job, he reported to the company's commander. Normally a Company's Commander is a Captain but this one was a Grand Major. That was done when they had officers with no post for them. Later he became the Battalion Commander. The Company's Commander, Major Brown, knew Adrie. He was the one who had punished him with three days light arrest for assuming watch duties with a dirty rifle. When Adrie told him what he was supposed to do Major Brown said: "Very well, I can sit at the table while you wax my desk."

Adrie started his job while he was wondering how long he should work on that stupid desk and how good a job he had to do. Major Brown was kind of talkative and said casually to him: "How are things?"

As he wasn't in the best of mood with the stupid job he had to do, he answered: "Terrible Major!"

That wasn't the answer Major Brown had expected, he had more or less expected that Adrie would say: "Good" or "Not bad." His curiosity was aroused and Major Brown asked: "Why is life so terrible to you, don't you have fun in your life?"

Adrie answered the Major: "Right now there is no fun in my life, there are no words to express my depression."

Major Brown was astonished with this reply and said: "Why don't you give it a try with the few words you know?"

Adrie started: "I had a good job as an electrician and made good money. All that I am good for now is scrub halls and wax desks. And then I come into all kinds of military offices in which I see giant posters on the wall, stating 'The Right Man, In The Right Place.' Do you really think that I am in the right place? I had a good trade; they could have used me with the technical engineers to build bridges. I even have a driver's license, which not many people have. They could have taken me as a chauffeur. Instead they take guys that they have to start from scratch. No, those posters don't make any sense to me!"

Major Brown had listened attentively to Adrie's complaints and said: "I can see your point; we should be able to get better use out of you. The problem is that we have enough chauffeurs, right now we are in need of cooks. Can you cook?"

"Yes Major, I can cook."

"Where did you learn to cook?"

"From my mother," Adrie replied. "During the Depression, my father was working in Government camps and my mother went working. I was six years old when my task was cooking supper and later I did some cooking when we went camping."

"I'll put you on the list for cooks," Major Brown said. "In a week or so you'll be called up for a medical examination to make sure you are in good health to work in a kitchen. Maybe we are getting the right man in the right place after all."

A week later the company administrator came to Adrie to tell him that he had to come to the military hospital in Utrecht for a medical. He was examined and re-valuated. They checked eyes, ears etc. and for everything they tested there was a number given from one to five to show what condition everything was. Number one was perfect and number five meant no good for the army. In between, a soldier could be used for different duties and be excluded from the infantry. When he got into the army he had all number ones. That was remarkable, considering that the Navy rejected him because of his flat feet. After his re-valuation he had now a three for his feet, all the other numbers were still number one. Everything used to be 'A One' but it wasn't anymore.

A week after his medical, he had to appear before Major Brown. Major Brown said: "From now on you'll be a cook, your medical examination states that you are good for kitchen duties. Go to the kitchen and report to the Sergeant for duties. And remember the saying that 'An army marches on its stomach.' Do a good job and hopefully you'll find that you are now the right man in the right place."

It seemed that the complaint about the right man in the right place had sunk in pretty good; Major Brown was mentioning it over and over again. Much happier than he had been for the last five months, Adrie replied joyfully: "Thank you major, I'm sure that I will feel more at home when I have a task to fulfil that suits me."

While he was walking to the kitchen, he thought: "What a luck that I was able to talk to the right man in the right place to tell him that I wasn't the right man in the right place at all."

He hurried to the kitchen to commence his new task. When he opened the kitchen door enough steam escaped to drive a train. It wasn't a very modern kitchen; there were six individual steam kettles which had to be independently stoked with coal. There were three civilian ladies who cleaned and prepared the vegetables. They had a machine to peel the potatoes which saved a lot of time. As the machine didn't take the eyes out of the potatoes, the ladies had to do that job themselves. There were also two civilian men whose task was mainly to debone meat and cut it into portions for the troops.

Corporal Peekstok needed somebody to fry the meat. As he couldn't remember Adrie's name, he shouted: "Say Charley, I have a job for you."

Everybody caught on and called him Charley which became his nickname in the kitchen. That was not the end of his nick name. There was a famous piano player in The Netherlands by the name of Charley Koontz and soon Adrie had a complete name change. He was now known as Charley Koontz and he loved his new name. First it was 'Fieldwebel' and now 'Charley Koontz.' He loved everything in the kitchen and started to purr like six kittens.

It was ten days before Easter and everybody was looking ahead for the extra-long weekend. Adrie had all kinds of plans for spending that time. Things had never looked better until somebody dropped a monkey wrench in the gears. In Tilburg there was an outbreak of smallpox and Tilburg was only 20 miles from the army camps. Somebody had returned from Africa and became very sick.

The doctor's diagnoses was smallpox. He informed the medical authorities, who took appropriate steps trying to avoid a smallpox epidemic. They traced all the people who had been in contact with the smallpox man since his return to The Netherlands and tested them for smallpox. The result was a disaster; there were eleven reported cases of the deadly illness.

As soldiers, everybody had received all kinds of inoculations and vaccinations but not against smallpox. Nobody in The Netherlands had been vaccinated against smallpox except the older people. It used to be law that children who went to school had to be vaccinated. They had to have a smallpox paper from the doctor, showing that the child had been vaccinated, in order to be registered. A few years before Adrie went to school this forced smallpox vaccination had been abolished. Nobody had been sick with smallpox for many years and the Dutch Government scrapped the program. It was too expensive to vaccinate all those children and moreover the Government was strapped for cash with the Great Depression.

That was in the early 1930's when hardly anybody was travelling. Most of the people never travelled more than fifty kilometres away from their home. Smallpox is spread by contact with other people who have the disease. If there is nobody in a country that has smallpox anymore, there will be no cases of smallpox. In the first post war years travelling was hardly possible. When things started to look up, more and more people started to travel. This man who had contacted the deadly disease had gone to Africa where smallpox was still occurring.

Nobody of the Medical Authorities in The Netherlands had expected an outbreak of smallpox and consequently there was not even any vaccine on hand for this emergency. In a heck of a hurry, the Government had to obtain some from abroad, to vaccinate all the people who had been in contact with the man that had smallpox. Moreover, the whole medical industry was put in high gear, to make vaccine from cow lymph containing the causative cowpox virus.

As soon as the news became known to the military authorities they closed all military camps. Nobody was allowed to leave the camps and only food supplies were allowed to enter the camps. There were some soldiers from Tilburg in the camps of s'Hertogenbos who had to report immediately to the doctor for tests. Luckily nobody had the dreadful smallpox disease and a vaccination program was set up right away. The military camps were privileged to receive the first available vaccine.

All military camps were vaccinated against smallpox four days before the cancelled Easter leave. The rumour went that the Camp Commander would let all vaccinated soldiers go home for the long weekend. That was only a rumour and nothing was for sure; the soldiers could only hope. Five more cases of smallpox were reported among the civilian population, which showed that the smallpox hadn't been contained and an epidemic could still happen. All detected persons were put in quarantine and doctors were busy bodies trying to vaccinate the entire population of The Netherlands.

Smallpox vaccination in young kids seldom causes a problem, that's why it used to be done before the kid would enter school. Vaccination of adults is an entirely different matter. Most of the adults get quite sick from a smallpox vaccination and if the infection hits the brain, they usually die.

A couple of days after the vaccination most of the soldiers were sick. Adrie didn't feel good at all; he was sweating like an angry God from fever. This would normally be a good excuse to get free from duties but not this time. He liked his new job and he had to fry meat for 1,000 soldiers. This had become one of his duties in the kitchen. Almost half way into his meat frying duties he could hardly stand it anymore. Finally he attracted the attention of Corporal Peekstok, who had seen him drinking extra ordinary quantities of fluids. Corporal Peekstok said: "If I were you I would go to bed and maybe you'll feel better tomorrow."

Adrie rejected that idea: "It's not all that bad."

Corporal Peekstok became resolute and said: "I order you to go to bed and I'll call the doctor right away, you are in no condition to do any work. Don't worry about frying meat, we'll get it done, just go to sleep it off and wait for the doctor."

The doctor came, armed with a thermometer to check the fever. His temperature was high, in the forties and medicine was needed to break the fever. The only remedy the doctor had was aspirin, he advised to take four at a time, three times a day. And there was an order to drink lots of fluids.

Corporal Peekstok came with some food and tea for lunch. The food was tasteless; when he chewed it, it became a ball in his mouth. With his high fever, the tea was welcome; he could drink lots of that.

When at night Corporal Peekstok came with coffee and supper Adrie was sweating out gallons of water. He was soaked and the steam was visibly going up through the blankets. Corporal Peekstok left and came back with the doctor.

When the doctor took his temperature again, he said: "There is very little I can do at this stage, with taking aspirin the fever should break."

The doctor was talking to Corporal Peekstok about all the sick soldiers, he said: "More than half the soldiers are in bed today and the other half will probably be in bed tomorrow as well. It can take about four to five days before most of the soldiers will be back to normal. Some will take a week or longer to recover."

On Saturday morning, everybody was wondering if the Camp Commander would let the soldiers go home for the Easter long weekend. At about 10.30 a.m., the Camp Commander's order came out that all vaccinated soldiers could go home. Soldiers who hadn't been vaccinated had to stay in the barracks.

That was great news; everybody was all of a sudden busy with cleaning his rifle and other equipment. Since Adrie was in the kitchen, he had no inspection of his rifle and other equipment anymore. He made sure not to be around when the sergeant came to inspect everybody.

When Adrie heard that he could go home, he felt better already. He jumped out of bed for a shave, a shit and a shoe polish. There was work to be done if he was going to be ready by 1.00 p.m. to go home. When he looked in the mirror, he looked horrible. There were circles around his eyes and he had a beard that could suit a sea pirate. While he was shaving, he was trembling on his feet from the fever that wouldn't let up. It was difficult not to cut yourself, Adrie thought, when your hands are trembling like a leaf in the wind. Moreover it was a very difficult shave, he hadn't shaved since he was sent to bed, which was four days ago. He could almost leave his moustache which was allowable for a soldier. As he didn't like a cookie duster under his nose, the moustache had to go.

First of all he had to tell Corporal Peekstok that he was leaving for the Easter long weekend and at 1.00 p.m. he walked out of the gate to the train station. This was a weekend with a free travelling pass and even if he had had no free travelling, he would have taken the train anyway in his condition.

Adrie was glad when he was sitting in the train; he just felt awful and was very thirsty. Luckily, there was food service in the train which gave him a chance to quench his thirst. When the waiter came by with bottles of cold drinks he stopped him, took a bottle of Seven Up off his tray and paid him.

That tasted great but when you are really thirsty there is not much in a bottle. When the waiter came by again, he took one more Seven Up and four more after. Every time the waiter came by he took another Seven Up and consumed a total of six bottles.

After the train ride, it was only twenty minutes by bus before he was home. Unfortunately, there were no soft drinks in the bus. With nothing to drink for half an hour, he was very thirsty by the time he got home. At home, he drank lots of coffee and his mother brought him some strawberries. When he tried a cheese sandwich it tasted terrible, he felt very sick and decided to go to bed. First, he checked his temperature and found it still almost 41 degrees. "Phone the military doctor right away and tell him about my high fever," Adrie instructed his mother.

Ordinary people had no phone in those days. In order to make the phone call, his mother had to go to a store. When she came back, his mother said: "The military doctor wasn't in, as soon as he returns his wife will give him the message. Then I phoned Doctor Meerkerk, our own doctor, because you need a doctor as fast as possible. However, Doctor Meerkerk was out for the night and his wife was going to try to reach him."

About 10.00 p.m. the military doctor came, he checked Adrie and said: "Keep taking aspirin and stay in bed."

He had a long sleep and woke up at 9.00 a.m. Amazingly, he felt good and very hungry. His temperature was now a little under 37 which meant no more fever. A hearty breakfast would do the trick to get him going again. Soon he was eating some more strawberries and the cheese sandwich which had tasted like shit the night before tasted as good as caviar.

It was Sunday and the sun was shining, it looked like a very nice day for a stroll. When he came outside, he saw his neighbour Kees Meuzelaar, who had heard from his mother that he was very sick. Of course he was curious about how he was doing, and soon the two were in a conversation. Kees said: "Come in for some coffee." Soon they were drinking coffee and had a good time.

When Adrie came back home his mother said: "Dr. Meerkerk was here to have a look at you. I told him that you were all of a sudden free of fever and had gone out. He said that you should be very careful when you get sick from smallpox vaccination, you could die."

The weekend was over and Adrie went back to his garrison. Most of the soldiers were better; there were a few who hadn't returned from their leave because of illness. Everything seemed to be under control in the barracks and also in The Netherlands. Luckily for the Dutch Health Department, a smallpox epidemic had been avoided. However, the Dutch Health Department didn't take any more chances. Anybody who left the country had to be vaccinated and all new soldiers had one more vaccination added to the many they were already receiving.

Adrie sure liked his new job, he liked to do different things in his life and this was right up his alley. He had been a motor mechanic, became an electrician and now he was a cook. What a change that was, he loved all of it. He worked hard for the one guilder per day and he really didn't care. Everybody had to serve his time in the army and now he had a responsible job that he liked, he could handle the army.

It didn't take long for Corporal Peekstok to start him on early shifts. It meant he had to get up two hours earlier to make tea and prepare breakfast. Often the troops went out for the entire day which meant they had to have extra food for lunch and needed a bottle of coffee. Most of the work, like slicing bread, sausage and cheese was done the night before. All the slicing machines had to be turned by hand, there were no electrical machines for that in the kitchen.

Now that he was in the kitchen, he didn't have to perform watch duties anymore. Instead, he had to take turns to stay for the weekend, to cook for the people that stayed in the barracks. There was only skeleton staff remaining in the barracks during the weekend. Most of it was for security and there were also soldiers who were punished and couldn't go home. There were two army camps not far apart and those two camps worked together on the weekends. Only one kitchen was open in the two camps and food was prepared for both camps in one kitchen. A military truck transported the food to the other camp.

There were quite some perks with his new job. In the first place he was treated with respect and was rid of the childish behaviour of under officers and officers who supplied the training.

The Sergeant of the Week had a lot of responsibilities. He was responsible that everybody woke up in time and that all the soldiers would get to eat. Therefore he had to furnish a list of how many soldiers each platoon had, for feeding them the next day. The cooks would make the required portions of butter, cheese, meat etc. in stainless steel containers. It could happen that the cooks made a mistake when they were counting the portions but the Sergeant of the Week was responsible regardless. He was supposed to count the portions for the platoons to see if he received the correct number.

It could also happen that the designated soldiers, who were distributing the portions, pulled a fast one and benefited their buddy with an extra portion of meat. In either case there was a shortage and the Sergeant of the Week had to go to the kitchen to ask for more food. There was never a problem; there was enough food in the kitchen to do this, provided that the Sergeant of the

Week wasn't an asshole who had a big mouth to the cooks. They thought twice before they said anything wrong to a cook, they hated to be blackballed.

Sometimes there were soldiers returning late from the hospital or chauffeurs came late home from transport duties. Even with the kitchen closed, there was never a problem to get food. Everybody knew where to find Adrie to supply some food. There was no problem for him to get the key to the kitchen. All he had to do was going to the watch commander and ask for it. It was easy enough to whip up some food for the latecomers, there was always meat and fruit left overs. Even when he was already in bed, he would get out making something to eat for a hungry soldier who had just come in.

The staff scratched each other's back; if a chauffeur or hospital soldier needed food, Adrie would get it for them. On the other hand whenever they could be of service to him, they made sure he received it. With different shifts he could go to the movies in the afternoon and he didn't have to walk twenty five minutes. All he had to do was ask one of the chauffeurs and an army truck was waiting whenever he was ready to go. When the movie was finished, he walked to the corner of the street and there was the truck waiting for him. The chauffeur knew when the movie was about finished and made sure he was there. It looked like a regular taxi service.

Hospital soldiers, who took care of the sick in the barracks, had most of the time about 8 patients, with light ailments. Any seriously ill patients were transported to the military hospital. Whenever the hospital soldiers needed food, all they had to do was ask. On the other hand, when Adrie wanted to see the doctor he told the hospital soldier. Whenever the doctor had time to see him, the hospital soldier would come to the kitchen to get him and he never had to wait. This was service at its best; the entire staff enjoyed the perks which they supplied to one another.

Normally, cooks have to go three months to cooking school before they start to work in the kitchen. Because of the shortage of cooks, the military command had requested more cooks and Adrie was one of them. When the additional cooks had been picked, the cooking school was already two weeks on the go and moreover they needed cooks right away. Therefore he started in the kitchen without cooking school training. It didn't matter at all; he got practical training from the outset and when the cooks returned from the cooking school Adrie had one up on them, maybe more than one.

At the cooking school, the future cooks were pumped full of all kinds of theory. When the new cooks came to the kitchen, Corporal Peekstok had almost a fit. He watched them figure out on paper how much salt they had to put on the potatoes. If he hadn't stepped in the potatoes would have been salter than the water of the sea.

In the military camp the myth went around that the food of the soldiers was mixed with camphor. That would make them less horny so that they didn't have to run around in the camp with a hard on. When the new cooks came from the cooking school, one of them asked Adrie when they had to put the camphor in the food.

Adrie had a good laugh and asked: "Do you believe everything they tell you?"

The new cook said: "No, not really, but the food has a peculiar taste here; if it isn't camphor where does that taste come from?"

"Indeed the food tastes different than back home," Adrie explained. "That comes because your mother cooks for maybe two to five people. Here we cook for 1,000 soldiers and it is cooked in steam kettles. That makes a world of difference and that's why it tastes a little different but you'll get used to that."

The cooks who had the early shift had to get up two hours before reveille. Reveille was at six o' clock which was the time that a bugle player blew his bugle. It was the signal that all the regular soldiers in the camp had to get up. Most of the soldiers didn't know the difference between a bugle and a trumpet and called the bugle a trumpet. Therefore the trumpet players were called 'The Doomsday Serenade Players' and they all went by the nickname Gabriel. Thus when a cook had the early shift he had to get up at 4.00 a.m. That required a wakeup call which was booked by the watch commander.

Some of the new cooks thought it was terrific to have a wakeup call even if they didn't need one. Instead of getting up they could simply turn around and say: "The hell with it."

It never had entered Adrie's mind to ask for a wakeup call if he didn't need one. In a way he could sense that it was nice to wake up and go back to sleep. One of the new cooks and Adrie booked a wakeup call. Everything went like planned, there was a wakeup call in the morning and they turned around to get back to sleep. Then things started to go wrong, the sergeant who had woken the two cooks checked back after ten minutes. Finding them asleep made him mad and he started to take the blankets off their bed. Then they told him that they had the late shift and didn't need a wakeup call. They only wanted the pleasure of not having to get up when they were called.

The sergeant wasn't amused at all, he shouted: "If you assholes think it's fun to have me come to your room to wake you up, we'll see about that. I'll report you to the commander to smarten you up."

Wow, what a sore head that was, the sergeants before woke up the cooks and left, if they didn't get up that was their problem. This guy was too good to be true, he wanted to make sure. When the story went around in the kitchen, Corporal Peekstok said: "Don't worry; he wouldn't dare to report on cooks for a stupid little thing like that. If he does he'll cook his own goose." Corporal Peekstok was right; the incident was never mentioned again.

All the cooks, chauffeurs, hospital soldiers and technical troops were now in the staff company. It made it easier to make a deal with somebody; everybody was in the same building. In the staff company everybody took longer leave than he was supposed to. Any weekend started at 1.00 p.m. Saturday afternoon. That was the earliest a soldier was free to go, provided he didn't have any punishment. A lot of the staff disappeared Friday night and others left Saturday before 10.00 a.m. On one Saturday morning the Captain, who was the company's commander of the staff company, said to the lieutenant of staff: "I want a meeting with all the officers and under officers as soon as you can get them together."

The lieutenant replied: "Let the meeting begin, all the officers and under officers of the company are together."

The Captain said: "You mean everybody else buggered off already? Well in that case we'll have to have the meeting as soon as everybody is back from the weekend."

There were also arrangements made for the cooks to have longer leave. The lieutenant in charge of the kitchens and food supplies was a very nice officer, he said: "I don't give a damn how much you fix among one another with extra leave. I'll stick up for you as long as there is food of high quality at the prescribed time. If we get complaints there will be hell to pay."

There was only one long weekend per month when the soldiers returned on Monday night with the last train, all other weekends were what they called 24 hour weekends. That meant you were home Saturday night and on Sunday night you had to return. When it was arranged, only two cooks returned on Sunday night and the rest returned Monday morning, or in case it was a 48 hour weekend they returned on Tuesday morning. The two cooks who returned in time on Sunday night, left on Friday night. That way everybody had a longer weekend.

The two cooks who returned on Sunday night had their hands full to get everything in order for Monday morning. When they returned they went straight to the kitchen and worked all night. There was a lot to do; even if there was only food needed for breakfast. However, Monday was a day that there were always companies that went out all day and they needed lunch parcels and extra coffee for their field bottles.

Slicing bread, cheese and sausage for 1,000 people was quite a chore. Making tea and coffee wasn't that hard, the cook knew how much water he needed and how much tea or coffee to use. Milk to taste was put in the coffee when it was finished. Drinking black coffee couldn't be done unless you worked in the kitchen.

As soon as the other cooks returned Monday morning, the cooks who had worked all night went to bed. They returned to the kitchen by 4.00 p.m. to help out with the workload that had to be done for supper. All the cooks were happy with the arrangement and everybody worked as long as needed at night.

There was also an under officers kitchen and an officers kitchen. When they needed a cook for the officers kitchen, they took the cook from the under officers kitchen. Now they needed an experienced cook for the under officers kitchen. Adrie had already been in the kitchen for more than three months which made him the most experienced cook.

There was always a temporary shortage of cooks and chauffeurs. When a new draft came up, all recruits had to take a three months basic infantry training. In that time they learned how to shoot different weapons and how to throw hand grenades. Even when you are a cook, during war you have to be able to defend your kitchen. For that purpose, all cooks had to go once a month to the rifle range for target practise. When the infantry training was done and over with, the selected cooks and chauffeurs had to have three months training.

It took half a year before a new draft had their own cooks and chauffeurs. In the meantime they borrowed cooks from other regiments who were longer in the army. Once they had their own cooks and chauffeurs, other drafts came up with no cooks and chauffeurs for the first half a year. Consequently, the new regiments borrowed cooks from them. There were always cooks and chauffeurs moving to different camps and in the camps there was a movement as well between the different kitchens.

Even without cooking school Adrie was selected to cook in the under officers kitchen. Ah, promotion comes fast in the army, he thought, and it wasn't even war. During the war promotions come when many people are killed. When you are a soldier and your corporal got killed, you might find that you are the corporal all of a sudden. Then when the sergeant dies you'll become the sergeant. If enough people get killed you might be the General some day. Well, he didn't become a corporal yet, he was in the under officers kitchen.

Cooking for the under officers was more an art than in the soldiers kitchen. There were less than 100 under officers to cook for and he had been cooking for 1000 men. He didn't forget Corporal Peekstok and the other cooks in the soldier's kitchen. As whole cows and pigs were butchered and cut up in sizeable portions, there were extra good pieces of meat which were consumed by the cooks. Filet Mignon was on the menu most days of the week. And Adrie, who was appointed to look after the meat every day, could whip up a gorgeous meal with filet mignon just for the cooks. After the food was handed out to the troops, the kitchen was cleaned and then it was supper time for the cooks. That was usually an hour after the soldiers had their meal.

A lot of times when there were punishments handed out, the soldiers were given the duty of helping to clean the kitchen. That wasn't much of a punishment, actually everybody liked it. After they were finished there was always something good to eat for them and lots of coffee.

Another draft had been called up and all those recruits went to the military camps in Roermond and Venlo, which were two small cities in Limburg, one of the southern provinces of The Netherlands. Most of the recruits came from Limburg; that was probably done to save on travelling costs.

A military camp without cooks meant that they had to borrow from other camps again. Four cooks had to come from s'Hertogenbos, two had to go to Roermond and the other two had to go to Venlo. Adrie was ordered to go to Roermond with one of the new cooks.

On arrival, they reported to the kitchen and were assigned duties for the next day. The military camp in Roermond was built much later than the one in s'Hertogenbos and was consequently quite a bit more modern. All the cooking kettles were on steam, you didn't have to stoke them all individually. Adrie did miss the under officers kitchen where he had been able to experiment more. However, it was one more experience and working with modern equipment was enjoyable as well.

One day, Adrie went to his room to get some rest and soon he had a discussion with the new recruits of the Roermond Camp. One of the recruits was talking about eine stunde when he was talking about an hour. Adrie knew enough German to understand it but he remarked: "Where did I cross the border that I'm suddenly in Germany?" Some of the recruits were living very close to the German border and they spoke more German than Dutch.

With the smallpox incident in Tilburg the inoculation program had changed for the soldiers and they had to be vaccinated against smallpox. It went the same way as in s'Hertogenbos; most of the recruits got pretty sick and experienced high fever.

One of the recruits had been in the barrack hospital and was released before the weekend to go home for leave. He got sick at home and didn't return from leave. After four days the military doctor sent him back to the barracks although he felt lousy. Soon after his arrival, the doctor put him back in the barrack hospital. When the infection went to his brain his situation deteriorated very fast and his life was in jeopardy. He needed special medication and he needed it fast. When the doctor checked around, he found that it was available in The Hague. One of the military chauffeurs was told to go and get it on a special order which was marked with three crosses. Three crosses meant that his order was of extreme importance. It meant that the chauffeur must drive at the fastest speed possible and ignore speed limits totally.

Even at ultra-high speeds it took the chauffeur six hours before he returned. Unfortunately he was too late; the recruit had died in the meantime. There was quite a commotion about this incident, especially the parents weren't impressed with the way the army had handled it. They charged that it was criminal to have a chauffeur driving from Roermond to The Hague to pick up urgently needed medicine. It could have been picked up and delivered by helicopter, or the time could have been cut by half if the medicine had been ordered by telephone and a chauffeur had driven from The Hague to Roermond, instead of back and forward. The parents sued the Army for neglect and everybody was up in arms.

Army officials replied that everything in their power had been done. The Hague wasn't a garrison city, and consequently there were no military chauffeurs or helicopters available to deliver the medicine. The outcome of the trial was never revealed by the press. It was probably a trial behind closed doors.

Adrie was hardly used to Roermond and his work when an army order was issued that he had to go to Schalkaar, near Deventer, to cook in the officer's kitchen. His head start on the other cooks got him those jobs all the time.

During the five weeks he had been in Roermond there hadn't been extra days of leave. They never had heard about a thing like that. It was no s'Hertogenbos; he was shit out of luck without extra leave. Adrie wondered if he could revive longer weekends in Schalkaar, he was alone in the officer's kitchen with a civilian cook. He didn't think his Captain would go for that, which made him talk it over with the civilian cook. It was decided that Adrie was going to take all early shifts to give the civilian cook a break in the morning. Lunch and supper was a lot of work, and Adrie would always be there. He had to eat anyway and as long as he was in the camp there wasn't much to do except eating, sleeping and working.

There were sixteen officers and besides the cooking, they had to be served. Most of the days he got up one hour before reveille at 5.00 a.m., prepared and served breakfast to the officers and when the civilian cook came at 9.00 a.m., he went back to bed for a couple of hours. Around 11.00 a.m. he got up again and helped the civilian cook to make lunch and serve the officers.

The deal was that the civilian cook would take a day off every Wednesday and in turn Adrie would take off Saturday mornings and twice a month he would return on Monday as well. It could easily be done, nobody checked up on him. He was sleeping in a room with the new recruits and if he wasn't in his room, he could be in the kitchen or perhaps downtown when he wasn't working. When on Wednesday the civilian cook took his day off, Adrie had to cook and serve lunch and supper by himself. That was no problem, he knew all the officers; all he had to do is ask one of the captains to send him a recruit to help out. It worked perfectly like it had worked in s'Hertogenbos.

Cooking for the officers was quite different; they didn't go for the regular army fare the soldiers had to put up with. The officers wanted extras. With lunch there was always soup and pudding beside bread and with supper there was always soup and dessert. All officers paid thirty guilders per month for extras that had to be purchased which included cooking wine, eggs and spices.

Soup was made most of the time with an egg and wine in it and meat was always prepared with wine as an extra ingredient. In order to be able to make fancy dishes, Adrie had bought a good cook book; it had cost him 8.50 guilders. That was eight and a half days of his wages. It didn't matter at all, he wanted to stay in the officer's kitchen and if they liked his cooking, they would like to keep him. Besides, with his extra days of leave, he could make a few bucks with photography and radio repair. The days of despair in the Army that he had experienced in the beginning, and all the silly jobs he had to do were in the past. Whenever he was home, he tried out some new recipes to make another fabulous dish. Adrie told his mother that he was doing the cooking which was alright with her.

For five months everything went alright with taking extra days of leave but that was about to change. One Monday night when he returned to his barracks at 10.00 p.m., one of his roommates said that the Captain had been looking for him. That wasn't very good news when he should have returned on Sunday night. He was puzzled, why in the world would the Captain be looking for him? Nobody ever checked up on him so why now?

All the questions were answered the next morning. The civilian cook had had an attack from gallbladder stones and was in the hospital. That attack came early on Monday morning when Adrie was home. With no cook in the kitchen, there was nobody to prepare breakfast for the officers. Of course the question was asked 'Where is our army cook?' Nobody knew and a cook from the under officers kitchen had taken charge. When he saw Adrie on Tuesday morning in the kitchen, he went back to the under officers kitchen and let him handle it.

Of course, the Captain wanted to see Adrie and wanted to know if he was doing that all the time. If he would say 'yes' there certainly would be hell to pay so he had to lie a lot. "Well no, we had a celebration back home and I got too drunk to return to the barracks on Sunday night, and Monday morning I had a terrible hangover."

The Captain said: "Party or hangover doesn't give you the right not to return in time to your barracks; that will cost you four days light arrest."

That was a very light punishment for the offence and it didn't hurt at all. Friday was his last day of light arrest and he could go home on Saturday for the weekend. This time and all other next times, there was no extra leave anymore. It was nice while it had lasted; it seemed that good things had come to an end. The civilian cook dropped in the next day, to tell that he had to have surgery and wouldn't be back for about six weeks.

Adrie had been surprised that the Captain had accepted his reason for late returning that well. Since his story had fit in with what the civilian cook had told the Captain, he had no reason to doubt him at all. The Captain had talked to the cook and had asked why Adrie wasn't in the barracks. The civilian cook had said: "You mean Adrie didn't return on Sunday night? He always returns in time. I haven't got the foggiest idea what happened to him."

With the civilian cook under the knife, Adrie had his work cut out for him. It didn't matter; he had help all day from recruits. They washed the dishes, set the table and did as much as they could. Adrie was glad to have his cookbook now he was in charge alone, he tried all kinds of dishes and the officers praised him often when a special dish had turned out superbly. Everybody was happy with the arrangements.

When the cooks from the army camp returned from their training in cooking school, Adrie knew that he could expect to be used elsewhere. One of the cooks from the cook school was added to the officers kitchen and the civilian cook had returned after his surgery and recuperation. There were now three cooks in the officer's kitchen. It meant that everybody could take it easier with three experienced cooks to do the work.

It seemed that Army Headquarters had forgotten about a cook called Adrie. There was an explanation for this. In the meantime when Adrie was in Schalkaar, the army camp in s'Hertogenbos had been cleared out. All the soldiers of the same draft as Adrie had gone to Oorschot. Oorschot was a very large army camp with soldiers who had finished their military training and were ready for war. They now received the status to be in the Third N.A.T.O. Division. Adrie had no war destination and was kept in the reserves. However, after the camp was cleared, a new draft came under the weapons and the old problem occurred again, the new recruits didn't have any cooks for the first half a year. That's where Adrie came in; he received his orders to go back to his old garrison city.

Back in s'Hertogenbos, Corporal Peekstok was happy to see Adrie and vice versa. He was assigned to run the soldier's kitchen when Corporal Peekstok wasn't on duty. One day he would get up at four in the morning to take the early shift and Corporal Peekstok would come at 10.00 a.m. At 1.00 p.m.

Adrie was finished for that day and could go to the movies if he wanted. Most of the time he would go back to the kitchen at 4.00 p.m. to help out. He didn't have to, but he did it anyway. It was something he did beyond the call of duty, although he never received a medal for it.

The next day he would have the late shift and Corporal Peekstok took the early shift. He slept long that day and got up around 10.00 a.m. He ate late breakfast and after he started to help again, while his actual time was 1.00 p.m. Adrie was very happy to be back with his old Captain and sergeant major who allowed extra leave on the weekends. For extra-long weekends he was willing to do anything to keep things moving smoothly.

Life was beautiful even in the Army, it seemed one happy merry go around. Just when Adrie thought that he had it made in the Army, the proverbial fly landed in the ointment. He had been moved around from one garrison city to the other and moving people around wasn't restricted to soldiers. His Captain of the staff company with his sergeant major got the word. They said good bye and left. Another Captain took his place and instead of the faithful sergeant major, there was now an adjutant in charge as an administrator assistant to the commanding officer.

Everybody wondered how that would affect their extra leave. The new Captain left no doubt about it, he said: "I've heard how the staff company was run before. Under my command there are no extra leaves, everybody is equal and a twenty four hour leave constitutes just that and nothing more."

A talk with the adjutant revealed that he didn't care what the staff did as long as everything went smoothly. The first few weeks, everything went alright with extra days of leave. One weekend when Adrie, with another cook, had taken an extra day of leave, the Captain checked up on the staff and found that there were two cooks missing. A mad Captain told the lieutenant of supply to phone the Military Police to get the two cooks back. The lieutenant was a very good guy who knew that the two cooks had taken an extra day off. He pleaded with the Captain to let the cooks come back by themselves and then punish them, instead of the Military Police throwing them in jail for not being on duty. He said to the Captain: "You can throw them in jail, as long as you don't forget that we won't have enough staff in the kitchen if you do that."

When the two cooks came back Monday afternoon instead of Sunday night, it didn't take long to become familiar with the devastating news. Corporal Peekstok had been asked by the Captain if he knew where the two cooks could be. Corporal Peekstok said: "They don't have their shift till 4.00 p.m. this afternoon and I don't know what they are doing in their free time."

The adjutant had also been questioned and he too denied having any knowledge of the whereabouts of the cooks. "Very well then", the Captain said: "Tell them to report to me immediately when they return."

It was Tuesday morning when the two cooks had to appear before a very mad Captain. Adrie went first, reported to the Captain and waited patiently till all hell broke loose. The Captain had slanted cat like eyes, a flat nose and thin lips, he cast Adrie the disdainful look of an ill-tempered bureaucrat and asked: "And where did you come from, if I may ask?"

"From Home, Captain."

"From Home", the Captain thundered, "You were supposed to be back Sunday night."

"Yes Captain, I know, but I had the late shift on Monday so I returned on Monday."

The Captain started to raise supreme hell and asked: "To whom do you have to go if you want leave?"

"To you, Captain."

"Well then," the Captain shouted, "I see in your file that you never learn, you returned late from leave in Schalkaar and you were punished with four days light arrest. You are not getting off that easy this time."

Adrie thought that the Captain would throw him in jail because he was a second time offender.

The Captain said quite agitated: "This time I'll give you four days heavier arrest and if it happens again I'll throw you in jail and throw the key away, is that understood?"

Very timidly Adrie muttered: "Yes Captain, thank you Captain."

His buddy in crime was waiting outside in the hallway for his turn to get shit and punishment. When he came to the kitchen, Adrie thought that he would maybe have light arrest as it was his first offence. To his surprise he found out that he had the same punishment of four days heavier arrest.

They decided that they came off pretty good considering the seriousness of their offence. It actually didn't bother the two cooks very much, their punishment was finished on Friday and they could go on leave on Saturday again. This time and every other time they had to be back in time or they would end up in jail. It seemed that Adrie had seen this movie before, first in Schalkaar and now in s'Hertogenbos. It was definitely the end of an era; longer leaves were no more among the perks the cooks had enjoyed.

Heavier arrest means that as soon as your service is finished for the day, you have to report to the watch commander who will lock you in a cell. You can sit and read the Bible if you want, that's all the literature that's available when you are in a military jail. At ten o' clock, your roommates can bring your mattress for your beauty sleep till reveille. With reveille you are released to do your daily duty and after report at night, it's back to jail again.

Normally a soldier's duty ends at 5.30 p.m. They give him half an hour to eat and then he has to report to the watch commander to be locked up. But when is the cook's duty finished? Adrie knew that very well, it was at ten o' clock at night and his duties started at reveille. Nobody ever questioned that arrangement; those guys were cooks who work long hours.

The two cooks would sit in the kitchen till ten o' clock, smoking cigarettes and drinking coffee with the kitchen door locked. If somebody banged on the kitchen door, they pretended that they were working. As soon as the coast was clear, they continued smoking cigarettes and talking a lot of bull.

It was ten o' clock and time to go to bed. The two cooks went to their room, put the two mattresses on top of one another and marched to jail. With reveille they got up, put the two mattresses on top of one another and brought them back to their room.

The next morning they had early duty at 4.00 a.m. They told the watch commander to wake them up early. At 4.00 a.m. it was wakey wakey. The watch commander entered Adrie's cell, woke him up and grabbed the Bible which is present in every cell. Adrie asked: "Are you going to read me a story out of the Bible?"

"Fat chance," the watch commander said, "I was only checking that you haven't torn any pages out of the Bible."

"Now why would I tear pages out of the Bible?"

"One time when I was a civilian they threw me in jail for smuggling cigarettes. My girlfriend put a package of cigarettes in her panties to smuggle it inside. I saved the cigarette butts to roll my own cigarettes when my cigarettes were finished. As I had no cigarette papers I tore a page out of the Bible."

The cooks loaded the mattresses on top of one another and decided to run to their building. They both had wooden shoes on which made a hell of a noise on the cobble stones. It was fun to make a lot of noise early in the morning when everybody was still sleeping. They made sure that they stamped their wooden shoes hard on the pavement to make extra noise.

In the afternoon the officer of the watch came to the kitchen. He was looking for the two cooks and told them: "What the heck is that for an ordeal at 4.00 a.m. in the morning? I heard a heck of a noise this morning and when I looked out of the window to see what caused the disturbance, I couldn't believe my eyes. Guess what? The cooks came out of jail." For the rest he didn't say much but the message was understood, it was fun while it lasted.

After nineteen months of military service, the Government decided that they could go home for the time being. They had to come back every year for repeat exercises. Corporal Peekstok asked Adrie if he wanted to stay and become a professional military cook.

"Are you crazy with wages of one guilder per day?"

"As a professional you'll get much more money right from the start and I can ask to promote you after half a year of professional services."

"Thanks but no thanks; I would like to go back to work as an electrician."

There were only six people in s'Hertogenbos who could go back to civilian life. All the other soldiers of Adrie's draft were in the military camp at Oorschot. There they went in great numbers back to civilian life. In s'Hertogenbos there was only one cook, two chauffeurs, one hospital soldier and one administrator who could leave. Corporal Peekstok and the vegetable ladies had a party planned for Adrie to say goodbye. After all, military service had worked out not that badly.

To step back into civilian life requires a lot of adjustments, most of them pleasant ones. More money and more freedom were easy to adjust to. Adrie didn't know if his former employer would take him back. A lot of people had come back from Indonesia as well and it seemed that there weren't that many jobs available.

Rietschoten and Houwens was a very big business; they wired many big ships and land installations. The company employed over three thousand electricians and Adrie had been one of them before he went into the Army. He wondered if there was a job for him again. Soon he was sitting, chatting with the big boss, who asked how he had liked it in the army.

"Not too bad, I was a cook and consequently I always had lots to eat. The only problem was that the pay of one guilder per day was inadequate."

When Adrie asked if he could work again for Rietschoten and Houwens the boss said cordially: "Well of course we have a job for you, when do you want to start?"

And so Adrie became a civilian again but only for half a year. He started back to work on February 10 and in March he got a notice in the mail; that he had to return for repeating exercises, on September 3rd, for an entire month. Adrie was very unhappy with this message, yet, there was nothing he could do about.

After making some money in civilian life for half a year, he went back to one lousy guilder per day. 'It was hard to get ahead in this world,' he thought. Adrie's unit had to report in Roosendaal, which was the place they had to go to if trouble started and mobilization was necessary.

The staff company was directed to a Roman Catholic school which was registering for classes a week later. Only for six days could the Army use the school, which was ample time to assemble the troops for manoeuvres in Germany.

First of all the soldiers had to listen to a directive from the Captain. There had been an outbreak of polio with many young people being victims.

The Captain said: "A polio virus has struck the world. Desperate efforts have been made with road blocks on the highways, to keep travellers out of towns. In spite of the efforts it has spread at an alarming rate. Polio paralyses the muscles and affects the spinal cord. Many people have landed in an iron lung. Nobody knows where the virus came from and how it is spread. One of the worst affected places is Winnipeg in Canada. In Winnipeg there are over one thousand victims from which 100 people have died. The Medical Association warns that it seems to be spread mainly through sewers. Washing hands is a must after using the bathroom. Don't touch your food after you have touched your tart."

Adrie, with another seven soldiers, were still in reserves. They were not assigned any duties, and would be called if they were needed. The Military Command wanted to see the units operate with their allocated staff. That was fine with the reserve soldiers; they went outside to the square to do some sun tanning.

Next to the school was a monastery where young Roman Catholic men were educated into Priesthood. They were playing soccer for exercise and kicked the football across the fence where the reserve soldiers were sunning. The reservists kicked the ball back to the future Priests to enable them to continue their game. One stuck his head over the fence and said: "Thank you, if you have nothing to do, come and play soccer with us."

That was an invitation they couldn't refuse and soon the reserves were playing soccer. The future Priests had only one hour in the morning and one hour in the afternoon for exercise. In the afternoon they were looking for the idle soldiers again.

After five days, all troops were transported to Germany to a military camp for some more training. Adrie was now needed and took up his old cook job again. He was actually glad to have something to do. There were no Priests here to play football with and doing nothing is actually very boring.

After thirty days in the army, Adrie had made a whopping thirty two guilders and thirty cents. That was one guilder per day plus ten cents extra for each day they were in Germany on foreign soil. That part of being on foreign soil Adrie liked, it was the first time that he crossed the Dutch border. The army hadn't taken him to Indonesia; they had kept him a bit closer to home.

All married soldiers were getting paid the wages they made with their civilian job, from the Government. Moreover, they were getting paid that one guilder per day as well. To the married soldiers that was extra beer money. Poor unmarried Adrie got paid only one guilder per day. It must be a curse for being a bachelor. Maybe in future he could write a best seller, 'The Curse of the Bachelor,' to make up for all his lost money. Regardless of his poor pay, he had no intentions of getting married as yet. He first had to see the world before he got into that venture. At least, he had made a start to see the world; the army had taken him all the way to Germany. "Big deal," Adrie thought, he was planning to do some travelling without the army before marrying.

After the conflict in Korea was finished, it seemed that the Cold War had been put on the back burner. Apparently everybody had better things to do. People started to feel more relaxed, now the chances of war had diminished. Devastating news that shocked the world was forthcoming on November 1, 1952.

U.S. EXPLODES HYDROGEN BOMB.

The U.S. acknowledges that the Hydrogen bomb explosion was a great success. The Hydrogen bomb is one thousand times more powerful than the Atomic Bombs which were dropped on Hiroshima and Nagasaki at the end of World War II. It was a very powerful explosion which was the equivalent to 10 million tons of T.N.T. Since it is certain that the Soviet Union will have a Hydrogen Bomb as well in the near future, it will put the whole world at risk in case of a Third World War."

Everybody saw doom with the new development of more powerful bombs. Leen Willemstein's opinion was "Now they can annihilate the entire world population."

And the good old Reverend saw real doom as well; he preached that the Bible stated that the world will perish in fire. "It all becomes possible and people will do it themselves."

In spite of the threat of a devastating war, the world kept turning and Adrie kept working and studying hard between military manoeuvres. Barely back to normal and making some money again, there was another letter from the Government that he had to come back for another military manoeuvre in May, 1953. Every half a year they wanted his services for one guilder per day.

This time there was a real problem. When Adrie shifted jobs from motor mechanic to electrician, he had decided not to start studying for his journeymen papers right away. It normally took four years to complete the studies and he had only two years. Then he had to quit for two years and pick up where he had left off after he came out of the army. At that early stage, the military service prevented him from working on his civilian career. However, he wasn't that worried about it and was planning that winter to get the first two exams out of the way.

The first exam was strictly theory, which included Arithmetic, Algebra, Geometry, Dutch language and Electricity. For that exam he didn't attend evening classes, he had borrowed a book from his friend Anton who had already passed that exam. Adrie looked at the book and decided that he could study by himself, he was very good in all subjects and he had a whole winter to study.

The second exam was only practical; it included metal working, ground cable working and an electrical switching diagram. He decided to take classes for that. Working on ground cable wasn't easy, you needed proper instruction to do it right.

With passing those two exams, he would be a certified electrician's helper, which qualified him to precede for two years journeymen classes with two exams. Normally it takes four years to become a journeymen and Adrie was taking a short cut to do it in three years.

Everything worked out as planned; he passed the theory exam with flying colours. There was Dutch language, Electrical problems and a combined exam on Arithmetic, Algebra and Geometry. Adrie surprised himself; he had 85% on Electrical problems, 75% on Dutch language and 100% on the combination of Arithmetic, Algebra and Geometry. And he had just studied at home from a book. Of course, a person has to be lucky not to make any mistakes to score 100 percent but you have to be good at it too or else it will never happen. With those results he was very optimistic that he would pass his practical exam as well, all in one year.

That was nice thinking; he didn't doubt it for a moment that he could get his second exam out of the way within the prescribed time that he had allotted himself. That dream flew out of the window when the mail arrived telling him that his fatherland needed him again. They wanted him to come for three weeks and his practical exam fell within those three weeks. "Well," Adrie thought, "that's alright, I'll get a day off to go for my exam and the Army will have to give me free travelling to go to my exam."

Unfortunately, he had severely miss-figured on the generosity of the Army. After writing to the military commander for arrangements to write his exam, the reply was negative. The commander wrote: "The military training and manoeuvres are of the greatest importance to the security of the country. They cannot be interrupted no matter for what reason."

"We'll see about that," Adrie thought and wrote a letter to the Electrical Education Department to complain about the stupid army which interfered with his education. With their reply came a solution to the problem. He could be transferred to Amsterdam where the exams were on a different date.

That was an expensive solution to the problem, especially to his pocket book. His train ticket to Amsterdam wasn't free, he had to pay that out of his own pocket, and all to make one guilder per day. Adrie was furious, the very little bit he had felt for the army because of his cook career, died right there and then.

Early in the morning, he travelled to Amsterdam for his exam. The first order was to make a little wrench. When he went to his workbench he didn't find a piece of metal he could make that wrench from. When he asked one of the examiners, he couldn't believe it. Everybody had started and Adrie was just waiting for his material to arrive. It looked like a bad omen, there was only one hour allotted to complete this piece of work and precious minutes were lost. He finished just in time.

Next on the agenda was the ground cable. That was a difficult task; the cable had a lead mantle on which he had to solder a copper ground wire. The trouble with lead is that it oxidizes right away after you scrape or sand it. Therefore you had to drop candle wax on the lead mantle while you were scraping it, to prevent oxidation.

The last piece of art was an electrical switching diagram. For all three subjects only one hour was allotted for each. The entire exam took only three hours. The beauty was that you could wait for the result, you didn't have to wait weeks before the mail would tell you whether you had passed or not.

It took half an hour before everybody received his marks. Adrie had three sixes as marks which meant 60%. It was a passing mark but just. Less than 60% meant failure. Adrie was convinced that he had deserved better than three 60 percent marks. Anyway he passed, which was good enough for a celebration. All the candidates who had passed were heading for the beer parlour to talk things over.

Most of the marks of the other chaps who took the exam weren't high either. Everybody agreed that one cannot expect proper evaluation of your work, if they only need half an hour to judge work from twenty one candidates. Adrie said: "That's why I like theory exams, if you have it right; they have to give you the proper marks. With my theory exam I had a 100% mark and here I get three lousy marks of 60% for all my troubles."

With little enthusiasm Adrie went for another session of soldier games. It was hard to believe that he couldn't have taken time off to do his exam. He was blooming mad especially that he had to pay the train ticket to Amsterdam. As soon as he saw his Captain he complained bitterly about it.

Adrie said very much disenchanted: "The Army is preventing me from completing my studies which could jeopardize my future."

The Captain replied: "I wouldn't complain too much about it, you and I have to keep the Russians out of The Netherlands. If we don't succeed and the Russians occupy The Netherlands, you won't have a future at all."

The post war years had made the U.S. a land of plenty. It finally spilled over to Europe and people started to travel. Adrie wanted to see the world and go to far away places. He wanted to start with this plan right away because the world is a mighty big place.

> I am heading for somewhere,
> To a place far away.
> It's on a road called tomorrow,
> At the crossroads of today.

After working and studying so hard, Adrie decided to go on holiday with his friends Anton and Joop. He didn't have a heck of a lot of money, for which the army was partly to blame. On the other hand he had to start seeing the world before he got married. If he didn't get married, he would be forever stuck with his one guilder per day in the army.

To go to a place far away, had to wait till he would have more money but he could start closer to home. Most of the trip had to be done on their bikes; that was the cheapest. The three of them biked to Valkenburgh in the Southern province. From there on they took two day trips by touring bus, to Germany and Belgium. Germany was an eye opener when they visited Cologne. It was one of the hardest hit cities in Germany and was nothing but ruins. It seemed that the only building that was saved from the bombardments was the famous Cathedral of Cologne. It was blackened by the fires around from the burning city. The sturdy construction with basalt blocks, which didn't burn, saved the cathedral.

"What a destruction," Adrie said.

Joop replied: "Yes, Pompey is in comparatively good condition, if you look at this."

It was in 1954, nine years after the war had ended, that the newspaper revealed

BRITAIN BACK TO NORMAL.

For the first time since 1939, when the Second World War started, rationing has ceased and life is as in pre-war years.

Rationing had stopped in The Netherlands in 1950. It showed the poor condition that Britain was in after the war. For a welcome change, the next call for military manoeuvres was to be in December 1954. Almost one and a half year after the last call in 1953. You could smell that NATO was getting ready for a possible war with the Soviet Union and that this manoeuvre was designed to test the military equipment for winter use. It also became clear that the veto use of the Soviet Union was crippling the United Nations. This made everybody believe that the only way to settle arguments was another war and NATO got ready for it.

Early in December 1954, the military units reported at a military airport in North Brabant. Winter came early that year with freezing temperatures of ten degrees below zero with snow on the ground. It looked as if winter was in cahoots with the military establishment and was collaborating with the military high command.

The first three days were spent in tents with the first test of the winter equipment being a disaster. Insufficient ventilation of the sleeping bags made the soldiers sweat and consequently the bottom part of the sleeping bags became wet. With ten degrees of frost overnight, the wet sleeping bags froze up solidly. It meant back to the drawing board.

Next, everybody including the cooks and chauffeurs had to dig a foxhole, around the airport, to stay in for the next four nights. The ground was frozen solidly which made it that much harder. First there was a lot of picking to do. Luckily the ground was quite sandy which made the job easier. The sergeant who came looking at the progress said with a grin on his face: "You guys are lucky that you don't have to dig a trench because we don't have trench diggers in the army, except you guys."

Some straw was obtained from the farmers to put in the bottom of the hole to keep it warm. Overnight, with a clear sky, the temperature dropped rapidly and when Adrie looked up he could study the Big Dipper. He hoped that if he had to go to Siberia to fight the Russians that it would be in summer. The German winter campaign during the Second World War had been disastrous; it had destroyed the German army. Napoleon didn't fare any better in 1815 and lost out as well.

After all this excitement, the troops had to go to Germany to join up with the rest of the NATO forces. It was dark at five o' clock and the packing had to be done before dark. All equipment had to be ready for transportation to the railroad station.

During the daytime there was a lot of public transportation on the railways. Therefore the military train could only operate during the night and could not leave before one o' clock a.m. In order to get ready they could start boarding the train at midnight on a side track. Army trucks were going to transport the troops after 10.30 p.m. which left everybody in the cold for about four hours. Luckily there were a few cafes around the airport and soon everybody was enjoying the good things of life.

By ten o' clock everybody had to get out of the cafes to be transported to the railway station. After drinking for three solid hours, the troops were not in the best of shape and the truck ride didn't improve the delicate situation.

As a soldier you get used to waiting and the troops were waiting in front of the railroad station in the middle of town. It didn't take long for most of the troops to lie down on the street to take forty winks. Quite a few soldiers were throwing up and in no time it was a hell of a mess.

If Russian spies had seen NATO's decadent troops, they would have reported that it would be a piece of cake to beat NATO. Every time that the troops were called up, the drunkenness was worse. Most of the soldiers had made sure that they had a few bucks in their pocket to ensure a good time whenever it was presented. Somehow the troops survived the winter exercise, they returned home in time to sing Christmas Carols underneath the Christmas trees.

It seemed that NATO wasn't getting anywhere; they were outnumbered by the Soviets in troops and tank divisions by ten to one. All the West European countries were broke and could contribute little to get the troops to match the Soviet Union. After the war the U.S. came out with the Marshall Plan to help the countries in Europe to rebuild and to prevent them from going bankrupt. The Marshall Plan could be expanded to help those countries to increase their military strength, to contribute to NATO. Under the Marshall Plan the U.S. supplied a lot of money for that purpose.

The Dutch Navy received a lot of money. There was a deal in which the Dutch Government would build two cruisers and 32 mine sweepers. One cruiser and 16 mine sweepers were completely paid for by the U.S. The other half was paid by the Dutch Government. It seemed that The Netherlands got one cruiser and 16 mine sweepers from the U.S. and they were all built in Dutch shipyards.

That of course provided work from which the Dutch economy benefited. This plan received some opposition because all of the minesweepers and cruisers would be included in the NATO forces. The argument was that NATO received 32 mine sweepers and two cruisers for which they only paid half. That was of course very true; it was a clever ploy of the U.S. to have the European countries contribute to the U.S. war effort against the Soviet Union. On the other hand it provided jobs and jobs were needed to get the country going again.

(Under the Marshall Plan, participating countries received over $37 billion in economic aid in four years' time.)

One day the boss said to Adrie that he had to get a pass photo for a Navy pass. There were about 500 electricians that needed a pass for working on Dutch Navy ships. There was a special photo shop where everybody had to go to get his picture taken. The boss probably had a special deal for that many photos.

Not everybody who applied got a Navy pass. Your application with your picture went to the Navy and security decided whether you would get a pass or not. If you had been a member of the Communist Party or had had anything to do with the Nazis during the war, you were a security risk and you were rejected. Even if you had been in Russia or Yugoslavia, both Communist countries at the time, you were not allowed on Dutch Navy ships lest you might blow them up. Also if you wanted to go to the U.S. for a visit you didn't get a visa if you had been in Yugoslavia or Russia.

As soon as Adrie had his Navy pass he was sent to one of the minesweepers that were being built. When he reported to the shipyard boss of Rietschoten & Houwens, the boss said: "I have a problem finding somebody to wire the switchboard."

"What's so difficult to wire a switchboard?"

"Actually nothing, the only problem is to get the work passed by those darned Navy inspectors. They are a bunch of nit-pickers and quite a few electricians don't want to work for the Navy anymore because they are never happy. I don't give a damn how long you take to wire the switchboard, as long as the Navy inspectors pass the work. Do you think you can do it and make them happy?"

"I can try and I'll give it my best shot, if time is no object, I can't see a problem."

The boss continued: "Those Navy inspectors are ridiculous in their inspections; they count the windings of yarn that are wound on the cables to finish them. They demand that all cables have twelve windings on the cable and eight windings of yarn on the individual wires. Don't think that if you put one more winding of yarn on the cable that it's even better. Only work to the exact specifications will pass their inspection. They also demand that the yarn is lacquered all around. They come with a mirror and a lantern to check the back of the mounted cables, to see if the back is lacquered as well. That's where the problem comes in, the yellow oil stocking that you shove on the cable gets black marks on it and that means rejection."

Adrie went to work and took his sweet old time. He did one cable at a time, put the correct number of windings of yarn on it and lacquered them all around. After the cable was lacquered he didn't touch it any more that day and put the final straps on the next day. It looked real good, it was a beauty and it should satisfy any silly inspector. After three weeks of work, he was finished with the switchboard and it was ready for inspection. Two inspectors spent two days checking the switchboard and making up a report. The report included sixty corrections which had to be made. Most of them were more lacquer on a certain cable or an extra strap. Adrie looked at it and told the boss that he could do that in half a day.

The boss said: "Don't! Take at least four days, if you do it in half a day, they won't think that you really did a good job. To them if you put a lot of time in it, it should be good."

"And what am I going to do the three days that there is nothing to do?"

"I don't care," the boss said, "sit behind the switchboard and smoke a cigarette as far as I'm concerned. If the inspectors come back pretend you are working hard."

"You can't kill three days by smoking a cigarette," I'll need a carton to kill that much time."

Most of the three days were spent with talking to other electricians who had different jobs. A lot of jokes were cracked to make the three days pass. Killing time became a habit but if you can fool a Navy inspector who cares?

When that was done the boss had another critical job for Adrie, installing the minesweeper cables. Again, time didn't matter as long as the Navy inspectors were happy, that's all that counted. The 32 mine sweepers were built on different dockyards and when they were ready for the installation of the switchboard, they called on Adrie again. And of course, it amounted to being another time killing job.

Since the Navy was happy with his work, the boss sent him to the submarine base. He already had a Navy pass, which was not good enough for this top secret place. A special pass for working on the submarines was needed. In spite of all the security, the control at the gate bungled it. Adrie had to go to one of the Navy warehouses to get some sonar equipment which he had to install. There were eight warehouses and they were marked A,B,C to warehouse H. There was a window where a security officer was supposed to sit and everybody had to report there. When Adrie passed there was nobody, he got his equipment and when he tried to leave he was stopped by the Sergeant in charge of security. The Sergeant wanted to know where he was going with that stuff he was carrying. When Adrie told him he was working for Rietschoten & Houwens, the sergeant checked the list of visitors to the base. He couldn't find Adrie's name and the Sergeant asked how he got on the base. When he told him that he had come normally through the gate, the Sergeant said: "That's impossible, if you had entered through the gate you would have been on the list."

He took Adrie to the security officer who was a Captain. The Captain looked him over with suspicion and started to ask questions. Adrie got tired of this Mickey Mouse game and said: "Look, I have a special security pass for the submarine base. It will let me through the gate of the base and it is also good for the warehouse area. Now why would I want to sneak in without reporting? If there had been somebody behind the window I would have had no choice but to report. However, there was nobody there to stop me and ask me anything. All I did was to get the stuff I needed. Maybe you should check up on the security people; obviously they don't do a very good job."

The Captain saw that it made a lot of sense and let Adrie go through. When he walked through the long isle of the submarine with his parcels, carrying them in front of him, he didn't see that they had opened the floor to do some work and stepped right in the hole. He hurt his leg and said some unfriendly words about the stupid idiot that had not provided a barrier. One of the Navy officers heard all the commotion and came to check his leg. It seemed alright with only a few minor scrapes. The officer gave him a royal tour and explained a lot about the operation of a submarine. "When you are sailing underwater with a submarine and you walk from the front to the back or vice versa, you have to report to the dive helmsman. Then he can pump water equal to the weight of the person to the back or front. This is done to keep the trim of the boat under control."

There were also two cruisers built in The Netherlands, one of them was also wired by Rietschoten & Houwens and the other one was wired by a different company. Whenever the boss didn't know where to send an electrician, he sent him to the Cruiser 'The Seven Provinces.' When all the special equipment had to be installed, there were as many as 450 electricians working on the cruiser. There was all kinds of equipment and new and better radar equipment was introduced all the time. It meant that a whole bunch of cables had to be taken out and others had to be installed.

Another time consuming thing was that aluminium cables were used instead of lead cables. That was to reduce the weight of the cruiser; the lighter the cruiser was the faster it would go. The wires themselves were of course all copper and were covered with a rubber insulation and the outer core was aluminium to protect the cable from damage and sea water. Those cables came in all kinds of sizes, there were thin cables, thick ones and all sizes in between. When a bend had to be made there were special moulds to bend the cable around to make all the bends look the same. After a considerable time that was out of this world, it looked like a work of art. However, time and money seemed no object to the Navy.

Off and on Adrie worked a week or so on the cruiser and for a few weeks he worked on a destroyer. Everything that was brought aboard the cruiser had to be weighed, it was very important that they knew the weight of the cruiser. There was also a security problem on the cruiser. At one time, somebody had drilled a couple of holes in the steel wall for the purpose of putting a strap on the wall to hold a cable. On the other side of the wall was a bundle of cables. The bit went right into the bundle of cables, damaging one of the cables.

When the work on the cruiser came to an end everything had to be tested to see if all the equipment was working. There was one radar detector that didn't work and when the problem was in one of the cables, the cable had to be taken out and replaced. It happened to be a very long cable that went from the engine room to the bridge. It was suggested to put a junction box where the cable was broken. That idea was promptly rejected by the Navy; it was out of the question for such an all important piece of equipment.

Moreover, the Navy security moved in to find the culprit who was responsible for this act of sabotage. Somebody had sabotaged the radar equipment of the cruiser. Everybody that had been working in that section was questioned. Eventually they found the culprit, who had drilled the holes through the wall and had drilled into the bundle of cables by accident. The Navy security couldn't see that it was an accident and the boss in charge of the electricians on the cruiser argued with the officers for over two hours. For two solid days the security officers didn't do anything but make up reports. They had to show to their superior that they were doing a good job.

Most of the time Adrie was working for the Navy as an electrician and when he was called up every year for big manoeuvres, he was working for the army as a cook. Jokingly he said: "I am a very important man for NATO, I spent my entire life working for the defence of Europe."

In view of political unrest during the Cold War, NATO wanted a big manoeuvre with all of NATO's troops involved, to see if they were ready. This time it was an exercise of a pretended war. Half of NATO's troops were in defence and half were in the offence. The Dutch, Belgian, Danish and Norwegian troops had to go to Germany first to a forested area. They had to set up camp and camouflage to make sure that the so called enemy could not discover them. The attackers were going to use reconnaissance planes to take photographs of the area to find out the exact location of the various units. When they had a good idea about the whereabouts of the enemy they were going to attack. It was supposed to be a real war and referees, with white armbands, were travelling through the area to determine who was dead and who was alive.

Since this big war game took place in the month of September, 1955, the trees were loaded with ripe fruit. You could say, the timing was right especially for Adrie's staff unit that had its hide out at a farm surrounded with orchards.

The staff had to make camp in the orchards and use their little field tents. That part already buggered up. Every soldier had half a tent in his backpack and you needed two soldiers to make one tent in which two could sleep. In the middle the tarps were buttoned together and on the bottom were a few loops, to put some stakes in the ground to hold the tent down. Everybody had to sleep on the ground in his sleeping bag, except the Captain who slept in a nice warm bed between the farmer's daughters. At least that's what the soldiers thought.

Dick was another cook who was looking for a buddy to make one tent out of two halves. Adrie needed also half a tent to make a whole tent. Soon they were putting up their tent underneath the fruit trees. One of the administrators couldn't find a partner to make a tent. He was the odd man out. Very conveniently, there were an uneven number of soldiers, which left him out in the cold. As he couldn't sleep in half a tent, he found his solace in the hay of the barn. Adrie didn't think much about the organization and said to Dick: "What if there is no hay, where does a guy sleep then?"

Dick answered: "Maybe he could join up with the Captain to put up a tent."

Adrie didn't believe that the Captain had a back pack with half a tent, at least not here. Dick and Adrie were masters in putting up their tent, when they lifted the flap on one end, they could pick pears and when they lifted the flap at the other end; they could pick plums. All they had to worry about was not to overdo the fruit eating, to prevent diarrhea from sneaking up on them. There was another great thing about their camping spot at the farm. In the morning they went after the chickens to collect some fresh eggs for breakfast. It wasn't bad for camping at all, Dick and Adrie had seen worse.

As for the soldiers, they could live off the land as well and help the farmers out with the fruit harvest. Sufficient food was supplied to the troops; it might be not as tasty as back home but nobody would starve. In the morning breakfast was taken to them with army trucks. And at the same time lunch parcels were supplied. There was tea for breakfast and coffee for their field bottle to use with their lunch.

Supper in the field was different than in the barracks. Pretty well everything was dried. There was dried corned beef, dried fish and dried potatoes and vegetables. Some bacon and beef came salted and there was lots of egg powder to make some kind of scrambled eggs. For supper you could only make mashed food out of the dried potatoes and dried meat.

Dick and Adrie went for a walk between the preparations of food. They found lots of loaded blackberry bushes, loganberries and even wild strawberries. When they walked back to their orchard, some reconnaissance planes came over to make photographs for the intended invasion. It was an open road with not much cover. Dick and Adrie were not impressed with the planes and kept walking. A little behind them, on the gravel road, was the Captain who had gone out for a walk as well. He started shouting to take cover and jumped into the ditch which was half full of water, stingy bushes and nettles. Dick and Adrie had a good laugh about that scene and they huddled at the edge of the ditch making sure they wouldn't get wet. The Captain got hysterical and shouted: "If you were in a real war that ignorant attitude of you guys could cost us all our lives."

By then the planes were gone and it was safe to continue the stroll. The Captain caught up with them and gave the two cooks a lecture on the dangers of war. Adrie said: "But this is not a real war, it's only training."

Adrie knew already what the Captain was going to answer and indeed the Captain replied: "This is a serious training; we have to be prepared for the real McCoy."

One of the farmers had watched all this commotion, he shook his head and said: "What a stupid army this is. When we were in the army, we had to stand in rigid attention, even if we talked to a Corporal, and you guys talk to your Captain with your hands up to your elbows in your pocket."

"Tell me about it," Adrie answered, "I've seen the German army during the war; they were a lot better disciplined than we are but they still lost the war."

Alarming news came from the front the next day. The British and American armies had attacked, which had resulted in a couple of wounded Dutch soldiers. They had been stabbed with bayonets when the Americans stormed. They probably had been over excited and thought the Dutch army was a real enemy.

Since the battle had started, the Captain decided that the staff post had to be protected and ordered sentries around their positions. It meant that all the staff, cooks and soldiers had sentry duties. Nobody was impressed.

There was a railway line about a ten minute walk from the commando post. The Captain said: "This is a very likely place our enemies could come. They could even come with tanks on a railway track, we have to protect it. A machine gun, a bazooka and sentries with rifles will have to be on their post twenty four hours a day. The sergeant major is in charge to see to it that this is organized right away."

Dick said to the Captain: "I thought we had to keep the troops fed, how can we defend a stupid railway line and cook at the same time?"

"If there was a real war, you cooks would have to defend the staff company too. Our men are depending on us and how can we supply food to the troops if they ambush us?"

Dick mumbled to Adrie: "Great show; but this is not a real war. I would hate to confront those stupid Americans when they stick the bayonet into our belly."

Most of the staff was taken to the railway line to put up a machine gun nest for the defence of the staff company. The sergeant major found a spot that suited well and appointed one of the staff for the first hour. He said: "Normally there should be at least two sentries on duty but we have to guard the road as well. All our staff has other jobs to do too, like preparing food and administrative duties. We are really understaffed to do this job."

Adrie grumbled: "What else is new?"

"When it gets dark", the sergeant major continued with his instructions, "we can't see one another so we need a password. For tonight the password is 'Objection.' If you hear somebody you ask 'Password?' and if it isn't given, you have to consider that you are dealing with the enemy."

One of the staff asked: "If the other party doesn't give the password, do we shoot him?"

The sergeant major said: "Well no, you only take him prisoner."

None of the staff soldiers were very enthusiastic about the war game, especially now they were included in the fight.

The sergeant major stretched in his instructions that there were barbed wire entanglements on which they had hung some empty cans. He said: "When the enemy tries to cut the barbed wire he will give himself away with the noise he makes."

Adrie wasn't too sure; he found the cans a hindrance instead of a help; when the wind blew the cans made the necessary noise and he just wondered if it was the wind or an enemy. In spite of the war, a message was dispatched that an army truck had collided with a semi. The chauffeur had died and his co-chauffeur was in serious condition in the hospital. The Captain said: "It's very unfortunate that those things happen; in big manoeuvres like this we can expect casualties in dead and wounded. If the casualties stay below one in a thousand soldiers we can't complain. In a big manoeuvre like this, we always take body bags along to put the stiffs in."

Nobody liked the attitude of the Captain; he just had pictured himself as a guy who was not human at all. This was just an exercise and granted that accidents can happen no matter what you do. It sounded alarming that one in a thousand soldiers would die, plus the wounded.

As long as it was light there wasn't too much to do and one could find usually four soldiers in the machine gun nest instead of one. That was arranged by the soldiers for the purpose of playing Kaiser. Sleeping is essential for any soldier and moreover it's hard to play Kaiser in the dark. Therefore during the night one soldier on watch duty had to do.

Since the war had become a serious business, a double password had to be used during the night when you couldn't see anybody. The password was, "Nice weather today." Whenever in doubt, the watchman would say: "Password? Nice weather today." The other party had to answer: "Today is good but tomorrow might be worse." That had to satisfy both parties.

When Dick returned from his sentry duty during the night, the Sergeant

Major was checking the camp for security. When he heard Dick, he stepped in front of him and said: "Password?"

Dick hadn't figured that somebody would jump in front of him like that and realizing that it was the Sergeant Major he said: "I'm Dick, don't you know?"

The Sergeant Major shouted: "I want to hear the password! Nice weather today."

Dick replied: "Why don't you f...off instead of shocking people with your stupid check-ups." This incident prompted another lecture the next day about security, which nobody seemed to care for. The Sergeant Major said in the next day's briefing: "By the way, the password is not 'Go to hell with your password!' The new password is 'What's for dinner?' and the answer is 'Delicious pea soup.'"

It was Friday and the cooks were preparing supper. It was loaded in an army truck and Bob, Dick and Adrie were going to deliver it to the hungry troops in the field. They followed the highway up to the bridge, where they were stopped by a referee with a white band around his arm. The referee said: "Turn around, the bridge has been bombed, there is no bridge anymore."

The chauffeur asked: "And what are the troops going to eat tonight if we are not allowed to deliver food?"

"It's no use," the referee said. "It's war and supplies can't get through. There is no bridge so you can't cross the river."

The chauffeur replied to that attitude: "Maybe you have shit in your eyes because I see a bridge very clearly."

It was no use, the truck had to turn around and when they came back in the camp, they gave the food to the farmer to feed to his pigs. In spite of all the work they had done to feed the farmer's pigs, Adrie had to go on watch duty again at the hated railway. He crossed the field in the ghostly light of the new moon and reached his post. After a while, the skies darkened and it looked like rain. Finding your way to the machine gun post became a difficult task in the dark. In spite of a warning not to use lights, the lantern was used regularly.

That night when Adrie was taking his turn, it was raining steadily and after a while it started to pour. After enduring the elements for a while, he decided that this was absolutely insane and took the bazooka and machine gun on his back and headed for his tent. He woke Dick up and said: "It's raining cats and dogs, I came back for shelter. Here is the bazooka and machine gun, your sentry turn is about in half an hour. If you stay in the tent, make sure that you take the weapons to the next sentry."

Adrie crawled into his sleeping bag and in no time at all he was in dreamland. It was just getting light when he woke up; he looked dazed at

Dick who was lying with the machine gun and bazooka in his arms in the tent. "Holy smokes," he thought. "If the sergeant major finds out about this, there is going to be a lot of shit flying around."

He woke Dick up and said: "Wake up Bob; it is his turn to be sentry. I'll take the bazooka and machine gun to the post. Tell Bob to come immediately to relieve me."

Luckily the Sergeant Major wasn't around and the soldiers who missed their sentry duty turn didn't complain at all. Later on when Adrie saw the Sergeant Major he was complaining bitterly about his arthritis. "This kind of camping is alright when you are young and in good health. Once you get arthritis you should be able to sleep in a nice warm bed instead of a little tent."

Adrie thought to himself, "It's probably very lucky that he has arthritis, if he had felt better, he might have been checking up on security which wasn't there."

Saturday's news brought enough excitement. The enemy had managed to break through the lines. Consequently, an encounter with the enemy could be expected at any time. At night the sentries decided to double the men on their post. Not that they wanted to stop the enemy; that was the last thing on their mind. All they could think about was to get the hell out of there when they came. The enemy might take the bazooka and machine gun and they might have a hard time to get them back. With two guys it's easier to take to your heels when you have to carry weapons.

Luckily nothing happened during the night. An intelligence report was issued in the morning, stating that an enemy tank column was heading the direction of the Dutch division camp. In spite of the continuing rain, the Captain ordered taking the bazooka and machine gun to the highway to stop the tanks.

In the rain, on wet ground, they were waiting in ambush for the tanks. When the tanks came, Adrie started to shoot the bazooka. According to his calculations, he had already put three tanks out of action. To his surprise it made no difference, the tanks kept going as if nothing had happened. When Adrie saw one of the referees he shouted at him: "How come that after I have destroyed three tanks they still keep going?"

The referee answered: "You can't destroy tanks, you are dead. This morning your camp has been shelled for three solid hours and you are all dead."

Adrie got cheesed off about the whole thing and said to the referee: "Why don't you say that we were dead; then we wouldn't have to lie down in the rain for nothing."

Actually, it was alright with him that he was dead; at least they couldn't expect that he was supposed to do anything. He said to Dick: "We are dead, let's go to our tent to sleep it off. Maybe later we will have a resurrection of some kind when this stupid war game is finished."

A couple of hours later, the enemy infantry that had followed the tanks came screaming and yelling across the fields. It was English troops; they came with wire cutters and cut all the barbed wire fences. Dick and Adrie were standing on the side to watch all this commotion. When the English troops moved in their direction Adrie said: "Don't shoot, we are dead. Just ignore us."

The farmers weren't exactly amused that all their cattle and horses took off after the fences had been cut. Nobody seemed to care for the pissed off farmers. During the war there was a lot of damage done by the Germans in The Netherlands. They cared less then, so why should the Dutch care about damage done to them now? They only received some of their own medicine.

Well, the war was a great success, the Americans and English had won the war and the Dutch, Belgians and Norwegians had lost. Most of them were dead according to the referee. Adrie remarked: "What makes me think that the Americans always have to win the war? They wouldn't have it any other way."

It was Monday now and payday. The troops were getting paid to give them an opportunity to celebrate in the nearest town. That the Dutch had lost the war didn't deter the Dutch soldiers from celebrating. They celebrated that it was all over. All army trucks were at the disposal of the troops for transportation to town and back at night. It was a town that had about 25,000 inhabitants, with enough cafes to drink and stores to buy whatever you wanted.

Before the handing out of money started, the Lieutenant made a little speech about the success of the operation. Next, he said: "We have all received hospitality from the farmer here, and we all have eaten his apples, pears and eggs. To do something nice in return, we have decided that if every soldier gives up one guilder of his salary, we'll give it to the Captain who will give it to the farmer as a gift for the losses he has sustained."

One of the soldiers said: "Why don't you ask the farmer if he wants to contribute one guilder for the bike the Germans took from me during the war?"

The Lieutenant replied: "By now you should have forgotten about those things, we can't hate one another for things that happened a long time ago."

All soldiers were lined up and everybody had to report for his money. When it was Adrie's turn he counted his money and said: "I thought that I made one more guilder than you have given me."

The Lieutenant answered: "Yes but we took that guilder to give to the farmer as I just have explained."

Adrie was furious and said: "You have no right to do that against my wishes, I made that guilder and I am entitled to receive it. The Germans took our radio and no German has ever offered us compensation for that. Besides the hospitality that we have received, the Germans didn't have a choice. And if they have any damage, the respective Governments and NATO are responsible for this. Every bloody year I am called up, to do this for my fatherland, to be paid one guilder per day. I am not married so I don't get my wages paid. I'll be damned if I will give up one guilder, that's a whole day's wages."

The Lieutenant sounded cheesed off when he said to the Adjutant, who was handing out the money: "Give this childish sore head who is full of hate and anger, his one guilder."

When Adrie joined the others again everybody had heard the argument and most of them said: "You are right."

Adrie was still mad and said: "Why then don't you stand up for your right like I did?" Nobody gave an answer to that question.

Adrie thought about the boys who had been lucky not to be drafted for minor medical reasons, or because they had two brothers in the army. Yes, those people were the lucky ones; they lived perfectly normal lives and made a lot more money than a guilder a day. Even from the guilder a day, he was expected to give up a guilder so the Captain could present it to a German farmer.

That night all the stores were open to give the soldiers an opportunity to spend some of their hard earned money. Adrie bought a few souvenirs for his collection and one for his mother. As there was nothing else to do, he went with Dick to the pub to have a few beer. When it was time to return to their tent in the orchard, they walked back to the point where the army trucks were waiting to transport them.

There was an obstacle on the way to the trucks; it was controlled by the Military Police. Dick and Adrie were both searched and they were asked where they got the souvenirs. After they showed their receipts they had saved to cross the border, they were allowed to continue to the trucks. Neither Dick nor Adrie understood what was going on. This was no border crossing, so why the search?

It was the next morning when they heard what was going on. A lot of Dutch soldiers had not objected that they were deducted one guilder for the farmer. On the other hand, when they came in the stores, they were going to get even with the Germans. Twenty five expensive cameras had been stolen, 28 watches, a lot of jewellery and a host of other articles. Dick said to Adrie: "Actually the Germans are better off with you; you didn't give them a guilder in compensation for the apples you ate. On the other hand, you didn't steal cameras or watches either."

Going back home was exiting; everybody was looking forward resuming their civilian duties. First they had to cross the German border though. The border station contained an army of military police. They came to inspect the train and especially the belongings of the returning soldiers. It took two hours to clear the train; they emptied all the soldier bags and looked at everything the soldiers had on them. In spite of the thorough search, no stolen cameras or watches were found. Apparently the thieves were smart enough not to have it on them or in their bag, they probably had it hidden in the train or they had sold it in Germany, who knows?

NATO had another brilliant idea to test the readiness of their forces. It was 1956 and the Cold War was at its height. Several times there had been a close call with all kinds of incidents. Luckily, war had been avoided this long. Maybe next time all hell would break lose on short notice. There was one question among the Generals of NATO. 'How long would it take to mobilize all their divisions in various countries?' NATO was going to find out.

Early April, Adrie received a letter from the Ministry of War. From past experience, he knew what that meant. Another great manoeuvre would come up in which he was needed. When he read the hated letter he couldn't believe his eyes. This time they were going to call up the army unexpectedly to check the time needed to get the troops ready for combat. The recall of the Army was going to take place during the month of August. Any day of August, the troops could be recalled. It was only going to be a 15 day deal, but it buggered up the entire month of August and half of September. The call could come the last week of the month and spill into September.

Holidays had to be taken before August and then he had to sit tight. The call could come during the night as well, which was alright with Adrie, he wouldn't know about it till he got up. He expected the call back in the first two weeks of August, with a finish of the manoeuvres before the end of the month.

Adrie's father and mother were going on holiday the first week of August; they wouldn't be home if the call came early in the month. He said to his mother: "It seems that my whole life is controlled by the army and all for one guilder per day."

Since August was out for holidays, Adrie went for two weeks in July with his three friends to the French Riviera. They rented a car and were going to camp with a tent on the various campgrounds. After they arrived at the Riviera, they put up their tent and enjoyed a glass of good French wine. Adrie was trying to tune in on a radio station of The Netherlands to hear some news from back home. When he succeeded, his friends came to listen as well. First there was some music which was interrupted with a special news bulletin.

"Israel has attacked the Egyptian army in the Sinai Desert today. In support of Israel, the English and French air force have bombed strategic targets at Port Said, the Suez Canal city. After the privatizing of the Suez Canal, England and France are hell bent to take the Suez Canal back from Egypt.

Meanwhile President Krushchev from Russia has warned England and France to stop bombing any targets in Egypt or Russia will retaliate by bombing London and Paris. Egypt has sunk several ships in the Suez Canal and blown up bridges to make the Suez Canal unusable for shipping. President Nasser states that if Egypt cannot have the Suez Canal, nobody will. It puts the oil supplies of Western Europe in jeopardy, as all of the oil coming from the Persian Gulf transits the Suez Canal. Consequently a severe oil shortage will be the result now the oil tankers will have to round Cape of Good Hope in Africa. It will take several weeks longer for the oil tankers to reach their destination. An emergency session of the United Nations will take place tomorrow to avoid a Third World War happening."

Joop said: "Holy sheep shit, the shit hit the fan blade today."

Adrie replied: "I guess when I come home after this holiday; I can put my military uniform on and report for duties to NATO command. They wanted to call us up on an unknown date to check how long it would take to get all the troops under the weapons. With those new hostilities on the go, it doesn't seem that they have to recall the Army for exercise, it seems that it's going to happen ahead of the scheduled time."

"You could be right," Joop replied. "The Government of Israel is convinced that they can't lose any war or they'll be history. Millions of Jews died during the war without fighting. They needed a home land to escape persecution. The walking Jews finally came home and they are there to stay. Israel is surrounded by enemies and the Arabs are trying to run them into the sea.

After the last revolt against Rome they were scattered over the earth in Diasporas over the world. Finally they have a homeland and they are never to have a repetition of being a homeless nation. They'll fight to the last man."

Probably the whole world was listening all day for special bulletins from the U.N. security meeting. When news finally came, it gave hope that this incident could be contained to the Middle East.

The newscast said: "The session of the United Nations Security Council has ordered all involved parties to end all hostilities and return to diplomatic ways to resolve the crisis."

Luckily everybody backed off and a hostile peace settled over the Middle East. It remained a time bomb ready to explode at any time.

It was August 3rd and Adrie was working in Schiedam by Wilton

Feyenoord, one of the biggest shipyards in The Netherlands. Nobody had a car, which meant that you went by public transportation or on your bike to work. It was a full one and a half hours of biking and from the bike shed to the office of the electricians was almost fifteen minutes walking. He had to get up at 5.15 a.m. to be at work at 7.30 a.m. He worked all day till 5.00 p.m. and it was a quarter to seven before he was home.

That night when he came home, he came to an empty house. Any other time his mother would have his supper ready. With his parents on holiday there was no supper waiting and Adrie had to fend for himself. That was not a big deal for a cook from the army to whip up a good meal. He grabbed the newspaper out of the mailbox to glance at the headlines. There must be some terrible mistake, he thought when he read: "Third NATO Division now completely under the weapons." That couldn't possibly be, he was still home and without him the division wasn't complete, unless they had counted him out.

Instantly there were a whole bunch of problems. His toolbox, with about three hundred guilders worth of tools, was aboard of the ship he was working on. He couldn't even retrieve his toolbox that night; they would stop him at the gate and not let him in the yard. All he could do was to get his toolbox the following morning at 7.30 a.m. After that he had to bike back, put his uniform on, go by bus to the train station and take the train. With a little bit of luck he could be at his military destination by 4.00 p.m. the next day. Of course, he could have gone that night which meant that he would have to write off his toolbox. By the time he came back the boat would have sailed with his toolbox. "No way how say" Adrie thought, "You can all go to hell; I'm not going to take another three hundred guilders licking for the Army."

The next morning, followed the same routine as always and at 7.30 a.m. he was at his work. He told the boss that he had to go to serve his country and was on his way pedalling back home. Back home he might as well have a cup of coffee and something to eat before he went, he was late anyway.

At 4.30 p.m. he checked in. The other cooks had missed him and were all glad to see him again. He hadn't even finished shaking everybody's hand, when the Sergeant Major came to inform him that the Captain wanted to see him right away. "Of course," Adrie said to the other cooks, "the Captain wants to shake my hand too."

There was no handshaking in the Captain's office, only a lot of shouting coming from the Captain. As soon as Adrie had entered, the Captain asked: "Where the hell did you come from?"

That was a very simple question which needed only a simple answer. "From home Captain."

"And how did you happen to get this late, everybody was in the barracks last night and you are a day late to report?"

"I came home last night at 8.00 p.m. and that's the first time that I heard that the army had called."

The Captain interrupted and said: "You must have heard the announcement; it was broadcast on the radio at 8.30. A.M. in the morning and from there on, every half an hour the message was repeated."

"For your information," Adrie replied, "my father and mother were on vacation and I was just home by myself. I read in the paper that soldiers had sisters who were good enough to go to their brother's work, to get them. My sister is married, has two children and lives in North Brabant. I work at a shipyard and there are no radios there."

The Captain countered: "You must have come with a snail train that you managed to come at the end of the next day."

"My toolbox with 400 guilders worth of tools was on a ship. I couldn't retrieve it last night, as the gate was closed. All I could do was picking it up this morning or I would have lost it."

The Captain had an answer to that statement: "Even if that was so, you should have left your tools; your country comes before your tools."

Adrie said cheesed off "Yes, and then I could have easily bought new tools from the guilder you pay me per day."

The Captain replied: "You just didn't give a damn, that you are the last one to report for duty."

Adrie snapped back: "Well somebody has to be the last one." There was nothing to be said anymore and Adrie left for his room.

When the manoeuvre was all over, he was looking forward going home and going back to work to catch up on money making. Before leaving everybody got paid. Adrie received one guilder less than the other soldiers because he had missed a day. 'See if I care' Adrie thought, he had worked an extra day and had made a lot more money than that one lousy guilder.

Everybody received his train ticket to go home except Adrie. The Sergeant Major said: "I don't have a train ticket for you, the Captain took it."

"In that case," Adrie said, "could you get me an appointment to see the Captain?" The Sergeant Major said he would arrange it.

He wasn't too sure about the outcome of this meeting. You never know what those military bosses have up their sleeve. A silly thing he remembered about the song of the soldier in Vienna. That soldier was condemned to death. When he asked the Emperor for a pardon, the Emperor gave him four riddles and promised to set him free if he gave the right answers. Luckily the soldier knew all the answers and he got off the hook.

Adrie thought that if the Captain was going to condemn him, he always could ask a pardon from Prince Bernhard. Maybe he could guess four riddles that he already knew to get free. Well, luckily there was no war on, they couldn't shoot him. On the other hand they might keep him a while to smarten him up. His thinking was interrupted by the returning Sergeant Major, who told Adrie that the Captain could see him.

Innocently, the Captain asked, "What can I do for you?"

Adrie favored the direct approach and answered: "For a starter you could give me my train ticket."

The Captain shot a poisonous look at Adrie through a haze of smoke and said teasingly: "Oh, now you are in a hurry to get home, you weren't in such a hurry to come here. You were the very last one to report for duty."

Adrie knew that all this bullshit was going to be repeated and said: "As I already said before, somebody had to be the last one and I am sorry it was me. Can I please get my ticket to go home and get on with my life to do some work for my boss?"

"You don't seem to be sorry at all," the captain replied, "that you buggered up the appearance of your company. When your Fatherland calls you, you leave your tools behind because you have an important duty to fulfil. Our company has been disgraced and you were the one to disgrace it."

Adrie knew that he had to be careful not to bugger it up. If he said a wrong word, he sure wouldn't come home that day. He prepared a last ditch effort, full of bullshit, to convince the Captain that he was sorry. He started with his defence as a skilled lawyer: "I didn't know that I was that important to the army, I've never been important in my life so I'm not used to that. On second thought, I was wrong not to come when I was called, if I could do it over again, I would leave my tools and come right away to defend my Fatherland. I'm sorry that I was a disgrace to my company. I've had some tough times and I have been struggling to make something out of my life."

He looked hopefully at his Captain, who didn't seem too much convinced about his sincerity. Adrie wouldn't have been a bit surprised if the Captain had said: "Liar, Liar your pants are on fire."

For a brief moment the Captain glanced at Adrie as if he was testing him, then he opened the drawer of his desk and threw the train ticket to Adrie and said: "Go out of my sight before I change my mind."

Adrie grabbed his ticket hastily and said: "Thank you Captain," saluted and disappeared in a hurry.

NATO was formed to combat the Russians. In spite of all the manoeuvres that NATO had, they couldn't see how they could effectively defend Western Europe without the help of West Germany. They allowed West Germany to have an army to stop the Russians. France was the main opponent to that move, only ten years after the war had ended; German boots were marching through Europe again.

On October 23rd 1955, it was a great day for West Germany when the occupation by the U.S., England and France was lifted. West Germany joined NATO and was now an ally in the stand against Communism. Germany contributed 12 divisions with a total number of 450,000 men.

Before the year 1956 came to a close there was another incident that could have developed into World War Three. There was the Hungarian uprising. Russian tanks moved into Budapest and suppressed the uprising with a lot of blood spilling. The United Nations failed to pass a resolution condemning Russian interference in Hungary. Russia vetoed the resolution and stated that it was an internal affair under the Warsaw Pact, of which Hungary is a member. Hungary called on NATO for help and World War Three was looming again.

It was April 1957 when Adrie received the next letter from the Department of War. Reluctantly he opened the letter, expecting that he was needed again to save the world. He was too late to save the Christians from the lions and too late to prevent the sinking of Atlantis, but for a guilder per day he could save the world. For a welcome change, it was good news. He had to appear in army headquarters, only to bring back his army stuff. Younger draftees were now taken to do military manoeuvres and the old ones were just in reserves. They could be recalled if need would arise.

It was another day wasted to get rid of his uniform and all his other military clothes. That day he didn't even get one guilder, that guilder was probably supposed to be a donation for his Fatherland. Luckily they weren't very fussy when they took back the clothes. An undershirt was an undershirt, it didn't matter if it was full of holes or that it wasn't one from the army at all. One of the soldiers had a couple of pink undershirts which were from his wife. The quarter master sergeant didn't blink an eye; to him it was an undershirt. All the underwear was probably destroyed anyway so it didn't matter.

Hopefully this was the end of his military career. With the Cold War still raging, there was always the possibility of mobilization of all reserves. Several times that possibility became very real instead of remote. Luckily Adrie's fear was never realized.

The May 1957 news told the world that the Soviet Union had launched the Sputnik, which was orbiting the earth. This was not received as welcome news in the West. All world newscasts admitted that Communism had won the missile race. The Communist Police State had shown the world that their system was superior to the American Democracy. The worst thing was that the Sputnik had enough capability to have a warhead, which could be used against the United States.

The U.S had come out of the war as the most powerful nation on earth with the atomic bomb. In spite of that they bungled and Russia beat them with the Sputnik. When Russia put also the first space station and first man into space, the U.S. knew that they had to spend a lot more money if they wanted to keep up with the Soviet Union. This was serious and the U.S. had to scramble once more to catch up with the enemy. They were at least two years behind.

A Way Out of the Housing Problem.

In spite of all the hassle in the Army, Adrie with all the other soldiers of NATO's Third Division, together with all the other divisions, had kept the Russians out of The Netherlands. According to his Captain, if he didn't keep the Russians out he didn't have a future. Well, he had kept the Russians out so he should have a future.

Looking the situation over, he couldn't see that he had much of a future at all. He hadn't been particularly in a hurry to get married; he wanted to see the world first. After he had seen some of the world, with his holidays to the Riviera, Switzerland, Spain and Austria he was already 27 years old. At that time he decided to heed the call of Noah to come in pairs and got himself a girlfriend.

Housing for marrying couples was non-existent with the severe shortage of houses after the war. Some people who were lucky to have a little room without space felled like Jonah in the belly of the whale. After due consideration the choice was to emigrate to Canada. It took quite some preparation for a move like that. Nevertheless, on April 5, 1958 Adrie left for Canada and his girlfriend came three months later.

Adrian married his girlfriend after she arrived and they tried to make a go of it. It was a pleasant surprise that there was no housing problem at all in Canada. The Americas had never seen any bombardments and destruction like Europe had experienced.

Canadians had a problem to pronounce Adrie's name, they called him Audrey which is a feminine name. Adrie got tired of being called Audrey and decided to change his name to Adrian. That was an improvement; at least, he had a name that every Canadian could pronounce.

While they were struggling with the problems that a new country presents, the world kept turning and the Cold War didn't stop for a moment. It was January 1959 when the Western world was shaken by some alarming news. Newspapers, T.V. and radio brought the news about expanding Communism in the world.

CUBAN REVOLUTION A SUCCESS.
Castro takes control of Havana. Cuba joins
Soviet Block and becomes Communist."

The one least amused was the United States, as Cuba was in the backyard of the U.S. In 1962 it came to a head-on collision between Russia and the U.S. Newspapers, radios and T.V.s spread the news around the globe.

SOVIET MISSILE LAUNCHES BUILD IN CUBA.
President Kennedy of U.S. demands
immediate removal of missiles."

Three days later, the U.S. Navy put a blockade around Cuba to stop all ships that were heading for Cuba. It was in the interest of the U.S. to prevent more missiles from entering Cuba. The U.S. Army was on high alert and was preparing to invade Cuba. President Kennedy knew that if he would take Cuba, Russia would take West Berlin and perhaps all of West Germany.

For the sixth time, the world was confronted with a possible nuclear war which could annihilate the human race. Luckily President Krushchev backed down and by the end of 1962 all missiles on Cuba were dismantled by Russia. Again the chances of World War III diminished and the world relaxed once more. How many more incidents would the Cold War provide or would the Cold War change into a real war?

The Cold War was in progress, the U.S. and the U.S.S.R. worked around the clock to make ever more powerful bombs. In 1963 alone there were over 700 atomic explosions for testing purposes increasing the radiation level by over 7%. Both sides saw this as a threat to living on earth and put a Treaty in effect moving atomic testing underground. That was much safer, was the thought, until one of the biggest underground explosions in Alaska raised the earth's rock surface by 20 feet. It also raised the bottom of the sea by 50 feet permanently.

Green Peace and other anti-nuke groups were formed to protest atomic testing but nobody listened. Adrian started an electrical contracting business in 1963. He did rather well and in 1964 he clinched a maintenance contract with the Department of Defence. In cooperation with the U.S. there were two rings of radar towers built, for early detection of missiles fired from the Soviet Union to destroy the U.S. The rings overlapped each other and maintenance could only be done when the tower was closed down. One of the rings was far up North and the other ring had a radar tower in Dana, which was about 55 miles from Saskatoon.

Adrian didn't think much of the security on the radar base. Whenever he came he got a temporary pass, the gate went open and he pulled up to the tower. His truck could have been loaded with explosives to blow up the radar tower.

He had the contract until the radar tower closed down in 1990. Better radar equipment had made the tower obsolete and the inner ring of radar towers was abolished.

Another defence job came Adrian's way in the military camp in Dundurn. He had to put emergency lighting in all ammunition bunkers. One bunker was loaded with missiles, and again nobody ever checked the truck. There wasn't even anybody watching when the work was performed. The only security that was in place was a briefing by the security officer about the escape route in case bunkers started to blow up. If it had been in Russia, there would have been a minimum of five soldiers watching the working crew. In Canada they don't seem to think that sabotage is possible.

In 1964 the likelihood of a nuclear war kept increasing. The newspapers reported:

CHINA JOINS NUCLEAR ARMS RACE WITH SUCCESSFUL TEST OF ATOMIC BOMB.

More and more people started to build nuclear bomb shelters. Some contractors saw a way to make a buck and started to peddle their nuclear shelters. One contractor approached Adrian if he was interested in such a shelter. A good shelter completely covered in lead could be built for about $13,000. A three bedroom house could be built for $15,000. The shelter would cost almost as much as a house. With the possibility that people had to stay in their shelter for months after a nuclear attack, the shelter came with a large area for food stock piling. Radiation levels had to be back to the allowed maximum before people could leave their shelter. Adrian turned it down; he told the contractor that he wouldn't like to live in a world that was polluted with radiation in order to die from Leukaemia. *(There were over 100,000 nuclear shelters built in Canada during the Cold War. Luckily they were never used.)*

Some people seemed to be ignorant of the danger of a nuclear war. Adrian was wiring houses for various building contractors. One of those contractors was a German going by the name of Heintz. He was building good houses but his conversation was the pits. When the building boom slowed down one year, Heinz said: "They are always talking about a nuclear war. If that ever happens most of the major cities will be in ruins and just think of it how many houses we have to build. We will be plenty busy."

Adrian had never heard a guy talking that stupid, he replied: "If a nuclear war happens you wouldn't be around to build the houses, besides there will be not much need for housing after most of the people have croaked. If they use Neutron Bombs it won't destroy the houses because the neutron bomb kills people by radiation and leaves the buildings intact. There is nothing new under the sun, the Romans had already such a weapon that killed people and left the buildings intact, by 100 B.C. They called it bow and arrow. They killed one man with one arrow and never damaged a building."

It was 1965 when war returned to Asia. That was far enough away but it had repercussions all around the world. Vietnam was a former French colony and after World War II was finished, the French wanted to re-establish their authority in Vietnam. However, there was the Vietcong who opposed colonial rule. The U.S. had financed most of the war expenditures to halt Communism in Asia. In 1965 the French had enough of it and pulled out.

The U.S. had a theory that if one of the Asian countries falls to Communism, they all will fall like dominoes. They had made a stand in Korea to prevent the Communists from taking over South Korea. That struggle had ended in an armistice and South Korea remained a Democracy. The threat of a takeover of South Vietnam by the Communists was real and after the French pulled out, the U.S. took over to make a stand.

The U.S. started to land marines in Vietnam and by 1969 there were 600,000 troops fighting in Vietnam. This war needed a lot of copper and other materials for shells, bombs, grenades etc. Material became very scarce and basic material cost soared by the day.

Jungle covered Vietnam was a different war than the U.S. was used to. There was South Vietnam and North Vietnam with the Vietcong but in order to defeat the Vietcong they had to be found first. A South Vietnamese looked exactly the same as the North Viernamese Vietcong. The Vietcong fought the U.S. very successfully. All the fighters had was a pair of sandals and a rifle. People working the land had anti-aircraft weapons. Whenever a U.S. plane came over, they shot at it and hid their weapons right after.

The U.S. dropped more bombs on North Vietnam than all the countries in World War II. When that didn't give them victory they resorted to chemical warfare and dropped over seventy million litres of Agent Orange on the jungles to kill all plant life. Some important areas were sprayed twice daily and plants died within hours. It was figured that the Vietcong were mainly hiding in the jungle and after killing everything; the Vietcong would be exposed and couldn't hide in the jungle anymore.

They managed to kill the jungle alright but it didn't give them victory. It was guerrilla warfare; the Vietcong struck fast at weak points and disappeared in minutes. The Soviet Union charged that the Americans were a bunch of aggressors in Vietnam and had become grossly inhumane.

President Nixon of the U.S. replied: "We didn't go to Vietnam as aggressors, we went to destroy aggression. We didn't go to Vietnam to destroy freedom, we went to defend it."

The Vietcong had a complete underground city with living quarters, workshops and ammunition storage. They had a 200 mile long tunnel complex around Saigon that enabled the Vietcong to survive U.S. shelling and Agent Orange spraying. In case the U.S. detected it, they would be welcomed with booby traps and poisoned bamboo spikes.

For the U.S. 1968 was a bad year with over 15,000 marine casualties which created much unhappiness in the U.S. Protest marches were the order of the day and a real big protest march was heading for the Pentagon. The army was called in to provide safety for the Government. The more the Government pleaded for reason, the more unreasonable the protesters became. Finally, the U.S. pulled out of Vietnam which sealed the fate of South Vietnam.

After the U.S. pulled out of Vietnam, South Vietnam was on its own to fight the Vietcong. South Vietnam was beaten and all of Vietnam turned Communist. Saigon, the South Vietnamese capital, was renamed to Ho Chi Minh City after the leader of the Vietcong who had been the brain and the unsung hero in the war against the U.S. The Vietnamese were a war hardened breed, they had expelled the Chinese, Japanese, the French and they managed to kick out the U.S.

President Nixon had said: "In the 190 years history of our country, the U.S has never been defeated and we will never be defeated in Vietnam." He was wrong! After 58,000 U.S. marines had died and billions of dollars had been spent, it was all over.

For the U.S. citizens, the war in Vietnam brought many hardships. It was not only the tremendous cost of that war which had to be carried by the people. There was also conscription of all young men who reached the age of 20 years. Many young men refused to report for military duties and escaped to Canada. Some young men didn't succeed in crossing the Canadian border and were imprisoned for defying the law. A few years after the war in Vietnam was finished, the draft dodgers who had escaped to Canada were pardoned by the U.S. Government and could safely return to their country.

After World War II ended, the U.S. became the Good Samaritan; they had liberated Europe and were feeding the hungry countries. In Vietnam they became the 'Ugly American,' they lost the war against Communism after they resorted to chemical warfare.

Many of the Vietcong got killed by Agent Orange but it killed also wild life and affected half a million children who have birth defects and cancer. Vietnam has asked for compensation, but the U.S. refused as it was done to combat Communism. No country suffered more in the battle against Communism than Vietnam.

By 1968, the U.S. had 7,000 nuclear weapons and the Soviet Union was close to that figure. During that episode of the Cold War, there were a host of Western leaders who tried to let it not get out of hand. This Cold War could easily have escalated into a hot war. Prime Minister Trudeau of Canada was the first one to head for Russia and President Nixon of the U.S. followed. Nixon tried desperately to cover up that the Soviet Union was ahead of the U.S. in missiles. He said to Kruschev, who was the President of the Soviet Union: "The Soviet Union is ahead in missiles but the U.S. is ahead in T.V.'s."

Kruschev said while the entire world was watching: "We beat you in missiles and we'll beat you in T.V. as well. Wait and see!"

Bob Stanfield was the leader of the Progressive Conservative Party when Trudeau was Prime Minister. As the official Leader of the Opposition, Stanfield decided that he had to put his two cents worth in it as well and made a trip to the Soviet Union. There he was introduced as the 'Leader of the Opposition.' That became a real joke because in the Soviet Union they don't have any opposition; they killed it many years ago.

A large caricature picture featured the newspaper describing the puzzled Soviet Union Government. They tried to figure out what a leader of the opposition was. The head of the K.G.B. and President Kruschev were looking in the dictionary for the word opposition in vain. If you don't have a certain thing, you don't have a word for it.

The cold war was heating up with a possible nuclear strike. The U.S. and U.S.S.R. both had submarines in place to retaliate in case the other power would launch a nuclear strike. The U.S.S.R. had twice as many submarines as the U.S. and could destroy most of the U.S. in minutes which would mean total annihilation.

Even the U.K. had the submarine Victoria in place somewhere in the World's oceans to strike if necessary. It could deliver 16 missiles with accuracy on targets 6500 miles away and each missile had the power twenty times greater than the atomic bombs that had been used on Hiroshima and Nagasaki.

Both super powers acknowledged that using nuclear weapons would mean self-destruction by retaliation of the opponent. World War III was quite well possible, but if it happened, it would be the final war. There would be no World War IV, it would be the end. This knowledge created a "Balance of Terror."

To prevent such a war that would have no victors and few survivors, the super powers started 'Strategic Arms Limitation Talks.' (SALT).

The U.S. was the leader in the fight against Communism. It seemed that they were fighting a losing battle; China, Cuba and Vietnam had turned Communist and all of Europe from Trieste to Stettin was firmly under Soviet control. Several attempts in Eastern European countries to get rid of the Soviets had been crushed in a blood bath.

In a desperate struggle in an ever decreasing Free World, the U.S. turned to unpopular measures inside its own country to battle Communism. They saw Communists everywhere in their imagination. In spite of U.S. Democracy, the Communist witch hunt was on. Especially Hollywood was the target of the U.S. Government. Many prominent movie stars saw their movie career ended by false accusations.

Lucille Ball, one of the great movie stars of Hollywood, was accused of being a Communist. A special panel was set up to investigate the life of Lucille Ball. After a thorough investigation, the panel pronounced: "The only thing that's red on Lucille Ball is her hair and even that is not her natural color."

Within the U.S. a battle took place among the politicians and military leaders. At the end, the Army Chief of Staff resigned and wrote a book, "The Uncertain Trumpet." In his opinion, American defense policy was like the trumpet described in One Corinthians which reads: "For if the trumpet gives an uncertain sound who shall prepare himself for the battle?"

That's the way it was when Ronald Reagan became the U.S. President. In his inauguration speech he expressed dismay with this unfavorable situation: "The U.S. has been constantly in a lose lose situation and we are going to turn this into a win win situation."

When he was asked what he meant he simply said: "We are going to beat Communism. We win and they lose."

It sounded great but could he do it? Ronald Reagan was a former movie star but could he play his most important role with a happy Hollywood ending?

First of all he needed an electrician. A lot of people need an electrician but Ronald Reagan wanted a specific electrician by the name of Lech Walesa who lived in Poland.

The fortunes and mis-fortunes of Poland were remarkable. In 1616 when Poland was at the peak of its power they took Moscow. After a steady decline, things turned for the worst in 1870 when Prussia won the war against France.

Poland was divided between Germany, Russia and Austria and was completely wiped off the map.

Poland was revived after Germany had lost the First World War in 1914 and the big powers decided that there had to be a buffer zone between the big countries. That lasted to 1939 when Russia and Germany divided Poland between them. After the defeat of Germany in the Second World War, Russia didn't want to give up the piece of Poland they had taken in 1939 and Poland was given a piece of Germany to make up for it.

Unfortunately when the 'Big Three' were re-drawing the map of Europe, Poland fell behind the Iron Curtain. Poland was 80% Roman Catholic and was now ruled by the Communists. Stalin himself said that trying to make Poland Communist would be like trying to saddle a cow.

In the post war world, Poland didn't do well at all; there was constant poverty, food shortages and for ever increasing food prices. People started to revolt against Communism and an electrician by the name of Lech Walesa at the Gdansk dock yards started a Union called 'Solidarity.' He was fired by the shipyard for creating unrest among the laborers and after he was fired, he received monetary support from the U.S.

Only when the entire country was paralyzed by a strike did the Polish Government negotiate with Lech Walesa and gave him the right to have a Union and the right to strike. That was quite an accomplishment, it was the first Union in the Communist bloc, but when the Union became more and more militant and made demands for more freedom, the army stepped in. They put Poland under Martial Law, arrested Lech Walesa with 400 other unruly Polish citizens and outlawed the Union Solidarity.

If the Polish Government had thought that was the end of the trouble, they were wrong. To the Polish people it was a great honor when a Polish Cardinal was elected to be the new Pope, but the Government could do without honors like that. It was the first Polish Pope in history and it was not just by accident that the Vatican had elected a Polish Pope. The Vatican was always heavily involved in politics and figured that a Polish Pope would make a difference to the people in Poland.

The Polish Government was Communist and Atheist, they neither believed in God nor his Commandments. With the election of a Polish Pope, the Cold War became instantly a Holy War. The new Pope took the name of John Paul and made plans to visit Poland. With an eighty percent Roman Catholic population, the Government wasn't amused at all, they could sense trouble and the Pope wasn't welcome. On the other hand it was hard to keep the Pope out. That would create a revolution instead of a riot.

The Pope's visit was a great success. Not only Tom, Dick and Harry came to listen to what the Pontiff had to say, everybody else came too. The address of the Pope to the devout Roman Catholics was something the Government could do without. His message was: "It's a sin to God to prevent people from worshipping and to deprive them of their religion."

He closed his message with saying that the people of Poland should maintain solidarity among themselves rather than telling them to join the Solidarity Union. The Vatican had scored the first goal and the Polish Government could have killed the Pope for stirring up the unruly people some more. Not in Poland could they kill the Pope, it had to be elsewhere. President Brezhnev of the Soviet Union said: "This is nothing less than a counter revolution; something has got to be done about this."

Apparently, he did something to even the score. A couple of months later an attempt was made on Pope John Paul's life. The Pope was only slightly wounded and survived the attack. It couldn't be proven that the K.G.B. had ordered the killing of the Pope; apparently they had covered up their tracks very well. An investigation revealed that a Bulgarian extremist group was responsible. That could very well be possible but who had asked this group to kill the Pope?

President Reagan saw that he wasn't the only one who was fighting Communism and visited the Pope. All of Reagan's policies were approved by the Vatican and in an upbeat mood the Pope said: "All of Europe will be free before the end of the Century."

It was a powerful alliance between two of the most powerful people in the world. Pope John Paul was preaching and praying in the Vatican, Reagan was fighting in the U.S. and Lech Walesa was struggling in Poland.

It was an alliance that eventually scored a great victory against Communism. The battle was won by sheer economic pressure, showing the world that Communism could be beaten. Indeed Ronald Reagan had turned a 'lose lose' situation into a 'win win' situation for the U.S. It was the beginning of the end of the domination of Eastern Europe by the Soviet Union when free elections were held in Poland after the Soviet troops had been removed.

In a land slide election, Solidarity won 99 out of 100 seats and the electrician Lech Walesa became President of Poland. It was only a one time victory for Solidarity. The Polish people weren't all that happy with the performance of Lech Walesa who was dancing to the pipes of the Vatican. The Roman Catholic Church was dictatorial as well; they didn't know how to play a good hand of cards when they had one. Sex shows, free sex and birth control were called out of order and so were condom sales and abortion. In spite of the support of the Roman Catholic Church, Lech Walesa was defeated by a former Communist boss in the next election.

Despite lavish expenditures on armaments and national defence, the Western World experienced unprecedented material prosperity. Some industrialist had made an awful lot of money on the Cold War and hoped that it would last forever. Those were the people that tried desperately to make negotiations fail between Russia and the U.S..

In 1979 the U.S.S.R. showed their real intentions when they invaded Afghanistan. It was the final nail in the Communist coffin. Stalin had predicted that by 1980 the Soviet Union would have the highest living standard in the world. However, the enormous cost of the Cold War did him in. The enormous military spending was affecting the prosperity of the Russian people and the Soviet economy was faltering under a corrupt Russian Government.

When Gorbachev became President in 1985, the Soviet Union was in deep trouble. More and more militants were bred by unfavourable economic circumstances. Gorbachev was trying desperately to get the Soviet economy back on track again by promising 'Glasnost' (openness) and 'Perestroika' (restructuring) which amounted to severe cutbacks.

In spite of his efforts, Russia was broke which called for draconian steps. To Gorbechev; Afghanistan was a Russian Vietnam; many soldiers were killed and billions of rubles were spent needlessly. First of all, he called the Soviet troops out of Afghanistan, followed by cancelling all foreign aid to Cuba and other countries. Gorbachev wanted to end the Cold War, he couldn't afford it.

Western World Leaders loved to do business with Gorbechev but when he asked for money they turned him down flatly. Nobody wanted to loan him money except one party. It was West Germany that wanted to re-unite with East Germany. As long as Soviet troops were there it couldn't happen.

There was a problem in getting the Soviet troops to go home. For extensive loans Gorbachev was willing to pull his troops out of East Germany, but there were enormous costs involved to relocate his troops that had made East Germany a permanent home. The Soviet Union was broke with no money to pay for such a tremendous enterprise.

West Germany was hell bent to become one Germany again and picked up the tab of relocating the Russian army to the tune of $7 billon. It was a high price to pay, but to West Germany it was worth every penny of it.

The official date of unification was January 1st 1991. When the clock struck twelve, East Germany ceased to exist, German flags were raised, church bells were ringing and a dazzling fireworks lit the sky. Forty six years after defeat in World War II, Germany was one again.

The jubilant German people started to take the most hated wall in Berlin down. It had been put up by President Honnecker to keep the East German people in West Berlin and he had said: "This wall will stand for a hundred years." During the 28 years of the wall, eighty people paid with their lives for trying to scale the wall and escape to West Berlin. Luckily there were more than 5,000 East Berliners who had been successful to escape to the West.

Thousands of souvenir wall peckers came from all over Europe armed with hammer and chisel (not with hammer and sickle which are emblems in the Soviet flag.) to secure a piece of the wall that once divided the city for a souvenir.

When the most hated wall came down it was hard to believe that East Berliners would shout "Bring back the wall!" but it happened. When Berlin was divided, many people had lost their houses or buildings. It was stipulated that Berlin people who had lost businesses or houses due to Communism could make a claim to get it back. Some East Berliners were forced to hand over a house or a building in which they had lived for many years. Those people weren't amused at all and shouted: "Bring back the wall."

In the meantime Ronald Reagan had ordered to provide defence against a possible missile attack of the U.S.S.R. Those missiles had to be destroyed with laser beams before they reached U.S. territory. He called it 'Star Wars.'

Gorbachev didn't like it a bit and tried to persuade Reagan to cancel his Star War program as a base for disarmament. Reagan knew he was playing a good hand and refused. Finally in 1988 Gorbachev went to Washington to sign a nuclear arms treaty with Reagan that led to the removal of warheads in the U.S. and U.S.S.R. This was the signal that the Cold War came officially to an end. A Third World War had been threatening with the use of atomic weapons that could have annihilated the entire world population. The U.S. had spent 5.8 trillion dollars on the nuclear arsenal alone.

They also had built the Ronald Reagan aircraft carrier at the cost of $50 billion dollars. Its life span was fifty years and it only was fuelled with atomic energy once during its life. There were 5500 people aboard. In spite that the cold war had ended it was still a mighty power display.

An advertising on a service station announced: "Win the Cold War with our new anti-freeze coolant." They were too late with this new secret weapon to have any impact on the Cold War. The Cold War had been won without it.

Eastern European countries were like colonies after the war, they only cost money. Gorbechev pulled out his troops and let them become independent from the Soviet Union. He had allowed the Eastern countries to become independent but when the 15 republics of the Soviet Union wanted independence Gorbachev refused.

When the Soviet Union became Communist, everything became 'njet.' (no.) Free elections, njet. Democracy, njet. Free speech, njet. Only blind obedience to the State was 'Yes.' In a last ditch effort, Gorbachev tried to end the absolute power of the Communist Party by allowing other parties to participate in Government. It was in vain, everybody had enough of being part of the Soviet Union.

Boris Yeltzen was the leader of the opposition and wanted to pull Russia out of the Soviet Union. The Soviet Union became a madhouse with food supplies plummeting by 40% and industry came to a halt because of the chaos. A revolution was threatening. The Communist Party declared Gorbechev and Yeltzen Judasses. Not bad for Atheists who are not supposed to read the Bible. They put Gorbachev under house arrest and moved the tanks to Moscow to deal with Boris Yeltzen who was holding out in the Kremlin.

Yeltzen was faxing messages across Moscow to stop the tanks and put barricades up. The tank commanders had been ordered to restore order in Moscow with force. It was their own people, whom they had to shoot and they refused to do so.

It was December 1991 when the Soviet Union States gathered for the last time in order to end the U.S.S.R., so that all States could become independent. A Common Wealth of independent States was set up for the purpose of trade. Participation was voluntarily. The largest country in the world had collapsed into 15 independent Republics. Nine of the Republics joined the Commonwealth.

Fortunately there was some good statesmanship during the Cold War. Even Stalin backed away from an all-out nuclear war. I'm not saying that I liked Stalin; that would be like Red Riding Hood saying that she liked the wolf that ate her grandma. However, the monstrous man of steel, Stalin, saw the writing on the wall; he could see a total destruction of Russia and luckily he wasn't as crazy as Hitler.

The Green Soldiers and the Red Soldiers.

On one of the fishing trips that Adrian had with his son Michael, they had experienced a hectic day and while they were having a drink, Adrian started to yawn. He said: "I wonder why I'm so darned tired and sleepy? Maybe we should go horizontal in the tent to sleep it off."

As usual Adrian was sleepy but Michael wasn't. He said: "How about a bedtime story?" Only on camping trips would he ask for a bedtime story knowing that his father would dream up some crazy story. Usually, Adrian changed the contents of the fables to make it crazy.

This time he couldn't think of any crazy story, there are only so many crazy stories to go around. Besides he was just too sleepy and drew a blank. There was the story about Ali Baba and the Forty Thieves. This story could be made as long as you wanted it to be. It went as follows:

It was dark, a very dark night when Ali Baba and the forty thieves were sitting in their hide-out. Ali Baba rose to his feet, looked outside and told a story. 'It was night, a very dark night when Ali Baba and the forty thieves were sitting in their hide out. Ali Baba rose to his feet, looked out of the window and told a story. It was night,' and so on.

At one time he had told the story long enough for Michael to fall asleep. The following night Adrian said teasingly: "Maybe you want to hear the story about Ali Baba and the forty thieves."

Michael said: "No thank you, it is too boring."

Adrian replied: "You fell asleep and you didn't hear the unhappy ending."

Michael got curious enough to ask: "Why was the ending unhappy?"

Adrian started his story: "I'll tell you the conclusion of the story. 'It was night a very dark night when Ali Baba and the forty thieves were sitting in their hide out. Ali Baba rose to his feet, looked outside and told a story. "It was night a very dark night", but then Ali Baba saw a light that came closer. All of a sudden, the police jumped in front of them and said: 'Aha, Ali Baba and the forty thieves. Hands up, you are under arrest.' And Ali Baba and the forty thieves lived very unhappily in jail for a long time to come."

Adrie found the story boring himself and was sure to fall asleep if he told that story again. He had told the story about the wolf that was hired as a sheepdog. The wolf did remarkably well playing sheepdog. At the height of his career he thought he could get away with murder. Then he got very smart, so smart that he outsmarted himself. He cut his own throat and lived very unhappily ever after."

That was a good one. When he told it to Trudy from across the street, she said: "That's not the way my mother tells this story."

Adrian had answered: "You tell your mother that she is short changing you, she keeps the best stories for herself."

Of course Trudy had to tell her mother that and her mother had said: "You tell Adrian that he is full of bull to tell you those crazy stories."

All those stories had been told over and over again, it seemed that the story teller had come to the end of his rope. He yawned once more, by golly was he tired and sleepy, he could not dream up any crazy story. Michael was waiting and asked: "Why don't you tell a story about when you were a soldier?" Here was an idea; that was an area he had not covered yet.

Adrian started: "When we were at war, we were the Green Soldiers and we had to fight the Red Soldiers." *(That was based on the fact that Adrian was in the army and their potential enemy was Russia. Russia was Communist and they were flying a red banner. Actually all soldiers are green soldiers, at least they have a green uniform on to blend in with nature. That way the enemy doesn't discover them as fast. But Michael wouldn't know about that at the time.)* There was no comment from Michael; he took all of it as a kid takes to a candy.

Adrian continued his story: "The war had run into a stalemate and there was little activity on the front. Our High Command wanted to force a victory and ordered an all-out attack to clobber the red soldiers. When we attacked, the red soldiers had positioned their machine guns well and fired one round of ammunition after another. Piles of dead bodies from the green soldiers covered the battle field. When we wanted to withdraw the commander ordered a renewed attack. Again we were fighting a losing battle with many more casualties. The corpses were now laying three high and were a problem for the green soldiers, they had to clamber over the dead bodies of their comrades. Wave after wave of green soldiers was stopped by the murdering machinegun fire of the red soldiers.

Finally at night the commander saw that there was no way to get through the enemy lines and we were allowed to withdraw. At night; the Generals came together to plan new strategy. It was decided to attack the red soldiers with pussycats. A cat has nine lives so if the cat is shot he can get up and live his next life. He can do that nine times before he is finished for good.

We strapped a package of explosives on the cats' backs and let them storm the lines of the red soldiers. The red soldiers had no problem to kill all the cats the same way they had killed our green soldiers. To their surprise the cats got up to start their next life. Again all the cats were shot but they were closer to the positions of the red soldiers. After being downed again the cats would get up again and again they stormed the red soldiers. Time after time the cats died on the battlefield. Six times the cats were gunned down but the seventh time when they got up they were close enough to the trenches from where the red soldiers were shooting. The cats got up and jumped right in the trenches of the red soldiers blowing them all to hell.

Without machine gun fire across the battlefield from the red soldiers, it was a piece of cake to cross the field to kill the remaining red soldiers. As for the cats, they had still two lives left, which they lived very happily catching those miserable mieces, they hate to pieces."

(This story was based on the Battle of the Somme during the First World War. The English troops that were attacking the German lines were wiped out time after

time. The English army had 60,000 deaths in one day, before they were allowed to withdraw their troops. Unfortunately, they never thought to let the pussycats handle the problem of blowing the Germans out of their trenches.)

No Forgiveness in Fifty Years.

When the years go by things change and all we have left is memories. Nothing is lost, yet everything is past they say, but is it?

Fifty years is a long time for people who went through the war and lost friends or family members. Memory and hatred go a long way; people never forgot and didn't forgive either. There were immense celebrations in Europe to celebrate the liberation fifty years ago but hatred against Germans and Japanese remained strong. Leave it to teenagers; they'll rub it in when they possibly can. Teenagers would shout when they saw a German: "Say, when are you going to return my bike that you stole during the war?"

Of course they didn't know anything about the war; they weren't even born when the war ended. When the war ended in 1945, Queen Wilhelmina returned from England, she said: "Forever we will celebrate the liberation of The Netherlands on May 5th."

Forever was exactly five years. Right after the war everybody celebrated. That went good till 1948 when Queen Wilhelmina abdicated in favor of her daughter Juliana. Queen Wilhelmina's birthday had been on August 31st and Queen Juliana's birthday was on April 30th. The Queen's birthday was always a day off. This meant that April 30th was a day off and May 5th was another day off. Working people thought that was great, there never could be enough holidays. Only the bosses complained bitterly that they had to pay for too many holidays. It was decided to join the two holidays into one celebration on April 30th. So much for eternal remembering and celebrating, as soon as it costs money they don't like it.

Of course fifty years after the war it is even worse. The younger generation wants to cancel the memory of the war dead. Fifty years of memory is enough memory they say. They also think that the Germans suffered too and enough is enough.

Naturally, the older generation who lived through the war don't want to hear about it. They say: "The Germans are responsible for 230,000 dead

Dutch people and the destruction of 150,000 houses. Moreover they stole one million bikes, half a million radios and caused 25,000 million guilders damage. The damage is repaired but the dead people are still dead. During the two minutes prescribed silence to honor the soldiers who died fighting for freedom, the traffic keeps going.

Hirohito, the Japanese Emperor, visited The Netherlands in 1971. Furious people were throwing rotten eggs, tomatoes and stones at his cavalcade. Queen Juliana was planning a visit to Japan in 1987. Infuriated people in The Netherlands wanted to have nothing to do with Japan and Queen Juliana scrapped her visit.

Prince Alexander, the heir to the throne after his mother Queen Beatrix, is President of an organization promoting good will between The Netherlands and Japan. Very few Dutch people are buying it. They say: "Prince Alexander wasn't even born yet and has no idea of the brutality of the Japanese. They built the Burma railroad with P.O.W.'s. As many as 12,000 of the prisoners succumbed in the immense jungle and the ones that survived returned skin over bone.

Japanese intern camps in Indonesia were a sheer disaster as for human rights, the treatment they received was plain monstrous. The Japanese had it in for the former white masters of the colonies and made them bow. Even in women camps, the women had to assemble every day three times on the camp square. The women had to stand at attention for fifteen minutes, next they had to bend forward and shout: "Long Live the Emperor." To conclude those sessions, the women had to leap like frogs around the camp. Whenever they passed a Japanese soldier, they had to make a very deep bow. All Japanese military were representatives of his Imperial Highness Hirohito. If they didn't bow deep enough they would receive a spanking.

When the atomic bombs were dropped on Hiroshima and Nagasaki, the Japanese saw the Americans as barbarians that had destroyed two cities and punished the women. They had to stand at attention for 12 hours and had to jump like frogs for half an hour. Nobody can ever understand the cruelty of the Japanese. Dolls look more like Japanese people than any other kind of people. In the real world, during the war, they were monsters instead of dolls.

On the other hand, the Japanese of today denounce the U.S. for dropping the two atomic bombs. The Japanese state that they declared war out of self-defence. The Soviet Union covers one sixth of the earth's surface and Japan is overcrowded. They also objected against the white man having all the colonies and wanted to liberate those colonies. When they wanted to colonize parts of China, the U.S. put a stranglehold on Japan with an oil embargo.

In the year 1600, a Dutch ship called 'Love' was stranded in Japan. It was the start of a long friendship which was interrupted by W.W.II. To celebrate this occasion that happened 400 years ago, Emperor Akihito, Hirohito's son, is going to visit The Netherlands and hopes to renew the friendship.

The Dutch people are still very angry; there are still survivors of Japanese P.O.W. camps who worked on the Burma railway. And the Dutch Government expects an apology from Japan in order to get back their friendship.

Colonel Tibbits who dropped the bomb on Hiroshima said: "We saved more lives than we took. We were bombing Tokyo at the time and if we hadn't ended the war with the atomic bombs, we would have flattened some more of Japan.

When Hiroshima vanished in a cloud of smoke and dust there were a lot of innocent victims. Many movies have been made about Hiroshima; the one I like is about the little Japanese girl Satako who died at the age of twelve. A Peace Memorial was put up in Hiroshima to honor her and the other children who died with the atomic blast.

Satako was only two years old when the bomb was dropped on Hiroshima. Her mother carried her to safety after the damage was done. She grew up to be a strong healthy girl but nine years later she was diagnosed with leukaemia.

According to a Japanese legend, 'If you fold a thousand paper cranes you will always be healthy.' Satako believed in it and started to fold paper cranes. She accomplished her arduous task but died at the age of twelve.

The movie was made more dramatic than the story already was. It was geared to create more suspense and was not factual anymore. In the movie, Satako started to fold her paper cranes. When she had still one hundred cranes left to fold; Satako got seriously ill. In spite of her illness she kept folding cranes while she was in much pain and agony. She folded another fifty paper cranes. At the end she could hardly sit up anymore but kept folding her cranes. Finally there were only ten more cranes needed. She kept going in agony and died when she was completing her last crane.

August 15, the capitulation of Japan is not much celebrated. On the contrary May 5th, the liberation of The Netherlands, is. It doesn't matter whether we hate the Germans and Japanese or not, one thing is for sure, the dream of 'Deutschland uber alles' ended fifty years ago. However, in the last decade of the century, Germany and Japan have become economic giants and are on top of the world. Did Germany and Japan really lose the war? The answer is 'Yes, they lost the war but they reached their objective. It was a war against colonialism and colonialism has disappeared. Moreover in the second half of the 20th Century Europe's might dwindled and Japan is on top of the world. That's what they always wanted!'

Japan has made a lot of money and is in everything. The only things Japan isn't in is aviation and movies. According to the peace treaty they are not supposed to build aircraft, yet Japan wants to build civilian aircraft. Of course the next step is military aircraft. The Japanese Ambassador says: "We won't do that, we have no ambition to become a military power anymore. Once we were a military power and we have learned our lesson." Of course we have to believe that promises are never broken and that the next generation will act the same.

In 1995 the world celebrated that 50 years ago World War II ended. Believe it or not Canada is still deporting former Nazis. Finally the Canadian court decided that 'Orders are orders' is not a valid excuse for atrocities committed.

For ninety years England had been producing top model cars in its Rolls Royce plant. In the final years of the century, a German auto maker B.M.W. bought up Rolls Royce. And then to think that Germany lost the war.

When Hitler overran Western Europe in 1940, they were stopped at the coast of the North Sea. They were singing "Wir gahn fahren gegen England." It never happened then but after the Germans were thrown back into their homeland they returned to The Netherlands in hordes. The cat came back and so did the Germans with plenty of money in their pockets. They say that the sea attracts them and they are staring across the sea. In their heart they still sing "Wier gahn fahren gegen England." And they did, they didn't conquer England by military force, they did it by economic force.

And how long were the people of Europe happy that they were liberated? Not very long. As soon as it was business as usual competition ended friendships. Canada had sent many troops to liberate Europe but in the 1970's Canada was blackballed by Western Europe. The newspapers had terrible headlines.

Barbarian Seal Hunters In Newfoundland.

There were many T.V. programs that showed how Canadian seal hunters clubbed baby seals to death. Other programs showed that some seal hunters skinned the baby seals alive. All of Europe became alarmed and boycotted baby seal fur from Canada. Consequently the baby seal hunt died and thousands of people in Newfoundland lost their livelihood. People in Canada became apprehensive about Europe, they said: "Many Canadians sacrificed their lives to liberate Europe and now they put Canadians out of business. How soon they forget."

Winning Three Times.

As the author of this book I have tried to tell one more war story, a personal story of how our family coped with the tragedies of war. For the ones who haven't lived during that time it's hard to imagine the hardships that were experienced. When I told my son about conscription, how young people were forced into the army and had to fight for their country. Michael said: "I won't go!" I said: "You had no choice; if you didn't go they would shoot you as a deserter. Even born cowards took a chance and entered the army when they were called. The real coward at all times shuns nothing so much as death. At the front a man can die, as a deserter he must die."

When he heard that I was drafted and made one guilder a day, he said: "You are crazy to accept such a lousy tip for wages."

My reply was: "In the 1970's a union came into being to defend the rights of the drafted soldiers and for the first time since history the soldiers received minimum wages. It came too late for me."

All centuries have provided warfare. The 19th Century saw the Napoleon and the France-Prussian war. People thought those wars were dreadful, unfortunately they hadn't seen anything yet.

People of the 20th Century saw the most remarkable century with two world wars engulfing Europe within a single generation. Those two world wars were greatly responsible for the unbelievable changes. It happened a few times that things changed twice and went back to where they were when the 20th century started. At the beginning of the century there was one Germany and one China. After the Germans were defeated there was a West and East Germany. However, Germany was re-united and Berlin was once more the capital of all of Germany except the piece of Germany that went to Poland. We've seen China divided into a Communist China and a Nationalist China. Even China is trying to become one again, they succeeded in getting HongKong incorporated but Taiwan is still on its own.

Things have changed but the more change we have the more things stay the same when they come full circle. However, during this century some things changed that will never be the same again.

We have seen how the super powers confronted each other and how Capitalism won over Marxism, with Gorbachev as a casualty. The Red Flag was lowered for the last time on the Kremlin building and the East European satellite countries went on their own. Even the Ukraine became independent for the first time. Before they only had been independent for a couple of years after they proclaimed independence with the Russian Revolution in 1917.

At one time we were honorable guests of the Ukrainian pavilion at Folk Fest. The chairman of the committee came to have a talk with me. He said that they were trying to get the Ukraine independent from Russia. I figured that would never happen. However, in 1991 the Ukraine became independent and independence was obtained without firing a shot.

Other than China, the lone holdout of Marxism is Cuba.

Many questions remain. Why did the people of Korea and Vietnam die and why were we there in the first place? The walking Jew came home but the Middle East is a powder keg.

Never was there a party like the Victory Party in Europe in 1945. It was the party of the century, even more so than the Y2K celebrations. The victors celebrated and the vanquished feared for their future. At the end of the Century the vanquished have lots to celebrate and the victors have lots to fear. The Third Millennium will see a United Europe. It all started with the energetic Belgian politician Henry Van Spaak, who started the Benelux right after the war. People from Belgium, The Netherlands and Luxemburg didn't need a pass when they were travelling in those three countries. A proof of citizenship was sufficient. In 1960 Henry Van Spaak formed the Common Market which was very successful and now a new Europe is emerging without trade barriers when independent countries become obsolete.

Famous and infamous names were in the news: Hitler and Stalin; the worst mass murderers of the century, Mussolini, Churchill, Roosevelt, Eisenhower, and Montgomery. Some insignificant countries or islands became important when they were holding a strategic position, or an important battle took place right on their door steps. When the war was over they returned to their slumbering state of unimportance being only a household name in the history book.

We have heard a lot about important places like Verdun and Pearl Harbour. Some pieces of coral in the Pacific became important as well during the Second World War. After the war was finished they returned to oblivion again.

On November 11th we commemorate two World Wars. The First World War ended in an armistice on November 11th at 11.11 a.m.

In Flanders fields the poppies grow,
Between the crosses row on row.

World War I was mainly fought in France and Belgium in Flanders. Many monumental graveyards were the result in Flanders. Because of the poppies growing on the graveyards we wear red poppies on November 11th.

After World War II ended, Canada's Remembrance Day remembers and honors the people who gave their lives during the wars. Usually the wreath is laid in Ottawa by a mother who lost two sons during the Second World War. Since we are running out fast of mothers who lost two sons during the Second World War, we now take a mother who lost her son in a peace keeping mission in Bosnia.

At the end of this century of war which has seen so much bloodshed, we all hope that a lasting peace will be obtained. The Twentieth Century could have been the annihilation of mankind. Both sides had weapons of mass destruction during the cold war. Neither side used them because of the consequences called M.A.D. which means Mutual Assured Destruction. The cold war went out with a whimper; it could have gone out with a big bang. Despite of man's worst effort at annihilation we survived the Cold War.

With all the wars during the 20th Century we didn't accomplish much. There are five times as many conflicts on the go as there were when the Century started and we also have nuclear bombs that make the bombs on Hiroshima and Nagasaki look like nuclear popguns.

We are now entering the Twenty First Century and we are still here. Even if we don't have an atomic war, the survival of the human race is still in question. Can we survive terrorism, pollution and killer viruses?

With the millennium bug under control we start the Third Millennium with cautious optimism. At the turn of the century; that is from the Nineteenth Century to the Twentieth Century, most people were rather optimistic that the Twentieth Century would be a century of peace and prosperity. Unfortunately their optimism wasn't realized. Many people in Europe went through three calamities which were never experienced before. Two World Wars and a Great Depression. Let's hope that history doesn't repeat itself and that the Twenty First Century has no Depressions and World Wars.

At the beginning of a new millennium and century, let's hope that world leaders will give peace a chance. One thing is for sure; the 21st Century will offer no shortage of challenges. In spite of Quebec wanting to separate, globalization is upon us and affecting us all whether we like it or not. During the Twentieth Century Imperialism came to an end and for the Twenty First Century we are looking towards space travel.

The Twentieth Century had been a blood drenched century with two World Wars and one Cold War. With tremendous destruction, an unprecedented loss of lives and unnecessary suffering, the Allies won all three wars. They almost didn't win any war. The First World War was a close call when the Russians were defeated by Germany. The U.S. entered the war almost too late and had to pick up the slack to replace the many Russian divisions that had fought Germany.

The Second World War didn't go any better. A well trained and armed

German Army conquered almost all of Europe, thanks to Prime Minister Chamberlain and his kin who couldn't even run a Hottentot village let alone an Empire. For the second time in a row the U.S. joined the War effort almost too late again. The Germans were way ahead with the atomic weapons and it was a race against time to beat Germany before they would have the bomb ready.

Even the Cold War didn't go that well, this time the better part of Europe was overrun by Communists and the U.S. lost its longest unpopular war in Vietnam. The Americans didn't do well at all but luckily the Russians fared worse. Next came the missile crisis in Cuba and the world edged ever closer to a nuclear war. The turnaround came in the late 1980's and again the Allies were the victors. The Cold War was won with enormous costs of money and lives for the sake to be free.

All three wars turned out in favor for the West and proudly we can say that we were on the right side and on the victorious side. We could boast that we fought two World Wars and a Cold War and we won all three times. It looks as if we are born winners; however, when there are winners there are losers. It seemed that we were the lucky ones who can proudly proclaim that we were **"Winning Three Times."**